DATE DUE

N0 05 '09			
DE 14 '09			
DE 08 '11			

Marriages & Families

Marriages & Families

Intimacy, Diversity, and Strengths

Sixth Edition

David H. Olson
University of Minnesota

John DeFrain
University of Nebraska

Linda Skogrand
Utah State University

McGraw-Hill
Higher Education

Boston   Burr Ridge, IL   Dubuque, IA   New York   San Francisco   St. Louis
Bangkok   Bogotá   Caracas   Kuala Lumpur   Lisbon   London   Madrid   Mexico City
Milan   Montreal   New Delhi   Santiago   Seoul   Singapore   Sydney   Taipei   Toronto

The McGraw·Hill Companies

MARRIAGES AND FAMILIES: INTIMACY, DIVERSITY, AND STRENGTHS
Published by McGraw-Hill, an imprint of The McGraw-Hill Companies, Inc., 1221 Avenue of the
Americas, New York, NY 10020. Copyright © 2008, 2006, 2003, 2000, 1997, 1994 by The McGraw-
Hill Companies, Inc. All rights reserved. No part of this publication may be reproduced or distributed in any form or by any means, or stored in a database or retrieval system, without the
prior written consent of The McGraw-Hill Companies, Inc., including, but not limited to, in any
network or other electronic storage or transmission, or broadcast for distance learning.

This book is printed on acid-free paper.

1 2 3 4 5 6 7 8 9 0 DOW/DOW 0 9 8 7

ISBN: 978-0-07-338004-9
MHID: 0-07-338004-0

Editor in Chief: Michael Ryan
Publisher: Frank Mortimer
Sponsoring Editor: Gina Boedeker
Executive Marketing Manager: Leslie Oberhuber
Developmental Editor: Larry Goldberg
Production Editor: Melissa Williams
Production Service: Rochelle Bogatz, Newgen–Austin
Manuscript Editor: Frances Andersen
Text Designer: Susan Breitbard
Cover Designer: Andrei Pasternak
Photo Research: Emily Tietz, Editorial Image, LLC.
Media Project Manager: Thomas Brierly
Production Supervisor: Dennis Fitzgerald
Composition: 10/12 Palatino by Thompson Type
Printing: PMS 562, 50# Pub Matte, R. R. Donnelley & Sons/Crawfordsville, IN

Cover Photo: Copyright © Zia Soleil/Getty Images.

Credits: The credits section for this book begins on page C-1 following the References and is considered an extension of the copyright page.

Library of Congress Cataloging-in-Publication Data
Olson, David H. L.
    Marriages and families: intimacy, diversity, strengths / David H. Olson, John DeFrain, Linda
        Skogrand.— 6th ed.
        p. cm.
    Includes bibliographical references and index.
    ISBN: 978-0-07-338004-9; ISBN: 0-07-338004-0 (alk. paper)
    1. Family—United States—Psychological aspects. 2. Marriage—United States—Psychological
        aspects. 3. Intimacy (Psychology). I. DeFrain, John D. II. Title.
    HQ536.O46 2008
    306.8'0973—dc22   200703699

The Internet addresses listed in the text were accurate at the time of publication. The inclusion of
a Web site does not indicate an endorsement by the authors or McGraw-Hill, and McGraw-Hill
does not guarantee the accuracy of the information presented at these sites.

www.mhhe.com

Dedication

This book about marriages and families is dedicated to our marriages and families.

Brief Contents

Preface xxi

A Visual Preview xxviii

PART I — The Social Context of Intimate Relationships 1

Chapter 1   Perspectives on Intimate Relationships 1

Chapter 2   Cultural Diversity: Family Strengths and Challenges 30

Chapter 3   Understanding Marriage and Family Dynamics 64

PART II — Dynamics of Intimate Relationships 99

Chapter 4   Communication and Intimacy 99

Chapter 5   Conflict and Conflict Resolution 126

Chapter 6   Sexual Intimacy 151

Chapter 7   Gender Roles and Power in the Family 187

Chapter 8   Managing Economic Resources 215

PART III — Stages of Intimate Relationships 243

Chapter 9   Friendship, Intimacy, and Singlehood 243

Chapter 10   Dating, Mate Selection, and Living Together 273

Chapter 11   Marriage: Building a Strong Foundation 302

Chapter 12   Parenthood: Choices and Challenges 328

Chapter 13   Midlife and Older Couples 362

PART IV — Challenges and Opportunities 386

Chapter 14   Stress, Abuse, and Family Problems 386

Chapter 15   Divorce, Single-Parent Families, and Stepfamilies 426

Chapter 16   Strengthening Marriages and Families 466

APPENDICES

Appendix A   Couple and Family Scales A-1

Appendix B   Family Science and Family Research Methods A-7

Appendix C   Contraception and Abortion Options A-13

Appendix D   Pregnancy and Childbirth A-25

Glossary G-1

References R-1

Credits C-1

Name Index I-1

Subject Index I-9

Contents

Preface xxi

A Visual Preview xxviii

PART I The Social Context of Intimate Relationships 1

1
Perspectives on Intimate Relationships 1

Three Themes of Intimacy, Strengths, and Diversity 2

Defining Marriage and Family 3
What Is Marriage? 3
What Is a Family? 4

Trends in Marriage and the Family: Change and Continuity 6
Trends in Marriage and Cohabitation 7
Trends in Divorce and Remarriage 8
Trends in Family Structure 10
Continuity in Marriage and the Family 12

Focus on Marital and Family Strengths 12

BOX 1.1 Putting It Together: *Learning to Focus on Strengths 13*

Advantages of Marriage 13

Impact of the Social Environment on Relationships 16
Stress, Change, and Materialism 17
Lack of Time for Oneself and Significant Others 18
Increasing Use of Child Care Outside the Family 19
Instability of Couple and Family Relationships 19
Violence, Criminal Victimization, and Fear 20
Use of Alcohol, Tobacco, and Other Drugs 20
The Internet and Human Relationships 21

Changing Gender Roles and the Balance of Power 23
Urban Migration and Overcrowding 24
Financial Problems and the Global Economy 24

Changing the Social Environment 26

Positive Responses to the Social Environment 26

Summary 28

Key Terms 28

Activities 28

Suggested Readings 28

2
Cultural Diversity: Family Strengths and Challenges 30

Diversity and Strengths in a Cultural Context 31

Intimacy in Diverse Cultures 31

Cultural and Ethnic Identity 32

Race: An Antiquated Concept 33

BOX 2.1 Diversity in Families: *Race Has No Place 34*

U.S. Demographics and Future Trends 36
The Hispanic Population 36
The African American Population 37
The Asian American Population 38

The American Indian and Alaska Native
Populations 38
What the Future Will Bring 38

**Challenge to Researchers and
Practitioners 39**
Research 39
Practice 39

Cultural Competence 40
Awareness 40
Knowledge 40
Skills 41

Kin Relationships Across Cultures 42

**Family Strengths and Sociocultural
Characteristics Across Various Ethnic
Groups 44**
Three Family System Characteristics 44
Three Sociocultural Characteristics 45

**Family Strengths and Challenges Across
Ethnic Groups 46**
Strengths of White Families 46

BOX 2.2 Self-Assessment: *Rate the Strengths in
Your Family 47*
Strengths of African American Families 48
Strengths of Latino Families 50
Strengths of Asian American Families 52
Strengths of American Indian Families 54

Cross-Cultural Family Studies 56

BOX 2.3 Diversity in Families: *The Tables Are
Turned: Going from the Majority to the
Minority 57*

Challenges for Ethnic Families 58
Assimilation, Acculturation, and Segregation 58
The Advantages of Being in the Majority 59
Marriage Outside the Group 59
Relationships Between Men and Women 60
Relationships Between Parents and Children 61

Summary 62

Key Terms 62

Activities 63

Suggested Readings 63

3

*Understanding Marriage and
Family Dynamics 64*

Family Science: A Growing Profession 65

Models of Couples and Families 67
Family Systems Theory 67

BOX 3.1 Putting It Together: *Reorganization of the
Family System After a Car Accident 70*

BOX 3.2 Diversity in Families: *Cultural Conflicts for
a Female Chicana College Student 72*
Family Strengths Framework 73
Family Development Framework 79
Symbolic Interaction Framework 80
Social Construction Framework 81
Feminist Framework 82

Three Key Relationship Concepts 83
Cohesion in Couples and Families 83
Flexibility in Couples and Families 87
Communication in Couples and Families 88

Couple and Family Map 89
Balanced Versus Unbalanced Families 89
Balanced Relationships More Healthy 90
Value of Couple and Family Map 91

Family Dynamics in Television and Movies 92
Everybody Loves Raymond: A Rigidly Enmeshed
Family 92
What About Bob?: A Rigidly Connected Family 93
The Osbournes: A Chaotically Enmeshed Family on
MTV 93

**Dynamics Change in Relationships Over
Time 94**

Summary 95

Key Terms 96

Activities 96

Suggested Readings 98

PART II Dynamics of Intimate Relationships 99

4
Communication and Intimacy 99

Couple Strengths and Issues in Communication 100

Perspectives on Communication 101
Gender Differences in Communication 101
BOX 4.1 Self-Assessment: *Your Gender Communication Quotient 105*
Cultural Differences in Communication 106
BOX 4.2 Putting It Together: *All Together at Family Mealtimes 107*

Using Communication to Develop Intimacy 108
Communication as a Cooperative Endeavor 109
Content and Relationship Messages 109
Nonverbal Communication 110
Mixed Messages and Double Binds 111
Metacommunication: Clarifying Your Communication 112

Using Communication to Maintain Intimacy 113
Speaking: The Art of Self-Disclosure 113
Listening: A Difficult Skill 117
Assertive, Passive, and Aggressive Communication 119

Positive and Negative Communication Cycles 120
BOX 4.3 Putting It Together: *Using Communication to Increase Intimacy 121*
The Positive Influence of Assertiveness 122
The Negative Influence of Avoidance 122

Summary 123
Key Terms 124
Activities 124
Suggested Readings 124

5
Conflict and Conflict Resolution 126

Couple Strengths and Issues in Conflict Resolution 127

Conflict and Anger: An Overview 128
The Hierarchy of Conflict 128

Anger and Conflict Taboos 130
Myths, Theories, and Facts About Anger 131

Intimacy and Conflict 132
Intimacy Breeds Conflict 132
BOX 5.1 Putting It Together: *Anger: Myths and Facts 133*
Love and Anger in Balance 133
The Dance of Anger 134
Conflict and Supportiveness in Heterosexual, Gay, and Lesbian Couples 137
BOX 5.2 At Issue: *Determining Styles of Conflict Resolution in Happy Versus Unhappy Couples 138*

Approaches to Conflict Resolution 138
Fighting Fairly 138
Constructive and Destructive Approaches 143
Styles of Conflict Resolution 143
Resolving Conflict: Six Basic Steps 145

Summary 149
Key Terms 149
Activities 149
Suggested Readings 149

6
Sexual Intimacy 151

Intimacy, Strengths, and Diversity 152

Couple Strengths and Sexual Issues 152

Sex and Society: An Overview 154
Sexuality, Sex, and Gender 154
Historical Perspectives on Sex and Society 154
Gay and Lesbian Couples 155
Sexuality Across Cultures 157
HIV/AIDS—More than 25 Years Later 159

American Sexual Behavior 160
National Survey of Sexual Behavior 161
The ABC News Survey 164
Sexuality in the Later Years 166
Gay-Male and Lesbian Sexual Behavior 167

Sexuality Education 168
Consequences of Inadequate Sexuality Education 168
Sexuality Education Programs 168

BOX 6.1 Self-Assessment: *Testing Your Knowledge About Sex* 170
Sexuality Education and Parents 170
Is Sexuality Education Effective? 172

Premarital Sexual Behavior 173
Sexual Behavior Among Adolescents 173
Sexual Behavior, Alcohol, and College 174

Marital and Extramarital Sexual Behavior 176
Sex Within Marriage 176

BOX 6.2 Putting It Together: *Advice from Masters and Johnson on Sexual Health* 177
Marital Styles and Sexual Behavior 178
Infidelity 178

BOX 6.3 Diversity in Families: *Extramarital Sex Around the World* 180

Toward Sexual Health 181
Sexual Problems and Dysfunctions 182
Sex Therapy 183

Summary 185

Key Terms 185

Activities 186

Suggested Readings 186

7

Gender Roles and Power in the Family 187

Intimacy, Strengths, and Diversity 188

Gender Roles 188

Gender Roles and Marriage 190
Distribution of Family Work by Gender 191
Emotion Work in Marriage and Family Life 191
Two Gallup Surveys of Male and Female Traits 192
Traditional Versus Contemporary Views of Gender Roles 193

BOX 7.1 At Issue: *The Work–Family Interface* 194
The Move Toward More Egalitarian Roles 195
An International Perspective 197

BOX 7.2 Diversity in Families: *Gender Roles in Japan* 199

Gender Roles Across Ethnic Groups 199
Mexican American Culture 199
African American Culture 200
American Indian Culture 200
Asian American Culture 202

Theories About Gender Roles 202
Social Learning Theory 202
Cognitive Development Theory 203

Family Systems Theory 204
Feminist Framework 204

BOX 7.3 At Issue: *Gender Inequality as a Global Problem* 205

Power in Families 206
The Three Faces of Power 207
Types of Power Patterns 209
Egalitarian Roles and Marital Satisfaction 210
Communication and Power Dynamics 211
Suggestions for Minimizing Power Issues 212

Summary 213

Key Terms 213

Activities 214

Suggested Readings 214

8

Managing Economic Resources 215

Money and Happiness 216

Couple Strengths and Financial Issues 217

Diversity and Financial Style 218

BOX 8.1 At Issue: *The Effects of Debt on Newlyweds* 218

The Stresses of Finances 220
Finances: A Family Problem 220
Coping with Financial Stressors 221

The Cost of Divorce 222

Why Do Finances Cause Problems? 223
Money: A Taboo Topic 223
The Meaning of Money 224

BOX 8.2 Self-Assessment: *Money—What Does It Mean to You?* 225

Family Income and Expenses 225
Family Income 226
Annual Household Expenses 230
Family Net Worth 231
Does It Pay to Work Outside the Home? 231

Smart Money Management 232
Creating a Budget 232
Pooling Money: Pros and Cons 233
How to Save Money 234

Credit: Uses and Abuses 235
Credit Cards—Dangerous Plastic 235
Advantages and Disadvantages of Credit 235
BOX 8.3 At Issue: *The Credit Card Trap and How to Avoid It* 236

Purchasing a Home 237
Credit Overextension 238
Avoiding Debt and Bankruptcy 240
Financial Counseling 240

Summary 241

Key Terms 242

Activities 242

Suggested Readings 242

PART III   Stages of Intimate Relationships 243

9

Friendship, Intimacy, and Singlehood 243

Friends Versus Lovers 244
  The Fabric of Friendship 245
  The Tapestry of Love 245

  BOX 9.1 Putting It Together: *Ten Traits of Love* 246
  Contrasting Friends and Lovers 247
  The Love Triangle 249
  Three Perspectives on Love 251
  Jealousy: A Green-Eyed Monster or Real Love? 251

Exploring Intimacy: From Experience to Relationship 253
  Paths to Intimacy Differ in Males and Females 253
  Intimacy and Communication 253
  Intimate Experiences Versus an Intimate Relationship 254
  The Paradox of Marriage and Intimacy 255

Developing Intimacy 255
  Traits of Intimate and Nonintimate Relationships 255
  Couple Relationship Strengths 256

Intimacy Games 258
  Constructive Intimacy Games 259
  Destructive Intimacy Games 260
  Limiting Destructive Games 262

Being Single 264
  Increase in Singlehood 265

  BOX 9.2 Diversity in Families: *New Definitions of Singlehood* 266
  Singlehood as an Alternative to Marriage 266
  Characteristics of Successful Singles 268
  Making Singlehood Work 269

Summary 270

Key Terms 271

Activities 271

Suggested Readings 271

10

Dating, Mate Selection, and Living Together 273

Courtship Patterns 274
  Parent-Arranged Marriages 274
  Dating: An American Creation 277
  Hooking Up: The Contemporary Trend 278
  Internet Dating and Matchmaking Services 280

  BOX 10.1 Putting It Together: *Dating Do's and Don'ts* 281
  Dating Among Older People 282

Criteria for Choosing a Mate 284
  Physical Attractiveness 284
  Age and Finding a Mate 285
  Interracial and Interfaith Marriages 286

Theories of Mate Selection 289
  Homogamy Versus Complementarity 289
  The Stimulus–Value–Role Theory 290
  Reiss's Wheel Theory of Love 290

Conflict and Violence in Dating 292

Living Together 293
  Cohabiting's Dramatic Increase 293

  BOX 10.2 Putting It Together: *How to Tell If a Date or Mate Is a Potential Batterer* 294
  Why Cohabitation Is Increasing 295
  Types of Cohabiting 295
  Living Together Is Replacing Dating 297

  BOX 10.3 Putting It Together: *Ten Ideas to Consider Before Cohabiting* 297
  Cohabiting as Preparation for Marriage? 298

  BOX 10.4 Self-Assessment: *How Realistic Are Your Ideas About Cohabitation?* 298

Summary 300

Key Terms 300

Activities 300

Suggested Readings 301

11

Marriage: Building a Strong Foundation 302

Intimacy, Strengths, and Diversity 303

Perspectives on Marriage Today 303
The Benefits of Marriage 303
Marriage and Black Americans 304

BOX 11.1 At Issue: *Gay Couples Entering Civil Unions 305*
When Marriages Do Not Work 306
The Decline in Marriage 306

Components of a Successful Marriage 307

Marriage Education 308
Premarital Education 309
What Constitutes an Effective Premarital Program? 310

BOX 11.2 Putting It Together: *The PREPARE Program for Premarital Counseling 311*
Predicting a Successful Marriage 312

BOX 11.3 At Issue: *Predicting Marital Success 312*

Importance of Families of Origin in Marriage 313
Kathy's Family of Origin 313
Jim's Family of Origin 314
Goals for the Marriage 315

The Wedding and Newlywed Years 315
The Wedding 315
The Transition to Marriage 316

Keeping Marriages Strong 319
Five Types of Marriage 319
Changes in Marital Satisfaction Over Time 320
Why Marriages Drift Apart 322
Keeping Your Marriage a Top Priority 322
The Role of Forgiveness in Marriage 323
The Role of Sacrifice in Marriage 324

Federal Healthy Marriage Initiative 324
Changes in Policy and State Laws to Strengthen Marriage 325

Summary 326

Key Terms 326

Activities 326

Suggested Readings 327

12

Parenthood: Choices and Challenges 328

Roots and Wings 329

Couple Strengths and Issues in Parenting 329

The Challenge of Parenthood 330
Conventional Wisdom About Parenting 331
The Transition to Parenthood 333
Financial Issues and Children 334

Adoption 336

The Child-Free Alternative 337

Styles of Parenting 339
Democratic Style 340
Authoritarian Style 341
Permissive Style 341
Rejecting Style 341
Uninvolved Style 341
Democratic Parenting Works Best 342

Theories of Childrearing 343

Issues in Parenting 345
Discipline and the Lack of It Today 345
Corporal Punishment and Its Consequences 346
Child Care 348

BOX 12.1 Diversity in Families: *Child Care Issues for Hispanic Families 349*
Coparenting 350

BOX 12.2 At Issue: *Looking for a High-Quality Early-Childhood Program 351*
Single Mothers 352
Gay and Lesbian Parenting 352
Fatherhood and Motherhood Today 354
When a Child Dies 356
Parent Education and Family Therapy 357

Summary 359

Key Terms 360

Activities 360

Suggested Readings 360

13

Midlife and Older Couples 362

Intimacy, Strengths, and Diversity 363

Family Life in the Middle Years 364
Defining Middle Age 364

BOX 13.1 At Issue: *Family Stress in the Middle Years* 365
Middle Age: A Crisis or Opportunity? 367
The Middle-Aged Person and the Working World 367
Sexuality in Middle Age 368
The Middle-Aged Marriage 370
Increasing Divorce During the Middle Years 371
Empty Nest, Spacious Nest, or Cluttered Nest? 372
Caught in the Middle: The Sandwich Generation 373
Grandparenthood 373
Grandparents Raising Grandchildren 374

Family Life in the Later Years 376
Defining Old Age 376
Conventional Wisdom About Old Age 377
Retirement 380
Long-Term Marriages 382
Changes in Family Dynamics in the Later Years 383

Summary 384

Key Terms 385

Activities 385

Suggested Readings 385

PART IV Challenges and Opportunities 386

14

Stress, Abuse, and Family Problems 386

Intimacy, Strengths, and Diversity 387

Cross-Cultural Perspectives on Couple and Family Stress 388

Characteristics of Stress 388
The Curvilinear Nature of Stress 388
Stress and Life Events 389
Stress Pileup 390
Boundary Ambiguity and Family Stress 391

Stress Across the Family Life Cycle 392
Common Stressful Issues 393
A Roller Coaster Course of Adjustment 394
Family Systems Changes Before and After the 9/11 Attacks 396
Posttraumatic Stress Disorder and War 398

BOX 14.1 At Issue: *The Impact of War on Families Left Behind* 398

Family Coping Strategies 400
Theoretical Perspectives 401
Coping with 9/11 402

BOX 14.2 Putting It Together: *Strategies for Managing Stress* 403

Domestic Violence 403
Incidence of Domestic Violence 404
Diversity and Domestic Violence 405
National Survey of Domestic Violence 405
Relationship of Physical Abuse and Psychological Abuse 406
Factors Contributing to Domestic Violence 407
Patterns of Domestic Violence 410
Treatment and Prevention of Domestic Violence 410

Physical Abuse and Neglect of Children 411
Incidence of Child Abuse 411
The Impact of Abuse on Children 413
Transcending Abuse 413
Families at Risk 413

BOX 14.3 Putting It Together: *Surviving and Transcending a Traumatic Childhood: The Dark Thread* 414
Treatment and Prevention of Child Abuse 416

Sibling and Child-to-Parent Abuse 417
Sibling Abuse 417
Child-to-Parent Abuse 418

Alcohol Problems in Families 418
Alcohol as a "Cause" of Family Violence 419
The Family's Reaction to Alcohol Abuse 420
Treatment and Prevention of Alcoholism 421
Acknowledging the Dangers of Legal Drugs 422

Summary 423

Key Terms 424

Activities 424

Suggested Readings 424

15

Divorce, Single-Parent Families, and Stepfamilies 426

Intimacy, Strengths, and Diversity 427

Divorce in Today's Society 428
Statistical and Historical Trends 428

BOX 15.1 Diversity in Families: *The Globalization of Divorce* 430
Legal Trends 430

Understanding Divorce 434
  The Culture of Divorce 434
  Why Couples Divorce 434
  Unhappy Versus Happy Couples 435
  The Impact of Divorce on Parents 437
  The Impact of Divorce on Children 438
  Divorce in High-Conflict Versus Low-Conflict
  Marriages 439

Adjusting to Divorce 441
  Emotional Divorce 441
  Legal Divorce 442
  Economic Divorce 443
  Coparental Divorce 443
  Community Divorce 445
  Psychological Divorce 446
  How Long Does It Take to Adjust? 446

Single-Parent Families and Stepfamilies 447
  The Increase in Single-Parent Families 447
  Family Terminology 448
  Growing Family Complexity 450
  Differences Between Nuclear Families and
  Stepfamilies 451

Types of Single-Parent Families 452
  Mothers with Custody 453
  Fathers with Custody 454
  Split Custody 456
  Joint Custody 457
  Coping Successfully as a Single Parent 457

Stepfamilies 458
  Stages in the Formation of a Stepfamily 458
  Boundary Ambiguity in Stepfamilies 459
  Stepfamilies in Later Life 460
  Strengths of Stepfamilies 460
  Guidelines for Stepfamilies 461

  BOX 15.2 Putting It Together: *The Stepping Ahead
  Program* 462

Summary 463
Key Terms 464
Activities 464
Suggested Readings 465

16
Strengthening Marriages and Families 466

Couple and Family Strengths 467

Premarital and Marriage Programs 469
  Premarital Programs for Marriage 469
  Couple Education Programs 470

Marital and Family Therapy 471
  Common Problems in Couple Relationships 472
  Problem Related to Closeness and Flexibility 472
  How Effective Is Marital and Family Therapy? 474
  Choosing a Marital and Family Therapist 475
  Keys to Family Resiliency 476
  Family Therapy Case Study 476

Strengthening Your Marriage and Family
Relationships 479
  Building a Stronger Marriage 479

  BOX 16.1 Putting It Together: *Building a Stronger
  Marriage* 480
  Building a Stronger Family 480

  BOX 16.2 Putting It Together: *Building a Stronger
  Family* 481
  The Future of Your Family 482

Summary 482
Activities 483
Suggested Readings 483

Appendices

Appendix A
Couple and Family Scales A-1

Appendix B
*Family Science and Family Research
Methods A-7*

Appendix C
Contraception and Abortion Options A-13

Appendix D
Pregnancy and Childbirth A-25

  Glossary G-1
  References R-1
  Credits C-1
  Name Index I-1
  Subject Index I-9

Boxed Features

Box 1.1 **Putting It Together:** *Learning to Focus on Strengths 13*

Box 2.1 **Diversity in Families:** *Race Has No Place 34*

Box 2.2 **Self-Assessment:** *Rate the Strengths in Your Family 47*

Box 2.3 **Diversity in Families:** *The Tables Are Turned: Going from the Majority to the Minority 57*

Box 3.1 **Putting It Together:** *Reorganization of the Family System After a Car Accident 70*

Box 3.2 **Diversity in Families:** *Cultural Conflicts for a Female Chicana College Student 72*

Box 4.1 **Self-Assessment:** *Your Gender Communication Quotient 105*

Box 4.2 **Putting It Together:** *All Together at Family Mealtimes 107*

Box 4.3 **Putting It Together:** *Using Communication to Increase Intimacy 121*

Box 5.1 **Putting It Together:** *Anger: Myths and Facts 133*

Box 5.2 **At Issue:** *Determining Styles of Conflict Resolution in Happy Versus Unhappy Couples 138*

Box 6.1 **Self-Assessment:** *Testing Your Knowledge About Sex 170*

Box 6.2 **Putting It Together:** *Advice from Masters and Johnson on Sexual Health 177*

Box 6.3 **Diversity in Families:** *Extramarital Sex Around the World 180*

Box 7.1 **At Issue:** *The Work–Family Interface 194*

Box 7.2 **Diversity in Families:** *Gender Roles in Japan 199*

Box 7.3 **At Issue:** *Gender Inequality as a Global Problem 205*

Box 8.1 **At Issue:** *The Effects of Debt on Newlyweds 218*

Box 8.2 **Self-Assessment:** *Money—What Does It Mean to You? 225*

Box 8.3 **At Issue:** *The Credit Card Trap and How to Avoid It* 236

Box 9.1 **Putting It Together:** *Ten Traits of Love* 246

Box 9.2 **Diversity in Families:** *New Definitions of Singlehood* 266

Box 10.1 **Putting It Together:** *Dating Do's and Don'ts* 281

Box 10.2 **Putting it Together:** *How to Tell If a Date or Mate Is a Potential Batterer* 294

Box 10.3 **Putting It Together:** *Ten Ideas to Consider before Cohabiting* 297

Box 10.4 **Self-Assessment:** *How Realistic Are Your Ideas About Cohabitation?* 298

Box 11.1 **At Issue:** *Gay Couples Entering Civil Unions* 305

Box 11.2 **Putting It Together:** *The PREPARE Program for Premarital Counseling* 311

Box 11.3 **At Issue:** *Predicting Marital Success* 312

Box 12.1 **Diversity in Families:** *Child Care Issues for Hispanic Families* 349

Box 12.2 **At Issue:** *Looking for a High-Quality Early-Childhood Program* 351

Box 13.1 **At Issue:** *Family Stress in the Middle Years* 365

Box 14.1 **At Issue:** *The Impact of War on Families Left Behind* 398

Box 14.2 **Putting It Together:** *Strategies for Managing Stress* 403

Box 14.3 **Putting It Together:** *Surviving and Transcending a Traumatic Childhood: The Dark Thread* 414

Box 15.1 **Diversity in Families:** *The Globalization of Divorce* 430

Box 15.2 **Putting It Together:** *The Stepping Ahead Program* 462

Box 16.1 **Putting It Together:** *Building a Stronger Marriage* 480

Box 16.2 **Putting It Together:** *Building a Stronger Family* 481

About the Authors

David H. Olson, Ph.D.

David Olson is professor emeritus of family social science at the University of Minnesota, where he has been for more than 25 years. He is founder and president of Life Innovations. He is a past president of the National Council on Family Relations (NCFR) and a past president of the Upper Midwest Association for Marriage and Family Therapists (UMAMFT).

He is a fellow and clinical member of the American Association for Marital and Family Therapy (AAMFT) and a fellow of the American Psychological Association (APA). Olson is also a member of the editorial boards of six family journals. He has received numerous awards, including the Distinguished Contribution to Family Therapy Research Award from both AAMFT and the American Family Therapy Association (AFTA).

Olson has written or edited more than 20 books, including *Empowering Couples, Building Relationships, Families: What Makes Them Work, Circumplex Model, Power in Families, Treating Relationships,* and 10 volumes of the *Inventory of Marriage and Family Literature.* He has published more than 100 articles with the theme of bridging family research, theory, and practice.

Olson and his colleagues at the University of Minnesota have developed the Circumplex Model of Marital and Family Systems and a variety of couple and family assessment tools, including PREPARE, ENRICH, FACES, PAIR, and AWARE.

He is happily married to Karen Olson, who has provided companionship and support throughout this and numerous other projects. They have three terrific children (Hans, Amy, and Chris), a great son-in-law (Daniel), and five wonderful grandchildren (Adrienne, Evan, Chelsea, Alex, and Ava). Olson has been blessed with a fun-loving and caring family that continues to sustain and support him.

John DeFrain, Ph.D.

John DeFrain is an extension professor of family and community development at the University of Nebraska and has focused his professional energy for the past 35 years in better understanding how families learn to live happily together.

He cofounded the National and International Symposium on Building Family Strengths, which grew into a consortium of groups organizing 35 allied conferences in the United States and around the world since 1978. Recent gatherings have been held in Australia, China, Mexico, and Korea, and upcoming conferences are planned for southern Africa, the Middle East, the Mediterranean, and the United States. His research with a team of investigators around the world has collected data on family strengths from more than 21,000 family members in 27 countries.

DeFrain has served as consultant to courts, universities, churches, agencies, and individual families on marriage, parenting, grief, divorce, and child custody issues. He recently received the Outstanding New Extension Family Specialist

Award, and the MISS Foundation Phoenix Award for service to bereaved parents who have lost children.

He has co-authored more than 60 professional articles on family issues and 18 books, including *Secrets of Strong Families, Sudden Infant Death: Enduring the Loss, Stillborn: The Invisible Death, On Our Own: A Single Parent's Survival Guide, Building Relationships*, and *Parents in Contemporary America: A Sympathetic View*. His most recent books are *The Family Strengths Perspective: Strong Families Around the World, Surviving and Transcending a Traumatic Childhood: The Dark Thread*, and *Creating Strong Marriages and Families: A Strengths-Based Activity Book*.

He and his wife and best friend, Nikki DeFrain, M.S., have three grown daughters connected to two sons-in-law and a boyfriend-in-law, and a grandson. Nikki was especially important in the development and writing of this textbook, offering support in innumerable areas of the project and expertise in her own areas of study. The DeFrains are very interested in understanding family strengths and challenges from a global perspective, and have traveled and studied family relationships in 17 countries.

Linda Skogrand, Ph.D.

Linda Skogrand is an assistant professor and family life extension specialist at Utah State University in Logan, Utah. She began her professional career as a social worker in the inner city of St. Louis, Missouri, and throughout her career has enjoyed a balance between academic institutions and social service organizations. Her current position as an extension specialist allows her to take knowledge and research findings and make them available to people in communities in Utah and throughout the nation.

Skogrand's social service experience includes providing HIV/AIDS education programs for street kids, people in prison, and gang members, and overseeing the design of an AIDS house for the Latino population. She also taught family courses at St. Olaf College in Northfield, Minnesota, for 17 years and was adjunct faculty at the University of Minnesota for several years.

She has published articles focusing on values in parent education, the lives of families who have experienced sudden infant death syndrome, transcendence of traumatic childhoods, spirituality, strong Latino marriages, and debt and marriage. She has co-authored several books, including *Surviving and Transcending a Traumatic Childhood: The Dark Thread, Coping with Sudden Infant Death*, and *Sudden Infant Death: Enduring the Loss*. Her current research focuses on strong marriages in the Latino and American Indian cultures, and she is currently conducting a national study with John DeFrain of what makes "great" marriages.

Skogrand has been married to her high school sweetheart, Steven Gilbertson, for the past 7 years and resides in Logan, Utah. She has three adult children, Aaron, Jennifer, and Sara. Her children's multiracial heritage has taught her much about diversity.

Preface

Our colleague and friend, the late Dr. David R. Mace, once said, "Nothing in the world could make human life happier than to greatly increase the number of happy couples and strong families." Throughout six editions, our goal in writing *Marriages and Families: Intimacy, Diversity, and Strengths* has been to provide students with information about marriage and family relationships that will help them move toward Mace's goal.

We have tried to make the concepts and ideas presented in this book useful and meaningful so students will be able to apply them to their own lives. We hope to help students integrate intellectual ideas and personal experiences, thereby enriching both. Although the text deals with some complex ideas and materials, it is written in a style that is accessible to students new to the field of family studies and to those wanting to learn more about intimate relationships.

Intimacy, Strengths, and Diversity

Three distinctive themes have guided our efforts in writing this book, and they are woven throughout the text. The first is intimacy, and our focus is on how to develop and maintain close relationships. Most people seek connectedness and want to be involved in intimate relationships, the most intimate being marriage and family. This book is full of ideas, principles, and suggestions for building and keeping intimate relationships in your life. As a result, this is a book that you will want to keep and refer to throughout your life.

The second key theme is marital and family strengths. The family strengths perspective is based on the premise that if you approach relationships from a "problem" perspective, you will find problems. If you look for strengths, you will find strengths. Growing numbers of family educators and family therapists are using this approach today, helping families recognize their own strengths and use them as a foundation for positive growth. In Chapter 1, we identify a number of strengths that have been found to be present in healthy marriages and families all over the world. Throughout the book, we show how these strengths help families provide healthy and nurturing settings that promote the growth and well-being of individual family members, better enabling them to face the challenges and solve the problems they encounter.

Although the theme of family strengths is integrated throughout the book, three chapters focus especially on this theme: Chapter 2 highlights the couple and family strengths of diverse ethnic and cultural groups; Chapter 14 examines how families can use their strengths to manage stress, abuse, and other family issues; and Chapter 16 looks at how families and societies can work together to build healthier societies in the future.

The third key theme is diversity, and, wherever possible, we consider how concepts, research, and theories about the family apply to couples and families of diverse ethnic and cultural backgrounds. We also focus on the diversity in structure that characterizes families today, looking at the many different forms that "family" can take. Diversity in sexual orientation—gay and lesbian relationships and families in our society—is a third type of diversity we explore. The theme of diversity is introduced in Chapter 1, discussed in detail in Chapter 2, and integrated into discussions throughout the book. One of the four categories of the box program is dedicated to exploring diversity in families.

Family Systems and Family Strengths

We present many theories of family in this book, but we focus especially on family systems theory. Recognizing that the family unit is a system of interdependent parts, we look at how families maintain themselves, yet change; how family members can be separate, yet connected; and how communication facilitates the processes of change and growth. We focus on communication and conflict resolution skills as essential tools for creating healthy intimate relationships. We also look at how families can learn to function well within the larger systems of community and society.

The family strengths perspective was developed by Nick Stinnett, John DeFrain, and many of their colleagues across the country. We use this perspective throughout the text as a model for understanding and evaluating families. With it, we identify and focus on six key qualities of healthy families: commitment, appreciation and affection, positive communication, enjoyable time together, spiritual well-being, and the ability to cope with stress and crisis. The research driving this model has involved thousands of family members in the United States and other countries around the world.

In Chapter 3, we introduce the Couple and Family Map, an assessment tool that was developed by David Olson and his colleagues. The Couple and Family Map is based on concepts from family systems theory, and it focuses on the three dimensions of cohesion, flexibility, and communication. It has been used in hundreds of studies to help researchers understand and evaluate families. Throughout the text, we cite studies that have used the map as a theoretical base. An ongoing family case study, described in the Instructor's Manual, can be used to show students how the Couple and Family Map is applied. Appendix A contains the instructions and materials to apply the map to couple and family relationships.

Updates in the Sixth Edition

Like a healthy couple and family, a good textbook needs to identify major issues and change over time. We have tried to describe the current issues in marriage and families today and identify changes in these relationships.

The field of relationships, especially marriages and families, is increasingly changing and becoming more diverse and complex. Marriage is being preceded and/or replaced by cohabitation, and two-parent families are becoming less common. Same-sex couples are increasing, as are single parents and people who are choosing not to marry. We will now highlight some of the changes we have made in each of the 16 chapters.

Part I: The Social Context of Intimate Relationships

In Chapter 1, Perspectives on Intimate Relationships, we have updated the latest statistics from the U.S. Bureau of the Census on trends in marriage, family, and cohabitation. We have added new material on same-sex marriage, cohabitation, and the use of the Internet for dating and viewing pornography.

In Chapter 2, Cultural Diversity: Family Strengths and Challenges, we describe the growing diversity in ethnic groups and the dramatic increase in Hispanic families in the United States. We describe in more detail why the concept of "race" is an antiquated concept. We present new material on cultural competence that includes three components: awareness, knowledge, and skills. We emphasize the importance of family strengths in various ethnic groups, and we have added information showing there are more differences across social classes than across ethnic groups.

In Chapter 3, Understanding Marriage and Family Dynamics, we have updated information on the importance of family strengths across ethnic groups and with other countries around the world. More clarity and examples are provided regarding the Couple and Family Map and the three core concepts of cohesion, flexibility, and communication.

Part II: Dynamics of Intimate Relationships

In Chapter 4, Communication and Intimacy, we have added more research from John Gottman and Howard Markman about how communication can help build intimacy. We have added new research on self-disclosure with the same sex and opposite sex, along with studies that demonstrate the value of family mealtime for increasing couple and family closeness.

In Chapter 5, Conflict and Conflict Resolution, we have updated research on overfunctioning versus underfunctioning from Harriet Lerner, and we have added more studies on conflict resolution from John Gottman and other marriage researchers.

In Chapter 6, Sexual Intimacy, we have added more information on gay and lesbian relationships and on how their life experiences differ from those of heterosexual couples. Updated information on HIV/AIDS around the world is provided along with newer surveys of sexual behavior. New studies on the prevalence of sex before marriage and marital infidelity have been added that demonstrate how these aspects of sexuality are increasing in our society.

In Chapter 7, Gender Roles and Power in the Family, we present new research on the distribution of family work (housework, child care) and emotion work (attending to feelings of family members, offering encouragement) by gender. An expanded section on work–family balance has been added because more dual career and dual working families struggle to balance work, family, and their personal life. More information about gender roles across ethnic groups has also been added to this edition.

In Chapter 8, Managing Economic Resources, we have added new information about money and happiness, the effects of debt on newlyweds, and the cost of divorce. We have added a new section on diversity and financial style that compares the individualistic style of the middle and upper classes and the collectivist style of the lower class, where significant others more often help and support each other. The collective style is more common among Hispanic and African Americans compared to Caucasian families. We have also provided updated statistics on annual income and expenses across ethnic groups and by education level. A revised section on smart money management provides suggestions about how to avoid common financial issues such as overuse of credit cards and a lack of plans for saving money.

Part III: Stages of Intimate Relationships

In Chapter 9, Friendship, Intimacy, and Singlehood, we have updated the information on singles, who are increasing in number because they are now cohabiting and delaying getting married. We have provided more information on jealousy and on how it can negatively impact current relationships.

In Chapter 10, Dating, Mate Selection, and Living Together, we expand the discussion of Internet dating and matchmaking services, which have grown dramatically in popularity but have serious limitations. We provide more information on the increasing amount of conflict and violence in couples dating and cohabiting. Major updates on cohabitation are provided because of its growing popularity, along with new studies revealing the pros and cons of cohabiting. We have added a new box titled "Ten Ideas to Consider Before Cohabiting."

In Chapter 11, Marriage: Building a Strong Foundation, we identify the decline in the number of persons getting married. Most couples are now much older when marrying than they were two decades ago, showing that they are delaying marriage. We provide updated information about the value of premarital preparation. We also describe some of the new marriage education programs and state policies that reward couples who complete a premarital program.

In Chapter 12, Parenthood: Choices and Challenges, we provide more information about the importance of family cohesion (also called parental support) and family flexibility (also called parental control) in understanding parenting style. There is increasing evidence about the value of the democratic style of parenting versus a more authoritarian approach for children academically and socially. A recent problematic trend in parenting is "permissive parenting," where parents let children control the family. We have expanded the discussion of the increasing number of single mothers and their struggles. A growing trend is the increase in gay and lesbian parents. We describe their parenting style and its impact on the children compared to that of heterosexual parents.

In Chapter 13, Midlife and Older Couples, we highlight the growing "boomer generation" who have to deal with both caring for their elderly parents and launching their own children. We have added a new section on grandparents raising grandchildren because of this growing trend. As people delay retirement and live longer, there are also more issues for older couples to handle.

Part IV: Challenges and Opportunities

In Chapter 14, Stress, Abuse, and Family Problems, a new section on posttraumatic stress disorder (PTSD) and the Iraq War describes a major problem facing many of the troops returning from the war. We have added a new section on diversity and domestic violence, with updated information on domestic violence. A new box, titled "Surviving and Transcending a Traumatic Childhood," describes the stories of children who have survived and thrived after major trauma.

In Chapter 15, Divorce, Single-Parent Families, and Stepfamilies, we begin with a new section on statistical and historical trends in divorce. Newer studies on the impact of divorce on children provides a more reasonable perspective on the resiliency of children. A new section describes divorce in high-conflict versus low-conflict marriages and how, surprisingly, the impact is more detrimental for children in low-conflict marriages. A new section on boundary ambiguity in stepfamilies highlights the lack of clarity regarding who is in and not included in a stepfamily.

In Chapter 16, Strengthening Marriages and Families, we begin with a new section on couple and family strengths, which demonstrates that a strengths perspective is growing across other social sciences fields. We highlight the value of a variety of marriage education programs that are becoming more popular across the country.

In summary, these updates demonstrate the dynamic changes, increasing ethnic diversity, and growing complexity taking place in couple and family relationships in our society. There is also a growing literature that provides new data and useful insights into the couples and families in our society. We have tried to capture these new trends and dynamic changes in relationships so that people can be more proactive than reactive as they create their own couple and family relationships.

Ancillary Materials

The sixth edition of *Marriages and Families: Intimacy, Diversity, and Strengths* is accompanied by a number of supplementary learning and teaching aids. Learn more by going to the Online Learning Center Web site at www.mhhe.com/Olson6.

For the Student

AWARE Online. AWARE is a computerized assessment that contains 15 categories that match the chapters in the book. After completing the AWARE Online assessment, the student receives a 19-page *AWARE Personal Report* that identifies relationship areas and issues that are strengths for the student and problematic issues they need to consider. AWARE helps personalize the course by showing students how their current relationship attitudes compare with professionals in the field. It also stimulates students' interest and involvement in the class by highlighting current relationship issues. To learn more about AWARE, go to the Online Learning Center Web site at www.mhhe.com/Olson6.

Student's Online Learning Center (OLC). The Online Learning Center Web site that accompanies this text offers a variety of resources for the student. In addition to various study tools, students will find chapter objectives, chapter summaries, interactive chapter quizzes, annotated lists of Web links, Internet exercises, flashcards of key terms, and census updates. Please visit the text OLC site at www.mhhe.com/Olson6.

Reel Families Interactive Movie CD-ROM. Available as a separate package option, *Reel Families* is a professionally produced, interactive movie on CD-ROM that demonstrates concepts and issues that are important in the study of marriages and families. Each viewer assumes the role of one of the characters and influences key plot turns by making choices for them.

For the Instructor

The password-protected instructor side of the Online Learning Center Web site includes AWARE Online, the Instructor's Manual, Test Bank, Computerized Test Bank, and PowerPoint lecture slides. Go to www.mhhe.com/Olson6.

Instructor's Manual. For each chapter of the text, the Instructor's Manual provides a chapter outline, learning objectives, a chapter summary, a list of key terms, lecture notes, suggested activities, and suggested readings. The manual also includes strategies for using Family Quads (groups of four students who meet throughout the course) in classes, and instructions for the Family Case Study assignments. The Instructor's Manual also can be downloaded from the Instructor's Online Learning Center.

AWARE Online. AWARE is an acronym for **AW**areness of **A**ttitudes and **R**elationship **E**xpectations. AWARE contains 15 categories that match the chapters in the textbook. After the students have completed the AWARE Online assessment, the instructor can view online and print a 20-page *AWARE Instructor Summary.* The summary provides an overview of the background areas, along with the strengths and issues for the class on 15 categories and the Couple and Family Map. There are several advantages for using AWARE with a class.

- First, the instructor can quickly and efficiently learn about the relevant relationship attitudes of the students in the class.
- Second, by knowing the strengths and growth area for the class, the instructor can tailor the class to better serve the needs of that class.
- Third, AWARE provides background information about the students that an instructor could not easily ask in a class.
- Fourth, the instructor can provide the class with summary feedback about their relationship attitudes for each chapter in the book.
- Fifth, AWARE personalizes the class for the students and stimulates their interest and involvement in the class.
- Last, AWARE helps engage the students in the class and facilitates greater class interaction. For more information about AWARE, go to www.mhhe .com/Olson6.

Test Bank. The Test Bank, significantly revised and expanded, offers multiple-choice, true/false, short-answer, and essay questions for each chapter in the text. The Test Bank can be downloaded as a Word file from the Online Learning Center Web site at www.mhhe.com/Olson6. A Computerized Test Bank is also available on the Web site.

PowerPoint Slides. A collection of tables and figures from the text, augmented by additional graphics, allows instructors to add visual content to their lectures. The PowerPoint slides are also available on the Web site.

Instructor's Online Learning Center (OLC). Password-protected, the Instructor's side of the OLC offers chapter objectives, chapter summaries, interactive chapter quizzes, annotated lists of Web links, Internet exercises, flashcards of key terms, and census updates. The Instructor's Manual, PowerPoint slides, and more can be accessed on this Web site at www.mhhe.com/Olson6.

PageOut: The Course Web Site Development Center. Online content for *Marriages and Families* is supported by WebCT, eCollege.com, Blackboard, and other course management systems. Additionally, McGraw-Hill's PageOut service is available to help instructors get their course up and running online in a matter of hours, at no cost. (No programming knowledge is required.) When you use PageOut, your students have instant, 24-hour access to your course syllabus, lecture notes, assignments, and other original material. Students can even check their grades online. Material from the Online Learning Center (OLC) can be pulled into your Web site. PageOut also provides a discussion board where you and your students can exchange questions and post announcements. To find out more about PageOut, ask your McGraw-Hill representative for details or go to http://www .mhhe.com/pageout.

Acknowledgments

We are grateful to the following reviewers for providing us with their helpful comments and suggestions during the development of the sixth edition:

Kevin Bush, Miami University
Scott Gardner, San Diego State University
Cody S. Hollist, University of Nebraska
Kyle L. Kostelecky, University of Northern Iowa
Anna Netterville, Fayetteville Technical Community College
Stacy Ruth, Jones County Community College
Xiaolin Xie, Northern Illinois University

David Olson
John DeFrain
Linda Skogrand

a visual *preview*

Olson, DeFrain, and Skogrand offer students an easy-to-comprehend introduction to the couple and family field. They take a positive approach, focusing on intimacy and diversity from a strengths-based, multidisciplinary perspective. This is reflected in their pedagogy. They present concepts and ideas in a useful and meaningful manner that enables students to *apply* them to their lives.

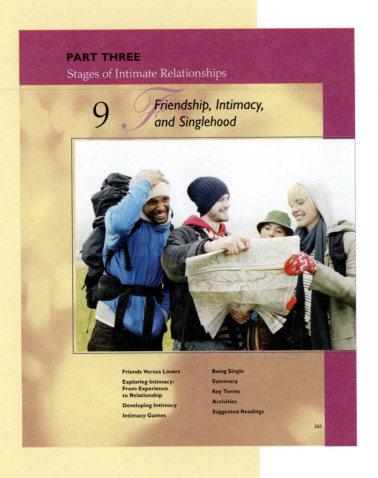

PART THREE
Stages of Intimate Relationships

9 *Friendship, Intimacy, and Singlehood*

Friends Versus Lovers
Exploring Intimacy: From Experience to Relationship
Developing Intimacy
Intimacy Games

Being Single
Summary
Key Terms
Activities
Suggested Readings

243

Chapter Opener and Outline

Each chapter opens with an outline of the major chapter headings, allowing students to preview at a glance the material to be covered.

Thematic Box Program

The box program is organized into four thematic categories that promote and strengthen the authors' emphasis on intimacy, diversity, and strengths.

Self-Assessment Boxes

These boxes allow students to test themselves in a number of areas and thus gain insight into their personal and family relationships. With this insight and knowledge, students are better able to maintain and strengthen these relationships.

Putting It Together Boxes

These boxes provide students with skill-building tools to help them in the development and maintenance of personal and family relationships.

At Issue Boxes

These boxes focus on topical issues affecting individuals and their relationships.

Diversity in Families Boxes

These boxes examine marriage and family issues across cultures and around the world.

Photographs, Illustrations, and Tables

Full-color photos bring the topics and concepts alive for the student. Tables and illustrations, for example, bar graphs and pie charts, bolster the text discussion and encourage critical thinking.

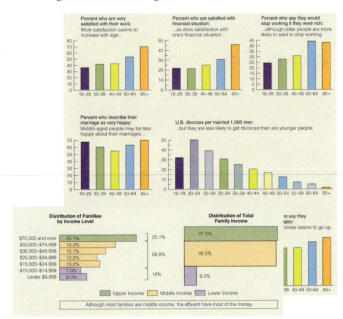

Ethnic Income Differences. While the average annual income for all groups was $42,100, there are considerable income differences across ethnic groups in the United States (Table 8.3). For example, among all types of family households, the median income for Asian families is $55,521; for White families, $45,856; for Black families, $30,439; and for Hispanic families, $33,447. Table 8.3 also indicates that for these three ethnic groups, married couples earn substantially more income than the average in their group and single parents make significantly less.

FIGURE 8.1
Income Levels of U.S. Families, 2002.
Source: U.S. Bureau of the Census, 2003b.

TABLE 8.3	Income Levels by Ethnic Group and Family Structure
Ethnic Group/Type of Family	**Median Income**
All Groups	
All families	$42,100
Married couples	47,129
Female householder, no husband present	21,348
Asian	
All families	$55,521
White	
All families	$45,856
Married couples	47,608
Female householder, no husband present	24,431
Black	
All families	$30,439
Married couples	
Female householder, no husband present	
Hispanic	
All families	
Married couples	
Female householder, no husband present	

Source: U.S. Bureau of the Census, 2

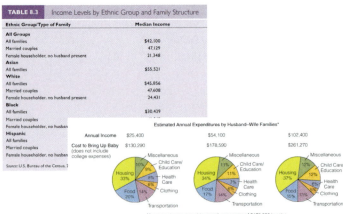

Estimated Annual Expenditures by Husband–Wife Families*

New parents can expect to spend an average of $178,590 to raise their newborn babies to age 17, up from $25,229 in 1960.

*Based on 1990–1992 Consumer Expenditure Survey data updated to 2003 dollars using the Consumer Price Index.

Conflict and Violence in Dating

The incidence of reported violence is 25% for women and 10% for men in dating relationships (Luthra & Gidycz, 2006). Jealousy and differences in level of commitment are only two of numerous causes for conflict between dating partners. These conflicts sometimes result in violent behavior, which can then lead to spouse abuse after marriage.

One young woman from Chicago recounts her experience before and after her wedding:

"I thought it would get better after the wedding. We had planned so long and carefully for it, and I knew the wedding would be wonderful. But even on the day of the wedding, Marty slapped me in the face. I don't know. He was frustrated about something my brother said or something. I don't know.

"After we got married, it really got bad. He would stay out with his friends till all hours and when he came home, if I said even one word about it, he would hit me. Hard. I stayed with him 2 years, but when he pushed me down when I was 7 months pregnant, I couldn't stand it anymore and I left for the domestic violence program shelter. He would have hurt the baby, and I would never have forgiven myself. I ended up leaving town, moving to my sister's in Indianapolis. I didn't have hardly anything . . . Alexis's baby clothes and her toys, my clothes, a small stereo system.

"I didn't have anything, really, but I was free and that was what counted."

Summary

- Communication, the process of sharing messages, is an integral part of intimacy.
- In a national survey of couple communication strengths, happy couples agreed more often than unhappy couples that they were satisfied with how they talked to each other as partners, had no trouble believing each other, felt their partners did not make comments that put them down, were not afraid to ask their partners for what they wanted, and felt free to express their true feelings to their partners.
- The top five communication issues identified by couples in a national survey were the following: They wished their partners would share their feelings; they had difficulty asking their partners for what they wanted; their partners did not understand how they felt; their partners often refused to discuss issues/problems; and their partners made comments that put them down.

- Men and women tend to have different communication styles as a result of culturally established gender roles. Although communication styles can vary greatly from one individual to another, in general, men tend to be more competitive in their communication and women tend to be more focused on connecting emotionally with others.
- Basic principles of communication include the following: One cannot not communicate; the message sent is often not the message received; when communication fails, both people are responsible for the failure; all messages convey both content information and relationship information; nonverbal communication carries about 65% of the meaning in an interpersonal exchange; incongruent verbal and nonverbal communication can cause misunderstanding; and metacommunication (talking about talking) is useful for unbinding double binds.
- Self-disclosure—individual revelations of personal information or feelings—is a key to the development of intimacy.

Chapter 4 | Communication and Intimacy   123

- Assertiveness and self-confidence are key elements of a positive communication cycle. A negative communication cycle is characterized by avoidance and partner dominance.
- The more assertive, and less avoidant partners are, the more satisfying their relationship will be.

Key Terms

communication	directive listening
linear causality model	attentive listening
circular causality model	assertive communication
nonverbal communication	passive communication
mixed message	aggressive communication
double bind	assertiveness
metacommunication	self-confidence
self-disclosure	avoidance
persuasive listening	partner dominance

Activities

1. Study Jane Tear's chart, Conversational Style and Gender, in Table 4.3. In small groups, discuss the hypothesis that men tend to use conversation in a competitive way in an effort to "win," whereas women tend to use conversation to build relationships. Is this true, or is it a stereotype? What are the values and limitations of each style?
2. Because males and females are socialized differently, adult male culture differs somewhat from adult female culture. What can parents do for their children in the early years to minimize confusion and misunderstanding between the sexes later on?
3. Use the Couple and Family Scales in Appendix A to rate the communication in your family of origin now or at some time in the past. Identify the most positive and most negative aspects of that communication.
4. Use the Couple and Family Scales in Appendix A to rate the communication at various stages of a current relationship (friendship, dating, cohabiting, marriage).

passively)
c. Assertive and assertive (both people are assertive)

Suggested Readings

Axtell, R. G. (1999). *Do's and taboos of humor around the world: Stories and tips from business and life.* New York: Wiley. Instructive and highly entertaining.

Christensen, A., Eldridge, K., Bokel Catta-Preta, A., Lim, V. R., & Santagata, R. (2006). Cross-cultural consistency of the demand/withdraw interaction patterns in couples. *Journal of Marriage and the Family, 68,* 1029–1044. A study of couples in Brazil, Italy, Taiwan, and the United States finds that constructive communication was positively associated with relationship satisfaction, whereas demand/withdraw types of communication were negatively associated with relationship satisfaction.

Gottman, J. M. (2001). *The relationship cure.* New York: Three Rivers Press. This book provides information on how to develop "emotional connections" and a stronger couple relationship.

Gottman, J. M., Schwartz Gottman, J., & DeClaire, J. (2006). *Ten lessons to transform your marriage: America's love lab experts share their strategies for strengthening your relationships.* New York: Crown. The latest book from the University of Washington research team.

Knapp, M. L., & Vangelisti, A. L. (2005). *Interpersonal communication and human relationships.* Boston: Allyn & Bacon. Many useful ideas.

Markman, H. J., Stanley, S. M., & Blumberg, S. L. (2001). *Fighting for your marriage.* San Francisco: Jossey-Bass. A very useful book to help build positive communication skills.

Markman, H. J., Stanley, S. M., Jenkins, N. H., & Blumberg, S. L. (2004). *12 hours to a great marriage: A step-by-step guide for making love last.* San Francisco: Jossey-Bass. Most recent popular book from Markman, the marriage communication authority, and his colleagues.

Miller, S., & Miller, P. A. (1997). *Core communication: Skills and processes.* Littleton, CO: Interpersonal Communica-

---

Personal Observations and Accounts

Integrated throughout the chapters as excerpts, these personal observations and accounts help to bridge the gap between the concepts discussed and real-life experiences. They illustrate family dynamics in a variety of situations, settings, and life stages, touching upon such issues as single parenting, sexual intimacy, family violence, managing money, dividing chores, expressing emotions, and adjusting to the death of a family member. They are intended to help students realize how much they share with families elsewhere.

Chapter Summaries, Activities, and Suggested Readings

Each chapter concludes with a bulleted chapter summary highlighting the key points made in the chapter, a list of key terms, activities that students can complete inside and outside the classroom, and suggested readings to encourage further study.

Key Terms and Glossary

The key terms listed at the end of each chapter are defined in the glossary at the end of the book. By visiting the text's Web site, students can test their understanding of these terms by using the chapter-by-chapter flashcards and doing the crossword puzzles.

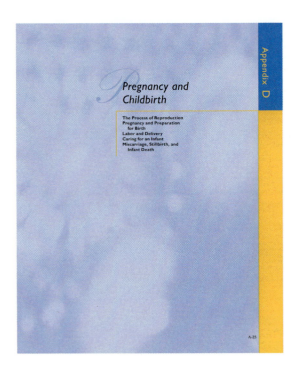

Glossary

A

ability to manage stress and crisis One of the six major qualities (commonly found in emotionally healthy families) identified by researchers working within the family strengths framework.

abortion Expulsion of a fetus from the uterus before it is sufficiently developed to survive on its own; commonly used to describe only artificially induced terminations of pregnancy.

accommodating style A style of conflict resolution characterized by nonassertive but cooperative behavior; accommodators subjugate their own wants and needs to those of others.

acculturation The intermeshing of cultural traits and values with those of the dominant culture.

afterbirth The placenta and fetal membranes, which are expelled from the uterus during the third stage of labor.

ageism A form of prejudice or discrimination in which one judges an older person negatively solely on the basis of age.

aggressive communication A style of interpersonal communication that attempts to hurt or put down the receiver while protecting the aggressor's self-esteem.

agreeing to disagree A negotiating strategy in which two people are unable to agree on opposing courses of action and decide to take neither course of action.

Al-Anon A self-help group for families of alcoholics.

Alateen A support group for young people with alcoholic parents, based on the Alcoholics Anonymous model.

alcohol abuse A generic term that encompasses both alcoholism (addiction to alcohol characterized by compulsive drinking) and problem drinking (alcohol consumption that results in functional disability).

Alcoholics Anonymous (AA) A self-help group for alcoholics.

alcoholism Addiction to alcohol characterized by compulsive drinking.

alimony Court-ordered financial support to a spouse or former spouse following separation or divorce.

ambiguous loss When a family member is physically absent but psychologically present, the family experiences highly stressful feelings. People need to find ways to accept a loss before they can move on through the grieving process, but this is difficult when there is

significant ambiguity in the situation. *See also* boundary ambiguity.

amniotic sac The membrane that encloses the fetus and holds the amniotic fluid, which insulates the fetus.

androgen Any of the hormones that develop and maintain male secondary sex characteristics.

anorgasmia A sexual dysfunction that prevents a woman from having an orgasm.

appreciation and affection One of the six major qualities (commonly found in emotionally healthy families) identified by researchers working within the family strengths framework.

arranged marriage *See* parent-arranged marriage.

assertive communication A style of interpersonal communication that involves expressing one's self-interests and wishes without degrading or putting down the other person.

assertiveness A person's ability to express her or his feelings and desires.

assimilation Adopting the cultural traits and values of the dominant culture.

attentive listening A style of listening focused on fully understanding the speaker's point of view; characterized by encouragement rather than trying to direct or control the speaker.

authoritarian parenting A parenting style characterized by the demand for absolute obedience to rigid rules and the use of punitive, forceful disciplinary measures.

autonomic power pattern A power pattern in a marriage in which both partners have about equal authority but in different areas of life; both make decisions in their particular domains independent of each other.

avoidance A person's tendency to minimize issues and a reluctance to deal with issues directly.

avoidance style A style of conflict resolution characterized by nonassertive and passive behavior; avoiders often withdraw from the conflict or change the subject.

B

balanced families Families who fit into the four central categories of the Couple and Family Map: families who are flexibly connected, flexibly cohesive, structurally connected, or structurally cohesive. *See also* midrange families, unbalanced families.

G-1

Appendix on Pregnancy and Childbirth

This appendix provides information on the process of reproduction; pregnancy and preparation for birth; labor and delivery; caring for an infant; and miscarriage, stillbirth, and infant death.

Appendix D

$\mathscr{P}$*regnancy and Childbirth*

The Process of Reproduction
Pregnancy and Preparation for Birth
Labor and Delivery
Caring for an Infant
Miscarriage, Stillbirth, and Infant Death

A-25

A Dynamic Web Site

Visit our Online Learning Center Web site at www.mhhe.com/olson6 for comprehensive resources. Students will find information on and optional access to AWARE Online, a computerized assessment, as well as a variety of tools such as chapter summaries, interactive chapter quizzes, Web links, Internet exercises, and flashcards of key terms. The password-protected instructor side of the Web site includes the Instructor's Manual, AWARE Online (optional access), Test Bank, Computerized Test Bank, and PowerPoint lecture slides.

PART ONE
The Social Context of Intimate Relationships

1 *Perspectives on Intimate Relationships*

Three Themes of Intimacy, Strengths, and Diversity

Defining Marriage and Family

Trends in Marriage and the Family: Change and Continuity

Focus on Marital and Family Strengths

Advantages of Marriage

Impact of the Social Environment on Relationships

Changing the Social Environment

Positive Responses to the Social Environment

Summary

Key Terms

Activities

Suggested Readings

Three Themes of Intimacy, Strengths, and Diversity

Most people need *intimate relationships* with other people. Intimacy is sharing intellectually, physically, and/or emotionally with another person. In this text we will focus on intimacy in marriage and family relationships and on how they are maintained and how they become broken.

Intimacy usually occurs when individuals disclose information about themselves, allowing themselves to become vulnerable, and involves trusting the other person will not use that information to cause harm. Sharing information that involves intimacy usually results in receiving support from that person or persons.

Intimacy will be discussed throughout this book in terms of dating and courtship, sexual relationships, communication, dealing with conflict, and other aspects of marriage and couple relationships. Intimacy may look different at different times in the life cycle. In addition to having intimacy in couple relationships, intimacy occurs in parent–child relationships, relationships with extended family, and relationships with others who take the place of family. Most intimate relationships go through periods when that closeness is threatened or destroyed. Our goal is to provide you with ideas and exercises to help you improve your ability to develop and maintain intimate relationships over time.

Identifying and focusing on *strengths* and building on those strengths are essential for developing and maintaining marriage relationships. Studies conducted by John Gottman and colleagues demonstrate that focusing on strengths is critical for healthy marriage relationships (Gottman & DeClaire, 2001; Gottman & Silver, 1994b, 1999). In fact, Gottman suggests that in happy marriages partners give each other at least five compliments for each negative comment.

The family strengths perspective provides evidence from the United States and 27 other countries from around the world that families that do well have qualities that contribute to making families strong (DeFrain, 2006). All families can identify their strengths—and all families have strengths—and those strengths can be a foundation for continued growth. When one only looks at problems in marriages and families, that is what one will find. In addition, looking for what makes families strong helps us use that knowledge to help other families. The strong families become the experts in teaching others.

Focusing and building on strengths in relationships will be evident throughout this book in relation to couples, marriage relationships, single-parent families, gay and lesbian relationships and families, parenting practices, relationships in diverse cultures, and life in the middle and later years.

There is more *diversity* in family and couple relationships than ever before. There are a variety of family structures that are described in this book, including married couples, cohabiting couples, gay and lesbian couples, single-parent families, stepfamilies, and grandparents raising grandchildren. There is also greater cultural and ethnic diversity in the United States than ever before, with minority cultural groups becoming a greater proportion of the total population. These cultural groups bring a wide array of values, beliefs, and practices to our understanding of how marriages and families work. It is increasingly challenging to understand the diversity of couple and family relationships that exist today and will continue to increase in the future.

The three themes of intimacy, strengths, and diversity are critical in understanding couple and family relationships today. These themes and the research and literature surrounding these themes are critical for developing healthy and happy relationships. Knowledge about the latest research in each of these areas will help you develop healthy relationships and better understand and appreciate those around you.

Defining Marriage and Family

Not as many people today live in the so-called traditional family, with a dad at work and a mom at home with the kids—only about 25% of all families in the United States match this model. In addition to the diverse types of family structure, families may vary in cultural or ethnic background, income, size, and longevity. There are many possible family structures rather than one "right" way for a family to be organized.

What Is Marriage?

Marriage is by nature a multifaceted institution. We define **marriage** as *the emotional and legal commitment of two people to share emotional and physical intimacy, various tasks, and economic resources.*

The following nine characteristics of marriage were identified by Carlfred Broderick (1992, 1993). A former president of the National Council on Family Relations, Broderick found these characteristics to be common across income levels, educational levels, and ethnic and cultural groups in the United States:

- *Marriage is a demographic event.* Each marriage creates a social unit in society.
- *Marriage is the joining of two family and social networks.* When individuals marry, they marry not only each other but their partner's family and friends. Their social network may comprise friends of both partners, but only those friends liked by both partners tend to remain friends of the couple.
- *Marriage is a legal contract between the couple and the state.* Each state specifies the rights and responsibilities of the partners.
- *Marriage is an economic union.* A married couple usually becomes a single financial unit for most purposes. As a group, married couples are probably society's most important financial decision makers—buying, selling, borrowing, and sharing resources as one.
- *Marriage is the most common living arrangement for adults.* Few people choose to live alone. Marriage is by far the most popular living arrangement for adults.
- *Marriage is the context of most human sexual activity.* Most married couples rate sexual activity positively, especially in the early years.
- *Marriage is a reproductive unit.* Most married couples become parents and see parenting as an important goal and a valued purpose in their lives.
- *Marriage is a unit that socializes children* (although children can also be raised by single parents, extended families, grandparents, and other caregivers).
- *Marriage is an opportunity to develop an intimate, sharing relationship.* Although many marriages fail, many others provide a supportive context in which people develop and maintain intimacy.

Same-sex couples have full marriage rights in several European countries, including the Netherlands, Belgium, and Spain, and in Canada (Herek, 2006). Currently, Massachusetts is the only state that allows same-sex marriages.

In the United States gay and lesbian families rose 300% between 1990 and 2000 (Deen, 2005). In 2005, gay and lesbian households accounted for 4.2% of all households (Family Focus, 2005). Whether these same-sex couples should be allowed to have couple relationships equal to marriage is controversial. There have been legal battles in many states as proponents of same-sex marriages have come up against religious groups who have tried to pass statutes and constitutional amendments banning same-sex couple relationships.

Several states have sanctioned civil unions, which do not provide the same privileges as marriage, but allow for limited couple benefits, such as access to group health insurance plans, parental and adoption rights, and inheritance rights. Although civil unions are considered acceptable by most of the public (53%), a minority (36%) are in favor of allowing same-sex couples to marry (Pew Research Center for the People and the Press, 2005). The debate over same-sex marriages is likely to continue for several years to come.

What Is a Family?

Family can be defined in many ways. One dictionary offers the following definitions (*American Heritage Dictionary of the English Language,* 2000):

1. A fundamental social group in society typically consisting of one or two parents and their children.
2. Two or more people who share goals and values, have long-term commitments to one another, and reside usually in the same dwelling place.
3. All the members of a household under one roof.
4. A group of persons sharing common ancestry.

There are innumerable other definitions of family and following is a collection that represents a diversity of definitions:

- The term *family* refers to a group of two or more persons related by birth, marriage, or adoption and residing together in a household. A family includes among its members the householders (U.S. Bureau of the Census, 2002c, p. 6).
- Family is a group of people who love and care for each other (conventional wisdom).
- A family is defined as two or more persons who share resources, share responsibility for decisions, share values and goals, and have a commitment to one another over time (American Association of Family and Consumer Sciences, 2004).
- Families provide emotional, physical, and economic mutual aid to their members. Ideally, such families are characterized by intimacy, intensity, continuity, and commitment among their members (Alliance for Children and Families, 2004).
- The definition of a family "should not rest on fictitious legal distinctions or genetic history" but instead should be based on the functional and psychological qualities of the relationship: the "exclusivity and longevity" of

Strong families are good for raising healthy and happy children. Extended families are a great source of support in raising children.

relationship; the "level of emotional and financial commitment"; the "reliance placed upon one another for daily family services"; and how the couple (members) "conducted their everyday lives and held themselves out to society" (New York State Administrative Regulations, 1995).

- Definitions of the family vary along a continuum with biological conceptions on one end of the continuum and social conceptions on the other

(Holtzman, 2005). Having a child through birth would be on the biological end and adopting a child would be on the social end of the continuum. Both are legitimate definitions of family.

• Call it a clan, call it a network, call it a tribe, call it a family. Whatever you call it, whoever you are, you need one (Howard, 2002).

Any definition of **family** should be broad enough to encompass a range of family structures, dynamics, and functions. *Our definition of family is two or more people who are committed to each other and who share intimacy, resources, decision-making responsibilities, and values.* This definition is inclusive and allows for diversity in family structure, family values, and ethnic groups. At a Wimbledon tennis match, sisters Venus and Serena Williams were going to play each other and a sports writer asked, "Will this match hurt your relationship with your family?" The immediate answer was: "Tennis is just a game. Families are forever."

Trends in Marriage and the Family: Change and Continuity

What are marriage and the family like today? Current trends include fewer marriages, later age of marriage, fewer children, continued flattening of divorce rates, more single-parent families and stepfamilies, a greater need for day care, more child abuse, more spouse abuse, and less connection to kin networks (Popenoe & Whitehead, 1999b, 2005).

Statistics on divorce, domestic violence, and alcohol and other drug abuse, as well as stories of families in crisis, paint a rather negative picture of marriage and family life today. These snapshots of troubled families may be newsworthy, but the situations they describe are not new. For decades, many respected social scientists have predicted that the institutions of marriage and the family would not

Strong families enjoy leisure activities together.

survive. For example, in 1927, psychologist John B. Watson predicted, "In 50 years, unless there is some change, the tribal custom of marriage will no longer exist." He believed marriage would disappear because family standards had broken down. In 1937, Pitirim Sorokin, a respected Harvard sociologist, wrote, "The family as a sacred union of husband and wife, of parents and children, will continue to disintegrate." Ten years later, Carl Zimmerman, also a Harvard sociologist, noted, "There is little left now, within the family itself or the moral code, to hold the family together" (Bernard, 1970, p. 42).

Although some professionals emphasize the decline of marriage and the family, others see them as being in a state of transition. As Ernest Burgess and his colleagues stated in 1954, "Certainly marriage and the family in the U.S. are in the process of rapid change. But is it change for the worse? Perhaps it may be for the better" (Bernard, 1970, p. 43). In a similar vein, David and Vera Mace, pioneers in the marriage and family enrichment movement in Great Britain and the United States, argued that "marriage has not failed—it is simply in transition" (Mace & Mace, 1980, p. 260). Skolnick and Skolnick (1977), in their classic study *Family in Transition*, clearly illustrated the dramatic changes in family life over the centuries. In fact, one of the salient characteristics of the family is its ability to adapt to changing times and new challenges.

Pessimists and optimists disagree about how to interpret these trends and what to do about them. The pessimists see recent changes as an indication that marriage and family are in serious trouble and are declining in their significance to society. They believe that we need to return to a more traditional value system to curtail these negative trends. The optimists, on the other hand, see recent changes as a reflection of the flexibility of marriage and family and the ability of these institutions to adapt to the increasing stresses of modern life. They believe marriage and the family will survive and thrive.

In fact, marriage and the family have survived over time despite all the predictions of their imminent collapse. Moreover, marriage remains the most popular voluntary institution in our society, with about 85% of the population marrying at least once (Popenoe & Whitehead, 2004).

Trends in Marriage and Cohabitation

There are several important trends in the United States that will be briefly described in this section: a decline in the percentage of those who are married, an increase in the number of those delaying marriage until they are older, an increase in the number of the never married, and an increase in the number of couples who choose to cohabit before—or instead of—marrying.

Marriage. Although marriage remains popular in the United States, it is not as popular as it once was. The percentage of people over the age of 18 who are married has steadily declined. In 1970, 68% of adults were married; in 1980, 66%; in 1990, 62%; and about 60% in 2000 (see Figure 1.1). In 2006, homes headed by married couples dipped to 49.7% (Roberts, 2006). This is the first time that married-couple households dipped below 50%, thus making married couples a minority in the United States. There are two reasons for this change: Many couples are choosing to stay single longer or are choosing to cohabit. There are also increased numbers of elderly people who have lost their spouse, which is adding to the number of single-family households. In addition, there are increasing numbers of same-sex couples who are not typically counted as being married.

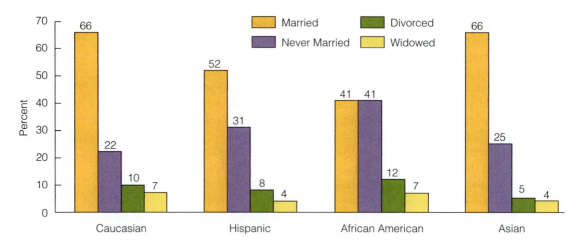

FIGURE 1.1

Marital Status of U.S. Population

Source: U.S. Bureau of the Census, 2005e, table 54.

More individuals are delaying marriage until their late 20s. Today, the median age for first marriage is 27 years for men and 26 years for women, the oldest in U.S. history (Popenoe & Whitehead, 2005). Age at marriage has been on the increase for more than four decades. In 1960, the median age for a first marriage was 22.8 years for men and 20.3 years for women.

Cohabitation. More than half of all couples cohabit before marriage, and cohabitation is becoming more acceptable. Although cohabitation was once rare, a majority of young men and women of marriageable age will live together without being married for some time, and about 40% of all children before reaching age 16 will spend some time in a cohabiting family (Bumpass & Lu, 1998, 2000a). The number of cohabiting couples has increased 800% since the 1960s, when fewer than 500,000 were cohabiting. There were 2.5 million couples living together in 1988, 3.5 million cohabiting in 1993, 4.7 million couples cohabiting in 2000, and 5.5 million couples in 2003 (U.S. Bureau of the Census, 2003b, 2004c). Recent research indicates that measurements to determine cohabitation are probably inadequate and that the percentage of couples who cohabit is actually underreported because the language used for reporting is not universally understood (Manning & Smock, 2005).

Trends in Divorce and Remarriage

Although marriage is still popular, it is not necessarily lasting, with about half of all recent marriages in the United States ending in divorce. However, the majority of those getting divorced will remarry.

Divorce. Almost 20 million Americans—about 9.9% of the U.S. population—are currently divorced (U.S. Bureau of the Census, 2001g). On the basis of current trends, about 50% of all recent U.S. marriages are likely to end in divorce (U.S. Bureau of the Census, 2001g). And even though 50% survive, the quality of some of those marriages may be poor (Popenoe & Whitehead, 1999b). In many lasting marriages, one partner is unhappy; typically, it is the wife who is more unhappy than

Cohabitation was once rare, but today a majority of young men and women of marriageable age live together without being married for some time, and about 40% of all children before reaching age 16 will spend some time in a cohabiting family.

the husband. A respected sociologist, Norval Glenn (1996), predicted that after 10 years of marriage only about 25% of the couples will still be happily married, which is a substantial decrease from the past.

The divorce rate climbed during the 1960s and 1970s, but it has stabilized today at about 50% for first marriages (Popenoe & Whitehead 2005). About 75% of those who divorce will later remarry, but approximately 60% of those remarrying will get divorced again (U.S. Bureau of the Census, 2000b). Because of this marriage–remarriage cycle, marriage patterns in our society are increasingly moving toward what anthropologist Margaret Mead originally described as serial monogamy.

Why are there so many divorces and unhappy marriages in our society? First, many people enter marriage with unrealistic expectations. Second, many marry the wrong person for the wrong reasons. Third, marriage is a challenging type of relationship, even if one chooses a partner wisely. Fourth, little time or effort is put into developing the relationship skills needed to maintain a strong marriage.

Remarriage. Only 54% of those who marry each year are doing so for the first time. In 23% of marriages, both the bride and the groom have been married before, and in the remaining 23%, it is the first marriage for one partner and a remarriage for the other person (U.S. Bureau of the Census, 2001g).

After divorce, men tend to remarry more quickly and more often than do women. The majority of younger divorced men and women, however, do remarry. According to one survey, 72% of recently divorced women remarried (Glick, 1989), but the rate of remarriage decreased as the number of children increased. About 81% of divorced women with no children remarried, 73% of women with one or two children remarried, and only 57% of women with three or more children remarried. In other words, the more children a woman has, the less likely she is to remarry. Table 1.1 provides some statistics on marriage and divorce trends. Divorce and remarriage will be discussed in greater detail in Chapter 15.

TABLE 1.1	Statistics on Marriage and Divorce

- Marriage is still very much a part of American life. The vast majority of men and women in 2000 had been married by the time they reached age 35, and by age 65 about 95% of men and women had been married (U.S. Bureau of the Census, 2002c).
- There were 2.3 million marriages and 1.2 million divorces in 2000 (U.S. Bureau of the Census, 2002c).
- People marrying today have a 50% chance of divorcing (Popenoe & Whitehead, 2004).
- The median age for first marriage is 27 years for men and 26 years for women (U.S. Bureau of the Census, 2005b).
- The average age of remarriage is 36 years for men and 33 years for women (U.S. Bureau of the Census, 2005b).
- First marriages for both the bride and the groom account for only 54% of marriages each year (U.S. Bureau of the Census, 2003b).
- Most divorces involved children, and more than 1 million children are affected by divorce each year in the United States (U.S. Bureau of the Census, 2003b).
- Most divorced individuals eventually remarry. For younger divorced individuals, this remarriage typically occurs within 5 years of divorce (U.S. Bureau of the Census, 2003b).

Trends in Family Structure

Family structure is becoming more complex through divorce and remarriage, which creates new kinship relationships. Contemporary families are more varied today than ever before. There are stepfamilies, same-sex parents and couples, child-free couples, grandparents raising grandchildren, surrogate parents, foster care families, families with disabled parents and children, and a variety of informal family arrangements (Halpern, 2005).

The following trends illustrate some of the changes in family structure in the United States:

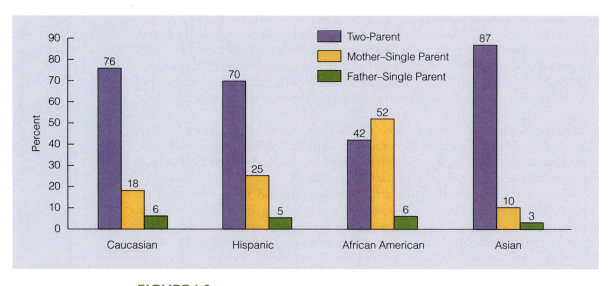

FIGURE 1.2
Family Structures with Children Under 18
Source: U.S. Bureau of the Census 2005b, table 62.

Single-parent families with children under the age of 18 have dramatically increased since 1970.

- In 2002, 69% of all children lived in a nuclear family in which two parents were present. The percentage of two-parent families varies by ethnic/cultural group (Figure 1.2): 76% of Caucasian children live in two-parent homes; 70% of Hispanics; 42% of African American children; and 87% of Asian American Children (Fields, 2003, pp. 3, 5; U.S. Bureau of the Census, 2005b).
- Single-parent families with children under the age of 18 have dramatically increased in number. In 1970, only 12% of children lived in a single-parent home. In 1980, this number had increased to 22%; and by 1990, to 28%. In 2005, the number of single-parent families had risen to an all-time high of 37% (Hamilton, Martin, & Ventura, 2006).
- About half (52%) of all African American families are headed by a single mother, while 25% of Hispanic families, 18% of Caucasian families, and 10% of Asian American families are headed by a single mother (Fields, 2003, p. 5). A small but growing number of families in the United States (3% to 6% of families across ethnic/cultural groups) are headed by a single father (Fields, 2003, p. 5; U.S. Bureau of the Census, 2005b). Some social scientists have predicted that 60% of children in the United States will have lived in a single-parent household by the time they are 18 years old if current divorce and remarriage rates hold.
- Families are typically having fewer children today, compared to earlier generations. A woman in the early 1900s in the United States could expect to give birth to about four children during her childbearing years, considered

to be ages 15 to 44. A woman living during the Great Depression of the 1930s could expect to have only two children. After World War II, the number of births per woman climbed to 3.7 in 1957, but fell to 1.8 by the mid-1970s. Since then, the birth rate in the United States has hovered around two births per woman over the past 20 years. This is a rate that is slightly below the long-term replacement level (U.S. Bureau of the Census, 2004b, p. 4-1).

- The number of stay-at-home moms has been on the decline since the 1950s, with more and more women choosing to enter the workforce. There has been a recent reversal of that trend, however, with 55% of mothers with infants in the labor force in 2002, down from 59% in 1998 (Family Focus, 2005).

Continuity in Marriage and the Family

Although we tend to focus on how marriage and the family have changed, in many ways these institutions have remained the same over several decades and continue to provide stability in our lives. For example, most people in the United States want to marry, and most couples who do so see marriage as a lifelong commitment and do not plan to divorce. Many couples want to have an egalitarian marital relationship, but equality does not mean that they will share exactly the same roles around the house. Rather, equality means that they work together to accomplish the many tasks and responsibilities required by family life on a regular basis and divide these responsibilities fairly.

Most couples who marry want to have children. Parenthood is an important goal for many couples, a fact that becomes more evident when a couple is not able to have a child. Most parents want their children to have a good education and to be at least as successful as they, the parents, are in society. In fact, most parents would like their children to do better than they have in all aspects of life.

Most family members also have a commitment to each other, although they might not always get along. They have an emotional connection to their immediate and extended family network and feel it is appropriate to call on them in times of need. This family network is an important support system, although it is often taken for granted until a crisis arises. The family is an interdependent system of people who are emotionally connected to each other.

Most families also have a value system that encompasses spiritual and/or moral beliefs that provide the foundation for their attitudes and behaviors. These values become even more important to couples after they have children or in times of crisis. Also, there is an ongoing commitment and connection between parents and their children, even after divorce. This is particularly true if the parents are given joint custody of their children. Most people also feel that the family is the most effective and efficient way of socializing children.

In summary, marriage and family provide significant continuity in our society. Unfortunately, emphasis on marriage and family problems can overshadow the stability and continuity that these intimate relationships offer us in our daily lives.

Focus on Marital and Family Strengths

A major theme of this book is strengths and the importance of focusing on strengths in a marriage and a family. This means paying attention to the good things your partner or children do and giving praise for the things you appreciate. Too often,

BOX 1.1 Putting It Together

Learning to Focus on Strengths

Over the past 30 years, researchers looking at couples and families from a strengths perspective have developed a number of propositions derived from their work with families around the world that they believe merit serious consideration:

- Families, in all their remarkable diversity, are the basic foundation of human cultures.
- All families have strengths. If one looks only for problems in a family, one will see only problems.
- It's not about structure, it's about function.
- Strong marriages are the center of many strong families.
- Strong families tend to produce great kids, and a good place to look for great kids is in strong families.
- If you grew up in a strong family as a child, it will probably be easier for you to create a strong family of your own as an adult.

- The relationship between money and family strengths is shaky, at best.
- Strengths develop over time.
- Strengths are often developed in response to challenges.
- Strong families don't tend to think much about their strengths, they just live them.
- Strong families, like people, are not perfect.
- When seeking to unite groups of people, communities, and even nations, uniting around the cause of strengthening families—a cause we can all sanction—can be a powerful strategy.
- Human beings have the right and responsibility to feel safe, comfortable, happy, and loved. Strong families are where this all happens.

Source: DeFrain, 2006.

married couples and family members tend to shift their focus from the positive to the things they do not like about each other.

Box 1.1 summarizes a number of important observations about relationship strengths. This includes the idea that all families have strengths and you will observe them if you look for them rather than look for problems. A strong marriage is the foundation for a strong family. This does not mean that single-parent families cannot be strong, but it is often harder for one parent to manage all the stressors and maintain the strengths. Strengths develop over time and are tested by struggles and ongoing issues that inevitably arise in marriage and parenting. Strengths also provide a framework for dealing with crises and for growing and changing over time.

Advantages of Marriage

Although people are delaying marriage and some are choosing not to marry, most people still value marriage. In a recent survey of adults, 93% rate having a happy marriage as one of the most important or very important objectives (Waite, 2001, 2003; Waite & Gallagher, 2000; Waite & Lehrer, 2003). For college freshmen, 94% said they personally hoped to get married and they had a negative view of divorce. Over 70% agreed that children do better with both parents, and over 60% felt that children develop more emotional problems if their parents divorce.

But until recently, the positive impacts of marriage on the persons in the marriage have not been emphasized. Linda Waite and Maggie Gallagher (2000) made a major contribution in that regard in their book *The Case for Marriage* where they summarized over 200 studies that clearly demonstrated the major positive impacts of marriage.

First, Waite and Gallagher (2000) found that married people live longer than unmarried or divorced people. In fact, Waite and Gallagher stated, "Not being married can be hazardous to your health" (2000, p. 47). Nonmarried women have 50%

higher mortality rates than married women, and nonmarried men have a 250% higher rate than married men.

Married people live longer partially because they lead a healthier lifestyle. Single men typically engage in more risky behavior, including drinking, smoking, and drug use. Although single women typically have lower levels of risky behavior compared to men, being married also lowers the rate at which women participate in unhealthy behaviors. In addition, marriage improves a man's health as well as a woman's health. Married partners also tend to monitor each other's health more closely than cohabiting couples.

Married people are happier than single, widowed, or cohabiting people. About 40% of married people said they were very happy with their lives, whereas only 18% of divorced people, 15% of separated people, and 22% of widowed and 22% of cohabiting people were very happy.

On the basis of two national surveys, married couples have sex more frequently and find their sexual relationship more satisfying physically and emotionally than singles (Waite & Gallagher, 2000). In one study, 43% of the married men reported having sex at least twice a week, whereas only 26% of the single men who were not cohabiting had sex this often. The findings were similar for women; very few married women reported never having sex. Almost half (48%) of married men said sex is extremely satisfying emotionally compared to 37% of cohabiting men who found sex satisfying. There was less of a difference for married women compared to cohabiting women (42% for married versus 39% for cohabiting) who reported that sex was extremely satisfying.

Married sex is better sex because of four factors that include *proximity, a long-term contract, exclusivity, and emotional bonding* (Waite & Gallagher, 2000). In terms of proximity, being married means your partner is more available and partners are more comfortable with each other. Because they plan to remain married, married couples are often more willing to invest time, money, and energy in the relationship. By being more sexually exclusive, married couples are more willing to develop a mutually agreeable relationship. Emotionally, married couples feel more connected to each other than cohabiting couples.

Being married is also good for men in regard to their career and financial earnings, according to Waite and Gallagher (2000). They argue that marriage is almost as important as education in predicting a man's success in a career. Their explanation of why this is so may raise the hackles of some readers, so let's discuss what they are saying in some depth. Why would marriage statistically predict a man's success in a career as much as his level of education? Waite and Gallagher propose that many married men are more successful because they can focus more on earning money and know that other tasks such as meals, laundry, and child care will be handled by their wives. Also, a wife often contributes ideas about her husband's job and generally supports the career of the husband.

The controversy ignites when wives don't feel equally supported in their careers, of course. And if an egalitarian relationship is not created—a genuinely 50/50 marriage—a couple runs the risk of ending up with two marriages, rather than one. Jessie Bernard, an eminent family sociologist explained her two-marriages concept quite compellingly more than three decades ago in her classic book *The Future of Marriage* (1972). Bernard argued that marriage was simply better for men than for women, because women take care of men but men in a male-dominant society aren't as willing or capable or inclined to take care of women. She argued that in many cases there are two marriages: *his* marriage and *her* marriage, and his marriage is a much better deal because the wife attends to the husband's needs with more energy and interest than the husband attends to her.

The argument looks like this behind closed doors, and it is still being fought today:

She: "Well, I took your suits to the laundromat and got them cleaned and pressed. And I got a great present for your secretary's birthday. Oh, your Mom called, and I told her you were too busy to go out to dinner this week, but I would take her to lunch Friday."

He [distracted as he looks through the mail]: "Oh, yeah, thanks. . . ."

She [miffed as blood pressure rises]: "I could use a good wife!"

He [startled and angered by her sarcasm, responds in kind]: "You couldn't afford one!" And on and on.

The concept of two marriages helps explain why women today are more likely to file for divorce than men: In essence, more women feel let down by marriage than men. The solution, of course, is not to bog down in *his* marriage and *her* marriage, but to work together to create *our* marriage. This, however, is no simple task.

Waite and Gallagher (2000) also argue that married couples accumulate more financial wealth, which is a total of their assets (home, car, investments, savings) after deducting their debts (mortgages, other loans, credit card debt). Married couples are able to combine their incomes, which is helpful in as much as more women work outside the home and increasingly are earning as much as or more than the husband. This pooling effect is worth 12% to 14% for couples at the age of 30 and it increases to 30% for retired couples compared to single individuals. Married couples are also more responsible in their spending because they have another person involved in the decision about spending. Conversely, if a person gets divorced the wealth is divided and each person starts over again.

Married people, especially women, are less likely to experience domestic abuse than cohabiting and separated women. The abuse rate for separated women is about 3 times higher than that for divorced women and 25 times higher than that for married women. Also, arguments between couples tend to lead to physical abuse in 4% of married couples compared to 13% for cohabiting couples.

Children generally fare better in families where their parents are married (Manning & Brown, 2006). Children from homes where the parents are married tend to be more academically successful, more emotionally stable, and more often assume leadership roles. This is, in part, because of the stability and guidance of two parents. Also, a married couple can model communication and collaborative behaviors, which helps childhood learning.

Marriage is much different from cohabitation (Waite & Gallagher, 2000). Cohabitation is seen by society and partners as a temporary arrangement, whereas marriage is still seen as a lifelong commitment. Marriage is seen as a sexually exclusive relationship, and cohabitation is perceived as more sexually open to others. People who are cohabiting are typically less willing than married couples to be financially responsible for their partners. For married couples there are higher expectations to be seen and to operate as a couple socially than is true for cohabiting couples. Cohabiting couples have less-positive attitudes toward marriage and more-positive attitudes toward divorce than married couples.

In summary, marriage seems to have multiple benefits for both the husband and the wife. Married people live longer, are healthier and happier, and feel better emotionally. They also have more sex and a better sexual relationship. Married people are also more successful in their careers, earn more, and have more wealth.

Married women experience less domestic abuse. Children raised by married parents tend to be more emotionally stable and academically successful. So, in many ways, married persons do experience numerous positive outcomes from being married that single and cohabiting couples do not receive.

Impact of the Social Environment on Relationships

Human beings do not live and love in a vacuum. Just as we are connected to the special people in our lives—our friends and loved ones—so we are inextricably embedded in our social environment. The **social environment** comprises all the factors in society, both positive and negative, that impact on individuals and their relationships, such as the mass media, the Internet, changing gender roles, and growing urban crowding. As individuals, we have a modest influence on society, yet society clearly shapes our personal attitudes and behaviors and ultimately our couple and family relationships.

There is emerging interest about the interface between individual and family lives and community life. For example, one study showed that when neighborhood factors were controlled, African American students were less likely to drop out of school than White students (Van Dorn, Bowen, & Blau, 2006). Bámaca, Umaña-Taylor, Shin, and Alfaro (2005) found that psychological outcomes for Latino adolescents were related to community assets, with more positive outcomes occurring in neighborhoods that had more assets. This occurred even when parenting influences stayed the same. Other researchers found that problem behaviors for African American children decreased when social assets in the neighborhood increased (Caughy, O'Campo, Nettles, & Lohrfink, 2006). It has also been found that the incidence of teen cohabitation and nonmarital births increased as ties with the community decreased (Houseknecht & Lewis, 2005). These studies make it apparent that there is an interface between families and the communities in which they live.

We may be drawn to the Western ideal of rugged individualism—going boldly where no man or woman has gone before—but the reality of our lives is probably closer to the East Asian notion that each of us is but a drop of water in the ocean of life. Cultural norms and expectations have a powerful impact on us, especially if we try to behave against these norms. Visiting another culture is one way to experience the pervasive influence the social environment has on our lives, as the following personal account illustrates.

"When my husband and I were living in China, everything was so different from what we were used to: the language, the food, the music, the dress, everything. Now this is a hard thing to explain to someone who has not already experienced it, but being out of my own culture, my own environment, I started to feel after a few months in China like my identity as a person was disappearing.

"It was like I was shrinking. Without my family and my friends at home, without our dog Jessie, without my music, without my food, without our crummy old car, I felt so disconnected, so insignificant. One day I would have given $50 for a cheeseburger. It sounds crazy talking about it now.

"We both finally did adjust pretty well to China. After about a year or so I kind of turned an emotional corner. And after 2 years I felt like an old hand at surviving culture shock. Today, I love China. But we also love home. And I learned something very important from all this: The social environment I'm used to is very, very important to me. I felt like a fish out of water for a while when taken away from what's familiar to me. I'm not the great individualist I thought I was."

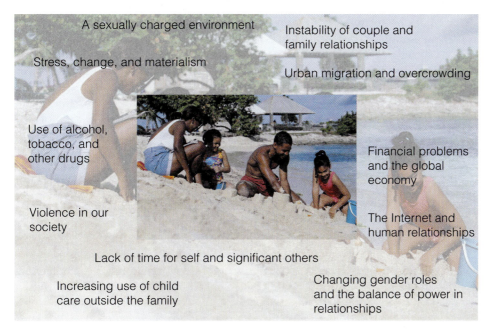

A sexually charged environment

Instability of couple and family relationships

Stress, change, and materialism

Urban migration and overcrowding

Use of alcohol, tobacco, and other drugs

Financial problems and the global economy

Violence in our society

The Internet and human relationships

Lack of time for self and significant others

Increasing use of child care outside the family

Changing gender roles and the balance of power in relationships

Although families work
and play together to create
a haven in a sometimes
bewildering world,
countless elements in the
social environment can
challenge a family's drive
for balance and stability.

In general, the social environment shapes us much more than we can shape the social environment. However, we are not puppets of the social environment. Growing up in an alcoholic family is not an excuse for being an alcoholic. Similarly, being abused as a child does not justify abusing one's own children. Countless people grow up in violent families but are able to rise above those life experiences. Individuals can make positive choices in their lives, regardless of their past lives.

The good news is that people are beginning to be more proactive in building stronger marriages and family. Surveys regularly indicate that the majority of Americans think their marriages and families are doing well. There are many elements in our social environment today that pose difficult challenges for couples and families. In this section, we will discuss a variety of issues that affect our close relationships (Figure 1.3) and describe some ways you can counter these negative influences with more positive approaches.

Stress, Change, and Materialism

"Whatever you're doing," one anonymous observer noted, "it's not enough." The velocity of life in this country appears to many people to be increasing exponentially, and our inner demons press us to perform, to produce, to consume, to move. These voices accelerate as social change presses upon us. **Stress** is the body and mind's reaction to life. Stress is directly related to change, and the greater the change, the higher the level of stress. The continuous cascade of new developments in society today can be defined broadly as progress, but many of these developments add stress to our lives.

We now want and expect things to happen fast. We now have voice mail and e-mail and we even call regular mail snail mail. We used to have telephones in our homes and offices. Now we carry them in our pockets, purses, packs, and attached to our belts. We also do multiple tasks at one time. We drive cars, talk on the phone, put on our makeup, sing along with the CD player, eat a cheeseburger, and plan our day. Not only have these technological changes increased the volume of information we receive and must respond to, but the time in which we are expected to respond has been shortened—from a few days to return a letter to a few hours to return an e-mail to seconds as we answer our ubiquitous cell phones.

As a society, we also have a great appetite for material possessions—for *stuff*. In fact, everything has to be new, if we were to believe media sales pitches: We need new cars, new houses, new clothes, perhaps a new nose. The business world is brimming with stories of corporate takeovers and downsizing. Companies come and go every day, and workers are cast off like old furniture. In this kind of consumer culture, it's not such a stretch to imagine that finding a new partner is the easiest option when there are problems with the old relationship.

Combined, technology and materialism increase our level of stress in all areas of life. We feel pressured to do more and to have more—and to run faster while grasping for all of it. The first casualty in such an environment is our individual sense of well-being. The second casualty is our bond of affection and closeness with each other.

You can counter these trends by being more proactive in your personal life. You can look for ways to be less materialistic and less caught up in the hectic pace of life. This is a personal choice that you can make, which will influence how much you let these factors affect you.

Lack of Time for Oneself and Significant Others

According to family researchers, one of the most difficult qualities to develop in many American families is the ability to spend enjoyable time together. Not only do we find ourselves challenged by a busy and competitive social environment outside the home, but once we return home, we need time to unwind from a hectic day before reconnecting with others.

For many in today's society, the boundaries between the home and work are being blurred. As sociologist Arlie Hochschild (1997) observed, work becomes more like home and home becomes more like work. Caught in the time bind, the more time we work, the more stressful home life becomes. The more stressful home life becomes, the more we want to escape back to work. Hochschild argues that we must challenge the economic and social system that invites or demands long hours at work, and focus our efforts on investing less time in the job and more time in one's couple and family relationships.

Families that have discretionary income can purchase labor such as child care and people who care for the household in order to free up time for families to eat out or engage in recreational or leisure activities. Low-income families may not have the option to purchase services and experience greater challenges in finding time for themselves and other family members. Researchers have found that low-income families are less likely to spend time in activities outside the home but instead intentionally build relationship time into mealtime and other household activities (Tubbs, Roy, & Burton, 2005).

You can counter these trends by purposefully setting time aside for yourself and also time to be with your significant others. Some people have found their alone time is to have 15 minutes with coffee in the morning; others look for time alone at the end of the day, going for an hour-long walk or exercising at the recreation center. For couples, it is important that they purposefully find time to reconnect after a hectic day, even though on some days it might be for only 10 to 15 minutes together. Families also need time to be with each other, and although it is often hard to find time, more families are taking time to set up regular rituals, eating together as often as possible, and not allowing the world to steal their time together.

Increasing Use of Child Care Outside the Family

What do we do about our kids when both parents work outside the home? This is one of the most challenging questions our society faces today. In 1940, only 10% of American children lived with a mother who was in the labor force. By 1990, nearly 60% of American children lived with an employed mother. This sixfold increase of mothers in the workplace over a 50-year period (Hernandez, 1997) fueled the steady increase of child care outside the family and the extended family, even for infants.

The most recent figures indicate that there are about 19.2 million children under 5 years of age (U.S. Bureau of the Census, 2001g). Research indicates that parents regularly care for about 40% of these children; 21% are cared for by other relatives; 31% attend child care centers; 14% are enrolled in family day care centers, and 4% are cared for by sitters in the child's home. These figures total more than 100% because 10% of the children receive more than one manner of care during a typical day, such as going to preschool in the morning and being with a parent in the afternoon.

Mothers and fathers struggle with questions about day care:

- Do I need to work outside the home? Is employment essential for our family's well-being? For my well-being? And how will it affect our child's well-being?
- Will I be able to develop a bond with my child if she spends so much time away from me?
- Will I spend more money on child care, extra clothes, lunches, and transportation than I make on the job?
- How will the stresses of the job affect me personally? Our family? Can all this be balanced effectively?
- How will our child adapt to outside care? Will he receive good care? Will it be as good as the care we can give him?
- Will our child enjoy being with other children? Will the child's social development be enhanced by these opportunities?

For parents, finding satisfactory answers to these and countless other child care–related questions is a considerable challenge.

Parents now are becoming more active in finding ways to balance time away from their children and quality child care. Parents are checking out day care centers more carefully and are looking more critically at teachers and their relationship with their child.

Instability of Couple and Family Relationships

Many observers have argued that our fast-moving and competitive social environment is directly responsible for the high rate of marital dissolution and the increase in single-parent families and stepfamilies. Although personality conflicts and troubles within a marriage clearly contribute to marital breakdown, societal factors and values also influence our intimate behavior.

Rather than come home from work and sit on the front porch to talk with family and neighbors, we often hide behind closed doors in a cocoonlike atmosphere, plopped down in front of the television or a computer. As a result, many of our personal impressions come from the media. We may know more about our favorite actor's marriage than we know about how the couple is doing next door. Perhaps we are choosing to live like this, of course, in the name of personal privacy. But married life on television and in the tabloids is far different from the average couple's life.

It can be argued that the steady diet of extramarital affairs and marital conflict we receive from the media helps create a "culture of divorce" in this country.

But we are now finding that more people are feeling the need to maintain their close personal relationships. People are seeking more stability in their relationships and are trying to stay more connected. Married couples are more interested in building a stronger marriage, and families are trying to find ways to spend more quality time together.

Violence, Criminal Victimization, and Fear

Violent and abusive behavior continues to be a major cause of death, injury, and stress and fear in our country. Crime victimizes millions annually. Suicide took the lives of 29,350 Americans in 2000 (National Center for Injury Prevention and Control, 2005). Approximately 25.9 million violent and property victimizations also occurred that year (U.S. Department of Justice, 2005).

Data from the recent National Crime Victimization Survey (NCVS; 2002) indicate there were 691,710 nonfatal violent victimizations committed by current or former spouses, boyfriends, or girlfriends of the victims in 2001. These crimes—intimate partner violence—usually involve female victims; in 2001, 85% of the victimizations by intimate partners were against women. By contrast, intimate partners in the same year committed 3% of all nonfatal violence against men.

In 2000, 1,247 women and 440 men were killed by intimate partners. Data from recent years indicate that 33% of female murder victims are killed by intimates, and 4% of male murder victims (Rennison, 2003).

Nationwide, an estimated 903,000 children were victims of abuse and neglect in 2001. The youngest children, ages birth to 3 years, accounted for 27% of the victims (Administration for Children and Families, 2003).

In 2001, there were 29,573 firearm-related deaths in the United States. In the same year, 56% of all homicides and 55% of all suicides resulted from firearm use (Centers for Disease Control and Prevention, 2005). The rate of gun homicides in the United States per 100,000 people is almost 7 times higher than Canada, 28 times higher than England and Wales; and 198 times higher than Japan. In 1999/2000 when the United States recorded 10,828 gun homicides, Canada had 183; Germany 103; England and Wales 73, Australia 65; Switzerland 36; Sweden 33; Austria 27, Japan 27; and New Zealand 3 (Educational Fund to Stop Gun Violence, 2005).

Use of Alcohol, Tobacco, and Other Drugs

Our social environment today is dominated by advertising and a consumption-oriented approach to living. Complex issues are reduced to sound bites; the sitcom family's problems are resolved in a half hour (that is, 22 minutes of dialogue serving as a grabber for 8 minutes of commercials).

More deaths and disabilities in the United States each year are attributed to substance abuse than from any other cause. Approximately 18 million Americans have alcohol problems, and 5 to 6 million more have other drug problems (Brandeis University Institute for Health Policy, 1993, 2001). More than half of all adult Americans have a family history of alcoholism or problem drinking, and more than 9 million children live with a parent who is dependent on alcohol and/or illicit drugs (Brown University Center for Alcohol and Addiction Studies, 2000). Alcohol contributes to the death of about 85,000 people each year in the United States, making it the third leading cause of preventable mortality in this country after tobacco

and diet/activity patterns (Centers for Disease Control and Prevention, 2004c). A study of high-school seniors in 2002 indicated that 71.5% had used alcohol in the past 12 months, and 48.6% had used alcohol in the past 30 days; 36.2% had used marijuana in the past 12 months, and 21.5% in the past 30 days (University of Michigan, 2003).

There is a relationship between alcohol use and relationship functioning (Roberts, 2005). Heavy alcohol use is associated with marital difficulties such as infidelity, divorce, violence, and conflict. Drinking can also affect marriage and family functioning by cutting into economic resources, creating communication problems, contributing to sexual problems, and causing difficulties at work. There is also evidence to suggest that the relationship between alcohol use and marriage and family functioning is bidirectional; that is, increased drinking can be a response to marital and family difficulties (Roberts, 2005).

Deaths caused by alcohol are dwarfed by deaths caused by tobacco in this country. In 2000, 435,000 people died from smoking tobacco, chewing tobacco, and breathing other people's smoke (Centers for Disease Control and Prevention, 2004b). Illicit drugs, which receive so much media attention, claimed the lives of 17,000 Americans (Centers for Disease Control and Prevention, 2004a). Thus, legal drugs (alcohol and tobacco) killed 520,000 people, more than 30 times as many as those killed by illegal drugs.

You can counter these trends by limiting or eliminating altogether your use of tobacco and alcohol, which is easier if you choose friends who also have a similar lifestyle. By limiting your use, you can minimize the addicting quality of these drugs, which are very difficult to stop using once addicted. Because drugs negatively affect your body in the short and long run, adopting a lifestyle without them will bring you a healthier life.

The Internet and Human Relationships

In our continuous quest to market technological solutions to human problems, much has been made of the computer's potential for connecting human beings. In the movie *You've Got Mail*, Meg Ryan and Tom Hanks fall in love via e-mail. It is a charming notion, but the research tells a different story.

Too much time on the Internet can create problems in relationships for many people.

The Internet is used extensively by people of all ages. Some of the trends we see for adults using the Internet include the following (U.S. Bureau of the Census, 2005d):

- People 35 to 54 years of age use the Internet more than other adult age groups.
- Men and women use the Internet about equally.
- Married people use the Internet more than single people.
- College graduates are more likely to use the Internet than people who do not have college degrees.

Current research shows that 59% of families with children have Internet access, with parents and children e-mailing, text messaging, listening to music, reading the newspaper, and shopping online (Wang, Bianchi, & Raley, 2005). Monitoring children's use of the Internet is increasingly difficult as young people rely on it to do homework, which means they also have access to unsuitable Web information.

According to a study by Wolak, Mitchell, and Finkelhor (2006), one in seven youths received unwanted sexual solicitations on the Internet, one in three have experienced unwanted exposure to sexual material, and one in eleven have been subjected to threatening or other offensive behavior. The good news is that these numbers are lower than they were 5 years ago, as a result of national Internet safety programs.

Pedophiles often use the Internet to lure children into participation in sexual behavior (National Coalition for the Protection of Children and Families, 2007). Sexual exploitation of children on the Internet is an increasing concern for parents, law enforcement agencies, and legislators (Wolak et al., 2006). Recent studies show that parents have made efforts to monitor young people's use of Internet sites, with one study indicating that 61% of parents regulated their teen's Internet use (Wang et al., 2005).

What about adult access to pornography on the Internet? What affect does it have on marriage and family lives? It is estimated that 15% of individuals visiting Internet porn sites develop sexual behaviors that interfere with their lives (Gustafson, 2005). On a very basic level, pornography is viewed in secret, which creates deception in marriage and contributes to divorce (National Coalition for the Protection of Children and Families, 2007). In addition, Dr. Mary Anne Layden, a psychotherapist and expert on sexual addiction, concludes that involvement in pornography is the common theme in sexual violence. Layden says that pornography increases the likelihood of sexual addiction, and 40% of sex addicts will lose their spouse, 58% will have financial difficulties, and 27% will lose their jobs or be demoted (Gustafson, 2005).

Sex is big business, and some say it has become a national obsession. This trend has been fueled by an increase in Internet sex reaching deep into our homes, causing problems for children and for marriage and family relationships.

Researchers have found that individuals who spend even a few hours a week online experience higher levels of depression and loneliness than those who spend less or no time on the Internet (Kraut et al., 1998). They also found that individuals who use the Internet more tend to decrease their communication with other family members and reduce the size of their social circle. Internet use in itself appeared to cause a decline in psychological well-being. According to Robert Kraut, a social psychologist, "We are shocked by the findings, because they are counterintuitive to what we know about how socially the Internet is used." He noted, "We are not talking here about the extremes. These were normal adults and their families, and on average, for those who used the Internet most, things got worse" (Harmon, 1998).

Changing Gender Roles and the Balance of Power

There has been a dramatic increase in the number of mothers working outside the home. This development has helped fuel an ongoing discussion of the roles of women and men in America and how power should be allocated in society as a whole and between household partners in particular.

Although women have served as leaders of more than 20 countries around the world, a woman has yet to serve as president of the United States (Porter, 1999).

Nevertheless, women are serving as associate justices in the Supreme Court, as senators and representatives of Congress, and in countless other positions of power and influence in both government and the business world. With the emergence of women in traditionally male roles, particularly in positions of power, **gender roles** (the traits and behaviors assigned to males and females in a culture) are being redefined.

Just as "supermoms" struggle to find a meaningful balance between work and family, so too men are challenged by their own changing world. Years ago, a man's home may have been *his* castle; today it's an "egalitarian haven." Just how fairly power and work should be shared in American households is a topic of considerable discussion today. Some observers suggest that men still have a long way to go before true equality is reached in the home.

Many maintain that women have been the true pioneers of the gender revolution, arguing that wives have more quickly changed their roles *outside* the home than men have changed their roles *inside* the home. Still others question how equal we really want males and females to be in our society. They assert that females and males are biologically different and that wives should stay at home to better socialize our children. Regardless of one's position, it's impossible to deny that gender roles and relationship power balances are evolving in today's society.

Urban Migration and Overcrowding

"The history of American agriculture," according to Rex Campbell, a rural sociologist at the University of Missouri at Columbia, "is the history of technology in rural areas" (cited in Graham, 1998, p. 9). When farmers depended on animals for work and transportation, small towns dotted the rural landscape in the heartland about 6 miles apart. Eventually, trucks and tractors replaced horses and mules, farms got bigger, and the number of farmers and farm families declined steadily over the years. Small towns also shrank in size.

What do we lose when a small town vanishes? What do we lose when the kids grow up and leave the farm or ranch for the city? A realist, focusing solely on harsh economic forces, might say that the young person is leaving the farm to find work and a more stable life in an urban environment. An idealist might argue that we lose a little bit of the fabric of America, a small piece of the American dream. American rural societies tend to be caring environments in which many honest and hard-working individuals live and join together to help each other and their communities to succeed (Struthers & Bokemeier, 2000).

Another trend is that more people are moving away from the large cities to smaller communities within commuting distance. Although it may take a village to raise a child, a villagelike atmosphere can also be created in an urban neighborhood, in an apartment building, or among relatives and friends scattered about a city. The impersonal forces of urban living can be countered by the creation of villagelike social structures in the neighborhood, in the workplace, in religious institutions, and in community settings.

Financial Problems and the Global Economy

Financial issues are the most common stressors couples and families face, regardless of how much money they make. Researchers have consistently found that economic distress and unemployment are detrimental to family relationships (Gomel, Tinsley, Parke, & Clark, 1998). Over 1 in 6 children in this country live in poverty, and almost 4 out of 10 of all poor people are children (U.S. Bureau of the Census, 2004b). And though the rate of hunger in America dropped during the economic boom times of the late 1990s, 27 million people, including nearly 11 million children, were hungry or at least food insecure in 1999 (U.S. Department of Agriculture, 2000). The National Coalition for the Homeless argues that it is very difficult to estimate how many people are without a home in the United States, but the best approximation comes from a study conducted by the Urban Institute (2000), which found that 3.5 million people are likely to experience homelessness in a given year, and 1.35 million of these people are children (National Coalition for the Homeless, 2004).

Many Americans today are doing well financially, and yet many other Americans live close to the edge, lacking savings and chronically spending more than they earn. Easy credit lines have contributed to mounting debt, especially credit card debt, which carries extraordinarily high interest rates. Debt threatens not only individuals but also the well-being of the lenders and, eventually, the economy as a whole.

The number of children living in poverty is related to a high degree to life in a single-parent versus a two-parent household in the United States but less so in other countries (Figure 1.4). In the United States, nearly 60% of the children from single-parent households live in poverty, as compared to only 11% of children from two-parent households. The unfortunate fact of single parenthood in the United States is the lack of government support for these families that other countries provide.

Although economic survival is challenging for many people in the United States, residents of many countries around the world are in far worse straits. Nonetheless, their economic problems do not exist in isolation; as business commentators and politicians frequently point out, we are living in a global economy. The strength of the American economy is inextricably linked in complex ways to the economies of many other nations.

Thus the employment situation in Asia, Europe, or Latin America influences marriage and family relationships not only in those corners of the world but in this country as well. For example, if American farmers can't find markets for

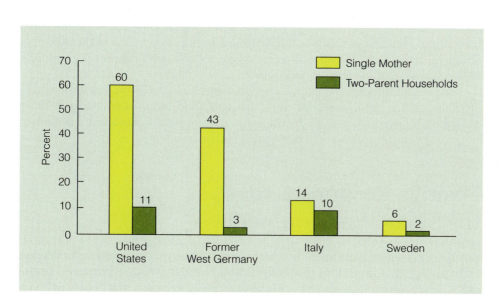

FIGURE 1.4

Percentage of Children Living in Poverty by Family Structure

Source: Adapted from "Family Decline and Child Well-Being: A Comparative Analysis" by S. K. Houseknecht and J. Sastry, 1996, *Journal of Marriage and Family, 58,* p. 734.

their produce in the United States or elsewhere, they aren't going to be able to buy American cars, Japanese televisions, or shirts crafted in Malaysia. Likewise, if the Japanese or Malaysians can't find markets for their products at home or abroad, income and employment will drop in those countries and Malaysians won't be going to college in California and Japanese won't be vacationing in Hawaii.

Although individuals cannot directly influence the economic changes in the United States or internationally, they can control their own spending. The most positive approach is that people should have a saving and investment plan, which is only possible if a person stays out of debt by limiting credit card spending and other overspending.

Changing the Social Environment

Recently, there have been a number of initiatives with the goal of improving the social environment in order to improve the lives of individuals and families in communities. An example of one of these initiatives is the Search Institute in Minneapolis, Minnesota, a nationally known organization that conducts research and creates programming around assets that promote healthy growth and development of young people (Search Institute, 2006). Twenty of the 40 assets that have been known to help youth have to do with positive experiences that young people receive from interactions in their communities. Several communities have enhanced community assets, such as schools, neighborhoods, and youth organizations, with the goal of ultimately improving the lives of young people.

William Doherty, a family scholar at the University of Minnesota, has developed the Families and Democracy Model, which provides strategies to engage citizens to make changes in their communities (Anderson & Doherty, 2005). The model provides direction to family professionals and community citizens to come together to solve problems that affect individuals and families. After hearing from a family professional about the loss of family time in today's busy society, community members in one neighborhood decided to do something to change this societal trend. Using the Families and Democracy Model, the community developed and implemented the Putting Family First initiative, which encourages families and community institutions to make family time a high priority. One of the outcomes of this initiative was the cancelation one night a week of all community activities so that families could spend time together.

Some communities have schools, organizations, and religious institutions that provide positive experiences for the individuals and families who live in those communities. Even when those institutions are not present, community initiatives can create a social environment that will benefit its residents.

Positive Responses to the Social Environment

Because the social environment in which we live poses many problems for couples and families, it is important that couples and families be more proactive, beginning with their own relationships. There is growing evidence that people are happier, healthier, and wealthier if they are in a marriage (Waite & Gallagher, 2000). And a strong marriage brings even more positive benefits for the individuals, the couple, and their family.

Fortunately, there are countless ways to provide for oneself and one's close relationships and at the same time help make the world a better place. There are types of work and lifestyle that provide not only financial security but also emotional satisfaction and the comfort of knowing that one's life actually makes a difference. The following account illustrates the reciprocal value of giving to others. This is what Raedene, 20, an undergraduate student and volunteer in a Big Brothers Big Sisters program, had to report:

> "I felt it was my job as a college student as well as a citizen to give something that I had always received, a little love and attention. I signed up for training in the program and was contacted by one of the organizers. After attending many long hours of training, I wondered if I had gotten myself into something more than I had bargained for. They required me to spend at least 5 hours a week with my match. I didn't think that I possibly had time but decided to give it a shot.
>
> "About 5 days after training, I received a phone call that I was going to be matched with a little 5-year-old girl. I met my supervisor at the home of Elizbeth, my new little friend. A little nervous, I walked into their home. It was really strange. The minute I sat down, Elizbeth jumped up on my lap like she had known me for years. 'Could you read this book to me? ... Watch this! ... Come into my room!' She just couldn't stop talking.
>
> "I did know from that minute on that this young child needed my love and attention more than 5 hours a week. I felt a sense of warmth come over me. To think that I was second-guessing 5 hours a week to give to a child who needed me. We played for a couple of hours until her mom felt comfortable with the match. I told Elizbeth that I would phone her Monday. Her response was, 'Don't forget.' When I left all I could do was smile. I knew I was in for some fun.
>
> "Over the semester I have seen much growth in her, socially and intellectually. She's in kindergarten and is always telling me how much she likes it, and I always try to reinforce how much fun school is. I understand what she talks about, and I listen to what she has to say. I feel she has gained so much trust in me over the past 4 months.
>
> "I am able to communicate openly with her mother. I offer suggestions to her on many topics. I am very honest with her mother, and her mother trusts me a lot, too. I have learned how difficult a time their family has dealing with finances, stepparents, and stepsiblings. I have seen much growth in their family over the past 4 months. I am very happy that I chose to volunteer my time. I wish everyone would volunteer because not only does the child benefit from the experience, but you do, too."

Betty Friedan, a pioneer in the latest wave of the feminist movement, states, "People's priorities—men's and women's alike—should be affirming life, enhancing life, not greed" (Friedan, 1997). She argues for a basic restructuring of our economy and society, putting the lives and interests of people first. The restructuring cannot be accomplished in terms of women versus men, Blacks versus Whites, old versus young, conservative versus liberal. "It can't be done by separate, single-issue movements now, and it has to be political to protect and translate our new empowerment with a new vision of community, with new structures of community that open the doors again to real equality and opportunity" (Friedan, 1997; Selle, 1998, p. 51; Wolfe, 1999).

Summary

- The family today is not in danger of extinction, but it is changing. The American family is more diverse today, in terms of family structure and ethnicity, than ever before.
- About half the people marrying today will probably divorce at some time in their lives, often because they enter marriage with unrealistic expectations, marry the wrong person, marry for the wrong reasons, or have few skills to deal with the many challenges of marriage.
- Marriage is the emotional and legal commitment of two people to share emotional and physical intimacy, various tasks, and economic resources. A family is two or more people who are committed to each other and who share intimacy, resources, decision-making responsibilities, and values.
- Some of the major trends in family structure, marriage, divorce, and remarriage are the following: There are both more families headed by single women and more stepfamilies today than there were in the 1950s and 1960s; families are smaller today; women are more likely to work outside the home after marriage; both men and women are marrying at a later age; cohabitation before marriage has increased eightfold; the divorce rate increased but has now stabilized at about 50%; and about 75% of those who divorce later remarry.
- All families have strengths, and strengths develop over time. Strengths help families cope with stress and problems and help families better manage change.
- Marriage has many advantages for individuals including a longer life, better health and healthier lifestyle, more money and wealth, a better sexual relationship, less domestic abuse for women, and more successful children.
- Human beings do not live and love in a vacuum. Besides being connected to special people in our lives, we are inextricably embedded in our social environment. As individuals, couples, and families, we have little influence on society, but society has a great deal of influence on our personal attitudes and behaviors.
- There are many elements in our social environment that pose difficult challenges for couples and families. These include stress, change, and materialism; lack of time for oneself and significant others; the increasing use of child care outside the family; instability of couple and family relationships; violence; the use of alcohol, tobacco, and other drugs; the Internet's effects on human relationships; changing gender roles and the balance of power in intergender relationships; urban migration and overcrowding; and financial problems and the effects of the global economy on families.
- Community initiatives led by community members and family professionals have made some communities more supportive of youth development and building strong family relationships. These initiatives can be models for other communities.
- Surveys over the years indicate that the majority of Americans think their marriages and families are doing pretty well and that their lives are generally satisfying.

Key Terms

marriage	stress
family	gender role
social environment	

Activities

1. In small groups, write down your own definition of the family. Share your responses within the group and compare how your ideas are similar and/or different.
2. What is your definition of marriage? After writing your definition, compare it with the definition used in this book.
3. Interview a grandparent or a great-grandparent (or another older person you would like to get to know better) about family life in "the old days"—both positive and negative aspects. Some interesting areas to explore might be (1) growing up in a family, (2) a "woman's place" in the world 50 or more years ago, (3) gender roles, (4) the Great Depression of the 1930s, (5) World War II, (6) major family crises, (7) religion, and (8) philosophies of child rearing.
4. What are the major stressors in your social environment? Make a list and discuss it with others. How did you deal effectively with these stressors?

Suggested Readings

Bryant, J., & Bryant, J. A. (2001). *Television and the American family* (2nd ed.). Mahwah, NJ: Erlbaum.

Family Focus. (2005). American families: By the numbers. *Family Focus, 6,* 14.

Gottman, J. M., & DeClaire, J. (2001). *The relationship cure: A five-step guide for building better connections with family, friends, and lovers.* New York: Crown.

Gottman, J. M., & Silver, N. (1999). *The seven principles for making marriage work.* New York: Crown.

Halpern, D. F. (2005). Psychology at the intersection of work and family. *American Psychologist, 60,* 397–409.

Kraut, R., Patterson, M., Lundmark, V., Kiesler, S., Mukopadhyay, T., & Scherlis, W. (1998). Internet paradox: A social technology that reduces social involvement and psychological well-being? *American Psychologist, 53*(9), 1017–1031.

National Stepfamily Resource Center. (2006). Web site: http://stepfamilies.info.

Popenoe, D., & Whitehead, R. D. (2005). *The state of our unions.* Piscataway, NJ: Rutgers University, National Marriage Project.

Search Institute. (2006). *Introduction to assets.* Minneapolis, MN: Author. Web site: http://www.search-institute .org/assets.

Straus, M., Gelles, R., & Steinmetz, S. (2006). *Behind closed doors: Violence in the American family.* New Brunswick, NJ: Translation Publishers.

Subrahmanyam, K., Greenfield, P., Kraut, R., & Gross, E. (2001). The impact of computer use on children's and adolescents' development. *Journal of Applied Developmental Psychology, 22*(1), 7–30.

Waite, L. J., & Gallagher, M. (2000). *The case for marriage.* New York: Doubleday.

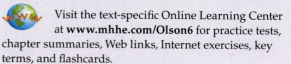 Visit the text-specific Online Learning Center at **www.mhhe.com/Olson6** for practice tests, chapter summaries, Web links, Internet exercises, key terms, and flashcards.

2 *Cultural Diversity: Family Strengths and Challenges*

Diversity and Strengths in a Cultural Context

Intimacy in Diverse Cultures

Cultural and Ethnic Identity

Race: An Antiquated Concept

U.S. Demographics and Future Trends

Challenge to Researchers and Practitioners

Cultural Competence

Kin Relationships Across Cultures

Family Strengths and Sociocultural Characteristics Across Various Ethnic Groups

Family Strengths and Challenges Across Ethnic Groups

Cross-Cultural Family Studies

Challenges for Ethnic Families

Summary

Key Terms

Activities

Suggested Readings

The United States is a gathering place of many cultures. Each cultural group that has come here has surrendered some of its past in an effort to build a new life in a new land. But the United States is not so much a "melting pot," in which these distinct cultures meld together, as it is a salad bowl, in which each of the ingredients retains its distinct flavor. The United States can also be likened to a symphony and its various cultural groups to instruments. Each instrument has its distinct part to play—its distinct contribution—but all must work together to produce beautiful music.

Diversity and Strengths in a Cultural Context

Our goal in this chapter is to point out some of the major strengths of various ethnic groups in the United States. One of the reasons our country has prospered is that the various groups have different strengths. The strengths of each of these groups can be seen at the individual level, family level, and cultural level. Some ethnic groups place a high value on the importance of kin networks and are very group oriented; other cultures emphasize more individual achievement. Some ethnic groups value both individual achievement and group connection relatively equally.

Diversity and strengths are also interconnected. There are strengths in diversity, and diversity helps build further strengths. The different abilities, interests, attitudes, and values of each ethnic group provide a broad range of options and ideas that can improve the ability to solve problems and create new ideas. These diverse strengths can help people at all levels of society from the personal level, to school, and at work.

When we see people from different ethnic groups, we typically do not focus on their strengths. The more common reaction is to notice how they are different from us. The next reaction can be that the difference is seen as interesting or it could be perceived as a potential problem. But after getting to know someone who is from a different ethnic group, you will be able to see that some of the differences can be both personal strengths and things you value about your relationship with them.

So one way to increase our appreciation of diversity is to seek out opportunities to talk with people who have ethnic backgrounds different from our own. Sharing feelings about one's cultural heritage with someone from another ethnic group can be a mutually rewarding experience, an opportunity to learn more about others and their unique cultures.

Intimacy in Diverse Cultures

While some cultural groups have relatively stable family lives evidenced by two-parent families, some do not. Poverty, prejudice, education level, and life experiences affect the ability to maintain intimate family relationships such as extended-family relationships, parent–child relationships, and couple relationships (Bent-Goodley, 2005; Perreira, Chapman, & Stein, 2006; Sarkisian, Gerena, & Gerstel, 2006).

Some cultural groups had historical experiences that have long-term effects on their ability to maintain intimate family lives today. For example, American Indians in the United States historically had land, language, and culture taken from them (Caldwell et al., 2005). In the mid-1900s, children were taken from their homes and put in boarding schools where they were to become "civilized" and adopt the ways of White Americans. These experiences created a legacy of trauma, which contributed to multiple psychiatric disorders such as alcoholism and violence (Caldwell et al., 2005). These issues affect intimacy in American Indian families.

How members of cultural groups entered the United States, when they entered the country, and how they were received may also impact their ability to develop intimacy among family members. Did they come as refugees with nothing but the clothes on their backs? If so, these refugees will need to focus on survival with little time or energy to develop intimate relationships. The following example is a real event that could impact close and intimate family relationships:

> Recently, there was a raid by immigration officials at a food processing plant in a small community that employed a large number of Latino immigrants. A significant number of Latino breadwinners were arrested for prosecution and deportation. Members of the Latino community were afraid to leave their homes, go to work, and send their children to school, and many had limited or no financial resources. In some cases both parents were arrested, and children were being cared for by friends of relatives.
>
> Financial, social, and emotional stress prevailed for these families. Survival and safety were foremost in the minds of these family members, which negatively impacted their intimate family relationships.

Cultural and Ethnic Identity

To put life in the United States into a more global perspective, Table 2.1 illustrates what the world village would be like if it contained 100 people. As you will notice, those from North and South America account for only 14 people. Over 70% of the people would be non-White and non-Christian. Most would live in substandard

TABLE 2.1	If the Earth Were a Village

The United States is a culturally diverse nation. To put cultural diversity in a global perspective, however, consider the following numbers from the late Dr. Donella H. Meadows, Dartmouth College. Meadows argued that if the earth's population were shrunk to the size of a village with 100 people, there would be:

- 57 Asians
- 21 Europeans
- 14 North and South Americans
- 8 Africans

And they would have the following characteristics:

- 51% would be female; 49% would be male

- 70% would be non-Caucasian; 30% would be Caucasian
- 70% would be non-Christian; 30% would be Christian
- 80% would live in substandard housing
- 70% would be unable to read
- 50% would suffer from malnutrition
- 1% would have a college education
- Less than 1% would own a computer
- 50% of the world's wealth would be in the hands of only 6 people, and all 6 would be citizens of the United States

Sources: World Citizen Update (Winter 1998). For more about Donella (Dana) Meadows, see the Sustainability Institute Web site: http://sustainer.org/meadows/; and the Geocities Web site: http://www.geocities.com/Heartland/Park/3252/Village.html.

housing, and 70% would be unable to read. At least half would suffer from malnutrition. Only 1% would have a college degree, and less than 1% would have access to a computer. An even more dramatic indication of the power of the United States is that 50% of the world's wealth is controlled by the 6 Americans.

One's cultural identity is an important aspect of being human. **Cultural identity** evolves from the shared beliefs, values, and attitudes of a group of people. It embodies standards of behavior and the ways in which beliefs, values, and attitudes are transmitted to the younger generation. Cultural identity also entails the ways in which kinship relationships and marital and sexual relationships are structured. Examples of the vast array of cultural identities in the United States include Anglo American, Italian American, African American, and Asian American—to name just a few.

Cultural identity can transcend **ethnic identity**, or ethnicity, which often refers to the geographic origin of a minority group within a country or culture. Whereas many people learn about their specific ethnic identities from their parents, many other children are born into families with roots in several ethnic groups. As this phenomenon increases in the United States, more young people are unclear about their ethnic identity and are simply calling themselves American.

A **cultural group** is a set of people who embrace core beliefs, behaviors, values, and norms and transmit them from generation to generation. Most cultures contain subgroups called **cocultures,** distinct cultural or social groups living within the dominant culture but also having membership in another culture, such as gay men and lesbians. An **ethnic group** is a set of people who are embedded within a larger cultural group or society and who share beliefs, behaviors, values, and norms that are also transmitted from generation to generation. Ethnicity "plays a major role in determining what we eat and how we work, relate, celebrate holidays and rituals, and feel about life and death and illness" (McGoldrick, Giordano, & Pearce, 1996, p. ix).

The United States today is one of the most culturally diverse nations in the world. Although the dominant culture of the United States is European American or Caucasian American, this country is home to many other ethnic and cultural groups. The major ethnic **minority groups** that are usually distinguished in the United States are African Americans (or Blacks), Latinos (or Hispanics), Asian Americans, and American Indians (Native Americans, Indigenous Americans, or First Americans). When discussing ethnic and other minority groups, however, it is important to remember that tremendous diversity exists among the people who are commonly grouped together.

Race: An Antiquated Concept

Race, which refers to the common physical characteristics of a group, is a problematic concept that is being dropped from scientific and popular use. The concept of race originally arose as a way to explain the diversity of the human population worldwide. As such, "race is a social, cultural, and political creation, a product of human invention" (Cameron & Wycoff, 1998, p. 279). Race has often been used as a psychologically and emotionally divisive tool, such as when Hitler and the Nazis identified Jews as racial scapegoats who needed to be eliminated from society.

Although race was once a core concept of cultural anthropology, scholars have dismissed its relevancy because it proved to be an unreliable and invalid measure of distinctions between people. Anthropologist Ashley Montagu argues in his

Box 2.1 Diversity in Families

Race Has No Place

The following are segments selected from a play called VOICES, created by Twin Cities Youth (in collaboration with Stacey Parshall) from Minneapolis and St. Paul for an exhibition on the concept of "race" at the Minnesota Science Museum in 2007.

"The words you hear, the stories, the definitions, the statements and wishes, are those of some of your teenage youth across the Twin Cities. A sacred space was created for them to write these words. They were told their voices are absolutely necessary for all of us to move forward, beyond the pain and confusion that the subject of race conjures up. . . .

Will you tell me about race. R. A. C. E. What does that mean to you? What does that stand for?

Respect All Colors Everywhere
Respect All Cultures Equally
Radical Awesome Cultures Everywhere
Rare Assortment of Color and Ethnicity
Rights And Confusion Expressed
Race Always Changes Everything
Rage Amongst Conflicting Ethnic groups

Revolutionize All Concepts that Enslave
Real Answers Can (help shape) Equality
Race Absolutely Costs Everybody

Race is just another word.
Race is just a title.
Race is not necessary.

Black, White, yellow, tan and they're just colors.
Color is what you get when White light is broken up.

Color defines merely what is on the outside.
Skin color? In my mind means nothing.
There is a saying, "it's only skin deep."
I always try to look deeper.

People are different races and come from different places, but we all have faces. Treat all with respect, no matter their races, even in tough cases. We are one human race."

Source: Adapted and used with permission from the Minnesota Science Museum, St. Paul, Minnesota, 2007

classic book *Man's Most Dangerous Myth: The Fallacy of Race* (1964) that similarities among ethnic groups are far greater than the differences among them. According to Montagu, "the term 'race' itself, as it is generally applied to man, is scientifically without justification, and that as commonly used, the term corresponds to nothing in reality" (p. 351). In a similar vein, anthropologist Conrad Phillip Kottak points out that racial classifications in this country are not based on biology but are arbitrary creations of American culture (2004). Selections from a creative play about the problems with the concept of race are provided in Box 2.1.

In the field of genetics, the term has also been dropped because there is so little (less than .001%) difference in all human beings in their genetic code (Cameron & Wycoff, 1998). In medicine, genetic differences between all people are so small that in many cases a Black donor can be a much better match for a White patient than can another White person.

The genetic theory of evolution assumes that humans were a genetically homogeneous group that began in one area of the world—Africa. This group of humans migrated to other lands and created more diverse groups as they adapted to their environment. Skin color and body size and shape changed over time in different environments. As these groups became more isolated, they appeared more homogeneous within their groups and more different when compared to other groups.

From a strictly scientific perspective, so-called racial characteristics do not exist (Root, 1992, 2002). Skin color, for example, can be defined only on a continuum, just as the colors black and white exist on a continuum, with gray in the middle and no clear-cut distinctions in between. As such, classifying people by racial groups

Because of increased diversity in the United States, opportunities for meeting and marrying someone from another race than your own have greatly increased. There are more multiracial marriages today than ever before.

becomes rather arbitrary. For example, consider the child of an Irish American mother and a Japanese American father. The child may have a skin color like her mother's and eyes like her father's. Genetically and aesthetically, she is an expression of both her father's and her mother's characteristics. Toni Morrison, the Nobel Prize–winning author of such novels as *Song of Solomon*, *Beloved*, and *Tar Baby*, puts it this way: "Race is the least reliable information you can have about someone. It's real information but it tells you next to nothing" (cited in Gray, 1998, p. 67).

What will the future bring? "More intermarriage will make it harder to figure out an individual's ancestry. But it can only hasten the approach of a color-blind society," according to Steve Olson (2001, p. 80). For the reasons just mentioned, we will try to avoid using the term *race* in this book; rather, we will use the terms *culture* (or *cultural group*) or *ethnicity* (or *ethnic group*) when referring to different groups of people. Because of the great diversity within groups, however, even calling them *ethnic* or *cultural* groups can be misleading. Jews, for example, are often classified as an ethnic group, but doing so stretches the imagination considerably, for a number of reasons: (1) Jews hold a wide variety of religious views, from very conservative to very liberal—some are Orthodox believers, and others are atheists; (2) Jews speak a variety of languages, and many Jews today cannot speak Hebrew, the language of tradition; (3) Jews are of many nationalities as a result of Judaism's expanding influence worldwide over the centuries; and (4) Jews exhibit a variety of physical characteristics, ranging from dark-skinned, black-haired African Jews to light-skinned, blue-eyed, blond European Jews. From a cultural viewpoint, a nomadic Jewish shepherd in Ethiopia has much more in common with other Africans than he does with a Jewish dentist in suburban Chicago.

Perhaps the key issue in determining membership in an ethnic or cultural group is whether the individual *believes* he or she is a member of that group. Clearly, human beings are diverse. Classifications cannot be based solely on religious views, language, ancestry, or physical characteristics.

U.S. Demographics and Future Trends

The United States is more ethnically diverse than ever before, with the Hispanic population making up the largest ethnic group, followed by African American, Asian American, and American Indian. For people reporting one race alone, 75% were White, 15% were Hispanic, 12% were African American, 4% were Asian American, and less than 1% was American Indian and Alaska Native (U.S. Bureau of the Census, 2005f).

Some states have become "majority–minority" states, which means that their total minority population is more that 50%. The states that have a minority population of more than 50% are Hawaii, New Mexico, California, and Texas, along with the District of Columbia (Bernstein, 2005).

See Figure 2.1 for some demographic characteristics of families from various ethnic groups.

The Hispanic Population

The Hispanic population, also referred to as "Latino," includes people from Spanish-speaking cultures. In 2005, the Hispanic population became the largest ethnic group, surpassing the African American population for the first time in U.S. history (U.S. Bureau of the Census, 2006a). The Hispanic population is the fastest-growing minority population, and growth is primarily due to new births and secondarily immigration.

The largest number of Hispanics in the United States immigrated from Mexico (64%), with the remainder coming from other Central American, South American, or other Hispanic countries (U.S. Bureau of the Census, 2006a). The Hispanic popu-

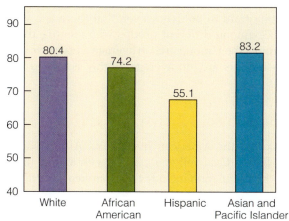

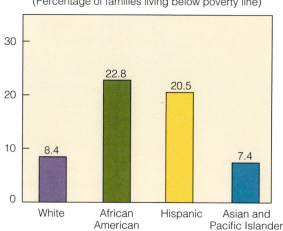

FIGURE 2.1

Characteristics of Families from Various Ethnic Groups

*U.S. Bureau of the Census, 2005f, tables 62, 677, 696.

**U.S. Bureau of the Census, 2005a, table 1a.

lation in this country is very young, with a median age of 27 years as compared with 36 years for the population as a whole (U.S. Bureau of the Census, 2006a).

The African American Population

The African American population is the second largest minority population in the United States. African Americans, or Blacks, refer to people having origins in any of the Black race groups of Africa. Although many African Americans came to the United States as slaves years ago, 7% of African Americans were foreign born in 2000 (McKinnon & Bennett, 2005). These new immigrants are very diverse and very different culturally from African Americans who have lived in the United States for several generations. These refugees and immigrants have come from the

Caribbean and African countries such as Nigeria, Ghana, and Ethiopia and have very little in common with their native-born counterparts (Batson, Qian, & Lichter, 2006). Because of this increasing diversity in the Black population, we need to be more aware of the diversity of cultural values and beliefs in what we once thought of as a relatively homogeneous cultural group (Batson et al., 2006).

In 2000, the median age for African Americans was 30 years, which was 6 years younger than the population as a whole (McKinnon & Bennett, 2005). Blacks have the lowest median income of any cultural group (DeNavas-Walt, Proctor, & Lee, 2006).

The Asian American Population

Asian Americans refer to people having origins in the Far East, Southeast Asia, or the Indian subcontinent. The Asian American populations differ greatly in their culture, language, and length of residency in the United States. More recent immigrants and refugees include Hmong, Vietnamese, Laotians, and Cambodians, while people coming from China and Japan typically have been in the United States for several generations.

The median age of Asian Americans is 33 years. Asian Americans have the highest income level of all the minority groups and higher than that of Whites (DeNavas-Walt et al., 2006). It is important to note, however, that there is a wide disparity in education and affluence among different groups who identify themselves as Asian American. For example, the Hmong are, on average, very poor with limited education, whereas Asian Indians are, on average, highly educated and affluent (DeNavas-Walt et al., 2006).

The American Indian and Alaska Native Populations

There are over 560 tribes that make up the American Indian and Alaska Native (AI/AN) population in the United States (Caldwell et al., 2005), with a wide range of tribal cultures. The largest tribes by population include the Cherokee and Navajo (Ogunwole, 2006).

One of the unique characteristics of the AI/AN population is that their communities are sovereign political entities with tribes having their own form of governance, culture, and history (Caldwell et al., 2005). Many AI/AN people live on tribal land or reservations (36%), with the remaining population living in rural and urban communities throughout the country (Ogunwole, 2006). The median age for American Indians and Alaska Natives is 29 years, which is lower than other U.S. minority groups.

What the Future Will Bring

Estimates have been made about what the White and ethnic populations might look like in the year 2050 (Figure 2.1). The minority populations will grow faster than the White population. The nation's Hispanic and Asian populations are predicted to triple over the next half century, and non-Hispanic Whites will represent about one-half of the total population (U.S. Bureau of the Census, 2004a).

If the trend of multiracial marriages and relationships continues to increase as they have in recent history (Qian, 2005), there will be increasing numbers of multiracial children in the country. This combined with the increase in minority groups means it is possible that by the year 2050 cultural groups may cease to be an issue that will be written about in marriage and family textbooks.

Challenge to Researchers and Practitioners

Most research that informs programs and services is based on White, middle-class families, and, yet, this research is typically used to provide programs and services for all ethnic groups (Skogrand, Hatch, & Singh, 2008). Most of these programs and services are not a good fit for families from other cultures, because the information is not culturally relevant. There is, therefore, a need for research to be conducted within a cultural context to inform programming for the members of diverse ethnic groups.

Research

Mohatt and Thomas (2006) indicate that we need to include members of diverse cultures in decision making about how we conduct research, analysis of findings, and interpretation of results. There are a variety of things we should be doing differently when conducting research with minority populations, which will take a shift in our thinking (Trimble & Fisher, 2006):

- We need to be respectful of the wishes of cultural groups regarding the research we do, how it should be used, and how those communities might benefit from the research findings.
- We need to collaborate with and develop partnerships with members and organizations in diverse cultures and accept the conditions imposed by the community when conducting research.
- We need to know about belief systems and show respect for these values in conducting research.
- Participants in research studies need to provide informed consent in a language and reading level that they understand.
- Interpretation of findings requires involving members of the population studied, because cultural meanings may not be understood by the researchers.

Practice

We might ask, "Why is it important to address the issue of marriage and family from the perspective of one's culture?" There are two responses to this question. First, if there is a cultural clash between the information and services provided and the values of a cultural group, people will usually not participate. If they do participate, they will not benefit from the information provided. Harm to members of the cultural may result if individuals embrace programming ideas that destroy aspects of their cultural heritage (Fowers & Davidov, 2006; Skogrand et al., 2008).

Second, there is evidence that relying on one's cultural heritage, the way one's people deal with struggles, is the most effective way for people to be resilient and capable of handling difficulties (Skogrand et al., 2008). Several studies have shown that a positive ethnic identity has a positive influence on the lives of youth (Kiang, Gonzales-Backen, Yip, Witkow, & Fuligni, 2006; Perreira et al., 2006; Spencer, 2006). Consequently, it is important to draw on and reinforce the existing family values that are evident in minority cultural groups. In addition, there is evidence that maintaining one's cultural heritage and also learning about the dominant culture contributes to positive mental health (Chapman & Perreira, 2005; Kiang et al., 2006; Perreira et al., 2006).

Cultural Competence

With the increasing numbers of people of diverse cultures becoming part of society, it is critical that professionals develop culturally appropriate ways to provide effective family education and services. This ability has been described as **cultural competence**. Cultural competence has been defined in a variety of ways. A general definition is that one is effective in working with a variety of cultural groups. Cultural competence is often viewed as having three parts: awareness, knowledge, and skills. Fowers and Davidov (2006) discuss these three components and also emphasize the importance of having an *openness* to learning about oneself and others throughout the process.

Awareness

According to Fowers and Davidov (2006), a person must begin with self-exploration, which leads to self-awareness. This is a process that starts with an understanding of one's own cultural heritage and belief system, which leads to the ability to recognize how one's own culture affects how one views those from other cultures. People who are African American have values and beliefs that come from a long history of racial and ethnic experiences, and a person who is African American sees others based on those cultural experiences.

People who are German or Norwegian also have cultural perspectives that affect how they view people from other cultures. Many who have a European ancestry see themselves as blending into the dominant culture in the United States and may not think of themselves as having a culture, but everyone has values and beliefs with which they grew up that affects how they view the world.

To better understand our own belief system, we might ask ourselves the following questions:

- What are my basic beliefs about family, children, and extended family?
- Do I think the individual or the collective group has the higher priority?
- How does religion and spirituality play into my belief system?
- What rituals do I carry out, and how and why have I developed these rituals?
- What foods do I eat and what kinds of clothes do I wear that make me feel like I am part of my family or community?

How we think about these questions may be influenced by a variety of things, but many of the answers might have resulted from our cultural experiences. Once we understand who we are and how our concept of self has been developed, we can think about how those views affect how we interact with those who are different from us.

Knowledge

The second component described by Fowers and Davidov (2006) is gaining the knowledge or factual information necessary to understand another person's culture. Knowledge may be general in nature and may include understanding discrimination, prejudice, and oppression and how these experiences affect a person or group of people. Specific knowledge about a cultural group might include the group's history, cultural beliefs and values, and family dynamics. The knowledge that one gains contributes to being more open to work with members of a culture because there is cross-cultural understanding. Not everyone within a cultural group is the same, but having knowledge about some cultural characteristics and features is necessary to become culturally competent. Once a person has knowledge about a culture as a whole, there can be additional learning about the subcultures within the larger group.

How does a person gain knowledge about a cultural group? Several strategies have been identified by Skogrand (2004) that are useful in learning about a cultural group. First, reading scholarly information that describes the history of the culture, beliefs and values, and family organization will provide much needed knowledge about a cultural group. A second strategy is to attend activities, markets, art galleries, or places of business that are frequented by members of the culture. For example, attending events such as pow-wows and Junteenth Day celebrations would help one learn about history and spiritual practices. Visiting markets, art galleries, or places of business would provide information about food preferences, clothing worn, and other cultural beliefs. Learning about family life will also occur as we pay attention to who goes to the market, how mothers and fathers interact with their children, and the presence or absence of extended-family members. Respectfully attending these events can contribute to learning about family life, customs, and heritage.

Skills

Developing and practicing appropriate skills in effectively working with people who are culturally different from us is the third component of cultural competency (Fowers & Davidov, 2006). Being aware and having knowledge is of little use unless it is put into action.

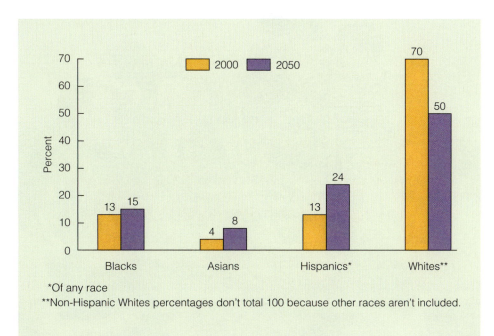

*Of any race
**Non-Hispanic Whites percentages don't total 100 because other races aren't included.

FIGURE 2.2

Increasing Diversity in America from 2000 to 2050

Source: U.S. Bureau of the Census, 2004a.

Cultural competence skills can be demonstrated by the language used and by showing knowledge of history, beliefs and values, and cultural practices in implementing programs and providing services. Fowers and Davidov (2006) make it clear that it is not easy to teach skills in being culturally competent, but, rather, these skills are an outcome and are expressed naturally and in individual ways once one is self-aware and has knowledge about a cultural group.

Kin Relationships Across Cultures

Most of us learn about kinship early in our lives, with little or no theoretical explanations. We learn, for example, about brothers and sisters and about aunts, uncles, and cousins; but we identify with them as people rather than focus on specific kinship principles. We know who Uncle Jack and Aunt Libby are long before we understand the concepts of "mother's brother" or "father's sister."

All cultures recognize **kinship**, the relatedness of certain individuals within a group, and have norms and expectations that structure and govern kin behavior. The diversity of these norms is wide ranging. These kinship concepts describe kinds of kinship groups and the norms that govern marital forms, family structure and organization, inheritance, authority, and residence.

Kinship groups range from nuclear families to various forms of extended families and may even include symbolic relationships. The **nuclear family**—the smallest, most elementary kinship unit—usually consists of two parents and their dependent children. Even in societies in which the nuclear family is embedded

As people get divorced and remarried, forming new stepfamilies, family and kin relationships become more complex.

within a larger group, it is recognized as a distinct entity. The nuclear family is a **conjugal family system**, one that emphasizes the relationships formed through marriage. Typically, a conjugal system comprises only two generations and is relatively transitory, dissolving when the parents die or the children grow up and leave. Because nuclear families are comparatively small and short lived, they are less likely to develop traditions that are handed down through the generations.

Many family functions are better performed by composite family groups, or **consanguineal family systems** which emphasize blood ties more than marital ties. In consanguineal systems, married couples and their children are embedded in a larger kinship group of three or more generations related by blood. Consanguineal systems can include extended families or families resulting from plural marriages. An **extended family** consists of a nuclear family and those people related to its members by blood ties, such as aunts, uncles, cousins, and grandparents.

A **plural marriage**, or **polygamy**, is a marriage in which a man has more than one wife (**polygyny**) or, more rarely, a marriage in which a woman has more than one husband (**polyandry**). In **monogamy**, a man or woman has only one mate. Although people from monogamous societies often perceive potential hazards in plural marriages, family patterns appear to operate in a relatively smooth fashion in groups in which plural marriages are the norm.

A third kind of kinship group is a **pseudo–kin group**, in which relationships resembling kinship ties develop among unrelated individuals. Relationships within these groups range in intensity, from close friendships to godparent–godchild connections to individuals living together and caring for each other without any legal or blood relationship.

Cultural norms influence family structure, but they also influence concepts of **lineage** or lines of descent; of who holds authority in a family; and of where newly married couples should reside. Lineage is important in determining membership in a particular kinship group, patterns of inheritance, and kinship obligations or responsibilities. In some societies, descent is traced by gender: **matrilineal societies** trace descent through females, and **patrilineal societies** trace descent through males. In a matrilineal society, for example, a man inherits group membership through his mother; lines of descent through his sister(s) are also important. Although a man may live with his wife or wives, he perceives the households of his mother and sisters as his true home. In a patrilineal society, a man's sister will be in his descent group but her children will not; they belong to their father's descent group.

Bilateral descent is common in many Western societies, with children tied equally to relatives of both the mother and the father. In this "family tree" approach to descent, in which ancestors and descendants multiply geometrically, true descent kinship groups are not formed unless limited by generation or to particular ancestors and descendants.

Norms for lines of descent may or may not be linked to lines of authority within a kinship group. If females exercise the authority, a kinship group is considered a **matriarchal group.** If males are dominant and exercise the authority, the kinship group is considered a **patriarchal group.** Note that these terms emphasize femaleness and maleness rather than motherhood and fatherhood. In a patriarchal group, for example, the grandfather is likely to wield more authority than the father of a nuclear family. But the criterion of gender always supersedes that of age in matriarchal and patriarchal kinship groups.

In **egalitarian groups**, such as those found in the United States, the ideals of democracy suggest that the rights and perspectives of both genders and all generations be respected. A given family's structure and interactions may lean toward the patriarchal or matriarchal, but the norms of the group would most likely be considered egalitarian.

Norms of residence for newly married couples can also be categorized by a society's emphasis on biological sex. In a **matrilocal society**, newly married couples normally live with or near the wife's kin, especially her mother's kinship group. Newly married couples in **patrilocal societies** are expected to live with or near the husband's kin, usually his father's kinship group. In a **neolocal society**, norms encourage newly married couples to establish a separate, autonomous residence, independent of either partner's kinship group.

Although a society may have norms regarding marital and family organization and interaction, diversity is generally also evident within that society's families and kinship groups. Understanding the concept of kin relationships, however, enables observers to compare and analyze the structure and dynamics of a broad range of kinship groups.

Family Strengths and Sociocultural Characteristics Across Various Ethnic Groups

Three characteristics of family systems are very useful for understanding and improving the quality of life for couples and families. These family system characteristics are cohesion, flexibility, and communication. Three sociocultural characteristics that also give us insight into families are the extended family, the social system, and the belief system. Figure 2.3 graphically illustrates how the family system characteristics and the sociocultural characteristics can be synthesized.

Three Family System Characteristics

There has been a great deal of research looking at the characteristics of strong families, focusing on their family system. The three dimensions (clusters of concepts) of family systems that have been found are cohesion, flexibility, and communication (Olson & Gorall, 2002; Walsh, 1998). These three dimensions also relate directly to the six characteristics of strong families described by DeFrain in the international family strengths model (DeFrain, 2006).

Family cohesion is *the emotional closeness a person feels to other family members*. Cohesion includes both commitment and spending enjoyable time together from the family strengths model. Commitment to the family includes trust, honesty, dependability, and faithfulness. Spending time together means committing a considerable amount of quality time to sharing activities, feelings, and ideas, and enjoying each other's company.

Family flexibility is *the ability to change and adapt when necessary*. Flexibility also relates to dealing effectively with stress and having helpful spiritual beliefs from the family strengths model. Coping abilities include using personal and family resources to help each other, accepting crises as challenges rather than denying them, and growing together by working through crises. Spiritual well-being includes happiness, optimism, hope, faith, and a set of shared ethical values that guide family members through life's challenges.

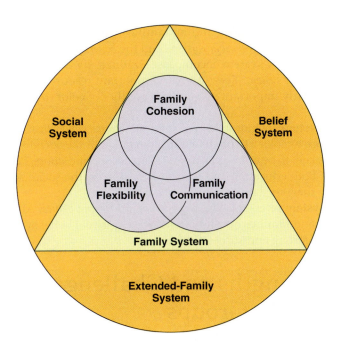

FIGURE 2.3
Sociocultural Context
and Family System
Characteristics

Family communication is *the sharing of information, ideas, and feelings with each other.* Communication is generally positive in strong families because angry outbursts and other negative interchanges simply don't work well. Appreciation and affection are regularly shared. Positive communication includes having open, straightforward discussions, being cooperative rather than competitive, and sharing feelings with one another. Appreciation and affection include kindness, mutual caring, respect for individuality, and a feeling of security.

Douglas Abbott and William Meredith (1988) studied over 500 successful families from five American ethnic groups—Native Americans, Hmong refugees, African Americans, Mexican Americans, and Caucasians—focusing on the three clusters (cohesion, flexibility, and communication). The study revealed more similarities than differences across the five groups. In fact, there were significant similarities among all the groups, with correlations in the range of .60–.85, except between the Hmong and the Native Americans and between the Hmong and the Caucasians.

All five groups agreed that strong families (1) use effective communication and listening skills, (2) are trusting and trustworthy, (3) are affirming and supportive, and (4) teach a sense of right and wrong behavior. Other common strengths were teaching respect for others, spending time doing things together, and feeling a sense of shared responsibility.

In summary, Abbott and Meredith noted that the most striking finding was the consensus among all five ethnic groups on the traits they considered most important to healthy family functioning. The researchers concluded that strong families are those that are high in family cohesion, family flexibility, and family communication.

Three Sociocultural Characteristics

In describing successful families, we have emphasized three important family system characteristics, but it is also important to consider the sociocultural context in which families live. The three sociocultural characteristics that are particularly useful in describing and understanding families from diverse ethnic groups are the *extended-family system*, the *social system*, and the *belief system*.

The **extended-family system** encompasses *relatives, kin, and other family members connected to the family system*. These are very important resources for most families and are a particularly important resource for families of color (McAdoo, 1997, 1999, 2002).

The **social system** includes *the economic, educational, and other related resources available*. Families of color are often at a disadvantage in the social system because they are more likely to be of middle or lower socioeconomic status. Because of their relative lack of both education and economic resources, the social system is often more a liability than an asset to families of color.

The **belief system** refers to *a family's spiritual beliefs and values*. All families have a value system, and families of color often have a spiritual belief system that helps them maintain a strong and successful family.

Family Strengths and Challenges Across Ethnic Groups

This section describes some of the most salient family strengths and family challenges of the major ethnic groups in the United States. The summary lists that follow were created from reviewing several hundred publications related to the various ethnic groups. We tried to rely on studies done by *insiders* rather than *outsiders*—studies done by researchers who were members of the particular ethnic group under study, rather than studies done by researchers on the outside looking in. Although the characteristics in each list are commonly found in a particular ethnic group, it does not mean that every family has these particular characteristics. Each family in the world is a culture all to itself. It is unique and different from all the other families in the world, even though it is quite likely to share many similarities with other families in its own ethnic group and similarities with families outside its ethnic group.

So that you may identify the strengths in your own family, we have put together a short quiz you can take. Box 2.2 lists 10 characteristics that you can use to rate your own family. We hope you find it a useful way to think about the good things in your family.

Strengths of White Families

Much of the early research on family strengths was done with a predominant focus on White or European American families and resulted in the family strengths framework of Nick Stinnett and John DeFrain (1985; see Chapter 3 of this text). In addition, David Olson and his colleagues completed a study of 1,000 couples and families across the family life cycle and identified strengths that helped families at each stage maintain high levels of marital and family satisfaction (Olson et al., 1989). Because these strengths will be described in more detail in Chapter 3, we will simply summarize them here (Figure 2.4):

- *Commitment to family.* Strong White families are very committed to one another and are able to give all family members the freedom and support they need to achieve their individual goals.
- *Enjoyable time together.* White families that remain strong throughout the family life cycle find ways to spend time together and enjoy each other.

Box 2.2   Self-Assessment

Rate the Strengths in Your Family

This Family Strengths Inventory was developed by researchers who have studied strengths as perceived by more than 21,000 family members in 27 countries. Put an "S" for *strength* beside the qualities you feel your family has achieved, and a "G" beside those qualities that are an area of potential *growth*. If the particular characteristic does not apply to your family or is not a characteristic that is important to you, put an "NA" for *not applicable*.

———   1. We enjoy expressing appreciation and affection for each other.

———   2. We are committed to our well-being as a family and the well-being of each individual.

———   3. Communication is usually positive, straightforward, and honest.

———   4. We share an adequate amount of enjoyable time together.

———   5. We share beliefs and values that give us meaning and a sense of belonging in the world.

———   6. We see challenges in life as opportunities for growing closer together.

———   7. We love one another.

———   8. Life in our family is satisfying to us.

———   9. We are happy as a family.

——— 10. All things considered, we are a strong family.

How Can a Family Use This Inventory?

Partners or family members can fill out a copy of this Family Strengths Inventory separately and then share their answers with each other. If discussed in a positive manner, they will be able to identify those areas they would like to work on together to improve, and those areas of strength that will serve as the foundation for their growth and positive change together.

Source: DeFrain, 2006.

Enjoyable time together is critically important for families in American society. In a fast-paced environment, loved ones need to s-l-o-w d-o-w-n and relearn why they care for each other so much.

- *Ability to manage stress and crisis effectively.* Although all families encounter marital and family stress, strong families see stress as a challenge and deal directly with issues as they occur.
- *Spiritual well-being.* Strong White families have spiritual beliefs and values, often including religious beliefs, that help them deal with ongoing life issues.

FIGURE 2.4
Strengths and challenges
of White Families

Strengths	Challenges
• Commitment to the family • Enjoyable time together • Ability to manage stress and crisis effectively • Spiritual well-being • Positive communication • Appreciation and affection	• Balancing work and family • Maintaining physical and emotional health • Creating healthy relationships in a society that glorifies winning, money, and material things • Learning about other cultures and being sensitive to the needs of those who are not in positions of power and authority • Preserving the natural environment in an economic system that is fueled by consumption

- *Positive communication.* One of the most important characteristics of healthy Caucasian families is that they feel good about their communication with one another.
- *Appreciation and affection.* Sharing the positive feelings they have about one another helps keep relationships positive in strong White families.

Strengths of African American Families

A number of family researchers have been interested in African American family strengths for more than three decades (Billingsley, 1992; McAdoo, 2007). A major book focusing on family life in Black America by Robert Taylor, James Jackson, and Linda Chatters (1997) provides an alternative to the more negative picture painted by past studies and writings about African American families. One of the classic studies of positive aspects of African American families was conducted by Marie Peters (1981). She reviewed her own work and that of other African American family investigators and identified five strengths of African American families (Figure 2.5):

- *Strong kinship bonds.* The extended family is very important to many African American families, and African Americans tend to take relatives into their households (Hunter, 1997; Padgett, 1997).
- *Strong work orientation.* Dual-job households are common among strong African American families.
- *Flexibility in family roles.* Role flexibility serves as an effective coping mechanism in healthy African American families. Because it has been necessary for many mothers to work outside the home, Black mothers tend to have considerable power in the family. The typical strong African American family is not matriarchal or patriarchal but is egalitarian in style. African American families have a longer tradition of egalitarian marriages than White families. Compared with African American couples, White couples as a group are relative newcomers to the dual-job arena (McAdoo, 1999).

Caring parenting has been identified as a strength of African American families. When parents take time to share recreational activities with their children, they make an investment in both the emotional development of their children and the future stability of the family.

Strengths	Challenges
• Strong kinship bonds • Strong work orientation • Flexibility in family roles • Strong motivation to achieve • Strong religious orientation • Caring parenting • Egalitarian marriages	• Being judged as a financial risk • Feeling powerless • Building self-esteem • Facing a high risk of being killed as a young man • Overcoming discrimination • Achieving higher levels of education • Violence against each other • Identifying male role models

FIGURE 2.5
Strengths and Challenges of African American Families

- *Strong motivation to achieve.* African American parents believe education is important, and many would like to see their children go to college.
- *Strong religious orientation.* African American churches provide emotional, spiritual, and intellectual satisfaction to African American families. Church work provides meaning and purpose for many African Americans. One study showed that Black adults who had church-based networks shared an emotional closeness to individuals in the church community, had frequent interaction with church members, and received substantial amounts of help from members of the church. These authors concluded that churches may function as families and supplement the efforts of the family network (Taylor, Lincoln, & Chatters, 2005).
- *Egalitarian marriages.* A sixth family strength is the observation that many successful African American marriages are defined as loving partnerships between equals. An egalitarian marriage does not necessarily mean that both partners contribute to the family in the same ways and that they both do the same things in life. In many couples, role responsibilities are somewhat different. For example, one partner might be especially good at cooking and the other might be especially good at balancing the checkbook. An egalitarian marriage, therefore, is marked by the fact that power and influence are shared between the partners, and each is held in high regard and respected by the other.

Researchers at Howard University (Gary, Beatty, & Berry, 1986) studied 50 strong African American families in Washington, D.C., and found that the strengths these families exhibited were very similar to the strengths reported in a study of strong families who were predominantly White. One difference between healthy families in these two groups is that religious values and kinship ties are somewhat more important in African American families (Lee, Peek, & Coward, 1998).

Strengths of Latino Families

Latinos, or Hispanics, encompass people from numerous Spanish-speaking cultures (Zambrana, 1995; Zambrana & Capello, 2003). About two-thirds are Mexican Americans, but even within this group there is diversity. Scholars Mario Garcia and Rodolfo Alvarez suggest that people of Mexican descent in the United States constitute several rather than a single demographic group (Shorris, 1992, pp. 95–100). Two such reference groups are Mexican Americans and Chicanos/Chicanas. The Mexican American group comprises people who immigrated to border states, such as California and Texas, following World War II. People who consider themselves Mexican Americans are generally older and more conservative than those who identify themselves as Chicanos or Chicanas, who are younger and more militant.

In one extensive overview of the strengths of Hispanic families, William Vega (1995) identified the six most important characteristics, which are very similar to those identified for families from other cultures in the United States (Figure 2.6):

- *Familism.* The family is a major priority; it is highly valued. There is a strong emotional commitment to the family.
- *High family cohesion.* Strong Latino families have very high cohesion, or closeness, although cohesion decreases across generations somewhat among Latino families living in the United States.
- *High family flexibility.* There is considerable role flexibility in Latino families, in contrast to the stereotyped view in which the male is seen as dominant.

Latinos in the United States have managed to preserve a strong family system in spite of the difficult challenges they face. As in other ethnic and cultural groups, Latino families are changing as mothers become more involved in the workforce and fathers become more involved in family responsibilities at home.

- *Supportive kin network system.* The large kin network system of most Latino families is very important as a supportive resource and is a strong tradition.
- *Egalitarian decision making.* Increasingly, families share roles more equally; decision making is egalitarian.
- *Strong ethnic identity.* The importance of the Latino culture and values binds families together and helps give them a strong ethnic identity.

Linda Skogrand and colleagues interviewed 25 Latino couples who had strong marriages to find out what made their marriages strong (Skogrand et al., 2008). The study was conducted using open-ended interview questions with the questions being developed within a cultural context. These couples indicated three things that were essential in making their marriages strong: children, communication, and religion.

Strengths	Challenges
• Familism • High family cohesion • High family flexibility • Supportive kin network system • Egalitarian decision making • Strong ethnic identity	• Remaining family centered • Maintaining traditions • Gaining financial resources • Overcoming the language barrier • Overcoming social and economic discrimination • Handling relocation issues • Achieving higher levels of education • Acculturating across generations

FIGURE 2.6
Strengths and Challenges of Latino Families

Children were important to these Latino couples because they were the reason for getting married and they were the "glue" that kept the marriages together. These couples saw there marriages subsumed within and a part of their family lives—marriage relationships were not separate, but a part of their family. Participants in the study also said communication was essential for a strong marriage. Finally, religion was important in making a marriage strong. Religion provided a strong base for the relationship with support from other congregational members. Religious beliefs were also the context for their strong sense of commitment in the marriage. Making a commitment before God and the church helped the couples stay in the marriage even through difficult times (Skogrand et al., 2008).

The Latino marriage study supported extensive literature identifying family and religion as important values in the Latino culture. These values provide resources and strength to Latino families.

Researchers have found that Mexican American families and Anglo families share two strengths. Using an assessment scale called FACES (Family Adaptability and Cohesion Evaluation Scales), William Vega and colleagues (1986) studied cohesion (togetherness) and adaptability (flexibility) in a group of low-income Mexican American parents and a group of middle-income Anglo parents. The researchers expected to find differences between the two groups, based not so much on culture but on social class. In short, they hypothesized that money helped family life run a bit more smoothly. They were surprised to find that even though the Mexican American families had the additional challenges that come with low income, their group scored no differently on cohesion and adaptability than the middle-income Anglo families.

Strengths of Asian American Families

Families of Asian descent are another very resilient group in this country. Although Asian Americans have faced prejudice and discrimination throughout their history in the United States, they have fared better than other ethnic minorities economically and have managed to preserve their family ties, traditions, and values (McLeod, 1986; Schwartz, Raine, & Robins, 1987; U.S. Bureau of the Census,

A tradition of hard work, discipline, high regard for education, and commitment to the family has translated into a valuable and important strength for many Asian American families. This graduate honors his family with his achievement, but he has probably also enjoyed their wholehearted support and encouragement as he worked toward it.

2000e). A period of disruption occurred in the 1940s. Following the bombing of Pearl Harbor, fear of further attacks by Japan led the U.S. government to resettle Japanese Americans—even those born in this country—in what were essentially prison camps until the war ended. Four decades later, the federal government agreed to modestly recompense surviving family members for the ill-treatment they suffered.

Although Asian Americans probably do not face the same level of discrimination that African Americans face in the workplace, a report by the Commission on Civil Rights was forced to conclude that "anti-Asian activity in the form of violence, vandalism, harassment and intimidation continues to occur across the nation" (Schwartz et al., 1987). Even today, there is a degree of discrimination against Asian Americans, fueled by a fear of competition from the economies in eastern Asia. Many Asian immigrants have come to this country in search of economic progress, which was unachievable in their homelands. Having reached their goals through hard work, Asian Americans are sometimes seen as a threat to those who have lived in this country longer and have settled into a comfortable, more easygoing life.

Many Asian Americans share a cultural heritage that values discipline, family commitment, hard work, and education (Qian, Blair, & Ruf, 2001). Young people reared in such an environment become challenging competitors in a society such as ours, which values competition and individual initiative. Asian American families are very diverse, but they commonly share many of the strengths of other cultural groups. Following are six major strengths of Asian American families, which are summarized in Figure 2.7:

- *Strong family orientation.* Both the nuclear and the extended family are very important historically and today.
- *Filial piety.* The great respect Asian American families have for their elders is noteworthy. It helps explain the high level of mutual support each generation receives from the other generations.
- *High value on education.* Asian American families emphasize the importance of education, from nursery school through college.
- *Well-disciplined children.* Traditionally, children are expected to be quiet, well behaved, and somewhat passive.
- *Extended-family support.* Financial and emotional support is provided by the extended family when the nuclear family needs it.
- *Family loyalty.* Family members support each other and protect each other's privacy.

Strengths	Challenges
• Strong family orientation • Filial piety • High value on education • Well-disciplined children • Extended-family support • Family loyalty	• A need to relax personal expectations somewhat • Maintaining ties with kin • Overcoming emotional vulnerability • Overcoming the stigma against seeking help • Trusting those outside the group • Relaxing the focus on work

FIGURE 2.7
Strengths and Challenges of Asian American Families

Recent immigrants from Southeast Asia (Vietnam, Cambodia, and Laos) have had a more difficult time adjusting to American culture than earlier immigrants from Japan, China, and Korea did. Although many recent arrivals have been farmers from rural areas, these immigrants often find themselves in poor inner-city neighborhoods, where their traditional values are challenged, making the adjustment to American culture difficult. To better understand the acculturation process of these families, one method used is the life history approach, in which elders told their stories rather than responding to questionnaires.

Strengths of American Indian Families

American Indians and Alaska Natives (AI/ANs) are people having origins in any of the original peoples of North and South America (including Central America) and who maintain tribal affiliation or community attachment (U.S. Bureau of the Census, 2000c). The greatest concentrations of American Indians and Alaska Natives are in the West, Southwest, and Midwest, especially in Alaska, Arizona, Montana, New Mexico, Oklahoma, and South Dakota. American Indian families in the United States are members of 569 federally recognized tribes, plus an unknown number of tribes that are not federally recognized (U.S. Bureau of the Census, 2000a).

About 4.3 million people in the United States are estimated to be American Indian and Alaska Native, or American Indian and Alaska Native in combination with one or more other ethnic/cultural groups. This is about 1.5% of the total population (U.S. Bureau of the Census, 2003a). Sixty-six percent of American Indians and Alaska Natives live in metropolitan areas in the United States. This is the lowest percentage of any ethnic/cultural group (U.S. Bureau of the Census, 2002c).

The 2000 Census classifies American Indians and Alaska Natives together. Native Hawaiians and other Pacific Islanders are included in a separate group. In this section on the strengths of American Indian families, we are looking only at the groups living in North America.

Six important strengths of American Indian families are listed here and summarized in Figure 2.8 (Carson, Dail, Greeley, & Kenote, 1990; Stauss, 1986, 1993):

- *Extended-family system.* The extended family is very strong in American Indian families.
- *Traditional beliefs.* The belief system of American Indian tribes focuses on harmony with nature and the value of contentment.

FIGURE 2.8
Strengths and Challenges of American Indian Families

Strengths	Challenges
• Extended-family system • Traditional beliefs • High family cohesion • Respect for elders • Bilingual language skills • Tribal support system	• Dealing with the conflicting values of the tribe and U.S. society • Maintaining family traditions • Staying cohesive and connected • Identifying role models • Achieving higher levels of education

- *High family cohesion*. The connectedness of the family is important. The family is broadly defined to include the nuclear family, the extended family, and the tribal community.
- *Respect for elders*. Elders are the most respected individuals in traditional American Indian tribes, and the family reinforces this attitude.
- *Bilingual language skills*. Most American Indians work hard to maintain their native languages, but this objective is becoming more difficult because the children attend school off the reservations and are increasingly exposed to television and other mass media.
- *Tribal support system*. Many American Indians rely on their tribal support system for all types of problems. Only when that is inadequate do they turn to outside support.

Although American Indian families are characterized by diversity (Stauss, 1993), some investigators have asserted that the family remains the basic unit of the American Indian community and that the American Indian family can be characterized as having traditional beliefs, practices, and languages and a unique history and lifestyle. American Indian families derive support from both individual family members and the clan or tribal group to which they belong.

Studies have found that many American Indian tribes emphasize mutual dependence among tribal members, responsibility, respect for others, courage, optimism, and contentment. This contentment comes from an identification with the cosmos (feeling one with the world), a spiritual orientation to life, and traditional religious practices. Living in harmony with nature and with other human beings is of utmost importance, nature being a powerful learning tool for family members and the tribe.

The extended family is still a source of strength for many American Indians, but this is changing as more family members leave the reservation to seek opportunities elsewhere. American Indian youths may have a wider array of people to whom they are attached than do non-Indians. In times of crisis, support from both

American Indian families have many strengths on which they rely, including a strong extended-family system, traditional beliefs that focus on harmony with nature and the value of contentment, high family cohesion, respect for elders, bilingual language skills, and the tribal support system.

the extended family and the tribal community helps people survive. Nuclear families are important, but the tribal community also acts as a safety net, assuming a great deal of responsibility for the welfare of its individual members. Many fathers actively care for their own children along with the mothers and serve as father substitutes for children whose fathers have died or deserted the family.

How an individual behaves, in both positive and negative ways, reflects upon the individual's family and tribe (Carson et al., 1990). The group is in part collectively liable for the transgressions of its individual members, so the group provides a collective conscience and consciousness that emphasize individual responsibility. Respect for elders is common among American Indian tribes, and grandparents often hold a unique position, passing on cultural values and beliefs to their grandchildren and educating the young about the physical, social, and spiritual world. Social shame (that is, embarrassment) is a common tool for disciplining children. In general, physical punishment is not encouraged or condoned. Parents usually praise their children only for special accomplishments. The young are not socialized to expect praise, and it is not given lightly.

A number of tribes stress marriages based not only on an attraction between two people but on the consensus of their relatives and the tribal community. This approach to marriage recognizes the fact that an individual marries not only another individual but also that person's family and cultural community. Research suggests that these officially sanctioned marriages are more stable than those not recognized by the couple's family members or the tribe.

The bilingual childrearing seen in some tribes and families is also identified as a strength of American Indian families. Although most American Indians learn English for survival in a White-dominant culture, they often find strength in sharing their own common languages. The family strengths and culturally adaptive patterns of American Indians deserve more extensive study in the years ahead.

Cross-Cultural Family Studies

Cross-cultural family studies tend to focus on two interrelated questions. First, how are families in the United States different from those in other parts of the world? Second, how are they similar? At first glance, people are often struck by the obvious differences between family cultures. Clothing styles, food preferences, religious beliefs, housing, music, education—all these aspects of culture vary from one society to another. When visiting a new culture, people often look for the differences between it and their own culture. Eventually, they also begin to see the similarities. When learning about another culture, then, the key is to look for both similarities and differences.

Cross-cultural family studies focus on how particular cultural contexts influence a wide variety of issues: family values and behaviors, courtship patterns and weddings, marital and parent–child communication, power and gender roles, work and the family, ethical and religious values, childrearing patterns, sexuality, the role of grandparents and the extended family, and the role people outside the immediate family play in helping families in crisis.

We are all ethnocentric to some extent; we see others through unique lenses that are shaped by our own culture. **Ethnocentrism** is the assumption that one's own culture is the standard by which other cultures should be judged. Our ethnocentricity influences the extent to which we judge other people, families, and

BOX 2.3   Diversity in Families

The Tables Are Turned: Going from the Majority to the Minority

In the following story, a father tells what it felt like when his family moved from being members of the dominant White majority in the United States to being members of the tiny White minority in the small country of Fiji in the South Pacific.

Living as a minority in another country was one of the most vivid experiences our family has ever had. It gave us all a great deal of insight into what it feels like to be an "outsider." We went from a city in which we were part of the 89% White majority and we were "insiders," to a village in which we were part of the 2% Caucasian minority.

We were used to being accepted, to being "normal," to "fitting in." When we arrived, everything was different to us, and it was clear that we just did not fit in. Instead of seeing the middle-class midwestern suburban neighborhood with well-kept homes, manicured yards, and new cars, we moved into an indigenous settlement. The settlement was set in a river valley ringed by low mountains that were covered with tropical rain forest. It rained 200 inches a year. The settlement was a 10-minute walk from a tropical lagoon where tiger sharks swam and women hunted for eels and shellfish to feed their large families.

The first evening we moved into our house we heard drums begin to beat a few hours after we had fallen into bed, exhausted; faint chanting was coming from the settlement. Lying underneath the mosquito netting in bed, we laughed about how the drums sounded like some kind of celebration. The islanders had given up cannibalism more than a century before: "Perhaps they're reviving the old ways to introduce us to the culture," we joked to each other, falling into cultural stereotypes that made us feel guilty for dredging them up. The next day we found out the drums were traditional instruments carved from large logs. They were being used to call members of the local church choir to Wednesday evening practice. We felt even stupider then.

The people of color who dominated the country had a different language than we did. They ate different foods, sang different songs, danced different dances, wore different clothes, held different religious beliefs, made different rules for their families and their communities and their government. And the color of their skin was different than ours. Frankly, everything was different to us.

At first these differences seemed exotic and interesting. After awhile, we were worn down by being different, and a kind of chronic fatigue set in upon us, sprinkled with occasional outbursts of anger that we felt we should not express. You could see the stress on the faces of other Whites who were either visiting the small island or had decided to live there. Being different meant that they didn't quite understand all the cultural rules—all the patterns of behavior and thought and speech, all the do's and don'ts.

Being a member of the 2% White minority in our little South Pacific country turned the tables on us. When we visited with other Whites on the island, the conversation often focused on how difficult it was to live in a culture dominated by people of color. "You can't trust them. They're always trying to take advantage of you. They run the government. They make the rules. There's no way we can get ahead in this country," and so forth. The minority Whites often seemed sick and tired and miserable, though they put on brave, smiling faces when around the majority.

Fortunately, my family and I met people of color there who took us into their homes and their hearts, and served as our cultural guides, helping us understand their world and the wonderful things about life the islanders knew that we didn't know. Without these cultural guides, our life on the island would have been much more difficult. Instead, it turned into an unforgettable experience in seeing the world from the perspective of an ethnic minority.

Source: John DeFrain.

cultures as similar to or different from us. Tolerance of the traditions and values of other cultural and ethnic groups is the first step in transcending our overconcern with human differences. Understanding other ways of looking at life and the world around us can lead to genuine, mutual appreciation among people of different backgrounds (see Box 2.3).

Related to the issue of ethnocentrism is what anthropologists have called *perspective*. When one looks at a society from the outside, or from an **etic perspective**, one sees its characteristics in isolation rather than as they relate to the structure of the society as a whole. On the other hand, when one looks at a society from the inside, or from an **emic perspective**, one analyzes behaviors in terms of the internal structural elements of the society. The etic perspective tends to focus on and exaggerate differences, whereas the emic perspective makes it easier to see similarities between cultures.

Family researchers attempt to combine these two perspectives, recognizing the differences between cultures but also trying to identify similarities. Researchers from one culture can never completely discard their personal lenses. They can, however, try to become more open to new ideas and behaviors by submerging themselves in another culture, even learning that culture's language and living within that culture.

Challenges for Ethnic Families

Ethnic families in the United States face many challenges. Among them are intercultural marriage, the issue of assimilation, and relationships between men and women and between parents and children. Ethnic families do not experience the "advantages of being in the majority" that White Americans in the predominant culture do.

Assimilation, Acculturation, and Segregation

Newcomers to any society face a difficult set of choices: Should they swiftly reject their former life and the culture from which they came? Should they downplay their ethnic origins in an effort to fit the mainstream view? Or should they build their own ethnic enclave and try to create a safe microworld that reflects their cultural heritage? These questions are extremely difficult to answer, and minority-group members often disagree on how to proceed. Some families are torn apart by controversies of this nature.

There are three important processes that help explain what happens when a cultural group from another country encounters the dominant culture of the new country. **Assimilation** is *the process in which old cultural traits and values are relinquished and replaced by those of the dominant culture.* **Acculturation** is *the process whereby cultural traits and values from one ethnic group become blended with those of the dominant culture.* **Segregation** is *the process in which an ethnic group isolates itself or is forced into isolation within the dominant culture.* All three of these processes can occur in an interactive way as a family adapts to living in another culture.

Members of the majority culture whose families have been in the United States for two, three, or more generations sometimes do not understand why immigrants are hesitant about assimilation—adopting the values of the dominant culture. But it is clear that immigrants are in a difficult psychological position. They see and are attracted by the strengths of American culture, especially its abundance of economic resources. But they also see the weaknesses of American culture—materialism, competitiveness, wasteful exploitation of the natural world, a fast-paced and often impersonal existence. Immigrants are in some ways in a better position to see America's strengths and weaknesses than are Americans, for they have another culture with which they can compare this one.

Unfortunately, most of what people know about ethnic and cultural groups other than their own is based on **stereotypes**—standardized, oversimplified, and mean-spirited views. When a person from one group describes people from another, the description is often a stereotype. **Prejudice**, which literally means prejudging, is also closely linked with stereotyping; both attitudes reinforce each other. As a society, we need to move beyond stereotypes and focus on each group's strengths and challenges. Recognizing others' strengths helps reduce prejudice.

Racism is closely related to ethnocentrism and may even be a by-product of it. All the various "isms" tend to distance human beings from each other by accentuating differences and ignoring fundamental similarities, which, in turn, leads to tension and conflict. **Racism** develops when the most powerful group in a society creates an elaborate mythology (a set of beliefs that grossly distort reality) about a minority group. These prejudices often endure because of the need of the dominant group to feel superior to others. These prejudices can be significant stressors for members of the minority group, having serious psychological, social, and physiological effects (Clark, Anderson, Clark, & Williams, 1999).

The Advantages of Being in the Majority

If you're a member of the predominant culture in any society, there are innumerable benefits that accrue to you. You receive these benefits every day of your life, regardless of whether you worked for them—and, thus, "deserve" them—or didn't do anything at all to gain them. They are a birthright, like being born into a wealthy family. If you're a member of the majority culture, you take these benefits for granted. In fact, you hardly ever think about them.

We're not just targeting American culture here; we believe this is a cross-cultural phenomenon. Many countries throughout the world have a dominant culture. The dominant culture does not necessarily have to comprise the largest population, but it does hold most of the power.

What, in essence, are we talking about here? If you're a member of the majority culture:

- People speak the same language you speak.
- The educational system is patterned after your ways of thinking and honors your history, your beliefs, and your values.
- The job market is more open to you because you are the "right" color, gender, religion, sexual orientation, political affiliation, or social class, and you don't have a disability that makes the majority culture uncomfortable.
- People will not discriminate in renting an apartment to you or selling you a house in their neighborhood.
- The laws, the police, and the courts are sensitive to your cultural values and tend to deal with you in a relatively open-minded fashion.
- Religious and spiritual values of the culture are ideals that you can agree on and live with.
- Music, literature, movies, and art reflect your tastes and values.

The list of advantages accruing to those in the majority culture is almost endless. What advantages can you add to this list?

Marriage Outside the Group

In many countries throughout the world, marriage is seen primarily as an agreement between two families. An alliance through marriage between two successful families can enhance the power, prestige, and well-being of all the members of both families. In this sense, one marries not just an individual but also that person's family.

Because American culture stresses individuality, the importance of a good "fit" between families is often overlooked, and individuals who wish to marry often purposely ignore advice from family members. Sometimes that advice is based on ignorance of the proposed partner's personal strengths and/or on prejudice toward the cultural group from which the proposed partner comes. The greater the differences between the two families, the more likely the chance for conflict.

As our society becomes more ethnically diverse, marriage across ethnic groups has increased and, in turn, expanded ethnic diversity. According to Qian (2005), who relied on the 2000 Census, 9% of African American marriages are multiracial, 39% of Hispanics, 56% of American Indians, and 59% of Asian Americans. Only 4% of Whites are in **multiracial marriages** (marriages between two people from two different cultural or ethnic groups). The pool for marrying within one's ethnic group is much smaller for minority populations than for the White population. Highly educated individuals are more likely to marry someone of another culture than those who have less education (Batson et al., 2006).

The number of multicultural couples cohabiting has increased and is approximately twice as high as the number of multiracial marriages (Batson et al., 2006; Qian, 2005). Some couples choose to live together to avoid disapproval from extended family. The number of multiracial marriages is increasing, and the trend is expected to continue as public attitudes become more accepting of such unions.

A survey conducted by *the Washington Post*, the Henry J. Kaiser Family Foundation, and Harvard University indicates that biracial couples report widespread tolerance and even acceptance of their relationships. The survey also found that an overwhelming majority of the 540 couples interviewed said they had introduced their partners to accepting parents and other family members, and felt comfortable talking openly about their partners. The survey also found that the majority felt their children are more advantaged than disadvantaged by having parents from different ethnic groups.

The researchers also conducted companion surveys with 1,709 randomly selected adults. They found that 53% of Whites, 77% of Blacks, 68% of Latinos, and 67% of Asians said it makes no difference whether a person marries someone of their own ethnic group or a different group. About 40% of those interviewed in the random sample said they had dated someone of another ethnic group. The researchers also found that 46% of Black–White couples said being married to someone of a different group makes married life harder, compared to 30% of Latino–White couples and 32% of Asian–White couples. And 65% of Black–White couples said a parent at first had a problem with the relationship, compared to 24% of Latino–White couples and 24% of Asian–White couples ("Biracial Couples Find More Tolerance," 2001).

Relationships Between Men and Women

Regardless of nationality or cultural background, friction occurs between men and women in intimate relationships. Although couples strive for mutual love and caring, different socialization processes and biological inheritances produce misunderstanding and conflict. Women in developed countries, because of greater education and more employment opportunities outside the home, tend to have more options. If they are dissatisfied with their marriages and can support themselves, they are not as likely to stay in these marriages. Women in rural areas and in developing countries have fewer options, even though they may be just as unhappy as their divorcing counterparts in developed countries. As a result, divorce rates tend to be higher in industrialized, urban-oriented societies around the world and lower in less-developed, agrarian societies. But the lower divorce rates in the more rural societies do not necessarily indicate happier marriages.

Relationships Between Parents and Children

Children often develop into adults much like their own parents. In the process of growing up, however, children and parents often experience much conflict. The younger generation strives to create a relatively independent life, and the older generation tries to maintain control of the children. These struggles are played out in countless cultures around the world. Family power structures in various cultures seem to change gradually over time, as societies move from agriculturally oriented economies to industrialized economies. In an agriculturally oriented family, the father, who is responsible for making sure the farm runs smoothly, has more control over his children. In the city, the father's influence lessens, and the influence of others (peers, school, the workplace) increases. Rural societies generally emphasize respect for the authority of the dominant males. In more modern societies, the rights of the individual, whether female or male, receive more weight because the family is more likely to succeed if all its members become well educated and find good jobs.

When a family moves from one culture to another, parent–child relationships can be especially strained, because the youngsters struggle to fit into the new culture and inevitably lose touch with past traditions. Kim, a 35-year-old woman who married an American and emigrated to the United States from Korea, explains why it is important for their children, born in Korea but being raised in the United States, to be able to speak not only English but her native language as well. It will be a delicate balancing act for the family to maintain connections to both Korean

Ethnic identity is a social construction rather than a biological fact. The children in this family are of mixed European American and Asian heritage; their ethnic identity depends not on their physical characteristics but on the tradition within which they are being raised. Many young parents such as these work to rear their children in a bicultural environment, respectful of both family traditions.

and American cultures, but the benefits of such an accomplishment can far outweigh the difficulties.

> "Of course, they need to know English. They're going to end up being Americans. That's obvious. We aren't going back to Korea to live, only to visit.
>
> "It's hard for them. They speak English in school and in the neighborhood, but in the home we speak Korean. They get confused sometimes and mix languages. Sometimes the neighbor kids tease them about it. It's especially difficult for Jared, our son, but Emily is doing great. I think they'll both catch on and see why it's important in the long run.
>
> "I want them to appreciate their roots, to remember the wonderful civilization they come from. And, most important, I want them to know me, their mother. I live in the United States but probably always will be Korean deep down, because that's where I grew up. I can't help it. That's home. The language of emotion, the language of love is your native language. How can I show my true emotions, my true love for my children if they cannot understand my Korean? How can they really know me?"

Summary

- Appreciating diversity and the strengths of diversity are major goals of this chapter.
- When viewing people from different ethnic groups, it is important to look beyond their physical qualities and get to know their personal and family strengths.
- Cultural identity evolves from shared beliefs, values, and attitudes.
- Ethnic identity refers to the geographic origin of a particular group.
- Race is based on the physical characteristics of a group of people and is a concept that is losing value.
- The Hispanic, or Latino, population recently became the largest minority population in the United States, followed by African American, Asian American, and American Indian and Alaska Native populations.
- Historically, research has been primarily conducted with White, middle-class populations. Not only is there a need to include minority population in research studies, but there is also a need to include members of these populations in all aspects of research, including planning, analyzing data, and interpreting results.
- Professionals need to become culturally competent in order to more effectively provide family education and services.
- Kin relationships—the structure of marital and family relationships—vary considerably across ethnic and cultural groups.
- Strong families share the three family system traits of cohesion, flexibility, and communication. Three sociocultural characteristics are also useful for understanding families: the extended-family system, the social system, and the belief system.
- The strengths of White families in the United States include commitment to the family, enjoyable time spent together, the ability to manage stress and crisis effectively, spiritual well-being, positive communication, and appreciation and affection for each other.
- The strengths of African American families include strong kinship bonds, strong work orientation, flexibility in family roles, strong motivation to achieve, strong religious orientation, and egalitarian marriages.
- The strengths of Latino families include familism, high family cohesion, high family flexibility, a supportive kin network system, egalitarian decision making, and strong ethnic identity.
- The strengths of Asian American families include strong family orientation, filial piety, a high value on education, well-disciplined children, extended-family support, and family loyalty.
- The strengths of American Indian families include an extended-family system, traditional beliefs, high family cohesion, respect for elders, bilingual language skills, and a tribal support system.
- Multiracial marriage can be challenging for families, but it can also be the source of considerable learning and personal growth.
- Male–female relationships and parent–child struggles are common issues in families from a variety of ethnic groups.
- The issues of assimilation, acculturation, and segregation must be faced by any new ethnic or cultural group.

Key Terms

cultural identity	minority group
ethnic identity	race
cultural group	cultural competence
coculture	kinship
ethnic group	nuclear family

conjugal family system
consanguineal family
  system
extended family
plural marriage
polygamy
polygyny
polyandry
monogamy
pseudo–kin group
lineage
matrilineal society
patrilineal society
bilateral descent
matriarchal group
patriarchal group
egalitarian group
matrilocal society
patrilocal society

neolocal society
family cohesion
family flexibility
family communication
extended-family system
social system
belief system
cross-cultural family study
ethnocentrism
etic perspective
emic perspective
assimilation
acculturation
segregation
stereotype
prejudice
racism
multiracial marriage

Activities

1. Make a list of your family's strengths. How do they compare with the strengths identified by family researchers?
2. For a week, observe and collect examples of racism in American society. Jot down in a notebook all the examples you find of prejudice and discrimination. Also collect examples of cooperation and appreciation expressed between different ethnic groups. Share these examples with others in a small-group discussion.
3. Find people in your class or on campus who have different ethnic backgrounds than yours. Talk with them about what positive and negative things they have experienced because of their ethnic group.

Suggested Readings

Cashmore, E., & Jennings, J. (2001). *Racism: Essential readings.* Newbury Park, CA: Sage. The long and complex intellectual history of the concept of racism and how powerful groups used racism as an ideology to advance social, economic, and cultural interests.

Chang, I. (2003). *The Chinese in America: A narrative history.* New York: Viking. The 150-year history of a people's search for a better life.

Garcia, A. M. (2003). *Narratives of Mexican American women.* Walnut Creek, CA: AltaMira Press. This is an insightful narrative of Chicana college students' struggle with their personal and family lives.

Graves, J. L., Jr. (2004). *The race myth: Why we pretend race exists in America.* New York: Dutton. Dr. Graves, an evolutionary biologist at Fairleigh Dickinson University in New Jersey, argues,
We have paid dearly for the policies of racism, and are continuing to pay in a currency of despair, unfulfilled dreams, and blood. . . . Every time we pay, we slide closer toward hell on a road paved with our racial misconceptions. We will continue to pay until we reject the notion that there are biological races in the human species, and that race determines an individual's worth.

McAdoo, H. P. (Ed.). (1999). *Family ethnicity: Strength in diversity.* Thousand Oaks, CA: Sage. Explores family ethnicity in five major cultural groups in the United States: African Americans, Latino Americans, American Indians, Asian Americans, and Muslim Americans.

McAdoo, H. P. (Ed.). (2007). *Black families* (4th ed.). Thousand Oaks, CA: Sage.

McCubbin, H. I., Thompson, A. I., & Fromer, J. E. (Eds.). (1998). *Resiliency in Native American and immigrant families.* Thousand Oaks, CA: Sage. A much-needed addition to the research literature.

Mohatt, G., & Thomas, L. (2006). "I wonder, why would you do it that way?" In J. E. Trimble & C. B. Fisher (Eds.), *The handbook of ethical research with ethnocultural populations and communities.* Thousand Oaks, CA: Sage.

Qian, Z. (2005). Breaking the last taboo: Interracial marriages in America. *Contexts, 4,* 33–37.

Rumbaut, R., & Portes, A. (Eds.). (2001). *Ethnicities: Children of immigrants in America.* Berkeley, CA: University of California Press, Russell Sage Foundation. Today's youth often find themselves straddling different worlds and receiving conflicting signals.

Skogrand, L. (2004). A process for learning about and creating programming for culturally diverse audiences. *Forum of Family and Consumer Issues, 9.* Online Journal: http://www.ces.ncsu.edu/depts/fcs/pub/forum.html.

Skogrand, L., Hatch, D., & Singh, A. (2008). Strong marriages in Latino culture. In R. Dalla, J. DeFrain, J. Johnson, & D. Abbott (Eds.), *Strengths and challenges of new immigrant families: Implications for research, policy, education, and service.* Lexington, MA: Lexington Books.

Willie, C. V., & Reddick, R. J. (2003). *A new look at Black families.* Walnut Creek, CA: AltaMira Press. This classic book uses the case study method to illustrate how Black families live in various social classes and to identify the strengths of highly successful Black families.

Visit the text-specific Online Learning Center at **www.mhhe.com/Olson6** for practice tests, chapter summaries, Web links, Internet exercises, key terms, and flashcards.

3 *U*nderstanding Marriage and Family Dynamics

PETTING ZOO OPEN
MON-SAT 10:00-4:30 SUN 12:00-5:00

Family Science: A Growing Profession

Models of Couples and Families

Three Key Relationship Concepts

Couple and Family Map

Family Dynamics in Television and Movies

Dynamics Change in Relationships Over Time

Summary

Key Terms

Activities

Suggested Readings

There are a variety of perspectives or ways of describing marriage and family dynamics. These perspectives are like different lenses through which we can observe the various aspects of close relationships. Each perspective, or framework, is built on different assumptions and has specific concepts that help define the relevant elements of each framework.

In this chapter we will present six major conceptual frameworks for describing marriage and family dynamics: *the family systems theory, the family strengths framework, the family development framework, the symbolic interaction framework, the social construction framework,* and *the feminist framework.* We will also take a look at three major dimensions of couple and family dynamics that integrate many of the concepts from the six frameworks; these three central dimensions are cohesion, flexibility, and communication. To conclude, we will discuss the Couple and Family Map, which helps integrate and apply these more abstract frameworks and concepts to specific couple and family relationships.

Before we begin exploring the conceptual frameworks, we will define some of the relevant concepts related to conceptual and theory development. A **conceptual framework** is a set of interconnected ideas, concepts, and assumptions that helps organize thinking from a particular perspective. A **theory** consists of general principles that are composed of interrelated concepts, and **hypotheses** are presumed relationships between variables. A **research study** can be designed to test one or more specific hypotheses.

Most family professionals maintain that there are many ways of looking at families. They use ideas and principles from several conceptual frameworks to help them understand marriage and family life. This open-minded approach to learning and to life is often termed an *eclectic* approach, and most family researchers, family life educators, and family therapists subscribe to it. However, professionals with an eclectic approach can sometimes be too open and accepting of contradictory ideas.

There are two contrasting approaches to understanding how individuals and families operate: the idiographic approach and the nomothetic approach. Some family scientists maintain that human beings are unique and that it is difficult to construct a broad conceptual framework or theory that applies to all couples and to all families. This view has been labeled the **idiographic approach**, which focuses on the unique aspects of individuals or families. Professionals who use this approach are more interested in individual case studies and tend to have a clinical focus.

On the other end of the theory spectrum is the **nomothetic approach**, which focuses on ideas that apply to the majority of individuals or families. Researchers using this approach try to develop a broader understanding of couples and families and to work toward a general theory. Both of these approaches have value and usefulness, because every marriage and every family *is* unique and yet has much in common with others.

Family Science: A Growing Profession

Family science is a relatively new multidisciplinary profession that began only about 50 years ago. It has grown primarily because professionals have become more interested in relationships, especially marriages and families. In the last 30 years, the profession has more clearly defined itself, and there are now research projects on almost any relationship topic you can imagine. The number of journal publications that deal with relationships, including marriage and the family, since the 1950s has grown to over 300,000 articles that have been published in over 300 professional journals.

One of the major characteristics of the family profession is that it is interested in applied issues related to relationships. The family field is also very interested in integrating theory, research, and practice. One major family organization that brings professionals together for integrating these three key areas is the National Council on Family Relations (NCFR). This organization has helped create the new profession called *family science*. Another important group of family professionals are *marital and family therapists*, who belong to the American Association for Marital and Family Therapy (AAMFT) and who focus on helping couples and families with problems. There are also *family life educators* who work in the public schools and in the community, conducting a variety of educational and prevention programs.

The growing impact of the family profession is indicated by how many other professional groups now focus on family-oriented topics. Table 3.1 illustrates the topics and issues that the traditional disciplines are now studying and are providing significant contributions. Increasingly, professionals from these other disciplines are now specializing in marriage and family. For example, there are lawyers who now specialize in family law. Even in the medical profession, there is a specialty that focuses on the family called *family practice*.

There is a growing awareness of the importance of close relationships in a person's life. Studies of personal happiness have consistently revealed that close relationships are the most important aspects of life and are essential to emotional well-being and good physical health (Berscheid, 2006; Berscheid & Reis, 1998). Conversely, many studies have documented that a troubled relationship, especially a distressed marriage and family, is the most common presenting problem of those seeking therapy.

While psychologists have traditionally focused on understanding individuals, family science is focused on *relationships*. The growing interest in relationship science was identified by Ellen Berscheid, a well-known social psychologist,

TABLE 3.1	Disciplines Contributing to Family Science
Discipline	**Topics in Family Science**
Anthropology	Cross-cultural studies; kinship; diversity in families
Biology	Conception and reproduction; growth, development, and aging
Child development	Development of infant and child; interpersonal skills
Economics	Family finances; consumer behavior
Education	Family life education; marriage preparation
English	Marriages and families in literature (present and past)
History	Historical perspectives on the family throughout time
Human ecology	Ecosystem perspectives on family, nutrition, housing, and clothing
Law	Marriage and divorce laws; child custody laws
Medicine	Families and health
Psychiatry	Family therapy
Psychology	Family psychology; assessment of couples and families
Social work	Treating problem families; family policy
Sociology	Marriage and divorce statistics; sociological theories about families

who emphasizes the importance of studying interactions and interconnections between people (Berscheid, 2006). Relationship science assumes that a relationship is dynamic and resides between people and not within a person.

Relationships are the essence of life. "We are born into relationships, we live our lives in relationships with others, and when we die, the effects of our relationships survive in the lives of the living" (Berscheid, 2006). It is for this reason that there is increasing interest in family science which focuses on studying, understanding, and helping all types of close relationships.

Models of Couples and Families

This chapter will describe a variety of models or ways of understanding couples and families, which are called *conceptual frameworks*. The most popular of the conceptual frameworks is the *family systems theory*, which focuses on the family as an ongoing system of interconnected members. (Because it is a broad and comprehensive set of principles, this perspective is referred to more often as a theory than as a conceptual framework.) The *family strengths framework* is becoming more accepted because it highlights the positive aspects of couples and families rather than their problems. The *family development framework* looks at how couples and families change over time. The *symbolic interaction framework* has historically been valuable to family professionals because it examines how family members learn roles and rules in our society. The *social construction framework*, which is growing in popularity, maintains that our views as partners and family members are shaped by our social world and that each of us has a different life experience and therefore a unique view of our own close relationships. The *feminist framework* is increasingly important to the family field because it emphasizes the value of women's perspectives on marriage and family life and on society.

Family Systems Theory

According to **family systems theory**, everything that happens to any family member has an impact on everyone else in the family (Goldenberg & Goldenberg, 2007). Because family members are interconnected and operate as a group, the group is called a **family system**. This approach to describing the family as a system has become very popular in both theory and practice, particularly with family therapists who work with couples and families having relationship problems.

A pioneer family therapist Carl Whitaker (1992) was fond of saying that in a metaphorical sense "there are no individuals in the world—only fragments of families." In other words, individual human beings are inextricably tied to their family. How people think and behave is deeply influenced by their family background, and people are best understood by understanding their family. From a family therapist's standpoint, an individual can most effectively change if his or her family also changes. If a family is in trouble, both parents and children need to become involved in family therapy.

When an individual has a problem, not only the family but also the whole community is often involved in finding a solution, an idea echoed in the popular statement "It takes a whole village to raise a child." A family simply cannot do it all alone. Troubled families often live in troubled communities, and if individuals are to be well, the community must find a way to create health for all its members.

Family systems theory grew out of the general systems theory, a conceptual framework developed in the 1960s by Ludwig von Bertalanffy (1968), and family therapists applied these ideas to marriage and family as a system. The **general systems theory**, a broad-based model used in a variety of fields, is a set of principles and concepts that can be applied to all types of systems, living and nonliving. The dictionary defines a **system** as (1) a set or arrangement of things so related or connected as to form a unity or organic whole and (2) a whole made of interacting parts.

Family systems theory was created by family therapists because family therapists working with troubled individuals over the years discovered that working with an individual alone did not produce long-term change in a child's behavior. A problem child might make some improvements in her or his functioning by working alone with the therapist, but the child often reverted back to problem behaviors unless the family changed. This is because the family system has such a powerful impact on a child's behavior.

Another important finding by family therapists was that when a child has problems, often there are problems in the family system. For example, family therapists have found that if there is a disturbed child in a two-parent family, there is often a troubled marriage which contributes to the child's difficulties.

A Hierarchy of Connected Systems. Proponents of the family systems theory have expanded on ideas and terminology developed by general systems theorists, and family therapists use these ideas in their practice. Several concepts of the general systems theory are particularly relevant to family systems. The idea of **multiple system levels** is that systems are embedded within other systems. Whenever attention is focused on a given system, a **suprasystem** (a larger system) and a **subsystem** (a smaller system) are usually also involved. If you are focusing on the couple as the system, the suprasystem is the family and the subsystem consists of the two individuals. If you are focusing on the nuclear family as the system, the suprasystem is the extended family and the subsystem is the couple or any other dyadic (two-person) unit, such as parent and child.

Systems are both connected to and separated from other systems by **boundaries**. The notion of a boundary also implies a hierarchy of interconnected systems, each system being separated by invisible boundaries from other smaller or larger systems (Goldenberg & Goldenberg, 2007). Considering the family, there is a boundary between the family and the larger kin system and a boundary between parents and the children.

Human systems have many different system levels that can be characterized as a set of concentric circles (Figure 3.1). For example, the smallest circle at the center would be the individual; encircling this in graduated rings would be the couple (a dyad, or two-person human system), the family, the local neighborhood (including businesses, schools, etc.), the town, the nation, the continent, the world, and so on. Families do not function in a vacuum because they are a part of larger systems.

Thinking about human systems is considered an ecological approach; **ecology** is the study of how all the organisms in a system are related to each other. As Figure 3.1 illustrates, all the concentric circles are connected to one another and the people in each of the circles influence the people in the other circles—creating a **human ecosystem**. To really understand a specific family system, you also need to consider the various system levels it influences and that influence it. For these reasons, helping a middle-class, suburban family through a crisis would be very different from helping a family living in poverty in the inner city.

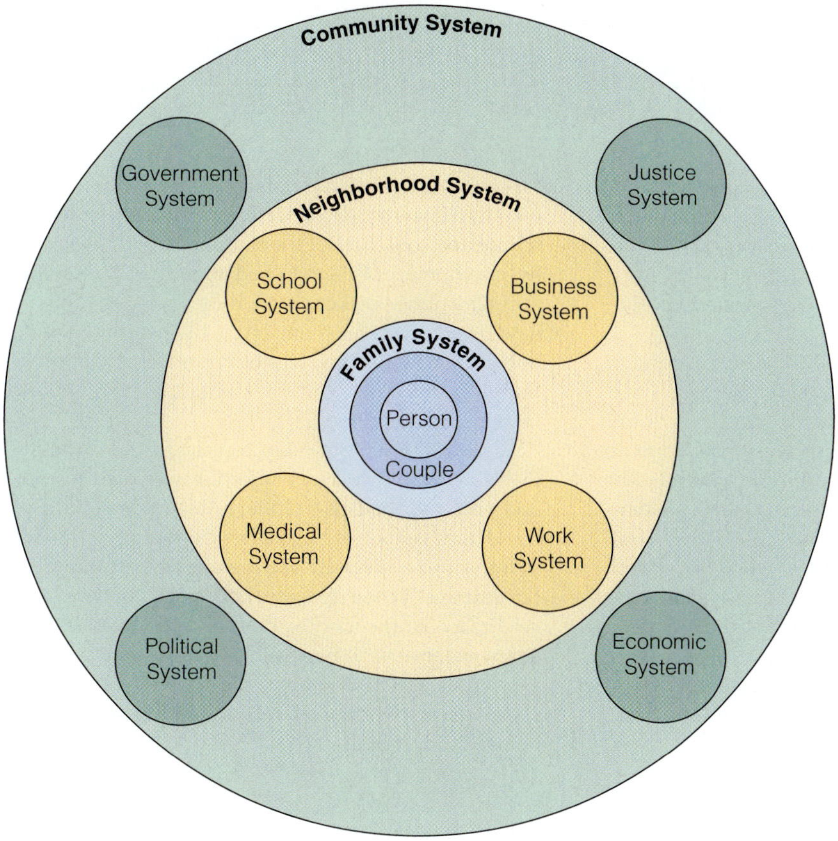

FIGURE 3.1
An Ecological Approach
to Human Systems

Another concept from general systems theory is **wholeness**, the concept that the whole is more than the sum of its parts. From a family systems perspective, the whole family is more than the total of all its individual members. This means that you cannot know the family simply by knowing each person as an individual because each individual will behave differently outside the family (Goldenberg & Goldenberg, 2007).

For example, Carla, a student living in an apartment, has a certain identity related to her life at college and another identity back home with her family. If you observe Carla very carefully in her college environment, you get a good understanding of what she is like at college. But when Carla goes home to visit her family for a holiday break, she becomes a different person in many ways. She is transformed into a daughter, a granddaughter, a big sister, a little sister. At home she may return to some of the ways she previously behaved at home, even though she does not continue that pattern at school. This is partly because although she might have changed in college, the family did not change and when the family is all together again she fills the role she played in the family to create the wholeness of the family.

A good cook takes individual herbs, spices, and vegetables and combines them to create a wonderful and zesty sauce that has flavors of the individual ingredients but is more than and different from the separate ingredients. The whole family system is also more than the sum of its parts, and the family's behavior cannot be predicted from knowing only the individual persons. Conversely, it is difficult to predict the behavior of the individuals by knowing about the family as a whole.

Like other families affected by sudden changes, Julia's family will probably never return to the way things were before an accident occurred. But as Julia's case shows, the nuclear family, with the help of extended-family members, is capable of establishing a more connected family system.

Julia was a single parent living with her two young children, Camille and Katy. Their life together was a hectic but satisfying round of school, work, family visits, and activities with friends. Last year, Julia was involved in an auto accident and was seriously injured. She could neither work nor care for her children. Her family's delicate balance was upset until her mother Eloise, her brother Tim, her sister Allison, and her best friend at work, Sheryl, all stepped in to help create a new sense of family balance.

These four adults spent countless hours at the hospital, reassuring Julia and listening to her express her uncertainty and pain. They also worked out some new arrangements to make up for her absence. Camille and Katy temporarily moved in with Eloise. She took care of them, prepared their meals, made sure they had clean clothes for school, and took over many details of their lives. Tim, who lived nearby, drove Camille and Katy to and from school and took care of them afterward. Allison, who still lived at home, got them to bed at night and took them on outings on the weekends. Camille and Katy took on some new responsibilities themselves, like walking the dog and doing their homework without prompting. Sheryl kept things going at the office by taking on several of Julia's responsibilities herself.

After an initial period of confusion and difficulty, all these individuals became familiar with their new roles and proud of their new skills. Julia was hospitalized for several weeks and had physical therapy for several months, but eventually she regained her strength and her courage. When she returned home, the whole family celebrated. In the months that followed, she established a new balance with her children, assimilating the experiences they had all had since the accident. She also had a stronger network of friends and family than she had before the accident.

Another concept of the general systems theory is the **interdependence of parts**: The parts or elements of a system are interconnected in such a way that if one part is changed, other parts are also affected (Goldenberg & Goldenberg, 2007). Visualize for a moment a mobile, an artistic creation suspended in midair, made up of many carefully balanced elements. Each element in the mobile is weighted and placed in such a way as to create not only an aesthetic effect but also a delicate system that can be easily set in motion by a slight ripple of wind or a soft touch. Anything stronger might knock it out of balance.

Healthy families, in a sense, are like a mobile: Each member fits into the whole in a unique way and adds to the beauty of the whole. If one individual changes—for better or worse—the total creation is affected. Consider how one event changed the family in the story presented in Box 3.1.

Flexibility: Balancing Stability and Change. Flexibility is the ability of a system to balance both stability and change. A flexible couple or family is like a flower in the wind because it is able to bend with the wind. General systems theorists use the term **open system**, or **morphogenic system**, when referring to a system that is open to growth and change. A **closed system**, or **morphostatic system**, is one that has the capacity to maintain the status quo, thus avoiding change (Goldenberg & Goldenberg, 2007).

Family therapists have discovered that many couples and families are highly resistant to change, even though they need to adapt to solve the problems they face. They are likely to want to maintain the status quo out of habit, lack of insight, or fear of something new. A common observation is when one family member changes, there is also change in the other family members.

As an example of a morphostatic system, consider the following story. By failing to deal openly and effectively with their relationship problems, Katherine and Ken are beginning a free fall into despair. They are an example of a morphostatic family system, unable or unwilling to change. A morphogenic system, one open to growth and change, might have been able to prevent such a scenario.

> *Ken and Katherine have been married for 15 years. Ken is an alcoholic, though he manages to hold onto his job as a floor supervisor at a printing plant. Ken has been having an extramarital affair with Winona, a co-worker at the plant, for 6 months. When Katherine discovers the affair, she tells Ken she is leaving him. He responds by begging for forgiveness and promising to give up the relationship with Winona.*
>
> *He wants to avoid divorce for a number of reasons: embarrassment at work, shame in his extended family, and financial consequences. Besides, although the thrill is gone from the marriage, he and Katherine have a long history together, and she is a good mother to their three children. Katherine is skeptical about Ken's promises. She tells him that she wants him to give up drinking as well. He says he can control his drinking and just drink "socially." He doesn't really need to go "cold turkey," he argues.*
>
> *Katherine remains skeptical; she has heard such arguments many times before. In spite of her skepticism, however, Katherine decides to forgive Ken, as she has before, and to stay. She genuinely loves him, even though she hates his drinking and, now, his seeing another woman. And he provides a good income for her and the children. Katherine also fears being on her own, both socially and financially. She dreads the thought of going back into the workplace after so many years at home. Whatever she has now, she feels, is better than what she would have as a divorced mother of three.*

The family systems framework assumes that systems operate on a continuum from extreme morphostasis to extreme morphogenesis. In a healthy system, there is a balance between these extremes. The couple or family needs to be open to change, but not to the point of being rootless or chaotic. Conversely, it needs to be centered and stable, but not to the point of being rigid.

Cohesion: Balance of Separateness and Connectedness. Couples and families need to find a balance between their separateness as individuals and their connectedness as a system. The dynamics that help systems maintain this separateness–connectedness balance are the opposing forces of centrifugal and centripetal interactions. **Centrifugal interactions** tend to push family members apart, thereby increasing separateness. **Centripetal interactions** pull family members together and increase family closeness (Goldenberg & Goldenberg, 2007).

Family therapists have found that a family crisis can push families to an extreme of either centripetal or centrifugal interactions. Faced with a death of a family member, one family may pull together and come out stronger as a result of the loss, whereas another family may find itself torn apart by the events. The first family resolves to hold onto each other, communicate about feelings, and help each other. These centripetal interactions strengthen the bonds of love and concern. The members of the second family are afraid, cannot talk with one another, and attempt to deal with the death as individuals. They separate from the family and look for comfort outside it, or they bury themselves in personal despair.

An important aspect of understanding cohesion is whether a family system permits family members to develop their own independence from the family. In the personal account of a young Chicana woman recounted in Box 3.2, you will see that in her close Chicano family, most of the family system is opposed to a female

BOX 3.2   Diversity in Families

Cultural Conflicts for a Female Chicana College Student

I am a Chicana graduate student who wants to complete a Ph.D. in family studies so I can teach at the college level and help the family field be more inclusive and up-to-date regarding Chicano families. Fortunately, the choices I've made are not in conflict with my family of procreation.

It was very difficult for my family of origin initially to understand why I wanted or needed to go to school for so long. Since my grandparents and parents struggled just to provide for adequate housing, food, and clothing, they find it difficult to see why education is so important. They were also somewhat threatened by the fact that I wanted to study families because I might learn too much.

Another conflict was regarding my interest in my own development versus their emphasis on the whole family. They felt I was focusing too much on myself and not giving back enough to the family. Also, they felt this was making me more competitive and less cooperative, which is a quality valued highly. Another issue is the use of the Spanish language and whether I would use both Spanish and English in my home. Since we decided to raise our children using English only, some family members viewed that choice as rejecting our heritage. Also, as my years of college education increased, my relatives tended to distance themselves more from me.

Fortunately, my husband, who is also Chicano, is totally supportive and is a house husband for our two small children. He takes care of the children, and I am the primary wage earner. This is not the traditional family model for most Chicanos, and so it does challenge some of our other family members and kin.

While I was not initially aware of the importance of my mother's support, I have lately become even more appreciative of her encouraging words. I have finally been giving her more credit for her support. She also served as a positive role model since she began working full-time when I was young. She also has strongly encouraged me to work outside the home and even to try to seek a career.

In general, I have made it because I am determined to have a professional career and have the strong support of my husband and my mother. My other relatives are less understanding and supportive since they question my goals and values. In spite of it all, education is necessary for me to help advance myself and my family.

Source: Unpublished manuscript by Julie Palacio, 1992, former graduate student in Family Social Science, University of Minnesota, St. Paul, MN. Reprinted by permission.

(Julie) getting too much education. However, her mother and her husband are very supportive and enabled Julie to continue graduate school and develop her own independence within a very close family system.

Family therapists agree that a healthy balance of separateness and connectedness works best for families in crisis. In the face of death, family members can draw on each other's strengths and skills for comfort and at the same time seek out positive people in the community who can be growth enhancing for the family as a whole. If family members choose to go their separate ways as a result of the crisis, the likelihood of a positive outcome for the family as a whole lessens considerably.

Feedback Within the System (Communication). Another basic principle of the general systems theory is that communication in the system is essential. No matter how hard one might try, one simply cannot *not* communicate (Becvar & Becvar, 2006). Even if we completely withdraw from our family, we are communicating an important message: the family is not a safe, healthy, or happy place to live.

Family systems function better when important information is regularly exchanged among the members, which is the essence of communication. General systems theorists talk about information feedback loops, which can be either positive or negative (Goldenberg & Goldenberg, 2007). **Positive feedback** in families is intended to create change, whereas **negative feedback** is designed to minimize

Families that spend time together and enjoy fun activities build stronger relationships.

change and keep things the same. Feedback can come either from family members or from people outside the family.

Positive and negative do not connote value judgments or indicate whether a change is good or bad but rather whether change occurs in the system or not. For example, Sandy suggests that the members of her family exchange jobs around the house to add variety and give everyone a better understanding of what the various jobs entail. If Sandy's family members accept this idea and change their routine, then Sandy's feedback to the system is considered positive. However, if they resist her idea of change, the system feedback is negative.

In sum, openness to change is a key concept in the family systems framework. A common reaction of some couples and families under stress is to pull inward and try to prevent new information or people from coming into the system. This would be an example of negative feedback because they are resisting change. When under stress, families would be helped if they were more open to change, which is an example of positive feedback.

Family Strengths Framework

The **family strengths framework** focuses on how couples and families succeed rather than on why they fail from a global perspective (DeFrain et al., 2006, DeFrain & Asay, 2007). This perspective arose from the notion that strong families can serve as models for other families wanting to succeed. One advantage of the family strengths framework is that it tends to change the nature of what one finds in families. Simply stated, if one studies only problems, one finds only couple and family problems. Similarly, if researchers and therapists are interested in couple and family strengths, they have to look for them. When these strengths are identified, they can be the foundation for continued growth and change.

Family therapists and other counselors are finding the family strengths framework helpful in treating family problems (Marsh, 2003). Many professionals have found that just solving problems is not enough. They need a model of healthy family development as a goal for troubled families to work toward. Identifying a family's strengths also boosts morale among family members.

The most extensive series of studies of family strengths has been conducted by Nick Stinnett, John DeFrain, and colleagues (DeFrain et al., 2006, DeFrain & Asay, 2007). In over 30 years of study, the researchers have collected data from more than 24,000 family members in every state of the United States and 27 countries around the world. Stinnett and DeFrain propose that six major qualities are commonly present in strong families (Table 3.2). These qualities are appreciation and affection, commitment, positive communication, enjoyable time together, spiritual well-being, and ability to manage stress and crisis.

All these family strengths are interrelated, overlap to some degree, and interact. Appreciation and affection for one another make family members more likely to spend time together, and time together is enhanced by positive communication. Communication enhances commitment, and commitment leads to spending more time together. A feeling of spiritual well-being gives people the confidence to weather a crisis, and the ability to manage crises makes family members appreciate each other more. Family strengths are thus interconnected like a large, complex puzzle. Let's look at each strength in more detail.

Appreciation and Affection. People in strong families care deeply for one another, and they let the others know this regularly. Many people, however, don't express **appreciation and affection** in their families. Consider the response of one

TABLE 3.2	Qualities of Strong Families
Appreciation and Affection	**Commitment**
Caring for each other	Trust
Friendship	Honesty
Respect for individuality	Dependability
Playfulness	Faithfulness
Humor	Sharing
Positive Communication	**Enjoyable Time Together**
Giving compliments	Quality time in great quantity
Sharing feelings	Good things take time
Avoiding blame	Enjoying each other's company
Being able to compromise	Simple good times
Agreeing to disagree	Sharing fun times
Spiritual Well-Being	**Ability to Manage Stress and Crisis**
Hope	Adaptability
Faith	Seeing crises as challenges and opportunities
Compassion	Growing through crises together
Shared ethical values	Openness to change
Oneness with humankind	Resilience

Source: DeFrain & Asay, 2007.

The family strengths framework focuses on the positive qualities of families. Apparent in this family are such strengths as warmth, caring, appreciation, affection, trust, commitment, and enjoyment of each other's company.

spouse: "She cooked dinner every evening, but it never occurred to me to thank her for it. She doesn't thank me for going to work every day." Such an attitude is unfortunate, because expressing affection and giving and receiving sincere thanks foster a positive atmosphere and help people get along better. A pat on the back, a smile, or a hug builds a bond of caring. One member of a strong family explained it this way: "He makes me feel good about me and about us as a couple. Very few days go by without him saying something positive."

People in dysfunctional families more often focus on the negative. These people gain energy by feeding off the self-esteem and good feelings of others. They believe that by putting other people down they can build themselves up. The approach usually backfires, however, often producing only countercriticism.

Researchers have found that sexual behavior in strong marriages is often a form of expressing appreciation for each other. "Foreplay does not begin at 10:30 P.M. on Saturday night," one husband explained. "It begins when I take out the garbage on Wednesday morning, when I cook dinner on Friday night, and when I help Jeannie solve a problem at her work on Saturday afternoon." Sex is a natural way to express warm feelings for the partner. Another person reported, "The times when sex was best have been times when we've felt especially close and in tune with each other, when we'd solved a problem or when we were working on a project together."

Commitment. Members of strong families generally show a strong **commitment** to one another, investing time and energy in family activities and not letting their work or other priorities take too much time away from family interaction. "My wife and kids are the most important part of my life," one father said in describing commitment. Another noted that "what we have as a family is a treasure." Commitment does not mean, however, that family members stifle each other. "We give each other the freedom and encouragement to pursue individual goals," one wife noted. "Yet either of us would cut out activities or goals that threatened our time together."

Commitment includes sexual fidelity. Some of the people interviewed by the researchers admitted to having engaged in an extramarital affair earlier in the marriage. Some believed the affair precipitated a crisis that in the final analysis led to a stronger marriage. But marriages can change for the better without a crisis of such major proportions. "Being faithful to each other sexually is just a part of being honest with each other," one young woman noted. Honesty, indeed, is the best policy.

Positive Communication. When people are asked to list the qualities they consider essential to a strong family, most list **positive communication**. Yet many families don't spend much time talking to one another. Although successful families are often task oriented, identifying problems and discussing how to solve them, family members also spend time talking with and listening to one another just to stay connected. Some of the most important talk occurs when no one is working at communication. Open-ended, rambling conversations can reveal important information. How does your teenager feel about sex? Her grades? Her future? When parents and children get comfortable with each other, important issues arise.

Communication does not always produce agreement in strong families. Family members have differences and conflicts, but they speak directly and honestly about them without blaming each other. They try to resolve their differences but may agree to disagree. Dysfunctional families, on the other hand, are either overly critical and hostile in their communication with each other or deny problems and avoid verbal conflict. Although verbal hostilities are not productive, neither is avoidance of problems.

Studies reveal that communication in healthy families has several important aspects. Members of strong families are good at listening. "I'd much rather listen to other people talk," one father explained. Family members are also adept at asking questions, and they do not try to read one another's minds. Members of strong families understand that people's views of the world change.

Humor is another important aspect of healthy family communication. Strong families like to laugh. A study of 304 mothers, fathers, and teenagers revealed that humor is a valuable source of family strength. Wuerffel, DeFrain, and Stinnett (1990) reviewed the scientific literature on humor and found that humor can be used in many different positive and negative ways. Humor can reduce daily tension, facilitate conversations, express feelings of warmth and affection, lessen anxiety, point out mistakes made by others, and entertain. It can also help put others at ease and help maintain a positive outlook on life.

The study found positive correlations between the use of humor and how strong the families were based on their responses to a family strengths inventory. The stronger the family, the more likely the family members were to use humor to maintain a positive outlook on life, to entertain each other, to reduce tension, to express warmth, to put others at ease, to facilitate conversations, to lessen anxiety, and to help cope with difficult situations. The stronger families in the study reported negative effects, however, when humor was used to put down other family members. Put-downs and sarcasm were used less often by the stronger families.

The study concluded that families benefit from humor that points out the incongruous aspects of life—the inconsistent, bizarre, silly, illogical things that happen to people every day. Families, however, do not benefit from humor that places someone in a superior position or from sarcasm aimed at demeaning a family member. Sarcasm is often an attempt to mask anger; it is rarely used out of love.

Enjoyable Time Together. "What do you think makes a happy family?" a researcher asked 1,500 schoolchildren. Few replied that money or cars or fancy homes or television sets made a happy family. The most frequent response? A happy family is one that does things together and spends **enjoyable time together.** Although the response seems simple enough, family therapists see many couples and families who haven't figured this out. "I don't have a lot of time with my family," many people like to say, "but I try to make it quality time."

Happy memories result from quality time spent together in considerable quantity: "I remember stories Mom and Dad told me when they tucked me into bed." "Going with Dad to work on the farm. I felt so important." "Singing together—we had an old piano, and I learned to play, and we would all sing corny old songs." "Vacation. We would go 50 miles to the lake and rent a cabin, and Dad would swim with us."

These happy memories share common threads. First, happiness often centers on activities that are shared as a family. Second, pleasurable time together often centers on simple activities that don't cost a lot of money. Strong families identified these popular family activities: meals together, house and yard chores, and outdoor recreation, including camping, playing catch and other yard games, canoeing, hiking, and picnicking.

Meaningful family rituals are one of the ways family members are brought together. Family rituals have been linked with positive outcomes for families, including greater marital and family satisfaction and better adjustment in children (Leon & Jacobvitz, 2003). Family rituals range from daily and weekly events like family dinners and weekend routines to family traditions like celebrating birthdays and holidays. These rituals contribute to a greater feeling of connection and stability in the family.

Spiritual Well-Being. Perhaps the most controversial finding of the family strengths researchers is the importance of religion or spirituality in strong families. Some families call this **spiritual well-being**. Others talk about faith in God, hope, or optimism about life. Some say they feel a oneness with the world. Others talk about their families in almost religious terms, describing the love they feel for one another as sacred. Others express these kinds of feelings in terms of ethical values and commitment to important causes.

Spiritual well-being can be the caring center within each individual that promotes sharing, love, and compassion. Spiritual well-being is the feeling or force that helps people transcend themselves. "I feel my family is a part of all the families of the world," said one respondent. An important aspect of membership in a religious or spiritual group is the caring, supportive community it provides. When illness strikes, a baby is born, or an accident occurs, friends in the group are often quick to help each other.

It is important to distinguish between "spiritual" and "religious" in talking about spiritual well-being (Erisman, 2004). While spiritual beliefs focus on private and more universal beliefs, religious beliefs emphasize the public and external system linked more with denominations than family dynamics. Families that are grounded spiritually often have integrated these beliefs into their family behavior and traditions.

Agreement by a married couple on spiritual beliefs has been found to be strongly linked to a more successful marriage (Larson & Olson, 2004). In a national study with 24,671 married couples who took the ENRICH couple inventory, couples with high agreement on spiritual beliefs not only were more happily married, but also had many other strengths in their marriages, including better communication, greater ability to resolve conflict, and feeling more couple closeness; they also had higher levels of couple flexibility.

Ability to Manage Stress and Crisis. Strong families are not immune to trouble, but they are not as crisis prone as dysfunctional families tend to be. Rather, they possess the **ability to manage stress and crisis**. Strong families are often successful at preventing troubles before they occur, but some stressors in life are inevitable. The best a family can do is meet the challenge as efficiently as possible, minimizing its damage and looking for any growth opportunities in the process.

What are the difficult family crises strong families face together? One study asked members of strong families to report the tough challenges they had faced in the past 5 years and rank each crisis in order of difficulty. The researchers found that serious illness or surgery was cited most often as the most difficult challenge, with 23% of adult respondents reporting their family had experienced this difficulty. A death in the family was next in order of frequency, with 21% seeing it as their most difficult crisis. Third in the rankings were marital problems, most of which involved adult children, in-laws, or brothers and sisters. A child's unwanted pregnancy, delinquency, or poor adjustment in school was also occasionally listed (DeFrain et al., 2006).

Fully 96% of the strong families said they were successful in meeting these crises. Among the strategies strong families use to weather crises is pulling together. Each person, even a very young child, has a part to play in easing the burdens of the others. Additionally, strong families seek help if they cannot solve the problem themselves. Although this may surprise some people, members of strong families do get counseling in an attempt to learn better ways of coping

Many cultures embrace a form of family and community life that reflects what theorists think of as extended family systems. Among many American Indian tribes, for example, significant life events are marked with community-wide ceremonies. Individual problems are considered problems that can be solved only within the context of the group.

with a crisis. In contrast, truly troubled families often do not have the strength to admit that they have troubles and need to seek advice (DeFrain, 1999; DeFrain & Stinnett, 2002).

Family Development Framework

Family development as a conceptual framework was originally designed to describe and explain the process of change in couples and families. Researchers and clinicians working from a **family development framework** are primarily interested in how partners and family members deal with various roles and developmental tasks within the marriage and family as they move through various stages of the life cycle. The family development framework assumes that the more efficient a family is at completing these tasks, the more successful the development of the various family members will be.

Evelyn Duvall, a major creator (with Reuben Hill) of the family development approach, has described some of the advantages of this framework (Duvall, 2001). For one thing, it focuses on development and change in individuals and the family over time. It also encourages attention to process. It approaches the family not as a static and unchanging group but as a dynamic system.

Some controversy surrounds the exact number of stages involved in the family life cycle. Duvall originally identified 8 stages; other family science professionals have identified 4 to 24 stages. The sequence of stages is clearest and easiest to apply when there is only one child in the family. The number of stages and the complexity of overlapping stages increase when there is more than one child or when the couple gets divorced and one or both partners remarry.

The family development framework is a useful framework for thinking about stages of the family life. However, it does not address the complexity of families today, which do not follow a traditional pattern of marrying, having a child or children, raising the children until they are launched, and retiring and becoming grandparents. Today's families often begin without marriage, and even those that begin with marriage often end in divorce. There is often remarriage that may include stepchildren from one or both parents, who might then have their own children. So while the family development model provides a model emphasizing changing structural composition in families, it is used less often today because families today to not follow such traditional and predictable patterns.

Symbolic Interaction Framework

As the name indicates, the **symbolic interaction framework** focuses on symbols, which are based on shared meanings, and interactions, which are based on verbal and nonverbal communication (Klein & White, 1996). This framework helps explain how we learn through communicating with each other about various roles in our society. The family is seen as a unit of interacting personalities, which according to Ernest Burgess (Burgess & Wallin, 1943) explains the importance of family interaction in creating an ongoing group.

A **role** is the expected behavior of a person or group in a given social category, such as husband, wife, supervisor, or teacher. Every family member plays a variety of roles at different times. For example, a man can be a parent, spouse, manager at work, and coach of a baseball team. A woman can be a parent, spouse, manager at work, and chairperson of a fundraising committee. A young girl can be a daughter, student, and musician.

Roles are learned in society by **role taking**, the process whereby people learn how to play roles correctly by practicing and getting feedback from others. **Role making** involves creating new roles or revising existing roles. For example, as a couple's relationship changes from husband led to a more egalitarian relationship, the partners need to change the way they interact with each other.

One assumption is that meaning arises in the process of interaction between people. Shared meaning helps people understand each other and learn how to play various roles. Another important concept is **definition of the situation**, developed by William Thomas: Each person subjectively interprets a given situation, and different people will interpret an interaction or situation in different ways. This helps explain why there are often different perceptions of a marriage; there can be "his" marriage and "her" marriage, as initially described by Jessie Bernard (1970).

Another assumption is that people learn about themselves and develop a self-concept based on their interaction with others. An early theorist, Charles Cooley (1864–1929), developed the concept of the **looking-glass self**, the idea that you learn about yourself based on the feedback you receive from others who are reacting to your behavior. In other words, your feelings about yourself are derived from how others react to you. Another important theorist was George Mead (1863–1931), who described how the self-concept emerges in childhood. The child plays out a certain role, which helps him or her learn to take the role of the generalized other—to understand and even predict the feelings of another person. This ability can be valuable in any situation because it enables a person to understand another's feelings.

Social Construction Framework

According to the **social construction framework**, human beings are profoundly immersed in the social world; our understanding of this world and beliefs about this world are social products. Similar to the earlier thinking of the symbolic interactionists, social construction theorists argue that because the self is a product of social processes, individuality is most difficult to develop because we live in a social environment: We are born into and live within social settings, as members of particular social groups. Our identities are shaped over time through our life experiences.

Social construction theories, which are compatible with the postmodernist and multicultural intellectual movements, are gaining attention today. **Postmodernism** has been described as a "thoroughgoing skeptical doubt in regard to questions of truth, meaning and historical interpretation" (Norris, 1990, p. 29). Rather than assuming that human reason should be or is the prime mover in developing our views of the world, postmodernist thinking emphasizes the notion that we live in a complex world and that multiple perspectives or "truths" are in constant interaction and conflict with each other. In a postmodern era, then, there is no objective, universal truth that can be seen, once and for all, and readily agreed upon; rather, there is a collection of subjective truths shaped by the particular subcultures in which we live. These multiple subjective truths are constantly competing for our attention and allegiance.

When we look at the world, we are looking through a lens colored by our own beliefs and values, which we have developed in our own particular social worlds. Any "truth statement" is a statement about the observer as well as about what is being observed. The various perspectives on life that we encounter are called *knowledge-positions*. When one knowledge-position gains more power than the others in a particular culture, it becomes dominant and its adherents sometimes refer to it as the truth with a capital *T*. Traveling around the world, however, we find that there are innumerable truths from country to country; even within a particular country or particular family there are many different brands of truth.

From a postmodernist perspective, a dominant truth in a particular cultural group is simply the most popular and widely accepted story or narrative explanation about the way life is or should be. This story serves two purposes: to reinforce and maintain the power and cohesiveness of the particular group and to eliminate or minimize the stories and explanations of competing groups. But because this story or truth or knowledge-position is socially constructed, as society changes over time and countless new influences emerge, the story continuously evolves: "The truth we see is a negotiated rather than a discovered one" (Sprey, 1990, p. 22).

From an individual family's perspective, the truth about who the family is and what the family does can change as time passes. A troubled family can learn how to create a new, more positive story about who they are and where their family is going. Narrative therapy, which developed out of social constructionist and postmodern thinking, seeks to develop a new story for the individual and the family that works better than the old approach (Cook & DeFrain, 2005; White & Morgan, 1990, 2007). The family, as storyteller, relates the current perspective on reality that the family holds. In addition, the family therapist, in concert with the family members, helps develop a new narrative, or story, that helps the family meet its goals in a more effective manner.

Finally, from a social constructionist and postmodernist point of view, this textbook represents not necessarily the truth about marriage and family today but rather the perspective of three family scholars who see the world through particular conceptual lenses and whose worldviews are shaped by the unique sociocultural context in which they live. The articles and books we choose to quote in this textbook and the personal comments we make all reflect the social environment that has heavily influenced us.

Feminist Framework

The feminist framework has grown in importance and has had a significant impact on theorizing about marriage and the family in recent decades (Fox & Murry, 2000; Switala, 2007).

Central to the **feminist framework** is the notion that women are exploited, devalued, and oppressed and that society should commit to empowering women and changing their oppressed condition.

The feminist framework grew out of the feminist movement, which began with the struggle for the right to vote, considered to be the first wave of the movement in the United States. The second wave was stimulated by women like Betty Friedan who wrote the important book *The Feminine Mystique* (1963). She argued that women needed a more active voice in decisions that affect them. She also pointed out that women are burdened by the guilt that they often feel because they are unable to balance motherhood and working outside the home.

The second wave occurred in the 1960s and 1970s, and the movement is now in the third wave, which is now led by women in their 20s and 30s. A clear difference between the second and third waves is that the former was more a collectiveness movement whereas the current wave is more an individualistic approach. There is currently some conflict between the second and third wave in terms of how the movement should proceed as well as how much effort should be put into individual versus collective efforts (Friedlin, 2002).

Feminist theories have a common interest in understanding the subordination of women with the goal of changing it (Fox & Murry, 2000). Feminists assume that women's experiences are central, not less important than those of men, and that gender must be explicitly used as a central focus. **Gender** is defined as the learned behaviors and characteristics associated with being male or female in a particular culture. Feminist theories examine gender differences and how gender-based distinctions legitimize power differences between men and women.

Feminists have also challenged the definition of family that is based on traditional roles. They see the family as a dynamic, changing, and open system that does not restrict roles and opportunities. They have criticized the "structural/functional framework," which prescribed the roles of males and females. Parsons and Bales (1955) assumed that the family was most functional if the male played the **instrumental role**, being in charge of tasks, and the wife played the **expressive role**, being nurturing. Feminists maintain that both men and women can play both roles. This perspective provides couples with more flexibility because both members can play roles based on their unique skills and interests.

Even though some men today are offended and threatened by feminist thinking, feminism may have certain benefits for both men and women in family relationships. It encourages men to express their feelings, to share wage-earning responsibilities, and to focus less on their careers and more on their children. For men, the pressure of being the only wage earner is reduced when both partners are working outside the home. At the same time, working outside the home helps women enjoy an identity separate from their role within the family. It also provides them with independent economic security. Sharing the responsibility for child rearing allows men to participate in their children's development and women to pursue professional and personal interests. When work and power are shared, both partners have more opportunity to develop their full potential.

Women's and men's roles continue to converge in American society, and distinctions between male and female activities are blurring. As this convergence continues, women and men will find more ways to work together. The feminist frontier now is the family and the problem is how to juggle work, love, home, and children.

Three Key Relationship Concepts

[Authors' Note: In order for you to more easily understand the three dimensions of family cohesion, family flexibility, and family communication, it would be useful to assess your own family of origin before reading the following section. Complete Activity 1 at the end of the chapter and then read the following section.

Also read about the Couple and Family Scales in Appendix A at the back of the book.]

There is considerable agreement among theorists who have studied couples and families that the dimensions of cohesion, flexibility, and communication are central to understanding relationship dynamics. Although the descriptive terms vary from theorist to theorist, the majority of concepts relate to the three dimensions of relationships that we will now describe in more detail.

Cohesion in Couples and Families

Cohesion is a feeling of emotional closeness with another person (Olson, 2003). Four levels of cohesion can be described in couple and family relationships: disengaged, connected, cohesive, and enmeshed (Figure 3.2). The extreme low level of

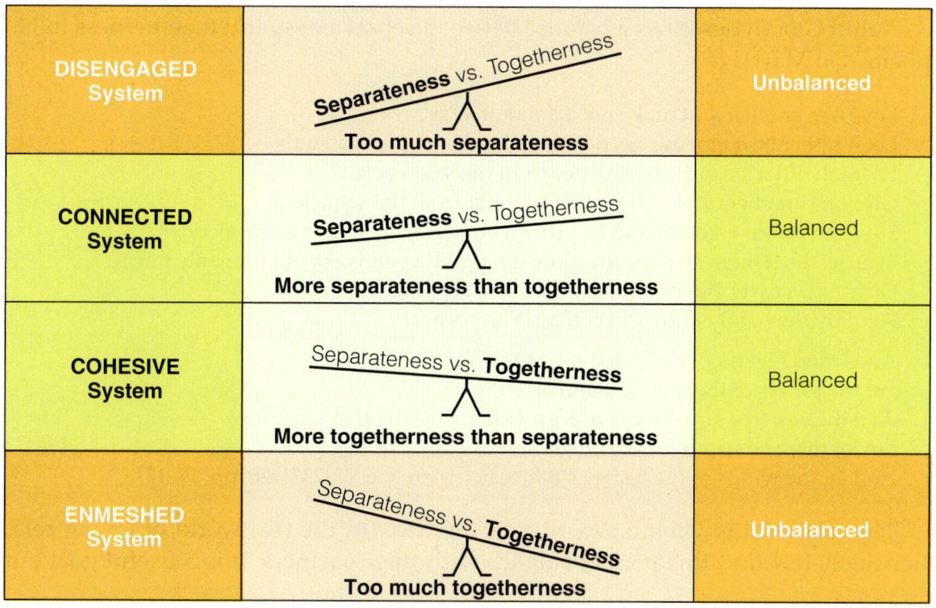

FIGURE 3.2
Four Levels of Family Cohesion: Balancing Separateness and Togetherness

cohesion is called *disengaged*, and the extreme high level, *enmeshed*. Although being disengaged or enmeshed is appropriate at times, relationships become problematic when they are stuck at one of these extremes. The two middle levels of cohesion—*connected* and *cohesive*—seem to be the most functional across the life cycle, in part because they balance separateness and togetherness. Both connected and cohesive relationships are classified as balanced family systems.

Balance Between Separateness and Togetherness. Balance between separateness and togetherness is the essence of family cohesion. Family members need to balance between being intimate with and feeling close to other family members and being independent from the family so that they can develop as individuals. The concept of balance entails both autonomy and intimacy—and the ability to move back and forth between the two. Establishing a dynamic balance between the two requires shifting back and forth on a weekly, daily, or even hourly basis.

Table 3.3 illustrates the four levels of family cohesion, from low to high. There is a balance between separateness and togetherness at both the connected and the cohesive levels of cohesion. *Connected relationships* place more emphasis on the individual than on the relationship. Levels of closeness are often low to moderate in a connected family system, with lower levels of loyalty; there is often more independence than dependence and more separateness than togetherness. *Cohesive relationships* place more emphasis on togetherness and less on separateness. There is some loyalty to the relationship, and there is often more dependence than independence.

Disengaged relationships (those with a low level of cohesion) emphasize the individual. There is often very little closeness, a lack of loyalty, high independence, and high separateness. *Enmeshed relationships* emphasize togetherness: very high levels of closeness, loyalty, and dependence on one another. Enmeshed relationships are often typical of couples in love. When this level of intimacy occurs between a parent and a child (for example, an enmeshed father–daughter relationship or an enmeshed mother–son relationship), the relationship often becomes problematic.

Kahlil Gibran describes a balance between separateness and togetherness in his poem "On Marriage":

> Love one another, but make not a bond of love:
> Let it rather be a moving sea between the shores of your souls.
> Fill each other's cup, but drink not from the same cup.
> Give one another of your bread, but eat not from the same loaf.
> Sing and dance together and be joyous, but let each one of you be alone,
> Even as the strings of a lute are alone though they quiver with the same music.
> Give your hearts, but not into each other's keeping.
> For only the hand of Life can contain your hearts.
>
> And stand together yet not too near together:
> For the pillars of the temple stand apart,
> And the oak tree and the cypress grow not in each other's shadow.
> But let there be spaces in your togetherness,
> And let the winds of the heavens dance between you. (1923/1976, pp. 16–17)

The relationship Gibran describes is an ideal. In the real world of loving relationships, few find this perfect balance with their partners. It is a useful goal but

Characteristic	Disengaged (Unbalanced)	Connected (Balanced)	Cohesive (Balanced)	Enmeshed (Unbalanced)
Separateness–togetherness	High separateness	More separateness than togetherness	More togetherness than separateness	Very high togetherness
I–we balance	Primarily I	More I than we	More we than I	Primarily we
Closeness	Little closeness	Low-to-moderate closeness	Moderate-to-high closeness	Very high closeness
Loyalty	Lack of Loyalty	Some loyalty	Considerable loyalty	High loyalty
Activities	Mainly separate	More separate than shared	More shared than separate	Mainly shared
Dependence–independence	High independence	More independence than dependence	More dependence than independence	High dependence

TABLE 3.3 Levels of Couple and Family Cohesion

one that is difficult to maintain for long. It is also important to note that in intimate relationships, people can experience and even enjoy, at least for a short time, both extremes on the togetherness–separateness continuum. Couples can remain in love with each other while also enjoying being apart for periods of time.

Extreme Togetherness and Extreme Separateness. Too much togetherness can lead to relationship fusion, or enmeshment. People "in love" often feel they need each other. Although this feels good for awhile, soon the enmeshment begins to prickle. After too much togetherness, lovers can get on each other's nerves.

Especially in the early stages of a relationship, couples enjoy being totally together. When two people are "falling in love," being away from each other for very long literally hurts. Each one aches and pines and feels pent-up emotion in the expectation of seeing the other again. Couples in this type of situation are enmeshed; being together so totally can be very exciting for a time. To expect to be totally sheltered from the storms of life by a loved one is a nice fantasy—but it *is* a fantasy. Judy Altura has expressed it poetically:

EXTREME TOGETHERNESS POEM

We do everything together.
I am here to meet all your needs and expectations.
And you are here to meet mine.
We had to meet, and it was beautiful.
I can't imagine it turning out any other way. (1974, p. 20)

Two of the most common reasons an enmeshed relationship becomes troublesome are jealousy and personification. People feel jealous when they fear they might lose their partner to another person. Tied closely to jealousy is **personification**, the notion that everything one's partner does is a personal reflection on oneself. A person who personifies his or her partner's actions will try to control the other's behavior. This may work in the short run, but it can destroy intimacy in the long run.

Enmeshment is problematic both for the people in the relationship and for the relationship itself because it romanticizes the relationship and puts impossible expectations upon the partners. It also tends to stifle individual development. One

Within every family, each member must find a balance between autonomy and intimacy. If their family is like other families, these five people will experience periods of greater and lesser separateness and togetherness over the course of their lives.

way to improve an enmeshed relationship is for each person to develop individual interests and abilities.

In the 1970s, one cultural theme in American society was "doing your own thing." Young people were dubbed "the me generation." This overfocus on self was problematic for relationships. "Doing your own thing" can lead to a disengaged relationship, in which there is very little emotional closeness.

A disengaged couple or family typically has very little emotional closeness. There is so much separateness that each person is mainly focused on himself or herself and not on each other. As a result, they have difficulty developing and maintaining intimacy with others. Most couples with marital problems have low levels of emotional connection as do families with problem children. Emotional closeness is the glue that helps couples and families stay connected even during difficult times. When emotional closeness is missing, individuals care more about themselves and there is little commitment and few resource to help the couple or family thrive.

A young former prostitute described the family she grew up in as very chaotic, saying, "It was like a sieve. Anybody could come into it, and anybody could leave, and anybody could fall through the gaps. The family wasn't safe or reliable for anybody at all."

Successful couples tend to be those who have figured out how to balance effectively between "I" and "we." Partners maintain both their own individuality and their intimacy as a couple.

Flexibility in Couples and Families

Flexibility is the amount of change that occurs in leadership, role relationships, and relationship rules (Olson, 2003). Like cohesion, flexibility has four levels, ranging from low to high. Those levels are rigid, structured, flexible, and chaotic (Figure 3.3). The extreme types of family systems—the *rigid* and the *chaotic*—can work well in the short run, but they have difficulty adapting over time. Conversely, the balanced types—the *structured* and the *flexible*—are more able to adapt to change over the family life cycle.

Balance Between Stability and Change. The essence of family flexibility is balancing stability and change. Families need a basic foundation that gives them stability, but they also need to be open to change when necessary. Change is particularly important when families are under stress and need to adapt in a crisis.

The two balanced levels of change are called *structured* and *flexible*. Of the two, structured relationships have more moderate levels of change, with leadership that is sometimes shared. Discipline is often democratic, and the roles are stable. In flexible relationships, there is more change. Often both the relationship between the couple and the relationships among family members are more democratic, and there is also more role sharing between the partners, as shown in Table 3.4.

The two extremes of change are described as *rigid*, indicating a very low degree of change, and *chaotic*, indicating an extremely high degree of change. Both extremes are unbalanced and problematic because families are often stuck at these extreme positions. In rigid relationships, the leadership is often authoritarian. As a result, the discipline is strict, and the roles are very stable. In chaotic relationships, there is too much change, often because there is a lack of leadership. Discipline is erratic and inconsistent, partly because there are often dramatic shifts in family roles.

Extreme Stability and Extreme Change. Families by nature tend to resist change; they are basically rigid. Most families function primarily to maintain the status quo: "When an organism indicates a change in relation to another, the

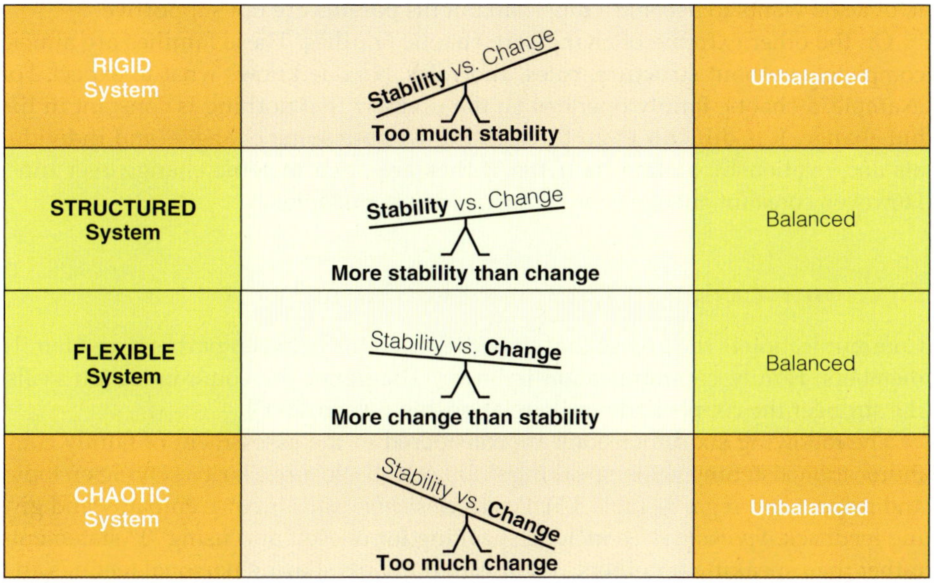

RIGID System	Stability vs. Change **Too much stability**	**Unbalanced**
STRUCTURED System	Stability vs. Change **More stability than change**	Balanced
FLEXIBLE System	Stability vs. **Change** **More change than stability**	Balanced
CHAOTIC System	Stability vs. **Change** **Too much change**	**Unbalanced**

FIGURE 3.3
Four Levels of Family Flexibility: Balancing Stability and Change

	TABLE 3.4	Levels of Couple and Family Flexibility		
Characteristic	Rigid (Unbalanced)	Structured (Balanced)	Flexible (Balanced)	Chaotic (Unbalanced)
Leadership	Authoritarian	Sometimes shared	Often shared	Lack of leadership
Discipline	Strict discipline	Somewhat democratic	Democratic	Lenient discipline
Negotiation	Limited discussion	Organized discussion	Open discussion	Endless discussion
Roles	Roles very stable	Roles stable	Role sharing	Dramatic role shifts
Rules	Unchanging rules	Few rule changes	Some rule changes	Frequent rule changes
Change	Very little change	Some change	Moderate change	Considerable change

other will act upon the first so as to diminish and modify the change" (Haley, 1959, p. 361; see also Zeig, 2001).

In short, when one partner tries to make changes in a relationship, the other partner's first reaction is often to defend against the change or at least to slow it down until he or she can better understand what is happening. People often fear that the change will bring more harm than good. The family, which is maintenance oriented and conservative in its approach to change, often creates even more problems for itself. As Lyman Wynne sees it, "Families that rigidly try to maintain homeostasis [the status quo] through successive developmental phases are highly disturbed and atypical. Enduring success in maintaining family homeostasis perhaps should be regarded as a distinctive feature of disorder in families" (1958, p. 89).

Extreme stability is seen in rigid families, those in which there is little room for change. The family rules are always the same, even though the game of life outside the family continuously changes. This rigidity manifests itself in such relatively trivial matters as scheduling family meals. Family members do not permit one another to make even the slightest changes, even if they helped one or more members. The rigidity may also be evidenced by resistance to changes in family roles. For example, a mother wants to find work outside the home but the father opposes it, or a son wants to become a musician but his parents are not supportive.

On the other extreme of change are chaotic families. These families are almost completely without structure, rules, and roles. No one knows what to expect. For example, a chaotic family operates on the premise that nothing is constant in life but change. It is difficult to go through life without some change—and individuals and relationships often do better if they are open to some change over time. However, constant change is problematic for most people.

Communication in Couples and Families

Communication is the grease that smoothes frictions between partners and family members. Family communication is linear: The better the communication skills, the stronger the couple and family relationship (Olson, 2003).

The following six dimensions are considered in the assessment of family communication: listening skills, speaking skills, self-disclosure, clarity, staying on topic, and respect and regard (Table 3.5). Positive *listening skills* involve empathy and giving feedback. *Speaking skills* include speaking for oneself and using "I" statements rather than speaking for others. *Self-disclosure* entails sharing personal feelings and

TABLE 3.5	Levels of Couple and Family Communication		
Characteristic	**Poor**	**Good**	**Very Good**
Listening skills	Poor listening skills	Appear to listen, but feedback is limited	Give feedback, indicating good listening skills
Speaking skills	Often speak for others	Speak for self more than for others	Speak mainly for self rather than for others
Self-disclosure	Low sharing of feelings	Moderate sharing of feelings	High sharing of feelings
Clarity	Inconsistent messages	Clear messages	Very clear messages
Staying on topic	Seldom stay on topic	Often stay on topic	Mainly stay on topic
Respect and regard	Low to moderate	Moderate to high	High

ideas openly. *Clarity* involves the exchange of clear messages. *Staying on topic* is another important aspect of interpersonal exchanges. Last, *respect and regard* reflect the good intentions of family members and keep communication positive.

Couple and Family Map

The **Couple and Family Map** is built on the three major dimensions of cohesion, flexibility, and communication. Four levels of cohesion and four levels of flexibility are integrated to create a model that is useful for describing and understanding couple and family dynamics. The Couple and Family Map (otherwise known in the field of family research as the *Circumplex Model of Marital and Family Systems*) was developed by David Olson and his colleagues at the University of Minnesota, especially Douglas Sprenkle and Candyce Russell, who worked on the original model. The model offers a way of mapping and understanding couple and family relationships. It can also be applied by therapists, counselors, and family members interested in understanding and changing the dynamics within a couple or family experiencing difficulties.

The Couple and Family Map is built primarily on principles and concepts from family systems theory, but it also has features in common with other frameworks. As a graphic model, it clearly represents the dimensions of cohesion and flexibility; the third dimension, communication, serves as a facilitating function.

It is through communication that family members identify and work out their concerns about cohesion—issues of spending time together versus having enough separateness to retain a sense of oneself—and flexibility—issues of adapting to the demands of change versus minimizing such demands if they threaten the stability of the relationship. Communication thus helps families move between the extremes of cohesion and flexibility to find a balance that works for them. If couples or families have good communication skills, they are more likely to be able to maintain their cohesive structure, adapt to change, and work out whatever problems confront them (Olson, 2003).

Balanced Versus Unbalanced Families

The Couple and Family Map identifies 16 types of couple and family relationships (Figure 3.4). The logic is quite simple: The dimensions of cohesion and flexibility are broken down into four levels each, and 4 × 4 = 16. A marriage or family

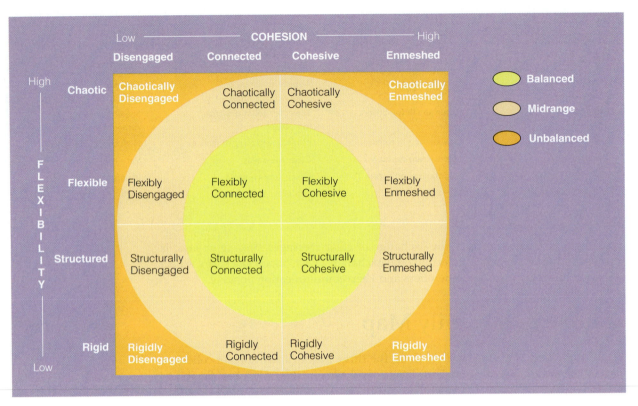

FIGURE 3.4
Couple and Family Map

relationship can be classified according to one of these 16 types depending on how a given family or couple relationship operates.

The 16 types of family relationships can be clustered into three general types of family systems: balanced families, midrange families, and unbalanced families. **Balanced families** are those that fit into the four central categories (yellow section) on the relationship map in Figure 3.4. Balanced families are labeled flexibly connected, flexibly cohesive, structurally connected, and structurally cohesive. **Midrange families** (orange section) are extreme on one dimension (e.g., cohesion) but balanced on the other (e.g., flexibility). **Unbalanced families** (red section) are those that score at extreme levels on both dimensions. In the Activities section at the end of this chapter, you will have the opportunity to classify your own family using the Couple and Family Scales.

Balanced Relationships More Healthy

The Couple and Family Map is a valuable model because it is scientifically verifiable; in other words, researchers can validate (or invalidate) the Couple and Family Map by testing hypotheses derived from it. A few of the most important hypotheses that have been developed and tested in numerous studies are discussed next.

One hypothesis is: *Balanced couple and family systems* (those that fall under two central levels of cohesion and flexibility) *generally function more adequately across the family life cycle than unbalanced types* (two extremes on cohesion and flexibility). Families balanced on cohesion allow their members to be both independent from and connected to the family. Families balanced on flexibility maintain some stability but are also open to change. Although balanced family types are located in the central area of the model, they can experience the extremes of the dimensions when necessary to deal with a situation, but they do not typically function at those extremes for long.

Conversely, couples and families with problems are more typically found at the extremes of the dimensions; they are unbalanced types. Problem families often experience too much separateness (disengaged type) or too much togetherness (enmeshed type) on cohesion. On flexibility, problem families tend to have too much stability (rigid type) or too much change (chaotic type).

There is considerable support for the main hypothesis derived from the Couple and Family Map: *Balanced family types are healthier and more functional than unbalanced family types.* One systematic study that found strong support for this hypothesis was by Volker Thomas and David Olson (1993). They tested four groups of families with an adolescent, videotaping each family while they discussed some family topics. The four samples included 35 families with an emotionally disturbed child, 25 families in family therapy for a variety of problems, 62 healthy families with a Down's syndrome child, and 60 healthy families.

The findings strongly supported the hypothesis (Figure 3.5). As hypothesized, only 16% of the families with an emotionally disturbed child and 12% of the families in therapy were balanced types, whereas about 78% to 80% of the healthy families were balanced types. Conversely, almost half (49%) of the families with an emotionally disturbed child and 40% of the families in therapy were unbalanced. Only 8% of the healthy families were unbalanced.

Value of Couple and Family Map

There are several advantages to using the Couple and Family Map to understand marital and family life. First, *the model provides a common descriptive language for talking about real couples and real families—a language the expert and the layperson can use to talk with each other.*

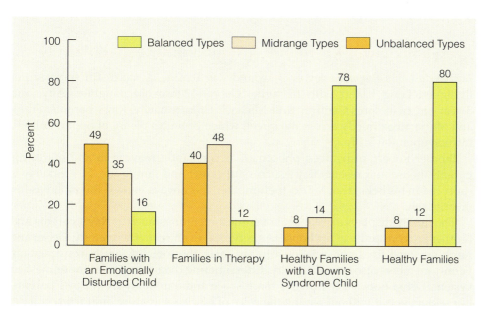

FIGURE 3.5
Degree of Balance in Problem and Healthy Families

Second, the Couple and Family Map *draws on concepts and ideas from three of the major frameworks we have discussed—family systems, family strengths, and family development*. It offers a means of bringing together and applying all three frameworks to the examination of real families and their interactions. It grounds theory in examples of relationships based on intimacy and commitment.

Third, the Couple and Family Map *can help describe how a couple relationship or a family changes as time passes or as stresses and challenges appear*. The relationship map provides information about the present dynamics of a couple or family's relationship and what actions are necessary to bring about change. It provides a means to visualize where one is and where one might wish to be.

Finally, the Couple and Family Map *turns concepts into working themes so one can observe and measure couple and family dynamics*. Just where is a given family on the relationship map? Is this relationship a rigid, inflexible, suffocating environment? Is it an unpredictable, unsafe, chaotic place to be? Or is it flexible and nurturing? Can family members communicate what their problems are and express what kind of family they would like to become? What changes must they make to move toward that ideal or maintain the aspects they wish not to lose as they change others?

Family Dynamics in Television and Movies

Movies and television shows often do an excellent job of portraying family types from the Couple and Family Map. Because they tend to be more dramatically interesting, the unbalanced family types are depicted more often than the balanced types. Some movies also illustrate how families change in response to a stressor or over time as people age. In this section we will take a look at some movies and television shows that vividly depict several family types. Many classic and current movie/television show families could serve as examples of the various family types. We chose the following selections, however, because they are particularly good examples of various family types in the Couple and Family Map.

Everybody Loves Raymond: A Rigidly Enmeshed Family

Everybody Loves Raymond revolves around Ray Barone, a successful sportswriter living on Long Island with his wife, Debra; 12-year-old daughter, Ally; and 8-year-old twin sons, Geoffrey and Michael. Unfortunately, Ray's parents, Frank and Marie, live directly across the street, which provides plenty of opportunity to intrude upon Ray's life.

Brother Robert, a divorced policeman, is constantly moving in and out of his parents' house and resents Ray's successful career and family life. His jealousy is captured in his belief that Marie, their mother, has always viewed Raymond as her favorite son.

The family displays a great deal of enmeshment inasmuch as Ray's parents and brother are constantly at his house. As is typical in an enmeshed family, Debra and Ray's personal lives and relationship are often the topic of family conversation. Family members also have difficulty differentiating themselves from the enmeshed system. Debra hopelessly pursues more space and autonomy from Ray's parents, but seldom gets it without paying the price of Marie's signature guilt trips.

Marie is the matriarch of the family, is in everyone's business, and has an unflappable urge to control others, a typical sign of a rigid system. In-laws have a hard time breaking into this family. The rigidity of their system is also seen in the inability of the boys to make any changes in their own lives or to ever go against their mother's wishes without paying a relational price.

As is characteristic of an unbalanced system, the communication is poor, filled with secrets, and characterized by indirect messages and put-downs. In fact, you rarely see examples of positive and healthy communication.

What About Bob? A Rigidly Connected Family

The Marvin family is headed by a prominent psychiatrist, Dr. Leo Marvin (Richard Dreyfuss), author of a popular book called *Baby Steps*. He and his wife, Fay (Julie Hagerty), have a teenage daughter, Anna, and a 9-year-old son, Sigmund. Leo is very self-confident and maintains strong control over his family. Fay is a warm and caring homemaker who tries to support her husband; both children are rather distant from their father. As a family, the Marvins operate as a *rigidly connected* system because the father is so controlling and there is a low level of emotional closeness in the family. Their communication skills are poor, mainly because the father controls the exchange of information and does not let others have much say.

The family experiences a great deal of change when Bob Wiley (Bill Murray) becomes a patient of Dr. Marvin. Bob becomes so dependent on Dr. Marvin that he follows him to the family's vacation home. About the same time, *Good Morning America* contacts Dr. Marvin and arranges to interview him at his lake home. Bob becomes involved in the production because he wants to share how helpful Dr. Marvin's counsel was. During the filming of the interview, Bob is very articulate; Dr. Marvin, on the other hand, becomes so flustered and frustrated that he is often speechless.

After the *Good Morning America* show, the family system changes. Bob encourages the family to express their feelings and have fun together. He helps the son, Siggy, learn to dive in the lake, something Leo had failed to do. The family becomes more *flexibly cohesive*, with good communication skills. Leo loses his total control over his family, and they enjoy the more flexible style of operating that Bob encourages. Leo becomes increasingly frustrated and disengaged from his family, which leads him to depression. Eventually he is hospitalized. But, in the end, the family changes and is more balanced as a result of Bob's becoming part of the family.

The Osbournes: A Chaotically Enmeshed Family on MTV

Ozzy Osbourne is the former lead singer of the heavy-metal rock band Black Sabbath. He is well known for his outrageous stage performances and excessive drug and alcohol abuse. He lives in a multimillion-dollar home in Southern California with his wife/manager, Sharon; their two children, Jack and Kelly; and several pet dogs that are not housetrained. The family has allowed MTV cameras into their home to produce a reality-based television program on their life. Some would suggest that the appeal of this show is watching the tattoo-covered rock star, who has been rumored to be a Satan worshiper, do everyday things like take out the trash and attempt to parent two rebellious teenagers. Both Jack and Kelly are using drugs and are involved with rehab. It is this "reality show" that provides viewers with a glimpse of the chaotically enmeshed family style.

Their *chaotic* style allows for regular alcohol and drug use, defiance, and family conflict within the household. Ozzy, who often appears to be confused and dis-oriented, commented in a CNN interview with Larry King (April 2, 2004) regarding his daughter Kelly's entrance into a drug rehabilitation center: "Well, being a drug addict and alcoholic myself, telling the truth . . . doesn't come very easy . . . I can't believe we were buying into it because she could tell instant stories, you know, and you'd go, am I getting too heavy with her?" The rules that Sharon and Ozzy lay down are often challenged and ignored, while consequences are haphazardly enforced.

Since the parents don't appear to actually work, and the kids rarely go to school, this family has plenty of time to spend under the same roof. Frequent family crises move them toward *enmeshment* as they are forced to deal with illness, drug use, and unexpected accidents. Sharon, the mother, was diagnosed with cancer, and Ozzy had a serious accident with his motorcycle. Their enmeshment is further revealed in their routine conflict, as they criticize and react to one another's lives and choices. The arguments reveal the concern they have for one another. Sharon not only attempts to manage Ozzy's career, but feebly attempts to manage the lives of the kids, their many pets, and the friends floating in and out of the picture. They are constantly involving themselves in each other's lives, another common characteristic of an enmeshed family.

Dynamics Change in Relationships Over Time

Another important characteristic of relationships is that they change over time. The Couple and Family Map is a useful tool that can help describe the changes in relationships, and they can be plotted onto the map. Figure 3.6 illustrates how a couple's relationship changed from the time they began dating, to marriage and as newlyweds, to the time when the couple became pregnant and had a baby.

What is apparent from viewing Figure 3.6 is the dramatic changes in the type of couple relationship over a few years. This level of change in a couple's relationship is typical as relationships deal with changes, particularly related to major events like parenthood. Jeff and Mary began dating in college as seniors and had a "flexibly cohesive" relationship that was open to change and growing closer. Two years later they got married and as newlyweds were "structurally enmeshed." They were very structured because they both were very organized and wanted to be like their families. Being enmeshed is a common characteristic of many newly married couples. During the first year to two of marriage, they each got busy with their own careers and had less time with each other. Emotionally, they moved apart more and changed from being enmeshed to being cohesive and then to connected levels of cohesion.

Mary became pregnant and the couple then had a "structurally connected" relationship. Once the baby was born, the couple moved to become a "chaotically cohesive" family. The birth of their first child brought them closer emotionally as a couple and new family. But the infant also added chaos to their typically stable life because life needed to revolve around the infant, which meant less sleep for both of them. As the child reached 1 year old, the couple was now "rigidly connected." The rigidity came from the need to establish a clear schedule for the child, and the child responded in a positive way to this structure by sleeping and eating at

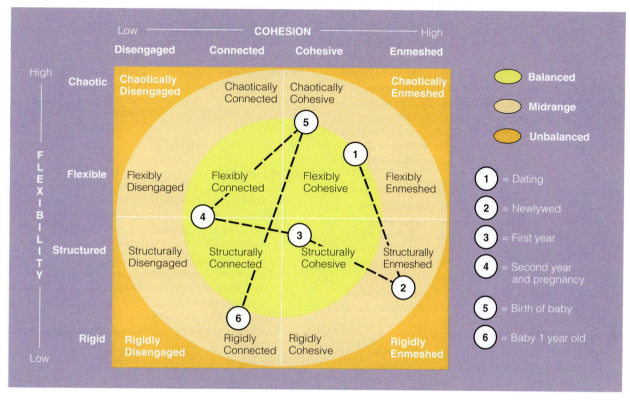

FIGURE 3.6
Couple and Family Map: Change Over Time

predictable times. But the couple became less close and moved from being cohesive to connected because Mary felt stuck with mainly child care, while Jeff continued to work and get more involved in his professional development.

In summary, this example illustrates how the Couple and Family Map can help a couple understand how their relationship changes over time. In terms of changes in the type of relationship over time, most couples and families simply experience the changes without knowing or thinking about them. But the model can also be used by couples and families in a more proactive way. Couples can jointly decide what type of relationship they want and they can work together to move the relationship toward that goal.

Summary

- Conceptual frameworks help describe different perspectives on couple and family dynamics.
- The family systems theory focuses on the family as a system of interdependent parts.
- The family strengths framework focuses on the positive characteristics of healthy families and couples.
- The family development framework examines how couples and families change across the life cycle.

- The symbolic interaction framework examines the internal perceptions of family members and how they learn social rules and roles.
- The social construction framework emphasizes the importance of multiple perspectives on reality and their use in helping families meet their goals more effectively.
- The feminist framework, which focuses on the world as women perceive it, aims to empower women in all aspects of their lives.

- Family theorists have identified three basic qualities that make couples and families stronger: cohesion, flexibility, and communication. These three concepts are central to the family systems theory, the family strengths framework, the family development framework, as well as other theories and frameworks.
- Cohesion focuses on the dynamic balance between the extremes of separateness and togetherness in both couple and family relationships. Balancing these two extremes entails maintaining both autonomy and intimacy but not remaining stuck at either extreme for long periods.
- Flexibility focuses on the dynamic balance between stability and change. The most functional couples and family systems have both characteristics, and they are able to move back and forth between them. Couples and families with problems over time tend to become stuck at one of the extremes, either too much stability (rigid) or too much change (chaotic).
- Communication is a facilitating dimension that can help create change in the levels of cohesion and flexibility when change is necessary.
- The Couple and Family Map is a tool for understanding couple and family relationships. It is based on the family systems theory and is structured on the three dimensions of cohesion, flexibility, and communication.
- The Couple and Family Map describes three general types of family systems—balanced, midrange, and unbalanced—and can illustrate how systems change over time.

Key Terms

conceptual framework	morphostatic system
theory	centrifugal interaction
hypothesis	centripetal interaction
research study	positive feedback
idiographic approach	negative feedback
nomothetic approach	family strengths
family systems theory	framework
family system	appreciation and affection
general systems theory	commitment
system	positive communication
multiple system levels	enjoyable time together
suprasystem	spiritual well-being
subsystem	ability to manage stress
boundary	and crisis
ecology	family development
human ecosystem	framework
wholeness	symbolic interaction
interdependence of parts	framework
open system	role
morphogenic system	role taking
closed system	role making

definition of the situation	expressive role
looking-glass self	cohesion
social construction	personification
framework	flexibility
postmodernism	Couple and Family Map
feminist framework	balanced families
gender	midrange families
instrumental role	unbalanced families

Activities

1. Use the Couple and Family Scales (Table 3.6 on page 97) to describe your family of origin. Select a time period when you were all together (e.g., when you were in high school). Make a list of the people you are including in your family. Then do the following:
   a. Review the six categories shown in the scales (Table 3.6) for assessing cohesion, flexibility, and communication.
   b. On a separate piece of paper, rate your family on a scale of 1 to 8 for each of the categories in the three dimensions.
   c. To determine a total score for each dimension, review the scores and select a number that represents the best average score. Record the score below, and indicate the level for each dimension (e.g., for cohesion, enter *disengaged, connected, cohesive,* or *enmeshed*).

Cohesion	Flexibility	Communication
Score: _____	Score: _____	Score: _____
Level: _____	Level: _____	Level: _____

   d. Now, plot the scores for cohesion and flexibility onto the Couple and Family Map (page 98) and identify the type of family system in which you grew up.
   e. After plotting your scores onto the model, consider the following questions:
   - What is/was it like to live in your type of family (e.g., flexibly connected, rigidly enmeshed, etc.)?
   - In what ways related to cohesion and flexibility is/was your family satisfying and in what ways is/was it frustrating?
   - How did your family change on cohesion and flexibility as you were growing up?
   - In what ways did communication affect your family's dynamics?
2. Plot on the Couple and Family Map (page 98) how your family changed over the years. Select at least three to five points in time and then plot them on the map. Then link those times and reflect on the changes. Also, were you and your family more happy at certain locations on the map than at others?

TABLE 3.6   Couple and Family Scales

COHESION

Characteristic	Disengaged (Unbalanced)		Connected (Balanced)		Cohesive (Balanced)		Enmeshed (Unbalanced)	
Score	1	2	3	4	5	6	7	8
Separateness–togetherness	High separateness		More separateness than togetherness		More togetherness than separateness		Very high togetherness	
I–we balance	Primarily I		More I than we		More we than I		Primarily we	
Closeness	Little closeness		Low-to-moderate closeness		Moderate-to-high closeness		Very high closeness	
Loyalty	Lack of loyalty		Some loyalty		Considerable loyalty		High loyalty	
Activities	Mainly separate		More separate than shared		More shared than separate		Mainly shared	
Dependence–independence	High independence		More independence than dependence		More dependence than independence		High dependence	

FLEXIBILITY

Characteristic	Rigid (Unbalanced)		Structured (Balanced)		Flexible (Balanced)		Chaotic (Unbalanced)	
Score	1	2	3	4	5	6	7	8
Leadership	Authoritarian		Sometimes shared		Often shared		Lack of leadership	
Discipline	Strict discipline		Somewhat democratic		Democratic		Lenient discipline	
Negotiation	Limited discussion		Organized discussion		Open discussion		Endless discussion	
Roles	Roles very stable		Roles stable		Role sharing		Dramatic role shifts	
Rules	Unchanging rules		Few rule changes		Some rule changes		Frequent rule changes	
Change	Very little change		Some change		Moderate change		Considerable change	

COMMUNICATION

Characteristic	Poor		Good		Very Good	
Score	1	2	3	4	5	6
Listening skills	Poor listening skills		Appear to listen, but feedback is limited		Give feedback, indicating good listening skills	
Speaking skills	Often speak for others		Speak for self more than for others		Speak mainly for self rather than for others	
Self-disclosure	Low sharing of feelings		Moderate sharing of feelings		High sharing of feelings	
Clarity	Inconsistent messages		Clear messages		Very clear messages	
Staying on topic	Seldom stay on topic		Often stay on topic		Mainly stay on topic	
Respect and regard	Low to moderate		Moderate to high		High	

3. If you are dating someone, are engaged, or are married, both you and your partner should answer the questions on the Couple and Family Scales twice: first, in terms of your families of origin (as in Activity 1) and second, in terms of your couple relationship. Compare your partner's description of your couple relationship with yours and discuss the similarities and differences. Then compare the descriptions of each of your families of origin with those of your couple relationship.

(For more details on using the Couple and Family Scales, see Appendix A at the back of the book.)

Suggested Readings

Goldenberg, H., & Goldenberg, I. (2007). *Counseling today's families* (4th ed.). Pacific Grove, CA: Wadsworth.

Goldenberg, H., & Goldenberg, I. (2007). *Family therapy: An overview*. Belmont, CA: Brooks/Cole.

Switala, K. (2007). The feminist theory Web site: http://www.cddc.vt.edu/feminism/enin.html. Research materials and information for students, activitists, and scholars interested in women's conditions and struggles around the world.

Walsh, F. (Ed.). (2003). *Normal family processes* (3rd ed.). New York: Guilford.

Walsh, F. (2006). *Strengthening family resilience* (2nd ed.). New York Guilford.

Visit the text-specific Online Learning Center at **www.mhhe.com/Olson6** for practice tests, chapter summaries, Web links, Internet exercises, film guides, key terms, and flashcards.

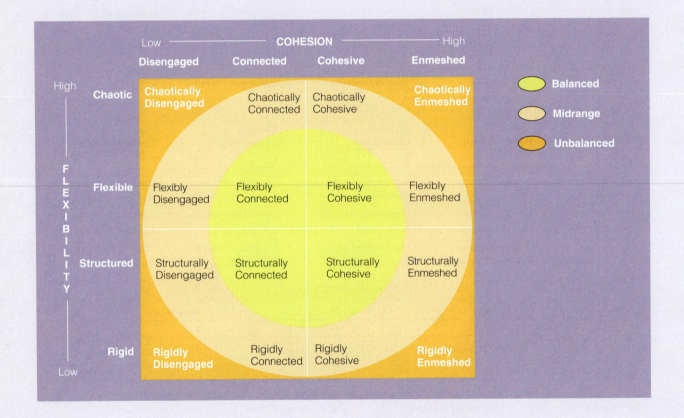

4 Communication and Intimacy

Couple Strengths and Issues in Communication

Perspectives on Communication

Using Communication to Develop Intimacy

Using Communication to Maintain Intimacy

Positive and Negative Communication Cycles

Summary

Key Terms

Activities

Suggested Readings

Communication is at the heart of intimate human relationships—it is literally the foundation on which all else is built. **Communication** is the way humans create and share meaning, both verbally and nonverbally. The ability to communicate is one of a handful of essential skills individuals must master if they are to enjoy close relationships. In fact, the ability and the willingness to communicate have been found to be among the most important factors in maintaining a satisfying relationship.

In this chapter we will look at the art of interpersonal communication, focusing on several important principles of communication, as well as gender and cultural differences in communication styles. We will examine ways for people to become more aware of their communication patterns and styles. Finally, we will explore various approaches and techniques people can use to improve communication in their relationships, thereby increasing the level of intimacy they enjoy with friends, partners, and family members.

Because communication is the key to a successful couple relationship, we will open this chapter with some findings from a national survey (Olson & Olson, 2000). The national survey included 21,501 married couples who completed a couple inventory called ENRICH. Some of the couples took ENRICH as part of a couple enrichment program, and others took it while seeking marital therapy. The total sample of 21,501 couples was divided into two groups: married couples in which both the husband and the wife were happily married ($n = 5,153$) and married couples in which both persons were unhappily married ($n = 5,127$).

This national survey identified couple strengths in communication by comparing the happy couples and unhappy couples. Responses from the entire sample of 21,501 couples were used to identify specific issues for married couples in terms of their sexual relationship. The quality and quantity of a couple's communication are the key to the quality of other aspects of their relationship.

Couple Strengths and Issues in Communication

In a national study (Olson & Olson, 2000) comparing the major communication strengths of happy couples with those of unhappy couples, researchers found that happy couples were six times more likely (90%) than unhappy couples (15%) to agree that they are very satisfied with how they talk to each other (Table 4.1). Most happy couples (79%) feel that their partner understands them, but this is true for only 13% of unhappy couples. Almost all happy couples (96%) feel that they can express their true feelings, whereas this is true for only 30% of unhappy couples. Happy couples are good listeners (83%) compared to unhappy couples (18%). Most happy couples (79%) do not make comments that put each other down, but few (20%) unhappy couples could say the same thing.

In terms of problematic issues for all married couples, the survey focused on all 21,501 couples regardless of whether they were happy or unhappy. As shown in Table 4.2, the vast majority of couples (82%) wish that their partner was more willing to share feelings. Over 70% of all couples had difficulty asking the partner for "what I want," do not feel understood by the partner, and feel the partner often refuses to discuss issues. About two-thirds (67%) of all couples felt that their partner put them down. So these are really common issues for all married couples; the difference is that happy couples are more able to resolve these issues.

TABLE 4.1	Communication Strengths of Happy Versus Unhappy Married Couples	
	PERCENTAGE OF COUPLES IN AGREEMENT	
Strength	**Happy Couples** ($n = 5,153$)	**Unhappy Couples** ($n = 5,127$)
Very satisfied with how we talk to each other.	90%	15%
Partner understands how I feel.	79	13
Easy to express feelings to partner.	96	30
Partner is very good listener.	83	18
Partner does not put me down.	79	20

Source: Adapted from Olson & Olson, 2000.

TABLE 4.2	Top Five Communication Issues for Married Couples	
Issue	**Percentage of Couples with Problems ($n = 21,501$)**	
Wish my partner were more willing to share feelings.	82%	
Have difficulty asking partner for what I want.	75	
Partner does not understand how I feel.	72	
Partner often refuses to discuss issues/problems.	71	
Partner makes comments that put me down.	67	

Source: Adapted from Olson & Olson, 2000.

Perspectives on Communication

Communication difficulties often arise when participants have divergent communication styles. This section sheds light on two significant sources of communication-style differences: gender and culture.

Gender Differences in Communication

Common gender-related differences in communication often cause conflict between men and women. It sometimes seems that there are two separate styles of communication: a masculine style and a feminine style. A better understanding of the differences between these styles can reduce some of the friction between men and women.

Jane Tear (cited in Meier, 1991) summarizes what many authorities believe to be common differences between male and female communication styles (Table 4.3). Men often use conversation in a competitive way, perhaps to establish dominance in the relationship, whereas women tend to use conversation in a more affiliative way, hoping to establish friendship. Females tend to use good listening behaviors (such as making eye contact, nodding frequently, focusing attention on the speaker, and asking relevant questions), whereas men seem less focused on listening and more focused on responding. Men also tend to talk more but to disclose

TABLE 4.3	Conversational Style and Gender		
LISTENING STYLE		**SPEAKING STYLE**	
Male	**Female**	**Male**	**Female**
• Irregular eye contact	Uninterrupted eye contact	• Few pauses	Frequent pauses
• Infrequent nodding	Frequent nodding	• May abruptly change topic	Connects information to previous speaker's information
• Infrequent use of "uh-huh"	Frequent use of "uh-huh"	• Speaks until interrupted	Stops speaking when information is delivered
• May continue another activity while speaking	Usually stops other activities while speaking	• Speaks louder than previous speaker	Uses same volume as previous speaker
• Interrupts in order to speak	Waits for pauses in order to speak	• Frequent use of "I" and "me"	Frequent use of "us" and "we"
• Questions are designed to analyze speaker's information	Questions are designed to elicit more information	• Personal self-disclosure rarely included	Personal self-disclosure often included
		• Humor delivered as separate jokes or anecdotes	Humor interwoven into discussion content
		• Humor often based on kidding or making fun of others	Humor rarely based on kidding or making fun of others

Note: This chart was developed by Jane Tear, a New York City–based consultant who specializes in gender dynamics in the workplace. She stresses that although most people have a speaking style fairly typical of their sex, each person's individual style reflects gender-typical tendencies to a greater or lesser extent.

Source: "War of the Words: Women Talk About How Men and Women Talk" by P. Meier, January 6, 1991, Minneapolis *Star/Tribune (First Sunday)*, p. 8. Copyright 1991 by Minneapolis *Star/Tribune*. Reprinted by permission.

less personal information about themselves. Women tend to speak as a way to connect with people and ideas.

Deborah Tannen's work complements Tear's synthesis of communication styles. In her book *You Just Don't Understand: Women and Men in Conversation*, Tannen (2001) reported a conversation between a couple in their car. The woman asked, "Would you like to stop for a drink?" Her husband answered truthfully, "No," and they didn't stop. He was later frustrated to learn that his wife was annoyed because she had wanted to stop for a drink. He wondered, "Why didn't she just say what she wanted? Why did she play games with me?" The wife was annoyed not so much because she had not gotten her way but because her husband had not considered her preference. From her point of view, she had shown concern for her husband's wishes but he had shown no concern for hers.

Tannen believes that in this instance the spouses had used different but equally valid styles of communication and that both need to learn how to decipher each other's approaches to communication:

> In understanding what went wrong, the man must realize that when [his wife] asks what he would like, she is not asking an information question but rather starting a negotiation about what both would like. For her part, however, the woman must realize that when he answers "yes" or "no" he is not making a non-negotiable demand. (2001, p. 22)

People forget what you say,
they forget what you do,
but they don't forget
how you make them feel!

—AUTHOR UNKNOWN

Competition Versus Connection. Men are generally socialized to be competitive; much of their life is spent in a hierarchical world in which each encounter with another person is seen as a challenge to their position. When the match is over, the man often evaluates himself as one-up or one-down. Male conversations are almost symbolic struggles in which the competitor tries to gain the upper hand, protect himself from threatening moves, and not allow himself to be pushed around. Men are therefore more uncomfortable talking about feelings than women are, because feelings can be interpreted as signs of weakness.

Women tend to approach the world not as competing, independent individualists but as individuals intimately interconnected with one another. Women tend to "network"; men tend to "compete." Tannen argues that, for women, conversations are "negotiations for closeness in which people try to seek and give confirmation and support, and to reach consensus" (2001). Women tend to seek out a community and to work to preserve intimacy and avoid isolation. Although they are also concerned with achieving status and avoiding failure, these are not their major focuses in life.

Although we all apparently need to have both a sense of independence from others and a sense of intimacy with others, men lean toward independence and women lean toward intimacy. The greater the difference in communication style between a man and a woman, the greater the potential for misunderstanding. A woman, needing closeness, will naturally want to tell her spouse where she's going, whom she'll be with, and when she'll return. A man, needing independence and control, may find it more difficult to see why it is important to share this information.

Similarly, a woman, being more concerned with building a close relationship, will want to tell her spouse about every purchase she would like to make—even those that are relatively inexpensive. Her husband may resist seeking permission from her for every little purchase, seeing any lessening of control over the family purse strings as a loss of control in life (Tannen, 2001).

Communication in an intimate relationship involves a continuous balancing of competing needs for intimacy and independence. Tannen points out that intimacy implies that "we're close and the same," whereas independence implies that "we're separate and different." Independence can also be the foundation of a hierarchy in a relationship—that is, "If I'm independent of you, and you're dependent on me, I'm higher on the totem pole. I have the power." Perhaps that is why men, socialized to pursue power and control, tend to place more emphasis on independence than women do. Independence fits better into the world in which men have been trained to live (Tannen, 2001).

Tannen explains women's "nagging" by arguing that it comes from a different approach to living. Women are inclined to do what people ask them to do, whereas men tend to resist even the slightest hint that someone else—especially a woman—has the authority to tell them what to do. Women tend to repeat their requests of men—to "nag"—because they assume men think like *they* think. "He would, of course, want to do what I'm asking if he only understood what I want."

So who's at fault? Neither. Both are simply reflecting masculine and feminine gender roles in their conversational styles. Tannen is careful to point out that women also value freedom and independence but tend to emphasize interdepen-

Gender differences in conversational style can lead to misunderstandings if people are not aware of them. Women tend to view conversation as an opportunity to connect with another person; men tend to view conversation as an arena for establishing dominance. These young women are probably able to communicate with each other more easily than with a member of the other sex.

dence and connection more. Similarly, men find comfort in closeness but are socialized to see independence as more important.

Affiliation Versus Action. Women are often seen as the "talkers" in the family, whereas men may play the "strong and silent" role (Tannen, 2001). This phenomenon also springs from differences between masculine and feminine gender roles. Women, seeking to affiliate, do so by talking. Men, being competitive, tend to be careful about talking. So when men go out with their friends, they are likely to do things together rather than to just talk. Women, on the contrary, tend to seek social situations centered around conversation, such as having lunch together. A good heart-to-heart talk builds intimacy and warm feelings. Many gay men also favor a conversational style that focuses on building intimacy.

In groups of people, men tend to be the talkers, but much of this talk is performance oriented, an attempt to establish dominance. When the topic is politics, sports, or other controversies that can be vigorously disputed, men lead the discussion. This performance-oriented talking is not really about establishing intimacy but about clarifying who has the power.

Men also tend to focus on solutions to problems, whereas women focus on sharing what they are feeling about problems. Because of this difference in focus, men often feel that women "only talk" about problems, and women often feel frustrated and misunderstood.

Male and female gender roles begin to influence boys and girls at a young age. Boys generally play outside more, in larger, hierarchically structured groups. Girls tend to play more in small groups or pairs, and their lives often revolve around

BOX 4.1   Self-Assessment

Your Gender Communication Quotient

How much do you know about how men and women communicate with one another? The 20 items in this questionnaire are based on research conducted in classrooms, private homes, businesses, offices, hospitals—places where people commonly work and socialize. The answers appear at the bottom.

	True	False
1. Men talk more than women.		
2. Men are more likely to interrupt women than they are to interrupt other men.		
3. There are approximately 10 times as many sexual terms for males as for females in the English language.		
4. During conversations, women spend more time gazing at their partners than men do.		
5. Nonverbal messages carry more weight than verbal messages.		
6. Female managers communicate with more emotional openness and drama than male managers.		
7. Men not only control the content of conversations, they also work harder at keeping conversations going.		
8. When people hear generic words such as "mankind" and "he," they respond inclusively, indicating that the terms apply to both sexes.		
9. Women are more likely to touch others than men are.		
10. In classroom communications, male students receive more reprimands and criticism than female students.		
11. Women are more likely than men to disclose information on intimate personal concerns.		
12. Female speakers are more animated in their conversational style than are male speakers.		
13. Women use less personal space than men.		
14. When a male speaks, he is listened to more carefully than a female speaker, even when she makes the identical presentation.		
15. In general, women speak in a more tentative style than do men.		
16. Women are more likely to answer questions that are not addressed to them.		
17. There is widespread sex segregation in schools, and it hinders effective classroom communication.		
18. Female managers are seen by both male and female subordinates as better communicators than male managers.		
19. In classroom communications, teachers are more likely to give verbal praise to female than to male students.		
20. In general, men smile more often than women.		

Answers: 1. T; 2. T; 3. F; 4. T; 5. T; 6–9. F; 10–15. T; 16. F; 17. T; 18. T; 19. F; 20. F.

Sources: "How Wide Is Your Communication Gender Gap?" by Hazel R. Rozema, Ph.D., University of Illinois at Springfield, and John W. Gray, Ph.D., University of Arkansas at Little Rock, Reprinted by permission.

best-friend relationships. Although they are attracted to each other, they have difficulty understanding each other. These difficulties continue throughout dating and into marriage. It is logical to argue that gender-role differences contribute to the unhappiness many people experience in marriage.

Tannen (2001) concludes that both sexes could learn from each other. Women could learn to accept some conflict and difference without considering it a threat to intimacy; men could learn from women that interdependence is not a threat to personal freedom. Tannen believes that the "best" style of communication is a flexible one: finding that delicate balance between separateness and connectedness. To determine your gender communication quotient, take the quiz in Box 4.1.

Tannen's work has generated a good deal of controversy. According to Elizabeth Aries (Tannen & Aries, 1997), the most common counterargument to Tannen's research is that Tannen unnecessarily polarizes the differences between men and women, deemphasizing the fact that men's and women's styles of communication overlap considerably. This argument is similar to the one that Sandra Bem (1995) makes in regard to gender roles: The differences between individual women and the differences between individual men are greater than the differences between women as a group and men as a group. In effect, even though men and women as groups may differ, there are countless individuals within each group who defy the stereotypes. The key is to recognize that the sexes do seem to differ to a modest degree on average but that averages do not tell the whole story by any means. As a friend of ours likes to say with a wry smile, "The meanest, toughest, most insensitive person in my office is . . . a woman!"

Cultural Differences in Communication

The uses and interpretations of both verbal and nonverbal communication vary widely from culture to culture. In England, for example, nonverbal gestures are considered brash and undesirable. But in Italy, France, and the Polynesian islands of the southwest Pacific, among other places, nonverbal gestures are common.

Culture influences many aspects of communication, including such nonverbal elements as eye contact, facial expression, physical proximity, and touching. These Latino men find it natural to greet each other on the street with a hug, whereas many other men in the United States would be more comfortable with a handshake.

Box 4.2   Putting It Together

All Together at Family Mealtimes

Researchers studying strong families have known for a long time that mealtimes together are one of the best ways to enhance communication and further develop family strengths (DeFrain et al., 2006). In recent years, family mealtime practices have been examined by researchers in a variety of disciplines, including family studies, psychology, cultural anthropology, history, and nutrition (Larson, Branscomb, & Wiley, 2006).

These researchers have been answering questions such as: What is the history of mealtime practices? Historically, how was mealtime different in differing socioeconomic classes? How does mealtime enhance the language skills of children? What role does mealtime play in the lives of those sitting around the dinner table?

For Linda Skogrand, mealtime on the farm in Minnesota in the 1950s and 1960s meant that work could stop and everyone could eat a large meal of meat, potatoes and gravy, vegetables, dessert, and coffee. The meal would have been prepared by the women in the family, including young girls, while the mean and boys did the heavier farm labor outside. The conversation would be about the quality of the crop, whether rain would fall to interrupt the harvest, and how Grandma was doing with her recovery from the flu. There were two major mealtimes, dinner (the noon meal) and supper (the evening meal). Of course, there were lunches between these major meals.

During this same time period of the 1950s and 1960s, immigrant families might be having a different mealtime experience. The newcomers to this country might have been domestic servants providing meals to more affluent families in urban communities (Cinotto, 2006). The family mealtime was a time to serve others, and the domestic help would eat in the kitchen after everyone else had been fed. Those eating at the kitchen table were the hired help, which could include the immigrant workers' own family members.

So, what is family mealtime like today, and what purpose does it serve for family members? We might expect that family mealtime has decreased with all the competition for valuable time. Although the frequency of family mealtimes together has declined somewhat since the 1950s, in more recent years it has remained constant and may have actually increased in the past few years (Larson et al., 2006). Family mealtimes today may be informal and may reflect the diversity of contemporary families today. A family member may have stopped at a restaurant on the way home from work, or families may go out to eat at a restaurant. Family mealtime may involve all members of the family participating in preparation of the meal to accommodate very busy schedules. Or an adult who has the major responsibility for homemaking may prepare the meal.

Mealtime activity can accomplish the goal of enhancing family well-being because family members can connect and share important happenings of the day. It provides opportunities for children to develop as they participate in conversations with other children and adults, solve problems, tell stories, and plan events (DeFrain, 2006; Larson et al., 2006). It is the place where communication skills are learned and cultural values are transmitted from one generation to the next (Ochs & Shohet, 2006). Although family mealtimes have changed over the years, this important time together is highly valued by most families today.

Cultural differences can affect not only how well a message is understood but also the way in which the messenger is perceived as an individual. A graduate student from India related the following incident, which occurred when he first arrived in the United States. The student was fairly fluent in English, but he was totally unfamiliar with American customs. One day he was walking down the street with a fellow student he had recently befriended. Without giving it much thought, he reached toward his friend and began holding hands with him as they walked down the street. Having assumed his friend was heterosexual, the American student was somewhat startled and asked his friend why he wanted to hold hands. The Indian graduate student became confused and said it was customary in India for two close friends to hold hands to show their friendship.

Clearly, actions may be interpreted quite differently in different cultures. The nature and scope of our nonverbal communication are largely determined by our cultural heritage, as well. For example, studies have documented the different ways in which men react to beautiful women around the world: the American male lifts his eyebrows, the Italian presses his forefinger into his cheek and rotates it, the Greek strokes his cheek, the Brazilian puts an imaginary telescope to his eye, the Frenchman kisses his fingertips, and the Egyptian grasps his beard.

Westerners consider direct eye contact important, but many cultures see it as a personal affront, conveying a lack of respect. In Japan, for example, when shaking hands, bowing, and especially when talking, it is important to glance only occasionally into the other person's face. One's gaze should instead focus on fingertips, desk tops, and carpets. In the words of one American electronics representative, "Always keep your shoes shined in Tokyo. You can bet a lot of Japanese you meet will have their eyes on them" (Axtell, 1999).

In most Latin countries, from Venezuela to Italy, the *abrazo* (hug) is as common as a handshake. Men hug men; women hug women; men hug women. In Slavic countries, this greeting is better described as a bear hug. In France, the double cheek-to-cheek greeting is common among both men and women. A traditional bow from the waist is the standard greeting for the Japanese, who are averse to casual touching. Many Americans, however, feel uncomfortable with bowing, but to the Japanese, it means "I respect your experience and wisdom."

Using Communication to Develop Intimacy

Good positive communication is a hallmark of successful close relationships (Markman, Stanley, Jenkins, & Blumberg, 2004). A man might say, "We're best friends. We talk about everything. I don't know what I'd do if she weren't around to listen to my problems. She lets me know, very clearly, when she's upset about something. But I don't feel attacked. We both just sit down and work out a solution." Poor communication, on the other hand, often minimizes the possibility of establishing a close relationship. People may say, "We don't communicate." "He never talks." "She always nags." "He doesn't understand me."

Communication is important in every stage of a close relationship. The seeds of marital failure are often sown early in a relationship—sometimes even before marriage. Poor communication before marriage is likely to continue after marriage. One study of premarital couples assessed individuals' feelings and attitudes toward communication in their relationships. The assessment focused on the level of comfort each partner felt in sharing feelings and in understanding each other. Couples who scored low on communication were more likely to be dissatisfied in their marriage or divorced 3 years later (Olson & Olson, 2000).

Communication is also important for families across the family life cycle. When children arrive, the complexities of family life increase, and positive communication becomes even more important. One of the challenges for families is parent–adolescent communication (Peterson, Steinmetz, & Wilson, 2005).

Communication is a complex process, but understanding certain principles can help individuals improve their interactions with others. For example, it is useful to know that people send subtle verbal and nonverbal messages to each other no matter what they say or do, even when they aren't consciously trying to say or do anything. Therefore, one important principle of communication is that "you cannot *not* communicate." Noncommunication is also a form of communication.

Communication as a Cooperative Endeavor

Communication depends on both the skillful sending and the skillful receiving of messages. Believing that you sent a clear message is no guarantee that it was decoded (understood) in the way you intended. The only way to know whether the message you sent is what was received is to ask the other person what he or she heard. Having the receiver restate what was said tells the sender whether the message was understood (Markman et al., 2004).

When disagreement and conflicts arise, there is a natural tendency to blame the other person and deny or minimize personal responsibility for creating and maintaining the conflict. For example, a couple has an argument over the husband's refusal to discuss issues in the relationship that are important to the wife. The more she pushes him, the more the husband withdraws. He says to her, in effect, "I wouldn't withdraw so much if you stopped nagging me." To which the wife retorts, "I wouldn't nag you if you would discuss these important things with me." The discussion finally ends with the husband's withdrawing even more, which only reinforces the wife's negative feelings. This potential dialogue ends in two monologues: Each blames the other for what has happened and neither accepts responsibility for the outcome.

One model of interpersonal communication assumes a linear cause and effect. In the battle just described, the husband blames the wife because she nags and the wife blames the husband because he withdraws. This is an example of the **linear causality model**, which states that there is a direct, or linear, relationship between cause and effect. Interpersonal communication that reflects this linear model is usually destructive rather than productive. Both people end up saying, in effect, "If it weren't for you, I wouldn't act this way."

A family systems model better explains both what has happened and how to escape this type of situation. According to the **circular causality model**, both people deny responsibility for what has happened and for changing it and preventing it from happening again. In the circular causality model, one person sends out a message, which causes a change in and a response from the other person. That response causes a new response in the first person, and so on. The communication cycle usually escalates into conflict. The husband's and wife's responses to each other's comments trap them in a vicious circle of causality: He says, "I withdraw because you nag," and she says, "I nag because you withdraw." Each spouse sees his or her behavior only as a reaction to the other's behavior, not as a determining factor in the other's response. In essence, they are both escalating the conflict.

It is best to avoid the "blame game" and to focus on working together to find solutions that are acceptable to everyone involved. Whereas blaming is a competitive endeavor in which one side tries to beat the other, genuine communication is a cooperative endeavor in which the participants focus on agreement. (See Chapter 5 for a detailed discussion of various approaches to conflict resolution.)

Content and Relationship Messages

When people communicate with each other, they send out two kinds of information. The most obvious component of communication is content—that is, the facts, opinions, and experiences people relate to one another. This is also called the *report* component of communication. The report component is usually relatively straightforward and for the most part is given verbally. The other component of communication is the message—that is, what the individual conveys about the relationship at hand—for example, whether it is a friendly relationship. This is called the *relationship*, or *command*, component of communication. More subtle than the report component, the relationship component is often conveyed nonverbally. Although the content of the message being communicated may be straightforward, it is always interpreted in light of the accompanying message about the relationship between the people involved in the communication.

Nonverbal Communication

In communicating with other people, it is important to pay close attention to nonverbal messages. In fact, some researchers estimate that nearly 65% of all face-to-face communication is nonverbal. It is ironic, then, that we select our words so carefully when they comprise only 35% of the communicated message and that we pay such little attention to the nonverbal messages we convey (Gottman & Notarius, 2000).

Verbal communication includes both spoken and written words. Spoken communication has various nonverbal aspects to it: tone of voice, volume, pitch, speed of speech, and rhythm of speech. Written communication also has nonverbal aspects: the style of writing (handwritten, printed, typed, sloppy, neat) and the medium (personal stationery, a card, a napkin).

Nonverbal communication takes a wide variety of forms. It includes facial expressions, eye contact, gestures and other body movements, spatial behavior (e.g., how far apart two people stand or sit from each other), body contact, nonverbal vocalizations (e.g., sighs, grunts), and posture. Nonverbal communication is just as difficult to interpret as verbal communication. Is that yawn boredom, or is it a reflexive action?

The relationship component of communication has a central influence on the accurate transmission and interpretation of nonverbal messages (Gottman &

People send some of their most powerful messages nonverbally. With his arms raised, his brow furrowed, and his eyes set in a fixed stare, the man on the right conveys an intense and intimidating presence. His conversational partner responds by turning her back and folding her arms. We don't know the content of their conversation, but we can guess something about their relationship.

Notarius, 2000). For example, if you saw two people hugging at the airport, you would assume that they have a close relationship. In other words, people make guesses about a relationship on the basis of nonverbal behavior and the context in which they observe the behavior.

Mixed Messages and Double Binds

People often send **mixed messages**—messages in which there is a discrepancy between the verbal and the nonverbal components. The receiver hears one thing but simultaneously feels something else. When the verbal and the nonverbal messages conflict, people tend to rely more on the nonverbal information. For example, a person collapses into his or her favorite chair to watch a favorite television show and says to another person, "Is there anything you want me to help you with now?" Although the verbal message conveys a willingness to help, the nonverbal actions express just the opposite. The person sending the message is hoping that the listener notices the discrepancy and responds to the nonverbal cues, enabling the speaker to watch the program while at the same time giving the impression of being willing to help out.

We all send mixed messages for a variety of reasons every day, but they often stem from an unwillingness to be direct and honest in our communication. Mixed messages can become a barrier to real understanding. Directness in communication minimizes misunderstanding and confusion.

Whereas a mixed message is a conflict between the verbal and the nonverbal components of a communication, a **double bind** occurs when the verbal and nonverbal messages (*interaction* component) relay information that causes some question or conflict about the relationship between the speaker and the receiver (the *relationship* component). The receiver is in a double bind when the speaker creates a situation—legitimate or not—that calls into question the type of relationship the receiver has with the speaker.

An example of a double bind is when one person tells a friend a secret and later learns from other people that the friend told them the secret. Because the supposed friend told a secret that was not to be shared, the speaker questions not only the trustworthiness of the friend but also the existence of the friendship. When one questions the relationship, one is caught in a double-bind situation.

Although a double bind can occur in any relationship, the probability of its occurring is greater if the relationship component is unclear. When the relationship between the two parties is established and clearly defined, the relationship component plays a less significant part in the interpretation of the message, and, consequently, the content can be more accurately understood. For example, if you say to someone, "You really are feebleminded," that message could be interpreted in a variety of ways, depending on the relationship you have with that person. If the person is a close friend, she or he would probably realize that you were just joking and might respond in a similar fashion. If, however, the other person was someone you just met, he or she might not only *not* know how to interpret what you said but also question whether he or she would want a relationship with you at all.

Furthermore, the potential for a double-bind message hinges on the quality and mood of a relationship. If a husband brings his wife flowers, for example, the way she interprets this behavior will depend on the mood of their current relationship. If she is feeling good about the relationship, she will likely interpret the flowers as a sign of affection. Depending on recent events, however, she might also see them as a bribe, an apology, or preparation for something to come. She might worry about what this act means, an indication that she is unsure or distrustful of her husband's behavior. Again, the interpretation depends on the quality and current mood of their relationship and on past experiences related to this event.

In summary, when the relationship between the two parties is established and clearly defined, the relationship component plays a less significant part in the interpretation of the message, and, consequently, the content is more accurately understood.

Metacommunication: Clarifying Your Communication

The original description of double-bind communications by Gregory Bateson (Bateson, Jackson, Haley, & Weakland, 1956) described a situation in which a mother visited her schizophrenic son in the hospital. When the man tried to embrace his mother, she stiffened, pulled away from him, and asked, "Don't you love me anymore?" On the verbal level, she was implying love, but nonverbally she was rejecting him. Because of his dependent relationship with her, he was unable to respond verbally to the double-bind situation she had created.

The primary way of preventing or unbinding a double bind is known as **metacommunication**—simply, communicating about communicating. It is sometimes easier for children to pick up and respond to conflicting messages than it is for adults, as illustrated in this exchange: A man was talking with an 11-year-old boy he liked very much. The boy was describing how much he disliked girls. The man commented that he really liked girls but disliked boys. After a moment of perplexity, the boy responded, "You're teasing!"—and they both laughed. In spite of the conflicting message about their relationship, the child was able to understand and to point out the incongruence. Because the man acknowledged the discrepancy, they were both able to see the humor in the situation. It did not turn into a double bind.

When a couple wants to really connect with each other, they have to use all their communication skills—speaking honestly, listening attentively, requesting clarification, giving constructive feedback. Such efforts pay off in high-quality moments like the one this couple is enjoying.

It is often more difficult to respond to a double-bind message that occurs within a close and dependent relationship. Because of the significance of the relationship, the possibility exists that metacommunicating might create more problems. Paradoxically, the more dependent the relationship in which the double-bind messages occur, the greater the resistance to clarifying these messages. The dilemma is this: In order to improve a relationship, one must be willing to risk losing it. Consequently, the more one has invested in a relationship, the less willing one is to discuss or change it, even though change is often necessary if the relationship is to remain vital or to grow. Because many individuals are not willing to take this "existential risk," their relationships become increasingly predictable and routine.

Although double binds are usually seen as detrimental to a relationship, they can also prove beneficial. They can, first of all, create a situation in which one person feels the need for a clearer definition of the relationship. This can be accomplished by discussing the nature of the relationship directly, to clarify and possibly to renegotiate its nature.

Using Communication to Maintain Intimacy

Developing and maintaining communication skills are lifelong processes (Gottman, Schwartz Gottman, & DeClaire, 2006). Being good at communicating takes time, practice, and attention to detail. In this section we will focus on specific speaking and listening skills.

Speaking: The Art of Self-Disclosure

It is very important that as a speaker you speak for yourself, not for others. Communication problems often occur when a person tries to speak for another person, especially in a close relationship. A good way to avoid unnecessary friction is to stay away from *you should's* and *we's*. Again, the issue is one of power and control.

Self-disclosure occurs when an individual reveals to one or more people some personal information or feelings that they could not otherwise learn. We acquire information about an individual in many ways—from mutual acquaintances, from the person's behavior, and even from the clothes she or he wears. Self-disclosure differs from these other ways in that the individual willingly and with some forethought discloses the information. (Self-disclosure does sometimes also occur inadvertently.)

Self-disclosure requires both an awareness of information (reactions, goals, feelings, etc.) about oneself and a predisposition to disclose that information. For example, an adolescent may want to discuss her vocational goals with her parents, goals that do not include college. Her parents, however, are set on her going to a particular college. The daughter complies with her parents' wishes to avoid conflict and never discloses her true feelings about going to college. Thus, although she is aware of her feelings, her predisposition to disclose does not overcome her desire to avoid conflict.

Females receive more disclosures than men. Females also disclose more than men. However, these differences in disclosure can be small and are moderated by the situation and the sex of the other person. Dindia (2000) completed a comprehensive review of studies on gender and disclosure and found the following:

- Females receive more disclosures than do males.
- Females disclose more to females than males do to males.
- Females disclose more to males than males do to females.
- Females disclose more to females than males do to females.
- Females that are attractive receive more disclosure from males.

In general, there is a strong relationship between the amount of disclosure and liking a person. People disclose more to people they like, and the more they disclose, the more the other person discloses in return. More disclosure between people leads to greater feelings of closeness. So self-disclosure helps to build closeness and intimacy between people.

Self-Disclosure and Intimacy. Patterns of self-disclosure vary with each type of relationship, but relationship type is not the sole determinant of self-disclosure. High and low levels of disclosure occur among strangers, friends, and intimates. But factors such as motivation for and frequency of disclosure are likely to be related to relationship type. Let's look at three different relationships—between strangers, between friends, and between intimates—and compare the patterns of self-disclosure among them.

If you were to ask your average city bus rider why he or she never reveals personal information to the bus driver, the answer you'd probably get is "that wouldn't seem right." What this means is that disclosure does not seem appropriate between people who don't really know each other. Personal disclosure to strangers seems inappropriate because there is no relationship history to serve as a foundation for the disclosure. There are, of course, exceptions to the general rule. When one stranger discloses to another, it may be because the discloser knows that he or she will never see the other person again and therefore feels there is little risk.

© King Features Syndicate. Reprinted with permission.

"I was on a plane trip from Texas to Chicago," related Lydia, a young art student. "I found myself seated next to a young man who, like myself, was a student. We talked casually for a few minutes, mentioning where we had spent our vacations. However, by the time the plane had reached cruising altitude, he began asking me questions about my relationship with my boyfriend, future plans for marriage, motivations for marrying, and a host of other pointed and personal questions.

"I was rather surprised to be asked to reveal such personal information, but I was even more surprised to find myself answering his questions. At first I was wriggling with discomfort at disclosing to a complete stranger. But although the questions were startling, his manner was not at all offensive. In fact, he seemed rather likable. Because he also revealed some information about himself, I revealed more personal information and feelings to him. I guess I felt I had nothing to lose because I would never see him again."

Strangers also engage in self-disclosure in structured support groups such as Weight Watchers, Alcoholics Anonymous, grief groups, or group psychotherapy. Here, self-disclosure is encouraged so that the group may help the person work through feelings related to a specific goal or task. Because the groups's purpose is to help the group member deal with problems that he or she might feel uncomfortable expressing in another situation, there is less concern about the appropriateness of self-disclosure.

Some couples, even though they are physically together, are less focused on each other than on their cell phones.

Self-Disclosure in Friendships and Intimate Relationships. Although self-disclosure is not expected between strangers, it is expected and desired between good friends. The discloser is usually aware of how the receiver will react to a disclosure on the basis of what has gone on previously in the relationship. Although self-disclosure between friends may be quite selective, it may also become quite intimate and personal as the friends increase their mutual trust and exclusivity. In a relationship between friends, self-disclosure increases the listener's obligations because the listener also feels compelled to self-disclose. Mutual disclosure helps the friendship develop more equally on both sides. Their close relationship and previous knowledge about each other allow friends to move quickly from impersonal to personal communication: One moment they may be talking about a mutual friend's wedding and the next about their personal feelings about their own marriages.

In some intimate relationships, including marriages and parent–child relationships, there is unfortunately less self-disclosure than in close friendships. Among married couples, partners often assume they know each other. Some even finish each other's sentences. But this assumption can be problematic, inhibiting communication. Also, couples often allow themselves only "leftover" time to share. At the end of the day, they may exchange pleasantries, review the day's activities, and talk about friends and the children, but they rarely take the time to talk with each other about their relationship, their hopes, and their dreams. Most married couples take their intimacy for granted. Consequently, they stop exploring new aspects of each other's personality and feelings. Some husbands and wives think that love alone will make the spouse understand all their needs and desires: "*If* she (he) loved me, she (he) would know what I want." However, spouses cannot guess their partner's inner feelings. Two people must *tell* each other what they need and want. Revealing new information allows the other partner to share in one's changes and increases the intimacy of the relationship. Failure to reveal changes can result in partners' "growing apart" from each other.

Figure 4.1 summarizes some research on self-disclosure, positive comments, and negative comments in various types of relationships. (The positive and negative comments were about the partner and sometimes about the relationship.) Interactions with strangers tend to involve low-to-moderate self-disclosure and

FIGURE 4.1

Self-Disclosure and Positive and Negative Comments by Relationship Type

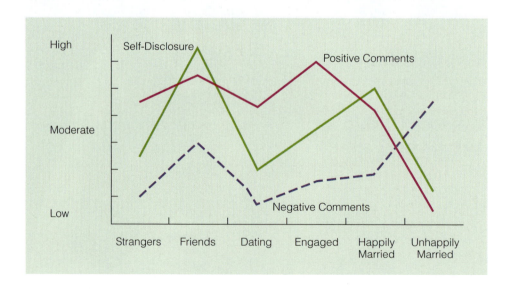

many more positive than negative comments. The greatest degree of self-disclosure and a high level of positive comments are seen in close friendships, which are also characterized by a moderate amount of negative comments. Dating relationships tend to have a higher level of expression of positive feelings and lower levels of both self-disclosure and negative comments. As couples move toward engagement, positive comments are at their highest, and both self-disclosure and negative comments increase. Happily married couples tend to be moderate to high on both positive and negative comments, as well as on self-disclosure. In contrast, unhappily married couples are very low on positive comments, very low on self-disclosure, and very high on negative comments.

Listening: A Difficult Skill

We hear only half of what is said to us, understand only half of that, believe only half of that, and remember only half of that.

—MIGNON MCLAUGHLIN, Journalist

Comedian Lily Tomlin urges us to "listen with the same intensity reserved only for talking." If one communication skill could be considered a foundation for intimacy, it would be listening. A very perceptive person once said, "Listening is really a lot more fun. When I'm talking, I'm not learning a thing."

People have a tendency to judge one another, listening to what others say and then deciding whether they are "right" or "wrong." "Being right" usually means that we agree with the other person, and "being wrong," that we disagree with the other person. Good listening skills require suspending judgment and spending more energy trying to understand other people. An important listening skill is to restate the speaker's ideas and feelings for verification. Although this approach slows down communication, it minimizes misunderstanding and conflict. When the goal of communication is to control other people, listening skills are of little importance. If the goal is to connect with other people and to develop genuine emotional intimacy, however, listening is essential.

Sherod Miller and his colleagues consider listening to be the process of developing a full understanding of another person's "story" (situation, concern, point of view). Effective listeners are aware of and make choices about how much they will attempt to direct or influence the speaker's telling of the story. Miller and his colleagues noted that the listener's motives are paramount and identified three basic motives, or goals, among listeners: (1) to lead by persuading, (2) to clarify by directing, and (3) to discover by attending (Miller & Miller, 1997).

The distinguishing factor of each of these three listening motives is the degree of control, or power, the listener desires over the situation. Does the listener follow the leader, allowing the speaker to relate the story in her or his own way? Or does the listener become the leader—getting the speaker to tell the story in the way the listener wants to hear it? Either approach affects the quality and integrity of the information that is exchanged.

Persuasive listening is hardly listening at all; the "listener" is really looking for an opening to jump in and control the direction of the conversation. Sometimes the persuader resembles a television reporter trying hard to get that 10- to 15-second sound bite for the evening news.

Directive listening involves less control than persuasive listening, but it does attempt to channel, or direct, the conversation. Studies indicate that excellent salespeople (those most likely to make the sale) ask four times as many questions

Attentive listening is a rare skill worth cultivating. It not only builds trust and intimacy in a relationship but also most efficiently allows the speaker to get a point across—without interruption or distraction.

as the average salesperson (Miller & Miller, 1997). The questions control the direction of the conversation, steering it where the directive listener wants it to go. Directive listening has certain advantages. It quickly focuses a conversation, and if the speaker cooperates, it allows the directive questioner to take charge of the dialogue. The major disadvantage of directive listening, however, is that in the interest of efficiency, crucial elements of the story may be lost. Directive listeners who use the approach in a very curt manner often fail to really understand what they are being told. By controlling the direction of the conversation, the directive listener may also lead the speaker down a blind alley into a trap.

Attentive listening is a mode in which the listener simply lets the speaker tell the story spontaneously and without interruption, encouraging rather than directing the teller. Busy people sometimes feel that attentive listening is too time consuming. In fact, it is more efficient than the other approaches because it lets the speaker get to the *real* point, avoiding misunderstanding and confusion. It is clearly the most effective listening mode for building rapport and trust. People who practice this skill, usually described as "good listeners," find this a positive trait to have in both their business and personal lives. Here's how one attentive listener, a retired newspaper editor, described the benefits of learning how to listen well:

> *"I hope I don't sound immodest, but I think the main reason people have always liked me over the years is because I'm a good listener. I really enjoy hearing what other people have to say. I don't have any desire to sit in judgment of them, or to feel superior, or to give out a lot of advice. I simply like to listen and try to understand how their world works. It's always very interesting.*
>
> *"People take this as a supreme compliment. They smile when they see me coming, and they're always coming up to me to tell me the latest story about their lives because they know I'll appreciate it if it's funny or sympathize with them if it's sad. It's really kind of fun. I always know what's happening, more than anyone else I know. My ability to listen served me well all those years in the newspaper business, too."*

Assertive, Passive, and Aggressive Communication

Researchers have identified three styles of responses in interpersonal communication: passive, aggressive, and assertive (Olson & Olson, 2000). Each response style has effects on both the respondent and the partner. Assertive statements were consistently found to be the most accurate, expressive, self-enhancing, and productive in terms of achieving a goal.

Assertive communication involves the expression of thoughts, feelings, and desires as one's right as an individual. Because it is self-expressive, assertive communication frequently uses the personal pronouns *I* and *me*. Assertiveness is associated with feelings of self-esteem, self-confidence, and determination to express opinions or feelings. Assertiveness, in sum, is giving yourself the right to be who you are without infringing on the rights of your partner to be who he or she is. Assertiveness enables people to feel good about themselves and increases the likelihood of achieving personal goals. Because assertiveness encourages expressiveness rather than defensiveness, it facilitates intimacy between partners.

Passive communication is characterized by an unwillingness to say what one thinks, feels, or wants. Passive behavior is frequently associated with feelings of anxiety about others' opinions, overconcern about the feelings of others ("I just didn't want to hurt her"), and fears about saying or doing anything that can be criticized ("I was afraid of saying the 'wrong' thing"). Passive responses reinforce feelings of low self-esteem, limit expressiveness, leave a well of hurt and anxious feelings, and make achievement of personal goals unlikely. Receivers of passive responses often feel anger at and lack of respect for the sender, realizing that their goals have been achieved at the sender's expense. Passive behavior does little to enhance either person's feelings about oneself or the other and creates distance rather than intimacy.

Aggressive communication aims to hurt or put down another person and to protect the self-esteem of the aggressor. Aggressive statements are characterized

TABLE 4.4	Communication Patterns and Intimacy			

COMMUNICATION PATTERN				
Person A	**Person B**	**Relationship**	**Who Wins**	**Level of Intimacy**
Passive	Passive	Devitalized/boring	Both lose	Low
Passive	Aggressive	Dominated	I win, you lose	Low
Aggressive	Aggressive	Conflicted	Both lose	Low
Assertive	Assertive	Vital/growing	Both win	High

by blame and accusation ("You always? . . . ," "You never . . ."). Aggressive behavior is associated with intense, angry feelings and thoughts of getting even. When people act in an aggressive manner with their partners, it reinforces the notion that the partner is to blame for the aggressor's frustration, that it is the partner's responsibility to make things "right." Aggressiveness is expressive behavior, but it is all too often self-enhancing at the other's expense. Goals may be achieved, but only by hurting and humiliating the other. The partner may also retaliate in kind. Because aggressive behavior focuses on the negative aspects of people rather than the negative aspects of the "situation," it generally escalates in negative spirals, leaving both partners feeling hurt and frustrated and creating distance in the relationship.

Assertiveness, passiveness, and aggressiveness are not personality traits; they are types of responses or behaviors. In most cases, it is inappropriate to label oneself or another an assertive, passive, or aggressive person. Some people use certain types of behaviors in specific situations or with certain people. For example, some women report that they have difficulty expressing their feelings or desires assertively in sexual relationships.

Because passive and aggressive responses affect intimacy negatively, becoming aware of the kinds of situations that elicit these nonintimate behaviors can enable individuals to practice more assertive responses. Table 4.4 illustrates how various communication patterns affect intimacy. For example, if both Person A and Person B have a passive style of communication, the relationship is likely to be devitalized and boring. In a conflict, both tend to lose because neither makes an effort to say what he or she thinks or wants. And in the end, the level of intimacy in the relationship is low, and the relationship is unsatisfying to both. Intimacy has the best chance of growing when both persons are assertive, because this combination of response styles creates a win–win situation. (Box 4.3 offers some excellent suggestions for improving intimacy through communication.)

Positive and Negative Communication Cycles

A study of over 15,000 married couples revealed that a positive communication cycle involves assertiveness and self-confidence and that a negative communication cycle is characterized by avoidance and partner dominance (Olson, 1997). The definitions of assertiveness, self-confidence, avoidance, and partner dominance are as follows:

Box 4.3 Putting It Together

Using Communication to Increase Intimacy

Using simple communication techniques like those listed below can help you increase and improve intimacy.

- Look for the good in your partner and give compliments.
- Praise your partner as much as possible.
- Take time to listen, listen, listen.
- Listen to understand, not to judge.
- After listening carefully, summarize your partner's comments before you share your reactions or feelings.
- Be assertive. Share your feelings by using "I" statements (i.e., "I feel," "I think," or "I would like").

- Share personal feelings.
- When issues arise, avoid blaming each other, and talk directly about how to deal with the issue differently.
- If issues persist, focus on creating as many new solutions as you can and then try them one at a time.
- If problems still persist, seek counseling early, when it's easier to find solutions.
- Give your relationship the priority and attention you did when you were dating.

Assertiveness is a person's ability to express his or her feelings and desires to a partner.

Self-confidence is a measure of how a person feels about herself or himself and the ability to control things in her or his life.

Avoidance is a person's tendency to minimize issues and a reluctance to deal with issues directly.

Partner dominance is the degree to which a person feels his or her partner tries to be controlling and dominant in their relationship.

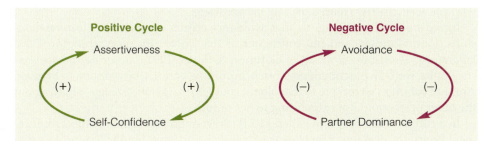

FIGURE 4.2
Positive and Negative Communication Cycles

In a positive communication cycle, as people become more assertive with their partner, they also tend to become more self-confident. This occurs, in part, because assertiveness often enables people to get more of what they want from others. Getting more of what they want tends to make them feel more self-confident. And as they gain more self-confidence, they tend to be more willing to be assertive. This positive cycle illustrates how communication skills can help people develop more positive feelings about each other (Figure 4.2).

In a negative communication cycle, as one person avoids making decisions, the other partner will take over and become more dominant, and as one partner becomes more dominant, the other partner may further withdraw (i.e., become avoidant). The combination of avoidance and partner dominance creates the negative communication cycle.

Research has found that couples in which both partners are assertive and self-confident tend to have very happy marriages. Conversely, couples in which one partner is dominant and the other is avoidant tend to have unhappy marriages.

The Positive Influence of Assertiveness

Assertive communication involves the expression of thoughts, feelings, and desires as one's right. It is self-focused and, therefore, favors "I" statements rather than "you" statements. An assertive person is able to ask for what she or he wants without demanding it or infringing on the rights of others. Assertive people tend to feel better about themselves because they are able to express themselves.

One goal in helping a couple improve their relationship is to try to help both people become more assertive with each other. Increasing assertiveness tends to increase each person's self-confidence and decrease avoidance and perceived partner dominance. Assertiveness generally has a positive impact on the person and on a couple's relationship.

Research has found a correlation (r) between assertiveness and the following personal and relational benefits (Table 4.5). As people became more assertive with a partner, they tended to be lower in avoidance ($r = -.72$) and lower in partner dominance ($r = -.50$). They also tended to like the personality of the partner more ($r = .49$) and to feel good about their communication with the partner ($r = .77$) and about how they resolved conflict with the partner ($r = .68$) (Olson, 1997).

In general, assertive individuals feel better about their partners and their relationships than nonassertive individuals. When both persons are assertive with each other, the level of intimacy increases because both partners are able to ask for what they want and, therefore, increase the probability that they will get what they want.

The Negative Influence of Avoidance

Avoidance, or a person's unwillingness or inability to deal with problematic issues, tends to be highest in people who are passive or nonassertive. Conversely, people who are very assertive tend to be low in avoidance.

Increasing evidence suggests that avoidance creates problems in close relationships. John Gottman and his colleagues at the University of Washington "love laboratory" (Gottman et al. 2006; Gottman & Silver, 1994a) describe the *avoidant style* quite well. Avoidant couples often minimize conflict by *agreeing to disagree.* Another common technique that avoidant couples use is *stonewalling*—shutting out the other person and not responding to her or him.

In a couple skills program called PREP (Prevention and Relationship Enhancement Program), developed by Howard Markman and Scott Stanley, counselors discovered that avoidance was very problematic for couples. In their book *12 Hours to a Great Marriage* (2004), Markman et al. describe the process of avoidance. They define avoidance as the reluctance to have any discussion that would raise problematic issues. When couples regularly avoid talking about risky issues, this is a sign that avoidance is becoming a more common style that will lead to problems in the long run.

TABLE 4.5	People High in Assertiveness

If a Person Is High in Assertiveness, He or She Tends to:
- Be low in avoidance
- Be low in partner dominance
- Like the personality of the partner
- Feel good about communication with the partner
- Feel good about conflict resolution with the partner

TABLE 4.6	People High in Avoidance

If a Person Is High in Avoidance, He or She Tends to:
• Be low in assertiveness
• Be high in partner dominance
• Dislike the personality of the partner
• Dislike communication with the partner
• Dislike conflict resolution with the partner

Researchers have found a positive correlation between avoidance and partner dominance ($r = .62$); this means that the more a person uses avoidance, the more that person perceives the partner as dominant (Table 4.6). People who are high in avoidance also tend to perceive their relationship with their partners in more negative terms. One study found that people high in avoidance tended to dislike the personality of their partners ($r = -.59$) and did not feel good about the way they communicated ($r = -.66$) or resolved conflict ($r = -.71$) with their partners (Olson, 1997).

In summary, it appears that assertiveness has a very positive impact on a couple's relationship, whereas avoidance has a negative influence. Learning assertiveness tends to help people overcome the more negative style of avoidance, so the more both people in a relationship can help each other become assertive with each other, the greater chance they will have in building each other's self-confidence and decreasing their feeling of being dominated by the partner. Couples in which both partners are high in assertiveness and self-confidence will feel better about their communication, how they resolve conflict, and, ultimately, how happy they are with their relationship.

Summary

• Communication, the process of sharing messages, is an integral part of intimacy.
• In a national survey of couple communication strengths, happy couples agreed more often than unhappy couples that they were satisfied with how they talked to each other as partners, had no trouble believing each other, felt their partners did not make comments that put them down, were not afraid to ask their partners for what they wanted, and felt free to express their true feelings to their partners.
• The top five communication issues identified by couples in a national survey were the following: They wished their partners would share their feelings; they had difficulty asking their partners for what they wanted; their partners did not understand how they felt; their partners often refused to discuss issues/problems; and their partners made comments that put them down.

• Men and women tend to have different communication styles as a result of culturally established gender roles. Although communication styles can vary greatly from one individual to another, in general, men tend to be more competitive in their communication and women tend to be more focused on connecting emotionally with others.
• Basic principles of communication include the following: One cannot *not* communicate; the message sent is often not the message received; when communication fails, both people are responsible for the failure; all messages convey both content information and relationship information; nonverbal communication carries about 65% of the meaning in an interpersonal exchange; incongruent verbal and nonverbal communication can cause misunderstanding; and metacommunication (talking about talking) is useful for unbinding double binds.
• Self-disclosure—individual revelations of personal information or feelings—is a key to the development of intimacy.

- Listening is the process of developing a full understanding of another person's "story" (situation, concern, point of view). Persuasive listeners and directive listeners try to control the conversation. Attentive listeners aim at fully understanding the other person's point of view, an approach that encourages the development of genuine intimacy.
- Assertive communication assumes that expressing thoughts, feelings, and desires is the right of the individual. Passive communication is characterized by an unwillingness to say what one thinks, feels, or wants. Aggressive communication aims at hurting or putting down the other person.
- Assertiveness and self-confidence are key elements of a positive communication cycle. A negative communication cycle is characterized by avoidance and partner dominance.
- The more assertive, and less avoidant partners are, the more satisfying their relationship will be.

Key Terms

communication	directive listening
linear causality model	attentive listening
circular causality model	assertive communication
nonverbal communication	passive communication
mixed message	aggressive communication
double bind	assertiveness
metacommunication	self-confidence
self-disclosure	avoidance
persuasive listening	partner dominance

Activities

1. Study Jane Tear's chart, Conversational Style and Gender, in Table 4.3. In small groups, discuss the hypothesis that men tend to use conversation in a competitive way in an effort to "win," whereas women tend to use conversation to build relationships. Is this true, or is it a stereotype? What are the values and limitations of each style?
2. Because males and females are socialized differently, adult male culture differs somewhat from adult female culture. What can parents do for their children in the early years to minimize confusion and misunderstanding between the sexes later on?
3. Use the Couple and Family Scales in Appendix A to rate the communication in your family of origin now or at some time in the past. Identify the most positive and most negative aspects of that communication.
4. Use the Couple and Family Scales in Appendix A to rate the communication at various stages of a current relationship (friendship, dating, cohabiting, marriage).

How has the communication changed over time on each aspect of the scale?

5. Focus on assertive, passive, and aggressive behavior in this exercise. Form groups of four. Two people will role-play the following styles for 2 to 3 minutes while the other two people observe. After each segment, discuss what it felt like to play the assigned role or to observe the role playing. When your group has role-played all three styles, compare and contrast the various styles.
   a. Passive and aggressive (one person acts passively; one acts aggressively)
   b. Assertive and passive (one acts assertively; one acts passively)
   c. Assertive and assertive (both people are assertive)

Suggested Readings

Axtell, R. G. (1999). *Do's and taboos of humor around the world: Stories and tips from business and life.* New York: Wiley. Instructive and highly entertaining.

Christensen, A., Eldridge, K., Bokel Catta-Preta, A., Lim, V. R., & Santagata, R. (2006). Cross-cultural consistency of the demand/withdraw interaction patterns in couples. *Journal of Marriage and the Family, 68,* 1029–1044. A study of couples in Brazil, Italy, Taiwan, and the United States finds that constructive communication was positively associated with relationship satisfaction, whereas demand/withdraw types of communication were negatively associated with relationship satisfaction.

Gottman, J. M. (2001). *The relationship cure.* New York: Three Rivers Press. This book provides information on how to develop "emotional connections" and a stronger couple relationship.

Gottman, J. M., Schwartz Gottman, J., & DeClaire, J. (2006). *Ten lessons to transform your marriage: America's love lab experts share their strategies for strengthening your relationships.* New York: Crown. The latest book from the University of Washington research team.

Knapp, M. L., & Vangelisti, A. L. (2005). *Interpersonal communication and human relationships.* Boston: Allyn & Bacon. Many useful ideas.

Markman, H. J., Stanley, S. M., & Blumberg, S. L. (2001). *Fighting for your marriage.* San Francisco: Jossey-Bass. A very useful book to help build positive communication skills.

Markman, H. J., Stanley, S. M., Jenkins, N. H., & Blumberg, S. L. (2004). *12 hours to a great marriage: A step-by-step guide for making love last.* San Francisco: Jossey-Bass. Most recent popular book from Markman, the marriage communication authority, and his colleagues.

Miller, S., & Miller, P. A. (1997). *Core communication: Skills and processes.* Littleton, CO: Interpersonal Communication Programs. An excellent, practical, and readable guide to better communication.

Olson, D. H., & Olson, A. K. (2000). *Empowering couples: Building on your strengths*. Minneapolis: Life Innovations. Contains national survey of strengths and issues and provides suggestions for improving couple relationships.

Seiler, W. J., & Beall, M. (2008). *Communication: Making connections* (7th ed.). Boston: Allyn & Bacon. An excellent resource.

Tannen, D., & Harness Goodwin, M. (2006). Family discourse. *Text, 26*(4). New thinking in the family communication literature.

Tannen, D., Kendall, S., & Gordon, C. (Eds.). (2007). *Family talk: Discourse and identity in four American families*. New York: Oxford University Press. The latest book from Tannen, one of the most prominent family communication specialists today.

Visit the text-specific Online Learning Center at **www.mhhe.com/Olson6** for practice tests, chapter summaries, Web links, Internet exercises, film guides, key terms, and flashcards.

5 Conflict and Conflict Resolution

Couple Strengths and Issues in Conflict Resolution

Conflict and Anger: An Overview

Intimacy and Conflict

Approaches to Conflict Resolution

Summary

Key Terms

Activities

Suggested Readings

Because people view the world from a wide variety of perspectives and have different goals, conflict is an inevitable part of intimate human relationships. In fact, the more intimate our relationships, the more chances there are for interpersonal conflict. Although conflict may be "normal" in a statistical sense, it does not have to escalate into verbal and physical violence. There are many constructive approaches to settling disagreements.

In this chapter we will begin with the results of a national survey (Olson & Olson, 2000) that identified the strengths of happily married couples versus unhappily married couples in how they resolve conflict. We will also review the five major conflict resolution issues reported by couples in this survey. These data set the stage for the rest of the chapter, in which we will discuss conflict and anger and the relationship between intimacy and conflict. We will also explore 16 rules for fair fighting and some basic approaches for constructive versus destructive conflict resolution.

Couple Strengths and Issues in Conflict Resolution

The results from a national survey of happy and unhappy married couples revealed the most common strengths for happy couples regarding conflict resolution (Olson & Olson, 2000). The most significant item distinguishing happy couples (87%) from unhappy couples (19%) was the feeling the partner understood them when they had problems. The survey also found that happy couples are almost four times as likely (85%) as unhappy couples (22%) to share feelings and ideas when they have disagreements. Happy couples were more than six times (71%) as likely as unhappy couples (11%) to feel that they are able to resolve their differences. About two-thirds (64%) of happy couples compared to 13% of unhappy couples have similar ideas about how to settle disagreement. Finally, happy couples were three times as likely (78%) as unhappy couples (26%) to feel that the partner takes their disagreements seriously (Table 5.1).

In terms of the most common conflict resolution issues for couples, the national sample of 21,501 married couples revealed that most (81%) of them end up feeling

TABLE 5.1	Conflict Resolution Strengths of Happy Versus Unhappy Married Couples	
	PERCENTAGE OF COUPLES IN AGREEMENT	
Strength	**Happy Couples** (*n* = 5,153)	**Unhappy Couples** (*n* = 5,127)
When discussing problems, partner understands my opinions and ideas.	87%	19%
Can share feelings and ideas with partner.	85	22
Able to resolve our differences.	71	11
Similar ideas about how to settle disagreements.	64	13
Partner takes our disagreements seriously.	78	26

Source: Adapted from Olson & Olson, 2000.

TABLE 5.2	Top Five Conflict Resolution Issues for Married Couples	
Issue		**Percentage with Issue** **(n = 21,501 couples)**
One person ends up feeling responsible for the problem.		81%
Go out of way to avoid conflict with partner.		79
Differences never get resolved.		78
Different ideas about best way to resolve conflict.		78
Have serious disputes over unimportant issues.		78

Source: Adapted from Olson, Fye, & Olson, 1999.

that they are personally responsible for problems (Olson & Olson, 2000). Seventy-nine percent of the couples reported that they go out of their way to avoid conflict with the partner, and most couples (78%) feel that their problems never get resolved and that they have different ideas about the best way to resolve their differences. Last, most couples (78%) feel that they have serious disputes over unimportant issues (see Table 5.2).

Conflict and Anger: An Overview

If conflict is not resolved, it continues to grow. In this section we will focus on the hierarchical process of conflict and discuss the value of early decision making in preventing problems and crises. We will explore some myths and taboos that limit our ability to express anger in a constructive manner and prevent us from establishing intimate relationships.

The Hierarchy of Conflict

The hierarchy of conflict, illustrated in Figure 5.1, can be thought of as a continuum, ranging from discussions of daily events to crises. The lowest three levels in the conflict hierarchy represent common reasons for individuals to get together to have a discussion: to chat about daily events, to discuss ideas, and to express feelings. These discussions generally operate at a low level of tension and usually entail little or no pressure for making decisions. The next four levels in the hierarchy involve increasing tension and the need for a decision. An awareness of the need for a decision precedes decision making. If a decision that should be made is not made, this could lead to the development of a problem, which would then need to be solved. If the problem is not solved, it could lead to a crisis, which is more difficult to resolve.

As an example of the hierarchical process of conflict, let's consider a couple, Joanne and Gary, who need to make a decision about birth control. The process involves three phases: the decision-making phase, the problem-solving phase, and the crisis resolution phase.

Decision-Making Phase. If Joanne and Gary are aware that they need birth control, then they need to make a decision about the type of method(s) to use. If they are not aware, then they won't make a decision; this could lead to pregnancy

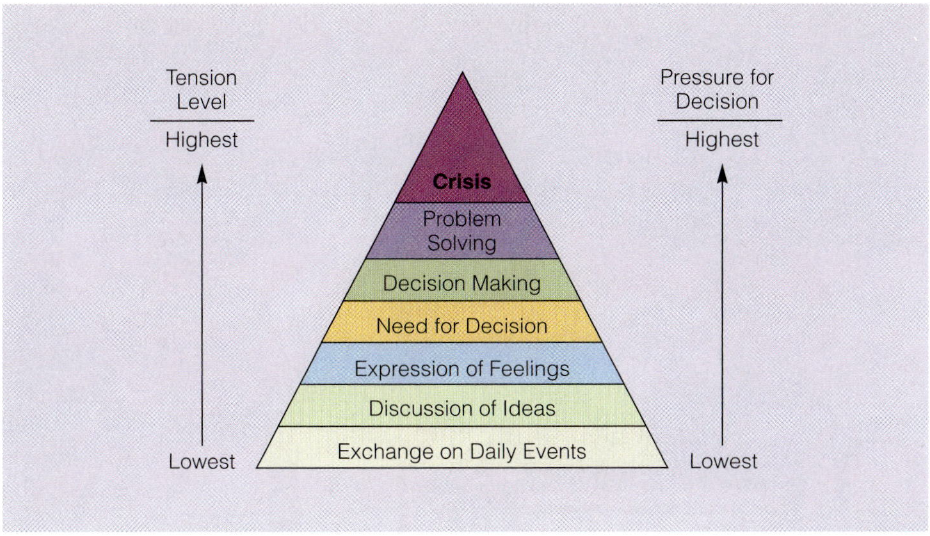

FIGURE 5.1
The Hierarchy of
Conflict

(a potential problem), and an unwanted pregnancy could become a crisis. Even if they are aware of the need for a decision, however, they may not be willing or able to make a decision, which could also lead to crisis. In other words, deciding not to decide *is,* in fact, a decision, but it is one that often produces undesirable consequences. Even if they do make a decision, it may be either effective or ineffective. An effective decision might be to use the birth control pill, which would greatly minimize the chance of an unwanted pregnancy. An ineffective decision would be to choose, say, withdrawal as their sole form of birth control.

Problem-Solving Phase. Problems can arise for Joanne and Gary if they made no decision or if the decision they made was ineffective. If Joanne becomes pregnant and neither Gary nor Joanne wants to have a baby, they have reached the problem level. In the problem-solving phase, Joanne could consider whether to have an abortion. If she does not want an abortion or fails to decide within 3 months, the problem becomes more serious.

Crisis Resolution Phase. Not dealing with the unwanted pregnancy could lead Joanne and Gary into a crisis. A crisis has the highest level of tension and creates the most pressure for a decision. Both tension and pressure increase the difficulty of making an adequate decision. The failure to make a decision earlier (to decide, for example, on a type of birth control) or the failure to make an effective decision (deciding, for example, to use a lower-risk, but relatively less reliable, method of birth control) forces Joanne and Gary to make a more difficult decision (whether to have the child or an abortion, whether to get married, whether to relinquish the child for adoption).

One would expect Joanne and Gary to be aware of potential problems and to therefore make an early effective decision to prevent problems and avert crisis. However, many individuals, couples, and families put off making easier, less complex preventive decisions. As a result, they are later faced with problems or crisis situations. This hierarchy of conflict model illustrates the sequential flow toward crisis and points up the importance of awareness and early decision making in preventing problems and crises.

If this couple is in a situation that requires a decision, they should deal with it as early as possible. When decisions are avoided, problems arise; when problems are ignored, crises develop.

Anger and Conflict Taboos

Most couples are afraid of negative emotions—anger, resentment, jealousy, bitterness, hurt, disgust, and hatred—and have a difficult time learning how to deal with them. A common tactic is to suppress negative emotions, hoping they will disappear with time. There are two predominant reasons for suppressing negative emotions. One is sociological in nature; the other is psychological.

Our culture and many others have a taboo against the expression of anger. This message, transmitted verbally and nonverbally from generation to generation, says that nice and competent people do not show anger, that anger is wrong, and that anger indicates that something is terribly wrong in a relationship. This message requires individuals to deny their genuine feelings and keeps them from being in touch with their true emotions. Repressed anger can lead to high levels of stress for individuals and their relationships, as Doris, a young woman married for 5 years, describes:

> *"I don't know what to do or think anymore. I know he loves me . . . I guess. He's just got so many rules he lives by, and so many rules I'm supposed to live by and the kids are supposed to live by. Maybe it's easier for him to live by these rules. Maybe he doesn't really think about them. I don't know. I just can't live by them anymore. The tension in me is volcanic. I find myself crying uncontrollably sometimes. I never have been able to express my feelings. My body expresses them. And now my feelings have built up so I can't seem to keep from exploding."*

The psychological reason for suppressing negative emotions has to do with human insecurity. Individuals think, "If I let other people know what I am really thinking and who I really am, they won't love me and I will be abandoned." In intimate relationships, partners struggle to find a delicate balance between dependence on each other and independence from each other. Some observers call that balance *interdependence.* In families, too, children and adolescents struggle to differentiate themselves from their parents and their siblings, to stake out territory and beliefs that are their own. People search for individuality while at the same time trying to maintain close relationships.

Some have been socialized to believe that all disagreements in a relationship are wrong, falsely assuming that the essence of marriage is harmony at any price. Such beliefs can be devastating to a relationship in the long run. Drew, a 30-year-old man, describes his relationship with his wife, Estelle:

> *"When I was growing up, my parents gave me the impression that fighting was wrong in a happy family and that kids should be shielded from it. When they wanted to have a good argument, they would wait until we kids were out of the house or asleep. I grew up believing that my mom and dad never fought."*

Fortunately, Drew and Estelle were both intelligent, creative, and committed to the marriage. They stuck with each other long enough to find out how to face and deal with conflict in a positive and productive way.

> *"Estelle, my wife, is from an alcoholic family. Her father would get drunk and pull the telephone cord out of the wall, push her mom around, and hit the kids. The meeting of these two approaches to conflict in one marriage was quite perilous for a number of years. My wife sometimes pushed and pushed until I blew up. She expected violence from men and pushed so she could get it over with and ease the tension. I would try to hold in my anger, but eventually I couldn't stand it any longer. One evening I got so mad I picked up a hamper full of clothes and was going to throw it at her."*

People tend to have negative attitudes toward conflict because of the popular assumption that love is the opposite of hate. Both love and hate are intense feelings. Rather than being opposites, however, they are more like two sides of the same coin. The line between the two is a fine one, with feelings of love often preceding those of hate. Nevertheless, when negative feelings are stifled, positive feelings also die. People often say, "I don't feel anything toward my spouse anymore. Not love or hate. I'm just indifferent." Indifference—lack of feeling—is the opposite of anger and love and hate. In the words of one loving father about his children, "If I didn't give a damn, I wouldn't get mad." Anger and love are connected; we often are angriest with the ones we love.

Rollo May (1969) described the dynamic connection between love and hate when he said:

> A curious thing which never fails to surprise persons in therapy is that after admitting their anger, animosity, and even hatred for a spouse and berating him or her during the hour, they end up with feelings of love toward this partner. A patient may have come in smoldering with negative feelings but resolved, partly unconsciously, to keep these as a good gentleman does, to himself; but he finds that he represses the love for the partner at the same time as he suppresses his aggression. . . . The positive cannot come out until the negative does also. . . . Hate and love are not polar opposites; they go together.

Myths, Theories, and Facts About Anger

In all matters of opinion, our adversaries are insane.

—MARK TWAIN (1907)

Bill Borcherdt (1996, 2000) offered an insightful perspective in his discussion of anger: "Of all the human emotions, anger has created the most harm and caused the greatest destruction within individuals, couples, families, and between social groups and nations" (1996, p. 53). Anger is a double-edged sword; just as it is directed at others, so it becomes internalized by the angry individual. As Borcherdt put it: "It is impossible to hate, despise, or resent somebody without suffering oneself." Although anger can sometimes make people feel good, it can also make them feel guilty and less positive about themselves.

Anger can also produce a feeling of strength and power. It deludes people into thinking that they are doing something constructive about the problems they face, when actually they are only making things worse. Anger lets people substitute feelings of superiority for those of hurt and rejection. It also allows them to think anything they want about another person without fear of retaliation.

Four common but false beliefs about anger are that it is externally caused, that it is best to express anger openly and directly, that it can be a helpful and beneficial emotion, and that it will prevent other people from taking advantage of you (Borcherdt, 1996, 2000). Let's take a closer look at these beliefs.

- *Anger is caused by others.* Many people believe that "somebody or something outside of you magically gets into your gut and makes you angry or gets you upset" (Borcherdt, 1996, p. 54). One's happiness or unhappiness, however, is not externally caused, Borcherdt points out. Anger, like any other human emotion, is self-created, usually when someone else does something we don't like.
- *The best way to deal with anger is to let it all out.* Although venting anger may make people feel better for the moment, it won't help them get any better. Letting it all out does not resolve the underlying issues. In fact, it tends to bring out those same feelings in others, increasing both people's anger.
- *Anger is a beneficial emotion.* This is simply not true. Individuals may find in the short run that they get their way by getting angry, but in the long run they will push others away from them or provoke them to get even.
- *You're a wimp if you don't get angry.* Some people believe that if they don't get angry, others will take advantage of them or consider them weak and inferior. Borcherdt urges people to decide how they want to feel, rather than how someone else is going to make them feel. Firm and assertive statements, such as "I disagree" or "I don't like that," let us take more control of situations. We do not have to get angry; we choose to get angry—and we can therefore choose a different approach.

Common myths and facts about anger are presented in Box 5.1.

Intimacy and Conflict

Someone once joked, "The major cause of divorce is marriage." Living together as a couple can be one of the most difficult challenges people face in life. In this section we will focus on how intimacy and conflict are bound together, the difficult balance between love and anger, the dance of anger that couples and families perform, and the sources of conflict in intimate relationships. We will also look at the significance of anger in all intimate relationships.

Intimacy Breeds Conflict

The more one knows about another person, the more possibilities there are for disagreement and dislike. If a relationship is to survive and thrive, each of these differences has to be worked through in some way. Folk wisdom tells us that "you

Box 5.1   Putting It Together

Anger: Myths and Facts

When it comes to anger, the ability to distinguish fact from myth helps to provide the insight needed to manage anger, promoting both emotional health and a positive and nurturing couple relationship. Below are some common facts and myths about anger to keep in mind:

Facts

- Anger is a feeling, with psychological components.
- Anger is universal among human beings.
- The nonexpression of anger leads to an increased risk of coronary disease.
- The venting of anger—"catharsis"—is of value only when it sets the stage for resolution.
- Aggression leads to further aggression, not resolution.
- Most anger is directed toward those close to us, not toward strangers.

- Depression, shyness, and suicide are expressions of anger at oneself.

Myths

- Venting (by yelling or pounding pillows) "releases" anger and therefore "deals with" it.
- Women get less angry than men.
- Some people never get angry.
- Anger always results from frustration.
- Aggressive behavior is a sure sign of an "angry person."
- TV violence, active sports, and/or competitive work "release" anger.

Source: Adapted from *Your Perfect Right: Assertiveness and Equality In Your Life and Relationships* (8th ed.) (p. 139) by Robert E. Alberti and Michael Emmons, 2001, Atascadero, CA: Impact. Adapted by permission of Impact Publishers, Inc., P.O. Box 1094, Atascadero, CA 93423.

always hurt the ones you love." Sociologists who have studied violence in America tell us that, statistically, it is safer to be with strangers than with your spouse or lover. Police officers report that domestic calls are among the most dangerous calls they respond to.

In their classic book *The Intimate Enemy: How to Fight Fair in Love and Marriage,* George Bach and Peter Wyden (1969) argue that verbal conflict is not only acceptable but highly desirable if it is constructive. According to Bach and Wyden, couples who fight together stay together, provided they know how to fight properly. Couples who don't fight and therefore don't resolve issues can become emotionally distanced from each other. Bach and Wyden's approach to conflict generated controversy when it first appeared; many felt the idea was too radical. However, the approach has helped many couples by encouraging them to discuss issues openly rather than denying them and assuming they would fade over time.

Love and Anger in Balance

In marriage counseling, couples commonly bring up the issue of balancing separateness and togetherness (the cohesion dimension on the Couple and Family Map). The challenge—or *growing edge* as family therapists call it—for couples is to preserve "a comfortable balance between the freedom of the individual partners to act independently and to develop their own individual patterns and abilities, while at the same time enjoying the rewards of a deeply shared life" (Mace, 1982, p. 113). With too much togetherness, marriage becomes a form of bondage. With too much separateness, the relationship dies from lack of attention.

Love and anger must also be kept in balance. "In every marriage the two dynamic forces are love, which seeks to draw the couple together, and anger, which

FEIFFER®

tends to drive them apart" (Mace, 1982, p. 115). Anger can be a healthy emotion if it helps a couple create an interdependent relationship.

Anger becomes an ally of the partners when they use it to attend to those areas in the relationship that need work. If the partners do not find a constructive way to use anger, however, they may gradually drift apart. The more common divorce scenario is not one of fireworks but one of a gradual loss of closeness (Mace, 1982, p. 116). In short, fear of anger can lead to disengagement, and disengagement can lead to emotional divorce, which often leads to legal divorce.

In a mature marriage, anger is seen not as an enemy but as a friend. Nevertheless, partners must use it carefully and at appropriate times. Experts suggest that couples make a contract never to attack each other when angry (Mace, 1982, p. 116). Feelings of anger signal that something is not right with the relationship. Rather than act on these feelings as they arise, partners should wait until they have calmed down and cooled off to calmly and rationally work things out. In other words, if they use anger as a barometer to signal an impending storm, partners can work together to prevent major damage to the relationship.

The Dance of Anger

It is our job to state our thoughts and feelings clearly and to make responsible decisions that are congruent with our values and beliefs. It is not our job to make another person think and feel the way we do or the way we want them to.

—HARRIET GOLDHOR LERNER (2005)

In her book *The Dance of Anger*, Harriet Goldhor Lerner urges people to closely observe how they manage anger. She graphically describes her own style of managing anger when she is under stress: "When stress mounts, I tend to underfunction with my family of origin (I forget birthdays, become incompetent, and end up with a headache, diarrhea, a cold, or all of the above); I overfunction at work (I have advice for everyone and I am convinced that my way is best); I distance from my husband (both emotionally and physically); and I assume an angry, blaming position with my kids."

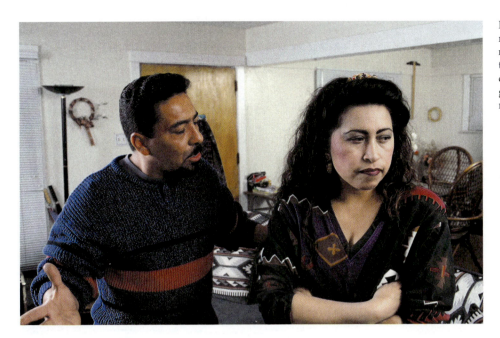

People send some of their most powerful messages nonverbally. We don't know the content of this couple's conversation, but we can guess something about their relationship.

Lerner developed a guide to various styles of anger management and labeled these styles pursuer, distancer, overfunctioner, underfunctioner, and blamer. Lerner's styles can be categorized in terms of the Couple and Family Map on the basis of the types of intimate relationships they tend to lead to.

In terms of the Couple and Family Map, **pursuers** tend to want to create connected or enmeshed types of intimate relationships that are very high in cohesion. Lerner describes pursuers as people who react to their anxiety by seeking greater togetherness in a relationship. Pursuers place a high value on talking and expressing feelings, believe other people should do the same, and tend to criticize a partner who can't tolerate feelings of closeness. When the partner wants more emotional space, the pursuer feels rejected and pursues the partner more vigorously before coldly withdrawing.

Distancers tend to create disengaged or separated types of intimate relationships that are low in cohesion. Distancers want emotional space when stress is high. They are private, self-reliant people rather than help-seekers. They have difficulty showing neediness, vulnerability, and dependency. Partners tend to describe them as being emotionally unavailable, withholding, and unable to deal with feelings. Distancers often manage anxiety by retreating into their work and may terminate a relationship entirely when things become too intense. Distancers tend to open up the most when they are not pushed or pursued.

The **dance of anger** is Lerner's metaphor to describe how human beings relate to each other. Think about the dance of a pursuer and a distancer. As the pursuer moves closer, the distancer retreats. Then, as the pursuer unhappily backs off, the distancer's comfort level increases and the distancer moves toward the pursuer. The pursuer warms up again and moves in on the distancer, who again begins to retreat. Back and forth, ebb and flow. Just as people have different tastes in food, clothing, and cars, so they have different needs and feelings about closeness. In terms of the Couple and Family Map, pursuers and distancers have difficulty finding a comfortable balance between separateness and togetherness. Left to their own devices, family relationships would move back and forth between the extremes of being enmeshed or being disengaged.

Although most people have an impulse to blame others when things go wrong, some people habitually avoid responsibility for their part in problems. "Blamers" such as this man tend to expend a great deal of energy trying to get others to change.

Lerner describes **underfunctioners** as people who in many areas of life just can't seem to get organized. These people are too high in flexibility (chaotic). Underfunctioners tend to become less competent under stress, letting others take over or fill in. These people are described at work and in the family as "the fragile one," "the sick one," "the problem," "the irresponsible one." Underfunctioners have difficulty showing their strong and competent side to intimates.

Overfunctioners, on the other hand, know what is best not only for themselves but for everybody else as well. These people are low in flexibility (rigid or structured). In difficult times, overfunctioners move in quickly to advise, rescue, and take charge. They can't seem to stay out of the way and let other people solve their own problems. In this way they avoid thinking about their own problems. Overfunctioners are commonly characterized as "always reliable" and "always together" people. They have difficulty showing their vulnerable, underfunctioning side, especially to people who are having troubles.

In terms of Lerner's dance metaphor, how would a couple composed of an overfunctioner and an underfunctioner dance? The overfunctioner would hide feelings of inferiority and incompetence by swooping in to "save" the underfunctioner, making the underfunctioner's task more difficult in the long run by depriving her or him of the opportunity to develop personal strengths.

Some may think that a couple made up of an overfunctioner and an underfunctioner would be a complementary couple, each helping to meet the needs of the other person. However, this type of relationship is actually quite tenuous. The overfunctioner eventually tires of saving the underfunctioner, or the underfunctioner tires of looking and feeling so incompetent. In both cases, the end result can be the breakdown of the partnership. For the relationship to endure and become strong, the partners need to find relative equality in terms of competence and functionality, both contributing a reasonable share to the common good.

Lerner's fifth style, the **blamer**, is a person who has a short fuse and responds in times of stress with emotionally intense feelings. Blamers often fall in the rigidly enmeshed category, an unbalanced type of family system. Blamers spend a lot of energy trying to change other people. They involve themselves in repetitive cycles of fighting, which may relieve tension but which also perpetuate old patterns. Blamers hold others responsible for their feelings and see others, rather than themselves, as the problem.

Lerner notes that women in our society are encouraged to overfunction in the areas of housework, child care, and "feelings work." In all other areas of endeavor, however, women are socialized to be pursuers and underfunctioners. Men, on the other hand, are socialized to be distancers and overfunctioners. Both sexes are good at blaming other people, but Lerner believes that women today do it more conspicuously than men because most women still feel they have less power in our society and resent their subordinate status.

All five ways of managing anger can be useful at times, but problems occur when one style dominates. It is important to find a balance between pursuing and distancing, underfunctioning and overfunctioning, blaming and taking the blame. In Lerner's (2005) words, "You will have a problem . . . if you are in an extreme position in any one of these categories or if you are unable to observe and change your pattern when it is keeping you angry and stuck". While many people do get stuck in their habitual styles of dealing with anger, Curt, a perceptive husband and writer, describes his experience with the dance of anger, noting that it *is* possible to change old patterns:

"I think dance of anger is a good metaphor for how we operated in the early years of our marriage. It almost seemed choreographed, it was so predictable. Eileen would do her part of the dance, and then I would respond with my part of the dance, back and forth, back and forth, and then all hell would break loose. It could get really ugly. I was so mad at her once, I thought I could kill her.

"I think a big part of the problem was we were simply replaying old videotapes of the families we grew up in. Her family in Puyallup was a soap opera par excellence. They loved to fight and did it well all their lives. My dad was an attorney in Bellingham, and he could really pour on the B.S. as well. He'd filibuster over the dinner table in his melodramatic way for ages, and my mother would finally crack and become a bitch on wheels. It was pretty predictable. It made me sick to my stomach. I left home when I was 17.

"Fortunately, Eileen and I could see the pattern in our own marriage. We read some books and articles about more positive approaches to settling our differences. We experimented and finally found better ways to get along. Luck probably played a part in it all—as did the fact that we mellowed a bit with age and just simply didn't enjoy a good brawl anymore. For whatever reason, we don't dance and brawl as much. Nobody's thrown anything for a long time. We don't fall into the old habits. We simply sit down and work things out. Thank God."

Conflict and Supportiveness in Heterosexual, Gay, and Lesbian Couples

Very few studies have compared couples with different sexual orientations (heterosexual, gay, and lesbian) in terms of their positive and negative communication. A recent study compared these three groups as the couples were videotaped while completing tasks designed to generate couple conflict and encourage supportive behavior (Julien, Chartrand, Simard, Bouthillier, & Begin, 2003).

The study found that there was no difference in the level of conflict or supportive behaviors between the heterosexual, gay, or lesbian couples. This was based on their observed communication patterns, and it is consistent with past studies in the field. A surprising finding was that for all the couples, positive communication during conflict was particularly important. Couples who had more positive communication during conflict resolved more issues and had higher couple

Box 5.2   At Issue

Determining Styles of Conflict Resolution in Happy Versus Unhappy Couples

How do the styles of conflict resolution differ in happy versus unhappy couples? Psychology professor John Gottman and his colleagues have been conducting scientific experiments for 20 years on more than 2,000 couples, using video cameras, EKG monitors, and specially designed instruments for observing what happens when couples interact. These researchers observe how couples talk to each other, examining facial expressions, gestures, fidgeting behaviors, and so on, as well as physiological clues such as changes in heartbeat and respiration during conflict. They also note listening skills and expressions of sarcasm and contempt. The results are like a "CAT scan of a living relationship."

The common denominator of a stable marriage is, according to Gottman, that the couples are "nicer to each other." The ratio of positive to negative moments in their relationship is 5 to 1. "Positive moments nurture the affection and joy that are crucial to weather the rough spots," Gottman says.

And what about divorce-prone couples? If there is a negative interaction for every positive one, the couple is divorce bound. Danger signs include *criticism* (attacking a spouse's personality or character), *contempt* (insulting and psychologically abusing a spouse), *defensiveness* (denying responsibility, making excuses, whining), and *stonewalling* (retreating from the conversation into stony silence). When these behaviors become routine, the marriage has serious problems.

To argue in a healthy manner, Gottman offers these strategies:

- Call a time-out and cool off.
- Edit the argument, responding only to constructive criticisms and ignoring the nastiness.
- Stay focused rather than wandering around verbally.
- Put the fight into perspective and be willing to see that most issues are not all that important.
- Be affectionate, understanding, empathetic, and validating.
- Use humor, and be able to laugh at yourself.

Source: Adapted from *Ten Lessons to Transform your Marriage: America's Love Lab Experts Share Their Strategies for Strengthening your Relationships* by J. Gottman, J. Schwartz Gottman, and J. DeClaire, 2006, New York: Crown.

satisfaction. So, for example, if a partner received positive comments when he or she was talking about a current problem, this helped them resolve the issue and maintain a happy relationship.

Box 5.2 summarizes findings on communication in stable and unstable relationships.

Approaches to Conflict Resolution

Grant me the serenity to accept what can't be changed,
The courage to change things that can be changed,
And the wisdom to know the difference.

—REINHOLD NIEBUHR (1951/1988, p. 600)

If anger is a normal part of intimate relationships, then fights and disagreements are likely to occur. The issue is how to fight fairly and constructively. In this section we will look at some suggestions for resolving conflicts in ways that preserve and enhance relationships.

Fighting Fairly

The terms *fight* and *fighting* are commonly used in our society to describe verbal disagreements between people. They are also used to describe boxing matches and other physically violent encounters. When family therapists talk about rules for *fair fighting*, they are referring to rules that govern verbal exchanges. Calling verbal conflict a fight is useful. It draws attention to the fact that verbal disagreements are serious business and should be treated with caution and good sense (Crosby, 1991). Tension and anger build up during these exchanges, and verbal conflict can turn into physical conflict.

People should observe certain conventions when arguing with each other; they will feel safer voicing disagreement if they know that it will not get out of hand. Crosby argues that "if we can trust—really believe—that our partner will not abandon us or take advantage of our vulnerability, we can then learn to interact in an aboveboard, straightforward manner" (1991, p. 170). Without this basic trust, people become defensive when they are accused or hide their defensiveness with a strong counterattack. The 16 ground rules for fair fighting (Crosby, 1991) are listed in Table 5.3 and explained below.

Negotiate from the Adult Position. Using terminology from transactional analysis, Crosby argues that each partner should make a firm commitment to negotiate from the *adult* position, rather than from the *child* or the *parent* position. Transactional analysis theorizes that people often replay old "tapes" in their minds and, under stress, are likely to act as they did when they were a child or as a parent acted toward them. Negotiating from the child position, a person acts vulnerable and often feels hurt or threatened. Negotiating from the parent position, a person rigidly repeats arguments and views held by her or his parents rather than interacting in new ways in this new situation. Negotiating from the adult position, however, the person can listen carefully to the other, respond assertively and rationally, and work with the other person to find a solution acceptable to both.

Avoid Ultimatums. An ultimatum is a nonnegotiable demand—"You do this or else"—and is a hallmark of dirty fighting. Fair fighting emphasizes negotiation, allowing each person room to bargain. Ultimatums generally lead to counterultimatums, leaving little room for genuine negotiation. An ultimatum puts the receiver in the child position and the sender in the parent position. Neither person gets a chance to negotiate from the adult position.

If One Loses, Both Lose. American society emphasizes competition in the marketplace, but in families competition can be problematic. Sometimes one partner is especially good at debating and may "win" most of the arguments. The other

TABLE 5.3	Sixteen Rules for Fair Fighting
• Negotiate from the adult position.	• Never use sex to smooth over a disagreement.
• Avoid ultimatums.	• Repeat the message you think you received.
• If one loses, both lose.	• Refuse to fight dirty.
• Say what you really mean.	• Resist giving the silent treatment.
• Avoid accusations and attack.	• Focus on the issue and focus on the present.
• Own your own feelings first.	• Call "time-out" and "foul."
• Always check out your perceptions.	• Use humor and comic relief.
• State your wishes and requests clearly and directly.	• Always go for closure.

Source: Illusion and Disillusion (4th ed.) (pp. 170–180) by J. Crosby, 1991, Belmont, CA: Wadsworth. Copyright © 1991 by J. Crosby. Reprinted by permission of Wadsworth Publishing, a division of International Thomson Publishing.

Couples need to observe certain conventions when arguing with each other; they will feel safer voicing disagreement if they know that it will not get out of hand. The goal is not winning the argument. The goal is to strengthen the relationship.

person may accuse the partner of using big words or sophisticated logic and may become unhappy with the situation.

The better debater may win arguments, but he or she will lose just as surely as the partner does. The relationship will become less open and cooperative. The goal of fighting fair in a family is not to win or lose the argument but to work together to find solutions that are acceptable to everyone.

Say What You Really Mean. As conflict increases, people often fail to say what they really mean. They may give in on issues when they don't really want to in order to protect the other person's feelings, but they are also protecting themselves from pain or embarrassment. The more people get in touch with and share their feelings, the earlier a solution can be found.

Take, for example, the issue of cohabitation. Two partners consider whether to move in together or to wait until marriage to live together. One person might feel positive about cohabiting; the other person might feel ambivalent, seeing both the positive and the negative consequences. Because cohabitation is a complex issue, the ambivalent partner should write down the pros and cons: "I love him"; "Mom and Dad will be mad"; "I'm afraid he will take advantage of me and I'll end up doing all the housework"; "I'm afraid I'll have to support him financially, and I can't even support myself now." The ambivalent partner can then see more clearly why she or he is feeling undecided and share these feelings with the other partner.

Avoid Accusations and Attack. When people are accused, they tend to react either by accusing the other person in turn or by withdrawing. "You" statements are implicit or explicit signals of attack: "You make me mad," "You always do that," or "It's all your fault." Most people become defensive and angry in response to statements of this sort.

Own Your Own Feelings First. Instead of attacking with "you" statements, use "I" statements: "I feel hurt," "I feel rejected," or "I feel disappointed." Although the difference between saying "I" and saying "you" may seem small, it is significant. By using "I" statements, the speaker is clearly pointing out that something is wrong in the relationship and is simply putting the issue on the table for discussion. The "I" statement indicates that the other person is innocent until proven guilty, rather than vice versa.

Always Check Out Your Perceptions. Miscommunication is often the catalyst for disagreements. Don't assume that you know what is really going on until you have talked with the other person. Also, don't try to guess what the other person is thinking or feeling. It is your responsibility to ask.

State Your Wishes and Requests Clearly and Directly. Dogs and cats often do a better job of communicating their needs than humans do. Because they are afraid of being turned down or rejected, people often do not say directly what they want. One common approach is to ask a leading question, one that hints at the desired result without directly asking for it. For example, someone who wanted to go to the movies might ask, "Wouldn't you like to see a movie tonight?" The indirect approach might work sometimes, but it is not a reliable way for people to get what they want.

Never Use Sex to Smooth Over a Disagreement. People sometimes use sex as a tool or a weapon in an argument. When people use sexual persuasion to get their mate to agree with them, the underlying issue or conflict often remains unresolved, or if the disagreement is about some immediate problem, it is likely that no decision will be made. Also, the partner who feels pressured into a decision might later resent the other partner.

Repeat the Message You Think You Received. Active listeners let their partner know that they correctly heard what the partner was saying. Active listeners don't repeat the message verbatim but simply restate it in their own words to show their partners that they understand it. Active listening does three valuable things: It forces people to listen; it slows down reaction time, which keeps the discussion calmer and more rational; and it aids in understanding the message.

Refuse to Fight Dirty. Dirty fighters lose the battle before they begin the attack. They prove their inability to deal positively and fairly with the situation. Crosby (1991) lists a variety of dirty-fighting techniques:

- *Gunnysacking.* **Gunnysacking** is an alienating tactic in which participants stuff their true feelings into a deep sack, thus preventing the other person from knowing what they are really feeling. The problem is that the gunnysack can hold only so much. When the sack overflows, gunnysackers may verbally or physically attack the other person.

- *Passive–aggressive behavior.* Like gunnysackers, people who engage in **passive–aggressive behavior** feign agreement or act like everything is okay when in fact they really disagree with what is happening. Over time, these people often become hostile and aggressive.
- *Rapid-fire questioning.* Rapid-fire questioning is an adversarial technique often used by police and lawyers to confuse a suspect or a witness. Some partners might try the same approach during arguments, but such techniques do not build intimate relationships or resolve conflicts.
- *Verbal abuse.* Name calling, yelling, pouting, and sulking all belong in the category of dirty-fighting techniques. None of them is helpful in resolving conflict.

Resist Giving the Silent Treatment. Refusing to talk—the silent treatment—is an attempt to get even with or to manipulate a partner. Shutting out another person emotionally in the hope that she or he will give in is a form of psychological torture and an approach that rarely resolves conflict. Disagreements don't go away by themselves; they may lie dormant for awhile, but they eventually resurface, often in a less manageable form than before. The shut-out partner's anger and frustration might also increase, even though that might not have been the intent of the "silent" partner.

Focus on the Issue and Focus on the Present. Constructive arguments focus on the here and now and stay on the topic. Arguments that leap from one issue to another accomplish very little. Bringing up the past usually is a ploy for placing blame. In a fair fight, the relevant question is not "Where have we been?" but "Where are we going from here?"

Call "Time-out" and "Foul." When verbal interchanges get too intense, a time-out can be useful. The length of the time-out depends on how emotionally overwrought the participants are. Sometimes a few minutes or an hour is sufficient; sometimes a day is needed. Time-outs shouldn't last too long, however, because one or both partners may refuse to deal with the issue again.

Another helpful tool is calling a "foul" when fair-fighting rules are broken. If one person brings up the past or uses a dirty-fighting technique, the other partner should call a "foul." This gives both partners a chance to calm down and think things through before trying again to resolve the disagreement.

Use Humor and Comic Relief. Sometimes laughing is just as beneficial as crying to relieve tension, but laughing is *always* better than yelling. Arguing people usually look and sound pretty foolish to an objective third party. In a conflict people need to step back, look at the situation from a new perspective, and laugh at themselves if possible. (Note, however, that sarcasm or laughing at a partner rarely helps resolve disputes.)

A useful form of humor is **incongruity humor**, which focuses on seeing the incongruous things in life—the things that don't fit together logically—rather than on blaming others or putting them down. Take, for example, a divorce court judge who had to listen for 3 hours to attorneys and the divorcing couple argue over who was to have possession of a 9-foot-long metal pipe. The judge tried to help the couple see the humor in the situation as a way of reducing tension.

Always Go for Closure. Closure is the resolution of an issue. Arguing couples should strive for closure as soon as possible or practical. Letting the argument drag on increases the likelihood of gunnysacking, passive–aggressive behavior, or the silent treatment. The sooner people reach genuine agreement, the better. Resolution lets the feelings of bonding and respect return to the relationship.

Constructive and Destructive Approaches

Peace cannot be kept by force. It can only be achieved by understanding.
—ALBERT EINSTEIN (1931/1988, p. 690)

In destructive approaches to conflict resolution, partners bring up old issues, express only negative feelings, reveal selective information, focus on people rather than on issues, and emphasize differences—all with the goal of minimizing change. There is often a winner and a loser, which decreases intimacy. Conversely, in constructive conflict resolution, partners focus on current rather than past issues, share both positive and negative feelings, provide information in an open manner, accept mutual blame, and search for similarities. Both partners win, and as a result intimacy increases and trust grows in the relationship. Table 5.4 compares constructive and destructive ways of resolving conflict.

Styles of Conflict Resolution

Learning how to deal effectively with conflict is one of the most important steps in creating strong relationships. Because conflict resolution is so critical, many therapists focus their efforts on understanding and describing useful approaches and identifying counterproductive ones.

TABLE 5.4	Constructive and Destructive Approaches to Conflict Resolution	
Area of Concern	**Constructive Approach**	**Destructive Approach**
Issues	Raises and clarifies issues	Brings up old issues
Feelings	Expresses both positive and negative feelings	Expresses only negative feelings
Information	Complete and honest information	Selective information
Focus	Conflict focuses on issue rather than on person	Conflict focuses on person rather than on issue
Blame	Accepts mutual blame	Blames other person(s) for the problem
Perception	Focuses on similarities	Focuses on differences
Change	Facilitates change to prevent stagnation	Minimizes change, increasing conflict
Outcome	Both win	One wins and one loses, or both lose
Intimacy	Resolving conflict increases intimacy	Escalating conflict decreases intimacy
Attitude	Trust	Suspicion

FIGURE 5.2

Styles of Conflict
Resolution

Source: "Interpersonal
Conflict: Handling Behavior as
Reflections of Jungian Personality
Dimensions" by R. Kilmann and
K. Thomas, 1975, *Psychological
Reports, 37*, pp. 971–980.
Copyright © 1975 Psychological
Reports. With permission from
the publisher and the author.

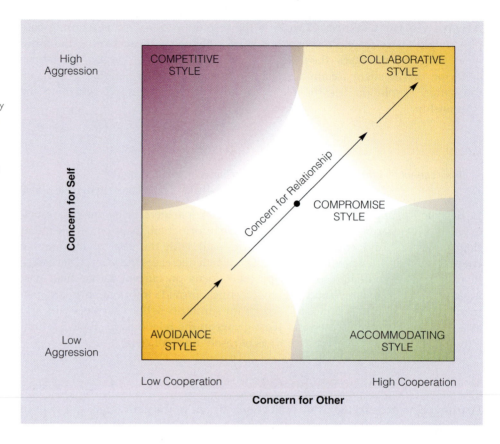

Figure 5.2 illustrates a useful model for comparing conflict resolution styles. The model is based on the belief that each style of conflict is composed of two partially competing goals: concern for oneself and concern for the other person. Concern for oneself is measured by how aggressive one is, and concern for the other focuses on the level of cooperation. This model of conflict resolution identifies five styles: the competitive style, the collaborative style, the compromise style, the avoidance style, and the accommodating style (Kilmann & Thomas, 1975). There are advantages and disadvantages to all five styles.

Competitive Style. People who use a **competitive style** of conflict resolution tend to be aggressive and uncooperative, pursuing personal concerns at the expense of the other. Those with a competitive style gain power by direct confrontation and try to "win" without adjusting their goals and desires in light of the other person's goals and desires. Life is a battleground for people with this type of style. They tend to identify with the following statements: "Once I get wound up in a heated discussion, I find it difficult to stop," and "I like the excitement of engaging in verbal fights" (Wilmot & Hocker, 2007). A competitive style is usually not conducive to developing intimacy.

Collaborative Style. People who use a **collaborative style** of conflict resolution are highly assertive in regard to reaching their goals but have a great deal of concern for the other person. Collaborators would identify with the following statements: "When I get into a conflict with someone, I try to work creatively with them to find new options," or "I like to assert myself, and I also like to cooperate with others" (Wilmot & Hocker, 2007). Collaborators tend to burn out on relationships because they invest so much energy into resolving conflict. Another problem with the collaborative style is that good collaborators are powerful and sometimes use their strength to manipulate others.

Compromise Style. People who use the **compromise style** (which is intermediate on both the aggression and cooperation axes, as shown in Figure 5.2) would identify with these statements: "You have to be satisfied with part of the pie," or "When disagreements occur, you each have to give a little" (Wilmot & Hocker, 2007). The compromise style is more direct than the avoidance style, but it does not push the issues as much as the collaborative style. Compromise is less time consuming than collaboration, but it also reinforces the notion that the relationship is one between equals. The downside of the compromise style is that it favors an easy "formula" for conflict resolution, which may not be the best solution for all involved.

Avoidance Style. Nonassertive and passive behaviors characterize the **avoidance style** of conflict resolution. Avoiders pursue neither their own concerns nor the concerns of the other person. They sidestep the issue by changing the subject or withdrawing from the conflict. The avoidance style has certain advantages: It gives the avoider time to think about whether any good will come from continuing the fight and about whether others could manage the situation better. There are several disadvantages of this style: It conveys the message that the avoider does not care enough to deal with the problem; it puts the problem on the back burner; and it reinforces the notion that conflict is bad and should be avoided at all cost. The avoidance style usually sets the stage for further conflict.

Accommodating Style. Nonassertive but cooperative behavior characterizes the **accommodating style.** Accommodaters put aside personal concerns to satisfy the wants and needs of the other. Accommodaters respond to conflict by giving in and being reasonable—both advantages, but only when the accommodater is in the wrong. Also, accommodation minimizes losses and possible harmful consequences in a losing situation. There are also disadvantages to this style: Accommodation tends to reduce creative options because it sacrifices genuine dialogue; it may also produce resentment and the desire to get even.

No one style of conflict resolution is automatically superior to another (Wilmot & Hocker, 2007). Each has advantages and disadvantages in certain circumstances and between different individuals. Clearly, there are no simple or easy ways to resolve human conflicts. Each situation must be approached with caution and thoughtfulness. People in conflict have to consider many factors, including the personalities of those involved, the merits of the argument, and the level of investment each has in continuing the relationship.

Resolving Conflict: Six Basic Steps

Let us begin anew, remembering on both sides that civility is not a sign of weakness, that sincerity is always subject to proof. Let us never negotiate out of fear, but let us never fear to negotiate.

—JOHN F. KENNEDY (1961/1990, p. 101)

Family therapists assume that most tension and fights between couples signal the need for conflict resolution. In this section we will examine the basic strategies authorities generally agree are useful for successful negotiation within intimate relationships. The steps are clarifying the issue, finding out what each person wants, identifying various alternatives, deciding how to negotiate, solidifying agreements, and reviewing and renegotiating. We will look at each of these strategies and pay particular attention to the communication skills necessary for effective conflict resolution. It is during periods of conflict that good communication skills take on additional importance.

Clarifying the Issue. Conflicts and fights are probably caused as frequently by misunderstanding as they are by genuine differences. Often people argue over something they don't really disagree on but only thought they did. Clarifying the issue helps; sometimes true differences get pushed aside or covered over by side issues. These types of misunderstandings can be minimized by using the following techniques:

- Both partners should spend some time alone to think through what is bothering them. During this time, they should ask themselves questions that focus on the issue and on their thoughts, feelings, and desires about the issue: What situation(s) triggered how I'm feeling? What was going on that made me feel uncomfortable? How would I like things to be different? What are some things I want for myself?
- Both partners should try to understand fully what the other partner is saying. Using good listening skills, the listener should repeat back to the speaker what is being "heard"—both its content and its feeling—until the speaker is satisfied that the listener has understood the message. In addition, the listener can ask questions to clarify or to elicit more information from the speaker. By focusing questions directly on what the speaker is sharing, the listener facilitates identification of the conflict.
- Each partner is responsible for keeping the discussion focused. This can be done by agreeing to talk at another time about side issues that may arise or by using reminders such as "Let's refocus" or "Now, where were we?" to keep the discussion from drifting.
- Each partner should sum up what the other has said after each person has had an opportunity to talk. Clearly identifying and echoing the problem ensures that both partners agree on what the issue is.

Finding Out What Each Person Wants. After both people are clear about what the issue is, the discussion should shift to identifying what each person wants. Omitting this part of the process often leads to unsatisfactory negotiations and repetitive fights. This step is important because it helps minimize hurtful exchanges between frustrated couples; each partner has to identify what he or she wants rather than recounting "how bad things have been." Identifying needs can be a difficult process for some couples, but it can be facilitated if both partners genuinely ask each other to express their desires. If one partner says, "I don't know what I want, but I just know I don't want things to be the way they have been," this is a straightforward signal that this part of the process has not been completed.

Brainstorming—thinking of as many solutions to a problem as possible—is a creative way to address conflicts in a relationship. Generating alternatives highlights the fact that many possibilities exist, even when partners think they're at an impasse.

Identifying Various Alternatives. During this step, partners look at the various options for achieving resolution. This step often leads to new insights. **Brainstorming** ideas can be a fun and creative process because both partners are working together to find ways to deal with an issue. Research indicates that brainstorming increases people's skill at identifying useful alternatives.

Deciding How to Negotiate. After the various alternatives have been identified, it's time to try to work out some agreements, or plans, for change. There are several strategies couples can use to negotiate differences. Each has advantages and disadvantages.

- *Quid pro quo.* A Latin term meaning "this for that," **quid pro quo** is a negotiating strategy by which parties agree that "I'll do this if you'll do that." For example, the Smiths have been bickering over the weekly household chores. Each feels that he or she is doing more than the other. After discussing the alternatives for dividing the tasks more equally, they readily move into a quid pro quo bargain. Jack agrees to do a certain number of the tasks, and Marlene agrees to do the rest. This strategy is effective because it clarifies what each person is going to do. The major disadvantage of this strategy is that it can easily break down if one person fails to keep her or his agreement. Another disadvantage is the difficulty of finding relatively equivalent divisions.
- *Quid pro quid.* A Latin term meaning "this for this," **quid pro quid** is an agreement to do something the other person asks you to do in exchange for being able to do something you want to do. For example, Brent's wife, Nancy, wants him to accept more responsibility for taking care of the children. He agrees to be fully responsible for the children for two nights in

exchange for a night out with his friends. This bargaining strategy has advantages over the quid pro quo method in that the consequences for not living up to the bargain are clear and are not based on what the other partner does. This strategy works especially well when one partner is asking the other to change because it enables the partner who agrees to the change to give himself or herself something he or she wants as well. This helps avoid power struggles in which one partner feels she or he has to change simply because the other demands that things be different. The disadvantage of this strategy is that many couples have difficulty reaching any type of mutually acceptable agreement.

- *Agreeing to disagree.* After exploring all the alternatives, a mutually agreeable solution is not always possible; the negotiating strategy then is **agreeing to disagree.** For example, Len wanted to invest the couple's savings in some lakefront property, and Lesley wanted to take a trip to Europe. After long hours of discussion, both felt even more strongly about what they wanted. Because they couldn't agree on either course of action, they agreed to disagree—and left the money in the account. When the issue is not critical to the maintenance of the relationship, agreeing to disagree leaves open the possibility of finding a solution later. When the differences are more basic, however (for example one partner wants children and the other does not), agreeing to disagree will only work in the short run.

Solidifying Agreements. Partners may need to try several negotiation strategies before reaching agreement. But when an agreement is reached, it is important that both people are clear about what has been agreed to and that both do indeed agree. Partners must be careful to avoid bulldozing the other into an agreement. Too often, in their haste to "get things wrapped up," people make agreements they know they can't stick to. Couples should take the time to fully explore what the agreement means for each person before giving it the final stamp of approval. They should be sensitive to each other's reservations. It's a good idea to avoid making agreements while either partner is upset. Pressure tactics, such as implied threats, often win the battle but lose the war. When both partners are in agreement, they should make a contract by writing down everything they've agreed to in simple, clear language. Couples should post the agreement as a reminder of what each is to do. They should also agree to review the situation within a short period of time.

Reviewing and Renegotiating. Once an agreement has been negotiated, it is easy to assume that the issue has been settled once and for all. Unfortunately, this is rarely the case. Carrying out an agreement often brings other issues to light. It is not unusual to discover that the agreement does not really resolve the problem. A timely review ensures that bad feelings about the agreement do not go on too long.

When agreements break down, partners distrust or are disillusioned about each other's genuine interest in working together. Broken agreements should be reviewed as soon as possible. Couples often discover that one or the other simply "forgot" to do what was agreed upon. It is important for people to remind themselves that change is rarely smooth and that it is also rare for any person to live up to any agreement completely. But if both partners are invested in each other's personal well-being and want their relationship to grow, couples can positively resolve just about any conflict.

Summary

- According to a national survey of married couples, happy couples are more able than unhappy couples to resolve their differences, to understand each other when discussing problems, to feel at ease expressing their feelings to each other, to reach consensus on ways to resolve their differences, and to share responsibility for their problems.

- According to the same national survey, the major conflict resolution issues that married couples experience are the following: serious disputes over unimportant issues, an inability to resolve differences, disagreement on the best way to resolve issues, an inability to voice concerns or feelings about problems, and a tendency to avoid conflict with their partners.

- Conflict is inevitable in any intimate relationship. It can be thought of as a process that moves from decision making to problem solving to crisis resolution; making decisions when they are called for helps prevent crises.

- Most couples are afraid of negative emotions and have a difficult time learning how to deal with them. A common tendency is to suppress anger for fear of damaging the relationship. Because love and hate are so closely tied, however, the suppression of anger can lead to loss of affection in a relationship.

- Popular myths about anger include the belief that anger is caused by others, that the best way to deal with anger is to let it all out, that anger is a beneficial emotion, and that you're a wimp if you don't get angry.

- Intimacy and conflict are inextricably tied together. Anger keeps people from developing unhealthy dependencies on each other. Interdependence, a balance between dependency and independence, seems to work best.

- People manage stress and anger in a number of ways: Pursuers seek greater togetherness in a relationship; distancers want emotional space when stress is high; underfunctioners become less competent under stress; overfunctioners tend to take charge in tough times; and blamers believe everyone else is responsible for their problems.

- People should observe certain conventions, or "rules for fair fighting," when they are arguing; these rules make the argument safer and more likely to lead to a satisfactory conclusion.

- Some styles of conflict resolution are the competitive style, pursuing personal concerns at the expense of others; the collaborative style, being highly assertive in regard to reaching one's goals while also showing great concern for the other person; the compromise style, an intermediate style between aggressiveness and cooperation; the avoidance style, avoiding conflict by changing the subject or withdrawing; and the accommodating style, which involves nonassertive and cooperative behaviors.

- Family therapists and other authorities generally agree on six steps for resolving conflict: clarify the issue, find out what each person wants, identify various alternatives, decide how to negotiate, solidify agreements, and review and renegotiate.

Key Terms

pursuer	closure
distancer	competitive style
dance of anger	collaborative style
underfunctioner	compromise style
overfunctioner	avoidance style
blamer	accommodating style
gunnysacking	brainstorming
passive–aggressive	quid pro quo
behavior	quid pro quid
incongruity humor	agreeing to disagree

Activities

1. Using Harriet Lerner's ideas about the various styles of managing anger, focus on someone with whom you have an important relationship. Does one of you tend to be a pursuer or a distancer? An overfunctioner or an underfunctioner? A blamer or a blame taker? Rate each of you on a scale from 1 (low) to 10 (high) on each of the dimensions. Are you performing any dance based on these style differences? If so, how might you create a healthier dance?

2. Use John Crosby's 16 rules for fair fighting as the basis for a small-group discussion. Group members should first rate themselves on each of the rules. Then members should discuss some practical things they can do to become fairer fighters.

3. Think of an ongoing disagreement you have had with someone in an important relationship, one that has been difficult for you both to resolve. Agree to discuss the issue. See if you can work out the disagreement using the six basic conflict resolution steps discussed at the end of this chapter.

Suggested Readings

Alberti, R. E. (2001). *Your perfect right: Assertiveness and equality in your life and relationships* (8th ed.). Atascadero, CA: Impact. An excellent resource.

Booth, A., Crouter, A. C., & Clements, M. (Eds). (2004). *Couples in conflict.* Mahwah, NJ: Erlbaum. A collection of insightful articles on conflict and conflict resolution in couples.

Borcherdt, B. (2000). *You can control your anger! 21 ways to do it.* Sarasota, FL: Professional Resource Press. A practical guide for people who would like to change.

Gottman, J., Schwartz Gottman, J., & DeClaire, J. (2006). *Ten lessons to transform your marriage: America's love lab experts share their strategies for strengthening your relationships.* New York: Crown.

Lerner, H. G. (2005). *The dance of anger: A woman's guide to changing the patterns of intimate relationships.* New York: Perennial Currents. A new edition of the classic.

Markman, H. J., Stanley, S., & Blumberg, S. L. (2001). *Fighting for your marriage.* San Francisco: Jossey-Bass. Provides an overview of the authors' PREP communication program for couples; contains very useful suggestions for resolving couple conflict.

Markman, H. J., Stanley, S. M., Jenkins, N. H., & Blumberg, S. L. (2004). *12 hours to a great marriage: A step-by-step guide for making love last.* San Francisco: Jossey-Bass. Sensual talking, friendship talk, hidden issues, enhancing loving relationship.

Olson, D. H., & Olson, A. K. (2000). *Empowering couples: Building on your strengths.* Minneapolis: Life Innovations. A self-help book that contains couple assessment and couple exercises to build relationship skills and a happier couple relationship.

Visit the text-specific Online Learning Center at **www.mhhe.com/Olson6** for practice tests, chapter summaries, Web links, Internet exercises, key terms, and flashcards.

6. $\mathcal{S}$ Sexual Intimacy

Intimacy, Strengths, and Diversity

Couple Strengths and Sexual Issues

Sex and Society: An Overview

American Sexual Behavior

Sexuality Education

Premarital Sexual Behavior

Marital and Extramarital Sexual Behavior

Toward Sexual Health

Summary

Key Terms

Activities

Suggested Readings

Intimacy, Strengths, and Diversity

The sexual relationship we have with another person is an aspect of intimacy, and sexuality plays a critical role in healthy couple relationships. Intimacy in relationships can be expressed in a variety of ways, and men and women differ in the importance they place on the sexual relationship versus emotional closeness. Men and women often view sex and love differently: Women are more likely to view sex and love as highly connected, and men are more likely to separate love and sex (Blow & Hartnett, 2005).

Sexual intimacy is an integral part of healthy marriage relationships. Studies show that martial satisfaction and the satisfaction of a couple's sexual relationship are related (Blow & Hartnett, 2005). The quality of the sexual relationship in a marriage or couple relationship strengthens a marriage, and the quality of the marriage relationship increases the couple's sexual satisfaction (Olson & Olson, 2000).

Although much of the discussion in this chapter is about sexual attitudes and behaviors in the United States, there is evidence that attitudes and behaviors differ in other countries (Blow & Hartnett, 2005; Scheinkman, 2005). There are also differences based on gender and the type of couple relationship (Blow & Hartnett, 2005; Scheinkman, 2005).

One of the changes that has occurred over time is that we increasingly talk openly about sex. References to sex are pervasive in the media—we hear about medications that address sexual dysfunction on prime-time television—and are evident in every aspect of our daily lives. We also educate our children about sex, HIV/AIDS, and other sexually transmitted diseases in our public schools. Couples talk about how to improve sexual satisfaction. We go to doctors and talk about what is not working and get information and treatment about how to make it work. This open communication about sex means young people and adults know more about sex than ever before in history. Following is a true story of one family mealtime discussion that illustrates this increased openness in communicating about sex:

> A family was having dinner with mom and dad and three children, ages 10, 11, and 12, present. The 11-and 12-year-olds were girls, and the 10-year-old was a boy. The mealtime discussion turned to the subject of sex, and the parents were delighted to have this opportunity to talk about sex with their children in a very casual way. The 10-year-old boy began talking about oral sex. The two girls began smiling and watching the expression on their parents' faces. The mother was surprised that her son knew anything about oral sex and asked if he knew what oral sex was. He said, "Sure I know what it is. It's when you sit around and talk about it!"

Couple Strengths and Sexual Issues

A major strength for a happily married couple is the quality and quantity of their sexual relationship. In a nationwide survey of married couples, researchers revealed distinct differences between happy couples and unhappy couples in terms of their sexual relationships (Olson & Olson, 2000). Happy couples agreed much more (85%) than unhappy couples (29%) that the sexual relationship was satisfying and fulfilling (Table 6.1). Most of the happy couples (72%) reported being satisfied with the amount of affection they received from their partner, whereas

TABLE 6.1	Sexual Relationship Strengths of Happy Versus Unhappy Married Couples	
	PERCENTAGE OF COUPLES IN AGREEMENT	
Strength	**Happy Couples** (*n* = 5,153)	**Unhappy Couples** (*n* = 5,127)
Sexual relationship is satisfying and fulfilling.	85%	29%
Are satisfied with the amount of affection they receive from their partner.	72	28
Feel partner does not use sex in an unfair way.	90	39
No concerns that partner will lose interest in me sexually.	88	37
Not worried partner would have affair.	92	43

Source: Adapted from Olson & Olson, 2000.

only 28% of unhappy couples reported being satisfied. Happy couples were more likely (90%) than unhappy couples (39%) to agree that their partner does not use or refuse sex unfairly. Almost three times as many happy couples (88%) as unhappy couples (37%) did not have concerns about their partner's disinterest in their sexual relationship. Likewise, most happy couples (92%) were not concerned about their partner's being interested in having a sexual relationship outside of their marriage, as compared to one-third (43%) of unhappy couples.

In this same study, the total sample of 21,501 married couples was used to identify the common issues across all married couples (see Table 6.2) (Olson & Olson, 2000). A majority of couples (70%) of all couples were dissatisfied with the amount of affection that they received from the partner. About two-thirds (62%) said they had to work on keeping the sexual relationship interesting and enjoyable. More than half (57%) felt that their sexual relationship was not satisfying or fulfilling, were dissatisfied (54%) with the level of openness in discussing sexual topics, or were reluctant (50%) to be affectionate because their partner may interpret it as a sexual advance.

TABLE 6.2	Top Five Sexual Issues for Married Couples
Issue	**Percentage of Couples** (*n* = 21,501)
Dissatisfied with amount of affection from partner.	70%
Difficulty keeping sexual relationship interesting.	62
Sexual relationship is not satisfying.	57
Dissatisfied with level of openness in discussing sexual topics.	54
Reluctant to be affectionate because partner may interpret it as a sexual advance.	50

Source: Adapted from Olson & Olson, 2000.

Sex and Society: An Overview

A person's sexual identity is an important part of who she or he is. A number of factors, including biology and culture, influence sexual identity. In this section we will discuss these factors, look at historical and cultural perspectives on sexuality, and explore the ways in which Americans receive information on sexuality.

Sexuality, Sex, and Gender

The formation of a person's sexuality is a complex process, involving continuous interaction among a wide variety of biological influences, family and cultural influences, and each individual's relatively unique set of personality characteristics. **Sexuality** is a broad term that encompasses the set of beliefs, values, and behaviors that defines each of us as a sexual being. One aspect of an individual's sexuality is whether a person identifies himself or herself as **heterosexual, homosexual, bisexual**, or **transgender**. This identity is otherwise known as one's **sexual orientation**.

Heterosexual means that one's sexual orientation is toward members of the other sex. Homosexual means that one's sexual orientation is toward members of the same sex. Bisexual indicates that one is sexually oriented toward both sexes. Transgender refers to people who believe they were assigned a gender at birth based on their genitals, but who feel that is a false or incomplete description of themselves. A majority of transgender persons are biological males who identify themselves as females, usually early in their childhood.

You will notice in these definitions that we did not use the term "opposite sex" because that term is imprecise. This is because males and females are much more similar than different, not only biologically but also in other ways. In fact, in the early phases of an infant's development, there is little visible difference in the genital development of the male and female. Other aspects of sexuality include a person's interest in having a variety of sexual partners or only one and a person's preference for specific types of sexual acts. There are countless beliefs, values, and behaviors associated with sexuality. Therefore, individuals vary widely in how they define themselves as sexual beings.

In our society, the term **sex** can refer either to being biologically female or male or to sexual activity. The term **gender** refers to the learned characteristics and behaviors associated with being male or female in a particular culture.

Historical Perspectives on Sex and Society

Throughout history, people's sexual behavior and thinking about sex have been guided by religious teachings and cultural beliefs. Many religions, Christianity among them, have attempted to regulate sex outside marriage by condemning it as sinful. Some religions, such as Islam, although also condemning sex outside of marriage, allow men to take more than one wife. Other ideas about sex evolve out of, and are part of, general cultural beliefs. For example, Western male-dominated culture has held the idea that women have little interest in sex. Other cultures—for example, that of the Inuit—consider female sexual activity to be on a par with that of males.

Advances in science as early as the 17th century led to a more technical approach to sex. Little was known about the biological aspects of sexuality until Dutch

In our society, most information about sexual behavior and intimate relationships comes from the media. Not surprisingly, many people have misconceptions and distorted ideas about both the physical and the emotional dimensions of sexuality.

microscopist Anton van Leeuwenhoek (1632–1723) and his student John Ham discovered sperm swimming in human semen. Oscar Hertwig was the first to observe fertilization of the egg by the sperm in sea urchins in 1875, yet the human ovum was not directly observed until the 20th century.

Today, we have a great deal of scientific knowledge about sex—about conception, contraception, and sexual functioning, as well as about how to treat infertility and sexual dysfunction. We talk openly about sex and are complacent about the ubiquity of sexual images in our society. Yet religion still plays a role in many people's sexual attitudes and behavior, and there is still conflict between those who espouse an open, objective, scientific, informational approach to sex and those who wish to regulate people's sexual behavior and their access to information on moral grounds.

Gay and Lesbian Couples

Historically, most of the focus on gays and lesbians has been on their sexual orientation and behavior, with little discussion of other characteristics of gay and lesbian couples. The number of gay and lesbian couples has risen dramatically in recent years, with a 300% increase from 1990 to 2000 (Deen, 2005). This change is likely due to the slow, but steady, more accepting societal view of gay and lesbian individuals. Gays and lesbians have increasingly moved in the direction of developing and maintaining ongoing relationships with one person (Kurdek, 1998, 2001, 2003). Increasingly, both gays and lesbians have had to struggle with coming out and have often experienced considerable rejection by their parents and other relatives. This struggle has helped some of them develop a variety of strengths that are valuable in relationships (Kurdek, 2000, 2001, 2003). In fact, a study using the Circumplex Model (Couple and Family Map) found that lesbian couples tend to have higher levels of cohesion, flexibility, and satisfaction compared to heterosexual couples (Green, Bettinger, & Zacks, 1996; Laird & Green, 1996). Some of the other characteristics that have been found to be strengths of gay and lesbian couples are:

- *High emotional connection with partner and others.* A common strength for many gays and lesbians is their ability to connect in an emotional way with people of both the same sex and the other sex.
- *High role flexibility.* In their same-sex relationships, they often have a flexible role relationship that gives them the ability to adapt to each other (Green et al. 1996; Laird & Green, 1996).
- *Egalitarian decision making.* The ability to negotiate and make decisions in a sharing manner enables them to establish and maintain an egalitarian relationship.
- *Positive parent–child relationships.* Gay and lesbian couples are on par with heterosexual couples when it comes to raising healthy, well-adjusted children (Chamberlin, 2005; Herek, 2006; Meezan & Rauch, 2005; Pawelski et al., 2006).
- *Psychologically perceptive.* Whether it is because they have had to struggle to come out or because of their lifestyle, they often tend to be very perceptive in terms of psychological dynamics.
- *Effective communication skills.* A common characteristic of many of the same-sex relationships is that they have been able to achieve very good communication skills.

It is difficult to study gay and lesbian couples for several reasons. First, many couples are not willing to be open about their sexual orientation and are less willing to be part of research. Second, laws and policies are still in place, along with prejudice and oppression, that impact the lives of gay and lesbian couples and families (Chamberlin, 2005; Herek, 2006; Pawelski et al., 2006). For example, in all states except Massachusetts, gay and lesbian couples are unable to have the benefits and security of legal marriage that is granted to heterosexual couples (Pawelski et al., 2006).

Even though there may be an expectation that gay couples function like heterosexual couples, this may be an unrealistic expectation. These differences regarding laws, rights, and the degree of acceptance make it difficult to compare gay and lesbian couples and families with heterosexual couples and families (Meezan & Rauch, 2005; Pawelski et al., 2006). Many gay and lesbian individuals have been in heterosexual relationships and have had children in those relationships. Their extended families may have disowned them, or, at best, they have strained relationships. These past and current life circumstances greatly affect one's family and other network relationships.

Third, we compare gay and lesbian couple relationships to heterosexual relationships with the assumption that heterosexual relationships provide the gold standard for how couple relationships should be—and this may not be a fair way to assess these relationships. Even though these issues are often identified in the literature, the majority of studies continue to compare gay and lesbian relationships to heterosexual relationships.

Kurdek (2006), in a large national study, compared gay couples, lesbian couples and heterosexual cohabiting couples to heterosexual couples with children regarding their relationship adjustment. The findings of this study showed that these couples did not differ markedly from each other in terms of relationship adjustment. Some relatively insignificant findings were reported. For example, Kurdek found that gay couples were more likely to rely on friends for support, and heterosexual sexual couples were more likely to rely on family for support. Kurdek also found that gay and lesbian couples and unmarried heterosexual couples were more prone to separation than married couples with children. What we know from current research is that children from same-sex couples typically fare about the same as children from other family structures (Chamberlin, 2005; Herek, 2006; Meezen & Rauch, 2005; Pawelski et al., 2006).

While gays and lesbians are increasingly visible in U.S. culture, homosexuality is often hidden and forbidden in many other cultures. For example, homosexuality among the men in Afghanistan was recently discovered and described because of the war in that country (Reynolds, 2002). While the Pashtun literature and the Muslim religion forbid sexual contact between males, it is increasingly happening and the rate could be as high as 50% in some cities such as Kandahar. Because young males are often unable to interact with women or even see their faces, they often turn to other males for sexual fulfillment. Also in the Pashtun culture, a man has to pay for the wedding and gifts for the family, and most men are unable to raise the $5,000 that is expected. So Afghan single men are more sexually involved with other men, and this is predicted to continue until economic conditions improve and women are given more freedom.

Sexuality Across Cultures

Attitudes toward sexuality and sexual behaviors vary markedly from one culture to another, and ethnocentrism encourages people to believe that their culture's thinking and practices are the only "right" or "natural" way to live. An important generalization cross-cultural researchers make about sexuality is that all societies regulate sexual behavior in some way, although the regulations vary greatly from culture to culture (Hyde & DeLamater, 2003). Sex is a powerful force, and societies around the world have found it necessary to develop some rules regarding sexual behavior. For example, **incest taboos,** which prohibit intercourse between parents and children and between siblings, are nearly universal; most societies also condemn forced sexual relations, such as rape (Hyde & DeLamater, 2003).

Standards of Attractiveness. Cultural standards of sexual attractiveness vary widely. In many non-Western cultures, a plump woman is considered more attractive than a thin woman. But in the United States, the ideal woman has a slim body, well-developed breasts, and long, shapely legs; the ideal man is tall and moderately muscular, with broad shoulders and narrow hips. Physical attributes are often more important for women in Western societies because women tend to be judged by their appearance, whereas men are judged by their accomplishments and power.

In some cultures, the shape and color of the eyes are most important; other cultures value good-looking ears. The Nawa of Africa value elongated labia majora (the pads of fatty tissue on either side of the vagina), and Nawa women reportedly tug on them to enhance their length. Although the specifics vary, most cultures identify certain physical traits as attractive and valuable (Hyde & DeLamater, 2003).

Sexual Behavior. Gender roles in sexual behavior differ considerably across cultures. In a few societies, including the Maori and the Kwoma of the South Pacific, females generally initiate love affairs. Although rape in American society is primarily committed by men, the anthropologist Bronislaw Malinowski (1929) reported groups of Trobriand Island women in the South Pacific who regularly

Standards for physical attractiveness, which we take for granted, are actually culturally determined. Although these two women are very different from each other in appearance, each is considered beautiful in her culture.

(a)

(b)

raped and sexually humiliated male strangers who were unfortunate enough to wander through the area near their village.

Sexual techniques also vary considerably from culture to culture (Hyde & DeLamater, 2003). Kissing is common in most societies; however, when the Thonga of Africa first saw Europeans kissing, they were amused and could not believe the Europeans were sharing saliva. In some societies, one partner inflicts pain on the other partner during lovemaking. Apinayean women of South America have been known to bite off bits of their partner's eyebrows; Trukese women in the South Pacific poke fingers in the man's ear when sexually excited; and partners in some societies draw blood and leave scars as a result of sexual passion.

The frequency of sexual intercourse varies from society to society (Masters, Johnson, & Kolodny, 1995, 1998). American society today is about average when compared with other cultures. The range of frequency of intercourse for married couples runs from a low of about once a month among the Keraki of the South Pacific to a high of a few times a night for young couples among the Aranda of Australia and the Mangaians of the South Pacific.

Sexual Attitudes. Attitudes toward **masturbation,** the self-stimulation of the genitals, vary widely from culture to culture. It is tolerated among children and adolescents in some societies but condemned at any age by other societies. Most societies tend to disapprove of adult masturbation; if it is discovered, the consequences range from mild ridicule to punishment.

Similarly, attitudes toward homosexuality vary widely from culture to culture. Although some cultures tolerate same-sex sexual activity among children, they disapprove when adults engage in it. Other societies force homosexual behavior on all their male members, most often during puberty rites. Despite variations in attitudes from culture to culture, investigators believe at least four generalizations can be made: (1) Homosexuality is universal, occurring in all societies; (2) homosexuality is more common among males than among females; (3) homosexuality is never the predominant form of sexual behavior for adults; and (4) only about 5% or less of the population of any culture tends to practice homosexuality (Whitam, Daskalos, Sobolewski, & Padilla, 1998).

Female Circumcision in Africa. The story of female circumcision is graphically told by the supermodel Waris Dirie in her book *Desert Flower* (1998; see also *Encyclopedia Britannica*, 2004). She was circumcised at age 5 in Africa as a member of a Somalian tribe and had an arranged marriage to an older tribal member when she was 13. In her teens, she served as a maid in London, England, to an ambassador family and then became a model. After a successful career, she became a special ambassador for the United Nations (UN) to promote cultural change away from female genital mutilation (FGM).

Most African cultures have practiced female circumcision for centuries. The UN estimates that it has been performed on over 130 million women. This still happens to at least 2 million girls a year and over 6,000 women a day. The practice varies by geographic location, cultural group, and tribe. At a minimum, the hood of the clitoris is destroyed. But in over 80% of women in Somalia, the most severe form is infibulation, in which the labia minora and labia majora are also removed, leaving only a small opening to urinate.

The practice of female genital mutilation has been promoted by men and maintained in the culture by women. Men demand a circumcised woman because they feel the woman is otherwise dirty and oversexed. The mothers support it because otherwise their daughters would not be selected by men for marriage. FGM is often done by gypsy women with dull and dirty knives under unsanitary conditions.

Female circumcision is dangerous because many women get infected and die from the surgery. They often suffer from immediate health problems from the surgery including infections and shock. They also suffer long-term problems like chronic urinary infection and depression. In addition, the surgery eliminates the possibility of achieving any sexual satisfaction. Waris Dirie continues to work to eliminate FGM.

Cultural Change. Cultural beliefs and attitudes regarding sexuality change, often dramatically, over time. In China, for example, economic and social reforms have spawned a new sexual permissiveness. The Shanghai Sex Research Center conducted a national survey of 23,000 people and found that the Chinese are having more sex outside marriage and are becoming increasingly adventurous in the ways they make love. The researchers also found an erosion of the strong tie between sex and marriage in the world's most populous nation. Of those surveyed, a vast majority of the people (86%) and about two thirds (69%) of married people approved of extramarital affairs. In the past, large families were revered in China, but today, China has a one-child policy (Liu, Ng, & Haeberle, 1997; see also China Internet Information Center, 2004).

HIV/AIDS—More Than 25 Years Later

In 2006, more than 25 years after AIDS was first identified among gay men in New York and Los Angeles, the epidemic still continues (Centers for Disease Control and Prevention 2006). The first case of a mysterious disease was identified in 1981 when researchers were trying to discover what was making gay men sick for no apparent reason. **Human immunodeficiency virus (HIV)** is the virus that causes acquired immunodeficiency syndrome (AIDS). HIV destroys some types of white blood cells and affects a person's immune system. Illnesses that once were fought off with a healthy person's immune system can no longer be fought off. A person with HIV will develop infections, which ultimately results in a diagnosis of AIDS, that make the person unable to work or cause death. People can carry HIV for years before they have any symptoms.

One of the reasons that HIV continues to be spread at alarming rates is that people do not know they are infected and pass it on to others. On average, people carry the virus for 8 to 10 years before they begin to have symptoms (Morbidity and Mortality Weekly Report, 2006). Currently, it is estimated that more than 250,000 people are infected with HIV but are unaware they are infected and therefore may be unaware that they are passing the virus on to others (Morbidity and Mortality Weekly Report, 2006). The rate of infection increased rapidly in the 1980s, peaked in 1992, and then stabilized in 1998 (Morbidity and Mortality Weekly Report, 2006).

During the 25 years of the epidemic, over 1 million cases of HIV or AIDS have been diagnosed and reported to the Centers for Disease Control and Prevention (Morbidity and Mortality Weekly Report, 2006). Racial and ethnic minority populations have been disproportionately affected by the epidemic, with the numbers in minority populations continuing to increase over time. From 2001 to 2005, African Americans had the highest proportion of people diagnosed with AIDS, followed by Hispanics, and American Indian/Alaska Natives (Centers for Disease Control and Prevention, 2006).

Most AIDS cases are men, with 73% of all diagnosed cases being men in 2005 (Centers for Disease Control and Prevention, 2006). Approximately 500,000 people in the United States died of the virus in the first 25 years of the epidemic. The survival rate began increasing in 1996 due to the development of new drugs that slowed the progression of the virus (Morbidity and Mortality Weekly Report, 2006). There is no cure, just treatment that helps people live longer with AIDS.

HIV is transmitted primarily through sex and injecting drug use. The modes of transmission of HIV/AIDS among men include men having sex with men (47%), injection drug use (25%); heterosexual sex (18%); and other (18%). The modes of transmission among women include heterosexual sex (75%) and injection drug use (25%) (White House, 2004).

The worldwide HIV/AIDS pandemic is staggering in its global scope: 37.8 million people worldwide are living with HIV/AIDS (almost 50% are women and approximately 1.4 million are children). Each year, an estimated 4.8 million people are newly infected with HIV. Each day, 15,000 people are infected, including 1,700 children. In the year 2003 alone, 4.8 million new people were infected with HIV. The cumulative number of AIDS deaths worldwide is more than 20 million. So far, sub-Saharan Africa has been hit the hardest: 25.3 million people are living with HIV/AIDS; approximately 3.8 million new people are infected each year. More than 12 million children have been orphaned in Africa, leaving whole villages decimated (United Nations AIDS, 2004; White House, 2004).

American Sexual Behavior

There have been a handful of large-scale sex surveys in the United States since Alfred Kinsey's landmark study in the early 1950s. These surveys reveal, among other things, information regarding the frequency with which Americans engage in sexual activity and the kinds of sexual activities they engage in.

The first sex survey we will discuss at length—the National Survey of Sexual Behavior—was conducted in the 1990s. We believe this is a landmark study that deserves considerable discussion in this chapter. We will also report the findings of a sex survey conducted by ABC News in 2004. Finally, we will summarize the study commissioned by AARP,* focusing on sexuality in the later years (AARP, 2005). These three studies are the most prominent large-scale studies of sexuality in the United States that we have found in our research literature investigations. Major studies of sexual behavior, as the reader can readily imagine, are not easy to conduct. These investigations are expensive, time consuming, and politically charged because they focus on sensitive and very personal aspects of people's lives. For these reasons, large-scale studies of sexual behavior are not conducted very often.

National Survey of Sexual Behavior

The most extensive study of sexual behavior in the United States was based on face-to-face interviews with 3,432 American women and men between the ages of 18 and 59. Researchers looked at how age, gender, and marital status are related to sexual behavior; how women's and men's sexual lives and attitudes are similar and different; and how social factors, including education, ethnicity, and religion, affect sexual behavior (Laumann, Gagnon, Michael, Michaels, & Kolata, 1995; see also Gagnon, 2004; Laumann & Michael, 2000; Laumann et al., 2004).

Although our country is awash in sexual images that suggest we live in a very promiscuous society, this study indicates that, in general, our sexual behavior does not measure up to those images. The researchers found that although 17% of American men and 3% of American women had had sex with at least 21 partners since the age of 15, the sex life of the average American is more mundane (Figure 6.1). As the mass media put it, "The sex lives of most Americans are about as exciting as a peanut-butter-and-jelly sandwich" (Cole, Dickerson, & Smilgis, 1994, p. 64).

Here are some of the results reported in the Chicago study (see Figures 6.1 and 6.2):

- People fall into three groups: One-third have sex twice a week or more, one-third a few times a month, and one-third a few times a year or not at all.
- People are largely monogamous. The majority (83%) have one or zero sexual partners a year. Over a lifetime, the average man reports he has had six partners, and the average woman reports two partners.
- Married couples, compared with single people, have more sex and are more likely to have orgasms when they do have sex. About one-third (36% for men; 32% for women) of those married reported that they had sex twice a week, whereas about one-fourth (25% for men; 23% for women) of singles said they had sex twice a week.
- Vaginal sex was ranked the most popular sex act (96% found it "very appealing" or "somewhat appealing"); watching a partner undress was ranked second in popularity; and oral sex was a distant third.
- Adultery is the exception, not the rule. Nearly 75% of the married men and 85% of the married women told interviewers they had never been unfaithful. Among the married people in the study, 94% said they had been faithful over the past year.
- Only 2.7% of the men and 1.3% of the women reported to the interviewers that they had had a same-sex sexual experience over the past 12 months.

*The American Association of Retired Persons officially changed its name to AARP in 1999.

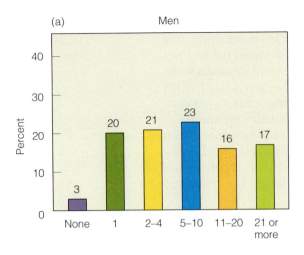

(a) Men

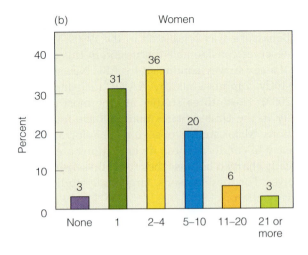

(b) Women

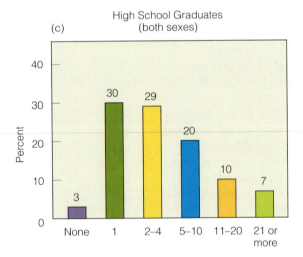

(c) High School Graduates (both sexes)

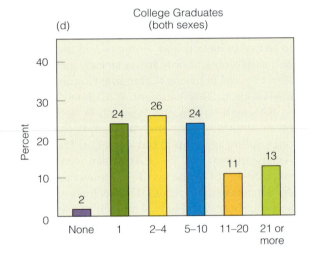

(d) College Graduates (both sexes)

FIGURE 6.1

Number of Sex Partners Among American Men and Women

Source: From Sex in America by Robert T. Michael et al., 1994, Boston: Little, Brown. Copyright © 1994 by CSG Enterprises, Inc., Edward O. Laumann, Robert T. Michael, and Gina Kolata. By permission of Little, Brown and Company.

Figure 6.2 indicates the frequency of sexual activity as reported in the study. The study sparked a wave of controversy. The most common counterargument suggested that the results were relatively conservative because people are likely to lie in a face-to-face interview about their sex lives. This U.S. study mirrored recent studies in France and England that reported low rates of both homosexual behavior and extramarital sex.

Although most observers felt the research was well done, the University of Chicago research team admitted that the findings will remain debatable. First of all, 4,369 people were scientifically sampled for the study, but many were reluctant to participate. The 220 interviewers were trained to persist in trying to gain people's participation; some individuals were visited 15 times before being persuaded to cooperate. In the end, 79% of those randomly selected for the research actually participated.

Second, even though people agreed to participate, they may not have told the truth. "There is no way to get around the fact some people might conceal information," team member Stuart Michaels noted. For example, some gay men and lesbians might not have disclosed their sexual orientation to an interviewer: "This is a stigmatized group. There is probably a lot more homosexual activity going on than we could get people to talk about" (Cole et al., 1994, p. 66).

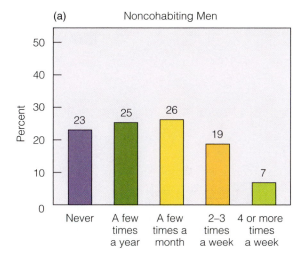

(a) Noncohabiting Men

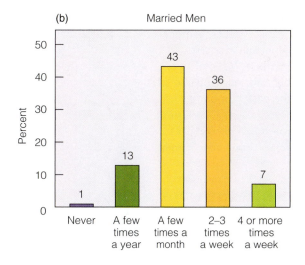

(b) Married Men

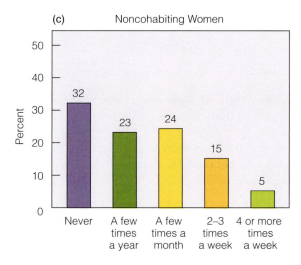

(c) Noncohabiting Women

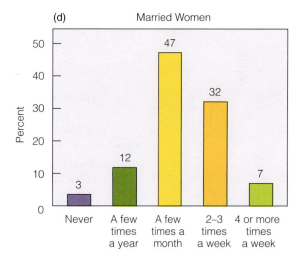

(d) Married Women

Figure 6.3 summarizes the various sexual practices reported in the study. Some of the other findings of the Chicago study included the following:

- The 1960s and the 1970s were a time of free love, compared with other decades; 40-something baby boomers were more likely to have had 21 or more sex partners, compared with respondents in other age groups.
- AIDS has changed sexual behavior to some degree. Among those who were especially active (five or more partners in the past year), 76% decided to slow down, use condoms faithfully, or get tested for HIV.
- The people who masturbate the most tend to be the people who also have sex the most. In team member John Gagnon's words, "If you're having sex a lot, you're thinking about sex a lot."
- Both men and women prefer receiving oral sex to giving it. White, college-educated men were more likely to have performed oral sex (80%) than Blacks (51%).
- Among women, 29% reported that they always have an orgasm during sex.
- Of women who had had an abortion, 72% had had only one.

FIGURE 6.2

Frequency of Sexual Activity in the United States

Source: From *Sex in America* by Robert T. Michael et al., 1994, Boston: Little, Brown. Copyright © 1994 by CSG Enterprises, Inc., Edward O. Laumann, Robert T. Michael, and Gina Kolata. By permission of Little, Brown and Company.

FIGURE 6.3

Sexual Practices Among American Men and Women. Types of behavior engaged in over the past 12 months

Source: From *Sex in America* by Robert T. Michael et al., 1994, Boston: Little, Brown. Copyright © 1994 by CSG Enterprises, Inc., Edward O. Laumann, Robert T. Michael, and Gina Kolata. By permission of Little, Brown and Company.

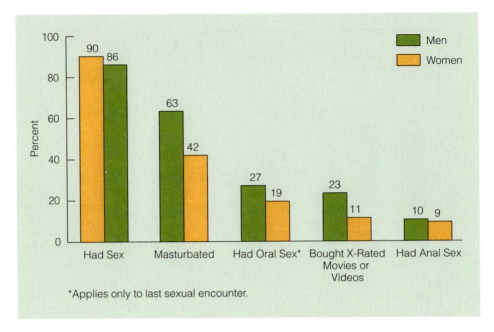

*Applies only to last sexual encounter.

- Fifty-four percent of men said they think about sex every day or several times a day; 67% of women said they think about it only a few times a week or a few times a month.
- Twenty-two percent of women said they had been forced by men to do sexual things they didn't want to do, but only 3% of men admitted to ever having forced themselves on a woman.

We will let humorist Garrison Keillor have the last word on the University of Chicago study:

> Despite all you may have read lately, there is an incredible amount of normality going on in America these days, and it is good to know. Our country is not obsessed with sex. To the contrary. We wear ourselves out working, we are surrounded with noise and distraction and all manner of entertainment, we indulge our children as they run roughshod over our lives, the ghosts of old aunts and beady-eyed preachers lurk in the shadows watching us. Considering what the American couple is up against, it's astounding to think that once a week or once a month or maybe just on Memorial Day and Christmas or whenever the coast is clear, they are enjoying this gorgeous moment that is, despite its secrecy and long, shuddering climax, essentially the same experience as everyone else has had. It's almost worth all the misery of dealing with real estate people, bankers, lawyers and contractors—to have a home that has a bedroom where the two of you can go sometimes and do this. It is worth growing up and becoming middle-aged to be able to enjoy it utterly (Keillor, 1994).

The ABC News Survey

We would also like to discuss the results of a recent study, the American Sex Survey, conducted by ABC News. The ABC survey confirms much of what the earlier research found, concluding, "the vast majority of Americans are monogamous and happy about it, expressing satisfaction with their sex lives and a broad prefer-

Young people become sexually active at an earlier age than in previous generations of Americans, and they also tend to have more sexual partners over a lifetime. But recently there seems to be a trend toward more conservative sexual behavior, perhaps because of the threat of sexually transmitted diseases.

ence for emotional commitment in sexual relationships. Most by far prefer marriage to the single life" (Langer, Arnedt, & Sussman, 2004, p. 1).

ABC conducted a telephone poll of 1,501 randomly sampled American adults. Differences between men and women were illuminating:

- Forty-three percent of the men in the survey said they thought about sex several times a day; only 13% of the women thought about sex that much.
- Eighty-three percent of the men said they enjoyed sex "a great deal"; 59% of the women said they enjoyed sex "a great deal"; women, however, were equally likely to say they were satisfied with their sex lives.
- Women, on average, reported that they had 6 sex partners in their lifetime; men reported 20. A better measure of sexual activity, however, was the median for both. (The median is the midpoint where half the participants scored higher, and half of the participants scored lower.) Women reported a median of three sex partners, and men a median of eight. ABC explained that the averages are higher than the medians because a small number of

individuals, especially men, reported a very high number of sex partners. Five percent of the men in the ABC sample said they had 99 or more sex partners, including four men who reported 200, three who reported 300, and one who reported 400. For the women, 1% reported more than 99 sex partners, and the high was 100 (reported by two women).

- Forty-two percent of the men reported having had sex on a first date, while only 17% of the women reported this.
- Women were more conservative than men on other sexual attitudes and behaviors as well: 84% said there was too much sex on TV, while 62% of the men agreed; 54% of the women condoned sex before marriage, compared to 68% of the men; 31% of the men said they slept in the nude, while only 14% of the women said they did; 51% of the women preferred sex with the lights off, while only 27% of the men liked it this way; 54% of the men thought participating in a sex chat room was cheating on the partner, while 72% of the women thought it was cheating; 15% of all men had paid for sex, and 30% of single men had paid for sex. None of the women reported this.
- About half the women said they had faked an orgasm.

Sexuality in the Later Years

AARP commissioned a research study of individuals age 45 years and older, focusing on attitudes toward and experience with sexual intimacy. The study was conducted in 2004 and included a representative sample of nearly 1,700 men and women. The data were gathered by way of a lengthy questionnaire (AARP, 2005).

The study indicated that, for more than half of those participating in the study, sexual activity contributed to their quality of life. Although we often think of older adults as having no sexual feelings, a vast majority of individuals in this study had a positive attitude about sex. One-half of the respondents said they were extremely or somewhat satisfied with their sex life. As one might expect, those in the younger age groups were more satisfied with their sex life than those who were 70 years and older, and women were more satisfied with their sex life than men.

Approximately one-third of all participants, approximately half of those with regular sexual partners, had sexual intercourse once a week or more. Two-thirds of the participants in this study were married or had a regular sexual partner, and most had been with their partner for more than 10 years (AARP, 2005). Not only do many individuals in the middle and later years of life view a satisfying sexual relationship as being important, approximately two-thirds of participants who had a regular sex partner said they discussed sexual satisfaction with their partner.

The health of the partners in the relationship had an important effect on sexual satisfaction, with health problems identified as the most significant factor affecting sexual satisfaction. Medical conditions and medication were often cited as the reason for sexual dissatisfaction. Some of the health conditions that had a negative affect on sex were high blood pressure, high cholesterol, arthritis or rheumatism, back problems, diabetes, and depression.

Many of the participants in this study wanted to improve their sexual satisfaction. One-fifth of participants, more men than women, have sought treatment for sexual dysfunction. Fourteen percent of the participants, again more men than women, have used medicines, hormones, and other treatments to improve sexual function and activity. Approximately two-thirds of the participants who had used treatments for sexual dysfunction felt it had increased their satisfaction and enjoyment of sex. In addition to health issues, less stress and more initiative from their partner were cited as things that could increase sexual satisfaction.

It is clear from the AARP study that the majority of individuals age 45 and older seek a healthy and satisfying sex life. They talk about improving their sex life with their partner, they seek out medical care for sexual dysfunction, and they take medications to enhance sexual functioning. Sexuality plays an important part in couple relationships.

Gay-Male and Lesbian Sexual Behavior

The *Janus Report* and the *American Couples* study reported different and sometimes contradictory data about lesbians and gay men. There are probably several reasons for these inconsistencies. One is the issue of definition and identity: Are you gay if you have one same-sex interaction? Or are you gay only if you identify yourself as gay?

Another issue is the stigmatization of same-sex relationships in our culture. Gay people are frequently the targets of prejudice and sometimes violence. Gay men and lesbians often experience discrimination in the employment and housing markets, and in most communities they hold little political power. Physical force is often used against them: Gangs of teenagers and young adults have terrorized homosexuals, and stories of brutality against gays by police and military personnel are not uncommon.

A study that appeared in 1989 reanalyzed data from a 1970 study of men and concluded that a minimum of 20% of the males had had sexual contact to orgasm with another male at least once in their lives. About 7% had had such contact in adulthood; approximately 2% had had such contact in the previous year. The researchers emphasized that these findings should be viewed as minimum estimates because people are likely to conceal such behavior (Fay, Turner, Klassen, & Gagnon, 1989; see also Binson et al., 1995; Gagnon, 2004). As we saw earlier, the Chicago study reported that only 2.7% of the men interviewed and 1.3% of the women said they had had a same-sex experience in the previous 12 months.

The AARP (2005) study reported that 4% of males and 1% of females had a same-sex partner.

In nearly all ways, gay-male and lesbian relationships are like heterosexual relationships. In general, gay men and lesbians have increasingly moved toward developing and maintaining ongoing relationships with one person. Because they have had to struggle with coming out and have often experienced considerable rejection by their families, gay men and lesbians, like other groups, frequently develop skills and strengths that are valuable in relationships. These include an ability to connect emotionally with other people of both sexes, flexible role relationships and an ability to adapt to a partner, an ability to negotiate and share decision-making power, caring and effective parenting among those who choose to become parents, psychological perceptiveness, and effective communication skills (Bepko & Johnson, 2000; van Wormer, Wells, & Boes, 2000).

Many gay-male and lesbian couples build satisfying relationships (Patterson, 2000; Peplau, 2001; Peplau, Cochran, & Mays, 1997; Peplau & Spalding, 2000; Peplau, Veniegas, & Campbell, 1996; Veniegas & Peplau, 1997). One study compared relationship satisfaction among comparable samples of gay-male, lesbian, and heterosexual couples and found no significant differences. All three groups rated their relationships highly satisfying (Peplau et al., 1997). Emotional expressiveness—"being able to talk about my most intimate feelings"—was cited by both heterosexual and homosexual women as very important. Lesbians placed a high value on equality in relationships; the most satisfying relationships were those in which both partners were equally committed, equally "in love," and equal in power.

Sexuality Education

To the young people of this nation
Who must find their way to sexual health
In a world of contradictions.
Where the media scream "Always say yes,"
Where many adults admonish, "Just say no,"
But the majority just say . . . Nothing.

—PEGGY BRICK (2001)

Where do Americans get their sex education? Unfortunately, the *Janus Report* found that most people learn about sex "on the street" from their peers. Home ranked second as a source of sex education, followed by school and, rarely, a religious institution.

Consequences of Inadequate Sexuality Education

Because so little of our sex education is adequate, we have become a country with major sexual and parenting challenges, such as AIDS and adolescent motherhood. Teen pregnancy rates are much higher in the United States than in many other developed countries: twice as high as in England and Wales or Canada, and four times as high as in France and Sweden (Alan Guttmacher Institute, 2002). Each year in the United States over 1 million unmarried women become pregnant, and of those, 10,000 are girls 15 years of age or younger (Alan Guttmacher Institute, 1999; Henshaw, 1999). Clearly, compared with other Western nations that have similar standards of living, levels of industrial development, and forms of government, the United States has a much higher rate of teenage pregnancy. This higher rate can be attributed to the irregular and ineffective use of contraception by American adolescents (Boonstra, 2000; Coley & Chase-Lansdale, 1998; Singh & Darroch, 2000).

The high rate of adolescent pregnancy in this country has a multitude of negative consequences. The problems associated with "children having children" are enormous. The father usually disappears from the picture, and the young mother ends up rearing the child alone. This often places an extra burden on the grandparents, forcing many into a second—often unwelcome—"parenthood." And although the young mother needs a decent education, she may find it difficult to continue in school. Young mothers often experience serious financial problems, inadequate housing, lack of transportation, loneliness, poor nutrition, physical health problems, and a cluster of other stressors that commonly foster child neglect and abuse (Bissell, 2000; Coley & Chase-Lansdale, 1998; Higginson, 1998; Pieve, 2001).

Sexuality Education Programs

The high rate of adolescent pregnancy and the long list of problems it causes in families have led to the development of a wide variety of sex education programs across the country. (To find out how good your sex education has been, take the

Because parents tend to be poor at providing their children with clear, useful information about sex, the responsibility for sex education in our society has fallen largely to schools and communities. Sex education is more effective when combined with access to a health clinic where contraceptives are available.

quiz in Box 6.1.) Most young people today receive sex education—whether on the street or in the classroom. The debate continues, however, on what precisely sex education means, and the controversy over abstinence-only versus more comprehensive approaches that discuss contraception continues as well.

These debates have a considerable impact on what is taught in the classroom, and some researchers have found that politicians who promote morality-based abstinence-only education are out of touch with what teachers, parents, and teenagers think should be taught. A national poll found that Americans overwhelmingly favor broader sexuality education programs over those that discuss only abstinence: 81% said young people should be taught about abstinence, pregnancy, and the prevention of sexually transmitted diseases (STDs); 18% said young people should be taught only abstinence; and 1% had no opinion (Henry J. Kaiser Family Foundation/ABC Television, 1998).

According to interviews the Kaiser Foundation conducted in 2000 with parents, 65% believed that sex education should encourage young people to delay sexual activity but also prepare them to use birth control and practice safe sex when they do become sexually active. Among the one-third of parents who said that adolescents should be told "only to have sex when they are married," the overwhelming majority said that schools should teach adolescents how to get tested for HIV/AIDS and other STDs (86%), how to talk with a partner about birth control and STDs (77%), how to use condoms (71%), and where to get and how to use other birth control methods (68%) (Dailard, 2001, p. 5).

More than four out of five adults in the United States favor sex education and want courses for children age 12 or older to deal with birth control information

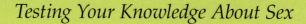

BOX 6.1   Self-Assessment

Testing Your Knowledge About Sex

For more than 40 years, the Kinsey Institute at Indiana University has been a pioneer in the scientific study of human sexuality. In a Roper poll conducted for the Kinsey Institute, 2,000 adults in the United States were asked a series of true-or-false and multiple-choice questions about sex. Only 45% of those tested answered more than half the questions correctly. See how you do on this sample of the questions.

Circle True or False and Fill in the Blanks

T F 1. Most women prefer a sex partner who has a large penis.

T F 2. Menopause does not cause a woman to lose interest in having sex.

_____ 3. When does the average American first have sexual intercourse?

_____ 4. Of every 10 women in the United States, how many would you estimate have ever masturbated?

T F 5. More than 25% of American males have had a same-sex sexual experience.

T F 6. Anal intercourse between uninfected people can cause AIDS.

T F 7. Most husbands have extramarital affairs.

_____ 8. What percentage of women engage in anal sex?

T F 9. Problems with erections are most often started by a physical problem.

T F 10. Almost all erection problems can be successfully treated.

_____ 11. What do you think is the average length of a man's penis?

T F 12. Lubricants like Vaseline Intensive Care or baby oil can cause microscopic holes in a condom or diaphragm.

T F 13. Homosexuality is usually difficult to tell just by people's appearance or gestures.

T F 14. A woman can get pregnant if she has sex during her menstrual period.

T F 15. A woman can get pregnant even if the man withdraws his penis before ejaculating.

Answers: 1. F; 2. T; 3. age 16 or 17; 4. 6–8; 5. T; 6. F; 7. F; 8. 30–40%; 9. T; 10. T; 11. 5–7 inches; 12. T; 13. T; 14. T; 15. T

Source: Adapted from *The Kinsey Institute New Report on Sex* (p. 45) by J. Reinisch and R. Beasley, 1994, New York: St. Martin's Press. Copyright © 1994 by The Kinsey Institute for Research in Sex, Gender, and Reproduction. Reprinted by permission.

(Janus & Janus, 1993). About three out of four adults want the courses to talk about homosexuality and abortion. Similarly, another nationwide survey indicates that 89% of Americans believe that sexuality education programs should focus on how to avoid unintended pregnancies and sexually transmitted infections, including HIV and AIDS, because these are such pressing problems in American society today. And, more than 8 out of 10 Americans reject the idea that providing sexuality education encourages sexual activity (Sex Information and Education Council of the U.S., 2001, 2004).

Planned Parenthood, a national private nonprofit organization, has developed a wide variety of presentations and materials to benefit young people. A sample of the organization's materials, displayed in Table 6.3, lists some common misconceptions young people have about sex—"ridiculous ideas" that can lead to trouble.

Sexuality Education and Parents

Although people disagree about sexuality, there is agreement on one issue—that education about sexuality should begin in the home (Jaccard, Dittus, & Gordon, 1998; Raffaelli, Bogenschneider, & Flood, 1998). The reason that schools, religious

TABLE 6.3	Ten Ridiculous Ideas That Will Make You a Father

- You can count on your partner to use birth control.
- Men have stronger sex drives than women do.
- Men need to have sex with different women to learn to be better lovers.
- If a woman uses birth control, then she has probably been sleeping around.
- A woman would do anything to keep from getting pregnant.
- It is easy for a woman to get on the pill.
- If a man hasn't gone all the way by the time he's 16, then something is wrong with him.
- I don't like condoms.
- When a woman says no, she really just wants to be talked into it.
- I could never talk to my partner about birth control.

Source: Adapted with permission from the brochure "Ten Ridiculous Ideas That Will Make a Father Out of You," © 2000, Planned Parenthood of Central Oklahoma, 619 N.W. 23rd Street, Oklahoma City, OK 73103–1457.

institutions, and agencies such as Planned Parenthood have become involved in sex education is that most parents feel incapable of or uncomfortable about talking seriously with their offspring about sexual matters. A subtle conspiracy of silence exists between parent and child. Parents tell themselves that they are willing to answer any questions their children might have about sex, but children sense that their parents really do not want to talk about these sensitive issues. Because both feel uncomfortable talking about sexuality, they avoid the subject.

Joyce, a 45-year-old single mother of three, describes growing up in a home in which her parents avoided any mention of sex, her early self-consciousness about her own sexuality, and her unease in talking to her own children about sex. Through sexuality education, she overcame her anxieties and can now talk freely about sexual matters.

"My parents were intelligent, sensitive individuals, and yet they treated the subject of sex like it was the plague. All I knew for sure was this must really be something if it was such a big secret! What happened with my brothers and sister (and me) was there were a lot of misconceptions and a lot of guilt.

"As a parent, what kind of message did I give my children? In my head I knew what I wanted to give them, but in my gut I was still at war with my own sexuality. So I, too, gave mixed messages to my children about sex. It wasn't until I went back to college full-time after my divorce and got into a human sexuality class that the shift really came for me internally. I began to stop feeling self-conscious and began to relax—to enjoy being human. I still have one child living at home, and I'm able to talk openly and honestly with him about any subject regarding sex.

"I feel strongly about good sex education for our children. Two years ago I would have been floored by the idea of showing films on sexual intercourse, masturbation, and gay and lesbian lovemaking to 12-year-olds and their parents in a church setting. Today, I would support it 100%. I wish sex education could be available to all children and their parents at least by the time kids are 12 years old."

Few children receive direct instruction from their parents in the areas of sexuality, sexual intercourse, or birth control (Miller, 2002; Miller, Benson, & Galbraith, 2001). This is sad because good parental communication about sex might forestall or postpone a child's sexual activity. Among those daughters who are sexually active, parental communication appears to help promote more effective contraceptive practices on the part of the adolescent. An interesting study of family interaction patterns in homes with teenagers found that adolescents who experienced open communication and satisfaction with family interaction also reported having received more sex education in the home (Baldwin & Baranoski, 1990).

There is less pregnancy risk if adolescents have intercourse less often or with fewer partners, as well as by using contraception at first or most recent intercourse and by using contraception consistently over time. Elevated risk of adolescent pregnancy is associated with living with a single parent and living in a lower socioeconomic status family. There is also more risk if a women has older sexually active siblings, has been a victim of sexual abuse, or is residing in a disorganized/dangerous neighborhood (Miller, 2002).

Sol Gordon and his colleagues concur that parents who accept their children's sexuality and help them learn to cope with it have a better chance of raising healthy and sexually responsible children than parents who avoid the issues. Gordon urges parents to become "askable," positing that young people who can talk freely with their parents about sex will be stronger and more able to make wise choices as they grow to adulthood. Surveying more than 8,000 students, Gordon found that fewer than 15% had received a meaningful sex education from their parents. Girls were usually told about menstruation; the balance of their teaching, however, could be summed up in one word: *don't*. And except for the occasional or single prepuberty talk with Dad, who used vague birds-and-bees analogies and ended by mentioning the use of a condom, the boys were on their own (Gordon & Gordon, 2000; Klein & Gordon, 1992).

Brent Miller and his colleagues studied how strictness of parenting was related to adolescents' sexual attitudes and behaviors (Miller et al., 2001). These researchers hypothesized and found a curvilinear relationship between flexibility in parenting and sexual behavior. Sexual promiscuity and the experience of intercourse were highest among teenagers who saw their parents as not being strict or as not having any rules (chaotic on the Couple and Family Map; see Chapter 3), lowest among those teens who reported that their parents were moderately strict (flexible on the Couple and Family Map), and intermediate among teenagers who saw their parents as being very strict and having many rules (rigid on the Couple and Family Map). The results of this study suggest that if parents are concerned about adolescent sexual behavior, they can err in two directions: by being either too lenient (chaotic) or too strict (rigid). The more balanced levels (being structured or flexible on the Couple and Family Map) are related to more responsible sexual behavior on the part of adolescents.

Is Sexuality Education Effective?

Most Western nations try to reduce adolescent pregnancy through programs that emphasize abstinence but also offer the alternative of effective contraceptives to those who choose to remain or become sexually active. In the United States, "Just Say No" programs are promoted heavily, but there is little research evidence to conclude that they are very effective (Christopher, 2001; Sex Information and Education Council of the U.S., 2001). As in Europe, the most effective American programs encourage abstinence but also offer an alternative for those who are already, or who choose to become, sexually active. Current research indicates that 95% of Americans have had sex before marriage, with 93% having had premarital sex before age 30 (Wind, 2006). This high number of people having sex before marriage calls into question the effectiveness of abstinence-only educational programs (Wind, 2006).

Sex is a powerful drive among human beings, and it is difficult for one course or program to have a major impact on a person's sexual behavior. A meta-analysis of the effects of 12 abstinence education programs on teen sexual behavior found that these programs had very little impact on the sexual attitudes and behaviors of young people (Silva, 2002).

Another research team reviewed 26 trials of sex education programs aimed at delaying sexual intercourse, improving birth control use, and reducing the incidence of unintended pregnancy in adolescents. This research team concluded that the interventions did not delay initiation of sexual intercourse in women or men; did not improve birth control use by either women or men at every, or at their last, intercourse; and did not reduce pregnancy rates in women (DiCenso, Guyatt, Willan, & Griffith, 2002). These researchers concluded that sex education programs do not seem to have a direct impact on sexual behavior of adolescents.

Premarital Sexual Behavior

In the 1960s, about two-thirds of American adults felt premarital or nonmarital sex was wrong, according to a Gallup poll. By the late 1980s, adults in this country were about evenly split, with half saying it was wrong "for a man and a woman to have sex relations before marriage" and about half saying it was not wrong. The pollsters believed this to be a dramatic turnaround in attitudes (Gallup, Inc., 1989). American attitudes continue to evolve, and recent data indicate that 60% of adults believe sexual relations between unmarried men and unmarried women are acceptable versus 36% who feel the practice is morally unacceptable (Gallup, Inc., 2004).

Sexual behavior among adolescents and young adults is of great concern to parents, educators, and policymakers. Risky sexual behavior can result in lifelong consequences of pregnancy and sexually transmitted diseases. Young people may not be mature enough intellectually or emotionally to make wise choices regarding sexual behavior, and adding alcohol or drugs to the picture can have devastating results.

Sexual Behavior Among Adolescents

The latest government research from the Centers for Disease Control and Prevention on teenagers in the United States reports national estimates of sexual activity, contraceptive use, and childbearing among males and females 15–19 years of age (Abma, Martinez, Mosher, & Dawson, 2004). Among the highlights of the study conducted in 2002:

- About 47% of female teenagers and about 46% of male teenagers had had sexual intercourse at least once.
- For never-married males, this was a significant decline from 55% in 1995 to 46% in 2002. Rates of intercourse for males 15–17 declined from 43% in 1995 to 31% in 2002. For males 18–19, rates dropped from 75% to 64%.
- For never-married females 15–17, there was a significant decline (from 38% to 30%), and for those 18–19, there was no significant change (68% in 1995 to 69% in 2002).

- Teenagers are delaying sex until older ages. In 2002, 13% of never-married female teenagers had had sex before age 15 compared to 19% in 1995; 15% of males had experienced sex in 2002 compared to 21% in 1995.
- The vast majority of teens had not had intercourse in the month before participating in the interview (72% of females; 75% of males), but 16% of the females and 12% of the males had sex four or more times in the past month.
- First intercourse was nonvoluntary for 9% of teen females.
- When asked how much they wanted their first intercourse to happen at the time it did, 13% of the females and 6% of the males said they really didn't want it to happen at that time; 52% of the females and 31% of the males had mixed feelings about the experience.
- Teen females most commonly have first sexual partners who are 1 to 3 years older than they are, and most commonly the partner is someone with whom they are "going steady," as opposed to a less-involved relationship.
- About one in four teen females and 18% of teen males used no method of contraception at the time of first intercourse. The most popular method was the condom (66% of the females and 71% of the males used this at first intercourse).

The researchers found that males and females whose first intercourse occurred between 1995 and 2002 were much more likely to be protected at first intercourse than their counterparts having first sex before 1990. Use of the highly effective injectable method of contraception (Depo-Provera™ and Lunelle™) increased from 10% in 1995 to 21% in 2002. Almost all sexually experienced females (94%) reported use of the male condom. Pill use, condom use, the use of new hormonal methods, and the use of dual methods all increased for sexually active male and female teens (Abma et al., 2004).

Sexual Behavior, Alcohol, and College

Most young people (75% of boys and 60% of girls) will have had sex by the time they graduate from high school, and the majority of those who have not will have their first sexual experience while in college. During this developmental period in life, the sexual experience tends to be sporadic, furtive, and poorly managed. Even sexually experienced students entering college therefore have much to learn in the sexual arena (Cooper, 2002).

In a culture that glorifies sex and drinking, it is of no surprise that the college campus is probably little different from anywhere else. Alcohol use and risky sexual behavior among college students are strongly linked. Cooper (2002) found that having multiple or casual sex partners, failing to discuss risk issues before having sex, the decision to have sex itself, and inconsistent use of condoms and birth control were all related to alcohol use.

One research team looked at sexual behavior, alcohol, and housing in a northwestern university in the United States (Dinger & Parsons, 1999). The team found that:

- 39.4 percent of students living in fraternity/sorority housing reported having six or more sexual partners compared to 22.8% of students in residence halls.
- 15 percent of students living in fraternity/sorority housing reported more than 20 acts of sexual intercourse prior to the study compared to 5% of students living in residence halls.

Recent estimates indicate that 400,000 college students between age 18 and 24 have had unprotected sex after drinking in a given year, and an estimated 100,000 had sex when they were so intoxicated they were unable to consent.

TABLE 6.4	Risky Sexual Behavior

Percentage of sexually active young people who say . . .

	Teens 15 to 17	Young Adults 18 to 24
Alcohol or drugs influenced their decision to do something sexual.	29%	37%
They did more sexually than planned because they had been drinking or using drugs.	24%	31%
They worried about STDs or pregnancy because of something they did sexually while drinking or using drugs.	26%	28%
They used alcohol or drugs to help them feel more comfortable with a sexual partner.	13%	16%
They had unprotected sex because they were drinking or using drugs.	12%	25%

Source: Substance Abuse and Risky Behavior: Attitudes and Practices Among Adolescents and Young Adults: Survey Snapshot by the Henry J. Kaiser Family Foundation and the National Center on Addiction and Substance Abuse at Columbia University, February 6, 2002.

- 38.2 percent of the students in the study reported drinking alcohol or using other drugs prior to their last sexual intercourse; students living in fraternity/sorority housing were more likely to report this behavior (50%) than students living in residence halls (30.4%).
- 60.3 percent of students reported using a condom at last sexual intercourse; condom use did not differ by residence or fraternity/sorority affiliation.

Recent estimates indicate that 400,000 college students between the ages of 18 and 24 had unprotected sex after drinking in a given year, and an estimated 100,000 had sex when they were so intoxicated they were unable to consent (Hingson & Howland, 2002). (See Table 6.4.) Another investigator looked at the connection between drinking and teen childbearing and found that teenage girls who binge drink are up to 63% more likely to become teen mothers (Dee, 2001).

Marital and Extramarital Sexual Behavior

Surveys indicate that most young people have intercourse before marriage; in fact, premarital relationships are often highly sexual. Current research shows that 95% of individuals have had sex before marriage, with 93% indicating they did so by age 30 (Wind, 2006). In fact, this study indicates that this high percentage of people having premarital sex has been evident for a long time, with nearly 9 out of 10 women born in the 1940s indicating they had sex before marriage. The fact that couples are waiting to get married until their late 20s means that individuals have more years available to have sexual relationships before they enter into marriage (Wind, 2006). After marriage, the sexual relationship gradually changes. Some people have jokingly asked, "Is there sex after marriage?" Research indicates there is.

Sex Within Marriage

Years ago when newspaper columnist Ann Landers asked her readers, "Has your sex life gone downhill since you got married?" 82% of the 141,210 people who responded said yes, sex after marriage was less exciting (Landers, 1989). However, intimacy—feelings of warmth and closeness between two people who love each other—does not appear to diminish with time. Within the intimate environment of a happy marriage, sexual experiences can become more satisfying and meaningful—and retain their excitement—over time.

The *Janus Report* indicated that married couples have higher levels of sexual activity than divorced people and single people. More specifically, 44% of the married couples reported having sexual activity at least a few times a week compared with 32% of singles and 33% of divorced people. Conversely, only 7% of married people rarely had sex, whereas the figure was 19% for singles and 22% for divorced people. In other words, married couples across the life cycle are even more active sexually than singles.

A hectic life often gets in the way of an active sex life. Long hours on the job, caring for children, continual interruptions, and countless other stresses tend to tire people out and decrease their sexual activity. For those couples with two jobs, the phenomenon has been called the **DINS** (double income, no sex) **dilemma**. Therapists have labeled it *inhibited*, or *hypoactive, sexual desire*. In addition to sheer fatigue, boredom is also a factor for some individuals. Most of the time, couples can resuscitate the sexual relationship with some tender care and concern, such as having dinner out together, seeing a movie, or going to bed early. Consulting a marriage and family therapist or a sex therapist may be useful for persistent sexual problems. The preeminent sex researchers and therapists William Masters and Virginia Johnson, along with Robert Kolodny (1998), argued that half of all American couples are troubled at some time by some type of sexual distress, ranging from disinterest to genuine sexual dysfunction. Some couples need therapy, but many others can benefit simply by heeding the 16 ideas outlined in Box 6.2.

For many people, sex is not the most important thing in life. A nationwide survey of 815 men found that the most important thing in a man's life is not sex, career, fame, or fortune, but marriage, according to 75% of the married men in the sample. About 90% of these husbands called their wives their best friends.

Friendship, based on trust and sharing of responsibilities, becomes more important as life's challenges mount and sexual energy decreases (Hellmich, 1990).

Although sex is clearly not everything, it is important to an intimate relationship. Barry McCarthy (2001, 2003) explained that when sex goes well, it is 15% to 20% of a relationship; but if there are sexual problems, then it has a much more powerful role of 50% to 75%, and it robs the marriage of intimacy and vitality. Sex is more than a simple physical need; it also impacts the quality of the marriage.

Different people have different needs for sexual intimacy, and those needs affect how they perceive their sexual behavior. For this reason, couples must communicate clearly about sex if they are to maintain a satisfying relationship. The classic movie *Annie Hall* depicts two lovers with different perceptions of their sexual relationship. When a therapist asks them (separately) how often they have sex, the character played by Woody Allen answers, "Hardly ever, maybe three times a week"; the character played by Diane Keaton replies, "Constantly, three times a week."

Overall, it appears that in many marriages sex is very important for long-term happiness. It has powerful symbolic value in a successful marriage, reaffirming the bond between the individuals. It is an indication that everything is still okay despite wrinkles, sags, and love handles. To keep the spark in their lovemaking, married couples need to keep the relationship alive through communication and sharing. It is very difficult to have a successful sexual relationship if each partner does not feel good about herself or himself or about other aspects of the relationship. Serena, a middle-aged woman in St. Louis, describes the "sexy relationship" she has with her husband, a relationship founded not just on physical attraction but on a number of elements that make her marriage strong and healthy.

"Our sexual relationship is great today. It's a lot better than it was early in our marriage. I don't know why exactly, but I think we're more used to each other, more comfortable with each other. Perhaps we really love each other more. As the years pass, you look back and see a long-term tradition of commitment and kindness, and recognize that you have really created a wonderful marriage together.

"That's very special, and it makes you feel so very close to each other. It's hard to explain, but we do have a very sexy relationship with each other. Perhaps not as often as before, but it sure can be full of fire and tenderness."

Marital Styles and Sexual Behavior

Four types of marital dynamics were identified by Barry McCarthy (2001, 2003), and he found that each style had sexual strengths and problems. The four styles were complementary couples, conflict-minimizing couples, best-friend couples, and emotionally expressive couples. These are not "pure" styles, and couples can sometimes change their styles over time.

Complementary Couples. This was the most common marital style (also called validating or supportive), and each partner has power in certain domains and moderate levels of intimacy. They validate each other's worth and value the marital bond. Sex for them becomes a low priority and often becomes routine, like watching the evening news. Usually the male is in charge of sexuality, and he overemphasizes intercourse at the expense of affection and intimacy. As the couple ages, sexuality drops considerably.

Conflict-Minimizing Couples. These couples are the most stable couple style (also called traditional) and usually have traditional roles. Strong emotional expression is discouraged. The male initiates sex and decides on the sexual style. Sex is very predictable and is rarely discussed.

Best-Friend Couples. This style values intimacy the most and considers friendship to be a strong foundation of their marriage. When the relationship works well, sex is an integral part of the marriage. Sex energizes the relationship and the marital bond is strong. The major pitfall is that it is a difficult style to maintain and it has a high rate of divorce. High expectations and disillusion rob the marriage of its excitement and pleasure.

Emotionally Expressive Couples. This style is full of feelings and can range from intense feelings of love and anger (also called volatile or explosive). Sex is often passionate, exciting, fun, and playful. A healthy pattern can be that sex occurs as a way of making up from conflict or a fight. The problem is that the conflict can often drive the couple apart and it could end in a "divorce from hell."

In summary, each marital style has both positive and negative consequences on the sexual relationship. Most couples develop a style that works for them and find it hard to change it over time, even when they are dissatisfied.

Infidelity

Where there is marriage without love, there will be love without marriage.
—BENJAMIN FRANKLIN (1733/1980, P. 347)

Extramarital friendships are common in American society. As one husband put it, "It doesn't make a whole lot of sense to deny friendships across-the-board to half the human race. If I enjoy talking with a person at work, it doesn't make sense to lose this friendship just because she's a female." Ideally, couples should allow each other the freedom to develop relationships outside the marriage. But if they are not properly handled, friendships with members of the other sex can harm a marriage. These friendships can sometimes develop into extramarital sexual relationships, which are commonly cited as one reason for divorce. Opinion is divided on whether men and women can be friends—loving, affectionate, accepting, and so on—without becoming sexually involved.

Blow and Hartnett (2005) reviewed the research conducted on infidelity from 1980 through 2005. They summarized the research from the perspectives of attitude toward infidelity, prevalence, type of infidelity, infidelity by gender, and several other demographic characteristics. Based on this review, they drew the following conclusions:

- Attitudes about infidelity are related to actions, and those with more positive attitudes about infidelity are more likely to engage in infidelity.
- Attitudes about infidelity differ based on culture, gender, type of couple relationship (e.g. heterosexual, gay/lesbian, dating marriage), behaviors that make up the infidelity (e.g., kiss, intercourse, emotional connection), and prior experience with infidelity.
- Internationally, differences in attitudes and behaviors vary by country and culture.
- Men are more likely to see a distinction between love and sex than woman, with men more likely to view infidelity as only sexual and not emotional.
- Men are more likely to engage in sexual infidelity than women.
- Over the course of married heterosexual relationships in the United States, extramarital sex occurs in less than 25% of committed relationships.
- Dissatisfaction with the marital relationship is related to increased incidence of infidelity.
- There appear to be at least three types of infidelity: emotional-only, sexual-only, and combined sexual and emotional infidelity. Most research is about sexual infidelity.
- Some studies show that gay men are less concerned about infidelity than heterosexual couples. Lesbian couples are less likely to experience infidelity than gay couples.

Emily Brown, a social worker, offers a different perspective on affairs. She identifies six stages in the process of infidelity (Brown, 2000b). The first stage occurs when a climate develops in which infidelity can germinate, such as a couple's allowing hurt, dissatisfaction, and differences to go unresolved. Betrayal occurs in the second stage. The more dissatisfied spouse "slides" into the infidelity. The unfaithful spouse denies it is happening, and the other spouse may collude by ignoring obvious signs. The infidelity is revealed in the third stage. At this stage, both partners realize they will never be able to picture themselves or their marriage again in the same way. According to Brown, this stage requires a lot of time for partners to process; both need to experience the shock and fury of what happened, why it happened, what it means, and what the underlying issues might be. The impact can be as severe as the revelation of sexual abuse. The fourth stage involves admission of a crisis in the marriage. Brown believes that too often the infidelity itself is seen as the crisis rather than the problem she believes underlies the infidelity. In the fifth stage, the partners make a decision either to address all of the issues involved or to bury them and get on with rebuilding the marriage. The sixth and final stage involves forgiveness. Brown believes this can take place only if the preceding five stages have been successfully addressed and resolved.

The American Association for Marriage and Family Therapy (AAMFT; 2004) argues that the disclosure of infidelity can be devastating to a relationship.

BOX 6.3 **Diversity in Families**

Extramarital Sex Around the World

Sex outside marriage is a concern around the world, and a global sample of research and commentary will give the reader a better understanding of how diverse cultures address the issue:

- Worldwide, as many as 60% of all condoms are used outside marriage (*Population Reports*, 1999).
- An extramarital affair is the top cause of divorce in Shanghai, the largest city in the People's Republic of China. A 25-year-old worker in a Shanghai computer company was the first person sentenced to jail for violating the Marriage Law enacted in 2001. Chen Yue, 25, was sentenced to six months in prison after being found guilty of having a live-in girlfriend only months after marrying another woman (China.Org.CN, 2001).
- "When a man is with a woman, it feels like electricity." Men in a rural community in central Mexico believe that male sexuality is a natural force that is difficult to control. For this reason, they are permanently suspicious about the fidelity of their wives and the paternity of their own children. Contraceptive use is experienced with some ambivalence by the men—contraceptives help relieve the economic burdens of a large family but promote the sexual freedom of women (Castro, 2001).
- Indonesia's Justice Ministry drafted laws to ban premarital sex, extramarital sex, living together without being married, reneging on a promise to marry, having sex with a prostitute, performing as a stripper, and witchcraft, among other things (*Gay & Lesbian Times*, 2003).
- Using data gathered from wives in the Philippines, researchers found that a number of factors were associated with husbands' sexual activity outside their marriage. Men who were more educated, who had been in the relationship longer, and who had sex before marriage were more likely to be engaging in sex outside the marriage. Men who were older, who were farmers, who lived at home, and who had more-educated wives were believed to be less likely to be having extramarital sex (Ahlburg, Jensen, & Perez, 1997).
- Two U.S. psychologists studied "human mate poaching," the efforts to romantically attract someone who is already in a relationship. The investigators argued that poaching attempts were relatively common (Schmitt & Buss, 2001).
- The Japanese are more accepting of extramarital sex than are Americans. Or, at least, they are more willing to admit this. While 45% of Japanese adults believed that "extramarital affairs are acceptable under certain circumstances," only 12% of Americans said they felt this way. There were few differences between men and women within each country: Only 14% of American men and 11% of American women agree with the 49% of Japanese men and 42% of Japanese women that extramarital affairs can be acceptable (Taylor, 1998).
- An Islamic court in Lagos, Nigeria, sentenced a 20-year-old woman to 100 lashes with a cane in public for having an extramarital affair (PlanetSave.com, 2001).
- Article 340 of the Jordanian penal code reduces or eliminates punishments for men who claim "honor" as their motivation for murdering a female relative. Women who survive such murder attempts face a life in protective custody, because they have nowhere else to turn. Extramarital sex is one breach of this ancient code (Husseini, 2000).
- Senegal's efforts to prevent AIDS have been successful because husbands have been increasingly likely to use condoms during extramarital sex (amFAR AIDS Research, 2004).
- Twenty-eight percent of husbands surveyed in southeastern Nigeria health care centers said they had engaged in extramarital sexual relationships during their wife's pregnancy. Some of the husbands believed that sex during pregnancy should be less frequent or could cause a miscarriage. Other husbands thought sex during pregnancy enhances fetal well-being (Onah, Iloabachie, Obi, Ezugwu, & Eze, 2002).
- Twelve percent of married or cohabiting men in Brazil reported having had at least one extramarital partner in the previous months, researchers found. Forty percent reported having used condoms during the last time they had extramarital sex. Men who belonged to an evangelical church were significantly less likely to engage in extramarital sex. Brazilian men who lived in the northern part of the country were three times more likely to have extramarital sex than men who lived in southern or central Brazil (Hill, Cleland, & Ali, 2004).
- A German medical researcher studying coronary heart disease and sex sees death in the extramarital bed as a significant problem (Neumaier, 2001).
- An academic studying adultery as it is represented in the literature of the Middle Ages (476 to about 1450) finds evidence for a wide variety of perspectives: from defense of adultery and approval through leniency to condemnation; from joyful sexuality on one side to a crass hostility toward sex on the other (Schnell, 2000).

Intense emotions and recurrent crises are the norm. But AAMFT also notes that the majority of marriages not only survive an affair but can become stronger and more intimate. Couple therapy can be a useful tool for helping this growth begin. Approximately 50% of couples who seek couple therapy do so because an extramarital involvement has occurred.

Family therapists counsel couples dealing with the crisis of infidelity and try to help them work through the situation in a cautious and rational manner. A professional therapist can be very helpful by encouraging spouses to be calm and honest in disclosing their motives. Infidelity can signal the end of a relationship, or it can be a catalyst for dramatic and positive growth in a marriage. (See Box 6.3.)

Toward Sexual Health

Sex is an important part of human life, health, and happiness. It's a crucial ingredient in individual well-being and in intimate relationships, especially marriage. Problems in sexual functioning therefore need to be addressed if people are to have successful relationships.

A survey of common sexual problems identified the most frequent problems for women and men (Laumann, Gagnon, Michael, & Michaels, 1994). About one-third (33.4%) of women reported a lack of interest in sex, as compared to only 15.8% of men (Figure 6.4). The second most frequent issue for nearly one-quarter of the women surveyed was an inability to reach orgasm (24.1%) and to find sex pleasurable (21.2%). In contrast, roughly one-quarter of the men reported that they reached climax too early (25.5%) or had anxiety about their sexual performance (17%). These symptoms are very similar to the common complaints heard from married

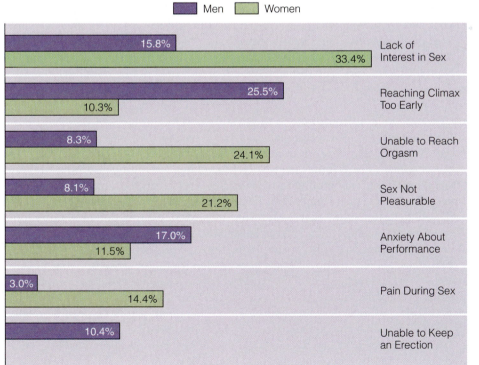

FIGURE 6.4

Frequency of Sexual Problems

Source: The Social Organization of Sexuality: Sexual Practices in the United States (pp. 370–371) by E. O. Laumann, J. H. Gagnon, R. T. Michael, and S. Michaels, 1994, Chicago: University of Chicago Press.

couples in which the male feels the female is not interested in him sexually—often because he climaxes too early and does not satisfy her needs. (See also Gagnon, 2004; Laumann et al., 2004; Laumann & Michael, 2000.)

Sexual Problems and Dysfunctions

Probably the largest sexual problem for both men and women as they get older is the lack of sexual desire. In a recent survey, 43% of women and 31% of men have problems with diminished sexual desire (Hart, Weber, & Taylor, 1998). In her book *Better Sex for You*, Helen Pensanti (2001) said: "The number one question I receive from thousands of people of every age, race, class and occupation worldwide is: 'Can you help me with my sex drive? I don't have one.'"

Related to the lack of sex drive is the fact that 45% of the women said that the greatest difficulty was finding the energy for sex. Raising children, lack of sleep, and exhaustion were the major reasons given for the lack of energy (Hart et al., 1998).

Other common sexual problems are, for men, the inability to achieve and/or maintain an erection and, for women, the inability to reach orgasm. Many sexual problems arise from beliefs and attitudes about sex that are narrow or incorrect (Leiblum, 2002; Leiblum & Rosen, 2000).

Nearly 1 in 3 American men and 4 in 10 American women suffer some kind of sexual dysfunction, ranging from lack of desire and performance anxiety to problems with arousal and orgasm and pain during intercourse (Herbert, 1999; Laumann, Paik, & Rosen, 1999). **Sexual dysfunction** has been defined as a state in which sexual behavior or the lack of it causes anxiety, anguish, and frustration, which can lead to unhappiness and distress in a couple's relationship (Leiblum, 2002; Leiblum & Rosen, 2000).

What Causes Sexual Dysfunction? There are two causative categories for sexual dysfunction, according to Masters and his colleagues (1995, 1998). **Organic sexual dysfunctions** are related to physiological factors; **psychosocial sexual dysfunctions** are related to psychological, developmental, interpersonal, environmental, or cultural factors. The researchers note that it may not be possible to identify the precise cause of a particular form of dysfunction and that some dysfunctions may have multiple causes. Organic factors cause 10% to 20% of all cases of sexual dysfunction and contribute to the dysfunction in another 15% of all cases, the researchers estimate. For example, a man may have difficulty achieving or maintaining an erection as a result of numerous medical conditions, including diabetes and alcoholism. Prescription medicines (e.g., drugs for high blood pressure) and street drugs (e.g., amphetamines, barbiturates, and narcotics) can also cause erection difficulties (Masters et al., 1995, 1998).

Psychological factors that can result in sexual dysfunction are numerous. Developmental factors include troubled parent–child relationships, negative family attitudes toward sex and sexuality, traumatic childhood or adolescent sexual experiences, and conflict over one's gender identity (one's sense of being male or female). Personal factors include a variety of fears: of poor sexual performance, of pregnancy, of venereal disease, of rejection, of pain, of becoming close to someone, of losing control, or even of success. Interpersonal factors that can be related to sexual problems include poor communication and frequent power struggles between partners; hostility, distrust, and deceit; lack of mutual physical attraction; and gender-role conflicts (Masters et al., 1995, 1998).

Sexual interactions can be a source of frustration and disappointment, but they can also be a source of happiness and great joy. A satisfying sexual relationship is an important ingredient in a healthy intimate relationship.

Types of Sexual Dysfunctions. Male sexual dysfunction is expressed in a variety of ways. **Erectile dysfunction** (formerly called impotence) is the inability to achieve or maintain an erection that is firm enough for intercourse. (Isolated episodes of the inability to achieve or maintain an erection are nearly universal among men.) **Premature ejaculation**, or rapid ejaculation, is difficult to define precisely, although it is a common sexual dysfunction. It causes problems in a sexual relationship when the woman is dissatisfied because the man reaches orgasm much more quickly than she does. **Retarded ejaculation**, the opposite of premature ejaculation, describes a dysfunction in which prolonged and strenuous effort is needed to reach orgasm. **Ejaculatory incompetence** is a man's inability to ejaculate in his partner's vagina despite a firm erection and a high level of sexual arousal. **Painful intercourse,** often believed to be a problem only for women, can also affect men. Pain can be felt in the penis and/or testicles or internally; the pain is often related to a problem with the seminal vesicles or the prostate gland (Insel & Roth, 2004; Masters et al., 1995, 1998).

There are also various female sexual dysfunctions. **Vaginismus** is a condition in which the muscles of the outer third of the vagina respond with involuntary spasms to attempts at penetration, preventing intercourse. **Anorgasmia** is the inability to have an orgasm. **Rapid orgasm**, reaching orgasm too quickly, is the much-ignored female counterpart to male premature ejaculation. And **painful intercourse**, including burning, sharp or searing pain, or cramping, is also a common problem in women (Insel & Roth, 2004; Masters et al., 1995, 1998).

Sexual dysfunctions are generally something people are uncomfortable admitting to themselves and discussing with others. We can laugh and leer about sex, but our culture has a difficult time talking honestly and openly about it.

Sex Therapy

Many people with sexual difficulties go without help for a long time. This is unfortunate, because most **sex therapy** is simply a process of education. Sex therapists instruct clients (people who seek sex therapy are not called patients) in the gentle art of lovemaking.

Reputable professional sex therapists are trained in the subjects of sex and sexuality and have experience working with many different people regarding sexual needs and dysfunctions. A national organization, the American Association of Sexuality Educators, Counselors, and Therapists (AASECT), has established criteria for certifying sex therapists who have met its training standards. AASECT has also developed ethical principles for the practice of sex therapy. For a small fee, AASECT will provide by mail a list of certified counselors and sex therapists.*

Sex educators typically work with relatively large groups of people and teach general information and principles that are useful to a variety of individuals. **Sex therapists** typically work with individuals, couples, or small groups of individuals and couples and focus more on individual concerns and problems. On the basis of content alone, a sex therapy session can be difficult to discern from a sex education session. The two approaches overlap considerably, so much so that some professionals do not distinguish between sex education and sex therapy.

Solving Sexual Problems. Sex therapy can involve a number of different components, including the following:

- Learning more about basic anatomy.
- Learning what one's true feelings are about the body.
- Learning what one's basic attitudes toward sex and sexuality are.
- Learning to relax with a partner and to get in a sexually responsive mood.
- Learning to sense one's own body and how the setting affects the body's responses.
- Learning sexual techniques.
- Exploring one's own and one's partner's body.
- Developing new sexual attitudes and techniques and maintaining them over time.

Sex therapists are quick to point out that couples with sexual problems should not rush into intercourse but should take time to enjoy each other's company and to touch each other in a variety of loving ways.

Two of the most common self-help techniques for overcoming sexual problems are body exploration and masturbation. Clinicians have found that masturbation exercises are helpful for treating orgasmic dysfunction in women and lack of ejaculatory control in men. Once a woman learns how to reach orgasm through self-stimulation, she can teach her partner the best ways to bring her to orgasm through intercourse. Self-help techniques that help men slow down during masturbation often help them delay ejaculation while making love with a partner (Kelly, 2004).

Behavioral exercises may also be prescribed to help couples enrich and expand their sexual awareness and enjoyment. These exercises include sensate focus, the stop-and-go technique, and the squeeze technique.

- *Sensate focus.* This technique teaches couples how to give each partner pleasure without expecting anything in return. The goal is not sexual arousal or intercourse but education. Each partner directs the other, showing her or him what kinds of touches are the most enjoyable and where the sensitive places are. The exercise helps people learn to communicate better sexually.
- *The stop-and-go technique.* This technique teaches men how to control ejaculation and orgasm. The man's partner manually or orally stimulates his penis until he is just about to ejaculate. Then, the partner stops the stimulation,

*AASECT, P.O. Box 1960, Ashland, VA 23005–1960.

resuming it only when the man is in control. Stimulation and rest may be alternated several times in a session before orgasm and ejaculation are triggered. Repeated sessions over weeks or months help men control rapid or premature ejaculation.

- *The squeeze technique.* In this variation on the stop-and-go technique, when the partner stops stimulating the man's penis, the partner immediately applies pressure to the penis, squeezing it with the thumb and two fingers until there is a tolerable degree of pain. This pattern is repeated seven or eight times until the man learns to tolerate intense stimulation while delaying ejaculation. The squeeze technique further shortens the time it takes to resolve the problem of premature ejaculation (Hyde & DeLamater, 2003).

Summary

- According to a national survey, happily married couples reported that they were satisfied with the affection they receive from their partners, did not have concerns about the partner's interest in sex, were not concerned that the partner was interested in having an affair, felt the partner did not use sex unfairly, and had a more satisfying and fulfilling sexual relationship as compared to unhappily married couples.
- The most commonly reported issues for married couples in terms of their sexual relationship were differing levels of interest in sex between husband and wife, dissatisfaction with the amount of affection received from one's partner, sexual disinterest between partners, difficulty talking about sexual issues, and an inability to keep the sexual relationship interesting and enjoyable.
- Attitudes toward sexuality, including sexual attractiveness and sexual behaviors, vary markedly from one culture to another.
- Sex surveys—such as the University of Chicago study and the AARP study—reveal useful information about the sexual behaviors of Americans.
- More than 25 years after AIDS was first Identified, there Is still no cure; however, new drug treatments have helped people live longer. Those infected with HIV can spread the virus to others because they may not know for years that they are infected.
- The most effective sex education programs are those that encourage abstinence but at the same time offer an alternative of effective contraceptives to those who choose to remain sexually active or become sexually active.
- Few children in the United States receive direct instruction from their parents on sexuality, sexual intercourse, or birth control. However, studies have shown that parental communication may forestall or postpone a child's sexual activity.

- Although sexual activity often decreases after marriage, this decline is not inevitable. Key elements in keeping the sexual relationship vital include communication, commitment, and investing time to enjoy each other.
- The majority of individuals age 45 and older seek healthy and satisfying sex lives. Health issues and medication were cited as reasons for sexual dissatisfaction.
- According to the National Survey of Sex, about 25% of husbands and 15% of wives reported having had an extramarital sexual affair. Infidelity can signal the end of a marriage, but it can also be a catalyst for dramatic and positive growth in the relationship.
- Types of male sexual dysfunctions include erectile dysfunction, premature ejaculation, retarded ejaculation, ejaculatory incompetence, and painful intercourse. Female sexual dysfunctions include vaginismus, anorgasmia, rapid orgasm, and painful intercourse.
- Sex therapy involves a number of different components, including learning more about basic anatomy, learning what one's true feelings are about the body, and discovering one's basic attitudes toward sex and sexuality.

Key Terms

sexuality	human immunodeficiency
heterosexual	virus (HIV)
homosexual	DINS dilemma
bisexual	sexual dysfunction
transgender	organic sexual dysfunction
sexual orientation	psychosocial sexual
sex	dysfunction
gender	erectile dysfunction
incest taboo	premature ejaculation
masturbation	retarded ejaculation

ejaculatory incompetence   rapid orgasm
painful intercourse   sex therapy
vaginismus   sex educator
anorgasmia   sex therapist

Activities

1. Is sex truly everywhere in our society? For a day, keep a log, noting what, when, and where you see or hear something with a sexual theme. Several people in the class can work together and report their findings to the larger group.
2. In small groups, discuss the following situation: You are the parent of a 15-year-old son. He is interested in your views on nonmarital sex. What would you tell him?
3. What are your personal beliefs about nonmarital sexual behavior? Write a brief essay articulating and supporting your views.
4. What are the challenges of being gay or lesbian?

Suggested Readings

AARP. (2005). Sexuality at midlife and beyond. Web site: http://www.aarp.org.

American Association for Marriage and Family Therapy. (2004). AAMFT is the key national organization for advancing the professional interests of marriage and family therapists, and it has excellent educational resources for professionals and laypersons on its Web site: http://www.aamft.org.

Berzon, B. (2004). *Permanent partners: Building gay and lesbian relationships that last* (Rev. ed.). New York: Penguin. Suggestions by a psychotherapist specializing in same-sex relationships for resolving conflicts over power and control, jealousy, differences in sexual desire, money, and family demands.

Blow, A. J., & Hartnett, K. (2005). Infidelity in committed relationships II: A substantive review. *Journal of Marital and Family Therapy, 31,* 217–233.

Brown, E. (2000). *Patterns of infidelity and their treatment.* London: Brunner/Mazel. A seasoned social worker offers her perspectives on affairs.

Centers for Disease Control and Prevention. (2006). *HIV/AIDS surveillance report, 2005, 17.* Atlanta: Author. Web site: http://www.cdc.gov/hiv/topics/surveillance/resources/reports.

Christopher, F. S., & Sprecher, S. (2000). Sexuality in marriage, dating, and other relationships: A decade review. *Journal of Marriage and the Family, 62,* 999–1017. A comprehensive look at research.

Florsheim, P. (Ed.). (2003). *Adolescent romantic relations and sexual behavior: Theory, research, and practical implications.* Mahwah, NJ: Erlbaum. What's wrong with love, and can it be fixed?

Glass, S. P. (2003). Not *"just friends": Protect your relationship from infidelity and heal the trauma of betrayal.* New York: Free Press. Good people in good marriages are having affairs. The most fertile breeding grounds for affairs are in the workplace.

Gordimer, N. (2004). The diamond mine. In *Loot and other stories.* pp. 120–132. New York: Penguin. A touching story of a young woman's first sexual experience, and a funny portrait of how out of touch parents can be in such situations. Gordimer, a South African, won the Nobel Prize in Literature in 1991.

Harvey, J. H. (Ed.). (2004). *The handbook of sexuality in close relationships.* Mahwah, NJ: Erlbaum. Enhances the dialogue about the centrality of sexual issues in close relationships.

Planned Parenthood Federation. (2004). Teen Web site: http://www.teenwire.com. Sexuality and relationship information, including a "note to parents."

Savin-Williams, R. C. (2001). *Mom, dad, I'm gay: How families negotiate coming out.* Washington, DC: American Psychological Association.

Sex Information and Education Council of the U.S. (2004). SIECUS conducts research, disseminates information, promotes comprehensive education about sexuality, and advocates for the right of individuals to make responsible sexual choices. Web site: http://www.siecus.org.

Wincze, J. P., & Carey, M. P. (2001). *Sexual dysfunction: A guide for assessment and treatment* (2nd ed.). Treatment Manuals for Practitioners Series. New York: Guilford. An excellent overview of sex therapy today.

Visit the text-specific Online Learning Center at **www.mhhe.com/Olson6** for practice tests, chapter summaries, Web links, Internet exercises, key terms, and flashcards.

7 *G*ender Roles and Power in the Family

Intimacy, Strengths, and Diversity

Gender Roles

Gender Roles and Marriage

Gender Roles Across Ethnic Groups

Theories About Gender Roles

Power in Families

Summary

Key Terms

Activities

Suggested Readings

Intimacy, Strengths, and Diversity

All animals are equal, but some animals are more equal than others.

—GEORGE ORWELL (1951)

Contemporary models of intimacy stress gender equality in marriage and other types of partnerships. Egalitarianism is the trend among many couples making a serious commitment to each other. But if women continue to make less money for the work they do outside the home and if men continue to avoid child care and household labor, the fabric of intimate relationships is threatened. The fragile bonds of intimacy can easily be damaged when one spouse is subordinate to the other, has more power than the other, or receives less respect and dignity in society.

Individual and couple strengths result when there is equality and a lack of power in important family relationships. This chapter provides a description of some of the gender differences between men and women, along with a discussion about the respective influences of nature and nurture to explain these differences. There are clearly cultural differences when it comes to gender roles. Does that mean strengths cannot exist when relationships are not equal? Or does it mean that there can be gender-role differences, but equal power? We will explore the complexity of gender roles and the quality of relationships in the United States and other cultures.

Gender Roles

The different ways in which men and women behave are linked to, but not necessarily determined by, their biological sex. Individuals are identified as male or female on the basis of physical structures, which are determined by chromosomes, gonads, and hormones. This labeling occurs at birth and is the first step in the process of developing **gender identity**—a sense of being male or female and what that means in one's society.

Although nature determines an individual's sex, culture determines the attitudes and behaviors appropriate for an individual on the basis of her or his sex. In each culture, individuals learn to adapt to these expectations as they shape their personal and professional lives. **Gender roles** are expectations about people's attitudes and behaviors in life based on whether they are male or female. When a child is born, **gender-role stereotypes** come into play. People comment, for example, that he is "a strong, healthy boy" or she is "a darling, adorable girl."

Labeling affects a child's psychological development in a variety of ways. The child begins to adopt personality traits, attitudes, preferences, and behaviors considered appropriate to his or her sex, and these affect how he or she walks, talks, eats, exercises, thinks, and later makes love. The gender-role patterns assigned to males and females influence all our roles in life.

Masculinity is the gender-linked constellation of traits that have been traditionally associated with men; **femininity**, the traits associated with women. In our society, the qualities stereotypically associated with masculinity include aggressiveness, independence, dominance, competence, and a predisposition for math and science. Qualities stereotypically associated with femininity include

Gender-role behaviors are less distinct today than they were in the past. One example is the degree to which girls play on sport teams that were historically restricted to males.

passivity, dependency, sensitivity, emotionality, and a predisposition for art and literature. These stereotypes are destructive because they imply that all males, and only males, have the so-called masculine qualities and that all females, and only females, possess the so-called feminine qualities. Obviously, any human being can have any of these qualities. Socially imposed gender-role stereotypes create inequality by prescribing—based on whether a person is male or female—certain qualities, behaviors, and opportunities and prohibiting or discouraging others.

Language is one of the most powerful tools people use both deliberately and inadvertently to establish and maintain rigid gender roles. The subtle ways we talk about people of the other sex reinforce stereotypes and segregate people by sex. We talk about men and women as being members of the "opposite" sex, reinforcing the notion that men and women are opposites and accentuating the differences rather than affirming the similarities.

Gender-biased language reinforces the misguided notion that men are more competent and rational than women. Terms used for men are more positive and affirming, whereas equivalent terms for women are more negative and degrading. These differences in terminology have an impact on how we perceive and feel about each gender.

Gender Roles and Marriage

The nationwide survey that focused on the strengths of married couples revealed that happy couples agree more often (87%) than unhappy couples (46%) that both partners are equally willing to make adjustments in their marriage (Olson & Olson, 2000). As indicated in Table 7.1, more happy couples (81%) than unhappy couples (41%) believed that both persons are satisfied with the division of housework in their marriage. Happy couples agreed more often (90%) than unhappy couples (54%) that both partners work hard to have an equal relationship. Happy couples also agreed more often (89%) than unhappy couples (57%) that they make most decisions jointly. Finally, this survey found household tasks were divided on the basis of preferences rather than tradition more often in happy couples (71%) than among unhappy couples (55%).

There is an interesting story about the role relationship of Bob and Elizabeth Dole (Fadiman & Bernard, 2000). When Elizabeth Dole was appointed secretary of transportation in 1985, the press was curious about their role relationship because Bob Dole was a senator and she would have a higher political position than him. A photo was taken of them making the bed together, and a man wrote to Bob complaining, "You've got to stop doing the work around the house. You're causing problems for men across the country." Bob responded, "You don't know the half of it. The only reason she was helping was because they were taking pictures." Perhaps his willingness to do more housework contributed to their still being a married couple in spite of all the stress and public scrutiny they are under as a couple.

Based on the national sample of 21,501 married couples, the major role relationship issue that couples faced (49%) was concern about unfair division of the housework (Table 7.2). Less than half of the couples (44%) disagreed on the issue of whether housework was based on tradition versus their interests. Another common problem (44%) was that the husband was not willing to adjust as much as the wife. They also disagreed (43%) about how much the wife handled housework, even though she worked outside the home. About 40% disagreed that they both worked to maintain an equal relationship.

TABLE 7.1	Role Relationships in Happy Versus Unhappy Married Couples	
	PERCENTAGE IN AGREEMENT	
Role Issues	**Happy Couples**	**Unhappy Couples**
1. Both are equally willing to make adjustments in marriage.	87%	46%
2. Both are satisfied with the division of housework.	81	41
3. Both work hard to have an equal relationship.	90	54
4. Couples make most decisions jointly.	89	57
5. Household tasks are divided on the basis of preferences, not tradition.	71	55

Source: Adapted from Olson & Olson, 2000.

TABLE 7.2	Top Five Role Relationship Issues for Married Couples	
		Percentage
		(*n* = 21,501 Couples)
1. Concern about unfair division of housework.		49%
2. Housework is based on traditional roles versus interests.		44
3. The husband is not willing to adjust as much as the wife.		44
4. Women are responsible for running the household in addition to working outside the home.		43
5. Disagree that both work to maintain an equal relationship.		40

Source: Adapted from Olson & Olson, 2000.

Distribution of Family Work by Gender

Extensive research has been carried out in the past several years about gender and the division of labor in the household. A summary of current findings (Meier, McNaughton-Cassill, & Lynch, 2006) include the following:

- Husbands and wives have both decreased the total number of hours spent on housework.
- Wives still do almost two-thirds of the work compared to husbands.
- Having children makes the imbalance even greater.
- Mothers spend twice as much time caring for their children as fathers.
- Even though fathers spend more time with children today than in the past, they still are often seen as "helpers" in providing care for their children.
- Perceptions of fairness regarding the division of household responsibilities are a more likely predictor of marital discord than actual behavior.

Husbands and wives disagree about how much housework each spouse does (Lee & Waite, 2005). These researchers found that wives typically make accurate estimates of husbands' time spent on housework, and husbands overestimated the time they spent. In addition, wives think they spend 13 hours more on housework each week, and husbands see the gap as only half as large. In addition, they found that wives overestimated the numbers of hours worked in the home. These authors concluded that what happens with housework depends on who you ask, and this gap in perception can lead to marital conflict. The authors also concluded that wives, in fact, do 9.4 hours more housework per week than their husbands, and the husbands perform about 40% of the work in the home.

Emotion Work in Marriage and Family Life

Although most research in marriages relating to gender has focused on housework and care of children, recent research has conceptualized emotion work in families (Erickson, 2005). Emotion work, according to this author, includes such things as listening closely to their spouse's thoughts and feelings, recognizes feelings, offers encouragement, and shows appreciation. Women are deliberate about paying attention to the emotional well-being of other family members. This author concluded that emotion work is a gender issue and looks different to men and women, in that women see emotion work as part of their family work role and they recognize that they are held accountable for performing this work in their families.

Other researchers talk about mental work that happens in families, and this work is also divided unequally, with women performing more mental work than men (Meier et al., 2006). Mental work includes worrying about children and household tasks, planning and monitoring children's activities, seeking solutions to child care problems, and managing the division of labor and the delegation of tasks (Meier et al., 2006). This mental work is invisible and is very difficult to measure, but it is estimated that women are doing most of the mental work in families. Meier and colleagues also indicate that the unequal division of mental work affects women's marital satisfaction but not men's marital satisfaction.

Two Gallup Surveys of Male and Female Traits

In a Gallup poll (2001) of how Americans see males and females, the words that most often were used by both sexes to describe males were aggressive, courageous, and ambitious. Females were most often described by both sexes as emotional, affectionate, talkative, patient, and creative. In 6 out of 10 traits, both genders agreed about the traits for males and females. The one that they both agreed applies more to one gender is men are more aggressive. The three traits that differed by less than 20% were ambitious, easygoing, and intelligent. Table 7.3 provides a summary of the differences on the major traits survey. It is clear that in most ways both sexes see the major traits of men and women as different.

In an international survey of 22 countries, the Gallup poll (1996) found conventional stereotypes of women and men. Women were perceived as more affectionate, emotional, talkative, and patient than men. In the United States, 76% of those surveyed considered women to be the more affectionate sex; only 6% named men the more affectionate. When asked which sex is the more emotional, 88% said women, and only 4% said men. Men were perceived across cultures as being more aggressive, ambitious, and courageous than women. In most cultures, women and men were perceived to be equally intelligent.

Although none of the 10 traits surveyed was seen solely as male or female, the trait considered predominantly male was aggressiveness. The country with the highest margin was China, where 81% identified aggression as most characteristic of men and only 3% as most characteristic of women, a difference of 78 points. The

TABLE 7.3	Traits of Males and Females from Gallup Poll		
Trait	**More True of Men**	**More True of Women**	**Advantage for Men**
1. Aggressive	68%	20%	+48%
2. Courageous	50	27	+ 23
3. Ambitious	44	33	+ 11
4. Easygoing	55	48	+ 7
5. Intelligent	21	36	− 15
6. Creative	15	65	− 50
7. Patient	19	72	− 53
8. Talkative	10	78	− 68
9. Affectionate	5	86	− 81
10. Emotional	3	90	− 87

Source: Gallup poll (Dec. 2000). © 2000 The Gallup Organization. All rights reserved. Reprinted with permission.

A person's sex is biologically determined, but the abilities, behaviors, activities, social roles, and other characteristics that are considered appropriate for males and females are determined by one's culture.

differences favoring men were 58 points for the United States and 60 points for Canada and Great Britain. Both men and women across most of the 22 countries surveyed tended to agree with the opinions reported here.

A consistent finding across hundreds of studies is that men of different ages, with different ethnic backgrounds and income levels, are less likely than women to seek professional help for physical and emotional problems (Addis & Mahalik, 2003). Even though women outlive men by an average of 7 years and have lower rates of most deadly diseases, men still do not typically seek outside help for their problems. Men are also much less likely to seek help for emotional and drug- related problems, even though they have higher rates than women (Addis & Mahalik, 2003).

Traditional Versus Contemporary Views of Gender Roles

In the traditional view of gender roles in our society, males are assumed to be superior to females and to have characteristics that are more desirable. The contemporary view holds that neither males nor females are superior; both have desirable—and undesirable—traits not based specifically on sex.

To counter the traditional view of men and women in our society, humorist Garrison Keillor ends his radio show *A Prairie Home Companion* with the statement that in Lake Wobegon: "All the women are strong, all the men are good looking, and all the children are above average" (Keillor, 2005).

A Traditional View. The traditional view of gender roles in our society grew out of our male-oriented culture, but specific theories have been put forth in its support. One of the best known is that of sociologist Talcott Parsons (1955, 1965), whose theory of the family assumed that highly contrasting gender roles were essential for families and society. Parsons believed that, in this modern family, society required that men be "instrumental" and women be "expressive." The man's instrumental role was to be the breadwinner, the manager, and the leader of the family. The

Box 7.1   At Issue

The Work–Family Interface

Much of the current gender research is centered on dual career couples as they balance their family and work lives. It is appropriate, then, that we explain what the work–family interface looks like.

Managing the responsibilities of work and family life began to be an issue for researchers in the 1970s, as women increasingly entered the workforce. At that time, approximately one-third of women with children under the age of 6 worked outside the home (Halpern, 2005; Raley, Mattingly, & Bianchi, 2006). The issues of work and family in the 1970s focused primarily on how to manage work and child care responsibilities (Halpern, 2005). Researchers found that women became employed but also continued to be the major caretakers of children and other domestic responsibilities.

The numbers of women with children in the workforce has increased dramatically. Approximately 50% to 66% of heterosexual couples, with and without children, are both employed today (Haddock, Zimmerman, Ziemba, & Lyness, 2006; Meier et al., 2006; Winslow, 2005).

Work-to-Family Influence

When we think about balancing work and family issues, we usually think about the effects of one's work life on one's family life. Work and family researchers often think about the multiple issues work places on family time and include such things as time-based demands and strain-based demands. Time-based demands focus on the idea that time at work means there is less time for family (Voydanoff, 2005). Therefore, when a person works extra hours, does shift work, or travels extensively, there is likely to be less time with the family. In addition, there are often strain-based demands that affect family life. Strain-based demands include such things as job insecurity, workload pressures, time pressures, or dealing with a demanding supervisor. Both time-based demands and strain-based demands have significant effects on family life.

Certainly there are times when both time-based demands and strain-based demands enter into one's work life. For example, when companies go through cycles of downsizing, which has happened in the past several years, employers will decrease the workforce with added responsibilities and longer hours for the workers who remain. In addition, there is the fear of additional downsizing, which also adds stress to the work environment. These stresses together can cause psychological spillover to the family (Voydanoff, 2005)

Family-to-Work Influence

Family-to-work influence refers to how family demands affect work performance (Voydanoff, 2005). The family demands drain one of time and energy to do well at work

woman's expressive role was to take care of the emotional well-being of the family through nurturing and comforting. Parsons saw these two roles as separate, one to be performed by the husband and the other by the wife.

Parsons's theory, which has been attacked by numerous critics, is no longer considered valid. His critics charged that it was a mistake to assume that the traditional family structure was both a universal and necessary social institution—that only this traditional family structure could fulfill the needs of the individuals within the family and of the greater society. They further argued that Parsons's theory focused on the positive aspects of this traditional family structure but deemphasized potential problems. The traditional model emphasized stability rather than change, focused on harmony rather than conflict, and identified function but ignored dysfunction. Parsons's theory also tended to stereotype masculine and feminine traits, reinforcing differences and denigrating women.

A More Contemporary View. Today, it is more commonly assumed that both sexes are capable and can be successful in a variety of roles at home and at work. Women can be independent, strong, logical, and task oriented; men can be nurturing, sensitive, cooperative, and detail oriented. However, men and women can ben-

and affect one's ability to take advantage of opportunities to advance or take on more responsibilities. The behaviors that might be evident at work because of family demands include such things as absenteeism and lack of ability to concentrate on work tasks.

When family stresses occur at home such as marital issues or divorce, child behavior problems, financial difficulties, or a death, there is less energy for one's work life. For example, a couple may be having marital difficulties. This couple may be fighting more often and constantly feeling stressed over what might happen to the marriage and family life. There is little rest, relaxation, and sleep. Because of the stress the couple is experiencing, there is less quality time for children, and the children feel the stress about what might happen to their family. As a result, the children's behavior deteriorates, and now there is even more stress in the family. As one can imagine, the adults in the family have very little energy for their work. According to Voydanoff (2005), there is a reciprocal and positive relationship between work and family life. It seems that when things go well at work, it positively affects family life, and when family life is positive, a person is more productive at work.

Current Issues That Affect Work and Family Life

Being part of a dual career family is very different today than it was in the 1970s. Today, people are living longer, and, in addition to caring for their own children, they are also likely to be caring for aging parents (Halpern, 2005). For example, approximately 50% of working adults plan to assume significant caregiving responsibilities for aging relatives during the next 5 years, and many more are already doing so. Although women are most likely to provide such care, approximately 25% of care is provided by men.

Currently, there are also more family forms than in previous years (Halpern, 2005). For example, there are stepfamilies, single-parent families, same-sex couples, cohabiting couples with children, and grandparents raising grandchildren. These family forms make the work and family relationship even more complex. A single parent balancing work and family will experience different stresses than a two-parent couple. In addition, there are cultural values with new and growing diverse populations that might view the work and family relationship very differently than is described by previous research (Halpern, 2005). For example, members of diverse cultures may utilize extended-family members as a source of childcare, which would affect the stress experienced by a dual-earner couple.

efit by learning from each other: Men can learn the value of being more sensitive and caring from women; women can learn the value of independence from men; and both can learn to work together and become interdependent.

Women may be at an advantage in this more cooperative approach to living. Traditional culture has encouraged them to be good listeners and to be empathic, understanding, helpful, and supportive. These caring values fit well with the more cooperative approaches to group decision making that are gaining strength at home and at work.

See Box 7.1 for a closer look at the work–family interface.

The Move Toward More Egalitarian Roles

American society in many ways is moving away from male dominance and toward **egalitarian roles** (also called *equalitarian roles*)—social equality between the sexes. The process of change has been long and fraught with controversy. The struggle not only occurs in society but is also played out each day in close relationships. Table 7.4 highlights some differences between traditional dating and marriage patterns and more contemporary practices. Looking back through the generations of one's own family illustrates how dramatically times have changed.

Working parents are under increasing stress as they try to balance time for their career and family. Too often, the marriage is what suffers.

TABLE 7.4	Contemporary Versus Traditional Dating and Marriage Patterns

Contemporary	Traditional
Both women and men initiate dates.	The man initiates dates.
The woman keeps her maiden name after marriage.	The woman takes the man's last name.
The partners cohabit before marriage.	The partners live apart before marriage.
Premarital sex is expected.	Premarital sex is not an option.
Both partners continue their education.	The wife supports the husband through school.
The birth of a child might precede marriage.	Children are conceived after marriage.
Both partners work, and both may have careers.	The husband's work is the priority.
Roles are flexible.	Roles are rigid.
Both partners share child care.	The mother is responsible for child care.
Both partners initiate sex.	The husband initiates sex.
Both partners select the couple's friends.	The husband's friends become the couple's friends.

Gender-role stereotypes limit people's choices by dictating what they are believed to be able to do. Today, however, it is more commonly assumed in the United States that both sexes are capable and can be successful in a variety of roles at home and at work.

One of the most telling indexes of change is the decline of the double standard, the social convention allowing men more sexual and social freedom than women. Women are claiming more freedom for themselves, although some don't realize or acknowledge they are doing so. A number of social scientists have commented that today many women shy away from calling themselves nontraditional or feminist but are clearly living very different lives than their mothers or grandmothers. What is apparently happening is that as women's roles change, the definition of *traditional* also changes.

An International Perspective

Perhaps the classic description of how gender roles are rooted in culture comes from anthropologist Margaret Mead. In *Sex and Temperament in Three Primitive Societies,* Mead (1935) looked at "maleness" and "femaleness" in three New Guinea tribes: the Arapesh, the Mundugumor, and the Tchambuli. In American society, two traditional attributes of females are gentleness and unaggressiveness. Among the Arapesh, Mead found both the women *and* the men to be unaggressive. Not far away, among the Mundugumor tribe, Mead found that both males and females displayed an aggressiveness that Americans would characterize as traditionally masculine. In both the Arapesh and the Mundugumor tribes, Mead found little contrast in temperament between the sexes.

© King Features Syndicate. Reprinted with permission.

The third New Guinea tribe Mead studied provided further evidence of cross-cultural differences. Among the Tchambuli, both men and women behaved in ways that are opposite to traditional behavior in Western societies. Tchambuli women were independent and aggressive, acting like traditional Western men; Tchambuli men were gentle and sensitive, like traditional Western women. Mead's conclusion was that the varieties in temperament she observed among these three "primitive" societies were not dictated by biology but were largely the creations of the societies.

Mead's conclusion has been vigorously debated since it was published. Psychologist David Buss believes, for example, that innate biological differences between males and females have more to do with the differences in their social behavior than the culture in which they live. He devised a questionnaire asking people to describe their ideal mate in five categories: earning capacity, industriousness, youth, physical attractiveness, and chastity. Buss then administered the questionnaire to 37 groups of men and women in 33 different societies around the world. Even though they came from different geographic and cultural areas, the people Buss surveyed consistently expressed the same patterns of preference. Females placed greater value on wealth and ambition, and males were more interested in signs of youth and fertility. Finding a mate who was a "good financial prospect" was more important to females in 36 of 37 groups. "Good looks" were more important to males than to females in all 37 groups (cited in Cowley, 1989, p. 56).

A comprehensive survey of gender roles and the family, the Gallup poll (1996) surveyed men and women in 22 countries with a combined population of 3.05 billion, or 53% of the world's population. The survey included countries in North America, South America, Europe, and Asia. The sampling error in the results is within 3 percentage points (plus or minus). Residents of nearly two-thirds of the countries polled felt that their society was biased toward men. In 15 countries, either a majority or a plurality of those surveyed said that society favors men over women. Countries in greatest agreement that society favors men are Japan (78%), Germany (76%), Iceland (76%), France (76%), the United States (73%), and Great Britain (72%). In seven countries, including El Salvador (63%), China (53%), and Thailand (52%), the consensus leaned more toward the belief that men and women are treated equally.

The survey showed some potential for change, however, because in five countries, about half those surveyed resented the gender-role expectations their society placed on them (Gallup poll, 1996). Those countries are Germany (52%), Japan

Box 7.2　Diversity in Families

Gender Roles in Japan

To understand the complex topic of power and gender roles in families in Japan, it is necessary to understand both the social system and the family system. The following overview, which applies to middle- and upper-class urban Japanese families, is provided by Shuji Asai (2004), a Japanese family therapist.

At the societal system level, Japanese culture is patriarchal. The male dominates; he plays the instrumental role in society and tends to be married to his work. Although women make up about 40% of the labor force in Japan, they face discrimination in terms of wages, assignments, and promotions.

Although Japanese society is patriarchal, the Japanese family is more of a matriarchal system, with the mother dominating. This is particularly true of child rearing and finances. Although the husband brings home the money, the wife controls it, often deciding how much spending money the husband receives each month. The woman's

financial power also entails making decisions about when and where to invest and how much to pay for a house or remodeling.

In most Japanese families, family cohesion and family communication are also controlled by the mother. Japanese mothers often develop a very strong emotional connection with their children and serve as the communication link between the children and the father; the father may remain disengaged from the family. As a result, the mother dominates the family system, and the father emphasizes his role at work.

Today, more Japanese women are seeking professional careers, and more are delaying marriage and even remaining single. These changes are moving Japan toward a more egalitarian society and are demanding that men and women renegotiate their traditional gender roles at work and at home.

(52%), Thailand (52%), Chile (46%), and Panama (46%). In those five countries, at least half the women and more than 40% of the men expressed resentment. (See Box 7.2, which focuses on Japan's traditional yet evolving gender roles.)

Gender Roles Across Ethnic Groups

What would it be like to have not only color vision but culture vision, the ability to see the multiple worlds of others?

—Mary Catherine Bateson (1994, p. 53)

It is commonly believed that gender roles do not spring from innate characteristics individuals possess. Rather, they are learned behaviors, rooted in the social context of the particular culture in which people live. The gender roles women and men play vary widely from culture to culture. This section examines some examples of cultural gender-role differences in the United States.

Mexican American Culture

Mexican American males are often stereotyped as being *macho*. Male exhibitions of aggressiveness—*machismo*—include bossing women around, being abusive to them, and having numerous extramarital affairs. But this macho attitude is not supported in the research literature (Vega, 1995). Even though some Mexican American males act macho, this is not the predominant pattern for this group. Researchers have found that warm, nurturing, and egalitarian male behavior is more likely in marriages in which the wife is employed, although it is also demonstrated in many more traditional marriages.

There are different interpretations as to why some Mexican American males display machismo (Falicov, 1996). One viewpoint holds that machismo is an unconscious attempt to overcompensate for feelings of inferiority, powerlessness, and inadequacy. This inferiority springs from the fact that the man's Mexican ancestors were conquered by Spaniards (Whites), producing a "hybrid Mexican people having an inferiority complex based on the mentality of a conquered people" (Baca-Zinn, 1995). Intermingling of the various cultures over the centuries produced a nation of mostly *mestizo* (mixed-"race") people.

Men are capable of exhibiting a macho, or aggressive, attitude as a way of asserting their need for respect and dignity (Falicov, 1996). Macho behavior becomes less acceptable when it attempts to deny the inherent rights of other family members, particularly women.

African American Culture

African American men may have an advantage over White men in developing and integrating the "feminine" qualities that foster egalitarian relationships with women. According to one African American scholar, displaying dominant, aggressive behavior in the greater society carries considerable risk for African American males. As a consequence,

> Black male socialization includes a range of very positive results that young white men do not typically experience. From peers, for instance, young black men learn the concepts of "brother" and "blood"—a deep sense of identification with other black men that cuts across age, class, and geography. . . . From the women who raise us, black men learn firsthand to respect the strength of so-called feminine qualities—intuition, warmth, cooperation, and empathy. (Franklin, 1989, p. 278)

One of the complexities in gender roles for African American families is that many African American men have been marginalized in their roles as a provider and as a marital partner (Hines & Boyd-Franklin, 1996). African American males have often grown up in single-parent homes where they do not have a male model to learn from. However, in a study of African American marriages, it was found that they have a very similar role relationship as compared with Caucasian marriages (Allen & Olson, 2001). African American marriages were most often egalitarian where the couple shared responsibilities and worked together to provide for their family.

Many African American women see feminism from a different perspective than do White women. African American women have rarely served only in the housewife role because economic circumstances have dictated that they work outside the home. African American women are also acutely aware of the disadvantages African American men have faced over the years, making it difficult for them to adopt a wholeheartedly feminist agenda. The dilemma: Am I more oppressed as a woman or as an African American? Because these two factors converge for African American women, life can be especially difficult for them.

American Indian Culture

Native American women confront many of the same problems that African American women face in American society (Sutton & Broken Nose, 1996). Native American cultures in the United States vary widely, but some are identified by a matrilineal tradition in which women owned or still own houses, tools, and agricultural land. Over the past three decades, there have been signs that American Indian women are beginning to regain some of the power and prestige they had historically. In 1985, a woman was elected chief of the Cherokee Nation, signifying "a revitalization of the role of women" in that tribe. In the 1986 Navajo elections, women won 72 of 327 local offices, and 62% of Navajo tribal scholarships were awarded to women (Robbins, 1987).

Many Native American families also face racism, unemployment, poverty, and the abuse of alcohol and other drugs (Sutton & Broken Nose, 1996). Native American women play an important role in keeping the family and the tribe together. Some tribal traditions make it difficult for Native American women to attain leadership roles, and some tribes have religious beliefs against both contraception and abortion. But it has also been argued that tribal traditions are a source of strength for American Indian women.

The value orientation of Native Americans has considerable impact on why role relationships in their culture are more complex and less clearly defined (Sutton & Broken Nose, 1996). Native Americans emphasize communal living rather than a nuclear family and communal sharing rather than focusing on individual possessions. As one tribal member commented, "When I was little, I learned very early that what's yours is mine and what's mine is everybody's" (Sutton & Broken Nose, 1996, p. 40). Native Americans also have a tribal identity that puts a high value on the group. Time is also seen differently by Native Americans in that it is cyclical rather than linear, so minutes and hours are less important than seasonal rhythms. In summary, these cultural values greatly influence their lifestyle and how they function as a group.

Wilma Mankiller, former chief of the Cherokee Nation, was the first woman ever elected to that position. Her election reflected the growing power of women in some Native American tribes.

Asian American Culture

Asian American families have been very successful in the U.S. culture. They value education highly, and they have the highest family income of any ethnic group. They value tradition and respect their elders (called *filial piety*), and their children are well disciplined (Lee, 1996).

Sex roles are very segregated so that the woman is very connected to the children, and the husband is most highly connected to his work. As a result, there is a very strong mother–child bond and a weak husband–wife bond (Asai, 2004). While marriage is important in Asian families, it is usually not as strong as the family system. Fathers tend be mainly involved with providing the economic base and are typically not very involved with child rearing. A Japanese family therapist described the communication in Japanese families as generally weak with the exception being the mother–child relationship (Vosburg, 2004).

In a study of 849 premarital couples in Japan, it was found that while both the male and the female had a traditional role orientation, the women were more traditional than the males (Asai, 2004). These premarital couples had a clear awareness of the importance of issues related to living arrangements and care of their parents as they age. These premarital couples had more conflict and less awareness of potential issues than premarital couples in the United States.

Theories About Gender Roles

Theorists interested in gender roles have focused on how children acquire gender-role identity during the early years of life and how changes in gender-role identity occur. Some observers believe that changes in gender-role identity are possible after early childhood, but it is generally assumed that once gender-role identity is formed, it remains stable and continues throughout adulthood. Four theories about gender-role development and change are described here: the social learning theory, the cognitive development theory, the family systems theory, and the feminist framework.

Social Learning Theory

The **social learning theory** is concerned with how individuals learn the behavior patterns considered appropriate for their sex. Social learning researchers have particularly focused on direct observation of behavior and how people reinforce each other's behavior. Early in life, reinforcement of sex-related behavior by others is of primary importance. As individuals grow and develop, they assess personal situations and develop standards and rules by which to live. In the case of gender roles, individuals begin as very young children to internalize the standards and rules for being a boy or a girl in our society.

Social learning theorist Jerome Kagan (1964) argued that children at a young age dichotomize the world as female versus male and have a strong desire to match their own personal characteristics with the gender-role standards they learn from parents and society in general. Kagan believed that all children want to develop a gender-typed identity and that they see variations from the gender-traditional ideal as failures. He noted that certain aspects of gender-role standards cause unnecessary anxiety and restrictions for individuals, and he proposed that perhaps these standards should be changed.

Cognitive Development Theory

The **cognitive development theory** links gender-role development (the progressive acquisition of gender typing) to the more general maturation of the child's thinking processes. Lawrence Kohlberg (1966), the developer of this theory, argued that children themselves actively create gender identity, gender-role stereotypes, and values in their minds in their efforts to understand the world around them (e.g., "I can't do that! Only boys do that!"). He argued that the stereotypes do not necessarily become more rigid over time but follow a curvilinear pattern. In early childhood, the stereotypes develop quickly and are quite rigid. When the child realizes that not all gender-typed characteristics (hair, clothes, sports, etc.) are crucial to maintaining gender identity, the child's thinking becomes less rigid. With increasing maturity, the child learns that variations are possible and becomes more flexible in his or her thinking.

Paul Mussen (1969) synthesized social learning and cognitive processes in looking at gender-role development. Mussen noted that labeling occurs early in the child's life and that the child must see the label as positive, rewarding, lovingly applied, and accepted by the labeler. This linkage between the label and love and acceptance helps motivate the child to perform gender-typed behaviors.

Both the social learning and cognitive development theories have been attacked in recent years. First, critics argue that these early theories erred by assuming that children of the same sex develop very similar gender-role identities (masculine for boys and feminine for girls). In fact, many boys engage in traditionally feminine behaviors, and many girls engage in traditionally masculine behaviors.

Second, the early theories were criticized for characterizing the traditional gender-role identities as desirable and a divergence from the norm as deviant. Today, many children enjoy the freedom to engage in a broad range of activities, despite the dictates of tradition.

Third, the theories were criticized for assuming that early childhood is a critical period in gender-role development and that an adult's gender-role characteristics spring directly from early-childhood experiences. Dramatic changes in gender-role

Among earlier generations of American women, relatively few had the opportunity to learn skills traditionally assigned to men. Today, people are not limited as much by gender-role stereotypes, though barriers still remain for those who cross traditional gender lines.

behavior can take place later in life such as a female homemaker going back to school to become a lawyer and a male engineer retiring early to take care of the home and garden while his spouse begins a new career outside the home. Subsequent theorists have explored human development after childhood and suggest that individuals retain the capacity for growth and change in their gender-role identity.

Family Systems Theory

Family systems theory, as presented in Chapter 1, suggests that the family functions as an interconnected system. A change in one family member necessitates compensatory changes in other family members if the family is to achieve a new balance.

According to family systems theory, change is a difficult process for both individuals and families. If the individual is successful in growing in new directions, sometimes other family members will attempt to bring the individual back "into the fold."

Consider, for example, a young woman who desires more independence in a family wanting to maintain traditional family roles. The daughter feels stifled by the family's long list of rules and beliefs and finds support in feminist writings and rhetoric, but when she expresses her views, her parents react emotionally. "Are you telling me my life has been worthless?" her more traditional mother asks. "Those damned feminists!" her father sputters. Her mother becomes defensive because she has made a career of her children and her marriage. Her father becomes defensive because he feels he has done the right thing by supporting his wife and children.

Family systems that are balanced (on the Couple and Family Map; see Chapter 3) tend to be more open to change and are more supportive of independence in family members. In contrast, some types of unbalanced family systems, particularly rigidly enmeshed types, are resistant to change and restrict independence in family members.

Feminist Framework

Traditional gender-role patterns—stressing the differences between men and women, masculinity and femininity—have been criticized by many observers of American society since the 1960s, including feminists. The gender-role constraints under which men and women traditionally have lived have been revised considerably. Many women are doing things their mothers would not have deemed possible. Many men are also gaining the freedom to function outside the traditional boundaries of masculinity. Making these profound changes in life is a struggle, and it would be difficult—if not impossible—for many people to go back to the traditional patterns.

Feminist scholars have focused on the contributions that women have made to society (Fox & Murry, 2000). Feminists point out that, although women have made countless contributions to culture and to human life, the omission of these achievements from the historical record reflects the low status in which women have been held in society. Feminists point out that women have been exploited, devalued, and oppressed. In addition, as a result of their own experiences, feminists tend to be sensitive to other oppressed people.

Another focus of feminists is a commitment to change the conditions of women. Feminists strive to empower women by documenting oppression so that people recognize it when they see and experience it. Feminists take an affirming stance toward women, challenging the status quo of devaluation (see Box 7.3, which

Box 7.3   At Issue

Gender Inequality as a Global Problem

Thanks in large part to the work of feminists and activists around the world, gender roles have broadened, and many constraints about what is possible and/or appropriate for men and women to do have been lifted in many places. However, even in contemporary American society, the reality is that gender inequality continues.

In 1963, the U.S. Congress passed the Equal Pay Act to "prohibit discrimination on account of sex in the payment of wages by employers engaged in commerce or in the production of goods for commerce."

The act was intended to level the playing field for men and women in the workplace. However, the AFL-CIO and the Institute for Women's Policy Research (1999) found that working families in the United States lose more than $200 billion each year because of the wage gap between men and women, which amounts to an average of $4,000 per year per family.

According to a report published by the U.S. Department of Labor (2003), American women were paid 77 cents for every dollar men received. For minority women, the figures were even worse: African American women earned 70 cents for every dollar men earned, and Latinas only 58 cents.

This kind of gender inequality is by no means exclusive to the United States. In Scotland, for example, the Scottish Trade Union Congress found that as of November 2004, women earned, on average, 19% less than men, and in one city—Aberdeen—the discrepancy was closer to 30% in favor of men in the same job (BBC News, 2004).

The United Nations International Labour Office (2004b), in a report titled "Global Employment Trends for Women 2004," estimated that in 2003 there were 2.8 billion workers around the world, of whom 1.1 billion—or 40%—were women. This represented an increase of nearly 200 million over the past decade. The United Nations International Labour Office (2004a) concluded that women's share of managerial positions in more than 60 countries ranges between 20% and 40%—a figure that has remained the same since 2001.

In almost every country in the world, women are responsible for most of the unpaid, "nonmarket" work. In most societies, women care for the children, the elderly, and the ailing. Women do most of the household chores, which in developing countries can mean walking many miles to fetch water and firewood.

Of course, gender inequality—which exists in every part of the world—isn't limited to gaps in earnings. In an essay published in *Frontline* (India's national magazine), Nobel laureate Amarta Sen (2001) delineated seven kinds of disparity between men and women:

1. *Mortality inequality.* In some areas of the world (e.g., North Africa and Asia), women suffer unusually high mortality rates due to gender bias in health care and nutrition.
2. *Natality inequality.* Where boys are considered more desirable than girls, modern technology can determine the gender of the fetus, and the pregnancy can be terminated if it is a girl. Sex-selective abortion has become a common practice in China, South Korea, Singapore, Taiwan, and several other areas of the world.
3. *Basic institutional inequality.* In many countries women are denied access to education and other social and cultural institutions.
4. *Special opportunity inequality.* In some countries where women do have access to *basic* education, they are denied access to higher education and/or professional training.
5. *Professional inequality.* Even in countries where special opportunities exist, women often encounter great difficulties trying to gain and advance in managerial positions.
6. *Ownership inequality.* In many societies it is very difficult, if not impossible, for women to own land or homes, thus making it much harder for them to become economically independent.
7. *Household inequality.* Family arrangements in most cultures place the burden of unpaid work squarely on women's shoulders and take for granted that, whether they work outside the home or not, they will perform such duties as child care and housework.

One positive note is that many countries exhibiting a high degree of gender inequality are initiating government-led programs to try to reduce the gender gap. However, because gender bias has such a long cultural history and appears on so many fronts, the process ahead to overcome it will no doubt take many more years to accomplish.

describes one woman's struggle against gender inequality). This affirmation of women does not imply a rejection of men or all things masculine. Instead, both men and women are accorded equal respect and value.

According to feminists, the boxes males and females are put in are too simple and too idealistic. In practice, many individuals—both men and women—feel stifled by the roles they have been assigned and have sought a way to transform the traditional family. The following poem by Nancy R. Smith sums it up nicely:

> For every woman who is tired of acting weak when she knows she is strong,
>
> There is a man who is tired of appearing strong when he feels vulnerable.
>
> For every woman who is tired of acting dumb,
>
> There is a man who is burdened with the constant expectations of "knowing everything."
>
> For every woman who is tired of being called an "emotional female,"
>
> There is a man who is denied the right to weep and be gentle.
>
> For every woman who feels "tied down" by her children,
>
> There is a man who is denied the full pleasures of shared parenthood.
>
> For every woman who takes a step toward her own liberation,
>
> There is a man who finds the way to freedom has been made a little easier.

Power in Families

The fundamental concept in social science is Power, in the same sense in which Energy is the fundamental concept in physics.

—BERTRAND RUSSELL

The words *family* and *power* are inextricably linked. Power, control, and authority are continuously exercised in families, and struggles for personal power in families are exceedingly common. Tradition has dictated that considerable power go to the males in the family, but women often have more power than they or anyone else admit.

Power is defined as the ability (potential or actual) of an individual to change the behavior of other members in a social system (Olson & Cromwell, 1975, p. 5). By extending this definition to families, we can define **family power** as the ability of one family member to change the behavior of the other family members.

Many of the characteristics of power in close relationships were summarized by Kathleen M. Galvin and Bernard J. Brommel (1986, p. 123). Power is a system property—a feature of a family system—rather than a personal characteristic of any one family member. Power is an interactive process involving one family member who desires something from one or more other family members; these members may affect all other members in the system. Power is also a dynamic process, not a static one. It creates reciprocal causation (i.e., family members react to power attempts) in which one move leads to another, which leads to another, and so forth. Power also changes over time, particularly when the family is under stress. Power has both perceptual and behavioral aspects: The same power issue may be perceived differently by each family member.

Educational level, occupational prestige, and income are all sources of power in our society—and in relationships as well. This college graduate is very likely to have more power in a marriage relationship than a high school graduate who chooses the role of full-time homemaker and mother.

The Three Faces of Power

Many disciplines have attempted to understand power, but it has proven to be a complex and elusive concept. "In the entire lexicon of sociological concepts, none is more troublesome than the concept of power. We may say about it in general only what St. Augustine said about time, that we all know perfectly well what it is—until someone asks us" (Bierstedt, 1950).

Three major aspects of power have consistently emerged in understanding couples and family power. These three areas can be considered different faces of power and they are bases of family power, family power processes, and family power outcomes (Olson & Cromwell, 1975).

Several important questions emerge when you try to assess couple and family power. Each of these areas can assess a different and important aspect of power, and yet there is no one single best way to identify power in relationships. Consider the following questions:

- Is power the actual ability to influence another person's behavior, or is it just the potential ability to do so?
- Is power an intentional or an unintentional process?
- Is power both overt and covert?
- Is power who decides or who does an activity?
- Is power who decides, or is it who decides who decides?
- Is power a process or an outcome?
- Does a power struggle mean there is a winner or loser, or is it possible for both individuals to win or lose?

Bases of Family Power. Interest in the study of family power by family-focused social and behavioral scientists was sparked by Robert Blood and Don Wolfe's classic study *Husbands and Wives* (1960), which developed a **resource theory of family**

power. The researchers argued that the balance of power in a marriage is related to the relative resources each spouse has in that relationship. Blood and Wolfe focused on the resources of money, educational level, and occupational prestige and found that these were statistically related to the extent of the husband's perceived power in the marriage. In short, whoever has the most resources in the relationship has the most power.

Recent studies of dual working households and also those where the woman makes more money than the husband have found that women's power has not increased proportionally to the increase in their income and job status (Tichenor, 1999). This is generally because women are less willing to take advantage of their growing contributions to the household income.

Some social scientists have argued that power in families is a function of more than income, education, and occupation. People find value in many different things, including intelligence, pleasing personality traits, personal appearance, skill in various areas of endeavor, social prestige, a sense of humor, and interpersonal skills. One husband, speaking of his intelligent, well-educated, professionally successful wife, half-jokingly admits that a big part of the power she has over him stems from her personality. The wife, on the other hand, says that one of her husband's most powerful resources is his sense of humor: "He's crazy, I admit. But he sure is entertaining!" The ability to make a partner laugh often translates into power in a relationship.

An important nonmaterial resource that needs to be considered in any discussion of power is the individual's interest in maintaining the relationship. This *principle of least interest* was described by Waller (1951), who believed that the individual who is least interested in maintaining the relationship has the most power. If one person is more dependent than the other or is more concerned about keeping the relationship alive, the most-interested partner is likely to defer to the least-interested partner. In short, the least-interested partner will have more power. Even if the least-interested partner does not exploit the situation, he or she will be more powerful, and this is likely to be demonstrated in a variety of subtle and not-so-subtle ways.

Other researchers have approached the bases of family power in a somewhat more abstract way. Raven, Centers, and Rodrigues (1975) identified six bases of power. *Legitimate power*, also called authority, is based on an individual's legitimate or normatively prescribed right to change another's behavior. Legitimate power stems from one person's acceptance of a role relationship, believing that the other person has the right to request compliance. *Reward power* is the ability to provide rewards for desired behavior changes. *Coercive power* is based on the perception that punishment will occur if the desired behavior does not happen. *Referent power* is based on identification with or attraction to another; people with referent power are role models or are physically attractive to others. *Informational power* is an individual's ability to use explanations and other persuasive communication to change someone else's behavior. The individual with informational power has carefully and successfully explained the necessity for change. *Expert power* is based on the perception that one person has superior knowledge or ability within a given area and the understanding and skill to lead another to the best outcome. Table 7.5 lists examples of these six bases of family power.

Family Power Processes. Family power processes are those interaction techniques that occur during general family discussions, decision making, problem solving, conflict resolution, and crisis management. *Assertiveness* and *aggressiveness* refer to ways in which people attempt to change the behavior of others. People are

TABLE 7.5	Six Bases of Family Power		
Type	**Resource**	**Definition**	**Example**
Legitimate power	Authority	Having the right to make a decision	A single woman's right to decide whether to have an abortion
Reward power	Rewards	Being able to reward for appropriate behavior	Praising a child for helping with household chores
Coercive power	Punishment	Being able to punish for inappropriate behavior	Punishing a child for staying out late
Referent power	Respect and/or love	Having others' trust	Following one's parents' advice about how to handle their funerals
Informational power	Knowledge	Having specialized knowledge	Following a husband's advice on buying a car because he has carefully researched the topic
Expert power	Experience in an area	Having experience and respect in a field	Following a wife's advice about finances because she is a financial counselor

Source: Adapted from "The Bases of Conjugal Power" (pp. 217–232) by B. H. Raven, R. Centers, and A. Rodrigues. In *Power in Families*, edited by R. E. Cromwell and D. H. Olson, 1975, Newbury Park, CA: Sage. Copyright © 1975 by David H. Olson.

being assertive when they express what they want or desire: "I would like you to pick up your clothes." People are being aggressive when they demand that others comply with their requests: "Pick up those clothes, or I won't fix dinner tonight." *Control* refers to the effectiveness of these attempts to change the behavior of others. The more often others are willing to comply with a person's request, the more control that person has.

Family Power Outcomes. The third area of family power—outcomes—centers on who makes decisions and who wins. There are several ways of measuring power outcomes. When doing observational research on power in families, researchers typically count the number of assertive statements individuals make and record how others respond to those statements. For example, in a family with two parents and an adolescent, if the husband makes 10 assertive statements and 8 of them are accepted by the rest of the family, the researchers calculate the husband's effective power in the family as 80%. If the wife makes 8 assertive statements but only 2 of them are accepted by the other family members, her effective power is 25%. If the adolescent makes 14 assertive statements and only 2 of them are accepted, the adolescent's effective power is 14%. On the basis of these observations, one could conclude that the husband in this family has more effective power than the wife or the adolescent.

Types of Power Patterns

According to one classic model (Herbst, 1952), the power balance in a marriage can be characterized in four basic ways: a **husband-dominant power pattern,** in which the man is basically the boss; a **wife-dominant power pattern,** in which the woman is basically the boss; a **syncratic power pattern** (in essence, "to decide

FIGURE 7.1

Power Patterns in
Marriages

Source: Adapted from "The
Measurement of Family
Relationships" by P. G. Herbst,
1952, *Human Relations,* 5,
pp. 3–35.

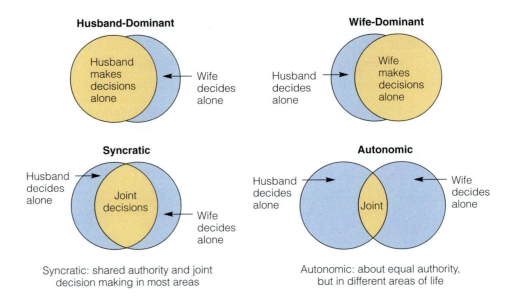

Husband-Dominant

Wife-Dominant

Syncratic

Autonomic

Syncratic: shared authority and joint
decision making in most areas

Autonomic: about equal authority,
but in different areas of life

together"), in which authority is shared and decisions are made on a joint basis in most areas of endeavor; and an **autonomic power pattern,** in which each spouse has about equal authority but in different areas of life and essentially makes decisions in her or his particular domain independent of the other. These patterns are illustrated in Figure 7.1.

In the early stages of a relationship, there can be a great deal of instability as the individuals struggle to work out the balance of power. As time passes, the partners assert themselves to establish some power in the relationship. A male- or female-dominant relationship, with one person leading and the other following, is difficult to maintain. Eventually, the dominant one may tire of leading, and the submissive one may tire of following. The result may be a change to another type of power sharing.

In a syncratic relationship, the sharing of decisions and tasks affords the family system a better power balance. The partners are relatively equal, and couples with children often encourage some sharing of power, especially as the children become older.

In an autonomic relationship, one spouse may have most of the power in one area, such as inside the home, whereas the other spouse may have most of the power in another area, such as outside the home. Both perceive the relationship to be relatively equal in power on the whole, because both domains of endeavor are perceived to be important.

Egalitarian Roles and Marital Satisfaction

When it comes to the importance of an equal relationship versus a traditional relationship to marital satisfaction, the national survey by Olson and Olson (2000) clearly demonstrated that more equal relationships are highly related to marital satisfaction (see Table 7.6). If both partners perceive their relationship as egalitarian, 81% of the couples describe their marriage as happy and only 19% are unhappy. Conversely, if both partners perceive their marriage as traditional, only 18% feel their marriage is happy and 82% are unhappy. These findings are rather dramatic and demonstrate the importance of an equal relationship for marital happiness.

| TABLE 7.6 | Egalitarian Roles and Marital Satisfaction |

	PERCENTAGE IN AGREEMENT		
Perception of Relationship	Happy Couples (n = 5,153)	Unhappy Couples (n = 5,127)	Total (n = 10,280)
Both perceive as egalitarian.	81%	19%	(n = 4,130)
Husband perceives as traditional; wife perceives as egalitarian.	50	50	(n = 1,267)
Wife perceives as traditional; husband perceives as egalitarian.	37	63	(n = 1,561)
Both perceive as traditional.	18	82	(n = 3,322)

Source: Adapted from Olson & Olson, 2000.

Two interesting patterns emerged when the partners perceived their relationship differently with one person saying it is equal and the other saying it is traditional. When the husband says the relationship is traditional and the wife says it is equal, half the marriages are happy and half are unhappy. However, when the wife says the relationship is traditional and the husband says it is equal, only about one-third (37%) are happy and two-thirds (63%) are unhappy. It is the wife's perception of equality that is most predictive of couple satisfaction.

Communication and Power Dynamics

Researchers who study communication have identified several ways in which spouses exert power in their interactions with each other or avoid the use of power in communication (Fitzpatrick, 1988, pp. 116–117). Conversations can be either symmetrical or complementary.

A **symmetrical interaction** is one in which partners send similar messages that are designed to control how the relationship is defined. Researchers further divide symmetrical interactions into three types: competitive, submissive, and neutralized. The three are similar in that both spouses adopt the same tactic: Both compete, both submit, or both are relatively neutral in the search for a solution to the issue. They differ in the tactic used and in the results.

In **competitive symmetry**, the conflict between partners escalates. He says, "I don't want to go to your relatives' birthday party. I'm real tired from work." She says, "You may be tired, but the real reason you don't want to go is you simply don't like my relatives. You never have." He says, "Well, I don't. They're boring and bigoted, and I've heard everything they ever had to say years ago." The discussion becomes a competition in which both aim to defeat the other. This win–lose approach sets the stage for escalating hostilities.

In **submissive symmetry**, both spouses try to give control of the situation to the other. He says, "Look at the checkbook. How will we ever get out of debt?" She says, "I don't know. We never seem to have enough money." He says, "I'm afraid they'll repossess the new car if we don't send in the payments on schedule." She says, "It would be a shame. I love that car. . . ." Both partners avoid taking control of the situation, attempting to win by passing responsibility to the other.

In **neutralized symmetry**, spouses respect each other and try to avoid exerting control over each other. She says, "I noticed the toilet has a little leak again. I

The quest for power, money, and material success in which so many men are immersed is accompanied by higher levels of stress, higher rates of heart disease, and shorter life spans. Some observers believe that over time as women continue to rise in the working world there will also be a concomitant increase in the stress-related health problems that women experience.

have a meeting this evening, but tomorrow after work I can fix it." He says, "You're better at figuring out mechanical things than I am, but I could pick up the parts." She says, "That would free us both up by 6:30 to go out to dinner together." These spouses have avoided a power struggle over the toilet by offering ideas in a gentle spirit, approaching the matter as equals on the same team instead of as boss and servant. Each gives a little, and both come out ahead. This win–win approach ensures that partners will have time to enjoy each other instead of fighting.

A **complementary interaction** differs from a symmetrical interaction in that the participants adopt two different tactics: One is dominant and one is submissive. He says, "Would you iron my shirt? I've got an important meeting tonight." She says, "Sure." If a relationship is to remain vital, it is important that partners try not to exert power over each other but, instead, work together for mutual benefit. Equality nurtures intimacy.

Suggestions for Minimizing Power Issues

Remember that power is a characteristic of relationships, not of people. Power is always relative, changing, and useful only to the extent that it is legitimate. Many of the conflicts that cause relationship stress are struggles over the power process (the way decisions are made) rather than disagreements about a specific issue. The person holding the authority to make each decision must have the responsibility for following through on the decision.

Decision making should be balanced by the value of the areas each partner controls, not by the number of areas each has. It is more efficient and more realistic to assign each partner primary responsibility for making decisions in certain areas, whether or not the other has veto authority, than to make all decisions a matter of mutual agreement.

Men may think they have a lot to lose by giving up some of their power over women and children, but, in fact, they have a great deal to gain. Men tend to die younger than women, often from a variety of illnesses related to stress and poor lifestyle choices. A macho, "win-at-all-costs" attitude is commonly thought to contribute to men's health problems. Rigid gender roles may have afforded men more power in our culture, but it is lonely at the top. The path toward intimacy is best walked side by side.

Summary

- According to a national survey, happily married couples agree more often than unhappily married couples that both partners are equally willing to make adjustments in roles, that they are satisfied with the division of housework, that it takes hard work to have an equal relationship, and that they make most decisions jointly and household tasks are divided on the basis of preferences rather than tradition.

- The most commonly reported issues for married couples in their role relationship were the following: concern about unfair division of housework, housework based on traditional roles, husband not willing to adjust, women too involved in housework, and lack of working to maintain an equal relationship.

- Gender roles—the expectations every society has about people's attitudes and behaviors based on whether they are male or female—are rooted in biology but heavily influenced by culture.

- A Gallup poll indicated that males were more often perceived as aggressive, courageous, and ambitious. Females were described as emotional, affectionate, talkative, patient, and creative. There was considerable agreement across genders on these descriptions of men and women.

- Sociologist Talcott Parsons espoused a traditional view of gender roles. His theory of family roles assumed that men should be "instrumental" and women "expressive." Parsons's theory has been vigorously challenged and is no longer accepted.

- Persistent gender-role patterns in marriage mean that women do much more of the housework in the family than men do, which often leads to relationship conflict.

- In Mexican American, African American, and American Indian cultures, as in White society, men have often been dominant in their families, but signs of change are also apparent in these cultures.

- Historically prominent theories of gender-role development include the social learning theory, which is concerned with how individuals learn the behavior patterns considered appropriate for their sex; the cog-

nitive development theory, which links the progressive acquisition of gender typing to the general maturation of the child's thinking processes; the family systems theory, which holds that the entire family must change when an individual member changes; and the feminist framework, which argues that women are exploited, devalued, and oppressed and affirms their equality with men.

- Family power is the ability of one family member to change the behavior of other family members. Researchers have looked at three areas of family power: bases of power, power processes, and power outcomes. Power in a family is related to how much money an individual earns, to educational level, and to occupational prestige, among other things.

- The power balance in a marriage can be characterized in four basic ways: a husband-dominant pattern; a wife-dominant pattern; a syncratic pattern, in which authority is shared; and an autonomic pattern, in which each spouse has about equal authority but in different areas of life.

- One way power is exerted or avoided in families is through patterns of communication. The most successful relationships appear to have a relatively even balance of power between the partners.

Key Terms

gender identity
gender role
gender-role stereotype
masculinity
femininity
egalitarian roles
social learning theory
cognitive development
    theory
power
family power
resource theory of
    family power

husband-dominant
    power pattern
wife-dominant power
    pattern
syncratic power pattern
autonomic power pattern
symmetrical interaction
competitive symmetry
submissive symmetry
neutralized symmetry
complementary interaction

Activities

1. In small groups, discuss whether American society will ever evolve into one in which one's sex is relatively unimportant, except in relation to reproduction. How far can we go in removing the old gender-role stereotypes?
2. Study Table 7.4, Contemporary Versus Traditional Dating and Marriage Patterns. If you are in an intimate relationship, decide which aspects from the "contemporary" list and which from the "traditional" list apply to your relationship. Have your partner do the same exercise and compare your answers.
3. In small groups, discuss family power. How was power distributed in your family of origin? How do you know? (Give examples.) How do you want power to be distributed in the family you hope to create in the future?

Suggested Readings

Barnett, R. C., & Rivers, C. (1996). *She works/he works: Two-income families are happier, healthier, and better off.* New York: HarperSanFrancisco/HarperCollins. A discussion of the rewards and concerns associated with women's and men's experiences as employees, marital partners, and parents and how these relate to mental and physical health.

Crose, R. (1997). *Why women live longer than men: . . . and what men can learn from them.* San Francisco: Jossey-Bass. A gerontologist's perspective on how much of the difference in life expectancy between women and men can be attributed to traditional, masculine high-risk behaviors that men could change if they wanted to.

Lippa, R. A. (2001). *Gender, nature, and nurture.* Mahwah, NJ: Erlbaum.

Meier, J. A., McNaughton-Cassill, M., & Lynch, M. (2006). The management of household and childcare tasks and relationship satisfaction in parenting couples. *Marriage and Family Review, 40,* 61–88.

Pitt-Catsouphes, M., Kossek, E. E., & Sweet, S. (2006). *The work and family handbook.* Mahwah, NJ: Erlbaum.

Schwartz, P. (1995). *Love between equals: How peer marriage really works.* New York: Free Press.

Thornton, J., & Lasswell, M. (1997). *Chore wars: How households can share the work and keep the peace.* Berkeley, CA: Conari Press.

Voydanoff, P. (2005). Work demands and work-to-family and family-to-work conflict: Direct and indirect relationships. *Journal of Family Issues, 26,* 707–726.

Visit the text-specific Online Learning Center at **www.mhhe.com/Olson6** for practice tests, chapter summaries, Web links, Internet exercises, key terms, and flashcards.

8. *Managing Economic Resources*

Money and Happiness

Couple Strengths and Financial Issues

Diversity and Financial Style

The Stresses of Finances

The Cost of Divorce

Why Do Finances Cause Problems?

Family Income and Expenses

Smart Money Management

Credit: Uses and Abuses

Summary

Key Terms

Activities

Suggested Readings

Financial issues are the most common stressors for couples and families across the life cycle, regardless of how much money they make (Rich, 2003). In addition, many couples planning to marry are unwilling or unable to simply talk about financial issues. As one couple commented: "Before we were married, we talked about every detail of our lives we could think of, but we never got around to asking how we felt about money. So we are doomed to act out those feelings." On a more positive note, however, research has consistently demonstrated that couples who handle their money and finances well also tend to be more happily married (Olson & Olson, 2000).

In this chapter we will focus on financial issues, particularly as they relate to intimate relationships and to families across the life cycle. Money problems are often related to an inability to develop an open and well-organized couple or family system. These financial problems then lead to more stress and conflict in the marriage or family. We will explore the field of financial resource management, whose aim is to achieve economic **goals** and harmony in intimate relationships. Finally, we will take a close look at the advantages and disadvantages of buying on credit and how to avoid the related financial pitfalls.

We will begin this chapter, as we have several others, with a look at a national survey that examined couple strengths and issues for married couples (Olson & Olson, 2000). In the following section, we will focus on couple strengths in terms of financial management, comparing happy couples with unhappy couples. We will also review the findings of this survey regarding the five most common financial-management issues married couples experience.

Money and Happiness

Money, of course, cannot buy happiness. As one observer noted, "The best things in life are not things." The media remind us of this almost daily with stories of rich but unhappy politicians, businesspeople, royalty, movie stars, and celebrities.

Most people believe that their problems would be resolved if they had more money. But there is little evidence that wealth and happiness are related (Csikszentmihalyi, 1999). Only among the very poor does money make a difference in happiness. Once people have a comfortable level of income, money has a diminishing impact on one's happiness. David Lykken (1999) found that "People who go to work in their overalls and on the bus are just as happy, on the average, as those in suits who drive to work in their own Mercedes" (p. 17). One reason for this is as your money increases, so do your expectations about spending. Second, people evaluate life not based on their possessions, but in terms of those who have the most. Third, one's focus on money distracts from other enjoyable aspects of life.

On the other hand, there seems to be little truth to the "poor but happy" scenario. Economic hardship and problems in couple and family relationships are often related. Researchers have found that divorce, marital separation, domestic violence, and the abuse of alcohol and other drugs are more likely among the poor than in any other socioeconomic group (Bowen, Pittman, Pleck, Haas, & Voydanoff, 1995). Earning an adequate income and managing money efficiently and effectively are important for a couple's and a family's well-being. If they have enough money to meet their basic needs, couples and families can turn their attention to enhancing the quality of their lives and their relationships.

TABLE 8.1	Financial-Management Strengths of Happy Versus Unhappy Married Couples		
		PERCENTAGE OF COUPLES IN AGREEMENT	
Strength		**Happy Couples** ($n = 5,153$)	**Unhappy Couples** ($n = 5,127$)
Agree on how to spend money.		89%	41%
No concerns about how partner spends money.		80	32
Satisfied with decision on savings.		73	29
Major debts are not a problem.		76	35
Making financial decision not difficult.		80	32

Source: Adapted from Olson & Olson, 2000.

Couple Strengths and Financial Issues

Based on a national sample of 5,153 happy married couples and 5,127 unhappy married couples (Olson & Olson, 2000), the financial-management item that most distinguishes happy couples from unhappy couples is how much they agree how to spend their money (happy couples 89%, unhappy couples 41%) (see Table 8.1). Over three-quarters (80%) of happy couples reported having no concerns about how money is handled in their marriage, as compared to only 32% of unhappy couples. Happy couples were also more satisfied (73%) than unhappy couples (29%) with their decisions about saving money. Happy couples were significantly less likely (76%) to have major debts than unhappy couples (35%). Furthermore, happy couples were more likely (80%) to find financial decisions easy to make compared to unhappy couples (32%).

The major financial issues for a national sample of 21,501 married couples surveyed by Olson and Olson (2000) are presented in Table 8.2. The two most common financial-management issues voiced by couples were wishing the spouse were more careful spending money (72%) and having trouble saving money (72%). About two-thirds (66%) of the couples had problems deciding what is more important to purchase. About half (56%) of the couples said major debts were a problem for them or they felt their partner tried to control the money in their household (51%). See Box 8.1 for a look at the effects of debt on newlyweds.

TABLE 8.2	Top Five Financial-Management Issues for Married Couples

Issue	Percentage ($n = 21,501$ couples)
Wish their partner were more careful spending money.	72%
Having trouble saving money.	72
Problems deciding what is more important to purchase.	66
Major debts are a problem.	56
Partner tries to control the money.	51

Source: Adapted from Olson & Olson, 2000.

BOX 8.1   At Issue

The Effects of Debt on Newlyweds

Is it finances in general, or specifically debt, that causes problems for couples? Much has been written about the stress of finances and money in causing problems for couples in their marriages. One study, however, found that it was debt that caused the most problems in newlywed marriages, rather than finances in general.

In a study by Skogrand, Schramm, Marshall, and Lee (2005) of approximately 1,000 randomly selected newlywed couples who had been married from 3 to 9 months, debt brought into marriage was identified as the second most-cited problem in their marriage by both husbands and wives. In this study, debt brought into marriage was separate from financial decision making, which was much farther down the list of 30 possible problematic areas for couples.

Couples in this study were asked to indicate their level of debt in areas of debt such as medical bills, credit card debt, auto loans, and school loans. Home mortgage debt was not included as a possible problem area in this study, because most newlywed couples do not own a home. Important findings of the study include the following:

- Seventy percent of husbands and wives brought debt into the marriage. Thirty-five percent of husbands and wives had more than $5,000 in debt when they married.

- Fifty-five percent of husbands and wives had automobile debt, 48% had credit card debt, 23% had school debt, and 12% had medical debt when they entered the marriage.
- Of the four kinds of debt, credit card and automobile loan debt had the highest correlation with lower marital satisfaction and adjustment scores for both husbands and wives.
- Higher levels of education were related to lower amounts of debt brought into marriage.
- Medical bills and school loans may have been viewed as necessary debt, because they did not have a high correlation with low levels of martial satisfaction and adjustment.
- The higher the debt brought into the marriage, the lower the marital satisfaction and adjustment scores of participants. Those who brought no debt into the marriage had the highest marital satisfaction and adjustment scores.

According to this study, debt is an important factor in marital satisfaction and adjustment. Why is this true? We suggest that debt and financial difficulties create stress, which takes away from developing and maintaining the marital relationship.

Diversity and Financial Style

Little has been written about how finances are handled by low-income families and families from diverse populations. A major difference between low-income and middle- and higher-income spending practices relates to the difference between a **collective worldview** and an **individualistic worldview** (Skogrand, Hatch, & Singh, 2008). Low-income families and families living in poverty usually view things from a collective worldview. This means a family often gets through life because someone—a family member, friend, or neighbor—helped them when they really needed it. It follows, then, that when this family has a little extra money, it will be shared with the same people who helped them. People with an individualistic worldview typically use resources to better themselves such as buying a bigger house, furthering their education, or investing their money in the stock market.

Diverse cultural groups are also likely to have a collective worldview rather than an individualistic worldview and see helping family and friends as a high priority. This would be true of many Latino families. Family is the highest priority, and family needs would come before personal needs (Skogrand et al., 2008). Family is also viewed as the primary source of financial support. This perspective may be viewed by European American, middle-class folks as being irresponsible when, in fact, it is a cultural strength.

Finances can create difficulties for couples. Discussing financial issues and reaching an agreement about these issues will help the couple relationship.

Low-income families may have had financial stresses in their lives to the point that they do not have a bank account because of bad credit. They use money orders to pay bills rather than writing checks or using debit cards. They may not have enough left over to have a savings account or envision a retirement account. Etta Norwood (1998) talks about being poor in this way:

> I notice that people with money talk about it a lot. I was sitting in a meeting with employees of my district and they began to discuss the "Rule of 90" [retirement formula] as though everyone knows what it means. Their failure to acknowledge [social] class in that room caused them to make this assumption. Then the words savings and annuity come up. It did not fit into my context of living: before, now, or in the future. I don't even think about those kinds of things. Because I started with not having enough, I didn't think about piling it up. Getting into neutral territory where you don't owe or you're not doing stuff to get around not having is as good as I can imagine. (p. 74)

Past life experiences also affect how one manages finances. For example, new Latino immigrants often do not use banks because they were not always trusted in the country from which they emigrated (Holzner et al., 2006). Instead, money may be kept at home—literally under the mattress or in the cupboard, because those are more trusted places than a bank. Having a savings account, investing in a retirement account, or using credit, which involves banks, may not be something Latino families would do. Only a small percentage of Latinos have investment accounts (Holzner et al., 2006). In addition, substantial amounts of money are often sent to family members in their country of origin, rather than being used for improving quality of life for the family that is in the United States. This affects the entire financial picture for this population and does not fit with what might be considered sound financial planning by financial counselors.

Couples and families use a wide range of strategies, however, that are dependent on social class, family structure, life experiences, and culture. Stepfamilies have to negotiate ways to manage finances that account for each spouse having individual financial responsibilities involving their own children. They may have to manage several pots of money that include yours, mine, and ours to accommodate a complex family system (Stewart, 2007). Child support and other types of financial commitments must be met that were made before the stepfamily relationship developed. Couples who have divorced and remarried later in life may not have young children to financially care for, but may have adult children who do not want their inheritance to go to a new spouse or that spouse's children.

The Stresses of Finances

To some people, money means power; to others, love. For some the topic is boorish, in bad taste. For others, it's more private than sex. Add family dynamics to the mix, and for many you have the subject from hell.

—KAREN S. PETERSON (1992a)

Although Americans make more money per capita than residents of many other countries, financial issues tend to dominate our lives. An enduring paradox about money is that no matter how much families have, they always seem to need more. And even when they have more, financial anxiety isn't necessarily relieved, as Paul, a contractor and writer, can attest:

"When our first daughter was a toddler 20 years ago, my take-home pay was about $3,100 a year. Adjusted for inflation today, that might be about $10,000. Things were tight, but we lived pretty well in many respects. We traveled a lot—cheaply, of course—and we enjoyed life. We were, for the most part, happy. Today, we have three teenagers and our family income is approaching $80,000 a year. Frankly, money causes me just as much anxiety today as it did way back then. And I really can't say we're any happier."

Most people, no matter what their income, would likely say that if they had only $5,000, $10,000, or $25,000 more a year, things would be better. There never seems to be enough money, whether one's income is $10,000 or $100,000; couples and families often find themselves with some debt each month. Many people assume that material things will bring them happiness but find instead that their possessions have a certain power over them: The house and car must be repaired, the clothes cleaned, the swimming pool maintained, any extra money invested wisely. As one observer said, "Everything you own owns you."

A major stressor for individuals and families is money and how to handle finances. Thomas Garman, a professor of personal finances, has found (Garman & Forgue, 2002) that about one-third of workers report financial stress being high to the extreme and that worrying about money hampers their job performance. More than half (54%) of the workers worry about how much they owe, and over half (53%) reported dissatisfaction with their personal financial situation. Garman recommends educational programs to help people deal with these financial issues. He has found that over 75% of those who have taken educational programs about finances have found that they are able to make better financial decisions (Garman & Forgue, 2002).

Finances: A Family Problem

For most Americans, money is a source of anxiety and discomfort that continues across the life span. Olson and Olson (2000) found in their study of 21,501 couples that money is the most commonly reported source of stress and strain that couples and families face. Many families at each stage of the family life cycle felt finances were problematic (Olson et al., 1989). The most difficult periods of the family life cycle financially were the childbearing stage, the adolescent stage, the launching stage, and the retirement stage. About half the families in the childbearing stage reported stress and strain related to finances. During the adolescent stage, money-related problems apparently peaked; 60% of the families reported feeling stress in this area. This dropped to 40% at both the launching and the retirement stages.

Money problems often have a negative effect on individual well-being and family relationships (Bowen et al., 1995). Stan, a middle-aged man living in Boston, recalls the anxiety and devastation he and his family experienced a decade ago when he was unemployed for months on end:

> "I was out of work for 26 months over a period of 40 months, but who was counting? It was probably the most devastating experience in my life. I applied for 205 jobs before I finally found one that worked out. People say, 'All you have to do is get off your butt and you can find work.' I used to believe that myself. But it's not that easy.
>
> "Now I know that they really were upset about my unemployment. My wife, Sally, was probably as upset about it as I was. But there was nothing any of them could do at the time but go on with their own lives. They tried to comfort me, but many times I was beyond comforting. Fortunately, I found a good job that I enjoy. It doesn't pay all that well, but I love having it. Being without work was terrifying. Even talking about it still upsets me today, 10 years later."

Family members simply don't get along as well with each other when they are suffering from economic distress. Employment instability—job loss or uncertainty over the future of a job—can be a major stressor. Those who are unemployed have an increased likelihood of suffering from depression, anxiety, and psychophysiological distress (stress-related physical problems). If a man is unemployed, his wife is also likely to experience psychological distress from trying to deal with the situation. Low income is also related to several types of psychological distress (Bowen et al., 1995).

Coping with Financial Stressors

Why do some couples and families survive economic hard times whereas others are torn apart? Researchers have focused on coping resources and coping behaviors in trying to answer this question (Bowen et al., 1995). Coping resources can come from oneself and from the family. Foremost among **personal coping resources** are self-esteem and mastery. To survive economic hard times, individuals need to feel good about themselves, to feel as if they are capable of standing up to the onslaught. They need a sense of mastery, confidence in their ability to learn new skills and techniques to meet changing situations.

Family coping resources include cohesion, adaptability, and a willingness to adopt nontraditional family roles in the face of changing economic circumstances—all characteristics of a healthy family system. Consider, for example, the following family: The mother has never worked outside the home, and her husband has lost his job at a manufacturing plant. He has been out of work for 6 months, and the family has used up its savings. To keep the family afloat, the wife finds a job as a clerk at a convenience store. In this crisis situation, the family coping resources include cohesion (the ability to stick together in tough times and to empathize with each other's plight) and adaptability (the ability to change to deal with the crisis).

Social support, or help from other people, can be critically important in times of economic distress. Major types of social support include instrumental aid (such as money, goods, and services), emotional support, and information (such as advice

and feedback). Social support can come from a variety of people, including a spouse or an immediate family member, extended family, co-workers, neighbors, self-help groups, and human services professionals. When social support is available and is used by an individual in financial crisis, it generally provides increased psychological well-being and improved quality of family life (Bowen et al., 1995).

When the major wage earner of a family loses his or her job, there are several options:

- Other family members can go to work outside the home.
- The family can increase its participation in the so-called informal economy, exchanging goods and services for cash or by barter.
- The family can decide together how to cut back expenditures dramatically.

Cutting the budget is not easy, and families have reported depression, low marital satisfaction, and high tension when forced to do so. Nonetheless, there are certain approaches that have been found to make things worse in times of economic distress. Denying that there is a problem; keeping feelings to oneself; and eating, drinking, or smoking to relieve tension tend to increase marital stress.

The Cost of Divorce

We have always known that there is a tremendous emotional cost to families who experience a divorce. One researcher recently identified the potential economic cost of divorce. Divorce is necessary and in the best interest of the couple and the family in many cases, and to stay in the relationship would be financially costly as well in terms of physical, emotional, and mental well-being (Schramm, 2006). This study was conducted in 2001 in a western state to determine the cost of divorce to the family and to the state and federal governments, with implications for social policy that would contribute to strengthening marriages.

The personal costs of divorce in the study were calculated based on legal and filing fees for the divorce, divorce education classes that were required in the state where the study was conducted, housing costs with required moves, and lost productivity due to distress (Schramm, 2006). Legal fees for a divorce vary, of course, but a conservative estimate of the costs was $7,000 per divorce for a couple with children, and a filing fee of $95 to start the divorce process. Some states have divorce education classes, especially for couples with children. Although this cost is somewhat minimal, in this western state it was $70 per couple.

Housing may be a substantial cost for divorcing couples. Schramm (2006) indicates that minimally there would be one geographic move in each divorce, and approximately one-third of the couples would have two geographic moves. It is estimated that the average housing cost for a family not going through a divorce would be $15,500, and the housing cost for a divorcing family is estimated to be almost $20,000. Based on estimates of other studies regarding lost productivity related to stress, it is estimated that approximately $3,000 per year per couple is the cost of lost productivity. These costs total approximately $14,000 for the year of the divorce (Schramm, 2006).

Although a personal cost of $14,000 is considerable for any family, this amount would be especially burdensome for low-income families, where the divorce rates are the highest. Many couples may see only the anticipated added benefit of getting out of a marriage without being aware of the added financial costs.

In addition to the personal costs of divorce, Schramm (2006) calculates the cost to communities and local and federal governments and concludes that each divorce has a total average estimated cost of $30,000. Schramm suggests that resources might be invested in education to strengthen marriages, which would result in less money spent than the potential costs of divorce. Couples may also consider the personal investment in marriage therapy and education as being less costly than a divorce.

Why Do Finances Cause Problems?

There are several reasons finances cause problems for families:

- Money is a taboo topic in many families.
- Many couples do not create and stick to a budget.
- Some families overspend and rely too heavily on credit.
- Partners have different styles of spending and saving.
- One partner uses money as a tool to gain power and control over the other partner.
- Partners have different ideas about the meaning of money.

Money: A Taboo Topic

In the dating phase, couples are more likely to talk about any topic other than their financial situations; it's not very romantic to talk about potential income, the use of credit cards, and views on savings. In contrast, among married couples, money matters are the most common sources of arguments. Money can symbolize different things to different people, and if couples don't recognize these differences, they are often unprepared for the resulting friction. That's the situation described by Marcia, a 42-year-old computer technician, in the following account:

> *"I thought we talked about everything before marriage. But we never seemed to get around to money—what it means to each of us and how it should be spent. Because I saw money as a symbol of security, I wanted to scrimp and save. I wanted to build a house, a nest, and feel safe inside. Because he saw money as a tool to achieve freedom and independence, he wanted to use it for adventure. We were doomed from the beginning to fight over money."*

Money is not just the paper, coin, or plastic used to buy things. It can also be a perceived source of status, security, enjoyment, or control. If partners have incompatible attitudes about money and its uses, extravagant purchases are likely to cause conflicts between them over deeply held beliefs and values.

It isn't just married couples, however, who lack communication skills when it comes to finances. The discussion of money between parents and children is often nonexistent. Nonetheless, many financial advisers and counselors argue that it is essential to break the family pattern of financial silence. If parents refuse to help their children learn how to manage money, it "creates people who depend on us," according to psychologist Jane Nelsen. "When we don't teach kids responsibility, their self-esteem suffers. They feel inadequate. That teaches them to manipulate us to get what they want. They don't develop their own capabilities" (cited in Peterson, 1992b). By setting a budget for adolescent spending, parents can prevent many emotional struggles with their teenagers.

The Meaning of Money

Arond and Pauker (1987) have identified four common orientations toward money:

- *Money as status.* A person with a status orientation is interested in money as power—as a means of keeping ahead of one's peers.
- *Money as security.* A person with a security orientation is conservative in spending and focuses on saving.
- *Money as enjoyment.* A person with an enjoyment orientation gets satisfaction from spending both on others and on himself or herself.
- *Money as control.* A person with a control orientation sees money as a way of maintaining control over her or his life and independence from a partner or other family members.

It is possible for a person to have more than one orientation but not two conflicting approaches—for example, enjoyment *and* security.

A questionnaire for assessing your money orientation is provided in Box 8.2.

BOX 8.2   Self-Assessment

Money—What Does It Mean to You?

Use the following scale to respond to each of the items below:

1 = Strongly disagree; 2 = Disagree; 3 = Uncertain; 4 = Agree; 5 = Strongly agree

_____ 1. It is important to me to maintain a lifestyle similar to or better than that of my peers.

_____ 2. In making a major purchase, an important consideration is what others will think of my choice.

_____ 3. Because money equals power, I am willing to work hard for money in order to have more power.

_____ 4. I really enjoy shopping and having nice things.

_____ 5. Saving money for a rainy day is an important principle to live by.

_____ 6. If I had a moderate amount of money to invest, I would be more likely to put it into multiple resources that are relatively safe than into one fairly risky source that has the potential to make a lot of money.

_____ 7. Being "flat broke" is one of the worst things that could happen to me.

_____ 8. Saving for retirement is an important financial goal for me.

_____ 9. If I suddenly came into a windfall of $1,000, I would use the money for something I have always wanted to do or have.

_____ 10. Since "You can't take it with you," you might as well spend it.

_____ 11. Money can't buy happiness, but it sure helps.

_____ 12. Few things in life give me greater pleasure than making a great buy.

_____ 13. I like/would like having my own business because I can/could control my financial destiny.

_____ 14. I like being able to make decisions about how to spend the money I earn.

_____ 15. It bothers me to be dependent on someone else for money.

_____ 16. I feel uncomfortable if someone offers to "pick up the tab" at a meal we have shared because I feel indebted to the person.

Scoring and Interpretation

After taking the quiz, add up your answers to the four questions for each category and record your scores below. Scores for each category can range from 4 to 20, with a high score indicating more agreement with that approach. It is possible to have high or low scores in more than one category. General guidelines for interpreting your scores appear in the table below. Record the interpretation for your score in each category on the scoring chart.

Category	Items	Your Score	Interpretation of Score
Money as status	1–4	_____	_____
Money as security	5–8	_____	_____
Money as enjoyment	9–12	_____	_____
Money as control over life	13–16	_____	_____

Score	Interpretation
17–20	Very High
13–16	High
9–12	Moderate
4–8	Low

Source: Adapted from *The First Year of Marriage* by M. Arond and S. L. Pauker, 1987, New York: Warner. Copyright © 1987 by M. Arond and S. L. Pauker. Reprinted by permission of Warner Books, New York.

Family Income and Expenses

In this section we will focus on the average income of U.S. families and on income variations among different ethnic and cultural groups and between men and women. We will also explore typical family expenses and differences in family net worth. Finally, we will examine the financial feasibility for both spouses to work outside the home, especially if they have children.

What does *living in poverty* mean? It means that people might not have adequate food or a decent place to sleep. (In the case of the homeless, it could mean living in a refrigerator box in an alley or under a bridge.) It means people cannot afford to see a physician when they are ill or to purchase medicine when they need it. Being poor may mean having no telephone, no radio, no television, no means of transportation. It often means that children attend substandard schools or that their parents move so often looking for work that the children do not attend school at all. Poverty is a very stressful state of affairs.

Lower-middle-income families, although not officially "poor" by government standards, also find it quite difficult to make ends meet. In both two-parent and single-parent lower-middle-income families, about three-quarters of all family expenditures can go for housing, food, and transportation. This leaves little money for anything else.

The number of people living in poverty continues to increase. In 2003, there were 35.9 million people in poverty, an increase of 1.3 million more people than in 2002. The poverty level is defined by the government and is based on the number of people in the family. For 2003, a family was considered to be living in poverty if a family of two had an annual income of $12,015 or less; a family of three, $14,680 or less; and a family of four, $18,810 or less (U.S. Bureau of the Census, 2004a).

The percentage of families living in poverty varied greatly across ethnic groups. While Whites had a poverty rate of 8.2%, Asians had an 11.8% rate, Blacks had a poverty rate of 24.4%, and Hispanics had a rate of 22.5%. About 18% of children under the age of 18 live in a household that is in poverty. The states with the highest poverty rates (about 19%) were Arkansas, New Mexico, Mississippi, Louisiana, West Virginia, and the District of Columbia (U.S. Bureau of the Census, 2004b).

Family Income

More than half the families in the United States are considered middle-income families. The U.S. Bureau of the Census currently defines the middle-income range as between $15,000 and $75,000 per year. Lower-income families make less than $15,000 per year, and upper-income families make more than $75,000. Figure 8.1 breaks the lower- and middle-income categories down into various subcategories (left side) and also illustrates the distribution of all the money in the United States (right side). This figure clearly illustrates that although most U.S. families (58.9%) are middle income, a disproportionate share of the money in this country goes to affluent families.

Roughly 47.3% of all income goes to only 25.1% of America's families and these families have an average income of $75,000 per year. By contrast, lower-income families comprise 16% of U.S. families but make only 6.2% of the money. The rich have gotten richer since the mid-1980s, and both middle-income and lower-income families have lost ground.

Internationally, the world is also controlled by the very rich. The world's 225 richest individuals have a combined wealth of $1 trillion dollars, which is what the bottom 47% of the world's population has in terms of money (Woodward, 2000). So, economic inequality is a problem both in the United States and throughout the world.

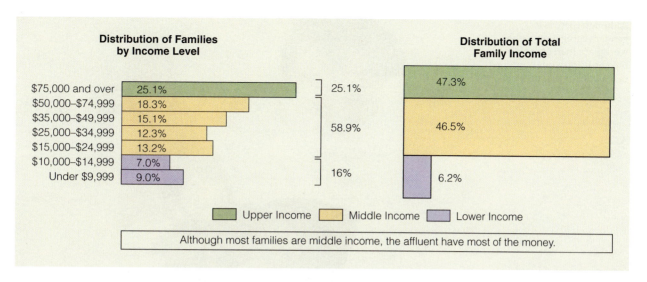

Distribution of Families by Income Level

Income Level	Percentage
$75,000 and over	25.1%
$50,000–$74,999	18.3%
$35,000–$49,999	15.1%
$25,000–$34,999	12.3%
$15,000–$24,999	13.2%
$10,000–$14,999	7.0%
Under $9,999	9.0%

25.1%

58.9%

16%

Distribution of Total Family Income

47.3%

46.5%

6.2%

Upper Income   Middle Income   Lower Income

Although most families are middle income, the affluent have most of the money.

FIGURE 8.1
Income Levels of U.S. Families, 2002.
Source: U.S. Bureau of the Census, 2003b.

Ethnic Income Differences. While the average annual income for all groups was $42,100, there are considerable income differences across ethnic groups in the United States (Table 8.3). For example, among all types of family households, the median income for Asian families is $55,521; for White families, $45,856; for Black families, $30,439; and for Hispanic families, $33,447. Table 8.3 also indicates that for these three ethnic groups, married couples earn substantially more income than the average in their group and single parents make significantly less.

TABLE 8.3	Income Levels by Ethnic Group and Family Structure
Ethnic Group/Type of Family	**Median Income**
All Groups	
All families	$42,100
Married couples	47,129
Female householder, no husband present	21,348
Asian	
All families	$55,521
White	
All families	$45,856
Married couples	47,608
Female householder, no husband present	24,431
Black	
All families	$30,439
Married couples	41,362
Female householder, no husband present	15,589
Hispanic	
All families	$33,447
Married couples	30,195
Female householder, no husband present	14,755

Source: U.S. Bureau of the Census, 2003b.

Although there is less gender segregation in the workplace than ever before, income differences between men and women still exist.

Gender Income Differences. There is a large difference in the average income of males and females at all educational levels, with men making more than women at each level (U.S. Bureau of the Census, 2000e). According to a 2002 U.S. Census Bureau report (2002a), in 2001 the average American male working full time earned $38,275, whereas the average American woman working full time earned only $29,215, a difference of about $9,000. The discrepancy between the incomes of males and females in Black and Hispanic families is smaller than that in White families.

Education pays off financially as shown in Figure 8.2. As education increases for both males and females, their income progressively increases (U.S. Bureau of the Census, 2001g). Individuals completing 9 years of schooling or less averaged $17,932, those with 9 to 12 years of schooling averaged $20,823, high school graduates averaged $28,106, and college graduates averaged $45,856. Individuals with professional degrees beyond college make even a larger increase in salary, some almost double those of a college graduate.

A continuing issue in our society is the large discrepancy in salary between males and females with the same education level (see Figure 8.2). Males consistently make more money than females across all education levels, and the salary difference increases as the level of education increases. While women earn about $8,774

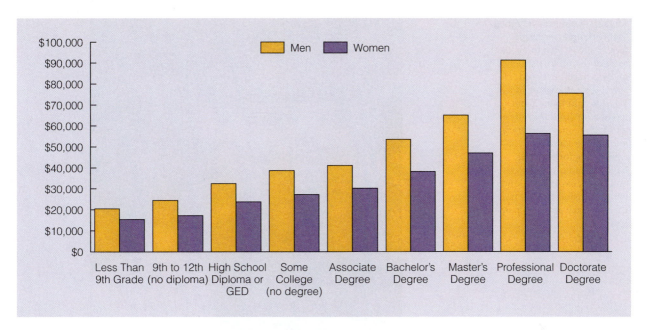

$100,000
$90,000
$80,000
$70,000
$60,000
$50,000
$40,000
$30,000
$20,000
$10,000
$0

Men   Women

Less Than 9th Grade | 9th to 12th (no diploma) | High School Diploma or GED | Some College (no degree) | Associate Degree | Bachelor's Degree | Master's Degree | Professional Degree | Doctorate Degree

less than males with a high school degree, this increases to $15,297 when both have a college degree, and to $34,979 when they both have a professional degree. While there are a number of factors that account for this difference, there continues to be a clear case of discrimination in the workplace.

Education is truly a great investment when you look at the total income individuals achieve in a lifetime of working full time. Individuals with a high school education earn about $1.2 million in a lifetime, while those with a college degree earn almost twice that amount, $2.1 million. Those with a master's degree earn about $2.5 million, with a doctorate (Ph.D. or Ed.D.) about $3.4 million, and with a professional degree (such as an M.D.), the total annual income is about $4.4 million over a lifetime.

Economists and other social observers cite a number of reasons for these income differences. Women often drop out of the labor force to have children and then stay at home to care for them for a few years. Meanwhile, men gain seniority in the labor force and get more job-related experience. Although it is illegal to pay women less for doing the same job, women have little legal recourse when they are paid lower wages for jobs that may require essentially similar skills. Also, salaries in fields traditionally dominated by women tend to be lower than those in fields traditionally dominated by men. Many people attribute these tendencies to discrimination and sexism.

The "equal pay for comparable work" approach takes a fresh look at "men's" and "women's" work. Proponents argue that pay should be based not on traditional gender-role assumptions but on the comparative difficulty of the job. How much should a secretary be paid in comparison with a plumber? A child care worker in comparison with a computer service technician? Some states have developed elaborate formulas. A job's worth, in terms of salary, is calculated on the basis of the number of years of education, training, and experience it demands and the difficulty or risk it involves.

Why do Whites tend to make more than African Americans and Hispanics, even when their educational levels are similar? Many observers argue that racism

FIGURE 8.2
Median Earnings of Men and Women Age 25 and Older Who Work Full Time, Year Round by Educational Attainment
Source: U.S. Bureau of the Census, 2001c.

As more women have joined the workforce and more families need two incomes to meet their expenses, debates have increased about the differences in salaries paid to men and women for similar kinds of work. If a female secretary and a male computer technician, for example, have the same amount of education, experience, and job responsibility, why is the secretary apt to be paid less?

still exists in the United States and that the difference in income can be traced to discrimination. Some believe, however, that a number of other factors also play a part. The first is urban residence. Many jobs sought by minorities have moved from the cities, where most people of color live, to the suburbs, where there are fewer African Americans and Hispanics. The second factor is the type of employment; minorities are more likely than Whites to work in service industries, where salaries are lower. The third factor is tenure; many college-educated minorities are relative newcomers to the labor market and have had less time than Whites to earn promotions and higher pay.

The controversy over the income gap between White males, females, and minorities in our country is not likely to end soon. The disparity in income between the haves and the have-nots is a problematic issue in a society where millions of people are living at or near the poverty level.

Annual Household Expenses

In terms of annual expenditures, couples and families spend the largest percentage of their income on three items: food, housing, and apparel (Duly, 2003). Figure 8.3 illustrates the income spent on these three items for couples and families across the life cycle. In general, people spend most of their income (about 23% to 30%) on housing, about 15% on food, and about 5% on apparel. However, the amount spent on these items varies by the family structure and stage. One-parent families spend the highest percentage of their income on housing (30%), while the average for other families is about 25%; two-parent households with young children spend the least on food (11%) compared to other families because they eat at home more often.

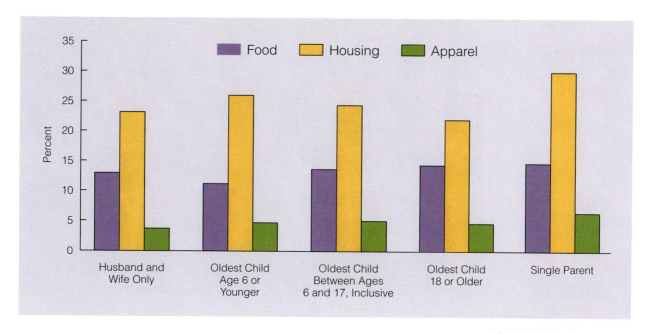

FIGURE 8.3
Annual Expenditures for Necessities
Source: U.S. Bureau of the Census, 2003b.

Family Net Worth

Net worth is defined as the sum of all your financial assets minus all your liabilities. Assets can be liquid (e.g., cash, savings, stock) or nonliquid (e.g., real estate or a trust account). Based on a survey of income by the U.S. Bureau of the Census (2003b), Whites have by far the greatest family net worth compared to Blacks and Latinos, and this difference has increased over time. In 2001, Whites had a median net worth of $117,722, while Blacks had only $18,510 and Latinos had $11,149 (Robles, 2003).

A revealing fact is the percentage in each ethnic group that had a zero net worth. While 11% of Whites had a net worth of zero, 27% of Latinos and 29% of Blacks had a net worth of zero. This means that when these families encounter any financial problem, they will quickly be in debt. These findings clearly demonstrate why families are so vulnerable to any financial situation.

Does It Pay to Work Outside the Home?

Financially and emotionally, there are both advantages and disadvantages for two parents of young children to both work outside the home. An estimated 70% of all women in the United States are working outside the home, up from 57.5% in 1990 and 43.3% in 1970 (U.S. Bureau of the Census, 2000b). This means that there will be more two-income families at all age levels.

One of the sobering facts of life for two-income families is that the second income often seems to disappear when the expenses associated with earning it are paid. A hypothetical example: Assume the second income in the family is a reasonably good one—$28,000 a year, or $2,333 a month. Each month, federal, state, and Social Security taxes could conceivably take about $942. Child care for two children under school age could easily take another $550 a month. Working outside the home also entails increases in clothing expenditures, say, $110 extra a month; personal-care and dry-cleaning bills may also go up an extra $45 a month. Lunch

The costs of professional child care can be a significant expense for couples in which both partners are working outside the home.

costs may rise about $110 monthly, and transportation to work could add at least $55 a month. After all is said and done, the $2,333 monthly salary is reduced to $521—about $3.25 an hour—in real income.

One woman who quit her $7-an-hour job in a family decision to rely solely on the husband's income said, "I had the feeling that all my money was going for clothes, lunch, and day care for my daughter." It is important to emphasize, however, that there are many reasons beyond financial ones for working outside the home, including personal and professional development, networking with others, and getting a break from child care at home.

Smart Money Management

Managing money requires knowledge of how to budget, which is really how one manages expenses considering income, and to do this taking into account personal, couple, and family values. It also requires consideration of how two-income couples manage the different pots of money that they bring into the relationship. Smart money management also involves a plan for saving money for future needs, including unexpected crises.

Creating a Budget

Budgeting is the regular, systematic balancing of income and expenses. It is a personal system for making sure there is enough money to cover the essentials and, one hopes, a few extras.

To construct a workable budget, individuals need to examine their personal values about saving and spending; they must also have a good idea of what things really cost. To begin with, couples need to establish how much income they can count on. They should then outline their expenses by category: shelter, transportation, food, clothing, and so forth. After developing categories that reflect their particular circumstances, they must estimate how much money they will need to pay for each category.

Finances are one of the most stressful areas for couples because they reflect couples' power dynamics and values.

Most people don't take the time to create a budget. An accurate budget requires that a couple or family record their expenses on a regular basis (e.g., monthly) so they know how much they are spending in each category. At the end of the month, the couple can look at the recorded expenditures and develop a budget for the next month. Individuals usually find budgeting easier than families do because they don't need to negotiate decisions and work out priorities that are appropriate for the entire family.

Budgeting is a continuous process of assessment and adjustment. A good budget is simple, realistic, and clear. A good budget builds in some personal control for each family member. It also distinguishes between wants and needs, with needs given priority but a few wants satisfied if possible. A good budget treats credit as debt, not income. Charging something or deciding to pay for it "on time" creates a fixed expense that adds to a family's debt.

Pooling Money: Pros and Cons

Should two-income couples pool their money? This is a difficult question that partners have to answer together, and one they should discuss before marriage. Many newly married couples feel obligated to pool their money, believing that a refusal to do so might be interpreted as a lack of commitment. Married couples tend to favor pooling more than cohabiting couples, but those who remarry after divorce are more likely to maintain separate funds, perhaps because they worry about the permanence of the new relationship.

Pooling is simpler because there are fewer accounts to balance. But because each spouse must keep the other informed about financial transactions, pooling entails some loss of independence. If one partner forgets to record a check written on the joint account and causes an overdraft, a conflict is inevitable.

Another approach is to pool some of the money from each person to cover joint expenses and for each person to also keep a smaller but separate checking account and credit card. The problem with each individual having more freedom is when the total from the joint expenses and the two separate expenses cannot be paid.

How to Save Money

Thrift used to be a basic American virtue. Now the American virtue is to spend money.
—DAVID BRINKLEY

Most poverty-level and lower-income families are incapable of saving much money. They spend a high percentage of their income to meet basic needs such as food, clothing, shelter, and utilities. However, middle- and upper-income families are in a good position to save something each month, and there are very good reasons for them to do so.

Perhaps the best reason for saving is to prepare for the possibility of a financial crisis. Accidents, illness, pregnancy, job loss, divorce, and many other crises are all too common—and they all have financial consequences. At least 6 months' salary should be saved for emergencies. By following a few simple guidelines, couples and families can save 10% to 20% of their income per year. Thomas Garman and Raymond Forgue (1997), experts in financial management, offer six guidelines for those who want to save money:

- *Don't buy on impulse.* Know what you're shopping for and don't buy anything you don't really need.
- *Avoid buying on credit.* The high interest rates credit cards charge can double the cost of an item.
- *Buy at the right time.* Avoid peak-demand, and therefore peak-price, periods. Watch for sales but don't buy something just because it's cheap. Look for quality.
- *Don't pay extra for a brand name.* Generic items are often as good as and are usually cheaper than brand-name goods. Again, look for quality.
- *Recognize that convenience costs money.* The local store may be handy, but a once-a-week trip to the discount center may yield savings.
- *Question the need to go first class.* Do you really need the "best"? Can you really afford the most expensive version of a given product or service?

Perhaps the most important fact of the financial world is that interest on savings compounds. Money invested in a safe place at a good rate of return grows at a steady rate. Albert Einstein is reported to have called compound interest "the

TABLE 8.4	The Results of Saving $100 a Month at Different Interest Rates			
		INTEREST RATE		
Years	Amount Invested	6%	12%	Difference
10	$12,000	$ 16,766	$ 23,586	$ 6,820
20	24,000	46,791	96,838	50,047
30	36,000	100,562	324,351	223,789
40	48,000	196,857	1,030,970	834,113

greatest mathematical discovery of all time." By saving a few hundred dollars a month over 30 or 40 years, a person can become a millionaire. It takes some planning and careful budgeting, but the result is relative financial gain and security. Table 8.4 shows the result of saving $100 a month and investing it at 6% and 12% rates of growth over various periods.

Credit: Uses and Abuses

There are both advantages and disadvantages to using credit. Buying on credit is easy, but it is important not to overdo it. Excessive debt can result in bankruptcy. Financial counseling can help those who have gotten into problems with credit.

Credit Cards—Dangerous Plastic

Having a credit card, actually several cards, has become the norm for most adults and with it has come credit card debt. The average credit card debt for the typical American family is now $9,205 (CardWeb.com, 2004). About two-thirds of families carry a monthly balance and the interest rate ranges from 15% to over 20%. These plastic cards are creating a society where having a savings account is rare compared to having credit card debt.

College students are now offered "interest-free" credit cards with unspecified spending limits and these cards are very easy to obtain. College campuses are flooded with a large variety of credit cards that students can sign up to use. Unfortunately, it is too easy to spend money and abuse these cards, and most students find themselves having credit card debt. A common sign of financial problems is when people sign up for additional credit cards, which they use to pay off past credit card debt. (See Box 8.3.) "Twenty-somethings" are the group of individuals who are most likely to get into credit card trouble because they have recently begun living on their own and have new financial obligations (Chu, 2006).

Some credit card companies are now even offering prepaid cards for teenagers from 13 to 17 years of age. The parents set the spending limits, and children learn how easy and fun it is to use a credit card like their parents. This could be a great opportunity for parents to teach their children the value of saving and being wise shoppers, but most parents do not follow through with these important financial lessons.

Just paying the minimum amount on a credit card can be very costly. Let us assume that the interest rate is about 17%, which is about the average rate on most credit cards. If you had a monthly balance of only $1,000, it would cost you $2,590 and 17 years to pay off the balance. If you had a monthly balance of $2,500, your total cost would be $7,734, and with a monthly balance of $5,000, the total cost you would pay over 40 years would be $16,305. So the goal should be to pay off your credit card balance every month; otherwise, you will be in a difficult financial position very quickly, which will be hard to resolve.

Advantages and Disadvantages of Credit

Buying on credit is very popular for a number of reasons. It is convenient, and it also allows people to enjoy something while paying for it, to take advantage of sales, and to have something in case of an emergency. The disadvantages of credit include the generally high interest charges and the potential for overuse. Credit should be used with caution. Unfortunately, it is a very seductive luxury.

BOX 8.3 At Issue

The Credit Card Trap and How to Avoid It

College campuses today are practically overrun with credit card offers. Some banks offer free T-shirts, water bottles, umbrellas, or other incentives to encourage students to sign up for their cards. Actually, many students already have cards before they ever set foot in a college dorm. In his report, "Credit Cards on Campus," Dr. Robert D. Manning (2001) notes that ". . . companies are approving credit lines for students at progressively earlier ages, including high school seniors. Most college freshmen now receive their first credit card before taking their first mid-term exam." And no wonder—marketing these cards to students is now a billion-dollar business, and there is no sign of a slowdown.

Having a credit card in hand makes it so easy, so convenient, to shop for clothes, eat out with friends, and enjoy the good life. But such convenience often comes at quite a price, and every year thousands of college students find themselves caught in the credit trap.

Here are some surprising statistics about college credit card users:

- In 2003, 54% of freshman students carried a credit card. By sophomore year, that number rose to 92% (Lazarony, 2002).
- 47% of college students have four or more credit cards (Lazarony, 2002).
- Between freshman orientation and graduation day, students double their credit card debt and triple the number of credit cards in their wallets (Lazarony, 2002).

- Three out of five students reached or exceeded their credit cards' limits during their freshman year (Singletary, 2003).
- Almost three-quarters of students used their student loans to pay credit card bills (Singletary, 2003).
- Student credit card holders are more likely (12.1%) to be more than 30 days late in paying their bills, as compared to older adult card holders (8.1%) (Singletary, 2004).

There are many reasons students get into trouble with credit cards. One reason is that banks and credit card companies, which used to require parental approval for student cards, no longer do so. Some teens, out from under parental authority for the first time and enjoying the sense of financial freedom that having their own credit card gives them, fail to realize the consequences of letting their spending get out of hand.

Another reason, according to James A. Roberts, associate professor of marketing at Baylor University, is that "research shows that when you use a credit card you overestimate your wealth, you are less sensitive to price and you are more likely to purchase compared to those who write checks or pay cash" (Singletary, 2004).

Students, and some parents as well, argue that it is important to have a credit card in order to build a good credit history so that after graduation they will be able to rent an apartment or finance a car. Thus, building a credit history—a good credit history—can be a good thing.

Buying a home is an important aspect of family life. A home can be a great unifying benefit for families and can also be a major cost.

However, problems with credit cards—like late or missed payments—stay on your credit reports for seven years. It isn't necessary to have a credit card to establish credit. Another way for students to establish credit is to sign up for telephone, utility, or retail accounts in their own names (i.e., not their parents') and pay their bills on time (Singletary, 2003).

The best way to *avoid* the credit trap is to be knowledgeable about credit cards before getting one. Think seriously about whether or not you really need one. Many people do just fine in life without them. And, be very cautious if you do choose to have a credit card.

Below are some tips for the wise credit consumer:

- Make sure you're ready to handle your own finances. Open a checking account before you get to school and learn how to track your expenses.
- Get a secured card or a debit card. A secured card requires a security deposit of a certain dollar amount, and that is your credit limit (which can be as low as $200 to $500). A debit card is linked to your checking account balance, so you can't overspend easily.
- Compare rates and fees before you sign up for any card. You can go to Web sites like www.cardtrak.com or www.bankrate.com to make comparisons.
- When comparing rates, look for details like annual fees, late fees, and charges for cash advances.
- Be sure to read the fine print of any credit card offer. Some cards offer a "teaser rate," which is an initial low interest rate that increases sharply after only a few months.
- Take responsibility for paying the card yourself. You're much less likely to rack up the spending if you're footing the bill rather than your parents.
- Negotiate lower rates. Call the credit card company and ask for a lower rate. Companies are competitive, and if you have a good credit history, the company may give it to you (Chu, 2006).
- Pay your bills on time. Finance charges and late fees quickly add up to much more than the cost of the original product or service.
- Visit the Federal Trade Commission Web site at either www.ftc.gov or www.consumer.gov for free information on dozens of topics relating to credit cards.

If you do fall into the credit trap, Poduska (2001) suggests ways to get out of it—for example, by paying cash for as many things as possible, using the credit card only for emergencies, paying off the debt as soon as possible to reduce the compounded interest over the long haul (even if this means asking your parents for help), and reducing your living expenses by buying only what you really need.

When it comes to the credit card trap, the most important thing to remember is that while it is easy to fall into it, getting out of it can prove very difficult.

Purchasing a Home

The family dwelling has psychological significance in virtually all cultures. It provides the family's space and binds them together as a unit. It can be a haven, a place of rest and enjoyment, somewhere to kick off one's shoes and escape the pretenses of polite society.

A home is usually the most expensive item Americans buy. Careful deliberation should go into its purchase. One rule of thumb is that, whether renting or buying, a family should spend no more than 1 week's take-home pay per month for housing expenses. Housing expenses are either rent or the total of all housepayment expenses (mortgage payment, insurance, and real estate taxes). Families who can find adequate shelter for 20% to 25% of their take-home pay are likely to be in relatively good financial health. Unfortunately, many lower-income families find themselves paying 50% of their income or more for housing.

Renting Versus Buying. Generally speaking, it is wiser to buy a home than to rent. Rent money is gone forever, whereas each mortgage payment gradually increases one's equity in the home and inflation increases the net worth of the dwelling. There are, however, many exceptions to this generalization, and families must carefully analyze their unique financial situation to decide if buying a home is the right choice for them.

There are numerous advantages to both renting and buying. The advantages of renting include mobility, perhaps some amenities (pool, tennis courts, party rooms, laundry facilities), and a lifestyle that involves fewer responsibilities. No large down payment is needed (only a security deposit), and the relatively fixed housing expenditure (rent) makes budgeting easier.

The advantages of buying include pride of ownership, a better credit rating, and a monthly payment that remains constant for many years (that is, with a fixed-rate mortgage). The federal income tax deductions for mortgage interest and real estate property taxes are a major advantage, as is the potential for the home to increase in value over time. Owning a house forces one to save; each payment represents an asset that is growing in value. A homeowner can also borrow against equity as the value of the home increases. Furthermore, owners can make home improvements and alterations, which can increase the value of the home and/or add to the enjoyment of the dwelling.

The disadvantages of renting are that it offers no tax deductions and no potential gain from the rising value of the property. Furthermore, rents rise with inflation, and many rental units have restrictions on noise level, pet ownership, and children. One disadvantage of buying is the substantial down payment that is needed; this can reduce available funds for other things. Also, the cost of maintenance and repairs can be high. A home is a big commitment in time, emotion, and money.

Table 8.5 illustrates the financial benefits of buying versus renting. The example is based on renting a home for $600 a month or buying a similar home for a slightly lower mortgage payment of $545.48 a month. Careful study of the table shows that renting in this particular situation costs more than buying by $2,154 a year.

The Cost of Home Loans. The average interest rate in 2006 for a 30-year home mortgage was only about 6%, a drop from about 9% to 10% in 2000. This drop has greatly increased the number of people purchasing homes. The difference in the monthly payment between a 9% and a 10% home loan might not be much, but over the life of the loan—which usually lasts anywhere from 15 to 30 years—the savings on interest payments can be substantial. A very modest 25-year mortgage loan of $60,000 will cost the borrower more than $151,000 at 9% interest but more than $157,000 at 10% interest. One percentage point makes a $6,000 difference over the 25-year life of the loan. These figures also show that a $65,000 or $75,000 home (assuming a $5,000 or $15,000 down payment plus a $60,000 loan) really costs more than double its price when the interest on the mortgage is considered.

Credit Overextension

Out of debt, out of danger.

—From a Chinese Fortune Cookie

Credit overextension, a situation in which excessive debts make repayment difficult, is a serious problem that can cause considerable stress on families. The following danger signs suggest credit overextension (Garman & Forgue, 1997):

- *Debt exceeds normal limits.* People who spend more than 15% to 20% of their disposable income to repay debts (excluding mortgage loans) are likely to be in trouble. If the percentage increases each month, the situation becomes even more serious.

	CALCULATING THE COST TO	
TABLE 8.5 Should You Buy or Rent?	Rent	Buy
Cash Flow Considerations		
Annual rent ($600/month) or mortgage payments ($545.48/month)	$7,200	$6,546
Property and liability insurance	270	425
Real estate taxes	NA	2,000
Maintenance	NA	320
Less interest on funds not used for down payment (at 5%)	−750	0
Cash flow cost for the year	**$6,720**	**$9,291**
Tax and Appreciation Considerations		
Less principal repaid on the mortgage loan	NA	−725
Plus tax on interest from funds not used for down payment (28% tax bracket)	210	NA
Less tax savings due to deductibility of mortage interest (28% tax bracket)	NA	−1,630
Less tax savings due to deductibility of real estate property tax (28% tax bracket)	NA	−560
Less appreciation on the dwelling (2% rate)	NA	−1,600
Net cost for the year	**$6,930**	**$4,776**

Source: Personal Finance (5th ed.) (p. 292) by E. T. Garman and R. E. Forgue, 1997, Boston: Houghton Mifflin. Copyright © 1997 Houghton Mifflin Co. Reprinted by permission of the publisher.

- *Monthly expenses exceed income.* When too much income goes to debt repayment, people may use credit cards to purchase things they would normally buy with cash. They may also use high-interest-rate cash advances from their credit cards. Both actions increase the overall debt load.
- *Using savings to pay for everyday expenses.*
- *Paying the minimum payment only.* Rather than paying each month's bills in full, people begin to pay only what they must, increasing their debt from month to month.
- *Reaching or exceeding credit limits.* People who are at or near the limits of their various lines of credit or those who are requesting increases in their credit limits may be in trouble.
- *Picking which creditors to pay.* As monthly bills mount and sources of additional credit are exhausted, people begin to pick and choose among creditors, paying a few one month and others the next.
- *Borrowing from one source to pay another.* People who use a cash advance from one credit card to pay the monthly bill on another credit card are likely to be in trouble.
- *Total debt is unknown.* People who cannot quickly estimate how much they owe often have multiple creditors to whom they owe large amounts.
- *Loss of a job would mean immediate financial disaster.* When a wage earner loses a job, it is a serious financial crisis for most families. But the full effects may not be felt immediately by families who have a savings cushion. Those who

are already overextended in terms of credit have no resources with which to weather any loss of income.

Avoiding Debt and Bankruptcy

Bankruptcy is a legal term indicating that a person is financially insolvent and unable to pay her or his debts. In 2003, more than 1.6 million people declared personal bankruptcy in the United States, and about 35,000 businesses filed for bankruptcy (U.S. Bureau of the Census, 2004b). Although bankruptcy offers some protection from creditors, it is not a solution to financial problems because bankruptcy blemishes one's financial record for many years, making many financial matters more difficult. In our society bankruptcy signifies an individual's inability to handle money wisely, and society exacts various punishments on those who declare bankruptcy.

To stay out of debt and avoid bankruptcy, it is helpful to know why some people assume too much debt. It is interesting that level of income is not clearly related to debt. Debt-free families and debt-ridden families alike come from all socioeconomic levels.

Excessive debt may be due to any or all of the following reasons: credit spending, crisis spending, careless or impulsive spending, and compulsive spending. Unwise *credit spending* can lead to overextension. *Crisis spending*—resulting from unexpected events in life such as unemployment, uninsured illness, and business income decline or failure—can throw personal finances into turmoil. *Careless or impulsive spending* includes overpaying for items that could be purchased for less, purchasing inferior merchandise that does not last, and buying things one does not really need. *Compulsive spending* occurs because some people simply can't say no to salespeople or because they have an uncontrollable impulse to acquire material things.

Fortunately, there are a number of time-tested strategies for families who have become overextended. Although these solutions are not easy, they are far better than the alternative of bankruptcy:

- Develop and stick to a balanced budget.
- Avoid making any new financial commitments. Do not incur any new debt.
- Destroy all credit cards or lock them up so that they can't be used.
- Develop a plan for repaying all debts. If the budget cannot handle the repayment schedule, try to negotiate lower payments and lower payback periods.
- Pay off debts with the highest interest rates first.
- Work to reduce the total number of debts.
- Make a plan to pay at least a small amount on each debt each month.
- Avoid debt consolidation loans. These can set the stage for new borrowing, especially on credit cards.

Financial Counseling

If they have made no progress in 3 to 6 months, people who are overextended should seek financial counseling. Many large employers have budget counselors available through the human resources department or an employee assistance program. When financial difficulties are a symptom of a deeper marital or personal problem (alcohol or other drug abuse, depression, violence), a therapist may be the best way to approach the crisis.

For example, a single parent continues to support her 25-year-old son, even though his cocaine addiction is dragging her down financially. The son deals cocaine to come up with some of the $3,000 or $4,000 a month he needs to support his drug habit. He regularly borrows money from his mother and even steals and pawns her possessions. Consumed by guilt, she covers up for him, pays the bills, and lends him money, denying his drug habit. This mother needs not only a competent financial adviser to help her deal with the mountain of debts she has accumulated but also a personal therapist to help her come to grips with her son's drug problem, for which he must take responsibility.

People seeking financial counseling should avoid "credit clinics," which charge fees of $250 to $2,000 or more for their services. Some of these businesses advertise that they will negotiate new repayment schedules with creditors, but people in financial trouble can work directly with their creditors or can find help from non-profit personal counseling organizations (Bauer & Wollen, 1990; Garman & Forgue, 1997). The human services section of most local telephone books lists resources. Another possible resource is the network of more than 1,000 Consumer Credit Counseling Service (CCCS) agencies across the United States. Each year about a million people seek credit and budget counseling advice from CCCS.

Summary

- According to a national survey of married couples, happy couples—as compared to unhappy couples—agree on how to spend money, have no concerns about how the partner spends money, are satisfied with decisions about savings, major debts are not a problem, and financial decisions are not difficult.

- People manage their economic resources in different ways, depending on their worldviews, life experiences, and family structures.

- The top five financial-management issues that married couples identified in a national survey were the following: wish partner was more careful spending money, have trouble saving, have problems deciding what is more important to purchase, major debts are a problem, and partner tries to control the money.

- Financial issues are the most common stressor for U.S. families across the family life cycle, regardless of their income level. The most financially trying periods are the childbearing, adolescent, launching, and retirement stages.

- Money problems are often related to a couple's or a family's inability to develop specific spending and saving plans. Some arguments are not really about money, however, but about power and control in the relationship.

- Personal and family coping behaviors that help people through difficult economic times include self-esteem, cohesion, and adaptability. Social support from family members and others and the use of family service agencies are also important resources. Coping strategies that make things worse include denying the problem and failing to disclose feelings.

- Although couples often think that things will get better after a divorce, divorce is financially costly, and couples need to be aware of those potential costs as they contemplate this important life decision.

- Finances cause problems for couples and families because people (1) consider the topic of money taboo, (2) do not create and stick to a budget, (3) overspend and rely too heavily on credit, (4) differ in their spending and saving styles, (5) use money as a tool to gain power and control over their partner, and (6) have different ideas about the meaning of money.

- More than half the families in the United States are considered middle-income families, defined by the U.S. Bureau of the Census as earning between $15,000 and $75,000 per year. However, a disproportionate share of the money in this country goes to affluent families, with 25.1% of families receiving roughly 47.3% of the personal income. About 16% of U.S. families are lower-income families, but they make only 6.2% of all personal income.

- White families in the United States make more money, on average, than Hispanic and African American families. Asian families have the highest median income of $55,521. The median income for White families is $45,856 and is considerably higher than that of African American ($30,439) or Hispanic ($33,447) families. Males make more money than females, and there is a clear relationship between educational level and income.

- Budgeting is the regular, systematic balancing of income and expenses. To budget successfully, individuals need to examine their personal values about saving and spending and to monitor their plan monthly.
- Couples who pool their money are neither more nor less satisfied with money management issues in the relationship than couples who have separate accounts.
- Most poverty-level and lower-income families are incapable of saving much money because they must spend most of their income to meet basic needs. Middle- and upper-income families should put aside at least 6 months' income in savings for financial emergencies.
- Monthly housing expenses should consume no more than 1 week's take-home pay. Generally, buying a home is a better investment than renting.
- Credit spending, crisis spending, careless or impulsive spending, and compulsive spending are four reasons people go into excessive debt. Families who cannot reduce their debt over a period of 3 to 6 months should seek financial and perhaps personal counseling.

Key Terms

goals	family coping resources
collective worldview	budgeting
individualistic worldview	bankruptcy
personal coping resources	

Activities

1. Go to the Web site for Crown Financial Ministries (www.crown.org) and click on Budget Guide and then the Credit Calculator. Borrow $10,000 on your credit card and then set up minimum monthly payments and see the consequences.

2. Write a few paragraphs describing how money was handled in your family of origin and how you handle money today. Then form groups of five or six for discussion. After having read the essays out loud, identify similarities and differences that emerge.

3. Are you a spender or a saver? How about your partner? Consider the similarities and differences between your style and your partner's style.

4. Pair off into "couples" and discuss the following questions as if you were planning to marry. Then report your discussions to the class.
   a. Do you expect to share equally in financial decisions? If not, how do you plan to make financial decisions?
   b. Do you plan to use a budget? Why or why not?
   c. How do you feel about each partner's having a personal allowance for which he or she is not accountable to the other?
   d. How do you feel about buying small items on credit? Large items?
   e. Who will be the treasurer? The check writer? The bookkeeper? The investor?

Suggested Readings

Anthony, J., & Cluck, K. (2001). *Debt free by 30: Practical advice for young, broke and upwardly mobile.* New York: Plume.

Bach, D. (2002). *Smart couples finish rich.* New York: Random House.

Holzner, C., Jameson, K., Maloney, T., Abebe, B., Lund, M., & Schaub, K. (2006). *The economic impact of the Mexico–Utah relationship.* University of Utah Study. Web site: http://www.ipia.utah.edu/utah_mexico_final_version.pdf.

Kobliner, B. (2000). *Get a financial life: Personal finance in your twenties and thirties.* New York: Fireside.

Schramm, D. G. (2006). Individual and social costs of divorce in Utah. *Journal of Family and Economic Issues, 27,* 133–151.

Skogrand, L., Schramm, D. G., Marshall, J. P., & Lee, T. (2005). The effects of debt on newlyweds and implications for education. *Journal of Extension, 43.* Web site: http://www.joe.org/joe/2005june/rb7.shtml.

Visit the text-specific Online Learning Center at **www.mhhe.com/Olson6** for practice tests, chapter summaries, Web links, Internet exercises, key terms, and flashcards.

9 *Friendship, Intimacy, and Singlehood*

Friends Versus Lovers

Exploring Intimacy: From Experience to Relationship

Developing Intimacy

Intimacy Games

Being Single

Summary

Key Terms

Activities

Suggested Readings

In this chapter we will explore various ways of defining love and the related concept of intimacy. We will also identify a number of constructive and destructive games people play in their intimate relationships. The goal of this chapter is to help you understand love and intimacy and learn how to enhance your own intimate experiences and relationships. To conclude, we will take a close look at singlehood, which for many is a legitimate, healthy, and happy alternative to marriage.

Love and friendship bind society together, providing both emotional support and a buffer against stress and thereby preserving our physical and psychological health. Love is clearly much more than friendship, and thus we treat love relationships more seriously. However, the strongest love relationships have roots in friendship. Satisfying and stable love relationships come from shared interests and values. When friends fall in love, they are adding passion to the emotional intimacy we call friendship.

Love means different things to different people. Definitions of love are almost endless (Table 9.1). No other topic demands so much attention and generates so much confusion in our society. We cannot turn on the radio or TV, pick up a magazine or book, or converse with a friend for long without being confronted with words about love, thoughts of love, acts of love, or images of love. Despite the ubiquitous nature of love, it remains a mystery to many. Many regard it as a strange force that can overpower us and at times take control over our lives: People speak of being "under love's spell" or being "swept away" with passion.

Friends Versus Lovers

Research over a 20-year span indicates that love and friendship are alike in many ways but that crucial differences make love both more rewarding and more volatile than friendship. After conducting several studies, Keith E. Davis and his colleague Michael J. Todd came to this conclusion:

TABLE 9.1	On Love
In love the paradox occurs that two beings become one yet remain two. —ERICH FROMM, *Psychiatrist* Love doesn't just sit there, like a stone, it has to be made, like bread; remade all the time, made new. —URSULA K. LE GUIN, *Writer* Being in love isn't ever really loving, it's just wanting. And it isn't any good. It's all aching and misery. —JAMES LEO HERLIHY, *Writer* Love is the history of a woman's life; it is an episode in man's. —MADAME DE STAËL, *Writer* He who knows nothing, loves nothing . . . But he who understands also loves, notices, sees . . . The more knowledge inherent in a thing, the greater the love. —PARACELSUS, *Philosopher*	The trouble with some women is that they get all excited about nothing—and then marry him. —CHER, *Actor* When the satisfaction or the security of another person becomes as significant to one as is one's own security, then the state of love exists. —HARRY STACK SULLIVAN, *Psychiatrist* Chains do not hold a marriage together. It is threads, hundreds of tiny threads which sew people together through the years. This is what makes a marriage last—more than passion or even sex! —SIMONE SIGNORET, *Actor* Love is a state of perpetual anesthesia. —H.L MENCKEN, *Journalist* There is only one happiness in life, to love and be loved. —GEORGE SAND, *Writer*

Typical love relationships will differ from even very good friendships by having higher levels of fascination, exclusiveness and sexual desire, a greater depth of caring about the other individual (which would be manifest in a willingness to give the utmost when needed), and a greater potential for enjoyment and other positive emotions. Love relationships will also have, however, a greater potential for distress, ambivalence, conflict, and mutual criticism. (Davis, 1985, p. 30)

Love, in short, runs deeper and stronger than friendship. And because the stakes are so high with love, the possibility of interpersonal difficulties increases, and we jealously guard this important relationship.

The Fabric of Friendship

Davis and Todd began their research by developing a classic model of friendship and love (Davis, 2004, 2007). In their original profile of friendship, they first assumed that two individuals participate in a reciprocal relationship as equals. The fabric of friendship included eight important elements:

- *Enjoyment.* Friends enjoy each other's company most of the time, although disagreements and friction occasionally occur.
- *Acceptance.* Friends accept each other for who they are and don't try to change each other.
- *Trust.* Friends assume that they will act in each other's best interest. "Even when he's hassling me, I know it's for my own good." "She would never intentionally hurt me, except in a fit of extreme anger."
- *Respect.* Friends respect each other; they assume the other has good judgment in making choices in life.
- *Mutual assistance.* Friends help and support each other; they can count on each other in times of need.
- *Confiding.* Friends share life experiences and feelings with each other.
- *Understanding.* Friends know each other's values and understand what is important to each other. "I know what makes her tick."
- *Spontaneity.* Friends feel free to be "real" around each other. They don't feel they have to play a role or hold back their true feelings.

The Tapestry of Love

Love is magical, changing, fragile, complex, and paradoxical. Amy and David Olson (2001) describe 10 traits of love that are common in our culture (see Box 9.1).

Davis and Todd assumed at the outset of their studies that romantic relationships would have the same characteristics as friendship but that they would also have additional, unique characteristics. The unique characteristics were grouped in two broad categories: the Passion Cluster and the Caring Cluster. The model of friendship and love that Davis and Todd developed is shown in Figure 9.1.

The **Passion Cluster** encompasses three related characteristics: fascination, sexual desire, and exclusiveness. Fascination is a preoccupation with the other person—a tendency to think about, look at, want to talk to, and want to be with that person. Sexual desire is the lovers' desire to touch each other and to make love, even though they may not engage in sexual intercourse for religious, moral, or practical reasons. Exclusiveness is giving the partner priority over other relationships in one's life.

The **Caring Cluster** contains two components: being an advocate for one's partner and giving the utmost. Being a champion and an advocate means defending

BOX 9.1   Putting It Together

Ten Traits of Love

Amy and David Olson (cited in Levine & Markman, 2001) describe 10 traits of love that are common in our culture. Learning to recognize and appreciate these 10 traits can be a major factor in honing intimacy skills.

1. **Love is a magical process that creates couple chemistry**. Like a chemical reaction, love creates a new entity when two people are in love. The whole is also greater and different from the sum of the parts. In chemistry, two molecules of hydrogen and one molecule of oxygen create water. So it is with couples. If one of the same people pair with a different person (like a different element in chemistry), the resulting product will be different.

2. **Love is often blind**. Love causes us to see things more optimistically than they actually are, which interferes with our knowledge and true discovery of each other. For this reason, family and friends can often know who is a better match for you than you do for yourself. This is because people outside of your intimate relationship are better able to more objectively "see" things that you may not be able to "see" because you are too close emotionally to the relationship.

3. **Love changes over time**. The beginning stages of love are typically very romantic and idealistic. Over time, love becomes more realistic. Some of the "excitement" that comes from the mystery and unfolding of getting to know another person will inevitably dissipate with discovery. But real love will continue to grow and mature in deeper and more meaningful ways as you nurture it and keep it alive.

4. **Love-based marriages are more fragile than arranged marriages**. Because the nature of love is always changing, a couple in a love-match marriage may feel threatened by the natural changes of love. They may interpret the change as "falling out of love" and may think about getting out of the relationship. And although love is an important ingredient in marriage, it should not be the only one.

    We know that in the United States where love-match marriages occur, the divorce rate continues to be about 50%. During the early stages of a relationship, it probably *appears* to both individuals that love is all they need to get them through any circumstance. Whether love will prevail no matter what problems you encounter will be determined by the quality of the relationship and each partner's commitment to it.

5. **Superficial love fades over time**. With superficial love, the best and most intense moments are at the beginning of the relationship—the "falling in love" stage. Reality inevitably dissolves and breaks down this type of unstable love, and the relationship becomes progressively less satisfying, either slowly or sometimes very quickly. Superficial love may feel intense, but it is really a delicate phenomenon. It tends to be equated with sex, attraction, security, and romance.

6. **Real love grows over time**. With real love, the positive feelings grow with time. Couples experiencing real love will often express that they love their partner more and more each day. Real love creates and enables both individuals to grow. Real love realizes that love does not just "happen" but is the result of the process of working on the relationship.

7. **Our language of love is inadequate**. We are limited by the language we have to describe love. Love is much more complex than what we often express. Can we possibly be expressing the same thoughts when we say, "I love pizza," "I love football," and "I love you"? Similarly, whereas Eskimos have many different words to describe what we simply call "snow," we basically have one word to describe love. How, then, do we describe love when love is infinite and beyond definition?

8. **Love is often misdiagnosed**. Related to the language barriers in describing love is a common misdiagnosis of love. People often make the mistake of using the word "love" when what they really are describing is passion, excitement, enjoyment, or need.

9. **Love is paradoxical**. Love is both limited and unlimited. Love can conquer anything, yet it often does not. In marriage and relationships, love helps get the relationship off to a good start because it energizes the couple to connect, but it is not sufficient in making the relationship last. Unless the couple have and use good relationship skills, love will fade over time.

10. **Giving love is receiving love**. In order to experience love, you must be vulnerable to it. When love is given away, it remains with you as well. In fact, love is unique in that the more you give, the more you will have to give and the more you will receive.

Source: Olson & Olson, 2001.

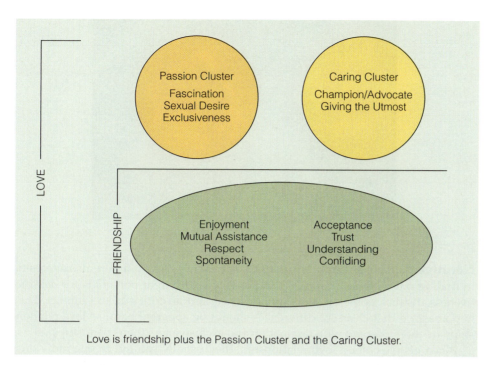

FIGURE 9.1

Love and Friendship

Source: "Near and Dear: Friendship and Love Compared" by K. E. Davis (February) 1985, *Psychology Today*, p. 24. Copyright 1985 by Sussex Publishers, Inc. Reprinted by permission from *Psychology Today* magazine.

Love is friendship plus the Passion Cluster and the Caring Cluster.

and supporting each other, even during difficult times. Giving the utmost is easy for people in love; sometimes they give to the point of self-sacrifice.

Contrasting Friends and Lovers

Davis and Todd found that love is friendship with a few added components, but they were surprised by a few other findings. In their survey of 242 friends, spouses, and lovers (two-thirds students, one-third community members), the researchers discovered specific similarities and differences between friends and lovers.

Positive Aspects of Friendship and Love. On the Caring Cluster, best friendships are similar to spouse/lover relationships in several ways: Both show virtually identical levels of acceptance, trust, and respect and similar levels of confiding, understanding, spontaneity, mutual assistance, and satisfaction and happiness with the relationship. On the Passion Cluster, however, there is much more fascination and exclusiveness in spouse/lover relationships than in best-friend relationships.

On the Caring Cluster, Davis and Todd hypothesized that spouses and lovers would be more willing than best friends to give the utmost when needed and would be more active champions and advocates of the loved one. They were surprised, however, to find that this was the case only on the give-the-utmost characteristic. They were also surprised to find that best friendships were perceived as being more stable than spouse/lover relationships. Spouses and, especially, unmarried lovers were more concerned that their relationships might break up. As a single woman in her early 30s put it, "Lovers come and go, but I can always count on my friends." The loss of friends and, especially, loved ones can lead to illness and even suicide. Although love is much more than friendship, both kinds of relationships are important in people's lives.

Love has much in common with friendship, but it is more intense and passionate. Like this man and woman, couples in love tend to be fascinated with each other, spending long moments gazing unselfconsciously into each other's eyes.

Negative Aspects of Friendship and Love. Davis and Todd were also interested in finding out whether friendship and love have different potentials for destructiveness, distress, possessiveness, ambivalence, mutual criticism, and conflict. They hypothesized that clear-cut differences should be apparent because love relationships are more charged with fascination and exclusiveness than friendships.

When people enter a love relationship, they usually commit to one individual and give up other, similar love relationships. Being a spouse or a lover also means closely coordinating activities with the loved one and giving the loved one's interests priority over relationships with others. This strong commitment can lead to such questions as, "Am I giving up too much?" "Did I do the right thing by committing to her?"

Davis and Todd found that because the stakes are so high, love relationships can easily become breeding grounds for ambivalent feelings and conflict. They also found that spouses and lovers were significantly less accepting of each other than were friends. Spouses and lovers had a greater desire to change each other; they were also more willing to criticize their partners than to criticize their friends.

Friendship Into Love. It appears that the strongest love relationships have roots in friendship. Many scholars maintain that satisfying and stable relationships come from shared interests and values, and "that's what love is about." According to Susan S. Hendrick (Hendrick & Hendrick, 2000), the following clues signal the end of a beautiful friendship and the beginning of love: You are suddenly aware of your friend's wonderful smile, great body, or cute freckles; you get dressed up when you know you're going to see each other; you feel excited at the thought of meeting; and you begin to feel shy and less spontaneous when you're together. Josh, a graduate student, recalls the transformation of his relationship with Jessica and his realization that the qualities that make up friendship can also be the foundation for love:

"I'm so happy we were friends for a long time before we became lovers. Passion is really great, but it clutters up a relationship a great deal. You don't know what you have underneath the passion if it drains away. But the friendship shines on and on, through good times and bad times.

"I didn't really think of Jessica in a genuinely sexual way until several months after I got to know her. She was just always that good friend down the hallway in the apartment building who I could talk to about anything. Sometimes she would counsel me on my girlfriends, and then one day I looked at her and thought, 'Wow, she ought to be my girlfriend!'"

Psychologist Robert Sternberg (2006, 2007; Sternberg & Weis, 2006) believes that when friends fall in love, they are simply adding passion to the emotional intimacy we call friendship. The temptation is to let oneself be swept away by romance, but Hendrick (Hendrick & Hendrick, 2000) argues that individuals should use some uncommon sense. This includes letting things develop slowly, being honest with the other person and with oneself, and keeping an open mind and a sense of humor. It is important to remember that it is easier to fall in love than to stay in love.

The Love Triangle

Although the phrase *love triangle* usually brings to mind a relationship in which one person has two lovers, another sort of love triangle was developed by Sternberg and Weis (2006). The three dimensions of the triangle are commitment (the cognitive component), intimacy (the emotional component), and passion (the motivational component) (see Figure 9.2).

A relationship can start off with intimacy (friendship) and develop into love. A relationship can also start off with only passion and later develop the other two components. A relationship (such as an arranged marriage) can also begin simply with a commitment between partners for economic reasons or for reasons dictated by the couple's families; even this type of relationship can later develop intimacy and passion and bloom into love.

Commitment is a cognitive attachment to another person. It develops over time, beginning slowly and increasing at a faster rate if the relationship is positive. If the relationship fails, commitment disappears. People express commitment when they move their relationship to a more advanced stage (from dating to engagement, from engagement to marriage), when they are faithful, or when they stay in the relationship during difficult times.

Intimacy involves sharing feelings and providing emotional support. It usually entails high levels of self-disclosure, the sharing of personal information not ordinarily revealed because of the risk involved. Intimacy gradually increases as closeness grows and deepens as a relationship matures. Few couples are likely to share everything with each other. People need some private space, a bit of their world that is closed to everyone else. But in a mature intimate relationship, most areas are open for discussion and sharing. By opening up, by earning each other's

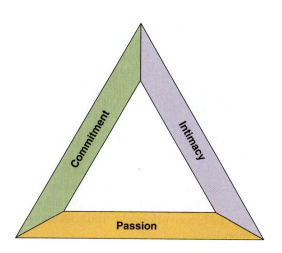

FIGURE 9.2

The Love Triangle

Source: The Psychology of Love (p. 37) edited by R. Sternberg and M. Barnes, 1988, New Haven, CT: Yale University Press. Copyright 1988 by Yale University Press. Reprinted by permission.

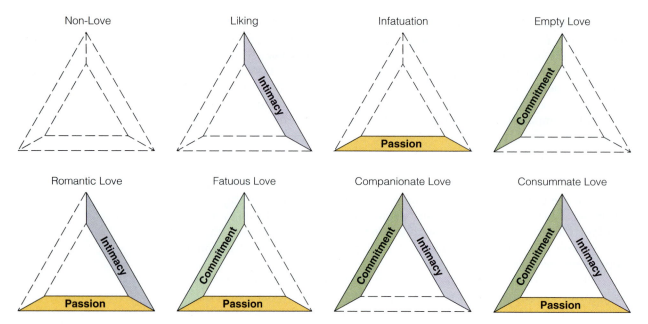

FIGURE 9.3

Eight Types of Love Relationships

Source: The Psychology of Love (p. 51) edited by R. Sternberg and M. Barnes, 1988, New Haven, CT: Yale University Press. Copyright 1988 by Yale University Press. Reprinted by permission.

trust and becoming vulnerable to each other, people can build a strong emotional bond of intimacy. The paradox is that by expressing feelings of weakness and vulnerability, individuals can gain support and strength from trusted loved ones.

Passion is usually expressed by touching, kissing, and being affectionate, which are linked to physiological arousal; it is also expressed through sexual interactions. Because of its intensity, passion develops quickly but can also fade quickly. Passion is like an addiction; when it ends, a person can experience withdrawal symptoms such as irritability and depression.

Combining the three dimensions of love in various ways, Sternberg identified eight types of love relationships: non-love, liking, infatuation, empty love, romantic love, fatuous love, companionate love, and consummate love (Figure 9.3). **Non-love** occurs when there is no commitment, intimacy, or passion. **Liking** begins when there is just intimacy, but no passion or commitment. **Infatuation** involves passion only. In **empty love** there is commitment but no passion or intimacy. **Romantic love** has both intimacy and passion, but it is lacking in commitment. **Fatuous love** occurs when a couple is committed on the basis of passion but has not had the time to develop true intimacy. (For example, two people fall in love and, after seeing each other only on weekends for 2 months, get married.) **Companionate love** is more characteristic of couples who have been married for years. These couples have both commitment and intimacy, but they lack the passion they had when they were first married. Finally, **consummate love** is complete love, containing all three dimensions. It is the goal of most couples.

Most people have experienced several of these types of love and can recognize that each of them feels rather different. Even within one relationship, it is possible to experience two or more types of love over time. A couple, for example, may start out as close friends (liking) and then 2 years later become sexually involved (romantic love); a year later they may decide to live together (consummate love). However, 3 months later he has an affair; she finds out about it and moves out, ending the relationship (non-love).

Three Perspectives on Love

Love is the only thing you get more of by giving it away.

—Tom Wilson

In his classic book *The Art of Loving,* Erich Fromm (2000) describes several important myths about love. He believes that too many people think love is simple; in reality, he maintains, finding the right person is difficult, requiring work and practice. Fromm believes that falling in love is very different from being in love, which involves facing the realities of living together. He also suggests that "being a loving person is the best way to be loved."

Love can also be seen as an addiction. In *Love and Addiction,* Stanton Peele (1991) suggests that, unfortunately, many people who are in love are addicted to love much as people are addicted to alcohol, tobacco, or other drugs. As with other addictions, people seek stability and comfort in the addiction and suffer withdrawal when it is not available. Infatuation generates a good deal of adrenaline in the body, causing an emotional high that people learn to seek. When the high ceases abruptly (because of a breakup, say), people can have a sensation of "crashing," similar to the feeling people experience when certain drugs wear off.

Peele developed several criteria for distinguishing a mature love relationship from an addictive love relationship. Answering yes to any of the following questions indicates a mature love relationship:

- Do you each value yourself?
- Are you both better people as a result of this relationship?
- Do you both have serious interests outside the relationship?
- Is the relationship not the totality of your life?
- Is neither of you possessive or jealous of your partner?
- Are you best friends?

James Dobson offered another perspective on love in his book *Love Must Be Tough* (1999). Dobson believes that *tough love* can help couples and families overcome serious problems and develop stronger relationships. He maintains that in couple conflict, one person is often more independent than the other; the dependent person panics if the other suggests he or she is unhappy or otherwise starts to withdraw from the relationship. Rather than pursue the partner, Dobson suggests, the more dependent person should also pull back from the relationship and be "tough" by demonstrating independence and putting some realistic demands on the relationship. The tough love concept has also been suggested for parents who are having little success dealing with troubled adolescents in more traditional ways.

Jealousy: A Green-Eyed Monster or Real Love?

He that is not jealous is not in love.

Saint Augustine

Love, jealousy, and abuse are all interconnected (McGinley & Sabbadini, 2006; Puente & Cohen, 2003). **Jealousy** is defined as an emotional response to a real or perceived threat to a valued relationship. When a person is in love with another person, there is always the possibility that he or she will feel some jealousy. In fact, some maintain that if there is no jealousy, there is no real love.

Certainly, some level of jealousy is functional in a relationship, but it can become problematic if it intensifies. It can be functional if it encourages a person to think about an intimate relationship and look for positive ways to develop a stronger relationship. But jealousy can be hurtful and can destroy a relationship as it creates more suspicion about the relationship. In the extreme, jealousy can lead to the greater probability of abuse and violence in an intimate relationship.

Both men and women become jealous when their partners become emotionally or sexually involved with other persons; there are no gender differences in the frequency, duration, or intensity of jealous feelings (Levy, Kelly, & Jack, 2006; Pines, 1998). However, there is often a sex difference as it relates to causes of jealousy. Men are more likely to feel jealous if the partner becomes sexually involved with a new partner, whereas women are more likely to be upset if the partner is emotionally connected with another person (Levy et al., 2006; Pines, 1998).

Jealousy is seen by therapists as a self-defeating emotion, and jealous people are often their own worst enemies. Jealousy leads to feelings of possessiveness, envy, and suspicion. The more jealousy takes over as a factor in an intimate relationship, the more it creates a vicious cycle of greater and greater jealousy. The jealous partner, who is often insecure about the relationship anyway, fears losing the relationship. When the partner tries to control the relationship and seeks greater closeness, the person they most fear losing is often driven away. Thus jealousy often leads to more problematic behavior, including various types of abuse (verbal, physical, sexual), and tends to push many couples apart.

Jealousy can be triggered by both external causes and internal causes. The external causes relate to behavior by a person that demonstrates the partner is (or appears to be) more interested in another person emotionally and/or sexually than in you. While you cannot control your partner's behavior, you can control how you perceive this external behavior. You can perceive it as a threat to your relationship, which will trigger jealousy, or as a sign that your partner is friendly and this person is not a threat to you. The greater your insecurity about the relationship, the greater the chances you will feel jealousy (Marelich, Gaines, & Banzet, 2003).

Jealousy is often related to internal factors that are under your control and relate to such factors as your level of self-esteem, how dependent you are in the relationship, your level of insecurity about the relationship, your past experience about trusting others, and your perceived alternatives for another relationship (Levy et al., 2006; Pines, 1998). Findings from a variety of research studies have demonstrated that the lower a person's self-esteem, the more easily that person will become jealous. The more dependent you are on your partner or the more involved in the relationship, the more you will tend to become jealous. If you have been emotionally hurt in past relationships, trust in your partner is often not strong, which can lead to feelings of jealousy.

If you are feeling jealousy in an intimate relationship, it is very important to confront jealousy directly and to talk about it with your partner. Jealousy is a warning sign that things are not going well, and it should not be ignored. The person feeling jealousy should find a time and place to fully discuss the topic, and each person should openly share what he or she is feeling about the relationship. One significant issue to discuss is how much each person is committed to the relationship and wants to maintain it over time. If there is agreement on commitment to the relationship, then the couple should talk about ways that they can both work together to build a closer and more intimate relationship. In other words, jealousy can be a signal that you need to talk about your relationship and explore ways to make it grow.

Exploring Intimacy: From Experience to Relationship

Like love, intimacy is also an elusive concept. The word generally brings to mind images of physical closeness and sexuality. But it is really much more than that. Intimacy is the closeness and feelings of warmth we have with certain people. It is an ongoing process of life with other people, and it has many components. Without intimacy with other human beings, life would be boring, cold, and lonely. Many people in our culture place a high value on intimacy. Although intimacy is not restricted to marriage relationships, most of us get married in our search to find and maintain intimacy. It is considered a reward and benefit of marriage.

Paths to Intimacy Differ in Males and Females

Although both males and females agree that the path to greater intimacy is one of greater personal self-disclosure, a variety of studies have found that females are more likely to follow that path (Fehr, 2004). In studying same-sex friendships, women consistently increase their intimacy with higher levels of self-disclosure about themselves. Males feel greater intimacy through doing activities together. So for many men, intimacy with other males is formed through attending sports events or doing activities together.

When seeking intimacy with those of the other sex, both women and men are often disappointed because they falsely assume that they will create intimacy the same way with the other sex that they do with their same-sex friends. So women often assume that they will achieve greater intimacy with a man by mutual self-disclosure, but many men are not very good at self-disclosure. Similarly, men often assume that it is by simply doing activities together that they will increase intimacy with a woman.

A more realistic goal for creating a more intimate relationship with the other gender is that there needs to be both higher levels of self-disclosure on the part of the male and greater participation in activities by the female. By participating in activities with the male, females will find that doing things together opens the male up for more self-disclosure. A male will also appreciate the participation of the female in joint activities because this creates a feeling of greater bonding and intimacy to a male. And if men can learn to be more open and share personal beliefs and feelings, say, over lunch with their female partner, they will also benefit from this new-found emotional intimacy.

Intimacy and Communication

Honest communication is essential to true intimacy. We cannot feel close to another person if we are hiding or withholding important thoughts or feelings about that person, or even about ourselves. This doesn't mean, however, that we should lay bare our every thought or emotion. High self-disclosure can be detrimental to the development of intimacy at the beginning of a relationship, and it can damage a more established relationship if the "brutal truth" is too brutal. In the former case, when a relationship is just beginning, opening oneself up may threaten a partner who doesn't have the same commitment to the relationship and who therefore would not share in return. In the latter case, when a relationship is established, "honesty" may be a thin disguise for hostility or anger against the partner or spouse.

The temptation is to let oneself be swept away by romance, but individuals falling in love should use some uncommon sense: Let things develop slowly, be honest with the other person and oneself, keep an open mind and a sense of humor. It's easier to fall in love than to stay in love.

Nevertheless, open communication in appropriate doses, at appropriate times, and with good intentions can enhance a relationship and lead to greater intimacy. A couple who tries to maintain peace and stability by glossing over disputes or ignoring problems is headed for trouble. Finding a productive way of resolving differences, by meeting them head on and negotiating a workable compromise, is key.

Intimate Experiences Versus an Intimate Relationship

One can feel close to another person in a variety of ways and in different areas of one's life. Some of these ways include emotional intimacy, intellectual intimacy, social intimacy, recreational intimacy, and sexual intimacy.

An **intimate experience** is one in which we feel close or share ourselves with another person. For example, a deep philosophic discussion can be a very intellectually intimate experience. Working together successfully on a project can also lead to an emotionally intimate feeling. The most commonly perceived type of intimacy is sexual intimacy. Nevertheless, people perceive experiences differently, and what one person perceives as an intimate experience may not seem so intimate to another.

An **intimate relationship** is one in which we share intimate experiences in several areas over time, with expectations that this sharing will continue. It is difficult to have and to maintain intimate relationships with more than a few people at once because intimacy is time consuming. For example, how many really good friends, intimate friends, do you have? Probably very few.

Also, it is quite clear from research with couples that no relationship can provide intimate experiences in all areas all the time. With apologies to Abraham Lincoln,

"You can please some of the people some of the time, but you can't please all of the people all of the time." This is certainly the case with love relationships. Intimate partners may be able to satisfy each other in a number of ways—emotionally, intellectually, sexually—but both partners will most likely satisfy other intimacy needs outside the relationship. We do not suggest sexual intimacy as one of these areas, because an extramarital affair can destroy intimacy in all other areas of the relationship. But both partners can have friends of either gender at work or in other areas of their lives, friends who are very special and who provide something that the mate does not or cannot provide. These friendships can add to each partner's happiness and thus be a positive force in the couple or marriage relationship as long as the partners can minimize feelings of insecurity and jealousy.

The Paradox of Marriage and Intimacy

Most people in our culture seek marriage in their quest for intimacy. Marriage is an important source of intimacy, but, paradoxically, intimacy too often declines, and sometimes is completely destroyed, after marriage. For many, marriage increases intimacy; for others, however, it becomes an intimacy trap and smothers the very thing the two people desperately seek to enjoy. On the one hand, marriage is extolled as the path to happiness; on the other hand, it can be a source of conflict.

The basic question remains: Does marriage provide intimacy on a permanent basis? The answer is a qualified yes. Marriage can provide intimacy, but the partners must work to make it happen. Marriage in our society has become the classic great escape. People escape into marriage to avoid loneliness and to find intimacy. Later, when the marriage feels stifling or empty, some people escape from it to maintain their sanity and independence. Single people can feel lonely. So can married people (Rokach, 2005, 2006). In the next section, we'll look more closely at how couples can develop and maintain intimacy.

Developing Intimacy

Researchers have identified 10 areas of marital and family dynamics that contribute to a couple's satisfaction or dissatisfaction with their relationship (Fowers, Montel, & Olson, 1996). Success in achieving intimacy in these areas increases the chances for success in the relationship as a whole. Most couples, of course, do not achieve complete satisfaction in all of these areas, but working toward a satisfactory level of intimacy in each area increases the chance of maintaining a healthy relationship.

Traits of Intimate and Nonintimate Relationships

In the national survey of 21,501 married couples (Olson & Olson, 2000), two groups were created, one group where the husband and wife were both happily married ($n = 5,153$) and a second group where they were both unhappily married ($n = 5,127$). All the couples completed a comprehensive marital inventory called **ENRICH,** which contained 10 categories of questions about the issues that are important in a married couple's relationship. The inventory is scored by comparing the responses of the two partners on all questions in each category, calculating the percentage of agreement for each of the 10 categories, and then averaging the results. The couples with high scores (i.e., a high percentage of agreement) on the ENRICH marital satisfaction scale were identified as high-intimacy couples, and those with low scores were labeled low-intimacy couples.

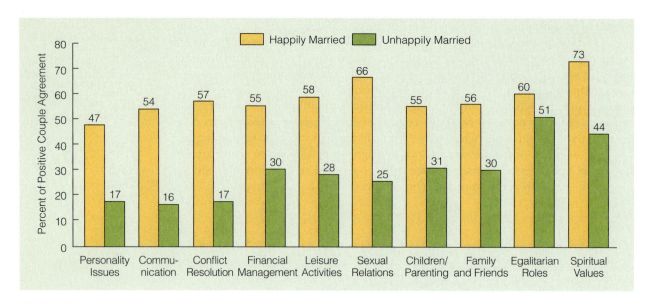

FIGURE 9.4

Happily Versus Unhappily
Married Couples

Source: Olson & Olson, 2000.

As hypothesized, the positive agreement scores of couples in the high-intimacy group were significantly higher than those of the couples in the low-intimacy group in eight ENRICH relationship categories (Figure 9.4). The categories showing the most significant differences were communication, conflict resolution, and the sexual relationship. These three areas have been identified repeatedly in various analyses as significant to maintaining intimacy in a relationship. It is also noteworthy that a high percentage (86%) of the couples in the low-intimacy group had considered divorce.

Couple Relationship Strengths

Some of the most important areas for developing and maintaining an intimate relationship, identified by Olson and Olson (2000), are described below.

Communication Skills. Although definitions of communication differ, there is considerable agreement that good communication is essential for maintaining an intimate relationship. Some people are more comfortable talking about their feelings than others, especially their feelings about their relationships. However, sharing even the most mundane thoughts or feelings can be a difficult experience for some people. Developing a satisfactory pattern of communication is critical to the development of an intimate relationship.

Conflict Resolution Skills. People have different attitudes about conflict—both acknowledging it and resolving it—in a relationship. Some partners are more open than others recognizing and resolving issues. Others believe it is better simply not to talk about problems and to hope they will somehow disappear. Couples who do well resolve conflict rather than avoid issues.

Sexual Relations. Sex is an emotional thermometer of the quality of a relationship. It is also an important aspect of human relations that couples generally have a difficult time discussing. When it comes to affection and sexual expression, differences are inevitable. Couples who have a good sexual relationship are able to

Open communication is an essential component of a successful relationship, but talking about feelings—especially feelings about the relationship—can be a difficult experience for some individuals and couples. Fortunately, communication skills can be learned.

express their affection freely and openly with each other and respect each other's needs and desires.

Couple Flexibility. Your ability to adapt to stress and to make changes when necessary is an important skill to have in a couple relationship. Flexibility in a couple has not been studied much in the past, but it has become an increasingly important relationship skill in this high-stress society.

Couple Closeness. Being emotionally connected is also an important characteristic of happy couples. As people get busy doing their own things during the day, they also need to have the ability to get reconnected when they come back together. Happy couples know how to maintain both intimacy and independence.

Personality Compatibility. Comfort with a partner's personality is important to a healthy relationship. The more we like and accept the personality traits and habits of our partner, the more satisfying the relationship. Conversely, personality traits such as tardiness, temper, moodiness, stubbornness, jealousy, and possessiveness are a few of the many traits that contribute to negative feelings and problems in a relationship. Couples need to realize that most of these traits will not change or disappear after marriage.

Good Relationships with Family and Friends. Relationships with relatives, in-laws, and friends can either strengthen or cause problems in a marriage. If the challenges of these family relationships and friendships are not handled carefully, they can compromise a couple's intimacy. Good friends, especially other couples,

Sharing leisure activities is one way couples can build and maintain the intimacy of their relationship. This couple has chosen an activity that allows for companionship and exercise.

can be a valuable resource. Brenda, the mother of two teenage sons, describes what friendship with other couples has meant to her:

> "We're friends with three other couples, and about every 6 weeks or so we get together at somebody's house for a potluck or whatever, just to talk. It's really good to hear what's happening to everybody. They're always short on money, short on time, and long on stress, just like our family. Charlie's veterinary business is extremely demanding for him, and I put in long hours, too, keeping the books.
>
> "It's comforting to share our lives. We laugh a lot. It puts my life into better perspective. Sometimes I get whiney and think, 'Woe is me.' But everybody's got problems, and our friends have a way of cheering me up."

Shared Spiritual Values. Religious teachings of traditional groups and more personal spiritual beliefs developed throughout life by individuals often bring comfort and build bonds between couples. When couples share similar values and belief systems, it can be a major positive factor in a relationship, but for some couples, spiritual issues can drive a wedge between them and become a source of long and explosive arguments. In studies of strong families, spiritual values are mentioned repeatedly as a core family strength (DeFrain et al., 2006).

In sum, attaining intimacy is a process that takes time, effort, intelligence, and dedication. Once achieved, it also takes effort to maintain. Couples must constantly search for ways to vitalize and revitalize their intimate relationship. Although it may be easy to fall in love, it is very difficult to stay in love. Nevertheless, achieving and maintaining intimacy is a challenge worth pursuing.

Intimacy Games

Two important aspects of any intimate relationship are honesty and straightforwardness. When one partner asks for or tells the other what he or she wants, the other partner is free to comply or not comply. But many people play **destructive**

intimacy games with their partner, concealing what they really want and attempting instead to manipulate the partner into doing or giving them what they want. (As we will see later in this section, there are also constructive intimacy games.) Because destructive intimacy games tend to be effective in the short run—people often get what they want using these techniques—they can be rewarding. But in the long run, they undermine relationships. Closeness and sharing suffer, resentment grows, and the relationship may ultimately be destroyed.

Along these lines is what family therapists refer to as the **zero-sum game.** In this type of game, there is a winner and a loser. Unlike more cooperative games in which both people win by working together, the competitive zero-sum game results in one person winning what the other person loses; hence the score of the game comes to zero. For example, if I win by six points and you lose by six points, it all adds up to nothing. In human relationships, zero-sum games usually lead to problems, especially if the rules are constructed so that the same person wins most of the time. One partner might say, for example, that he or she will make the final decisions about how the couple's money is spent because he or she works outside the home and the other spouse doesn't.

Why do people play destructive intimacy games? Sometimes people don't really know what they want from a relationship. Sometimes they're embarrassed or afraid to ask for what they want, or they assume they'll be turned down. Sometimes they perceive a situation to be so difficult that the only way they can see to handle it is by playing a game. Then, because playing games often works in the short run, people tend to play them again and again.

Destructive intimacy games share many elements of such games as chess, bridge, and football: goals, players, rules, and strategies. But in football, for example, everyone knows what the goal is, who the players are, what the rules are, what the rewards and penalties are, when the game is over, and what the outcome is. In a destructive intimacy game, many of these elements are hidden or unclear. Intimacy games can be identified and defined by asking the kinds of questions listed in Table 9.2.

Constructive Intimacy Games

Although most intimacy games are destructive, **constructive intimacy games** can enhance a relationship. Too often intimates focus on what they do *not* get from each other rather than on how often they benefit from the other person. This sets up a negative cycle: As one person becomes more negative and less willing to give, the other person reciprocates. Soon neither person in the relationship is giving to the other in a positive way.

One way to reverse this type of negative interaction is to focus on the positive, on what you can do for the other person and what the other person can do for you. Giving to another person in a positive way encourages the other person to do the same. Also, telling the other person what you want increases your chances of receiving it.

Marital therapists often find that when one partner does something positive for the other, the other will respond positively in return relatively soon. Over a period of 2 weeks, if one spouse did 10 positive things for the other, the spouse would be likely to receive about the same number of positive gestures in return. In contrast, when individuals are negative, they receive negative responses, and the negative pattern repeats itself. Marital therapists often ask partners to double the number of compliments they give to their spouses each day for a week. Although both

TABLE 9.2	Dimensions of Intimacy Games
Characteristic	**Relevant Questions**
Name of game	What name describes the game?
Players	Who were the players/opponents?
	Who were the spectators?
	Who were the referees?
Playing field	Where was the game played?
	When was the game played?
Objectives	What were the short-term objectives?
	What were the long-term objectives?
Rules	What were the rules?
	Were they implicit or explicit?
Strategies	How was the game played?
	What strategies did the offense use?
	What were the long-term objectives?
	What counterstrategies did the defense use?
Communication style	Did the participants express themselves verbally, nonverbally, or both?
Rewards and penalties	What were the rewards?
	What were the penalties?
Outcomes	How effective was the game in the short term? In the long term?
	How enjoyable was the game?
	Was there a winner and a loser?

spouses commonly feel it would be strange to exchange so many compliments, they find that the recipient not only accepts the compliments but returns about the same number over the next few days. This approach develops a positive complementary cycle. The Beatles put it more poetically when they sang, "In the end, the love you take/Is equal to the love you make."

Unlike destructive intimacy games, constructive games help develop positive cycles. In addition, constructive games have objectives that are specific, rules that are explicit, strategies that are cooperative rather than competitive, and outcomes that are mutually rewarding. A constructive intimacy game called "Giving Compliments" is available on the text's Online Learning Center. Couples who would like instruction in constructive intimacy games can enroll in a couples communication workshop. Research indicates that such training can lessen manipulative and competitive interchanges between partners (Olson & Olson, 2000). Constructive games can be especially enjoyable in intimate relationships, which allow for a greater variety of ways in which partners can reward each other and develop more positive feelings toward each other.

Destructive Intimacy Games

As mentioned, many intimacy games are destructive. Identifying and analyzing a few can illuminate their pitfalls and provide the basis for developing more constructive and positive ways of relating. Two destructive intimacy games are "I Don't Care; You Decide" and "The Ties That Bind."

Human relationships are too precious to risk by playing destructive games. Constructive interactions, positive feedback, and honest communication are the keys to successful, long-lasting relationships.

"I Don't Care; You Decide." Many times, when couples are involved in decision making, one partner genuinely wants the other partner to make the decision. However, when one partner knows what he or she wants but is afraid to tell the other person, or when the partner wants to make the decision but have it appear as if the other person has made it, the decision-making process can become a game.

The initiator often begins playing this game when he or she is relatively sure the other person will make the decision the initiator prefers. The initiator often opens the game with a loaded question, such as, "Do you want to stop here for dinner?" This really means, "I want to stop here, and I hope you will know that and make that decision." When the other player says yes, however, she or he can then be held responsible if the food is bad, the service is poor, or the bill is too high.

The following dialogue illustrates another common way this game begins. Jennifer and Tom have received an invitation in the mail from a couple they haven't seen in some time. The party-givers are primarily Tom's friends, whom he has known for years. Jennifer doesn't enjoy them because they argue so much.

Tom: What do you want to do about this party? Should we go?

Jennifer: I don't care . . . [even though she does].

Tom: Wouldn't you like to see them again?

Jennifer: Well . . . don't you have other things you'd rather do this Saturday?

Tom: No, I'd rather go. Okay?

Jennifer: Okay, but . . .

Tom: Are you sure you want to go?

Jennifer: Yes, I guess so.

When Jennifer and Tom go to the party, Jennifer will go reluctantly and will probably be frustrated by the experience. Jennifer had hoped Tom would realize she didn't want to go to the party and would decide they shouldn't go. But by not expressing her true feelings and not actively involving herself in the decision-making process, Jennifer failed to achieve what she intended. This is one of the negative consequences of playing games.

Another negative consequence might be that when she gets home from the party, Jennifer will feel so miserable or annoyed that when Tom wants to make love, she will say quite honestly, "I don't feel like it tonight." Tom, suspecting Jennifer's playing a game, might speculate, "She didn't want to go to their house all along, and now she's punishing me by withholding sex!" The merry-go-round continues, and both people feel frustrated.

"The Ties That Bind." The parent–child relationship is also fertile ground for destructive intimacy games, especially when the children become adults. Although supposedly played in the best interests of all concerned, these games are often disguised, and the players often do not enjoy playing them. Nevertheless, game playing between parents and their adult children is likely to exist. Giving up the role of parent is difficult. Although many parents would agree intellectually with Kahlil Gibran's observations on children, they often have difficulty living this philosophy:

> Your children are not your children.
>
> They are the sons and daughters of Life's longing for itself.
>
> They come through you but not from you,
>
> And though they are with you yet they belong not to you . . . .
>
> You are the bows from which your children as living arrows are sent forth.
>
> The archer sees the mark upon the path of the infinite, and He bends you with His might that His arrows may go swift and far. (1923/1976, p. 24)

The degree and type of involvement parents have with their married children causes difficulty in many families. The prevalence of in-law jokes attests to the significance of this issue in marital and family relationships. Some mutually agreed-upon degree of balance is important. But it can be difficult to successfully balance the dimension of separateness as individuals with that of connectedness to our families of origin. Some parents have difficulty accepting the fact that their children are grown up and desire a more independent lifestyle, one that is free from past traditions. Parents who are frustrated by their dwindling contact with their adult children often play games, such as the destructive intimacy game called "The Ties That Bind," which is also available on the text's Online Learning Center.

Limiting Destructive Games

Over the years, researchers and family therapists have devised a number of useful techniques for limiting gamesmanship in families and maximizing true intimacy. The four central techniques are (1) naming the game, (2) making implicit rules explicit, (3) identifying strategies and counterstrategies, and (4) discussing the disguised objectives and making them clear and specific. Each of these components is described in more detail below.

Naming the Game. Catching yourself and others playing intimacy games can be fun, as well as a way to increase intimacy in your relationships—as long as it is done in a playful and good-natured manner. A destructive intimacy game is a ploy someone uses to get something without directly asking for it. When you catch yourself or a loved one doing this, try very hard to describe what you see honestly. Encourage the loved one to be honest, too. Avoid blame or sarcasm. A matter-of-fact, caring approach is much more effective than a heavy-handed one.

Once the game playing is identified, try to give the game a catchy title. For example, everybody who has been in love is guilty at one time or another of playing the "If You Really Love Me, You'll Know What I Want" game. In this game we assume that the other person can read our mind at all times; if the loved one can't, then he or she must not care about us. Identifying and naming a game and focusing on the problem in a rational and calm manner are major steps in eliminating game playing.

Making Implicit Rules Explicit. Implicit (secret) rules are difficult to reveal, and they add confusion to the destructive intimacy game. Nevertheless, exposing implicit rules is an effective technique for ending the destructive intimacy game. The most common implicit rule is "Don't directly ask for what you want." This rule assumes that if you do ask directly, you will be refused. But playing by this rule puts you in a difficult situation. You don't ask directly because you think you'll be refused, but because you don't ask directly, people have to guess what you want. If they don't guess correctly, you won't get what you want.

By being direct, you give the other person a chance to choose how and when he or she might give you what you want. This places the responsibility for action on the other person and frees that person to give to you. And giving others what they want—making them feel good—makes the giver feel good also.

Unveiling Game Strategies. Withdrawing quietly and sullenly from an argument is a common strategy in destructive intimacy games. Its intent is to keep the other player in the argument from continuing on the offensive. The "opponent" may then respond with a counterstrategy by saying, for example, "What's wrong, Dear?" And the obvious counterstrategy to this ploy is for the quiet and sullen "Dear" to respond, "[Sigh] Oh, nothing."

Unveiling game strategies like this isn't easy because, as in cards or tennis, players often try to confuse their opponents. Your intimate opponent may set you up by unveiling one game strategy, only to substitute another. Nevertheless, unveiling strategies can be an important step in building intimacy in a relationship.

Identifying Disguised Objectives. Rather than directly asking for what they want, some people disguise their objectives. The loaded question is a common technique for disguising what one really wants and for making the partner think that he or she is making the decision. For example, suppose your partner asks, "Wouldn't you like to go to this movie?" To identify the hidden objective, you can ask your partner what movie she or he wants to see.

Being Single

Marriage is still very popular in the United States with the vast majority of people marrying at some time in their lives. The most recent Census data, for example, indicate that among Americans 70 years of age and older, 96.7% of the men and 96.7% of the women had been married during their lifetime. (See Table 9.3 for details on other age groups.)

Even though marriage is still in fashion, the Census data also show that 51% of American women were living without a spouse in 2005, up from 35% in 1950 and 49% in 2000. Married couples became a minority of American households for the first time. Explanations for these changes include the fact that women are marrying later or living unmarried with partners, and women are living longer as widows or delaying remarriage after divorce because they prefer their new freedom. Census data also indicate that about 30% of Black women are living with spouses, compared to 49% of Hispanics, 55% of White women, and more than 60% of Asian women. Family historian Stephanie Coontz notes that Americans are now spending half of their adult lives outside marriage. Demographer William H. Frey sees this as a culmination of post-1960s trends toward greater independence and more flexible lifestyles (Roberts, Sabar, Goodman, & Balleza, 2007).

Following are some other interesting statistics on singles from the U.S Bureau of the Census (2004d, 2006b):

- There are 95.7 million unmarried and single Americans.
- Fifty-four percent of the unmarried and single Americans are women.
- 14.5 million unmarried and single Americans are aged 65 and over.
- 28.8 million people in America live alone. These one-person households comprise 26% of all U.S. households.
- Thirty-three percent of births in 2002 were to unmarried women, varying from 89% for unmarried teenagers aged 15 to 19 to 12% for unmarried women aged 30 to 44.
- 683,000 unmarried grandparents are responsible for caring for their grandchildren.
- There are 120 single men who are in their 20s for every 100 single women in their 20s (for Hispanics, there are 153 men per 100 women; for Asians, 132 men per 100 women; for non-Hispanic Whites, 120 men per 100 women; and for Blacks, 92 men per 100 women).
- There are 33 single men aged 65 or older for every 100 single women of the same age.

See Box 9.2 for some new definitions of singlehood.

TABLE 9.3	Marital History of People Aged 15 Years and Over, by Age and Sex							
Characteristic	**15–19 Years**	**20–24 Years**	**25–29 Years**	**30–34 Years**	**35–39 Years**	**40–49 Years**	**50–59 Years**	**60–69 Years**	**70 Years and Over**
Men ever married	0.9%	16.1%	49.2%	70.5%	78.5%	85.8%	93.7%	95.7%	96.7%
Women ever married	3.7%	27.6%	62.7%	78.3%	84.4%	89.5%	93.6%	95.9%	96.7%

Source: U.S. Bureau of the Census, Survery of Income and Program Participation (SIPP), 2001 Panel, Wave 2 Topical Module.

Increase in Singlehood

Many factors have contributed to the increase in **singlehood** today. For one, education and career are delaying the age at which young people are marrying. Linked to this trend is an increasing recognition in our society that singlehood can be a legitimate, healthy, and happy alternative to marriage. Sociologist Arthur Shostak (1987) found in his groundbreaking interviews with young people that most would be "a little" bothered if they failed to marry.

Shostak concluded that marriage continues to be more important to young women than to young men. Although more and more young women are seeking jobs and careers, they still tend to value marriage and parenthood somewhat more than young men do. This is the case even though education and work opportunities have opened up for females in recent decades; if they choose to, women can make it on their own more easily than in the past. Evidence suggests that if an individual has experienced divorce in her or his family, that person is more likely to have both negative attitudes about marriage and positive attitudes about singlehood.

Some singles have been married before but are now in transition. About two-thirds of divorced people remarry, usually 2 to 3 years after they divorce. But researchers are finding that even though most people remarry after a divorce, the rate of remarriage has dropped by more than 25% (Coleman & Ganong, 2004; Coleman, Ganong, & Fine, 2000). The fact that individuals are not rushing back into marriage is another indication that the single lifestyle is becoming more and more

Once considered a sad fate to be avoided at almost any cost, singlehood is today recognized as a legitimate, happy, and healthy alternative to marriage. This single man in his 30s demonstrates some of the benefits of being single, including self-sufficiency and the time and space to cater to one's own tastes.

Box 9.2 Diversity in Families

New Definitions of Singlehood

Being unmarried in the United States, as well as in most other industrialized countries, is not what it used to be—especially for women. Only recently have the words "spinster" and "old maid" gone out of fashion. In the 1950s, for instance, if a young woman wasn't married by the age of 25, she was considered an oddity and was likely to be pitied. Most people were married soon after they graduated from high school or college. It's a different story today. According to the U.S. Bureau of the Census (2005c), the median age for getting married is now 27 years for men and 25 years for women, compared to 22.8 years for men and 20.3 years for women in 1960 (Glick, 1989).

In an article entitled "Singles Shall Overcome," Bella DePaulo (2004) reports that there are 86 million unmarried people now living in the United States, which represents more than 40% of the adult population.

For U.S. women, singlehood has its upsides and its downsides. On a positive note, increases in education and income have made single women the second largest category of buyers of condos, co-ops, townhouses, and single-family homes. RealEstateJournal.com, an online division of *The Wall Street Journal*, reported in November of 2004 that 21% of home buyers were single women (up from 15% in 1993), whereas only 11% were single men (Lisle, 2004).

However, the news for single women is not all good. Single women are often caught in the middle of two worlds. Like the four women on *Sex and the City*, they enjoy the freedom and sense of adventure that comes with being unattached, yet they spend much of their time searching for the perfect relationship. In an article in the *Journal of Mental Health Counseling*, Phyllis A. Gordon (2003) states that society does not prepare women for

singlehood and that "from an early age, most young girls are prompted to think of an adult life that encompasses marriage and motherhood." She also says that although it is fairly acceptable for a man to remain single, women who do so are usually seen as less loving and nurturing, less sexually attractive, and more selfish. They often see themselves as being "less than," as lacking something fundamental, and they frequently experience low self-esteem. Many women feel great societal pressure to be part of a couple.

Traditionally, people married to fulfill parental expectations, for social and economic security, and for religious reasons. Contemporary reasons for getting—or not getting—married are often more personal and include the rise of feminism and the sexual revolution, the fact that many young people are staying in school longer to earn graduate degrees, and the cultural changes that affect the way people search for mates. Many people are no longer so concerned about meeting society's expectations.

That is not to say that intimacy is not still an important issue. Many young adults are postponing marriage until they find that one individual who is just right for them. According to Whitehead and Popenoe (2001) in a report for the National Marriage Project at Rutgers University, young adults are "searching for a deep emotional and spiritual connection with one person for life." The authors went on to say that 94% of never-married men and women ages 20–29 are searching for their soul mates "first and foremost."

In a global context, waiting for Mr. Right is a particularly Western notion. In other places around the world, marriage is often seen as an alliance between families for

acceptable in our society. Nancy, a middle-aged divorced woman in Alabama, is content with being single, as she explains:

> *"I don't know, perhaps I'll never get married again. At first after the divorce I was very panicky, like, 'Oh, I've got to be married, I've got to be married!' And then after several months of looking for the ideal mate, I discovered that I liked myself quite a bit and actually was quite content having my own private space in the world. I'm a busy professional. Sure, it gets lonely sometimes. But I've got lots of friends, male and female. I get on the phone and call someone, and we get together and talk and laugh, and I think, 'Hmmm, it could be a lot worse. I could still be dealing with Jerome's drinking.'"*

Singlehood as an Alternative to Marriage

An increasing number of people in the United States see singlehood as a legitimate alternative to marriage. This outlook represents a major shift in our society's attitude toward marriage. Throughout most of American history, the failure to marry social, political, or economic reasons. The following are views of singlehood in several Asian countries:

- Phyllis A. Gordon (2003) reports in an article in The *Journal of Mental Health Counseling* entitled "The Decision to Remain Single: Implications for Women Across Cultures" that in Korea, choosing not to marry may reflect badly on the family, because it is perceived that the parents have been neglecting their duty to find a suitable mate for their child.

- In China, single women may face numerous problems, according to Philip A. Pan (2000) in a *Washington Post* article entitled "Thoroughly Modern Women Disconcert Many in China." Chinese men who are economically secure may choose to pursue extramarital affairs, but their wives usually choose to stay married to them, because divorced women in China are seen as tarnished. Single women in China are forbidden by law to bear children. And successful single Chinese women often find it difficult to find a mate. According to Pan, successful Chinese women want to marry men at least as successful as they are; however, Chinese men believe wives should be subservient, and ". . . less educated and less successful than their husbands, [and] university professors often advise their female students to get married before they pursue graduate studies, lest they end up 'overqualified' for marriage."

- In Japan, Anthony Faiola (2004) reports in an article in the *Washington Post* entitled "Japanese Women Live, and Like It, on Their Own" that Japanese women are entering the workforce in record numbers (with the percentage of women in the workforce hitting 40.8 in 2003). They are also becoming more financially independent,

and many are choosing to remain single. In 2003, according to Faiola, 54% of Japanese women in their late 20s were single—a higher percentage than that found in any other country, including the United States. For many years, their icon was Princess Sayako, daughter of Emperor Akihito, who chose to remain single until she recently announced her engagement at age 35 (although every year on her birthday she was asked by the press about her marriage plans). However, single Japanese women are often criticized strongly for not taking their traditional roles of wife and mother seriously. Faiola quotes former Prime Minister Yoshio Mori as saying, "Welfare is supposed to take care of and reward those women who have lots of children. It is truly strange to say that we have to use tax money to take care of women who don't even give birth once, who grow old living their lives selfishly and singing the praises of freedom."

- In Thailand, a young woman named Saovapa Devahastin, 38, won a beauty contest and became the first women ever to hold the title of "Miss Spinster." In an article in *The New York Times*, Seth Mydans (2004) reported that Miss Saovapa and ". . . a growing number of successful professional women like her are challenging not only the traditional imperative of marriage and family but also what they see as the delicate egos of Thai men." Not all traditions have changed, however. Before entering the contest, Miss Saovapa asked her father for his approval.

Throughout the world, marriage remains the norm. However, singlehood is increasing, and it is changing the makeup of many of the world's cultures.

(note how even the terminology is loaded) was considered undesirable. Of course, not everyone married in 18th- and 19th-century America, and many married in their late 20s or their 30s. But social circumstances or pure economics probably contributed to not marrying more than personal desires did, for marriage was highly valued. *Old maid* and *spinster* were certainly not flattering descriptions for unmarried women.

In colonial times in America (the 17th and 18th centuries), virtually all unmarried individuals lived in a family environment of some type—either in their parents' home or as servants in another's home. Unmarried people of all ages usually stayed dependent on the families with whom they lived until they married. Only then did they become fully independent members of society.

In the 19th century, the position of unmarried people began to change. They increasingly became involved in wage labor outside the family and often lived in boardinghouses. During the Industrial Revolution, many young people went to work in factories, often at some distance from the farms they grew up on. The boardinghouses exercised family-type controls but were still quite different from a traditional family environment. Although attitudes toward singlehood may have improved over the 19th and early 20th centuries, social custom held that marriage was by far the preferable state, and those who remained single were stigmatized.

The lifestyles of single individuals have changed in recent decades. More people are remaining single longer. Single young men and women are living together without being married—enjoying some of the benefits of marriage without the legal or religious commitments and with less stigmatization. There is at least one positive result of this trend toward longer singlehood and later marriage: The older one marries, the more likely one is to make a mature and permanent decision. Those who delay marriage until they have completed their education and found satisfying work increase their chances for marital stability.

Characteristics of Successful Singles

The adult single population today includes people who are single for a variety of reasons. One large and rapidly growing group of singles are professional and career-oriented individuals. Highly educated and achievement oriented, many of these people prefer to remain unmarried. Although employers used to believe that single professionals were less desirable employees (thinking perhaps that they could not adjust to marriage or were unstable or undependable), they are now beginning to appreciate the flexibility of "unattached" employees. Single individuals can transfer to new locations more easily than whole families, and they usually have fewer outside commitments, which can complicate a married employee's adjustment to a new locale. Single employees tend to devote extra hours to their careers. Furthermore, they are as highly trained and capable as married employees.

Although single women have been subject to discrimination in salary and promotions (often because of employer expectations that they might marry and resign), the widespread adoption of affirmative-action policies has contributed to a more equitable treatment of female employees. As a result, singlehood is losing its stigma within professional groups.

Women who remain single are likely to be high achievers of above-average intelligence. This can make it difficult for them to find an unattached man of equal status, because men sometimes prefer to marry "down." First-born girls (who are often achievement oriented) and "only" children are somewhat more likely to remain single than other children.

Although a few singles may lead the swinging lifestyle portrayed in Hollywood movies, the vast majority live very conventional lives. Career-oriented single people are likely to use the freedom their lifestyle provides to participate in a wide variety of experiences that individuals with families rarely have time for. They also like the flexibility to devote as much time as they like to career interests, to travel wherever and whenever the job demands, and to alter their lifestyles as they desire or when new opportunities arise.

One of the biggest problems singles face is developing a circle of friends and associates with whom they can share social activities. To meet this need, many churches, synagogues, and social organizations (as well as resort lodges and nightclubs) have created singles events. Most employed singles report that their social life is as active as they want it to be, and few middle-aged career-oriented singles report being lonely or isolated. Although single people may at times feel they have missed something in life by not creating a family and may perhaps

Women who remain single are likely to be high achievers of above-average intelligence. This can make it difficult for them to find an unattached man of equal status, because men sometimes prefer to marry "down."

fear the prospect of loneliness in old age, they often can satisfy these needs by networking with other singles.

Making Singlehood Work

Singles are an enormously diverse group; no stereotype can describe them. Individuals are single for many different reasons. In addition to younger, never-married individuals, there are divorced single people, separated single people, and widowed single people. Thus it is very difficult to generalize about singles. A 19-year-old college student who has never been married, a 33-year-old career woman who has just separated from her husband, a 27-year-old divorced father with custody of three young children, and a 78-year-old widow whose husband has just died of cancer are a few examples of the many faces of singlehood.

As mentioned earlier, singlehood can be a happy, healthy lifestyle. Nevertheless, for many single individuals loneliness can be a challenge. John C. Woodward (1988) offers the following seven suggestions for single individuals of all types to cope with loneliness.

- *Appraise your strengths.* What are the good things about yourself? If you have difficulty listing your attributes, ask some people who know you.
- *Develop a friendship network.* Spend time developing and connecting with a few close friends who can provide you with a caring network.
- *Take a chance.* Reach out and take risks. You must tell people how you really feel and what you need. Say, "I'm really lonely today. I wish I just had somebody to talk to." Until you do this, people can't help you.
- *Don't expect too much.* When you go out socially, go out just to have fun. Many lonely people go out with a different motive: to find the perfect

Single people have the same basic desire for sexual intimacy that married people have, but they must take different approaches to fulfilling that need. For some, clubs such as this one offer the right mix of sociability and opportunity. Other singles seek partners in more tranquil settings.

person, a lifelong friend. Convince yourself, instead, that you can enjoy relationships without long-term commitment.

- *Depend on yourself.* Looking for someone else to make you feel all right is seldom effective. You have to depend on yourself and participate in activities you enjoy.
- *Rejoin your family.* Your family can be a great support. Regardless of how you treat your family or how they treat you, you still belong to that family.
- *Find an outside interest.* Try to find something that really interests or excites you and then work at it. If you join an organization, for example, don't just sit in the corner. Take some responsibility. Volunteer for things; really get involved.

In summary, Woodward provides very useful suggestions not only for singles but also for anyone who wants to maintain healthy relationships with others. These time-tested ideas provide practical ways to live a happy and more connected life.

Summary

- Love and friendship are alike in many ways, but there are crucial differences that make love both more rewarding and more volatile. Love relationships differ from very good friendships in that they have higher levels of fascination, exclusiveness, and sexual desire; a greater depth of caring about the other person; a greater potential for enjoyment; and other positive emotions.
- The love triangle, developed by Robert Sternberg, has three dimensions: commitment, intimacy, and passion. Combinations of these dimensions are seen in eight different types of love relationships.

- Three noteworthy perspectives on love include Erich Fromm, who maintains that love is difficult and requires work and practice; Stanton Peele, who suggests that many people in love and addicted to love, just as people are addicted to alcohol or other drugs; and James Dobson, who argues that demonstrating some independence from a relationship can strengthen it.
- Jealousy is very connected with love and intimacy. Although jealousy can be both functional and dysfunctional in a relationship, it is more often seen as problematic. While both men and women get jealous, men are often upset when the partner has a sexual relation-

ship with another person, and women are more often upset when the partner becomes emotionally involved with another person.

- Even though both men and women agree that self-disclosure is related to greater intimacy, it is mainly women who are good at self-disclosure. Men seek intimacy by doing activities with others; women use self-disclosure to create intimacy with others.
- Intimacy involves feeling close to and sharing oneself with another. Although marriage is an important source of intimacy, intimacy often declines after marriage and sometimes disappears completely. Intimacy takes a great deal of time, effort, and hard work to develop and maintain.
- Ten essential couple relationship strengths are personality compatibility, communication skills, conflict resolution skills, financial management skills, shared leisure activities, sexual relations, consensus on attitudes about children and parenting, good relationships with family and friends, consensus on roles, and shared spiritual values.
- Intimacy games can be either destructive or constructive. To minimize destructive games, it's important to identify them, make their rules explicit, determine the hidden strategies, and make the disguised objectives clear and specific.
- Young people are staying single longer and marrying at a slightly older age than in the past, partly because of their pursuit of education and career.
- An increasing number of people in today's society see singlehood as a viable alternative to marriage. This represents a major shift in behavior in the last decade.

Key Terms

Passion Cluster	companionate love
Caring Cluster	consummate love
commitment	jealousy
intimacy	intimate experience
passion	intimate relationship
non-love	ENRICH
liking	destructive intimacy game
infatuation	zero-sum game
empty love	constructive intimacy game
romantic love	singlehood
fatuous love	

Activities

1. In a small group, discuss your friendships and how they are similar to and different from love relationships.
2. What does love mean to you? In a small group, share a description of an especially romantic time in your life. What are the similarities and differences among the descriptions group members provide?
3. Take a class survey—using anonymous written responses—to find out how many times each student has been in love. What is the average number? What is the range (lowest to highest)?
4. Interview a divorced or remarried person. Ask how the individual's definition of love changed as she or he went through the following phases: dating, engagement, marriage, marital dissolution and divorce, singlehood, and remarriage. To do this exercise well, spend 45 to 60 minutes with the person to get a good understanding of what happened to the marriage and why.
5. What intimacy games have you personally played? Pick an intimacy game you have played and respond to the questions in Table 9.2. Then discuss your experiences with other members of a small group.

Suggested Readings

Baumbusch, J. L. (2004). Unclaimed treasures: Older women's reflections on lifelong singlehood. *Journal of Women and Aging, 16*(1/2), 105–121. Lifelong single women strongly emphasize their independence and "ability to be alone" as significant benefits, while discussing drawbacks, including loneliness and the absence of a social support network, which became more important as they experienced increasing age and frailty.

Buono, A. J., & Weisenbach, S. (Eds.). (2004). *We met online! Stories of married Catholics who met their spouses on the Internet.* Philadelphia: Xlibris.

Buss, D. M. (2000). *The dangerous passion: Why jealousy is as necessary as love and sex.* New York: Free Press. Jealousy is described as an adaptive behavior based on studies of various species and humans from various cultures. The fact that more men than women want sex with multiple partners is seen from the perspective of cultural anthropology as functional for the long-term survival of human beings.

Chiriboga, D., Zettle, L., Connidis, I., Koropeckyj-Cox, T., Bluck, S., Luecking, G., Rook, K., Dykstra, P., DePaulo, B., Morris, W., & Hertel, J. (2004). The never-marrieds in later life: Potentials, problems, and paradoxes. *The Gerontologist, 44*(1), 145. A cross-national perspective on conceptual models and research findings, including discussions of social supports available to never-married men and women, advantages and disadvantages of never being married, how society views individuals representing this role status, and the variety of types of never-marrieds.

Ciaramigoi, A. P., & Ketcham, K. (2000). *The power of empathy: A practical guide for creating intimacy, self-understanding and lasting love in your life.* New York: Dutton. This book summarizes why and how empathy can lead to more healthy love relationships.

DePaulo, B. M. (2006). *Singled out: How singles are stereotyped, stigmatized, and ignored and still live happily ever after.* New York: St. Martin's.

Ferguson, S. J. (2000). Challenging traditional marriage: Never married Chinese American and Japanese American women. *Gender and Society, 14*(1), 136–159. Why do some heterosexual Chinese American and Japanese American women never marry? The four most significant reasons are the effect of their parents' marriages, their status as eldest daughter, their pursuit of education, and the lack of eligible suitors. Parents' traditional marriages and duties as eldest daughter caused many to have negative views of marriage and childbearing. The number of suitors was limited for 46 of 62 respondents because their parents placed strict restrictions on them concerning the types of men they are allowed to marry.

Heath, S. (2003). *Young, free, and single? Twenty-somethings and household change.* New York: Palgrave Macmillan.

Mashek, D. J., & Aron, A. (Eds.). (2004). *Handbook of closeness and intimacy.* Mahwah, NJ: Erlbaum. Written by scholars in the field, this book provides the most comprehensive summary of a wealth of ideas about closeness and intimacy.

Pines, A. M. (1998). *Romantic jealousy: Causes, symptoms, cures.* New York: Routledge. A revealing discussion of whether jealousy is a green-eyed monster or a shadow of love. This practical book provides useful suggestions on how to deal with jealousy.

Puente, S., & Cohen, D. (2003). Jealousy and the meaning of violence. *Personality and Social Psychological Bulletin, 29*(4), 449–460.

Sternberg, R. J. (1998a). *Love is a story: A new theory of relationships.* New York: Oxford University Press. Sternberg's latest work on love focuses on how the success or failure of a loving relationship can hinge on how compatible the partners' stories are, that is, how close their views of love match.

Sternberg, R. J. (1998b). *Cupid's arrow: The course of love through time.* Cambridge, UK: Cambridge University Press.

Sternberg, R. J., & Weis, K. (Eds.). (2006). *The new psychology of love.* New Haven, CT: Yale University Press. The latest hypotheses about love from the researchers studying it.

Visit the text-specific Online Learning Center at **www.mhhe.com/Olson6** for practice tests, chapter summaries, Web links, Internet exercises, key terms, and flashcards.

10 Dating, Mate Selection, and Living Together

Courtship Patterns

Criteria for Choosing a Mate

Theories of Mate Selection

Conflict and Violence in Dating

Living Together

Summary

Key Terms

Activities

Suggested Readings

Regardless of how intense a love relationship is, there are both good and bad reasons for getting married. Similarly, there are both good and bad reasons for remaining single. Today, marriage is a personal choice, not a social dictate. In this chapter we will examine theories that attempt to explain mate selection and the functions and stages of dating. We will focus on mate selection from a cross-cultural point of view, looking at arranged marriages around the world and comparing them with the customary couple-arranged "love matches" of more developed societies.

In American culture, physical attractiveness is the major factor in choosing a date but not necessarily a mate. We also tend to find mates who are like us in some way, people from our group—ethnic, religious, or socioeconomic. But many of these rules are changing as a result of our increasingly multicultural population. So-called mixed marriages are a growing phenomenon, causing many families to examine their attitudes and behaviors toward people outside their particular cultural group.

Later in this chapter we will take a close look at some serious problems in our society today: conflict and violence in dating and the relationship between premarital violence and violence after marriage. Finally, we will conclude with a discussion of the growing trend of couples living together—an arrangement that is becoming a new courtship stage but one with legal and relationship consequences.

Courtship Patterns

One of the chief reasons so many marriages fail is that the functions of a date and a mate differ radically—that of a date is to be charming; that of a mate to be responsible; and, unfortunately, the most charming individuals are not necessarily the most responsible, while the most responsible are just as often deficient in charm.

—SYDNEY HARRIS, Journalist

All societies have created some system for matching individuals for marriage and parenthood. These systems range from the practice of bride purchase, to the selection of a mate by the village shaman according to astrological signs, to contractual systems in which a mate may serve as an indentured servant to the bride's parents, to individual choice based on personal attraction and love. In some cultures, couples are matched while they are still infants; in others, the bride and groom must prove their fertility by producing children before they are eligible for marriage. Although the customs of mate selection vary widely, all perform the necessary function of matching a couple for marriage and eventual parenthood.

Parent-Arranged Marriages

Throughout much of world history, courtships were generally brief. In most cultures, the parents of the bride and groom selected the future spouse and made most of the arrangements for the marriage ceremony. If the prospective couple were granted any freedom of choice, they were expected to complete their arrangements in a few days. The pattern common in modern industrialized nations, in which a couple spends months or even years dating and choosing a mate, developed largely over the past century. Parent-arranged marriages, however, still occur throughout much of the nonindustrialized world; up to three-quarters of marriages in some cultures may be arranged (Bhopal, 1997; Remez, 1998; Sureender,

Khan, & Radharkrishnan, 1997). Although young adults in the United States today might view the practice as archaic and uncivilized, many people worldwide prefer parent-arranged marriages.

Parent-arranged marriages are based on the principle that the elders in a community have the wisdom to select the appropriate spouse. Parents or elders are more likely to base their decision on economic, political, and social status considerations—to enhance the family's status and position through their choice. Considerations of lineage and family status are generally more important than love or affection in such decisions, although the parents may take the couple's preferences into account to some extent. Arranged marriages thus serve to extend existing family units rather than to create new units. They reinforce ties with other families in the community, strengthening the order and organization of the community (Bhopal, 1997).

Advantages of Arranged Marriages. Parent-arranged marriages are usually very stable, because it is the duty of the whole family to help the new couple get established in life. Divorce is almost unheard of—except for the reason of infertility—because of the potential disapproval a couple would receive from the parents and members of the community who were responsible for the selection. Although love between the couple before marriage is relatively unimportant, affection and respect usually grow through the years; arranged marriages are often quite harmonious. Because there is not really a courtship period, premarital intimacy is minimal or nonexistent.

In parent-arranged marriage systems, couples avoid many of the problems of "American-style" dating. There is virtually no risk of being rejected or of losing one's true love, and one does not have to determine whether one's partner is committed to the relationship. Although many people might not view these factors as advantages, they effectively ensure a stable marriage. Remnants of arranged courtship and marriage systems are still found in our culture today; for example, a limited number of professional marriage brokers still operate among urban ethnic groups. Further, as most single people know, relatives and friends are often only too eager to help find that "perfect" partner.

Parent-arranged marriages are usually very stable, because it is the duty of the whole family to help the new couple get established in life. Divorce is almost unheard of—except for the reason of infertility—because of the potential disapproval a couple would receive from the parents and members of the community who were responsible for the selection.

Patterns of Change. The world, in general, appears to be moving toward freedom of choice in marriage. This approach is sometimes referred to as the *love match*, though love is not always the goal of marriage in Western industrial societies. Perhaps a better term would be **couple-arranged marriage.** Cross-culturally, the absence of economic means for women to gain financial independence leads to early marriage and little individual freedom. The ability of women to work leads to the decline of arranged marriages, enhances the possibility of love matches, and may slightly diminish the marriage rate. In general, the world is also moving toward monogamous marriage, although the rate of advance varies from country to country.

The movement away from arranged marriage appears to be related to industrialization. As countries shift from more rural to urban, industrial societies, love marriages become more common. Data from Africa, India, Israel, and Malaysia indicate that love marriages are more likely among people who marry at a later age, have a higher level of education, have a higher socioeconomic status (or the promise of a higher status), and live in an urban setting. A woman who can support herself financially is more likely to want to decide for herself whom she will marry.

Cultural Variations. The ways people find marriage partners vary from culture to culture. In developing countries that are moving away from arranged marriages, the influence of cultural tradition may be combined with modern sensibilities. In India, for example, it is commonly believed that there is one predestined mate who will share life with the spouse through reincarnation. Therefore parents believe they should supervise their children's marriage choices to avoid mistakes. But many young people are unhappy with this approach, and a compromise is often reached. Semiarranged marriages, in which parental approval is obtained before the marriage, are becoming more common. The case of Dipendra, an Indian sociology lecturer at a university in the South Pacific, provides an example:

> *"I suppose you could call our marriage a 'semiarranged' marriage. My parents had a girl in mind for me, but there was this other beautiful girl in my classes at the uni. I hadn't talked with her much, but she seemed good for me. So, I had my brother talk with her and then he talked with my parents, and the families got together and worked it out. She came from a good family, so my parents were quite pleased. Officially, it was an arranged marriage in the traditional Indian fashion, but I had a lot to say about it!"*

In China, there has been a dramatic change in mate selection from parent-arranged marriage to love-based marriage, as in the United States (Pan, 2002). Love-based mate selection happens more often in the larger cities than in the small towns and rural areas where parent-arranged marriage continues to occur. A common problem is that most of the young people in China do not know how to date or how to select a mate, and so dating is a challenging adventure for Chinese couples.

Japan, the industrial giant of the Pacific, has generally moved from arranged marriages to love-based marriages. The traditional *nakode*, or matchmaker, is still used in some rural areas of Japan, but the matchmaker's role has become increasingly ceremonial. As more women have entered the labor force and gained financial independence, they have moved away from marriages arranged by their parents. Japanese young people can find dating very awkward and uncomfortable, however, because they often do not have much social contact with members of the other sex.

The Scandinavian countries are perhaps the most liberal in the world in regard to marriage customs. Parent-arranged marriages disappeared decades ago in Scandinavia, and cohabitation has become the most common type of relationship until after the birth of a child. Research in Sweden indicates a steep drop in the marriage rate. Associated with this decline are an increase in cohabitation and an increase in state and parental support for children born outside of matrimony (Duvander, 1999).

Dating: An American Creation

Dating, historically speaking, is a creation of young people in the United States. It symbolizes couples' efforts to take more control over the process of mate selection. Because the United States was one of the first nations to industrialize, it serves as a good example of the changes in dating behavior that occur when a society evolves from an agrarian culture.

The Emergence of Individual-Choice Courtship. Early in U.S. history, parents typically exercised considerable influence over dating and the choice of a mate. Young people were usually tied to the home and the land, except for the occasional community social event, had little opportunity to escape the watchful eyes of their parents. Opportunities for dating were infrequent. Courtship was a rather formal event, often conducted under parental supervision. Males were expected to get the permission of the female's parents and to initiate the acquaintance. Although the couple were generally allowed the privilege of making up their own minds, family members usually announced their approval (or disapproval) before the relationship got too serious. But even then young people were granted much more freedom of individual choice than exists in a parent-arranged courtship system.

As America became more industrialized, families left the farm or ranch to find better opportunities in towns and cities. This has been a long-term trend in America, dating back to colonial times. When parents began to work away from the home, young people gained considerable freedom from parental supervision, as well as the responsibility for organizing their free time. **Dating,** or individual-choice courtship, emerged as an activity in its own right, creating a new institution within the culture. (See Table 10.1 for limitations on the current dating system in

TABLE 10.1	Limitations of Dating

Dating has become the predominant method of finding a potential mate in the United States and other industrialized societies, yet there are numerous limitations to the current dating system. In his book *I Kissed Dating Goodbye*, Joshua Harris (2003) identifies several shortcomings of dating:

- Dating leads to intimacy but not necessarily to commitment.
- Dating tends to skip friendship, which should be the foundation of a stable relationship.
- Dating focuses on romantic attraction, so it lasts only as long as the romantic feelings remain.

- Dating focuses on enjoying love and romance solely for their recreational value.
- Dating often mistakes a physical relationship for love.
- Dating often isolates a couple from other vital relationships, leaving important friendships in disrepair.
- Dating takes a lot of time and energy, which can distract young adults from their primary responsibility of preparing for the future.
- Dating creates an artificial environment for evaluating another person's character.

Source: Excerpted from *I Kissed Dating Goodbye*, © 2003 by Joshua Harris. Used by permission of Multnomah Publishers, Inc.

the United States.) This pattern, with some variation, appears to be common as societies change from agrarian to industrial.

Along with the emergence of individual-choice courtship and a defined period for dating, permissive behavior also increased. The term **permissiveness** refers to the extent to which couples are physically intimate before marriage. Historically, males were permitted greater freedom and privilege than females and tended to be more experienced in intimate relations than females. However, the same basic forces that revolutionized dating customs in industrial societies also fostered a decline in the **double standard**—different standards of sexual and social behavior for men and women. As customs changed, women engaged in more sexual experimentation. The amount of sexual intimacy women experience before marriage still does not match that of men, but because female sexual involvement has increased rapidly, the difference between male and female sexual behavior is much smaller today than it was in the past. Although many females still expect males to call them, to plan dates, and to propose marriage, females are more assertive and participate to a greater extent in the dating process than they did in earlier generations.

Hooking Up: The Contemporary Trend

A recent study of more than 1,000 college women (Glenn & Marquardt, 2001) discovered the newer trends of hanging out and hooking up as an alternative to dating. These women reported the following trends (see Table 10.2). First, marriage was a major goal of their life and they wanted to marry someone from college. They also felt that there was either no commitment in dating or else there was too much. Hooking up was a common term that had a vague definition on purpose so they would not have to reveal the specific details of their relationship. It could range from only kissing to oral sex to intercourse. About 40% of the women said they hooked up, and 10% had done it more than six times. Dating also had multiple meanings from hanging out, which meant just being together, to a more highly

TABLE 10.2	Hooking Up, Hanging Out, and Hoping for Mr. Right: College Women on Dating and Mating Today
National Study and In-Depth Interviews of More Than 1,000 College Women	• The ambiguity of the phrase "hooking up" is part of the reason for its popular appeal.
• Marriage is a major life goal for the majority of college women.	• "Hooking up" is widespread on most campuses.
• Most women would like to meet a spouse while at college.	• Dating carries multiple meanings from hanging out (being together) to a high level of commitment.
• Relationships between college women and college men are often characterized by either too little commitment or too much.	• It is rare for college men to ask women out on dates or to acknowledge when they have become a couple.
• "Hooking up" is a distinctive sex-without-commitment interaction between college students and has many levels ranging from only kissing to oral sex and intercourse.	• In areas such as marriage aspirations, getting advice from parents, and "hooking up," college women from divorced families differ significantly from women who grew up in intact families.

Source: Glenn, Norval, & Marquardt, Elizabeth, *Hooking Up, Hanging Out, and Hoping for Mr. Right: College Women on Dating and Mating Today*, pp. 4–6. Copyright © 2001, Institute of American Values, www. americanvalues.org. Reprinted with permission.

Couples may spend time together doing a variety of activities with others, or they many spend time together as couples.

committed relationship. Most college women said it was rare for college men to ask them out on dates. One-third of the women had two dates or less and half had six or more dates since college. So the scene on college campuses is changing from traditional dating to a greater variety of ways of relating, including hanging out and hooking up.

At Stanford University in California, journalist Marisa Milanese (2002) argued that it was a myth that no one dates there. The fact is that "it all depends on what you call a date." The writer noted that 70% of Stanford undergraduates reported having sex, compared to the national average of 72%, but the old adage on campus was that, "No one dates".

The problem may be partially one of semantics. For many students, the phrase "to date" sounds old fashioned, with "let's-split-a-malt-at-the-drive-in overtones." Those students who use the term can be referring to many different types of arrangements: to go out together twice, to be a genuine couple, to be a year away from engagement. The ambiguity of the term, and the ambiguity inherent in human relationships, make students skittish about labeling precisely what is happening.

Commenting on the Glenn and Marquardt study, one Stanford administrator stated that hookups "come with a lack of expectations about emotional depth," but that might not be the students' genuine preference. Stanford Student Health's regular health surveys on campus reveal that relationship concerns regularly top the list of anxieties. And Glenn and Marquardt had found that 63% of women enter college hoping to meet Mr. Right.

Why the confusion the campus dating situation? Many ideas have been advanced:

- An ever-increasing achievement ethic with rigorous schedules and ambitious goals leaves little time for dating.
- The women's movement eliminated traditional courtship rules but did not present alternative conventions, so that instead of women asking men out now, no one's asking anyone out.

- Coed dorms also figure in the explanation: Men and women brushing their teeth side by side at the sinks may start to see each other more as brothers and sisters rather than as dream dates.
- Finally, there are countless less formal ways to hang out together without generating the anxiety and high expectations of a formal date.

Some students do not consider that they are dating until they have become a solid pair (Milanese, 2002).

Internet Dating and Matchmaking Services

Although in an individual-choice courtship system young people make their own selections, many still want help in finding a mate. To fill this need, entrepreneurs all over the country have created a potpourri of dating services. The least expensive—and most risky—are the "Personals" or "Eligibles" sections in many newspapers and magazines. For a modest fee, individuals can run a small ad describing their qualities, the qualities they seek in a partner, and the type of relationship they desire. These personals make interesting reading, but they represent a less-than-safe way to find a dating partner.

Dating services are a more discreet but also more expensive approach. Some services call themselves "relationship services," and their approach is not too much different from that used by employment services. Dating services, popular in many major cities, charge a fee that can reach hundreds of dollars. Applicants fill out forms, describing their traits and the traits they want in a partner; some services videotape applicants' responses. Each customer's file (coded by number, not name, to ensure some privacy) is made available to those who have paid for the privilege. If questionnaire data on "Mr. X" look good to a woman, she might ask to see his videotape. If she is interested in learning more about him, the agency might

In the past, the pool of eligible partners was often limited by the difficulty of traveling long distances. Today, the Internet allows people from across the country to chat online, making the pool of potential partners less restricted by physical proximity. As in any dating situation, there are both rewards and risks associated with cyberdating, of course.

Box 10.1   Putting It Together

Dating Do's and Don'ts

Going out can be fun, but it can also be serious business. Here are some things to think about when dating:

- There are two main reasons for dating, for pleasure and to find a mate.
- Dating should be for fun and for mutual enjoyment. It gives two people a chance to get to know each other and enjoy each other's company.
- Take it slow. Don't jump into things. Gradually reveal more and more about yourself, rather than overwhelming the other person.
- Don't feel the need to become involved physically too soon because it is better for the relationship if you first become friends.
- Friendship is a better foundation to base a relationship on than sex. Sexual attraction and energy often confuse you and prevent you from getting to know each other in other ways.
- It's important to get to know a number of people before getting serious with one.
- In looking for good people to date, be very careful about using a dating service, the newspaper, the Internet, or going to a bar. Dating can be serious business, and you need to exercise caution in how you find prospective dates.
- Friends and relatives sometimes have good suggestions for dating partners.
- Friends and relatives also can give you good feedback about your dates. They often can be more objective about what is happening than someone who thinks he or she is falling in love.

- Get to know the friends and family members of someone you are getting serious about. You often can learn a great deal about a person by visiting with those who have known him or her intimately over a long period of time.
- How do your prospective mate's parents get along? This can give you some clues about how you will get along after marriage.
- Whatever you see that you dislike while dating someone is likely to become magnified after marriage. Small problems before the wedding can become large ones later.
- Be especially cautious about how the prospective mate deals with angry feelings. If the person takes anger out on others, it is only likely to get worse after marriage.
- Notice how your date treats other people. Look for someone who is respectful and kind to everyone.
- Be realistic. Don't look at your prospective mate through rose-colored glasses, seeing only the positives. Sometimes there are serious negatives that have to be considered carefully.
- Be sure to talk with each other about what you like and what bothers you. Being positive is easy, of course, but you need to be honest and express those thoughts that are more difficult to bring up.
- Falling in love is easy. Staying in love takes intelligence, creativity, commitment, and a good heart.
- Trust your feelings and use your brain.

contact him by phone or postcard, indicating the manner in which he can contact the interested woman. From that point on, what happens in the relationship is up to the individuals involved.

The most popular dating innovation is meeting people online, through subscription services or directly on the Internet. Some services offer chat rooms where strangers can get connected. As with personal ads, there are few safeguards to ensure the accuracy of the information people provide about themselves. Individuals often reveal only positive characteristics that they think will attract others to them. Although the subscription services and/or the Internet might be a simple and inexpensive way to meet someone initially, this approach to dating lacks intimacy and can be risky.

Some general guidelines about the do's and don'ts of dating are listed in Box 10.1. Basically, dating is a time to learn more about yourself and what you like and don't like in other people. These guidelines are suggestions that can help you make dating a more rewarding and useful experience.

Dating Among Older People

The term *dating* has a decidedly youthful ring, but single people over 65 also date and are sexually active. Dating offers the single older person romance, the most exciting form of intimacy for human beings, no matter what age. When it goes well, dating can boost an older person's self-confidence and offer the potential for happiness and companionship at an age in life when future prospects are uncertain. When it goes poorly, dating can destroy self-confidence. In sum, dating in the later years can be thrilling, nerve-wracking, and complicated, just as it was in the younger years of life. Older people on a date, just like younger people, can be interesting, smart, attractive, and complex, and they can also be boring, selfish, and superficial (Beers, 2007).

The proportion of older individuals in the American population has increased dramatically since 1900. About 12.5% of Americans are over 65 (almost 72% of these seniors are female) (He, Sengupta, Velkoff, & DeBarros, 2005). As life spans lengthen, the percentage of older individuals is expected to increase to about 20% by the year 2030 (U.S. Bureau of the Census, 2003b). People are not only living longer but are healthier and more active than in earlier generations. Also, the older they are, the less likely they are to have children at home. Subsequently, many generally healthy and active older adults are looking for meaningful relationships.

Older people date, fall in love, and behave romantically in ways similar to the young, as one fun, landmark study found (Bulcroft & O'Conner-Roden, 1986). While observing singles' dances for older individuals at a senior center, the researchers noticed "a sense of anticipation, festive dress, and flirtatious behavior that were strikingly familiar to us as women recently involved in the dating scene." They interviewed 45 individuals aged 60 to 92 in Minneapolis, Minnesota. One difference the investigators noted between older and younger daters was their

Although we usually think of dating couples as being young, today more older couples are dating, cohabiting, and marrying.

definition of dating. The older people defined dating as a committed, long-term, monogamous relationship, similar to going steady at a younger age. Unlike many younger individuals, who "play the field," the vast majority of the older people were not casual about dating.

But one facet of dating was similar for both older and younger daters: the "sweaty-palm syndrome." The elders turned "physiological and psychological somersaults" on their dates and experienced a heightened sense of reality, perspiring hands, heart palpitations, feelings of awkwardness, the inability to concentrate, and anxiety and longing when away from the loved one. The older individuals saw romance much as younger people do—candlelight dinners, long walks in the park, exchanging flowers and candy. For older men, romance and sex were closely linked: "You can talk about candlelight dinners and sitting in front of the fireplace," a 71-year-old widower explained, "but I still think the most romantic thing I've ever done was to go to bed with her."

What older people do on dates is similar to what younger individuals do but is often "far more varied and creative." In addition to pizza, movies, and dances, older couples went camping, enjoyed the opera together, and flew off to Hawaii for the weekend. Also, the pace of dating was greatly accelerated. Older people noted that they simply did not have much time to play the field. They favored a direct, non-game-playing approach in building relationships. Sexual involvements tended to develop, and sexual intimacy enhanced self-esteem. A 77-year-old woman explained, "Sex isn't as important when you're older, but in a way you need it more." For this woman, sex reaffirmed the fact that she was alive and important to at least one other person in the world.

Another major difference between older and younger daters was their definition of passionate love. Younger people tend to equate passionate love with real love; once the intensity fades, they think love is gone. Older daters looked at passionate love differently, having learned from experience that the early intensity of passionate love simply cannot be sustained for very long. Most of the older individuals had learned through their marriages the value of companionate love—the "steady, burning fire" that endures and deepens over time. As one older man explained, "Yeah, passion is nice—it's the frosting on the cake. But it's her personality that's really important. The first time I was in love, it was only the excitement that mattered, but now it's the friendship, the ways we spend our time together that count."

Like younger individuals, older people face a number of dilemmas and difficulties in dating. Fear of disapproval leads many to be secretive about their dating activities. As a 63-year-old man said, "My girlfriend (age 64) lives just down the hall from me [in a retirement home]. When she spends the night, she usually brings her cell phone just in case her daughter calls." And a 61-year-old woman reported that even though her 68-year-old boyfriend had spent three or four nights a week at her house over the past year, she had not yet told her family. "I have a tendency to hide his shoes when my grandchildren are coming over," the woman said.

Marriage is another dilemma for older people. They may initially seek a marital partner, but many decide as time goes on that they are not willing to give up their independence. Women, especially, often like the new freedom divorce or widowhood offers. Furthermore, older individuals are not involved in plans to raise a family together. Finally, many fear the burden of caring for someone in deteriorating health or being a burden themselves to someone else.

In general, family members and friends tend to support the older dater and to affirm her or his right to seek personal happiness. One 64-year-old woman summed up dating rather well: "I suppose that hope does spring eternal in the human breast as far as love is concerned. Individuals are always looking for the ultimate, perfect relationship. No matter how old they are, they are looking for this thing called love."

Criteria for Choosing a Mate

Americans tend to choose partners who are similar to them in a variety of ways—in ethnic and cultural background, age, educational and religious background, and socioeconomic status. Physical attractiveness also plays a large role in mate selection. This section discusses the criteria that influence mate selection in the United States.

Physical Attractiveness

Physical attractiveness is one of the most important components of mate selection; studies show that it is directly related to the frequency of being asked out on a first date (Berscheid & Reis, 1998). Researchers have been creative in devising rating scales to measure physical attractiveness. One method is simply to have

Appearance makes a difference in a person's life in several ways: Attractive individuals do better in school, believe they have a more promising future, and feel better about themselves than less-attractive individuals.

a panel of judges rate individuals on a scale of attractiveness from low to high. The more physically attractive a person was, the more likely she or he was to have friends of the other sex. At the same time, the more physically attractive a person was, the less likely he or she was to worry about the partner's involvement with other people. Among males, the more attractive the male, the more likely he was to desire involvements outside the relationship. The more-attractive women did not report a greater desire for relationships with men outside the partnership than did the less-attractive women. Couples of similar attractiveness levels were more likely to progress deeper into the relationship than were couples in which one individual was relatively more attractive than the other. Most of us are aware of how good looking we are compared with other people, and we tend to use this "attractiveness capital" as a bargaining chip in our negotiations with prospective partners.

Based on a sequence of studies over 50 years, Buss and colleagues (2001) found that there are several characteristics that both sexes consider very important in a potential marriage partner. Over time, physical attraction became less important for both sexes. Personal characteristics that grew in importance were whether the partner was dependable and had emotional stability and a pleasing disposition. Mutual attraction and love became more important for both sexes over time. The characteristics that were significantly different for males and females were that men placed a higher premium on physical attraction. Women placed a higher value than did men on ambition, similar educational background, and being a good financial provider.

Research also indicates that physically attractive people are more likely to be rated by others as possessing good personal and behavioral qualities (Berscheid & Reis, 1998). Overall appearance does make a difference in one's life in a number of ways: Attractive individuals do better in school, believe they have a more promising future, and feel better about themselves than do less-attractive individuals. Young people who are attractive also have lower rates of juvenile delinquency, suggesting perhaps that delinquency is lower among individuals who have a positive self-concept, good grades, and high expectations for the future. But physical appearance is not everything. Less-attractive males date and interact socially just as often as attractive males. Furthermore, less-attractive males are not any more angry or frustrated about life than are attractive males.

In a study of more than 728,000 Match.com members, it was found that being physically attractive was rated as the third most important characteristic; first was being intelligent, and second was being funny (Gardyn, 2002). The percentages that said it was more important to be intelligent were 79% for the total sample and 90% for people with a college degree. Being funny was rated as important by 70%, attractive by 34%, athletic by 12%, and wealthy by only 6%. So being attractive was much less important than being intelligent and funny.

Age and Finding a Mate

It has been estimated that in six out of every seven marriages in the United States, the man is as old as or older than the woman. Why is this the case? Physiologically, males mature more slowly than females and do not live as long. Furthermore, in the United States there are more males than females in their early 20s. Finally, there is the phenomenon social scientists have labeled the **mating gradient,** the tendency of women to marry men who are better educated or more successful than they are. Because men tend to "marry down" in terms of age and status, it can be difficult for successful older women to find an acceptable mate.

Although married men tend to be as old or older than their spouses, the age difference between partners marrying today isn't very pronounced, especially among younger people. In the United States in the 1980s, the median age for males marrying for the first time was between 23 and 25 years old, and the median age for females was between 21 and 22 years old. The age difference between the two was 2 to 3 years. By 2004, however, the estimated U.S. median ages at first marriage for women and men, respectively, were 25.8 and 27.4 years. The age for women had risen 4.7 years in three decades. The age for men at first marriage was up 4.3 years (U.S. Bureau of the Census, 2006). Age differences at the time of marriage are smallest between people marrying at younger ages and greater between those who marry at older ages. But in all age groups, men tend to marry younger women.

The term **sex ratio** indicates the relationship between the number of men and the number of women of a given age. Because of differences in birth and infant mortality rates, men have historically outnumbered—and continue to outnumber—women in the U.S. population. In 1910, there were 106 single men for every 100 single women; most recent Census Bureau (2000e) figures indicate there are 118 single men for every 100 single women. If every single man in this country wanted to marry, there wouldn't be enough women to go around. This problem is true for men across all age groups, except those 65 and older. At the present time, there are more men than women in almost all age groups so it is theoretically possible for women to have a greater choice in men.

An increasing dilemma for women who want to pursue a career is that it is challenging to develop a career while also trying to find Mr. Right. An insightful discussion of the many issues confronting women today is provided by Barbara Whitehead (2003) in a book entitled *Why There Are No Good Men Left*. As women reach their 30s, there are fewer men available who are personally acceptable and can also match the income and achievements of the women. As a result, many career women are frustrated with finding and developing a relationship that will lead to marriage and a family.

Interracial and Interfaith Marriages

Two other factors that influence mate selection are endogamy and exogamy. **Endogamy** is the culturally prescribed practice or tradition of choosing a mate from within one's own group. These groups might include ethnic, religious, socioeconomic, or general age groups. The principle of endogamy supposes, say, that middle-class Whites will marry middle-class Whites, Catholics will marry Catholics, and young people will marry young people. **Exogamy**—the practice or tradition of choosing a mate from outside one's own group—is typically discouraged in our society. There are no laws against marrying someone of a different socioeconomic status, religion, or ethnic group; however, outside groups tend to be off-limits or less desirable as a source of marital partners.

The growing ethnic diversity in the United States and the increasing rate of marriage across ethnic groups are changing the "unwritten rules" regarding exogamy. This change reflects a common belief that in the United States all ethnic and cultural groups can live and work together. This belief is true to a certain degree—we have developed a relatively stable society and share certain democratic values—but the United States is by no means a blended and homogeneous society. Although the ethnic and cultural mix often works rather well, the elements that make it up remain distinct. Ethnic values and identifications endure for generations. When people marry out of their ethnic group, problems can arise; the difficulties inherent in intercultural marriage often intensify if the partners do not anticipate them. We confuse the idea that we are all created equal with the belief that we are all the same.

The marriage rate between members of different ethnic groups is difficult to assess accurately because the concept of race is elusive, and many people cannot be easily classified into ethnic groups. The U.S. Bureau of the Census does, however, ask people to state their ethnic identity and thus has a means of calculating Black–White marriages, among other things. In 1970, the number of Black–White marriages was 65,000; by 1998, the number had increased to 330,000 (U.S. Bureau of the Census, 2000e, table 54, p. 51). Of those 330,000 couples, 64% were Black male–White female couples, and 36% were White male–Black female couples.

Parents are often hesitant to bless an intercultural marriage. They may be aware of the problems their children will face, both within the relationship and in our society. They may also think the young partners are naive, idealistic, or blinded by love and need the guidance of their more experienced elders.

Some of these concerns are legitimate. When people marry, they are often idealistic in their beliefs. One common—and unrealistic—belief is that love conquers all. Another is that true love means that the couple either has few differences or that one partner can change the other after marriage. In the words of one family therapist, "Spouses tend to perceive their cultural differences as failings—either badness or madness. With insight, people are able to get some distance from their hurt feelings and stop taking inevitable differences personally." Although differences can be a source of strength in a marriage, they can also cause problems.

Ethnically mixed couples are more likely to divorce and to have a variety of marital and family problems (McGoldrick, Giordano, & Preto, 2005). Children of intercultural marriages have more personal and relationship problems than children from ethnically homogeneous families. The greater the ethnic differences between individuals, the less likely they are to marry. After marriage, the greater the differences, the greater the difficulty the couple will have adjusting to each other. McGoldrick and colleagues (2005) identify eight factors that they believe most influence the degree of adjustment:

- *Values*. The greater the discrepancy in values between the cultural groups, the more difficulty the couple will have. For example, a Puerto Rican–Italian couple will probably have less difficulty because of disparity of values than will an Irish–Italian couple.
- *Acculturation*. The greater the difference in the levels of acculturation of each partner, the greater the probability of conflict. For example, a couple is likely to have more difficulty if one is a recent immigrant and the other a fourth-generation American.
- *Religion*. Adding religious differences to cultural differences can compound adjustment difficulties. An Irish–Italian couple will probably have an easier time adjusting to marriage than an Irish–Jewish couple because the Irish and Italian partners are likely to share a common Catholic heritage. This is one less area for misunderstandings.
- *Race (McGoldrick's term)*. Interracial couples are the most vulnerable of all couples, sometimes feeling isolated from both groups. The children of an interracial union are also sometimes subject to discrimination from both

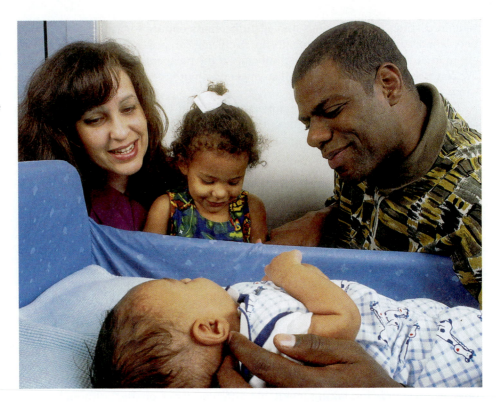

Marriages between individuals of different ethnic backgrounds involve special challenges. Partners must acknowledge and appreciate differences and make them a strength of the relationship rather than a source of conflict.

groups. As interracial children become more commonplace, however, this discrimination may decline.

- *Sex and sex roles.* Because women are generally reared to talk more about their feelings, an Irish wife, for example, will probably have an easier time adjusting to a Jewish husband than a Jewish wife would have adjusting to an Irish husband. Why? Because Jews are traditionally more verbal, and McGoldrick and colleagues presume that matching a verbal Irish wife and a verbal Jewish husband would work out better than matching a verbal Jewish wife and a relatively less verbal Irish husband.
- *Socioeconomic differences.* Partners from different socioeconomic circumstances have added difficulties adjusting to each other. The financial issues with which couples must contend can become even more problematic if the partners have different life experiences and expectations regarding them.
- *Cultural familiarity.* Partners who have some experience with each other's culture before marriage are more likely to understand and adjust to each other. Couples who live in a multiethnic neighborhood after marriage are also less likely to experience pressure and negative reactions from others.
- *Extended-family agreement.* If kin of both partners are supportive, the couple has a greater chance of success. If a couple feels forced to elope or if one partner's family refuses to attend the wedding, this can indicate future difficulties.

Every ethnic group has its own unique heritage, values, and behaviors that make it special. It is important for those who marry someone from a different group to be aware of these differences and to work toward making them an asset rather than a liability.

Theories of Mate Selection

Family researchers have developed a number of theories over the years to explain how and why individuals choose a particular partner. No single theory appears to answer these questions completely, but several shed light on the subject.

Homogamy Versus Complementarity

Family theorists from the early years of the field on down to the present have maintained that people tend to marry others like themselves (Blackwell & Lichter, 2000; Xu, Ji, & Tung, 2000). This tendency to marry someone of the same ethnic group, educational level, socioeconomic status, religion, and values is called **homogamy.** But the fact that exceptions occur—African Americans marry Whites and Catholics marry Jews—indicates that there is much more to the mate selection process than simple homogamy.

Homogamy is particularly prominent when you consider ethnicity and religion because only a minority of people marry persons from another ethnic group or religion (Gardyn, 2002). When 725,000 people from Match.com were asked if they would date outside their ethnic or religious group, about 70% to 80% of all males said that they would. However, only half (49%) of White women and 62% of Black women said they would date outside their ethnic group. Also, only about half (51%) of Muslim women, 58% of Hindu women, and 70% of Mormon women would date outside their religion.

Educational homogamy continues to be a major characteristic in dating and marriage in the United States (Gardyn, 2002). People tend to marry people from a similar educational level and social class. For example, less than 1% of the most-educated people married a person who did not complete high school. Also, about 94% of high-school dropouts were married to other dropouts or, at most, to people with a high-school education. So across various education levels, most people marry others who are generally similar to themselves in terms of education.

In a classic book, Robert Winch (1958) spurred debate among social theorists when he proposed that people are attracted to those whose personalities are very different from their own. Winch called his idea the **complementary needs theory** because it asserted that opposites attract—that people are attracted to someone whose personality complements their own. He proposed, for example, that a dominant person and a submissive person would be attracted to each other.

Many family researchers tried to resolve the two theories—homogamy and complementary needs—and found very little support for Winch's ideas. Although there is evidence that people are attracted to those with similar background characteristics, there is little evidence one way or the other that speaks to the influence of personality on mate selection. Perhaps one of the first to describe the importance of focusing on both similarities and dissimilarities was O. S. Fowler in his 1859 book *Matrimony*. Fowler advised, "Wherein, and as far as you are what you ought to be, marry one *like* yourself; but wherein and as far as you have any marked *excesses* or defects, marry those *unlike* yourself in these objectionable particulars" (cited in Murstein, 1980, p. 259).

All the studies cited earlier are consistent with the theory that "birds of a feather flock together." After reviewing the studies, individuals with high self-esteem or high self-acceptance perceive themselves to be similar to their partners and that people with low self-acceptance are significantly lower in both perceived and actual similarity to their spouses. In general, similar qualities and characteristics tend to attract people to each other. Very dissimilar people do not usually marry, and if they do, they are often among the couples who are likely to divorce.

The Stimulus–Value–Role Theory

One theory of mate selection is known as the stimulus–value–role (SVR) theory. Murstein (1987) theorized that people are attracted to each other by an initial *stimulus* and then test their suitability for establishing a permanent relationship by comparing their *value* orientations and agreement on *roles*. Let's take a look at Murstein's description of these three components:

- *Stimulus.* People are attracted to each other initially by a particular stimulus, such as an attractive physique or popularity. Each person evaluates how attractive the prospective partner is and how attractive he or she perceives himself or herself to be. The stimulus may act as a form of magnetism that draws the couple together, and that magnetism may be variously interpreted as love at first sight, magic, destiny, or infatuation. Whatever it is, the stimulus tends to energize the relationship beyond the bounds of simple friendship.
- *Value complementarity.* After a successful exchange during the stimulus stage of attraction, the partners begin to advance to the value stage of the relationship, in which they assess the compatibility of their basic beliefs and values. They often compare (in a very indirect, conversational mode) basic religious and political philosophies; attitudes toward money, work, and people; preferences for lifestyle and leisure activities; and feelings about character and personality. Although physical attraction is very important in drawing a couple together, it cannot overcome the strain of disagreement on many issues. Thus value complementarity becomes more important than physical attraction in selecting someone for an enduring relationship.
- *Role complementarity.* While comparing value complementarity, the partners also begin assessing role complementarity, or the extent to which they can establish a cooperative role relationship. Through interaction with each other, they discover each other's feelings and behaviors in terms of power and authority (who is going to be the boss), the division of labor (who will perform what tasks), and the expectations each has for the other in the relationship. Initially, each partner's separate values and roles emerge, but eventually negotiation may be necessary to achieve a workable balance.

The three components of SVR theory serve to help individuals evaluate a dating or cohabiting relationship and determine whether to continue or end it. When a potential relationship ends, one or both parties may observe, "It just didn't work out." Often, there was attraction, but value or role complementarity could not be achieved.

Reiss's Wheel Theory of Love

Another theory of how a love relationship begins, is nurtured, and grows is Ira L. Reiss's wheel theory of love (Reiss & Lee, 1988). This theory features four important components: rapport, self-revelation, mutual dependency, and intimacy need fulfillment. **Rapport** refers to the process of communication in which two people develop understanding and a sense of closeness. Two people have rapport when they are "on the same wavelength." Some people are quite skilled at building rapport with different types of people. They tend not to be excessively judgmental about others, and they listen so they can understand others. Good rapport between two people often leads to **self-revelation,** which is the disclosing of personal information about oneself. Self-revelation, of course, is a two-way street. When two people first meet, they are usually very cautious and reveal little. Gradually, one person lets a few "secrets" slip out, and the other person often reveals something very personal in return. Reiss notes that rapport encourages self-revelation, which, in turn, builds up what he calls **mutual dependency,** a relationship in which each person wants and needs the other person. This process takes time and can change over time. The fourth and final process in the development of love is what Reiss calls **intimacy need fulfillment,** the satisfaction one receives from having personal needs fulfilled, which leads to greater intimacy.

Reiss's wheel of love is graphically represented in Figure 10.1. Reiss describes his theory as a "wheel theory" of love because its four components are interdependent; that is, a reduction in any one of the components retards the development of a loving relationship. If, for example, a couple has an argument, self-revelation will diminish for a time. And if self-revelation diminishes in the relationship, the dependency and intimacy need fulfillment components will also diminish. The four components can also flow back and forth—even in the strongest of love relationships. In his model, Reiss indicates the movement of love in a positive direction (+) and a negative direction (−). Every relationship has its rocky times; love ebbs and flows. But in healthy relationships that survive and develop, the flow generally moves in a positive direction, toward increasing intimacy.

Surrounding the four components of the wheel of love are an outer ring, which Reiss labels "Social-Cultural Background," and an inner ring, which he labels "Role Conceptions." The four interpersonal components do not develop in a vacuum. Social-cultural background influences role conceptions, which, in turn, influence the four components, because role conceptions are how we define what we expect in a love relationship and determine what we do to meet these expectations. Our religious values, our educational background, the family values we grew up

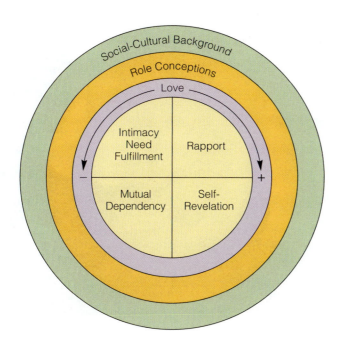

FIGURE 10.1
Reiss's Wheel of Love
Source: Adapted from *Family Systems in America* (4th ed.) (p.103) by I. L. Reiss and G. R. Lee, 1988, New York: Holt, Rinehart & Winston. Copyright by Wadsworth, an imprint of Wadsworth Group, a division of Thomson Learning. Adapted by permission of the publisher.

with—all these influence how we think about love relationships, and our thinking influences our actions.

Reiss notes that the wheel model applies not only to love relationships but also to other primary (close, intimate, face-to-face, and durable) relationships. It is useful for examining friendships, relationships with parents or children, and even casual relationships with colleagues, classmates, or roommates.

Conflict and Violence in Dating

The incidence of reported violence is 25% for women and 10% for men in dating relationships (Luthra & Gidycz, 2006). Jealousy and differences in level of commitment are only two of numerous causes for conflict between dating partners. These conflicts sometimes result in violent behavior, which can then lead to spouse abuse after marriage.

One young woman from Chicago recounts her experience before and after her wedding:

> *"I thought it would get better after the wedding. We had planned so long and carefully for it, and I knew the wedding would be wonderful. But even on the day of the wedding, Marty slapped me in the face. I don't know. He was frustrated about something my brother said or something. I don't know.*
>
> *"After we got married, it really got bad. He would stay out with his friends till all hours and when he came home, if I said even one word about it, he would hit me. Hard. I stayed with him 2 years, but when he pushed me down when I was 7 months pregnant, I couldn't stand it anymore and I left for the domestic violence program shelter. He would have hurt the baby, and I would never have forgiven myself. I ended up leaving town, moving to my sister's in Indianapolis. I didn't have hardly anything . . . Alexis's baby clothes and her toys, my clothes, a small stereo system.*
>
> *"I didn't have anything, really, but I was free and that was what counted."*

Conflict is an inevitable part of every relationship, but areas of conflict change as partners become more committed to each other. In the early stages of a relationship, jealousy and other personality issues are the greatest sources of conflict; later, conflict arises from such issues as differences in background, the balance of power in the relationship, and parent relationships.

A national survey by Jay Silverman (2001) of 4,163 high school students found that 22% of the girls were victims of nonsexual dating violence. Victimized girls were eight to nine times more likely to attempt suicide in the year previous to the survey, four to six times more likely to have been pregnant, three to five times more likely to use cocaine, and three to four times more likely to engage in unhealthy behaviors. It is unclear whether dating violence caused these teens to be involved in these activities or whether troubled girls selected more violent partners. It is clear, however, that many of the males felt that it was their right to control their girlfriends through violence.

In terms of handling conflict, all males and females (100%) used reasoning, and most (87% to 93%) used verbal aggression. In terms of physical violence, more men (32%) than women (29%) were on the receiving end of minor violence. This concurs with the fact that fewer men (3%) than women (19%) reported using severe physical violence. Men are less often hurt than women in violent encounters, however, because women are generally not as physically able to cause serious injury as men.

It is clear that if an individual is violent during dating, it is most likely this behavior will continue after marriage. In general, a violent date is a poor marriage risk. Violence breeds violence and quickly destroys an intimate relationship. It is important, especially for women, to watch for warning signals that a partner might become more abusive as the relationship becomes more serious. See Box 10.2, which lists several very useful warning signals.

It is important for people to trust their own feelings regarding abuse from a partner and not to confuse abuse with love. Following are four relevant questions to seriously consider before committing oneself to a relationship:

Does your love "turn you on" or "turn you off"?
Does your love "tune you in" or "tune you out"?
Does your love "make you sing" or "make you shout"?
Does your love "light your fire" or "put it out"?

Living Together

For many people, marriage is no longer considered a prerequisite for living with a romantic partner. **Cohabitation** is defined by the federal government as two unrelated adults of the opposite sex sharing the same living quarters. A broader definition would include same-sex couples who have an emotional and sexual relationship.

Cohabiting's Dramatic Increase

Between 1970 and 2000, the number of unmarried couples living together increased 10-fold from 500,000 to 5.5 million couples (U.S. Bureau of the Census, 2003b). Among cohabiting couples, about half (54%) the partners had never been married, about one-third (37%) had been divorced, and the rest were widowed.

Cohabitation is more popular than ever as a way for many Americans to move from being single to becoming married. While for many it is simply a transition from being single to being in a couple relationship, it is now becoming the norm to cohabit before marriage. In fact, the majority of all marriages are preceded by cohabitation with the rate being 60% to 75% for first marriages and up to 80% to 85% for remarriages (U.S. Bureau of the Census, 2003b).

Box 10.2 Putting It Together

How to Tell If a Date or Mate Is a Potential Batterer

Dear Ann: Please print this list of warning signals to help women determine if a mate or date is a potential (or actual) batterer:

- **Jealousy of your time with coworkers, friends, and family.**
- **Controlling behavior.** (Controls your comings and goings and your money and insists on "helping" you make personal decisions.)
- **Isolation.** (Cuts you off from all supportive resources such as telephone pals, colleagues at work, and close family members.)
- **Blames others for his problems.** (Unemployment, family quarrels—everything is "your fault.")
- **Hypersensitivity.** (Easily upset by annoyances that are a part of daily life, such as being asked to work overtime, criticism of any kind, being asked to help with chores or child care.)
- **Cruelty to animals or children.** (Insensitive to their pain and suffering, may tease and/or hurt children and animals.)
- **"Playful" use of force in sex.** (May throw you down and hold you during sex. May start having sex with you when you are sleeping or demand sex when you are ill or tired.)
- **Verbal abuse.** (Says cruel and hurtful things, degrades and humiliates you, wakes you up to abuse you verbally, or doesn't let you go to sleep.)
- **Dr. Jekyll and Mr. Hyde personality.** (Sudden mood swings and unpredictable behavior—one minute loving, the next minute angry and punitive.)
- **Past history of battering.** (Has hit others, but has a list of excuses for having been "pushed over the edge.")

- **Threats of violence.** (Says, "I'll slap you," "I'll kill you," or "I'll break your neck.")
- **Breaking or striking objects.** (Breaks your possessions, beats on the table with fists, throws objects near or at you or your children.)
- **Uses force during an argument.** (Holds you down or against a wall, pushes, shoves, slaps, or kicks you. That type of behavior can easily escalate to choking, stabbing, or shooting.)

Please tell women that help is as close as the telephone. Any woman who sees herself in this column should call the nearest women's crisis line and tell someone what is happening. She will be provided with support and safety options.

Identifying the warning signs is the first step in breaking the cycle of violence.

—Portland, OR

Ann says: Some women do not realize they are being abused until someone points it out to them. They have been made to believe that abusive treatment is what they deserve and that most women are treated that way.

I hope the women who see themselves in today's column will check out the nearest women's shelter and keep the phone number handy. They can also call the National Domestic Violence Hotline at 1-800-799-SAFE (TDD: 1-800-787-3224). It could save their lives.

Source: "How to Tell If a Date or Mate Is a Potential Batterer" by A. Landers, June 30, 1997, p. 16. Reprinted with permission.

Even for teenagers, a recent study of several thousand found that about 66% of the boys and 59% of the girls agreed that it is a good idea for couples to live together before marriage (Popenoe & Whitehead, 2004). Increasingly, young people were agreeing with the concept used in the title of the article about cohabitation—"Sex Without Strings, Relationships Without Rings" (Popenoe & Whitehead, 2000).

The length of time a couple cohabits varies considerably depending on whether or not they get married. While about half (55%) of cohabiting couples get married within 5 years of living together, 40% breakup and 10% stay together and choose not to marry (Smock, 2000). About 40% of cohabiting women have children with their partner, and many times the pregnancy was not planned (Bumpass & Lu, 2000b). It is predicted that about 40% of all children in our society will at some point in their life live in a cohabiting household.

Most of the research to date demonstrates that cohabiting is not a good way to prepare for marriage and that couples who cohabit before marriage have a higher risk for divorce (Popenoe & Whitehead, 2004). However, recent studies of cohabiting couples have found that if the cohabiting occurs after a couple has planned to marry or are engaged, there is no difference in marital success than with couples who did not cohabit (Kline et al., 2004; Skinner, Bahr, Crane, & Call, 2002).

The rate of cohabitation generally increases with age, but it is also related to the quality of an individual's parents' marriage. In a study of young people and their parents by Paul Amato and Alan Booth (1997), cohabitation increased as young adults got older. At each age level, the rate of cohabitation was lowest for adult children from stable families and was highest for adult children of divorced parents. More specifically, only 13% of the 20-year-olds from stable homes were cohabiting, whereas 30% of those from divorced families were cohabiting. For 26-year-olds, the rate was 30% for those from stable homes and 48% for those from divorced families.

The rate of living together is also related to religious orientation, according to James Duke (1999), professor of sociology at Brigham Young University. Based on several studies, Duke found that Mormons are the least likely to cohabit outside of marriage, with a cohabitation rate of 8.2%, as compared to 20% to 24% for Protestants, 23% for Catholics, 32.5% for Jews, and 44.8% for nonreligious Americans.

Why Cohabitation Is Increasing

Given the predominant rates of cohabitation, it is difficult to believe that only 30 years ago, living together for unmarried heterosexual couples was both illegal and considered immoral. This revolutionary change can be attributed to several factors. First of all, first marriages are occurring at a later age than ever before (median age for females, 25; for males, 27) (U.S. Bureau of the Census, 2000e). In addition, puberty and sexual activity begin earlier, resulting in an extended single-hood before first marriage. The social stigma that was attached to cohabitation in the recent past has significantly declined, in part because of the sexual revolution. The saturation of sexuality within the entertainment industry and the media has greatly contributed to this change. Another important reason for cohabitation's growth is the decline in the number of individuals who choose to marry. The number of Americans who marry declined more than one-third from 1970 to 1996 (U.S. Bureau of the Census, 2000e). Concern over the continuing high rate of divorce may lead couples to choose to live together as either an alternative to marriage or a precursor to marriage.

People cohabit for many reasons and have various types of cohabitation arrangements. Following are some common reasons that couples give for cohabitating:

- Living together enables us to spend more time together.
- Living together allows us to share sexual and emotional intimacy without the commitment of marriage.
- Economic advantage—"We can save money by sharing living expenses."
- We can better learn the habits and character of each other, and if the relationship does not work out, there is no messy divorce.
- We can "test" our compatibility for a potential future marriage—see how we operate on a day-to-day basis.
- Engagement—"We are planning to marry."

Types of Cohabiting

In a classic review of research and the observations of counselors, Carl Ridley, Dan Peterman, and Arthur Avery (1978) identified four common patterns of cohabitation: Linus blanket, emancipation, convenience, and testing.

- **Linus blanket.** Named after the character in the comic strip "Peanuts" who carries a security blanket with him, the Linus blanket cohabiting relationship occurs when one partner is so dependent or insecure that he or she prefers a relationship with anyone to being alone. The insecure partner often finds the open communication on which a successful relationship thrives to be difficult, and the stronger partner does not feel that he or she can criticize the more "fragile" partner. After shouldering the planning and decision-making burdens for too long, the stronger partner often becomes frustrated and leaves the relationship. When the relationship ends, the insecure partner's fragile self-esteem falls even lower, and the departing partner feels guilty.
- **Emancipation.** Some people use cohabitation as a way to break free from their parents' values and influence. Women who grew up in very conservative religious traditions sometimes seek sexual emancipation not permitted by their parents or their faith through cohabitation. Guilt often overwhelms these women, however, and they break off the relationship. But because the business of emancipation is not finished, they often enter into another cohabiting relationship. The partner suffers in this type of situation because the individual seeking emancipation brings too much unfinished business to the relationship and is trying to gain independence at another's expense.
- **Convenience.** Relationships in which one person is the giver and the other is the taker are often relationships of convenience. Cohabiting relationships of this type may involve a man who is in the relationship mainly for sex and to have a housewife (although women may cohabit for economic, sexual, and social reasons also). The woman supplies loving care and domestic labor—and hopes, but dares not ask, for marriage. It is obvious what the man gets out of the relationship. The woman gains a few hard-earned lessons: that unconditional giving can go unreturned and that reciprocity is essential for

Men have as much to gain from egalitarian relationships as women do. The quest for power, money, and material success in which so many men are immersed is accompanied by higher levels of stress, higher rates of heart disease, and shorter life spans.

Box 10.3 Putting It Together

Ten Ideas to Consider Before Cohabiting

1. Make the decision to live with another person with great care—remember it is much easier to move in together than to move out.
2. Before you move in together, clearly define what your expectations are for the relationship. Are you both interested in marriage or is this arrangement just because it feels right?
3. Keep your expectations reasonable. Do not live together to change the other person.
4. Define the amount of time you are planning to cohabit. Is it 1 month, 6 months, 1 year or whatever?
5. Draw up and sign a "living-together agreement" that clarifies how you plan to handle finances and property.
6. Use birth control and be clear about your interest in having children. Remember that an unplanned pregnancy is a common outcome of living together.
7. Take a couples education class together so that you can get to know each other and see if you can develop and maintain a healthy relationship together.
8. Ask your friends and family to honestly tell you what they think about your relationship and trust their opinion.
9. Remember that love "blinds you" and that love and your relationship will not always be like it is today.
10. Before you decide to marry, seek premarital counseling to build a stronger couple relationship.

Source: Adapted and revised from Solot & Miller, 2000.

the long-term survival and ultimate success of a relationship. The partners usually part company, older and wiser.

- **Testing.** Cohabitation can be a true testing ground for marriage if the partners are relatively mature and clearly committed to trying out their already mutually satisfying relationship in a situation more closely resembling marriage. If the test goes well, they marry; if not, they separate and go their own ways.

Living Together Is Replacing Dating

The growing rate of cohabitation among couples adds a new step in the mate selection and courtship process. Many counselors have severely criticized traditional courtship because it emphasizes recreation and avoids conflictual issues. Also the strong erotic needs of premarital couples tend to decrease their interest or ability to deal with problematic issues in their relationship. As one husband said in counseling, "When you're in love, you're willing to compromise on anything." Many believe that traditional courtship provides partners with idealized views of each other, making early marriage a period of more severe and difficult adjustments for most couples. In a cohabiting relationship, however, couples are able to experience the realities of life together before they decide to tie the knot.

Just as cohabitation has its supporters, so it has its detractors. Some argue against cohabitation on moral, religious, and philosophical grounds. Others question whether cohabitation is an effective predictor of marital success; because it is not truly a marriage, they contend, it cannot serve as a test of marriage. In the opinion of many observers, it is only "playing house"; to test marriage, they say, you need to actually get married.

Nonetheless, living together won't keep partners from experiencing pain and misery if the relationship breaks up. For most couples who have cohabited, dealing with the hurt of a broken relationship can be as difficult as it would have been if they had been legally married.

Box 10.4 Self-Assessment

How Realistic Are Your Ideas About Cohabitation?

Respond True or False

1. Cohabitation is the best way to prepare for marriage.
2. If we get married, our marriage will be similar to cohabitation.
3. Cohabitation will decrease the chances we will get divorced.
4. My partner and relationship will change after marriage.
5. Cohabiting will increase our commitment and closeness.
6. After cohabiting, couples become more critical of each other.
7. Premarital counseling can help couples better prepare for marriage and reduce the chances of divorce.
8. Cohabitation can create some issues with our parents.
9. Unresolved issues for cohabiting couples tend to increase after marriage.
10. The ability and skills of couples to communicate and resolve conflict tend to decrease during cohabitation.

Scoring

Count True for items 4, 6–10 ____

Count False for items 1–3, 5 ____

Total of above: ____

Interpretation	
9–10	Healthy and realistic perspective about cohabitation.
7–8	Generally realistic perspective about cohabitation.
4–6	Need more information about important issues regarding cohabitation and marriage.
1–3	You need to learn more about cohabitation.

Answers to Cohabitation Quiz

1. *Cohabitation is the best way to prepare for marriage.*

   False: Almost all studies of cohabitation find that living together is not a good way to prepare for marriage. A better way to prepare for marriage is to seek premarital counseling that will help you develop your strengths and overcome any ongoing relationship issues.

2. *If we get married, our marriage will be similar to cohabitation.*

   False: Most cohabiting couples report that being married feels different from cohabiting. Part of this is because marriage brings with it higher expectations that you operate as a couple. Each partner and others assume that since you are now married, you will more often be together as a couple.

3. *Cohabitation will decrease the chances we will get divorced.*

   False: A common myth of cohabiting couples is that living together can improve their chances of marital success. However, virtually all major studies have shown a higher divorce rate among couples who cohabited before marriage than those who did not. One goal of premarital counseling is to help couples work to improve their relationship so they will have a lower risk for divorce.

4. *My partner and relationship will change after marriage.*

   True: Marriage changes both the couple's expectations and other people's expectations about the relationship. For example, when cohabiting, the persons may have spent holidays apart, each spending time with their own families. However, once married, there is the assumption and greater

Cohabiting as Preparation for Marriage?

In a comprehensive review of cohabitation, David Popenoe and Barbara Whitehead (1999b) reported that more than half of couples marrying today have already lived together—a trend they foresee as continuing. Cohabiting relationships are, however, short lived for many couples. An estimated 40% do not result in marriage. In their report *Should We Live Together?* (1999a), Popenoe and Whitehead discovered that most couples believe it is a good idea to cohabit in order to decide if they should get married. Couples maintain that cohabitating enables them to share expenses and learn more about each other. If a couple chooses to cohabit, there are things a couple might consider (Box 10.3).

pressure that they attend more functions together as a couple.

5. *Cohabiting will increase our commitment and closeness.*

   False: Most studies have shown that commitment and closeness do not necessarily increase during cohabitation unless the couple is planning to marry. Once a couple has decided to get married, they have demonstrated their increased commitment, which then can lead to greater couple closeness.

6. *After cohabiting, couples become more critical of each other.*

   True: Living together enables couples to spend more time together, which makes them more aware of differences that were not apparent while dating. In addition to differences becoming more bothersome, there will inevitably be new issues that arise from living together. Thus couples often become more critical of each other after they cohabit with each other.

7. *Premarital counseling can help couples better prepare for marriage and reduce the chances of divorce.*

   True: There are many studies that clearly demonstrate that premarital counseling can improve the relationship skills (communication and conflict resolution) in a couple so that they can better deal with ongoing and future issues. A good premarital program includes taking a premarital inventory and four to six feedback sessions where relationship skills are taught.

8. *Cohabitation can create some issues with our parents.*

   True: While many parents are becoming more accepting of the idea that their son or daughter is cohabiting, they still have concerns about the value of cohabiting. One indication is that parents are often sensitive and often opposed to the couple sleeping together in their house when they visit.

9. *Unresolved issues with cohabiting couples tend to increase after marriage.*

   True: Issues that cohabiting couples hoped would disappear after marriage often increase in intensity. These issues generally escalate with time if not resolved. It is important that issues be worked on as a couple to get them resolved before marriage, but this rarely happens. After marriage, most couples also find new issues that they had not anticipated, in addition to the issues they already had as a cohabiting couple.

10. *The ability and skills of couples to communicate and resolve conflict tend to decrease during cohabitation.*

    True: Cohabiting increases the awareness and intensity of difference in personality, communication, and conflict resolution. Studies with cohabiting couples have found that their relationship skills tend to decrease and they tend to have more unresolved issues.

Nonetheless, Popenoe and Whitehead (2000) concluded from their review of many studies that cohabitation is detrimental to marriage and increases the probability of divorce. According to these researchers, living together increases the risk of domestic violence for women and the risk of physical and sexual abuse for children. Cohabiting is also potentially detrimental for children because the risk is high that the cohabiting couple will break up, thus making it difficult for the children to establish a close relationship with another adult. Also, women with children have higher levels of depression. Furthermore, cohabiting couples have lower levels of happiness and well-being than married couples. (See Box 10.4.)

In response to these findings, Larry Bumpass, a leading sociologist, feels that there are multiple causes of marital problems and divorce in our society. Bumpass

(1999) states: "It is inappropriate and simplistic to treat cohabitation as the major factor affecting divorce. The trend in divorce stretches back over the last hundred years, so clearly it wasn't caused by cohabitation" (p. 61). In fact, he maintains, cohabitation could have lowered the divorce rate by discouraging some couples from marrying who might eventually have divorced.

Summary

- Parent-arranged marriages remain common—and are effective—in many nonindustrialized cultures today, but in the United States, individual-choice courtship is the norm.
- Research on dating reveals that older individuals experience the same emotions as young people but that their dates are often more creative than those of younger people. Older couples do become sexually involved, but they look at sexual intimacy in a more realistic manner.
- Factors that influence mate selection are physical attractiveness, personality, age, life success, and the principles of exogamy and endogamy. The rise in ethnic diversity in the United States is changing the unwritten rules regarding mixed marriages.
- Theories about mate selection include (1) the homogamy theory, which proposes that people are attracted to others who are like themselves, and the complementary needs theory, which suggests that opposites attract; (2) the stimulus–value–role (SVR) theory, which holds that after the initial attraction (stimulus), value and role compatibility determine mate selection; and (3) the wheel theory of love, which explains the four interdependent components in the development of a love relationship—rapport, self-revelation, mutual dependency, and intimacy need fulfillment.
- Courtship violence, a formerly neglected area of research, has come under careful scrutiny in the past several years. Research shows that violent dates are likely to become violent mates.
- Cohabitation is increasing in popularity; in 2000, there were 5.5 million couples living together, as compared to 500,000 in 1970. Most couples see living together as a way to help them decide if they should get married. Experts disagree about the impact of cohabitation on the quality of a couple's subsequent marriage and whether it increases the chances for divorce. Living together is not a good predictor of whether a couple will have a good marriage or whether they will be at higher risk for divorce.

Key Terms

parent-arranged marriage
couple-arranged marriage
dating
permissiveness
double standard
mating gradient
sex ratio
endogamy
exogamy
homogamy
complementary needs
  theory
rapport
self-revelation
mutual dependency
intimacy need fulfillment
cohabitation
Linus blanket
emancipation
convenience
testing

Activities

1. Share your thoughts on these questions in a small group: What forces are pushing you toward marriage? What forces are pulling you toward marriage? What is pushing you toward singlehood? What attracts you to singlehood?
2. What initially attracts you to another person? Rank the following traits from 1 to 5 (1 being the highest and 5 the lowest): physical attractiveness, popularity, social status, personality, and character. Discuss your rankings in a small group.
3. Do opposites attract? Or do birds of a feather flock together? In a small group, discuss the theory of homogamy and the theory of complementary needs as they relate to friendships and love relationships.
4. Discuss violence in dating as a small group. Be sure to address these questions, among others: How frequently have you experienced abuse? What was your reaction to it? What can be done to reduce courtship violence?
5. What are the pros and cons of living together? Make a list of five advantages and five disadvantages.
6. Does cohabitation increase marital satisfaction and decrease the probability of divorce? Discuss this question in small groups.

Suggested Readings

Glenn, N., & Marquardt, E. (2001). *Hooking up, hanging out, and hoping for Mr. Right.* New York: Institute for American Values.

Larson, J. (2001). The verdict on cohabitation vs. marriage. *Marriage and Families,* pp. 7–12.

Popenoe, D., & Whitehead, B. (1999). *Should we live together? What young adults need to know about cohabitation before marriage.* New Brunswick, NJ: Rutgers University.

Popenoe, D., & Whitehead, B. (2000). *The state of our unions 2000: The social health of marriage in America.* New Brunswick, NJ: Rutgers University.

Waite, L., & Gallagher, M. (2000). *The case for marriage: Why married people are happier, healthier, and better off financially.* New York: Doubleday.

Visit the text-specific Online Learning Center at **www.mhhe.com/Olson6** for practice tests, chapter summaries, Web links, Internet exercises, key terms, and flashcards.

11. *M*arriage: Building a Strong Foundation

Intimacy, Strengths, and Diversity

Perspectives on Marriage Today

Components of a Successful Marriage

Marriage Education

Importance of Families of Origin in Marriage

The Wedding and Newlywed Years

Keeping Marriages Strong

Federal Healthy Marriage Initiative

Summary

Key Terms

Activities

Suggested Readings

Intimacy, Strengths, and Diversity

For those who marry, marriage is generally the most intimate relationship people have. It involves emotional and physical intimacy, which has the potential to make us feel happy and fulfilled. Intimacy involves good communication, which requires couples sharing feelings and experiences, and good communication helps couples solve problems and make decisions. Physical intimacy is also an important part of the closeness spouses feel toward one another. The degree of intimacy in a marriage is an important barometer of the health of the couple relationship.

Every marriage relationship has strengths, and it has been determined that focusing on strengths, rather than problems, is helpful for couples trying to make their marriages better. Marriage education inventories, such as PREPARE, help couples identify their strengths and also spend time addressing areas where they want to grow. Recently, there has been an increased interest in promoting healthy marriages through marriage education throughout the country.

Most research and marriage education is focused on White, middle-class couples. We know very little about the effectiveness of existing marriage education programs for low-income couples and couples from diverse populations. Because of the current interest in, and federal funding for, marriage education for such couples, it is likely that we will see an increase in culturally appropriate programming for diverse audiences in the near future.

Perspectives on Marriage Today

Next to parenthood, marriage is the most important, challenging and rewarding relationship we ever undertake. But what happens in this most private of all relationships can have powerful effects on others, and on society as a whole.

—THEODORA OOMS (1998, p. 6)

Based on the latest Census in 2000 of 221.1 million people over the age of 15, more than half the persons are married (120 million or 54.4%), about one-quarter have never been married (60 million or 27%), and about one-fifth are divorced, separated, or widowed (41 million or 18.5%) (U.S. Bureau of the Census, 2004c).

Both men and women are delaying when they marry to an older age. Males are now getting married at the average age of 27 years and 25 for women. In 1970, the average age for marriage for men was 23 and 20 for women (U.S. Bureau of the Census, 2004c). In 1970, 77% of women over the age of 15 were married but only 50% of women are currently married. Another indication of the delay in marriage is that for the age group of 25 to 34 years, in 1950 only 19% of men were never married but that increased to 39% in 2000. For women in 1950, only 11% were never married but that increased to 30% in 2000.

The Benefits of Marriage

Society has a large stake in strengthening marriages. Children should be our central concern and, in general, they are better when raised by two parents. Marriage also typically improves the health and economic well-being of adults, stabilizes community life and benefits civic society.

—THEODORA OOMS (1998, p. 4)

Because the media so often focus on the negative aspects of marriage (marital violence, divorce), many people often fail to see the positive effects of marriage, which are numerous. Linda Waite reviewed various studies that examined the positive effects of marriage on individuals (Waite, 1998; Waite & Gallagher, 2000). By and large, these studies included White middle-class couples. The benefits identified by Waite are as follows:

- *Married people lead a healthier lifestyle.* People who are married tend to avoid more harmful behaviors than do single, divorced, or widowed persons. For example, married people have much lower levels of problem drinking, which is associated with accidents, interpersonal conflict, and depression in women. In general, married people lead a healthier lifestyle in terms of eating, exercise, and avoiding harmful behaviors.
- *Married people live longer.* At every age level, married people live several years longer than do single, divorced, or widowed persons. This is often because they have emotional support in the partner, as well as more economic resources.
- *Married people have a satisfying sexual relationship.* Married couples have sex about six to seven times per month, as compared to an average of seven times for cohabiting couples and only three to four times for singles. In terms of sexual satisfaction, over half (54%) of the married males and 43% of married females are extremely satisfied with their sexual relationships. For cohabiting couples, about 44% of the males and 35% of the females are extremely satisfied.
- *Married people have more wealth and economic assets.* Because a married couple can pool their economic resources, they tend to be more wealthy. In fact, the median household wealth for a married couple is $132,000, as compared to $35,000 for singles, $42,275 for widowed individuals, $33,670 for divorced individuals, and $7,600 for separated individuals. Married couples have greater wealth in part because two can live for the price of 1½ persons by sharing the cost of housing, household appliances, furniture, utilities, and so on.
- *Children generally do better raised in a two-parent home.* Children from two-parent homes tend to do better emotionally and academically. They are half as likely to drop out of school; they have higher grades; and they are less likely to get pregnant. Children from two-parent homes also get more parental attention (such as parental supervision, help with schoolwork, and quality time with each child) than do children from single-parent homes. Also, children from single-parent homes have a much higher probability of growing up in poverty and experiencing a lower quality of life.

In summary, being married has a very positive impact on an individual's emotional and physical health. Some have suggested that the question isn't whether marriage has a positive effect on individuals but whether more healthy and happy people choose to marry rather than remain single. Nonetheless, an extensive analysis from a variety of studies demonstrates that selective factors in who marries do not explain the positive benefits of marriage (Waite & Gallagher, 2000). It is, in fact, the synergy of pooling a variety of resources that makes marriage beneficial to individuals. This pooling of resources can also occur as gay couples join in civil unions (see Box 11.1).

Marriage and Black Americans

Researchers have reviewed the studies conducted with Black American couples to determine if they benefited from marriage to the same degree as White Americans (Blackman, Clayton, Glenn, Malone-Colon, & Roberts, 2005). The review of the

BOX 11.1   At Issue

Gay Couples Entering Civil Unions

The New Jersey same-sex civil union law went into effect in February 2007. Although the New Jersey law does not call the union "marriage," it does provide the protections and benefits of marriage (Barry, 2007). Massachusetts previously was the only state to recognize same sex marriages, with California, Connecticut, and Vermont having laws allowing civil unions with benefits less generous than those of New Jersey. Forty-five states have laws in place to ban gay marriages (Mulvihill, 2007).

Many gay activists and gay and lesbian couples had hoped that the term "marriage" would be used so that such couples would have status equal to heterosexual couples. Many hope there will eventually be no distinction between unions of gay and heterosexual couples and that they will all be called marriages.

The law was a long time in coming. The enactment of the law began in 2002, when same-sex couples were denied marriage licenses. A lawsuit resulted, and the case went to the New Jersey Supreme Court. The court eventually ruled that the New Jersey state constitution guarantees same-sex couples all the rights and benefits of marriage. The court then passed the issue on to the New Jersey Legislature to determine what these unions would be called. Several months before the law went into effect, it was determined that they would be called *unions* rather than *marriages*. After the law went into effect, couples submitted applications for civil unions, which require couples to wait 3 days before the license is granted and the ceremonies can be performed.

The issue of same-sex unions continues to be controversial in the United States. Conservative groups, usually religious in nature, take the position that allowing same-sex unions takes away from the sanctity of marriage between a man and a woman. Gay and lesbian advocates think that all the rights and the title of marriage should be given to all couples.

While states are recognizing civil unions of same-sex couples, they are restricting the term "marriage" to heterosexual couples.

literature found many similarities but some differences with the findings of Waite and Gallagher (2000):

- Marriage for Black Americans was related to more income and less poverty, and couples were more likely to be happy and have better family relationship functioning.
- Physical health did not appear to improve for Black couples who were married.

- Black men benefited more from marriage than Black women in terms of family life and physical health.
- Children in Black families, especially male children, experienced great benefits from parents who were married.
- Black women who were married actually reported *poorer* health than unmarried women.
- Black women experienced no benefit in terms of quality of family life when they were married.

Why is it that Black men seem to benefit more in terms of health and quality of family life than Black women? The researchers speculate that Black marriages experience more conflict than White marriages, and women, in general, are more likely to experience stress from this conflict. Therefore, this conflict negatively affects the quality of family life and health for Black women (Blackman et al., 2005).

When Marriages Do Not Work

Even though, on average, individuals do better being married, people should not stay in destructive marriages. Marriages that involve physical abuse or substance abuse often are physically and emotionally damaging to individuals. Even though healthy marriages have positive effects on individuals, marriages with conflict result in negative effects on health and well-being.

Approximately one-third of divorces involve relationships with a high degree of conflict (Schramm, 2006). Couples may try therapy to improve the relationship, and certainly those efforts can have positive effects in developing a healthy relationship. However, if improvements cannot be made to make it a healthy relationship, couples may need to consider divorce.

It is also important to remember that it takes two people to make a marriage work. Even though one person is willing to make changes to improve the marriage, the spouse may not be willing to make changes. Ultimately, individuals must draw their own conclusions about whether the marriage is worth the effort and, sometimes, heartache.

The Decline in Marriage

The number of marriages in our society continues to decrease at the same time the number of singles and cohabiting couples increases. The number of marriages has reached its lowest level to date. The rate of marriage has declined from a high of 68% of the population in 1970, to 62% in 1980, to 52% in 2000 (U.S. Bureau of the Census, 2004c). This decline in marriage has occurred across ethnic groups, but it has most affected African Americans, of whom only 36% of women and 41% of men are married compared to 58% of White women and 60% of White men.

A second trend is an increase in the number of people who get divorced and choose not to remarry. The number of divorced people in the population has tripled from 3% in 1970 to 10% in 1996. Also, the number of adults who have never been married increased from 21 million (16%) in 1970 to 60 million (27%) in 2000.

A third major trend is an increase in the number of cohabiting couples in the United States. In 1970, only 500,000 couples were living together; the number rose to 3.7 million in 1996 and to 5.5 million in 2000. (More facts about marriage are listed in Table 11.1.)

As these statistics suggest, the popularity of marriage is decreasing. Although most individuals choose to marry at least once, it appears that fewer are choos-

TABLE 11.1	Facts About Marriage

• Approximately 1.8 million couples marry each year.	• Engagements last an average of 9 months.
• Approximately 1.0 million couples divorce each year.	• The average U.S. wedding costs about $15,000.
• In about half (47%) of all marriages, one or both people have been married at least once before.	• The average age at divorce is 36 for males and 33 for females.
• The bridegroom's average age was 27; the bride's average age was 25.5. In 1960, the average age was 22.8 for the bridegroom and 20.3 for the bride.	• Approximately half of all marriages end in divorce.
	• The average length of a marriage that ends in divorce is 7 years.
	• Over 1 million couples with children divorce each year.

Source: U.S. Bureau of the Census, 2004c.

ing to remarry and instead either stay single or choose cohabitation over marriage. Marriage has been on the decline for the last two decades, and it appears that increasingly fewer people will choose to get married or to remarry in future years.

Components of a Successful Marriage

A loving relationship can bring two people enormous benefits; it can help them grow as friends and lovers, and it can even heal wounds. Most counselors agree that the chances of marital success are greater if both partners enter marriage as friends; but the chances of achieving a successful intimate relationship are slim for a couple in which one plays the role of therapist and the other the role of patient. A careful review of research and clinical experience reported by many professionals indicates that a marriage has a better chance for success if potential partners meet the following conditions:

- *Both individuals are independent and mature.* The more mature and independent two people are, the easier it is for them to develop an interdependent relationship that can facilitate intimacy. Independence and maturity often increase with age, a good reason for waiting to marry. In fact, the single best predictor of a successful marriage is the age of the couple. This is partly because older people are typically more stable and know what they want in marriage.
- *Both individuals love not only each other but also themselves.* Self-esteem is very important in an intimate relationship. It is difficult to truly love another person without also loving oneself. People need to feel secure and self-confident before they can be truly giving and loving to another.
- *Both individuals enjoy being alone as well as together.* To balance the separateness and togetherness that an intimate relationship requires, partners need to enjoy separate activities and time apart. Time apart reminds partners of the value of the relationship and increases the importance and value of time together. Too much togetherness can lead to such negative behaviors as attempting to control one's partner and failing to appreciate the partner.
- *Both individuals are established in their work or occupation.* A stable and satisfying occupation or job fosters both financial and emotional security. When people's jobs are going well, they are able to devote more time and energy to

Independent and mature individuals are likely to have acquired the self-knowledge and self-confidence necessary for an intimate relationship and a successful marriage. Because they can express their needs honestly and assertively and respond unselfishly to each other's needs, such couples are more likely to be friends as well as lovers.

their relationships. Conversely, the greater the stress at work, the less positive energy there is for a relationship.

- *Both individuals know themselves.* An intimate relationship requires openness and honesty between partners. They must be able to evaluate their personal strengths and failings objectively and not blame their problems on other people. They must also know what they want from and can give to the partner.
- *Both individuals can express themselves assertively.* One key to developing intimacy is assertiveness—expressing oneself in a direct and generally positive manner. People who are not assertive in their communication often adopt a passive–aggressive approach. The more clearly partners can ask for what they want from each other, the better the chances for compliance. (See Chapter 9 for a detailed discussion on assertive communication.)
- *Both individuals are friends as well as lovers.* When people focus on their lover's needs, they find that the loved one tends to focus on their needs. This has been called the *law of enlightened self-interest*. Developed by social exchange theorists to describe successful relationships, the principle holds that being less selfish is in a person's best interest because it helps build cooperative and intimate relationships that benefit everyone. Nonpossessive caring encourages the partner to grow and to reach his or her potential. Both partners generally benefit.

Marriage Education

The dignity of a vocation is always to be measured by the seriousness of the preparation made for it. How then do we appraise marriage?

—R. Herbert Newton

Marriage education has had an interesting and sporadic history in the United States. In the 1970s, there were a significant number of marriage education programs. Such programs began with the work of David and Vera Mace, who founded the Association for Couples in Marriage Enrichment in 1973 (Doherty & Anderson, 2004). Marriage Encounter emerged during this time, which was used primarily by Catholics but by other denominations as well. Marriage Encounter became the largest national marriage education program during that time (Doherty & Anderson, 2004). Marriage Encounter was led by clergy along with laypeople, and marriage education was taught within the context of spiritual beliefs.

During the 1980s and 1990s, marriage education was less popular (Doherty & Anderson, 2004). Marriage was seen as promoting patriarchal norms and not allowing for the emerging gay and lesbian relationships that were becoming more and more publicly prevalent. In addition, cohabitation was becoming an acceptable partnership model. One program that continued to attract large numbers of premarital couples was PREPARE. During this time, however, new marriage programs began to emerge, such as the Prevention and Relationship Enhancement Program (PREP), Relationship Enhancement, and Couples Communication (Doherty & Anderson, 2004).

In the 1990s, research emerged about the negative effects of divorce and resulted in what we know today as the *marriage movement* (Doherty & Anderson, 2004). Healthy marriages were viewed as a necessary component of society for the benefit of the couples and their children. By 2002, there was the hope of federal funding to support marriage education nationally. Today, there are several well-known programs throughout the country that are being used to help couples develop marriage skills.

Most of the marriage education programs were based on research with primarily White, middle-class couples. As a result, the usefulness of these programs for low-income and diverse populations is unknown and currently being tested. Developing effective programs for these populations, where the divorce rates are highest, is one of the future challenges for marriage education (Skogrand, Hatch, & Singh, 2008).

Premarital Education

Failing to prepare is like preparing to fail.

—Anonymous

Before the wedding, couples spend hours talking about the wedding flowers, the size of the diamond and the design of its mounting, the color of the groomsmen's ties, and so on, but they rarely discuss such topics as finances, in-laws, and role relationships. Without instruction and preparation, people are no more expert at developing intimate relationships than they are at parenting. Writing about his own family-building experiences, Norbert Wiener, one of the original developers of the modern computer, said, "One has only one life to live and there is not time enough in which to master the art of being a parent" (Wiener, 1956, p. 224).

If it weren't for concerned clergy who insist that couples meet with them at least once before marriage, many couples would have no premarital preparation. About 40% of couples getting married for the first time in a place of worship (church, synagogue, or mosque) receive some type of premarital services or programs. Many of these couples meet only once or twice with their clergy to discuss marriage issues. Some premarital couples attend small-group couples' workshops or retreats where

A growing number of couples are now seeking premarital preparation. This is, in part, because they see the large number of divorced people around them, including their parents, relatives, and even friends who had only been married a few years.

they discuss marriage. Another group of couples complete a premarital inventory and receive some feedback in two or three sessions. However, very few premarital couples receive a comprehensive premarital program that includes all the components mentioned below.

What Constitutes an Effective Premarital Program?

It is evident from the research that there are at least five essential components to an effective premarital program:

- *The couple should take some type of premarital inventory and should receive feedback on the results.* A premarital inventory increases the couple's awareness of the strengths and potential problem areas in their relationship. It also helps them discuss their relationship. In addition, the process establishes a relationship with a clergy member, a counselor, or a married couple with whom the couple can consult should they need intensive counseling for serious problems. Finally, it prepares them for later marriage enrichment.
- *The couple should receive training in communication and problem-solving skills.* These skills help the couple deal with various relationship issues by teaching them empathy as well as techniques for self-disclosure, resolving conflict, and problem solving.
- *The couple should participate in a small discussion group in which couples share their feelings and experiences.* This increases a couple's ability and willingness to share with other couples, lets the couple see how other couples relate and deal with issues, and may foster friendships with other couples.
- *A good premarital program should start 12 months before marriage and last 6 to 8 weeks.* Unfortunately, most premarital couples do not begin marriage preparation until 2 or 3 months before their wedding. When a couple cannot complete a comprehensive program before marriage, they should enroll in some sort of program after marriage.

The PREPARE Program is offered by over 65,000 clergy and counselors in the United States and has been taken by over 2,000,000 premarital couples. The PREPARE Program consists of first taking the PREPARE Couple Questionnaire (165 questions) and then receiving feedback using the six couple exercises. During the four to six counseling sessions, the couple also learn how to improve their communication and conflict resolution skills.

The PREPARE Program has been demonstrated to be very effective in improving a couple's communication and ability to resolve conflict and has led to greater couple agreement (Knutson & Olson, 2003). By improving their relationship skills, they get their marriage off to a better start.

Six Couple Exercises

1. To help the couple explore their relationship strengths and growth areas.
2. To help the couple increase their communication skills (assertiveness and active listening).
3. To help the couple learn how to resolve couple conflict using the Ten Step Model.
4. To help the couple discuss their families of origin and what they want to bring, or not bring, from their families into their couple relationship.
5. To help the couple develop a workable budget and financial plan.
6. To help the couple develop their personal, couple, and family goals.

18 Important Relationship Areas (10 Questions Asked in Each Specific Domain)

Personality Areas

Self-confidence
Assertiveness
Avoidance
Partner dominance

Couple and Family System

Couple closeness
Couple flexibility
Family closeness
Family flexibility

Intrapersonal Areas

Realistic expectations
Personality issues
Spiritual beliefs
Marriage satisfaction

External Areas

Family and friends
Financial management

Interpersonal Areas

Communication
Conflict resolution
Role relationship
Sexual relationship

To Locate a Professional Offering the PREPARE Program (www.prepare-enrich.com)

To locate a professional trained to offer the PREPARE Program in your area, go to the Web site at www.prepare-enrich.com. You can insert your zip code and find professionals in your area. You can also take a Couple Quiz online, individually or as a couple, and learn more about your couple relationship.

- *A good premarital program should motivate the couple to want to continue marital enrichment after marriage.* Marriage is a process and one that takes continual effort to make it grow and deal with the stress and changes over time. Couples should ideally seek out couple enrichment programs after marriage to continue to sustain their relationship.

There are a variety of couple programs that contain most of the characteristics that are helpful to couples, both premarital and married couples. Several of these couple programs have been developed and tested over 20 years; they are each described in detail in the book *Preventive Approaches in Couples-Therapy* by Berger and Hannah (1999). The most highly recommended programs are Couple Communication, PAIRS Program, PREP Program, PREPARE/ENRICH programs, and the Relationship Enhancement Program. See Box 11.2 for more detailed

BOX 11.3   At Issue

Predicting Marital Success

We are taught, through fairy tales, TV movies of the week, romance novels, and our own fantasy lives, that love conquers all. And it does—in fairy tales, TV movies, novels, and fantasies. In real life, relationships (especially marriages) require continual care.

Couples often marry with unrealistic expectations of a life where both partners will always be happy, they will never fight, and conflicts will magically resolve themselves. They don't realize that fighting is an integral part of a relationship. In fact, in an article for *Psychology Today* entitled "What Makes Marriage Work," John Gottman and Nan Silver (1994a) state that fighting, "when it airs grievances and complaints, can be one of the healthiest things a couple can do for their relationship," and that ". . . a lasting marriage results from a couple's ability to resolve the conflicts that are inevitable in any relationship."

They also found that marriages tend to settle into one of three styles of conflict resolution:

1. *Validating*—couples argue, but they let each other know that they respect the other's points of view and emotions, even if they don't agree with them.
2. *Volatile*—passionate couples have intense fights and then intense make-up sessions; these couples see themselves as equal sparring partners.
3. *Conflict-avoiding*—couples often make light of their differences and learn to live with them.

Gottman and Silver concluded that no matter what the conflict resolution styles, the predictor of marital success is the ratio of positive-to-negative feelings and actions toward each other. "As long as there is five times as much positive feeling and interaction between husband and wife as there is negative," note the authors, "the marriage [is] likely to be stable over time."

On the other hand, Gottman and Silver have been able to predict which couples will get divorced by about 90% after watching and listening to couples' videotaped interaction for just 5 minutes. The following are the specific signs they used to identify couples who would later divorce.

1. *A harsh startup*—the couple begins the discussion by being negative and accusatory of each other.
2. *The four horsemen*—four ways of interacting that can sabotage communication:

   - *Criticism*—negative words that are global about the partner, attacking the partner's personality or character rather than a specific behavior.
   - *Contempt*—being overly critical and using such means of expression as insults, sarcasm, name calling, hostile humor, and mockery.
   - *Defensiveness*—denying one's own role in a problem or issue, thus blaming the partner.
   - *Stonewalling*—failing to respond, or tuning the partner out (85% of the time the male is the stonewaller).

3. *Flooding*—feeling overwhelmed by the partner's negativity leaves the person shell-shocked.
4. *Body language*—men are more physiologically and visibly overwhelmed by conflict than women are.
5. *Failed repair attempts*—failing to break the cycle of negativity or prevent the flood.
6. *Bad memories*—when a marriage isn't going well, the couple rewrites the past in a more negative way.

After finding the predictors of divorce, Gottman initially thought he would know how to save the marriages by overriding the four horsemen and eliminating the other negative signs. He concluded by stating, "But like so many experts before me, I was wrong. I was not able to crack the code to saving marriages until I started to analyze what went *right* in happy marriage . . . . The foundation of my (new) approach is to strengthen the friendship that is at the heart of any marriage (Gottman & Silver, 1999, p. 46).

---

information about the PREPARE Program. In addition to the book by Berger and Hannah, you can learn more about couple programs by visiting the Web site www .smartmarriages.com.

Predicting a Successful Marriage

Love is not enough to make a successful marriage. The truth of this can be seen in divorce statistics. Most people who marry are in love, but roughly half of those who marry eventually divorce. If love at the time of marriage is a poor predictor of marital happiness, what characteristics do predict a happy marriage? Studies demonstrate that the type of relationship a couple has before marriage is very predictive of whether they will have a successful and happy marriage.

Two different approaches to predicting a successful marriage were conducted by two different research teams. Both teams could predict marital outcome (happiness versus divorce) with about 80% to 90% accuracy. One team directed by John Gottman (Gottman & Silver, 1999) at the University of Washington focused on videotaping couples talking and resolving conflict based on microanalysis of the videotapes. The findings by John Gottman are summarized in Box 11.3.

The second team was directed by David Olson and colleagues (Olson & Olson, 2000) at the University of Minnesota, and they used couple questionnaires rather than videotaping couple interaction. The questionnaires are called PREPARE (for premarital couples) and ENRICH (for married couples). To identify factors that predict marital satisfaction, Olson and colleagues conducted two long-term studies of couples. Engaged couples were questioned 3 to 4 months before their marriages and then followed to a point 3 to 4 years after their marriages. The first study was done by Blaine Fowers and David Olson (1986); the replication study was done by Andrea Larsen and David Olson (1989).

Both studies found that 80% to 85% of the time it was possible to predict, on the basis of their PREPARE inventory scores *before* marriage, whether a couple would later be happily married or divorced.

Importance of Families of Origin in Marriage

When a couple gets married, each partner is also joining the other partner's family. As such, the Couple and Family Map can be useful for helping partners discuss and compare their **families of origin**—the families in which they were raised during childhood—before they marry. The case study that follows involves Kathy and Jim, a couple whose family backgrounds are quite different. They explored these differences in premarital counseling.

Kathy's Family of Origin

Kathy grew up in a *structurally enmeshed* family (Figure 11.1). She is the third oldest of six children, who at the time of counseling ranged in age from 18 to 27. Kathy's parents have been married for 28 years. All of the children except Kathy live and work in the town in which they grew up. Kathy's family is structured on the flexibility dimension of the Couple and Family Map for the following reasons: While growing up, the children knew what was expected of them. The parents were firm yet fair with discipline and enforcement of family rules. The mother was strong and a thorough organizer, and the father was equally strong and even stubborn at times. The father acted as the head of the household but respected his wife's education, contributions, and ability. The mother was comfortable playing a somewhat traditional role and worked hard at keeping the family organized.

Kathy's family is enmeshed on the cohesion dimension. They are a close-knit Catholic family from a small town. Except for 18-year-old John, all of the children have left home, and all except Kathy have settled in the local community. The children drop by the family home several times a week. On weeknights, they play cards or just sit around and talk. The whole family gets together at least every other

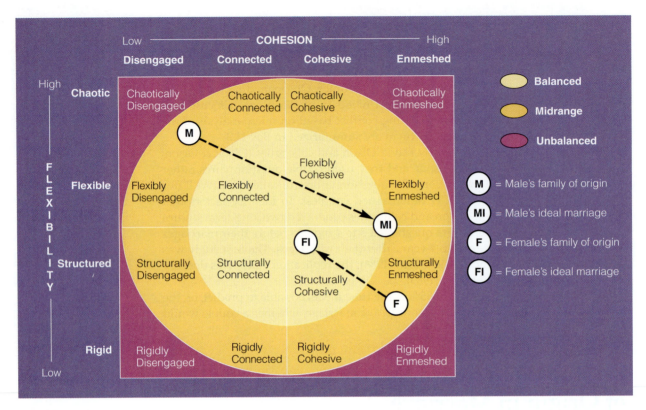

FIGURE 11.1
Family of Origin and
Ideal Type of Marriage

Sunday for dinner. The mother is heavily involved in each of her children's lives. She feels excited when they are excited and guilty when they are down, and she is always trying to help them. The father is less involved in the lives of his children but expects them to visit often, especially on weekends.

Jim's Family of Origin

Jim grew up in a *flexibly disengaged* family (see Figure 11.1). He is the older of two children; his brother is 4 years younger. His parents have been married for 27 years but are now separated. After several years of frustration, the mother decided that she had had enough and asked her husband for a separation; he moved out several months ago. He has been asking for a reconciliation, claiming he's changed, but she is suspicious of these "instant" changes and has decided to "wait and see" if they are permanent.

Jim's family is currently flexible in terms of how it functions, but over the past several years, it has undergone certain changes. For many years, it was closer to a structured family: The mother and father had traditional male and female roles; father handed down the rules, and mother backed him up. After 15 years as a homemaker, however, Jim's mother went back to school and got a 2-year certificate in bookkeeping. Her self-esteem improved, and she became more confident and assertive in her relationship with her husband. The family system became more flexible. Jim's father began helping out around the house. He became more lenient with the boys when he saw that they were fairly responsible and willing to pitch in around the house.

In terms of cohesion, the family is currently disengaged. When they were young, the boys were very involved in school activities, and the parents each had separate interests. The father hunted and fished, and the mother had her church activities. The father took the boys hunting and fishing when they got old enough, and they went on several canoe trips together. But these outings were the only times they were together. Most of the time, family members went their own ways and did their own thing. Each person in the family had his or her own friends, and these friends were sometimes more important to each person than family members were.

Goals for the Marriage

Kathy and Jim disagree somewhat on how cohesive (close) they want to be in their marriage, in part because of their families of origin. These two diverse family systems present some problems for this couple. Kathy would like a *cohesive* type of marriage but one in which she would have more emotional space and greater autonomy than in her *enmeshed* family of origin. Jim would like an enmeshed marriage, in reaction to his disengaged family of origin (see Figure 11.1). He has experienced a lot of pain and disappointment because of the breakup of his parents' marriage and has vowed not to make the mistakes they did. He doesn't want to be in another disengaged system in which people go their own way and do not connect emotionally.

This couple is struggling to negotiate just how much closeness they want from the relationship. Because it's hard for Jim to say what he is really feeling and to share his need for closeness in a direct way with Kathy, she sometimes interprets his desire for closeness as an attempt to control her. But Kathy wants to avoid the overcontrolling atmosphere of enmeshment that existed in her family. So she sometimes backs away from Jim when he is needy and wants closeness. Jim isn't always aware of how he tries to control Kathy or even why he wants to. He is more aware of the outcome of his efforts—her withdrawal.

What both Jim and Kathy have in common is the desire for a *structured* type of marriage. Although Jim sympathizes with his mother, he emotionally leans toward his father's value of a more structured type of system, with more stable male–female roles and predictable family rules and patterns. This is the level of flexibility with which he is most comfortable. Kathy would also like a structured marriage with fairly stable roles but with a distribution of responsibilities. She likes the predictability of a structured system but does not want it to become rigid like her family of origin. The desire for a structured system is a goal they both share and one they can work together to achieve.

The Wedding and Newlywed Years

In this section we will look at some guidelines for planning a wedding and at the difficult process of adjustment newlyweds face during the first few years of marriage.

The Wedding

Despite the great expense it often entails, a wedding is not a marriage. Today, the average wedding costs about $15,000. This figure includes the wedding ceremony, sit-down meals, reception, entertainment, gifts, honeymoon, and so forth. The

Whether a wedding is simple or extravagant, it is a milestone in the lives of two families and public testimony of a couple's love for each other. Decisions about the date, the place, the kind of ceremony, the size of the wedding party, the guest list, and the reception often require negotiation among the couple and their relatives so that everyone will feel that their preferences have been considered. Preparation for the wedding sometimes becomes the couple's first major challenge together in life.

average engaged couple spends about $4,000 of their own money on their wedding and honeymoon.

Although the wedding ceremony is an important celebration that also bonds friends and families, it can also create some problems. Decisions about the guest list and the kind of reception can create intense struggles between family members and the bride and groom.

Arond and Pauker (1987) have developed some useful guidelines for couples planning their wedding:

- Begin planning at least 1 year in advance.
- Try to consider the feelings of others, particularly family members.
- Consider what is important to you and what your budget is.
- Be assertive—it's *your* wedding.
- Use the preparations as a time to share and make decisions as a couple.
- Try to keep it simple so that you can enjoy it.

As the wedding approaches, many couples feel stressed out over all the planning and details surrounding the wedding. Arond and Pauker (1987) found that about two-thirds questioned whether they were making the right decision. About half were concerned about whether they would have enough money or whether they would get along with their in-laws or whether they would "goof up" during the ceremony. So, the wedding can be a very stressful event for most couples, and they are often exhausted by the time of their honeymoon.

The Transition to Marriage

The first years of marriage can be stressful, with spouses adjusting to the new relationship and with these marriages being especially vulnerable to dissolution. The newlywed years are also especially important for setting the tone that results in high marital satisfaction years down the road (Niehuis, Skogrand, & Houston, 2006; Schramm, Marshall, Harris, & Lee, 2005). Some of the difficulties that are

He likes to make a quick circuit of the store, picking up whatever appeals to him. She likes to make a list of what they'll need for the week and shop for bargains. Newlyweds discover differences in their habits and preferences and must find ways to accommodate these differences if their marriage is to succeed.

related to later divorce include difficulty with finances, emotional dependence, immaturity, difficulties with families of origin, infidelity, jealousy, and substance abuse—to name a few (Schramm et al., 2005).

In a random sample of over 1,000 couples who had been married for less than a year, Schramm and colleagues (2005) identified the problems most often faced by these newlywed couples. The problems faced by both husbands and wives in order of importance, were debt brought into marriage, balancing job and marriage, frequency of sexual relations, expectation about household tasks, in-laws, financial decision making, and communication (Schramm et al., 2005). It was interesting to note in this study that both husbands and wives generally experienced the same types of problems in the first several months of marriage, with debt brought into marriage and balancing job and marriage being the most commonly reported problems. Other newlywed research supports these findings in that things that affect marital stability and satisfaction are similar for husbands and wives (Kurdek, 2005). Table 11.2 shows how perceptions of the marriage relationship may look very different before the marriage a year or so than after the wedding day.

The study by Schramm and colleagues (2005) showed that between 8% and 14% of these newlywed couples scored in the distressed range of marital satisfaction and adjustment. According to this study, marital adjustment and satisfaction differences were clearly measurable even shortly after that wonderfully romantic wedding day.

Couples in the study by Schramm and colleagues (2005) also indicated that there were positive things going on in the relationship that provided protection from stress even when there were problems. These protective factors were respect, appreciation, commitment, mutual affection, and trust. When these factors were in place, problems did not result in as much marital stress.

The study also found that marriage education was an important variable in marital satisfaction and marital adjustment. Having formal marriage education

TABLE 11.2	Premarital Fantasies and Marital Realities
• She married him because he was such an assertive male; She divorced him because he was such a domineering husband.	• He married her because she was so quiet and dependent; He divorced her because she was so boring and clinging.
• He married her because she was so gentle and petite; He divorced her because she was so weak and helpless.	• She married him because he was the life of the party; She divorced him because he was such a dud at home.
• She married him because he could provide a good income; She divorced him because all he did was work.	• He married her because she was so sociable and talkative; He divorced her because she could only discuss trivia.
• He married her because she was so attractive all the time; He divorced her because she spent too much time in front of the mirror.	• She married him because he was such a good athlete; She divorced him because he was always playing or watching sports.
• She married him because he was so romantic and sociable; She divorced him because he was a fun-loving playboy.	• He married her because she was so neat and organized; He divorced her because she was too compulsive and controlling.

Happy couples learn to weather the stresses of life. They are, above all, best friends and enjoy spending time together. In fact, they are likely to find each other more interesting as the years go by.

in college resulted in higher marital satisfaction and adjustment. This study indicates how important it is to develop knowledge about issues that cause problems in marriage before the wedding day. Because many couples get married shortly after leaving high school, information about the findings of this study should be introduced in high school.

Keeping Marriages Strong

Five Types of Marriage

Using a national sample of 25,501 married couples, Olson and Olson (2000) described five significantly different types of married couples: *vitalized*, *harmonious*, *traditional*, *conflicted*, and *devitalized*. These five types of marriage are described in more detail, and the impact of the type on other aspects of their relationship is described elsewhere (Olson & Olson, 2000). These five types were created with largely White couples.

To see if the same types occurred in African American marriages, William Allen completed an analysis of 415 African American married couples from around the United States (Allen & Olson, 2001). He identified the same five types of couples in the African American marriages, and his findings demonstrate the similarity of these couple types across ethnic groups.

Vitalized couples had the highest levels of satisfaction across all the aspects of the marriage. Their positive couple agreement (PCA) scores were particularly high on marital interaction scales such as communication and conflict resolution. The couples in this group tended to be older and more educated, had higher-status jobs, and had been married longer. The majority (86%) of vitalized couples had never considered divorce (see Figure 11.2).

Harmonious couples were the second most satisfied type of couple, with moderately high PCA scores on the scales assessing marital satisfaction. Like vitalized couples, harmonious couples tended to be more educated and have higher-status jobs. Harmonious couples had the fewest number of children, yet they reported significant dissatisfaction with their parenting.

Traditional couples had high PCA scores in the traditional areas of children and parenting, egalitarian roles, and religion. These couples agreed that religion is an important aspect of their marriage. They had lower scores in the relationship skills areas of communication and conflict resolution, and they tended to dislike the personality of their partners. Most (92%) of traditional couples were either in their first marriage or had been married longer; they were also more educated. Fewer women in traditional couples were employed full time as compared to the women in other marital groups. Traditional couples also tended to marry younger, have more children, and have similar religious backgrounds. The most distinctive finding for traditional couples was that they tended to stay married even when they were dissatisfied with the marriage.

Conflicted couples had moderately low PCA scores overall, yet they had higher PCA scores in the areas of egalitarian roles and religious orientation. Furthermore, these couples had problems with communicating and solving problems. Conflicted couples tended to be younger, had been married fewer years, were less educated, and had lower job status. In 46% of conflicted couples, both spouses were dissatisfied, and in 42%, both spouses had considered divorce.

Devitalized couples had the lowest scores on all of the ENRICH scales. Couples in this group were characterized by pervasive unhappiness in almost all areas of

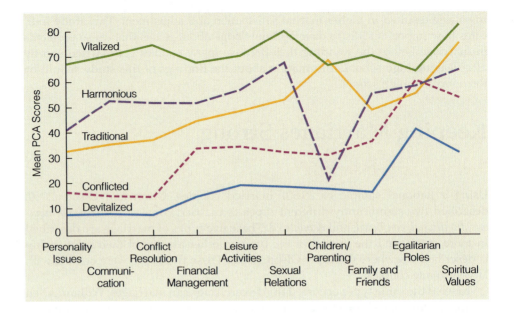

the marriage and were 10 times more likely to be separated than the other couple types. In 88% of devitalized couples, one or both of the spouses had considered divorce.

Interestingly, when the same analysis was done with premarital couples, four types of premarital couples were identified (Fowers & Olson, 1992; Olson & Olson, 2000). The devitalized type was missing, which makes sense because premarital couples are typically optimistic and happy with the relationship. The total sample consisted of 5,030 couples; there were roughly 25% to 30% of couples in each of the four types. Researchers subsequently conducted an outcome study to examine the relationship between the four premarital types (vitalized, harmonious, traditional, and conflicted) and the marital relationship 3 years after marriage (Fowers, Montel, & Olson, 1996).

Vitalized couples had the highest level of marital satisfaction, followed by harmonious, traditional, and conflicted couples, in that order (Table 11.3). More specifically, 3 years after marriage, 60% of vitalized couples were very happily married, and only 17% were divorced or separated. Conversely, 16% of conflicted couples were very happily married, and 54% were separated or divorced. Traditional couples were the least likely to divorce or separate, even though half of these couples were less happily married. These results clearly demonstrate that marital stability and satisfaction can be predicted on the basis of premarital relationship quality.

Changes in Marital Satisfaction Over Time

Researchers have consistently found that marriage satisfaction tends to decrease over time. In a longitudinal study of newlywed couples, Lawrence Kurdek (1998) found that over the first 4 years of marriage, the marital satisfaction for both males and females dropped each year and at a similar rate. As marital satisfaction dropped, there was an increase in the severity of depression, especially among women.

Another important study focused on change in marital satisfaction for couples who had firstborn sons; this study followed couples for 5 years. Using the *love scores*

TABLE 11.3	Marital Success of Four Premarital Types			
Four Premarital Types	**Very Happily Married**	**Less Happily Married**	**Separated/ Divorced**	**Total Couples**
Vitalized	60%	23%	17%	100%
Harmonious	46	29	25	100
Traditional	34	50	16	100
Conflicted	16	30	54	100

Source: Fowers et al., 1996.

from fathers and the *conflict scores* from mothers Jay Belsky and Kuang-Hua Hsieh (1998) found three distinct patterns of change. One group of couples, called the stays good group, maintained a good relationship over 4 years. In this group, the fathers' love level stayed high and the mothers' conflict level stayed low. In another group, the *good gets worse* group, the fathers' love level was initially high and then dropped and the mothers' conflict level was initially low and then became high. In the third group, the *bad to worse* group, the fathers' love level was initially low and went lower and the mothers' conflict level was initially high and stayed high. This typology of couples is very useful because it more clearly demonstrates the dynamics of change than an instrument can that only records average scores across

Some couples can maintain a healthy marriage with the advent of children, while others become less loving and more conflicted.

all couples, which is the typical approach to measuring change. What this study reveals is that some couples can maintain a healthy marriage in spite of having a child, whereas other couples' marriages become less loving and more conflicted.

Another type of marriage study examined how marriage changes before and after having a child. Audrey Bryan (1998) assessed married couples as they began a class on childbirth and then reassessed them after their child was born. She administered the ENRICH inventory at the beginning of the class and identified five types of married couples from most happy to least happy: vitalized couples (22%), harmonious couples (27%), traditional couples (8%), conflicted couples (23%), and devitalized couples (20%).

The percentage of couples who showed no change over time varied greatly by marital type. Over two-thirds (70%) of the vitalized couples stayed the same, and about one-quarter (26%) became traditional couples. For the harmonious couples, about one-quarter (27%) became happier, vitalized couples; another quarter (23%) became traditional couples; and one-third (35%) became less happy, conflicted couples. About half (55%) of the traditional couples stayed traditional, whereas 18% became vitalized and 18% became conflicted. For the conflicted couples, over one third (37%) stayed conflicted and another third (37%) became less happy, devitalized couples. About 70% of the devitalized couples stayed devitalized; 20% became conflicted; and 10% became traditional.

So, in general, most of the marriages changed as a result of having children. The least change was seen in the best marriages (vitalized) and the worst marriages (devitalized). The other three types experienced changes for better and worse.

Why Marriages Drift Apart

There are a number of reasons why couples drift apart over the course of the marriage. A major issue is that we begin to take marriage for granted and focus on other priorities in our life. William Doherty in his book *Take Back Your Marriage* (2001) identifies a variety of forces that negatively impact marriage: We are too busy for marriage; we get used to our mate; television and other media come between us; we stop dating, especially after having children; we don't know other couples' strategies for maintaining vibrant marriages; and the difference between spouses in their "work orientation" toward marriage gets resolved in the direction of less work.

This drifting apart is not usually done on purpose but gradually happens as a result of neglecting the marriage. William Doherty uses an interesting analogy in describing this process:

> Ever since I moved to Minnesota, I have thought that getting married is like launching a canoe into the Mississippi at St. Paul. If you don't paddle, you go south. No matter how much you love each other, no matter how full of hope and promise and good intentions, if you stay on the Mississippi with a good deal of paddling—occasional paddling is not enough—you end up in New Orleans. Which is a problem if you wanted to stay north. (Doherty, 2001, p. 11)

Keeping Your Marriage a Top Priority

One of the major things a couple can do to keep their marriage alive and growing is to make it a top priority—preferably number ONE. A good exercise for couples is to sit down and list the various important aspects of life and then rank them in terms of ideal priorities. Then rank them in terms of their actual priority in your life, which will probably be different from your ideal. The more you can keep your marriage the number one priority, the better your chances of marital success will be in the future.

There are a variety of specific things that you can do to keep your marriage a top priority in your life. Doherty (2001) offers these suggestions:

- If you are married, remind yourself repeatedly that your marriage is the foundation of your family and the cornerstore of your children's security.
- Remind yourself repeatedly that your children are apt to be better fighters for their needs . . . than you and your mate are at fighting for the needs of your marriage.
- Limit your family's outside activities so that you have two rare elements for today's families: time to hang out as a family and time to hang out as a couple.
- Have fixed bedtimes for your children, after which you are off duty and can be alone as a couple.
- Don't let children interrupt every conversation you have.
- Carve out private time for yourselves as a couple.
- Get sitters and go out on regular dates.
- Be open with your children about what you are doing for your marriage.

The Role of Forgiveness in Marriage

The importance of forgiveness in marriage has become recognized as an important part of couple relationships, and it contributes to marital happiness and stability (Fincham, Hall, & Beach, 2006). In fact, forgiveness is important in our overall well-being and general health in that it helps us deal with everyday hurts (Gordon, Baucom, & Snyder, 2005; Harris & Thoresen, 2005). This has become such an important topic today that a scholarly book entitled *Handbook of Forgiveness* has been published to describe the benefits of forgiveness in all aspects of life (Worthington, 2005).

Forgiveness does not mean you have to be religious or that you forget about or accept the transgressions of your partner (Fincham et al., 2006). A person forgives in spite of the wrongful nature of the transgression and even if the transgressor does not deserve forgiveness (Fincham et al., 2006). An important component of forgiveness can be reconciliation, which may be helpful in allowing a couple to move on to a more positive place in their relationship. Forgiveness is about decreasing the negativity and increasing positive feelings and goodwill toward one's partner.

Forgiveness contributes to marital satisfaction when it becomes a part of conflict resolution (Fincham et al., 2006). Forgiveness helps couples move on from a conflict without having resentments that spill over into future conflicts, resulting in escalation of conflict over time. Forgiveness on the part of the victim involves understanding the impact of the offense, finding meaning for what happened, and moving forward—which may mean a change in the relationship. Here is an example of what the process of forgiving looked like for one couple:

Mary and Louis had been having difficulties in their marriage because each had a stressful work schedule, and they had been unable to spend much time together. Mary was working long hours and spending a considerable amount of time with a co-worker. They ended up having an affair that lasted several months. Louis suspected the affair and confronted Mary. Mary had already ended the extramarital relationship, but admitted that it was true.

Mary said she was sorry and declared her commitment to the marriage. Louis also wanted to stay married, but he was so angry. He both loved and was angry with Mary for betraying his trust. He wanted to forgive Mary, but he wasn't sure he could ever trust her again and have a healthy marriage relationship. He wanted to hurt her as much as she hurt him.

After working with a therapist for almost a year, the relationship began to get back on track. Louis was able to forgive Mary and eventually, with the help of the therapist, was able to have positive feelings toward her. He shared with her how it had deeply wounded him since he had always been vulnerable when it came to being rejected. What happened would always cause him some pain.

Mary and Louis also began cutting back on the hours spent on work and created a relationship that was very different from the one they had before the affair. They would always set aside time to talk if either of them felt that things were not going well in their relationship. They fixed the problem rather than letting things go. Even though it took a long time, both Mary and Louis ultimately felt their marriage was better than before the affair. Forgiveness was definitely a necessary component of getting their marriage back on track in making their marriage healthy and stable.

The Role of Sacrifice in Marriage

Sacrificing for the other person in a marriage and how it affects relationship functioning has become an area of research in recent years (Stanley, Whitton, Sadberry, Clements, & Markman, 2006). There are two components of sacrifice. First, an individual can make sacrifices for his or her partner, which means that a person puts the partner's needs before his or her own needs. A second component of sacrifice is that the partner puts the relationship above selfish interests, which means a person places the couple or marriage relationship above personal needs (Morrill, 2006).

Stanley and colleagues conducted a longitudinal study of those who were newly married in 1980 and studied the effects of sacrifice on the long-term relationship. They were interested in following newlyweds through the first several years of marriage, because that is the time when many couples experience difficulties in their relationship. These researchers found that sacrifice predicted marital success when those behaviors began early in the marriage. Morrill (2006) also contributed to our understanding of the role of sacrifice in marriage relationships in her qualitative study of couples who had great marriages. She found that couples who thought their marriages were great regularly made sacrifices for their spouse. They gave up personal wants and desires for each other and for the good of the marriage relationship. Here is how one husband from Morrill's study described sacrifice for his wife and his marriage:

> The promise is to always be there, willing to do whatever is needed to help the partnership, and to provide continuous support for, and encouragement to, your mate. . . . You are not the most important, they are. (p. 49)

There is also evidence that sacrificial behaviors appear to be symbols of overall commitment to the marriage and result in mutual trust (Stanley et al., 2006). Sacrificial behavior, then, can be instrumental in affecting several aspects of the marriage relationship in that it can be a tangible way that partners can show commitment on a daily basis.

Federal Healthy Marriage Initiative

In 2006, the federal government passed legislation to fund the Healthy Marriage Initiative, which provided grant money of $100 million per year for 5 years to provide programs to promote healthy marriages around the country. According to the Administration for Children and Families (ACF), which is part of the U.S. Department of Health and Human Services, healthy marriages are the foundation of a successful society and promote the interest of children. Children do better when they are part of a family with two married parents.

Funding was granted to 126 organizations to provide programs for couples, especially those in low-income and minority populations who have high rates of single parents and divorces. The programs were to teach relationship skills and knowledge to couples with the goal of forming and sustaining healthy marriages.

This is what the federal government says about healthy marriages (Administration for Children and Families, 2007):

> "There are at least two characteristics that all healthy marriages have in common. First, they are mutually enriching, and, second, both spouses have a deep respect for each other."

> "It is a mutually satisfying relationship that is beneficial to the husband, wife, and children (if present)."

> "It is a relationship that is committed to ongoing growth, the use of effective communication skills, and the use of successful conflict management skills."

This initiative has been controversial. At a policy level, some question whether the federal government should be involved in something as personal as marriage. Some feel that the initiative is a way to promote marriage rather than promoting *healthy* marriages, and that promoting marriage could result in couples staying married when the marriage is harmful to the partners. Because this initiative is about marriage between a man and a woman, some believe it is a way to promote heterosexual marriage at the expense of same-sex unions and relationships. Because this initiative is supported by conservative religious organizations, some feel this initiative has a religious agenda.

However one feels about this initiative, it is an extensive policy change that can benefit many couples who want to have healthier relationships. Only time will tell if the funding and ultimate marriage education programming will accomplish the goal of couples having healthier marriages that will benefit children in those unions.

Changes in Policy and State Laws to Strengthen Marriage

Because of a growing concern over the rate of divorce (about 50%) in the United States, legislators are pushing for changes in the laws to impose more requirements on couples planning to marry (Ooms, Bouchet, & Parke, 2004). Florida was the first state to pass a comprehensive package of legislation designed to strengthen marriage and reduce divorce. Passed in the Florida State Legislature in 1998, the Marriage Preparation and Reservation Act became effective in January 1999. The bill had four key components:

- High-school students are required to take a course in marriage and relationship skill-based education.
- Engaged couples are encouraged to take a premarital preparation course of at least 4 hours. Those who do so qualify for a reduction in their marriage license fee. Each courthouse is to keep a roster of religious and secular approved courses.

- Each couple applying for a marriage license will be given a handbook prepared by the Florida Bar Association informing them of their legal rights and responsibilities as married partners to each other and to their children, both during marriage and in the event of marital dissolution.
- Couples with children who file for divorce must take a parent education and family stabilization course.

Other states are following this approach in order to develop policies and laws that support premarital education programs. Some of the states that have passed some form of premarital program are Arizona, Florida, Louisiana, Minnesota, Maryland, Oklahoma, Texas, and Utah (Ooms et al., 2004).

Summary

- Marriage offers a number of benefits. As compared to single or divorced individuals, married couples lead a healthier lifestyle, live longer, have a more satisfying sexual relationship, have more wealth and economic assets, and generally do a better job raising children.
- Three trends point to the changing role of marriage in the United States today. First, a decline in the popularity of marriage is indicated by a decrease in the number of marriages to an all-time low. Second, fewer couples who get divorced choose to remarry. And third, the number of couples living together has increased from 500,000 couples in 1970 to more than 5.5 million couples at present.
- Couples have a better chance for a happy marriage when both individuals are mature, love each other and themselves, enjoy being alone and together, are established in their work, are assertive with each other, and are friends as well as lovers.
- A very low percentage of couples in the United States enroll in a comprehensive marriage preparation program. The most useful programs include (1) a premarital inventory to assess strengths and areas of potential growth and a discussion of the assessment results with a trained counselor, (2) a small discussion group in which couples share feelings and concerns with each other, and (3) training in communication and problem-solving skills, which should start 12 months before marriage and last 6 to 8 weeks.
- Researchers have developed an inventory that couples can take before marriage to assess the strengths in their relationship. The inventory can predict a couple's chances of marital success or failure with 80% to 90% accuracy.
- A national survey identified five types of marriages: From most to least happy, they are *vitalized, harmonious, traditional, conflicted,* and *devitalized.* Studies suggest that these types exist across ethnic groups.
- Because of a growing concern over the high rate of divorce in our country, legislators are pushing for laws to strengthen marriage, such as offering incentives for engaged couples to attend premarital preparation courses; requiring high-school students to take courses on marriage and relationship skills; giving couples applying for marriage licenses a handbook informing them of their legal rights and responsibilities; and requiring couples with children who file for divorce to take a parent education and family stabilization course. Communities are also getting involved in developing a variety of premarital and marital enrichment programs.

Key Terms

PREPARE	traditional couple
family of origin	conflicted couple
vitalized couple	devitalized couple
harmonious couple	

Activities

1. List what you consider positive and negative reasons for getting married. Share the list with a partner or with others in a small discussion group.
2. How do you know if you are ready for marriage? Discuss this issue with a small group and formulate some guidelines to help people decide whether they are ready to marry.
3. For *dating or engaged couples:* Both partners should write down five things they like about the partner and five things that sometimes bother them. Then both partners should discuss the items on the lists very carefully and listen to each other so that the exchange is positive and constructive.
4. For those dating or engaged couples interested in taking the PREPARE Program, first contact a counselor

or a member of the clergy in your area. If you cannot locate someone trained in PREPARE, go to the Web site to locate one: www.prepare-enrich.com.

Suggested Readings

Administration for Children and Families. (2007). The Healthy Marriage Initiative. Web site: http://www.acf.hhs.gov/healthymarriage/about/mission.html#ms.

Berger, R., & Hannah, M. T. (Eds.). (1999). *Preventive approaches in couples therapy.* Philadelphia: Brunner/Mazel.

Doherty, W. J., & Anderson, J. R. (2004). Community marriage initiatives. *Family Relations, 53,* 425–432.

Gottman, J. M., & Silver, N. (1999). *The seven principles for making marriage work.* New York: Crown.

Knutson, L., & Olson, D. H. (2003). Effectiveness of PREPARE Program with premarital couples in a community setting. *Marriage and Family, 6*(4) 529–546.

McManus, M. J. (1995). *Marriage savers: Helping your friends and family avoid divorce.* Grand Rapids, MI: Zondervan.

Olson, D. H., & Olson, A. K. (2000). *Empowering couples: Building on your strengths.* Minneapolis: Life Innovations.

Ooms, T. (1998). *Toward more perfect unions: Putting marriage on the public agenda.* Washington, DC: Family Impact Seminar.

Schramm, D. G., Marshall, J. P., Harris, V. W., & Lee, T. R. (2005). After "I do": The newlywed transition. *Marriage and Family Review, 38,* 45–67.

Stanley, S. M., Whitton, S. W., Sadberry, S. L., Clements, M. L., & Markman, H. J. (2006). Sacrifice as a predictor of marital outcomes. *Family Process, 45,* 289–303.

Waite, L., & Gallagher, M. (2000). *The case for marriage.* New York: Doubleday.

Worthington, E. L. (Ed.). (2005). *Handbook of forgiveness.* New York: Routledge.

Visit the text-specific Online Learning Center at **www.mhhe.com/Olson6** for practice tests, chapter summaries, Web links, Internet exercises, key terms, and flashcards.

12 *P*arenthood: Choices and Challenges

Roots and Wings

Couple Strengths and Issues in Parenting

The Challenge of Parenthood

Adoption

The Child-Free Alternative

Styles of Parenting

Theories of Childrearing

Issues in Parenting

Summary

Key Terms

Activities

Suggested Readings

Roots and Wings

A parent's job is to give a child both "roots and wings," which is no easy task. Rearing children may indeed be life's greatest mixed blessing. It is full of good times and bad times, frustrating challenges and elating successes. A baby's first stumbling steps and first words, a teenager's first love, a grown child's first baby—all are important transitions that parents remember. At the same time, children bring heavy responsibilities and drain parents of energy, finances, and time.

When we did a search on "parenting" using the Amazon.com Web site, we found over 40,000 books listed in their database. Even so, we are quite confident that there is no book on rearing children that answers all the questions and no clear path to family happiness. The road is difficult, and there are no guarantees. In the words of Christine Todd Whitman in a commencement address at Wheaton College when she was serving as governor of New Jersey: "I don't mind saying that I have the most important and fulfilling job in the world. It demands responsibility, knowledge of finance, being on call 24 hours a day, combining firm leadership with careful negotiations, and keeping one's promise. That job is being a parent" (1995).

In this chapter we will examine the challenge of parenthood and take a look at some of the conventional wisdom that surrounds it. Among the challenges are the effects of parenthood on marriage, the decision whether to have children, and the financial burdens of raising children. We will discuss various parenting styles and how they relate to the family styles of the Couple and Family Map. We will also explore issues in parenting and some practical approaches to raising children, including coparenting. We will touch on the benefits of parent education and family therapy and conclude with a summary of the many satisfactions of parenting.

We will report on the national survey that examined couple strengths and issues for married couples (Olson & Olson, 2000). We will begin with the results of the survey regarding the parenting strengths of happy couples versus unhappy couples. Next, we will review the five most common parenting issues as reported by 20,151 married couples.

Couple Strengths and Issues in Parenting

In a national survey of married couples, Olson and Olson (2000) identified a number of parenting strengths. As Table 12.1 shows, happy couples were more than twice as likely (89%) as unhappy couples (36%) to agree on how to share the responsibilities of raising their children. Happy couples were three times as likely (63%) as unhappy couples (32%) to be satisfied with the amount of attention they focus on their marriage versus the amount of attention they focus on their children. Two times as many happy couples (59%) reported agreeing on how to discipline their children as did unhappy couples (30%). Sixty percent of happy couples believed that they agreed on how to provide financially for their children while only 38% of the unhappy couples agreed on this issue. Similarly, about 61% of the happy couples felt children did not create major problems for their marriage but that was less true (38%) for unhappy couples.

Table 12.2 identifies the top five parenting issues for a national sample of 21,501 married couples. The biggest issue for parents (84%) is that children had a negative impact on their marital satisfaction and they reported feeling more dissatisfied in their marriage since having children. The second most frequently reported parent-

TABLE 12.1	Parenting Strengths of Happy Versus Unhappy Married Couples	
	PERCENTAGE OF AGREEMENT	
Strength	**Happy Couples** (*n* = 5,153)	**Unhappy Couples** (*n* = 5,127)
Satisfied with how childrearing is shared.	89%	36%
Partner focuses as much on the marriage as on the children	63	32
Agree on discipline.	59	30
Agree on how to provide for children financially.	60	38
Children do not create major problems for the marriage.	61	38

Source: Adapted from Olson & Olson, 2000.

ing issue (68%) was that the father did not spend enough time with the children. Two-thirds (66%) of the parents were dissatisfied with how childrearing responsibilities were shared, they disagreed (66%) on how to discipline their children, and they felt (64%) their partner focused more on their children than on the marriage.

The Challenge of Parenthood

Many authorities have noted that parenthood is the last bastion of amateurism in our society. Plumbers, bookkeepers, computer analysts—all need some kind of formal training, certificate, or license. About the only job that doesn't require some special kind of education is nurturing the young to adulthood.

Our society tends to shy away from "intruding" into family matters, and rearing children is certainly a family matter. But some have gone so far as to argue that education and even something like an internship should be mandatory before people can become parents—that is, that a license should be required for parenthood—although such a proposal has little chance of becoming law. Nevertheless, its proponents underscore the importance of parenting: Society benefits from parents' successes but also suffers from their mistakes.

TABLE 12.2	Top Five Parenting Issues for Married Couples
Issues	**Percentage of Couples with Problems** (*n* = 21,501 couples)
Having children reduced marital satisfaction.	84%
Father not involved enough with children.	68
Dissatisfied with how childrearing is shared.	66
Disagree on discipline of children.	66
Partner focuses more on the children than on the marriage.	64

Source: Adapted from Olson & Olson, 2000.

Adults with problems often had problems as children, and many times they pass their problems on to the next generation. For example, one therapist described a counseling session with an abused woman who had fled from her husband after repeated beatings; the woman's 18-month-old son accompanied her. During the session, the toddler became angered over some minor issue and ran at his mother. In his frustration, he put his hands around her neck and tried to strangle her. He was imitating almost precisely what he had seen his father do a few days earlier. With counseling, this pattern could be changed so that the boy would not repeat his father's behavior.

Conventional Wisdom About Parenting

All societies have folk beliefs that are widely accepted and rarely examined. They may be commonplace, but they are not necessarily common sense. For the purposes of our discussion, we will call these common beliefs *conventional wisdom*. Although conventional wisdom often seems commonsensical, it occasionally gets us into trouble. As one observer noted, we do not need common sense at all; what we need is *uncommon sense.* Conventional wisdom on parenthood often sugarcoats the subject, romanticizing a task that is too important for people to undertake with rose-colored glasses. What follows is a list of commonly held folk beliefs in our society, along with some comments that offer a more balanced and realistic view:

- *Rearing children is nothing but fun.* Although childrearing can be fun, it is also a thankless and very demanding job. Parents have to *make* childrearing fun if they are to enjoy it.
- *Children will turn out well if they have "good" parents.* Parents are an important factor in a child's development, but they are only one influence among many, including siblings, schools, the mass media, and the child's peer group. The goal of parenting must be to instill values and model positive behaviors that children will internalize and use in their lives. But there are no guarantees. Some good parents work hard at parenting only to see their children get into great difficulty in life.
- *Children are sweet and cute.* Although children can be adorable, they can also be selfish and destructive, as well as extremely active. In fact, they possess the full range of human qualities—positive and negative—that adults must deal with in each other. Parents who have no break from watching over children can easily become exhausted.
- *Children improve a marriage.* Rearing children is a team effort. The bond between partners can intensify as they raise their children together. But children also put tremendous pressure on an intimate relationship, drawing energy away from the couple's time with each other in service to the child's needs.
- *Good parents can manage any child, no matter what the child's nature.* This myth is based on the notion that a human being is born a *tabula rasa*, a blank slate upon which the environment writes its script. But research on infants indicates that to some degree temperament is present at birth: Some babies are calm and content; others are cranky. Although the family environment that parents construct for their young is tremendously important, it is not, as mentioned earlier, the only influence or the sole determinant of a child's developmental outcome. It is important to note that children also strongly shape their parents' behavior. Parents, in sum, raise children. And, children also raise parents.

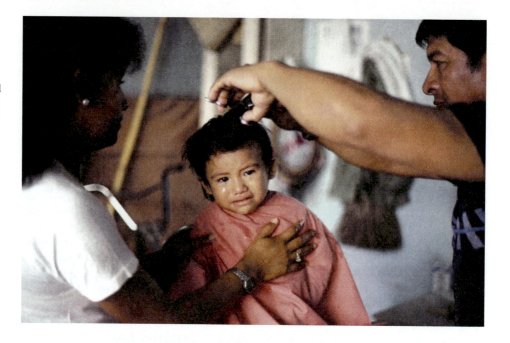

A first haircut is one of the many milestones that mark a child's growing up. Although this toddler may not remember the experience, his mother will likely remember this event in his transition from baby to little boy.

- *Today's parents are not as good as yesterday's.* Standards for raising children have gotten higher, making the challenge for today's parents even greater. Society now expects parents to be more democratic in their approach, to take the child's feelings into account when decisions are made, and to involve older children in the decision-making process.
- *Couples without children are frustrated and unhappy.* Many singles and couples without children are very happy and content. Many of them do, however, have close relationships with children of extended-family members or of friends.
- *One child is too few.* Although many believe that only children are spoiled and selfish, that is not necessarily the case. Studies have found that there are both advantages and disadvantages to having only one child. One child is less expensive to raise, is less demanding on the parents, places fewer limits on the parents' freedom, and receives more parental attention. On the downside, parents of only children sometimes focus too much attention on or overprotect the child, thus limiting the child's exposure to peer companions and possibly even causing her or him to feel lonely. Also, having brothers and sisters can be a great source of support and joy throughout life.
- *There are no bad children, only bad parents.* Most parents want the best for their children and do what they can to achieve that. Nevertheless, some fail at parenting because of ignorance, lack of support, or their own unhealthy family background.
- *All parents are adults.* As reflected in our nation's teenage pregnancy rates, many adolescents unfortunately become parents. Government statistics indicate that 11.8% of all birth mothers are teenagers (U.S. Bureau of the Census, 2000e, table 74, p. 63). Childrearing is difficult for adults, but it can be particularly challenging for teenage parents.
- *Children appreciate the sacrifices their parents make and the advantages they provide.* Most parents want to be appreciated for the sacrifices they make for

their children. Unfortunately, children often do not realize their parents' importance until they themselves become parents. Parents need to learn to enjoy the everyday pleasures and satisfactions of raising their children and to appreciate any small thanks they may receive along the way.

- *Parenthood receives top priority in our society.* Making money—not parenthood—receives top priority in our society. Parents are pressured to put their jobs first if they seek promotions—and sometimes even if they simply want to hold onto their jobs.

- *Love is enough to guarantee good parental performance.* Love certainly helps parents put up with the many difficulties of childrearing, but success at parenting also requires hard work and good parenting skills.

- *Single-parent families are problematic.* Single-parent families are often stigmatized in American society today, and the discussion of their efforts to create a happy life together too often focuses on the negative. There is little question that many single-parent families face considerable challenges, money and stress being very prominent on the list. The fact is, however, that there are countless strong single-parent families in which children are growing up happy and healthy. Simply knowing the structure of a family does not tell you how well a family is functioning.

- *Parenting gets easier as children get older.* Although most parents hope that parenting will get easier as their children mature, they typically find that their parenting issues change and become more difficult. Adolescence is the most challenging stage for a majority of parents because adolescents are seeking greater autonomy and freedom from parental control.

- *Parenting ends when the children leave home.* For most parents, parenting does not end when a child leaves home. Adult children often return home to live after a divorce, a job loss, or some other life crisis. Furthermore, parents are often called on to help with the care of their children's children; grandparenting brings joy, but it can also be exhausting.

- *The empty-nest syndrome leaves many parents lonely and depressed.* One observer noted, "After the kids leave home, some parents suffer from the empty-nest syndrome; others change the locks." Many parents enjoy the freedom that comes with not having adolescents at home. The middle-aged parent may get a job or change jobs, travel, or take up a new avocation. After they leave home, adult children are often surprised to watch their parents blossom and enjoy life in a variety of new ways.

- *Parents alone should rear the young.* Parents are ultimately responsible for raising their children, but society has a stake in children's development into adulthood and needs to support parents in this challenging process.

The Transition to Parenthood

Parenthood isn't something that happens gradually; the 9 months of a normal pregnancy should give prospective parents time to think about parenthood and to plan for the arrival of the baby. But many parents are unprepared for the challenges that will confront them when the infant arrives. They may take classes to prepare for childbirth, but few prepare for the responsibilities of parenting itself.

Parenthood as Crisis: Effects on Marriage. When the baby is born, parenting begins in earnest. For some it is a crisis. E. E. LeMasters gained prominence in the 1950s with his report in the *New York Times* of a study entitled "Parenthood as

Crisis." LeMasters argued that because of romantic notions about parenthood, people go through a process of disenchantment when they have children. LeMasters was flooded with letters from parents, most of whom agreed with his findings. In his research, LeMasters interviewed 46 couples and found that 83% defined the coming of a child as a "crisis" for their marriage (LeMasters, 1957). Other researchers have debated these findings ever since, and the definition of the term *crisis* remains controversial (Belsky & Kelly, 1994; Miller, 2000).

Becoming a parent is definitely stressful for most couples, and most find it harder than they anticipated. A major review of studies on the transition to becoming a family (Cowan, 1996) found that couples having a first child faced many issues in the marriage. The transition increased couples' stress level, increased the number of differences between partners, and lowered their marital satisfaction. In general, the decrease in marital satisfaction was twice as large for women as for men, and it was often attributed to the women's feeling that the partner was not as involved as they were in dealing with child care and household tasks.

Parenthood means that a married couple will have less time for each other. Before the baby, the couple could focus attention on their relationship and had time to enjoy each other's company. "Free" time markedly diminishes with the birth of a child, and a couple's focus shifts to nurturing the baby. Parents often find themselves exhausted after many nights awake with a hungry, crying, or sick infant. Few parents know much about caring for an infant until they have one of their own.

As a child grows older, the parents' job does not get any easier. Change only creates new challenges. The colic may end, but the curious and inventive child is soon toddling around, sticking fingers in wall sockets, emptying houseplant soil on the living room rug, or spreading Vaseline from the medicine cabinet all over the bathroom. Fortunately, most parents have a sense of humor and patience—and also realize the importance of covering sockets, locking cupboards, and putting many things out of the reach of a toddler.

The playfulness and pleasure of preparenting days disappear for some couples, and life becomes more serious. The couple's sexual relationship is often affected by the demands of raising a child. Most couples find that their sexual activity decreases because they are exhausted. Spontaneity in social patterns can also diminish. For example, parents of infants don't just drop in on friends when "dropping in" means packing baby bottles, diapers, plastic pants, and a change of clothes. (See Table 12.3 for a humorous look at some common challenges of parenting.)

Financial Issues and Children

One of the surprises for most parents is how much children cost, not just in terms of time and energy but also money. Raising children is a very expensive venture, no matter what a family's income. An analysis of the expense of raising a child, based on data from the Family Economics Research Group at the U.S. Department of Agriculture, was summarized by Mark Lino (2004). The data were broken down into six major categories: housing, food, transportation, clothing, health care, and education. As expected, the amount of money spent on a child varied with the income level of the family. For lower-income families, earning an average of $25,400 a year, the cost of raising each child from birth to age 17 was $130,290. For middle-income families, earning an average of $54,100 a year, the cost of raising each child was $178,590. And for upper-income families, earning an average of $102,400 a year, the cost increased to $261,270 (Figure 12.1).

TABLE 12.3	Mother Murphy's Laws for Raising Children

1. Parenthood is much easier to get into than out of.
2. If your spouse hasn't already driven you nuts, your kids will.
3. Nobody really wants your job, but everyone thinks they can do it better.
4. Those who think they can do it better messed up when they had the chance.
5. Bad traits are inherited from your spouse's side of the family.
6. Good traits are inherited from your side of the family.
7. By the time you've finally learned something about raising children, you're a grandparent.
8. Your mother knows best. About everything. And she'll never let you forget it.
9. You don't have to be a Supermom to succeed in both your career and childrearing. All you need is a $100,000 job and live-in help.
10. The day after you get a raise at work, your day care center will inform you that tuition is being increased.
11. The increase in tuition will exceed your raise.
12. Taking care of your baby is easy, as long as you don't have anything else to do.
13. The more experts you consult, the more solutions you'll find for any parenting problem.
14. Psychologists know best about writing books.
15. When you're pregnant, everyone gives you advice.
16. After you've had your baby, everyone gives you advice.
17. When your baby becomes a teenager, everyone gives you advice—especially your teenager.
18. When your teenager "leaves the nest," everyone gives you advice.
19. When you become a grandparent, you get to pass on all that good advice to your children.
20. By the time you can afford to start a family, you're too old to do it. (And you know enough not to.)

Source: Adapted from *Mother Murphy's Law* by B. Lansky, 1986, New York: Meadowbrook/Simon & Schuster. Copyright 1986 by Bruce Lansky. Adapted by permission of the publisher, Meadowbrook Press.

An important aspect of socializing children is helping them learn to understand and manage finances. Sharon Danes (1992) did a systematic study of 182 parents to learn when they thought it was appropriate to introduce their children to a variety of financial activities. About 70% of parents felt that children 8 years or younger were mature enough to receive an allowance, and 64% felt that they could open

FIGURE 12.1

Cost of Raising a Child
Source: Lino, 2004.

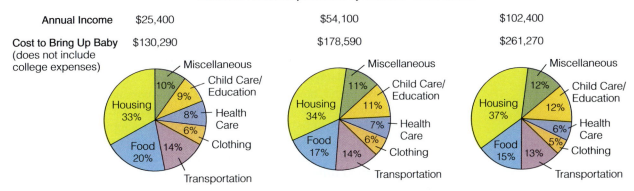

Estimated Annual Expenditures by Husband–Wife Families*

Annual Income	$25,400	$54,100	$102,400
Cost to Bring Up Baby (does not include college expenses)	$130,290	$178,590	$261,270

New parents can expect to spend an average of $178,590 to raise their newborn babies to age 17, up from $25,229 in 1960.

Based on 1990–1992 Consumer Expenditure Survey data updated to 2003 dollars using the Consumer Price Index.

their own savings account. Almost half the parents surveyed felt that 12- to 14-year-olds could be responsible for their own clothing budgets, and 29% believed that they were mature enough to be told the family's income. About half the parents felt that 15- to 17-year-olds should know about car insurance and have their own checking accounts. More than half the parents believed that by age 18 to 20, adult children should have and be responsible for their own credit cards and be able to apply for and make the payments on a loan.

Adoption

By most estimates, about 2 million, or 3%, of Americans are adopted. This is not a high percentage, but it has been estimated that 6 in 10 Americans have some kind of experience with adoption: A family member or close friend was adopted, or the individual had adopted a child or placed a child for adoption. Many other Americans consider adopting a child at one point in their life and spend a good deal of time discussing the issue with friends and relatives.

Since the mid-1970s, adoption practices in the United States have changed dramatically (Grotevant, 2003). In the past, confidentiality in adoption was the norm; today, the trend is toward "openness" in adoption, which means that there is increasing contact between adoptive families and birth parents. The contact may be either direct or mediated (e.g., through an adoption agency). Some adoption professionals argue that fully open adoption should be standard practice and that the secrecy of confidential adoptions has been harmful to all those involved. Others argue that openness is experimental and may prove to be harmful: Confidential adoption has worked well, so why change it?

To understand the issue of openness in adoption, Harold Grotevant and Ruth McRoy recruited a nationwide sample of adoptive families and birth mothers with a "target" adopted child between the ages of 4 and 12 when the first interview occurred between 1987 and 1992. The sample included 720 individuals: both adoptive parents in 190 adoptive families, at least one adopted child in 171 of the families, and 169 birth mothers. Families were sampled across the full range of openness in adoption: *confidential* (no information shared between birth parents and adoptive parents); *mediated* (information shared, with the adoption agency as the go-between); and *fully disclosed* (ongoing direct contact between birth parents and adoptive family members). Adoptive families were interviewed in their homes.

As predicted, when compared with parents in confidential adoptions, parents in fully disclosed adoptions reported higher levels of acknowledgment of the adoption, more empathy toward the birth parents and child, a stronger sense of permanence in their projected relationship with their child, and less fear that the birth mother might try to reclaim the child (Grotevant, 2003).

Researchers have found, however, that many adoptive parents fail to involve the child in mediated and open adoptions (Wrobel, Ayers-Lopez, Grotevant, & McRoy, 1996). In one sample, almost half the children in mediated adoptions did not participate in the contact their adoptive parents were having with their birth mother, but most of these children were not aware they were being excluded. However, most of the children in fully disclosed adoptions were included in meetings with birth parents.

It appears that couples who have greater openness in the adoption process also have better family communication (Mendenhall, Grotevant, & McRoy, 1996). In one study, adoptive couples' interviews were coded for communication skills using

Olson's Couple and Family Map Scale. Couples who had greater openness in adoption showed significantly higher levels of self-disclosure, listening skills, empathy, tracking, and respect.

Relationships between the adoptive family and the birth mother are also being examined through the lens of *boundary ambiguity* (Boss, 1999; Fravel, McRoy, & Grotevant, 2000). Boundary ambiguity occurs when a family member is physically absent but psychologically present or vice versa. Fravel (1995) examined the psychological presence of the birth mother in the adoptive family system. It appears that boundary ambiguity is almost inevitable in adoptive families. In many adoptive families, boundary ambiguity can exacerbate family stress because of an inability to determine who is inside or outside the family system. Adoptive families who have a higher level of tolerance for ambiguity, however, seem to handle open adoption more effectively. (For more on boundary ambiguity, see Chapter 14.)

Adoptees face unique challenges, and it is often assumed that these additional challenges increase psychological and interpersonal problems for them. Adoptees are sometimes stereotyped as being unhappy, poorly adjusted, and malfunctioning in life (Sharma, McGue, & Benson, 1998). But research comparing adoptees and a matched group of adult friends who were not adopted indicates more similarities than differences between the two groups. In many ways, adult adoptees "are navigating their adult years no differently than their non-adopted peers," and as a group doing reasonably well (Borders, Penny, & Portnoy, 2000, p. 415).

Another study that compared adopted and nonadopted adolescents found that adopted adolescents are at higher risk in all the areas examined, including school achievement and problems, substance use, psychological well-being, physical health, fighting, and lying to parents. The researchers concluded that their data showed that "more adopted adolescents have problems of various kinds than their nonadopted peers" (van Dulmen, Miller, Grotevant, Fan, & Christensen, 2000). Some observers believe there is a so-called "adopted child syndrome," which includes problems in bonding, attachment disorders, lying, stealing, defiance of authority, and acts of violence. These observers believe that adopted children are in an at-risk group for developing emotional problems because they are overrepresented in mental health caseloads (Smith, 2003).

The Child-Free Alternative

Various terms are applied to the choice not to have children, including *nonparenthood, voluntary childlessness,* and the **child-free alternative.** Many wonder whether a person or couple can be happy and fulfilled in life without having children (Hird & Abshoff, 2000; LaMastro, 2001; Lunneborg, 1999).

The percentage of childless women aged 40 to 44—those at the end of their childbearing years—has increased from 10% in 1976 to about 18% (Downs, 2003). Rates of childlessness in the United States, including both women who choose not to have children and women who cannot have children, have varied substantially over the years. For example, for White women born in the mid-1880s, slightly over 15% remained childless. For White women born in 1910 and who reached childbearing age during the Great Depression of the 1930s, the childless rate was more than 25%. For White women born in 1935 who reached childbearing age during the Baby Boom of 1946 to 1964, the childless rate dropped dramatically to 10% (Morgan & Chen, 1992). Since the end of the Baby Boom, the childless rate has increased again and has hovered around 18% since 1995 (Downs, 2003).

These fluctuations indicate that even when modern, relatively efficient contraception is not available, parents have responded over the years to changing economic and social conditions. Reviews of research revealed some interesting answers to common questions about childlessness (Hird & Abshoff, 2000; LaMastro, 2001; Lunneborg, 1999):

- *What long-term effects does voluntary childlessness have?* Although adult children are often very important to their parents in old age, older people without children also do quite well. (Aging parents may even find themselves rejected or neglected by their adult children.) Those without children often prepare for their later years by developing a network of friends and relatives to help meet their needs. They also learn how to cope with isolation if necessary (Skutch, 2001).

- *Is there something wrong with people who don't wish to have children?* The majority of studies on this topic concluded that nonparents exhibit no more psychopathology or deviance than a control group of randomly sampled parents. Culture affects one's attitude about whether or not to have children. For example, it has been argued that African Americans, American Indians, and Mexican Americans tend to be more family oriented than Whites and consider children an important part of marital life (Mindel, Habenstein, & Wright, 1988).

Parenthood is not for everyone. Couples who have decided not to have children can find happiness and fulfillment in life with each other, with their careers and avocational interests, and with friends and family.

- *Do people without children do better in their careers?* Apparently, many people without children do very well. Voluntary childlessness leaves people with time and energy that can be focused on career goals. A disproportionate number of high-ranking businesswomen and professionals are childless.
- *Is the quality of a child-free marriage as good as that of a marriage with children?* Studies have found more vital and happy relationships among child-free couples than among those with children (Olson et al., 1989; Somers, 1993). This is, in part, because child-free couples can devote more time to their marriages and because they are more likely to divorce if they do not have a good relationship than would a couple with children.
- *What are the advantages and disadvantages of voluntary childlessness?* A study of 287 childless individuals aged 55 and over found that 67% reported advantages to childlessness, and 64% reported disadvantages. Perceived advantages included fewer worries or problems, financial benefits, greater freedom, and career flexibility. The major disadvantages included lack of companionship/being alone/loneliness, lack of support and care when older, and missing the experience of parenthood (Connidis & McMullin, 1999).

Styles of Parenting

There are two key aspects of parenting: parental support (family closeness on the Couple and Family Map) and parental control (family flexibility on the Couple and Family Map) (see Figure 12.2). **Parental support** is defined as the amount of caring, closeness, and affection that a parent exhibits or gives to a child. **Parental control** is defined as the amount of flexibility that a parent uses in enforcing rules and disciplining a child.

There is considerable evidence that higher levels of parental support are related to positive outcomes in children, including better academic performance, higher self-esteem, more social competence, and better psychological adjustment (Amato & Booth, 1997; Bean, Barber, & Crane, 2006). However, when you look at the extremes of family closeness using the Couple and Family Map, where there is very low closeness (disengaged) or very high closeness (enmeshed), children from these extremes tend to have more problems emotionally, socially, and academically (Manzi, Vignoles, Regalia, & Scabini, 2006).

Regarding parental control (family flexibility on the Couple and Family Map), there is considerable evidence that parenting that is too lenient (chaotic on the Couple and Family Map) and too strict (rigid on the Couple and Family Map) results in children with more psychological and academic problems (Amato & Booth, 1997). Conversely, parents who have a more balanced style of parenting (central level of the Couple and Family Map where parents are "structured" or "flexible" in parenting) have more positive outcomes with their children (Bean et al., 2006).

Sons and daughters often have different experiences growing up in the same family because they are treated differently by each parent. Although it appears that mothers do not function that differently with sons than with daughters, fathers tend to pay more attention to sons. As a result, daughters often feel closer to their mothers than to their fathers. Both parents have a tendency to punish sons more than daughters, and many still tend to assign tasks on the basis of gender—more boys mow the lawn, and more girls clean the house. In general, parenting style has about the same impact on both the sons and the daughters (Amato & Booth, 1997).

Diana Baumrind (1991, 1995) identified four parenting styles and has done considerable work using those styles. Baumrind's four styles are the democratic

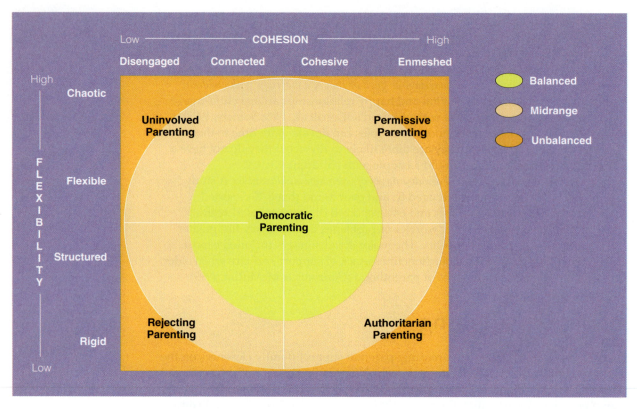

FIGURE 12.2

Parenting Styles and the Couple and Family Map

(authoritative), the authoritarian, the permissive, and the rejecting styles of parenting. To these four styles we have added the uninvolved style, which we identified using the Couple and Family Map (see Figure 12.2 and Table 12.4).

Democratic Style

In **democratic parenting,** parents establish clear rules and expectations and discuss them with the child. Although they acknowledge the child's perspective, they use both reason and power to enforce their standards. The democratic style is similar to the balanced type of system in the Couple and Family Map; these families tend to be *connected* to *cohesive* on the cohesion dimension and *structured* to *flexible* on the flexibility dimension. Considerable research on parenting has demonstrated that balanced family systems tend to have children who are emotionally healthier and happier and are more successful in school and life (Olson, 1996). Children of

TABLE 12.4	Parenting Style and Children's Behavior
Parenting Style	**Children's Behavior**
Democratic style	Self-reliant, cheerful, achievement oriented
Authoritarian style	Conflicted, irritable, unhappy, unstable
Permissive style	Impulsive, rebellious, underachieving
Rejecting style	Immature, psychologically challenged
Uninvolved style	Solitary, withdrawn, underachieving

democratic-style parents exhibit what Baumrind describes as energetic-friendly behavior. These children are very self-reliant and cheerful. They cope well with stress and are achievement oriented. Many other observers concur with Baumrind (Brown, 2003; Van As, 2003).

Authoritarian Style

In **authoritarian parenting,** parents establish rigid rules and expectations and strictly enforce them. These parents expect and demand obedience from a child. The authoritarian style is located in the lower-right quadrant of the Couple and Family Map; these families tend to be *structured* to *rigid* on the flexibility dimension and *cohesive* to *enmeshed* on the cohesion dimension. As the authoritarian style becomes more intense, the family moves toward the *rigidly enmeshed* style. This type of family system is particularly difficult for adolescents, who tend to rebel against authoritarian parenting. In Baumrind's observations, children of authoritarian-style parents are often conflicted and irritable in behavior: moody, unhappy, vulnerable to stress, and unfriendly. A study of authoritarian parenting (Rudy & Grusec, 2006) in several European countries and the United States found that children from these families have more serious problems in a variety of areas (lower self-esteem, more behavior problems, less academic achievement).

Permissive Style

In **permissive parenting**, parents let the child's preferences take priority over their ideals and rarely force the child to conform to their standards. The permissive style is located in the upper-right quadrant of the Couple and Family Map; these families tend to be *flexible* to *chaotic* on the flexibility dimension and *cohesive* to *enmeshed* on the cohesion dimension. As the permissive style becomes more extreme, the family moves toward the *chaotically enmeshed* style, a style characterized by constant change and forced togetherness, which is not healthy for children. Baumrind observed that children of permissive-style parents generally exhibit impulsive–aggressive behavior. These children are often rebellious, domineering, and underachieving.

Rejecting Style

In **rejecting parenting,** parents do not pay much attention to the child's needs and seldom have expectations regarding how the child should behave. The rejecting style is located in the lower-left quadrant of the Couple and Family Map; these families tend to be *structured* to *rigid* on the flexibility dimension and *connected* to *disengaged* on the cohesion dimension. As the rejecting style becomes more extreme, the family moves toward the *rigidly disengaged* style, which leaves children feeling uncared for even though they are expected to behave and have many rules to follow. As a result, children from these homes are often immature and have psychological problems.

Uninvolved Style

In **uninvolved parenting,** parents often ignore the child, letting the child's preferences prevail as long as those preferences do not interfere with the parents' activities. The uninvolved style of parenting is located in the upper-left quadrant of the Couple and Family Map; these families tend to be *connected* to *disengaged* on the

Democratic parents are actively involved with their children. They set standards and discuss them with the child. Children of these parents tend to be self-reliant and achievement oriented, and they cope well with stress.

cohesion dimension and *flexible* to *chaotic* on the flexibility dimension. As the uninvolved style becomes more extreme, it moves toward the *chaotically disengaged* pattern, in which children are left on their own without emotional support and a lack of consistent rules and expectations. The uninvolved style of parenting is not often discussed in published research, but it is in many instances combined with the rejecting style. Children of uninvolved parents are often solitary, withdrawn, and underachieving.

Democratic Parenting Works Best

Diana Baumrind (1991, 1995) completed several studies that linked the four parenting styles and outcomes with children. She has done considerable work using these styles. Baumrind described three styles of behavior in preschool children—energetic–friendly, conflicted–irritable, and impulsive–aggressive—and correlated those behaviors with her parenting styles (Table 12.4). In general, the democratic style resulted in children who were self-reliant, cheerful, and achievement oriented. Children raised with other styles, which are more extreme on cohesion and flexibility, had more problematic behaviors and less academic success.

In a major study of parenting that surveyed 11,669 high-school students, the democratic (authoritative) style of parenting had the most positive impact on an adolescent's development (Avenevoli, Sessa, & Steinberg, 1999). Democratic parenting was significantly related to lower psychological distress, higher self-esteem, a higher grade-point average, lower levels of drug use, and less-delinquent behavior. The importance of democratic parenting held up across ethnic groups and various levels of income.

In contrast to the positive outcomes of democratic parenting, authoritarian parenting was related to greater psychological distress, lower self-esteem, a lower grade-point average, and—interestingly—lower substance abuse (Avenevoli et al., 1999). Permissive parenting, considered the opposite of authoritarian parenting, was related to higher self-esteem, lower psychological distress, and lower substance abuse but also a lower grade-point average and some delinquency. Neglectful parenting was the most problematic parenting style. It was related to greater adolescent distress, lower self-esteem, a lower grade-point average, and greater drug use and delinquency compared to the other styles.

An important question concerns the importance of parenting style versus family structure (single- versus two-parent) and socioeconomic level (Avenevoli et al., 1999). Although they found that two-parent (intact) families from a variety of ethnic groups and socioeconomic levels were more democratic and less neglectful in their parenting style than were single-parent families, the differences between the two types of families were quite small and practically insignificant. The researchers concluded that the most important finding was "that family structure does not meaningfully moderate the relation between parenting and adjustment across a wide variety of socioeconomic and ethnic groups" (p. 87). The parenting style was the most critical variable in determining adolescent development and adjustment. Thus, regardless of ethnic background, socioeconomic level, or family structure, children of democratic-style parents have the best psychological and educational outcomes.

Theories of Childrearing

Parenting is a complex process that raises many questions: How shall we raise the children? How strict should we be, and how will we discipline our children? How soon should we begin toilet training? Will day care meet all our children's needs if both of us work outside the home? How can we share household and parenting responsibilities so that neither one of us feels overburdened or resentful? Before we tackle the issues surrounding these and other questions, let's take a look at some interrelated and complementary theoretical approaches to parenting.

The family systems perspective is increasingly being used by those studying the parent–child relationship. Earlier work focused on the influence of the parent on the child and some focus of the child on the parent. In the 1980s, a strong consensus developed by child development researchers about the need to study **bidirectional effects**—both the effects of the child on the parent and those of the parent on the child—in order to understand parent–child dynamics. The idea was not new to proponents of family systems theory, but it was a breakthrough for traditional child development researchers. The book by Richard Bell, who described the research in *Child Effects on Adults* (1977), helped stimulate interest in bidirectional research. The family systems perspective takes this one step further, viewing the parent–child relationship as an interactive cycle, a circular process of mutual influence.

Several theories of child development have had an impact on approaches to raising children. Freud and his followers focused on the importance of childhood, when the foundation for later life is laid down. Freudians and other proponents of the **psychodynamic theory** emphasized the importance of providing a positive emotional environment for the child, who needs to believe that the world is a safe and good place and that parents can be trusted to be kind and consistent. Although individuals who have suffered enormously in childhood can make dramatic, positive changes later in life, it is best if we can help children succeed from the very beginning.

Jean Piaget and proponents of **organismic theory** were interested in cognitive development, the development of the mind. Piaget held that the mind develops

Teaching a child appropriate behavior does not necessarily mean punishment for bad behavior. A more effective technique is reinforcing good behavior with praise and a hug.

through various stages over the course of childhood and adolescence. He observed that children think very differently than adults do. Child-thought is primitive and mystical; young children have only the beginnings of logical reasoning. Thought processes develop slowly toward higher forms into adulthood. This theory encourages parents to select toys and activities that are developmentally appropriate for their children and not to expect more than their children are capable of at any given stage.

The **behaviorists,** operating from **learning theories,** have developed some practical, positive approaches for dealing with children's behavior. Rather than focusing on punishment, behaviorists encourage "accentuating the positive," known as **reinforcement.** When a child does something positive, reward the child. Picking the appropriate reinforcer is not easy; "different strokes for different folks" often applies. Most children respond quite well to money, but praise and a hug are usually equally or even more effective. (Adults, too, appreciate praise from a boss for giving that extra effort.) A parent's job is to be creative in developing new reinforcers.

Perhaps the greatest positive reinforcement is simply enjoying each other's company. For example, when invited to speak about our research on strong families at a conference, John DeFrain often goes on a "journey of happy memories" with the audience. He asks people to recall the "best time" they can remember as a child: "Close your eyes. Think back to when you were a kid. Picture the best time you can remember with your family. Go right back to the scene as if you were there once again. What are you doing with your family? What's happening? Who's there? Get into it. Feel it . . . ." Then, we ask them to open their eyes, and we call for volunteers to describe what they just saw in their mind's eye.

Some people recall holidays:

"I'm in the living room. It's Thanksgiving. The whole family is gathered together, standing and sitting around the piano. We're all singing songs. Us kids are giggling and squirreling around, too. It's wonderful."

Some remember family nights together:

"I remember how we'd play games every Friday night. Just lie on the floor in the living room and play simple board games and laugh together."

Some tell about working together:

"When I was 12, my job was to scrub the kitchen floor with Mom every Saturday morning. We'd be on our hands and knees—just the two of us—scrubbing and laughing and flicking water at each other. It was great!"

Some remember times together outdoors in nature:

"We're on vacation. We're at the lake 2 hours north of our hometown. We're camping out. We're telling stories around the campfire."

We have gone on this journey of happy memories with literally thousands of people over the past 20 years, and the most remarkable thing we have found is that adults rarely recall something that cost a lot of money. On only a handful of occasions has anyone recalled an expensive event: a costly vacation to a theme park, a big meal in a fancy hotel. The vast majority of our happiest memories from childhood come from experiences that cost almost nothing. The key element is this: People who love one another are together, enjoying each other's company, being kind to one another.

It's very clear: Simple things can be tremendously reinforcing to a good relationship. These good times not only enhance the bond between parents and children, they also foster cooperation in children.

Issues in Parenting

Parents have become increasingly lax with disciplining their children and spoiling them (Doherty, 2000; Kindlon, 2001). There has also been less corporal punishment, but the impact of punishing your child is the continuing cycle of violence (Straus & Stewart, 1999). There is increasing use of day care as more mothers continue to work outside the home. Coparenting is becoming more popular as an ideal. Fatherhood continues to be a problem as fewer fathers stay connected with their children emotionally or support them financially.

Discipline and the Lack of It Today

There is increasing concern that parents today are becoming too lenient with their children and are letting the children take over more. *Time* magazine featured this topic with the theme "Who's in Charge Here?" (Gibbs, 2001). A Time/CNN poll indicated that 80% of parents felt that children are more spoiled today than 10 to 15 years ago. Seventy-five percent of the parents felt their children did fewer chores. Over two-thirds (68%) of the parents felt that children today are somewhat to very spoiled. Last, 71% of the parents felt that children are exposed to too much advertising, which increases their desires for more things.

In reaction to this trend, a variety of authors have identified the problem and offer some solutions. Bill Doherty (2000) in his book *Take Back Your Kids* describes how parents are almost afraid to discipline their children. He describes how parents are willing to sacrifice time so their children can have endless opportunities for community and school activities. He identifies ways parents can stand up to their children and take more control of their lives. He believes it is important to balance family time together and the needs of the individual children to achieve their personal goals.

Dan Kindlon (2001) sounds a similar theme of parents giving in too much in his book *Too Much of a Good Thing: Raising Children of Character in an Indulgent Age*. After surveying 1,700 teens and parents, he concluded that parents today want to indulge their children emotionally and with things. He even felt that he was too lax with his children and did not expect enough of them. He compared children where the parents were not indulgent with parents who were indulgent. The study found that the nonindulgent parents used the TLC approach. Time: They spent more time with their children at supper, after school, and at bedtime. Limits: They set firmer limits and expected more of the child in a variety of areas. Caring: They took an interest in all aspects of the child's life. Nonindulgent families also shared five traits:

- Families frequently ate dinner together.
- Parents were not divorced or separated.
- Children were required to keep their rooms clean.
- Children did not have phones in their rooms.
- Children did community service.

In summary, today's parents may be more indulgent and lenient with their children and this trend can be problematic. It is interesting that parenting styles change over time and that we are now operating in a more child-centered phase.

Corporal Punishment and Its Consequences

Corporal punishment is the use of physical force as punishment, correction, or behavior control. Corporal punishment usually refers to spanking or slapping but can also include grabbing, shoving, or hitting with an object. Corporal punishment is highest with younger children and decreases as the child reaches adolescence (Straus, 2002). Children aged 2 and 3 are hit about 16 to 18 times a year, and the frequency drops to about 10 times for 10-year-olds, and about 6 times for adolescents 13 to 16. In his research, Straus (1994) found that more men (58%) than women (44%) recall being hit as adolescents. Furthermore, adolescent sons are almost equally as likely to be hit by their fathers as by their mothers, whereas adolescent daughters are about a third more likely to be hit by their mothers (see Figure 12.3).

There is some evidence that the use of and support for corporal punishment in the United States is decreasing. This is congruent with the trend toward a more child-centered style of discipline that was previously described. Based on data merged from seven national surveys, the percentage of Americans who approve of corporal punishment declined from 94% in 1968 to 68% in 1994 (Straus & Mathus, 1996). Research findings also indicate differences in support of corporal punishment across sociocultural groups. Approval of corporal punishment is more common among African Americans, men, people who are less educated, older age groups, and individuals living in the southern United States.

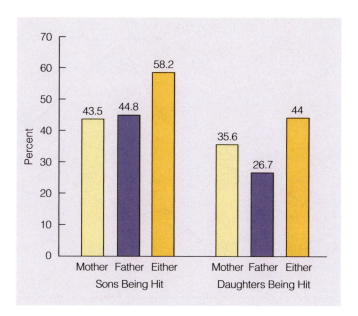

FIGURE 12.3
Frequency of Adolescent
Sons and Daughters
Being Hit by a Parent
*Source: Beating the Devil Out of
Them: Corporal Punishment in
American Families* by M. A.
Straus, copyright © 2001
Transaction Publishers,
New Brunswick, NJ.

Straus (2002) believes that all forms of physical punishment have long-term harmful consequences, not only for children and parents specifically but for society as a whole. By teaching the young that big people have the right to hurt smaller people, spanking contributes in some degree to the relatively high level of violence in American society. Straus (1998) found that the more corporal punishment experienced by the child, the greater the tendency for the child to engage in antisocial and impulsive behavior, and this pattern may contribute to the level of violence and other crime in our society.

In addition, the more corporal punishment experienced as a child, the greater the chance the person will hit his or her spouse (Straus, 1999). If a person experienced little or no corporal punishment as a child, the rate of hitting a spouse ranged from 8% to 14%. But if a child was hit 10 or more times a year, the rate of spouse abuse increased from 20% to 25%.

Several studies have found a direct linear relationship between corporal punishment received as a teenager and levels of adult depression in a sample of over 6,000 adults (Straus, 1994). Even when statistical analysis was controlled for other variables, such as poverty and witnessing violence between parents, it was found that the more corporal punishment teenagers experienced, the more depressive symptoms they had as adults. This relationship was stronger for women than it was for men (Figure 12.4). Also, adults whose parents hit them a lot as adolescents were more likely to have suicidal thoughts than adults who were not hit as adolescents.

Another researcher looked at the relationship between corporal punishment inflicted by parents and the perpetration of animal abuse by the children (Flynn, 2000a, 2000b). The research found that males who committed animal cruelty in childhood or adolescence were physically punished more frequently by fathers, both as preteens and teenagers, than males who did not perpetrate animal abuse. The relationship did not hold up for males spanked by their mothers or for females spanked by either their mothers or fathers.

In 1979, Sweden passed a law making it illegal for parents to spank their children. (Norway, Finland, Denmark, and Austria followed by forbidding corporal

FIGURE 12.4

Relationship Between
Corporal Punishment
Received as a Teenager
and Adult Depression

Source: Straus, 1994.

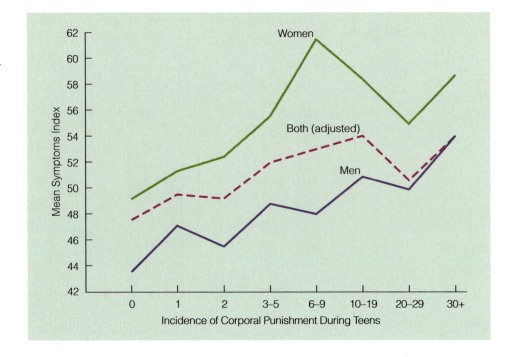

punishment as well.) The no-spanking law is not a criminal code; there are no criminal penalties for punishing parents who do spank their children. The law was designed instead to support, educate, and help parents rather than to label parents who use corporal punishment as "bad." After the law was passed, the Swedish government distributed to parents with young children booklets that listed alternative forms of discipline.

In American society, punishment of children by hitting and spanking has been an almost ubiquitous aspect of childhood. In fact, at least 90% of American children have been hit by a parent (Straus, 2002; Straus & Stewart, 1999). The sheer prevalence of corporal punishment alone demonstrates that social norms exist to legitimize it. But sometimes changes in public opinion are brought about by changes in social policy. As in the case of Sweden at the time the no-spanking law was introduced, many Swedes objected to and ridiculed the law. The dramatic decline in support for corporal punishment began almost immediately after the law went into effect, however, and a survey found that 71% of Swedes soon favored managing children without corporal punishment (Straus, 2002).

Child Care

As more mothers work outside the home, the need for child care in this country has increased. The most current government figures indicate that 63% of children under 5 years of age were in some form of regular child care arrangement in a typical week. Preschoolers (children under 5 years old) were more likely to be cared for by a relative (41%) than by a nonrelative (35%), whereas 12% were regularly cared for by both. Grandparents regularly cared for 21% of preschoolers, and 17% of preschoolers were regularly cared for by the father. Other relatives cared for 9% of preschoolers in a typical week, while siblings cared for 4% of the preschoolers and

Box 12.1   Diversity in Families

Child Care Issues for Hispanic Families

With so many mothers in the United States working outside the home, the issue of child care is a pressing concern. It is an issue that cuts across social and ethnic lines, as most families struggle to balance the need to work and the needs of their families.

Current statistics about Hispanic families provide information about Hispanic child care issues:

- The Hispanic population reached 39.9 million on July 1, 2003, accounting for about one-half of the 9.4 million residents added to the nation's population since the 2000 Census. The 13.0% growth rate for Hispanics over the 39-month period was almost four times that of the total population (*U.S. Census Bureau News*, 2004).
- While the median age for all Americans rose to 35.9 years in 2003, the median age for Hispanics was 26.7 years, the lowest of all single-race groups (*U.S. Census Bureau News*, 2004).
- Hispanics are the most likely to be preschoolers (under age 5), with more than 10% (or 4.2 million) in this age group (*U.S. Census Bureau News*, 2004).
- The number of Hispanic children as a proportion of all children in the United States has been increasing more rapidly than for non-Hispanic White and Black children for all age groups (National Child Care Information Center, 2004a).

- According to the March 2002 Current Population Survey (CPS), Hispanics experienced high rates of unemployment, earned less, and were more likely to live in poverty than non-Hispanic Whites. In 2002, 21.4% of Hispanics were living in poverty (vs. 7.8% of non-Hispanic Whites). In addition, Hispanic children under age 18 represented 17.7% of all children in the nation but constituted 30.4% of children in poverty (National Child Care Information Center, 2004a).
- By the year 2030, it is projected that Hispanics will make up 25% of the total school-age population (National Child Care Information Center, 2004b).
- By the year 2050, Hispanics and Blacks under the age of 5 will outnumber non-Hispanic Whites (National Child Care Information Center, 2004a).
- Although the Hispanic population is among the fastest growing and youngest segment of American society, families confront lower quality and lower supply of available child care in relation to the general public (National Child Care Information Center, 2004b).
- About 15.5% of Hispanic children of employed mothers were in organized care (child care centers, nurseries or preschools, Head Start programs, or other schools).

mothers cared for 4% while they worked (Smith, 2002). Care provided by extended family is especially common in Hispanic families (see Box 12.1).

About one in five preschoolers was cared for in organized facilities, with day care centers (12%) being more commonly used than nursery schools or preschools (6%). Overall, other nonrelatives provided home-based care to 17% of the preschoolers in this country, with 7% being cared for by family day care providers. More than one in three preschoolers had no regular child care arrangement (Smith, 2002).

One research team argued that employed mothers turn to relatives for child care not only for cost-saving reasons but also because they prefer care from extended-family members (Kulthau & Mason, 1996). These researchers suggest that public policies that encourage the use of relatives for child care might actually increase parental satisfaction with the quality of child care. Another research team found that parents who value developmental characteristics of child care programs tended to choose center care and that parents for whom hours, location, and cost of care were important chose care in a home. Additionally, parents who think it is important that the child know the caregiver were more likely to choose family care (Johansen, Leibowitz, & Waite, 1996).

The critical question is how day care affects children, both positively and negatively. An ambitious National Institute of Child Health and Human Development study offered some answers to this question. Researchers at 14 universities worked in 9 states and followed 1,364 children from birth to age 3—the largest and most diverse group ever studied. More than 20% of the children received full-time care from their mothers, and the rest were in day care centers or the homes of paid caregivers. Almost half the children spent 30 hours or more a week in these settings.

The researchers reported two significant findings. First, they found that high-quality day care—defined as settings in which adults speak with children a great deal and in a responsive way—had a slight advantage over day care settings in which the adults were less attentive: Children's language and learning abilities were somewhat enhanced in the high-quality settings. The second and most noteworthy conclusion of the researchers was that day care itself had far less impact on the emotional and mental development of the children than did the character of their family life (Lacayo, 1997).

The controversy over child care continues. Recent studies indicate that long hours in child care are related to children's later behavior problems and that child care may be physiologically challenging for young children (National Institute of Child Health Research Network, 2003; Watamura, Sebanc, & Gunnar, 2002). Explaining how all the pieces of the child care research puzzle fit together is a complicated task. Some researchers argue that results of studies will vary depending on the quality of child care offered (Greenspan, 2003). Some argue that children's stress responses to full-time, center-based child care may differ depending on the child's gender and temperament (Crockenberg, 2003). Some argue that family background affects children's responses in child care settings (Greenspan, 2003). Some argue that numerous studies indicate that many children thrive in day care, though we need to do some serious thinking about how to optimize the lives of young children under the conditions of modern life today in which so many parents must work outside the home (Maccoby & Lewis, 2003).

Although the interest and need for day care continue to rise, the United States is one of the few countries that does not have national day care policies or standards. Day care workers, who typically earn only minimum wage, often have little direct training. It is a sad commentary on our society that we fail to train and reward the people who are responsible for caring for, teaching, and nurturing so many of our children. See Box 12.2 for some thoughts on high-quality early-childhood programs from Marjorie Kostelnik, dean of the College of Education and Human Sciences at the University of Nebraska, and a former president of the National Association for the Education of Young Children.

Coparenting

A growing number of parents have adopted a cooperative approach to parenting, known as coparenting. Traditional family roles—in which dad was the provider and mom the nurturer; dad was "tough" and mom was "tender"—are changing. More mothers are working outside the home, and more men are sharing in parenting tasks. An increasing number of mothers are providing income for their families and enjoying their connection to the world outside the home. At the same time, an increasing number of fathers are experiencing the joy of watching their children grow and learn.

Some couples share the responsibilities equally: Mother and father each do half the child care, half the housework, and half the work outside the home. But most couples do not divide up the tasks exactly equally. One young father explained, "I'm a better cook, so I tend to do more of that. She likes to see a neat, clean

Box12.2   At Issue

Looking for a High-Quality Early-Childhood Program

This year, four out of five children below the age of 5 in the United States will be cared for outside the home. That means a lot of families are looking for people to care for their children and for programs in which to enroll them. In a recent national poll, 97% of the parents surveyed cited quality as their top priority in determining which early-childhood programs they wanted their child to attend. Yet there is a difference in the quality of education and care children receive. Only about 20% of our children will participate in high-quality early-childhood programs. High-quality programs benefit children and their families; poor-quality programs are detrimental to them. These outcomes compel us to better understand the difference between poor-quality early-childhood programs and ones that are high quality.

High-quality programs make a positive difference in children's lives. Children in high-quality programs demonstrate higher levels of language development, greater social competence, a better ability to regulate their own behavior, and better academic performance than do their peers in poor-quality programs. These results hold true in the short term and over time.

Poor-quality programs are worse than no programs at all. Poor-quality experiences lead to increased behavior problems and poorer academic progress in children. Such children are also more likely to have poor social skills.

These negative effects appear to be long lasting. Evidence of poor quality is still apparent up to 5 years later.

With so much at stake, it is critical to ask, "What do high-quality programs look like?" Fortunately, there is a growing research base we can draw upon for the answer. Here are some of the essential components of high-quality early-childhood programs:

1. Practitioners are well prepared and well compensated.
2. Staffing is stable.
3. Group sizes are small, and there are only a few children for each practitioner.
4. There are warm, attentive relationships between adults and children.
5. Environments are safe and healthy.
6. Environments are stimulating.
7. Families are treated as partners in the education and care of their children.
8. Programs are linked to comprehensive community services as a way to support families in their childrearing roles and as children's first teachers.

Source: Adapted from *What Is a High Quality Early Childhood Program?* by M. Kostelnik, 2005, Lincoln, NE: College of Education and Human Sciences, University of Nebraska. Reprinted by permission of M. Kostelnik, Lincoln, NE.

---

house, so she concentrates on that. We both like taking care of the girls, but I do baths and bedtimes because she's so tired at the end of a day of nursing." Flexibility is the key.

Researchers have found a number of advantages to the coparenting model. Parents report greater satisfaction with their marriage and family life than they had before they adopted the coparenting approach. They also report improved relationships with their children. Some partners even considered divorce before they changed their attitudes about childrearing. Coparenting frees men to spend more time relating to, caring for, and relaxing with their children and frees women to pursue outside interests. Both parents have much to gain from active involvement in their children's growth. Parenthood is much too important and much too time consuming to be left to one person (Dienhart, 2001; Risman & Johnson-Sumerford, 1998).

Another important benefit of coparenting is that it brings fathers into the family on an emotional level. Some observers have concluded that fathers often "draw on their life at home to take care of their emotional needs, but . . . distance themselves from the emotional needs of other family members" (Larson, Wilson, Brown, Furstenberg, & Verma, 2002). Some fathers enjoy being nurtured at home but don't want to nurture others in the home or don't have the capacity to do so. The experience of coparenting can help men learn how to attend to the emotional needs of others. This is a skill that has often been neglected because in our culture we tend to socialize men for competition, not cooperation.

A problem with coparenting is that sometimes the marriage gets lost in the shuffle. The mother is working outside the home, caring for the children, doing housework; the father is doing the same. Two outside full-time jobs and the job of maintaining a family and household add up to at least three full-time jobs for only two people. Often the marriage is neglected while the spouses concentrate on their employment responsibilities and their family and household tasks. The couple might be doing great at the office and great with the kids but still end up getting divorced because they forgot to focus on their relationship with each other. They need to remember that the foundation for the whole operation is a strong marriage.

Single Mothers

There is a growing number of single-parent mothers primarily because women are having children out of wedlock and, secondly, because of divorce from the father (Downs, 2003). The number of single-parent births is over 1 million each year, which represents 33% of all births. The rate of out-of-wedlock births is highest in the African American population (65%) and drops in Hispanics (36%), is lower in Asians (27%), and is lowest in Whites (25%). Younger women have by far the highest rates of out-of-wedlock births. About 90% of births to teenagers (15 to 19 years old) are out of wedlock, while the rate drops to 50% for women in their 20s and to 12% for women 30 years old and over.

What is common among all single-parent mothers is the high level of stress and the low level of economic and emotional resources that these mothers have in their lives. One qualitative study of single mothers ranging in age from 33 to 44 years old reports the various challenges they face, including time management, coping with sick children as the sole caregiver, and contending with the negative social stigma surrounding their choice. The support of friends and family, in particular, helps them meet the challenges they face and enhances their level of life satisfaction. All 15 participants in this study said they received life's greatest joys from motherhood (Fill, 2002).

In a study of midlife independent single women who intentionally decided to enter solo parenthood, the women said they felt entitled to be single mothers because of four attributes: their age and related maturity, the level of personal responsibility they demonstrated, their emotional security, and their financial capabilities. Presenting a variety of economic, moral, and religious justifications, these women saw themselves as competent mothers (Bock, 2000).

Gay and Lesbian Parenting

Nearly one-quarter of all same-sex couples (lesbian couples and gay couples) are raising children. Nationwide, over one-third (34%) of lesbian couples are raising children compared to 22% of gay couples (Herek, 2006). In contrast to same-sex couples, almost half (46%) of all married heterosexual couples have children.

After a major review of the studies comparing children of gay and lesbian parents to those raised by heterosexual couples, the American Psychological Association (2004) concluded that there was no difference in the children's adjustment, achievement, and overall well-being between the two groups. In another major review (Meezan & Rauch, 2005) on this topic, four conclusions were made

This is the first generation in the United States where gay and lesbian couples have openly raised children who are now reaching adolescence and young adulthood.

about same-sex parenting. First, when comparing lesbian mothers and gay fathers, few differences were found with children raised by heterosexual parents. In some cases, children with same-sex parents did better in that they were more tolerant of diversity and more nurturing toward younger children. Second, children of lesbian and gay parents are not confused about their gender identity and were not more likely to be homosexual. Third, there were no differences between children in cognitive abilities, behavior, and emotional development in the two types of families. Finally, there appears to be little difference in the parenting style and effectiveness of same-sex parents compared to heterosexual parents.

A relatively new trend is the increasing number of gay and lesbian couples who are having and raising children. Some of the children are the biological offspring of one of the persons, and some are from a previous relationship or marriage. Some lesbian couples have used donor insemination to have their own child, and more gay couples are choosing to adopt children.

This is the first generation in the United States where gay and lesbian couples have openly raised children who are now reaching adolescence and young adulthood. Studies have found that lesbian parents are very committed to creating a strong family (Herek, 2006). They are also concerned about the social challenges that their children will face when others learn that they are being raised by same-sex parents. The parents have generally found that they have had limited problems raising younger children, but some adolescents have felt embarrassed about their same-sex parents—especially among their peers.

In general, it appears that gay and lesbian couples are increasing their interest in raising children, and these families appear to be doing well. In addition to the normal challenges of raising adolescents, lesbian and gay couples and adolescents have to deal with the issue of social acceptance from others. The question about the eventual lifestyle and overall adjustment of the children will become more clear in the coming years.

Fatherhood and Motherhood Today

Coparenting may be gaining popularity as an ideal, but the reality in many cases is quite different (Doherty, Kouneski, & Erickson, 1998). Although the images of father as breadwinner and mother as nurturer are slowly breaking down, new images—especially for fathers—have not yet taken hold. More than half of American mothers with children under 18 are now in the workforce, but many fathers have not become proportionately involved in nurturing tasks. The value of fatherhood has not increased dramatically.

Margaret Mead once wrote that "motherhood is a biological necessity, but fatherhood is a social invention." James Garbarino explains that parenthood for women is clear, because it is tied to their essential biological role in the process of bringing children into the world. But the role of the father is ambiguous and relies on cultural prescriptions (Garbarino, 2000, p. 11).

Some scholars have gone so far as to ask, Is the father even a part of the family? David Blankenhorn (1999, 2004) has found that nearly 40% of children live in homes where the biological father is not present. Wade Horn (1995) estimates that 6 out of 10 children born in the 1990s will be "fatherless" before reaching adulthood. What forces are responsible for these trends? And what can be done about them?

The Absent Father. Two major threats to a father's presence in a child's life are divorce and nonmarital childbearing, both of which are increasing. Marriages are continuing to fail at a high rate, and a growing number of families are starting out without a father (U.S. Bureau of the Census, 2001a). One-third of births are to single women. Virtually all children born outside of marriage live with their mothers, and in two-thirds of these cases, the father never establishes paternity.

In 90% of divorce cases, the children reside with their mothers. Many fathers, no longer living with their children, struggle to stay involved with them. But research has shown a pattern of gradual withdrawal by nonresidential fathers and growing alienation between fathers and children. One large national study found that about two-thirds of children of divorce had poor relationships with their fathers; among children whose parents were not divorced, less than a third (29%) had poor relationships with their fathers (Nord & Zill, 1996). Conflict between the former spouses also affects the quality of the father–child relationship by creating strains on the child that may offset any advantages of having the father actively involved.

When fathers remain in frequent contact and when conflict between the parents is low, fathers are more likely to make regular child support payments. There is a strong association between a divorced father's economic support and the well-being of his children. So frequent contact, low parental conflict, and economic support have a positive effect on the child's well-being. Nevertheless, many fathers would like to have the opportunity to contribute to their children's lives in deeper and more meaningful ways.

The Father as Nurturer. Research in child development has shown that fathers are just as capable as mothers in performing nurturing tasks (assuming the fathers are living with their children). Children can establish attachment relationships with fathers as they do with mothers. Fathers respond to the needs of their infants, picking up on their cues, just as mothers do. When mothers are present, however, fathers tend to back off and defer to them.

Fathers are more likely to be involved in the care of children if the parents are dual earners, but only when the mother works different hours than the father.

Many fathers are fully capable of nurturing and caring for their children.

When parents work the same hours, mothers tend to come home to a "second shift" of family work (DeLuccie, 1995).

Some studies report that women want men to be nurturing in their families, whereas other studies have shown that many mothers do not want increased father involvement (Hogan, 1993). The home is said to be a place of power and control for women, whereas the workplace is where men have traditionally dominated. Some women do not want to share their power or their role as the "more important parent." Men's involvement as fathers can be shaped, positively or negatively, by the mothers' expectations and support.

In sum, it seems that fathers are fully capable of nurturing and caring for their children, but other factors—social, cultural, and interpersonal—tend to discourage them from doing so wholeheartedly. This is particularly unfortunate in light of the belief, put forth by some feminist scholars, that as more men become involved in nurturing tasks, inequalities in the workplace and the family will be reduced (Silverstein & Auerbach, 2000).

Responsible Fatherhood. What is the appropriate role for a father? It must first be acknowledged that every society constructs and defines roles for men and women; the role of father is no exception. In our society today, there is no single definition or description of this role. If a father is living at home with his children, he may be married and coparenting or single and parenting alone. Living apart from his children, he may be young and unwed, with or without paternity established. If divorced, he may have joint physical or legal custody or just visitation rights (Doherty et al., 1998).

Although single fathers and divorced fathers with custody have nurturing roles thrust upon them, it appears that many other fathers in our society are given quite a wide latitude in how involved they want to be in the family. Unlike mothering, fathering appears to be a choice that men make in the face of contextual pressures. They can be very involved—or they can walk away.

To develop new roles, fathers need the support of mothers. They also need the support of society in general—in the workplace, in the courts, and in the social service agencies that serve families. This support may be forthcoming. Recognizing the holistic nature of family health, family service programs now attempt to involve fathers when they work with families. Additionally, new community-based programs have emerged to support fathers in their efforts to be responsibly involved in their families. Jim Levine and Ed Pitt (1995), discussing their experience as practitioners who work with families, advance this definition of paternal responsibility: A responsible father waits to have children until he is prepared to support the child, financially and emotionally; he establishes legal paternity; and he actively provides physical and emotional care for the child, as well as financial support, in cooperation with the mother.

The best gift a father can give his children
Is to love their mother.
—ANONYMOUS

Good Fathering Makes a Real Difference in Children. Kristin A. Moore (1998) of Child Trends, a private organization that monitors research and policies related to children and parenting, conducted a major review of research on fathering. She found that fathers can have a very positive impact on their children's development—whether or not the father lives with the children or is a noncustodial partner. The specific conclusions from this review are as follows:

- The more fathers are involved in the routine activities of their children, the more likely the children will have fewer behavior problems, be more sociable, and do better in school.
- Fathers often promote children's development more through physical play, whereas mothers do it through talking and teaching.
- Across different ethnic groups, fathers tend to assume the important role of economic provider, protector, and caregiver.
- Fathers who provide economically for their children also stay more involved with their children, even if they live apart.
- Fathers who pay child support tend to have children who behave better and do better in school.

When a Child Dies

The loss of a child creates a unique crisis in a family. No individual experiences the crisis in the same way another does, and each family is different. Though common themes of grief and bereavement occur time and time again, each family experiences the crisis in its own desperate way.

We do not use the word *desperate* lightly here, because every parent we have talked with in our work as counselors and researchers over the past 30 years has been plunged into dreadful unhappiness in the aftermath of the child's death. Many parents consider suicide because of the death. Living becomes almost unbearable for most. Mothers and fathers have told us of slitting their wrists, trying to kill themselves in an automobile crash, trying to overdose on drugs, turning on the engine of the car in a closed garage.

The vast majority of parents who have experienced the loss of a child see the death as the most devastating crisis they have experienced in their lives. The child's death is clearly a catastrophe for families—mothers, fathers, brothers, sisters, grandmothers, grandfathers, and other close relatives and friends—and the responsibility falls to each of us in society to help these stricken people in any way we can. They are clearly crushed in a life-threatening and spiritually numbing situation.

And yet, parents do survive the loss of their child. They turn to each other for comfort, to their relatives and friends, and to professionals in their community. Many individuals suffering from the loss of a child say that their belief in God was helpful and that being able to tell themselves that their child was with God was one of the few comforts they received. But others caution that they sometimes couldn't sit back and wait for God to help, "You've got to get out of your rut yourself."

Commitment, togetherness, and the ability of partners and other family members to take turns being strong for each other are also seen as positive ways of enduring the loss of a child. A final common denominator seems to be a person's simple ability to survive—to get up in the morning and get through the day, to force concentration on tasks that may seem irrelevant to the situation. One woman found herself thinking, "How can I scrub this floor? My child is dead." But she knew she had to keep busy and involved, if even on such a basic level.

As the months and years after the death of the child pass, many parents and grandparents express surprise that they have survived the tragedy. Once the realization sinks in that they will live though their child did not, they find strength in themselves they never thought they had. Most of them grimly acknowledge the truth of one mother's words: "Now I can survive anything" (DeFrain, Ernst, & Nealer, 1997).

Parent Education and Family Therapy

In meeting the challenges of raising children, parents often turn to professionals for guidance, either for education or for therapy. **Parent education** usually involves a presentation of information in a group setting followed by a group discussion of generic parenting problems, such as communication, discipline, imparting values to children, sibling rivalry, and choosing adequate child care. In **family therapy**, a therapist typically works with a single family with one or more specific problems, including sexual abuse, spouse abuse, child abuse or neglect, a runaway child, a child's attempted suicide, a child's coming out as a gay man or a lesbian, or the abuse of alcohol or other drugs.

Both parent education and family therapy take place in a variety of settings, and fees range widely. Services through public agencies are often less expensive than those offered by private practitioners. Parent education programs are usually much cheaper than therapy, and many are free or cost very little. One of the main advantages of parent education programs is their ability to show parents that they are not the only ones having trouble figuring out how to raise their kids; this can be tremendously comforting to troubled parents. In an effective parent education session, a professional might present ideas to the group for 15 to 30 minutes and then let parents break into small groups to discuss their own family's trials and tribulations. Parents soon learn that they are all "in the same boat." Breaking the tension and discussing common issues can be the foundation for positive change and growth in the family.

An effective way to improve father involvement with their infants was to have them participate in a parenting program called STEEP (Steps Toward Effective

Enjoyable Parenting) (Doherty, Erickson, & LaRossa, 2006). It was assumed that by increasing a father's involvement with his infant, the father would become more attached to the child and that would increase his interest in fathering over time. The STEEP family education program had four 2-hour sessions before the birth of the child and four sessions after the child returned home. Fathers who participated in this program had more positive parenting skills and more involvement with their infant on workdays compared to a control group. The conclusion was that this brief educational program improved fathering and was a good investment in time and money.

Researchers Martha Zaslow and Carolyn Eldred (1998) conducted an important study of the New Chance parenting program; the sample consisted of 290 teenage mothers who lived under difficult situations. Zaslow and Eldred found that, although the program helped the mothers improve their parenting and nurturing skills, it had no effect on improving the cognitive and social development of their children. The study demonstrated the importance of the social context in the lives of the children. It suggested that ecological stressors such as poverty, unstable housing, and a mother's depression also had an impact on the children's development. The researchers recommended that to increase the effectiveness of the course, more training sessions should be added and parents should receive instruction that would help them improve their income and overall quality of life.

Parenting programs are increasingly using technology and other creative approaches to simplify parents' access to research-based information, services, and problem-solving support. Web sites, phone numbers to call for audiotaped information about parenthood, neighboorhood-based parent centers, and media campaigns are all being created to help improve the lives of parents and children (Mertensmeyer & Fine, 2000).

An enduring problem for parents is how to translate philosophy into action. One important goal is to provide children with a basic foundation upon which they can build, as illustrated by Kahlil Gibran's poem "On Children":

Your children are not your children.

They are the sons and daughters of Life's longing for itself.

They come through you but not from you,

And though they are with you yet they belong not to you.

You may give them your love but not your thoughts,

For they have their own thoughts.

You may house their bodies but not their souls,

For their souls dwell in the house of tomorrow,

which you cannot visit, not even in your dreams.

You may strive to be like them, but seek not to make them like you.

For life goes not backward nor tarries with yesterday.

You are the bows from which your children as living arrows are sent forth.

The archer sees the mark upon the path of the infinite, and He bends you with His might that His arrows may go swift and far.

Let your bending in the archer's hand be for gladness;

For even as He loves the arrow that flies, so He loves also the bow that is stable.

(1923/1976, pp. 18–19)

Each day, parents are confronted with difficult questions that have complex answers. To find these answers, parents must learn to relate their personal philosophy to what is actually occurring with their children:

- "I don't believe in spanking, but this kid is driving me crazy!"
- "I love to watch my children grow, but I also need a life of my own. How do I balance the two?"
- "One child has a soccer game, but we had all planned to go to a children's play."
- "He flunked his math test again. I told him I would help him study for it, but he didn't want to study. Should I let him suffer the consequences of failing?"
- "We have not gone out as a couple to the movies or for dinner for almost a year, but our kids always want more of us."

"What was life like before you had children?" Many parents respond, "I cannot imagine what it was like anymore. It has been such an emotional and overwhelming journey since the kids came along." Children take control of a parent's life and a parent's heart. They bring a considerable amount of stress to the parent's life; there is no question about that. But we cannot afford to discount the engagement and fascination and joy they spark in our lives. Each day is a new day for a child, and watching the story unfold can be a delight to loving parents. What will the next chapter of the story bring? What will the children do next? What will they become in life? As one father put it so well, "I suppose I could have concentrated on my career more if I hadn't had children, but love has always counted far more to me than money. You can't hold a $100 bill in your lap and read a story to it."

Summary

- A national survey of married couples revealed considerable differences in how happy couples versus unhappy couples handle parenting. Happy couples tend to agree more on how childrearing responsibilities are shared, to be more satisfied with the amount of attention they focus on their relationship as opposed to on their children, to agree on how to discipline their children, to agree on how to financially provide for their children, and to agree that children do not create problems for the marriage.
- According to a national survey, the top five parenting issues for married couples are the following: Children reduce marital satisfaction, the father is not involved enough with their children, dissatisfaction with how childrearing is shared, disagreement on discipline, and too much focus on the children versus the marriage.
- Paradoxically, parenthood is both very challenging and very satisfying emotionally.
- Conventional wisdom on the subject of parenthood in our society abounds. Although many people might believe the conventional "truths," research on parenthood indicates that the picture is more complex.
- Parenthood changes a couple's world: They have less time for each other and for individual interests; they may have money problems; and many find it physically exhausting, especially mothers.
- A middle-income couple (earning an average annual income of $54,100) will spend about $178,590 to raise each child through the age of 17.
- Researchers have found that voluntarily childless individuals and couples can have just as satisfying a life as those who have children. Child-free people have more time for intimate relationships and for their careers, and in old age they often rely on friends and relatives for support.
- Parenting styles differ, and some are more effective than others. The democratic style is favored today because it appears to produce self-reliant children who cope well with stress. Other parenting styles that are authoritarian, permissive, rejecting, and uninvolved tend to produce children with more behavioral and academic problems.
- Many parenting styles can be related to the cohesion and flexibility dimensions of the Couple and Fam-

ily Map. The democratic style falls into the balanced areas of the model because it exhibits dynamic balances on both the dimensions. Because other styles fall near the extremes of the model, they are less-effective approaches to rearing children.

- How to discipline children is a major issue for many parents, as well as a source of some debate in our society. There is increasing evidence that parents are currently too lenient and lack control over their children. This has stimulated a variety of new books designed to help parents take greater control over their children's lives.
- Corporal punishment is widely used in the United States; statistics suggest that 90% of all children have been hit by their parents and that 68% of Americans believe that spanking is sometimes necessary.
- Research on punishment has found that children who are hit are more likely to hit their partners and children later in life, to be depressed, and to exhibit learning impairments and delinquent behavior.
- In spite of the rising demand for day care, the United States is one of the few countries that does not have national day care policies or standards.
- Positive approaches to childrearing include (1) reinforcing (rewarding) children's positive behavior rather than punishing negative behavior and (2) coparenting, a sharing of traditional male and female roles between parents.
- Numerous studies demonstrate the important role a father plays in a child's development—whether he lives with the child or is a noncustodial parent.
- In the United States, many parent education programs have been developed as a response to the challenges of raising children and the diversity of American families. Many trained professionals provide both information and one-on-one therapy.
- Although parenting poses many challenges, it is also very gratifying for parents. A study on parental satisfaction indicates that parents enjoy watching their children grow, are proud of their children's achievements, enjoy sharing fun times with their children, feel self-fulfilled and needed, feel closer to their partner, and derive from parenting a purpose for living.

Key Terms

child-free alternative	psychodynamic theory
parental support	organismic theory
parental control	behaviorist
democratic parenting	learning theories
authoritarian parenting	reinforcement
permissive parenting	coparenting
rejecting parenting	parent education
uninvolved parenting	family therapy
bidirectional effects	

Activities

1. Read Kahlil Gibran's poem "On Children" carefully and write a brief essay analyzing his philosophy of parenthood. On what points do you agree and disagree?
2. Set a time and place to interview your father and/or mother about their beliefs on rearing children and the challenges and joys they have experienced over the years as parents. A good interview takes careful planning: Write down 15 to 20 questions you want to be sure to ask. Then write up your interview in a short paper and share it with the class or a small group. You might like to audiotape or videotape the interview. (These tapes might even become family treasures and make great gifts.)
3. Parenthood can be a thankless task; children are often too busy and too overwhelmed by their own problems and concerns to think about their parents' feelings. Write a letter to your parents, thanking them for all the things they have done for you and for their unique human qualities.
4. Spend an afternoon with some children you know—your nieces and nephews, a neighbor's children, or a friend's kids. Write down your reactions to this brief "parenting" experience.

Suggested Readings

Boyd-Franklin, N., Franklin, A., & Toussaint, P. (2000). *Boys into men: Raising our African American teenage sons.* New York: Penguin Putnam. "A convincing argument to parents that educating an African-American teenage son and keeping him alive, healthy, and out of jail past the age of 25 years is no small task."

Crittenden, A. (2001). *The price of motherhood: Why the most important job in the world is still the least valued.* New York: Metropolitan Books. "An easy, informative, enjoyable read."

Doherty, W. J. (2000). *Take back your kids.* Notre Dame, IN: Sorin. How parents can rescue their family from being taken over by outside activities.

Douglas, S. J., & Michaels, M. W. (2004). *The mommy myth: The idealization of motherhood and how it has undermined women.* New York: Free Press. Cultural forces are at work to "return women to the Stone age."

Helburn, S. W., & Bergmann, B. R. (2002). *America's child-care problem: The way out.* New York: Palgrave. A holistic overview of all aspects of child care in America.

March, K., & Miall, C. (2000). Special issue on adoption. *Family Relations,* 49(4). Focuses on the social context of adoption; adjustment and adoption outcome; openness in adoption; and transitions in adoption services.

M.I.S.S. Foundation. (2004). A nonprofit, 501(c)3, international organization that provides immediate and ongoing support to grieving families. Web site: http://www.missfoundation.org.

Nemiroff, M., & Annunziata, J. (2003). *All about adoption: How families are made and how kids feel about it.* Washington, DC: American Psychological Association. A book for children providing an understanding of how the adoption process works and the feelings many children have about being adopted.

Peters, H. E., & Day, R. D. (Eds.). (2000). *Fatherhood: Research, interventions, and policies.* New York: Haworth. Articles in the volume examine the many faces of fatherhood.

Tamis-LeMonda, C. S., & Cabrera, N. (2003). *Handbook of father involvement: Multidisciplinary perspectives.* Mahwah, NJ: Erlbaum. Experts from diverse scientific disciplines share their interests in the topic of father involvement in the lives of children.

Visit the text-specific Online Learning Center at **www.mhhe.com/Olson6** for practice tests, chapter summaries, Web links, Internet exercises, key terms, and flashcards.

13. *M* Midlife and Older Couples

Intimacy, Strengths, and Diversity

Family Life in the Middle Years

Family Life in the Later Years

Summary

Key Terms

Activities

Suggested Readings

Intimacy, Strengths, and Diversity

Intimacy in the middle and later years of life looks very different from intimacy in the earlier stages of the life cycle. Freedom from raising children for couples in the middle years of life may pave the way for new sexual and emotional intimacy. For those in later years, sexual intimacy in marriage or couple relationships may change with added health problems. Emotional intimacy in couple relationships, however, may be very solid as couples grow old together. There are strengths in couple and family relationships for people in the middle and later years of life. They have learned many of life's lessons and can pass this knowledge on to others.

Intimate emotional relationships with adult children may increase as these children have children of their own and they now have shared the life-changing experience of having children. Relationships with grandchildren may be deeper and take on new meaning as they see these young people providing a continuation of themselves to another generation.

Couples are likely to find themselves in the sandwich generation, which means they are caring for their aging parents and also have responsibilities for adult children who may have moved back into the home. This may create stress, but it also may create new opportunities to tap into family strengths and unexpected intergenerational family relationships (Skogrand, Henderson, & Higginbotham, 2006). Below is a true story about such a family:

> Sandra and Martin were in their mid-50s and for a couple of years they had been in an "empty nest." Their children were off to college, and the major responsibilities of raising children were done. It was great. They could go out when they wanted, take trips on the spur of the moment, or sleep late, with no major responsibilities except their jobs to tie them down. The spark was back in their relationship with limited stress in their lives and more opportunity to spend time together
>
> Several months ago, however, their son, Adam, dropped out of school and moved home to make a decision about career goals and decide where he wanted to continue his education. It was to be temporary, but there was much ambiguity about future plans. He quickly got a low-paying job and lived with Sandra and Martin. He was really not much bother. He took care of his own meals, picked up after himself, and got himself to work. Sandra and Martin were looking forward to spending time with their son who was now an adult.
>
> About the same time Adam moved home, the decision was made that Sandra's mother who lived 800 miles away would move to a nursing home in their town. Both Sandra and Martin viewed the move positively. For the first time in her adult life Sandra would be able to have quality time with her aging mother.
>
> Soon after the move, however, Sandra's mother's health began to decline. She needed daily visits and frequent medical appointments and conferences. Work for Sandra involved long days, ending with several hours spent at the nursing home in the evening. There were many 14- and 15-hour days for Sandra, who would drop into bed exhausted, only to do it again the next day. Martin's days also became longer as he picked up most of the household responsibilities in addition to his job.
>
> Although Adam generally took care of himself, he still counted on his parents' help in buying a new car and applying and making arrangements to enroll in school. He anticipated he would have his parents available to help him plan his future, but they were rarely available.

This sandwich generation family was experiencing stress and responsibility at a time when the middle-aged couple expected a less stressful time. As you read this true story, you may be feeling yourself tense up as you think about all the responsibilities in their lives. The couple reflected on this time a year after Sandra's mother died and their son had gone back to college. They said it had been stressful and they did not want to do it again. They also said, however, that there were many positive things that happened in their family relationships during this time. Adam got to know his grandmother as he sat by her bed in the last weeks of her life. Adam's grandmother had talked about how she loved getting to know her grandson as an adult—something that she had not anticipated before she died. Sandra developed that intimate relationship with her mother that she had hoped for. In fact, she says this special time was short and at times difficult, but was also one of the best times of her life. Martin and Sandra developed a closer couple relationship because they agreed that both generations needed them during this time.

The middle and later years of life are filled with surprises, some difficult and stressful, and also some positive things that they never anticipated. Individuals and couples in the middle and later years of life usually have developed skills to weather the storm and appreciate wonderful surprises.

In the middle years and later years of life there is diversity. Couples who have been married for 50 or more years—accepting and loving their children, grandchildren, and great-grandchildren who have been married and divorced, who are in stepfamilies, and who may be in gay or lesbian relationships. Many folks in these middle and later years have problems with these new family structures, but many embrace this diversity and show unconditional love to family members.

Family Life in the Middle Years

After the kids leave home, some parents suffer from the empty nest syndrome; others change the locks!

—Anonymous

What images does the term *middle age* conjure up? For most young college students, their mom and dad are the first to come to mind. Middle age can be a relaxing time, a time of thankfulness that the challenges and fears of youth have been overcome. But middle age can bring new pressures, new challenges.

"Life begins at 40," an old saying goes. The kids may leave the nest. Family income may reach a peak. But *middlescence* can set in. In the middle years, some people mourn lost opportunities, the road not taken, and wonder what their lives would have been like if only they had been bolder, smarter, or luckier. Middlescents also often yearn for a taut young body and freedom from the grind.

In Erik Erikson's classic schema, middle age can be a time for generativity or stagnation (1950). The question of middle age is, "Can we remain productive despite boredom and malaise? (Can an old dog learn new tricks?)" Millions of people transform their lives in the middle years by starting new careers or falling in love. Those who are flexible, who can adapt to new circumstances and "roll with the punches," will be much more likely to succeed. The inflexible ones may survive but will probably not excel—and they will be less likely to enjoy the process of living than those who are flexible. (Box 13.1 presents a broad-ranging study of family stress in the middle years. It details both the types of stressors families face and their strategies for coping with stress.)

Defining Middle Age

A popular societal definition of **middle age** is the period of life between ages 35 and 65, but age alone does not tell the whole story, especially when applied to the middle years. The eminent gerontologist Bernice Neugarten notes philosophically that the middle years are the time when people begin to think about how

BOX 13.1   At Issue

Family Stress in the Middle Years

We all go through many stages of life as we age; each stage brings with it both rewards and challenges. What brings us pleasure in our youth may not be the same thing that delights us in middle age. And, just as responsibilities change as we age, so do things we worry about and stress over. When researchers in nine states—Indiana, Iowa, Kansas, Kentucky, Louisiana, Michigan, Minnesota, Missouri, and Nebraska—wanted to determine what stressors most affected families and how they coped, they gave more than 1,900 families a 27-page questionnaire. The research (the largest study ever undertaken of family stress and coping in middle years) focused on intact families, consisting of a middle-aged husband, a wife, and at least one child still living at home.

Types of Stressors

Families in the study were asked to rank various stressors. The top 10 stressors identified by both husbands and wives were the following:

1. A family member's involvement with the judicial system.
2. A major financial loss.
3. Serious emotional problems.
4. A serious illness or accident involving a child.
5. A serious illness or accident involving the primary wage earner.
6. Marital separation.
7. The death of an adult brother or sister.
8. Loss of the primary wage earner's job.
9. The death of either spouse's parent.
10. The illness of either spouse's aged parent.

This list represents an average of the rankings reported by both husbands and wives. Wives perceived family-related matters to be more stressful, in general, whereas husbands considered job-related and financial concerns to be more stressful.

The researchers found that stressors have an additive effect. The greater the number of stressors, the more likely a family is to experience emotional, relational, and health difficulties. In short, the more troubles we have, the more likely we are to become physically and emotionally ill, and the more likely our family relationships are to suffer.

Stress-Related Symptoms

Reported symptoms of stress, from most common to least common, were:

1. Irritability.
2. Weight problems.
3. Muscle tension or anxiety.
4. Use of prescription drugs.
5. Difficulty relaxing.
6. Use of tobacco.
7. Depression.
8. Headaches.
9. Frequent colds or flu.
10. Difficulty sleeping.

Parents generally reported more symptoms of stress than children. Wives reported more symptoms than husbands.

Coping with Stress

The families were asked how they coped with life's stressors. They ranked their stress-management techniques in descending order:

1. Attending church services.
2. Sharing concerns with friends.
3. Facing problems head-on and trying to find solutions.
4. Participating in church activities.
5. Sharing difficulties and doing things with relatives.
6. Seeking information and advice from the family doctor.
7. Seeking information and advice from people in other families who had faced similar problems.
8. Asking for and accepting help from neighbors.
9. Seeking help from community agencies and programs.
10. Seeking professional counseling.

If the signs appear in a family, the family needs to find help. First and foremost, the results point to the importance of talking. The researchers found the most common coping skill to be talking to other family members, relatives, friends, and professionals.

Source: Adapted from "Stress, Coping and Adaptation in the Middle Years of the Family Life Cycle," by the Cooperative Extension Service, Iowa State University, Ames, on research conducted by the North Central Regional Committee 164. Agriculture Research Service, U.S. Department of Agriculture, Washington, DC, 1989.

many years they have left rather than how many they've already lived (1968). One middle-aged man described life as a rainbow: At the beginning are infancy, early childhood, adolescence, and young adulthood; around the very highest point of the rainbow are the middle years; and nearing the end of the rainbow are the later years of life. When one reaches the crest of the rainbow, the middle years, one can clearly see the remainder of life for the first time. "When I reached middle age," the man explained, "I saw the rest of my life clearly. It looked like more of the same old stuff I had grown tired of over the past 10 years. Some people might call it a middle-aged crisis," he continued. "I thought of it as a middle-aged opportunity, and I've been changing steadily ever since."

The post–World War II Baby Boom period ran from 1946 to 1964. Now this group of Americans is well into middle age. The U.S. Bureau of the Census takes detailed snapshots of the age of the population every 10 years and for analysis purposes divides people into 5-year age groups. One interesting finding from the 2000 Census data was the dramatic increase in the 50- to 54-year-old group. Between 1990 and 2000, this Baby Boomer group grew 55%, making it the fastest-growing group in America. The second-fastest-growing group for the same time period was the 45 to 49 age group, which grew 45% (U.S. Bureau of the Census, 2000a).

Because of the growing numbers of Baby Boomers, they will put increasing pressure on society to focus more on retirement, health care, and empty-nest issues. Their buying power will impact consumer goods and health care systems. While our society is often portrayed as a youth-oriented culture, Baby Boomers will have a growing impact on shifting more attention to their group.

One of the biggest changes of middle age is the children's departure from home for college or a job. Parents who are flexible usually enjoy the freedom from daily responsibility for their children and are likely to develop new interests or even start new careers.

Middle Age: A Crisis or Opportunity?

For some, **midlife crisis** is an apt term. During their 40s and 50s, many people will experience the death of a parent or family member, career changes, physical changes in appearance and health, and noticeable changes in relationships with a spouse and children. The realization that one's life is half over and that many goals have not been attained or that there is nothing new to look forward to can cause emotional upheaval.

Despite this common perception—and even the popularity of the term *midlife crisis*—evidence does not support the existence of a generalized midlife crisis. Although people do experience crisis and stress at important transition points in life, including midlife, data show that midlife is not any more stressful than other life stages. In fact, midlife is often a time of stability, freedom, and control, as well as a time to redefine life and relationships.

Statistically, midlife does not bring about an increase in divorce, depression, suicide, or alcoholism. In fact, a survey found that people in their 40s find life more exciting than younger or older adults (National Opinion Research Center, 1996). With age comes greater work satisfaction and satisfaction with one's finances, a reduction in depression, and a rise in one's general happiness. Additionally, older people are less likely to divorce than younger people, and suicide rates drop during middle age (National Opinion Research Center, 1996). In fact, the statistics in Figure 13.1 suggest that *early life* is more a time of crisis than midlife.

The Middle-Aged Person and the Working World

Many people in their 20s and 30s bounce from job to job. Sooner or later, however, these people (especially members of the middle class) settle into a relatively comfortable position—one that provides a reasonably good income, requires expertise, and involves interaction with amiable co-workers. The job, in short, becomes as comfortable as an old shoe. After 10 or 15 years, though, job satisfaction may level off because of **routinization**. It might be years (or possibly never) before there's any chance for a lateral move or promotion.

Middle-aged people can feel trapped by their work. Making a career change in midlife, however, can be risky: The tradeoff for a new, more interesting job may be a pay cut. If a person cannot figure out how to make the old job fulfilling again, however, boredom, anxiety, or anger may reach the boiling point. Fights with bosses and co-workers (and one's family) often have their roots in these common middlescent developments.

Women who return to college or to work outside the home when their children reach a more independent age find themselves at the onset of a second, distinct career in their lives. Middle-aged women returning to the work marketplace after a long absence are at a certain disadvantage because they lack up-to-date on-the-job experience. Although they may have acquired tremendous insights and skills from their work in the home and in the community that would translate well on the job, they sometimes experience discrimination. Employers may demean their talents. Worse yet, women themselves often do not realize how competent they are and suffer from feelings of inferiority.

The good news about this two-career approach to life is that just when one career, parenthood, is running out of steam and may be becoming burdensome, a new career in the working world is waiting in the wings. Delighted with her new job teaching at a community college, one woman stated, "I've been recycled. I've

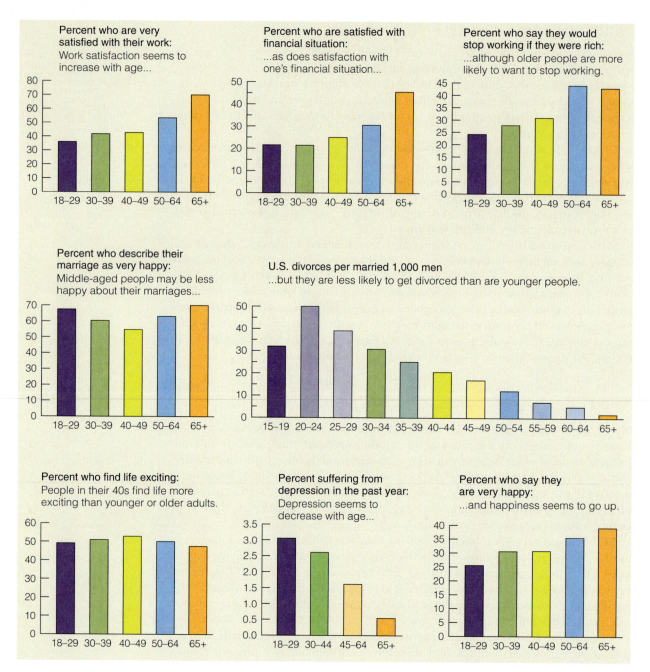

FIGURE 13.1

Personal Satisfaction of Adults by Age Group

Source: General Social Survey, National Opinion Research Center, 1996 University of Chicago. Used with permission.

been a mother of four children for 15 years. And now I'm a *person* again!" At age 42, to use a common expression, she was "born again."

Sexuality in Middle Age

As noted in Chapter 6, sexual activity often declines steadily over the years of a marriage, as stress and boredom take their toll. Fortunately, among couples who are creative and committed, sex can remain a source of intense pleasure throughout the middle years. Two issues of concern during this time are menopause and "male menopause."

People between the ages of 43 and 50 usually come to terms with life, and are able to more realistically assess their strengths and weaknesses.

Menopause. The most dramatic age-related change in female reproductive functioning, after puberty, is **menopause**, the end of monthly menstrual periods. Sheehy (1998) refers to menopause as the "silent passage" because it is so rarely discussed openly. Menopause occurs, on average, around the age of 50 but can begin as early as a woman's mid-30s or as late as her early 60s. Because of various hormonal changes, menopause signals the cessation of a woman's ability to have children. Reproductive organs shrink, and the amount of fatty tissue in the breasts and other parts of the body decreases. The vulva becomes thinner, losing its capacity to engorge with blood, and the vagina shrinks and loses some elasticity. Vaginal secretions that provide lubrication during intercourse diminish.

Many women experience distress—including irritability, insomnia, "hot flashes," headaches, and depression—during menopause. Some physicians recommend taking hormones orally, by injection, or by use of a transdermal patch to relieve these symptoms, which result from hormonal imbalances. Hormone replacement therapy is a common approach to relieving some of the discomfort that menopause can bring. It can also minimize the loss of bone mass that can occur after menopause. Recent evidence suggests that hormone therapy is not appropriate for all women and raises questions about long-term use of hormone therapy. Taking hormone therapy for more than 5 years is no longer recommended (Beers, 2003).

In general, most women perceive menopause as a transition period rather than a problem. Even though physical responses change, a woman's perception of pleasure and satisfaction during intercourse remain the same or may even increase. A number of factors may be involved, including freedom from fear of pregnancy and the fact that the couple may be rediscovering each other after losing contact during the challenging full-time parenting years (Beers, 2003; Hyde & DeLamater, 2003).

"Male Menopause." Sexual changes related to age also occur in men. Production of the male hormone **androgen** declines slowly and steadily in most men until about age 60, when it levels off. For most men, this decline in hormone production does not cause the emotional and physical changes that some women experience during menopause. In other men, the symptoms are so similar to those experienced by menopausal women that physicians label the condition **male menopause**, a term that generates some controversy in the medical community.

As men get older, the amount of fluid ejaculated with orgasm tends to diminish, as does the strength of the ejaculation. The testicles become smaller and less firm; erections become less frequent and also less rigid. By age 50, the average male may require 8 to 24 hours after orgasm before he is capable of having another erection. Most men also require more time to reach orgasm, but this can be viewed as a benefit, as a lengthening of the period of pleasure for both the man and his partner (Hyde & DeLamater, 2003).

The Middle-Aged Marriage

Many marriages are happier before children arrive and after they leave home. For many couples in the middle years, marital satisfaction may reach a low point and then increase as the adolescents leave home.

Strengthening Marriage in the Middle Years. A great deal can be learned about marriage from divorced people. Based on interviews with those who have experienced marital dissolution, here are some suggestions for strengthening marriage in the middle years:

- Establish priorities early in marriage, with the spouse at the top of the list. Do not allow parenthood to overshadow the marriage.
- Be alert for warning signs of marital problems, which include nagging, sarcasm, possessiveness, criticism, and personal discontent.
- Strive toward equality in all aspects of the marriage. Each partner should feel important and powerful.
- Seek a balance between togetherness and personal growth; either extreme can be harmful to a marriage.
- Good sex in a relationship in the middle years does not come naturally; it is a result of a positive daily life together.
- Develop a network of friendships with other couples who are concerned about maintaining a quality marriage.
- Evaluate the marriage from time to time and attend a marriage enrichment workshop.
- Avoid boring or frustrating work situations; a midlife career change may be beneficial.
- Consider a lifestyle change rather than a partner change in middle age to add pizzazz to the marriage.
- A happy marriage is the key to a content spouse. The best way to deal with infidelity is to prevent it from occurring.

Successful middle-aged couples tend to be those who have shared feelings and activities throughout their marriage, in spite of the competing demands of jobs and children. They continue to express love and concern both verbally and physically.

Increasing Divorce During the Middle Years

A study of middle-aged couples who got divorced found the participants emerged from the difficulties of later-life divorce far happier and emotionally healthier than most of them would have dared to hope at the beginning of their journey (Enright, 2004; Kornblum, 2004). They surveyed 1,147 men and women, ages 40 to 79, who divorced in their 40s, 50s, or 60s. The researchers found that 66% of the women said they had asked for the divorce, while 41% of the men said they asked for the divorce. More men were caught off guard by the coming divorce than women (26% to 14%). Men were likely to remarry sooner.

Sociologist Andrew Cherlin believes the number of people ending long-term marriages after age 50 is steadily increasing. "The divorce rate has risen for all adults at all ages over the past decades," Cherlin noted. Why? As people's prospects for a long life have increased over the past decades, many are leaving unhappy marriages in quest of many more happy years ahead (Enright, 2004).

There is no epidemic of divorce among middle- and later-year adults, though, according to Cherlin. "But compared to older people a generation or two ago, they are more likely to divorce. You had almost no divorce among the elderly a half-century ago; now you have a bit" (Kornblum, 2004).

An AARP study found the top causes of divorce for women were (1) verbal, physical, or emotional abuse (23%); (2) alcohol or drug abuse (18%); and (3) cheating. The top causes of divorce cited by men were (1) no obvious problems, simply fell out of love (17%); (2) cheating (14%); and (3) different values, lifestyles (14%) (Kornblum, 2004). About 70% of those who had initiated the divorce, looking back, felt they had done the right thing (Enright, 2004).

Empty Nest, Spacious Nest, or Cluttered Nest?

The term **empty-nest syndrome** describes the feelings of malaise, emptiness, and lack of purpose that parents sometimes experience when their children leave home. Some parents do suffer from these feelings, and most go through a period of adjustment when their children leave the nest. But the empty nest is a boon for many parents, giving them more time and energy to invest in their marriage. To emphasize the positive aspects of this time, we prefer the term **spacious nest**. There is more room in the home for the parents' things—and more money and time in the marriage for each other.

The opposite of the spacious nest is the parental nest refilled with **boomerang kids**—adult children who return home for economic reasons, because of divorce, the need to find a safety net, extended education, drug/alcohol problems, or during a temporary transition period. The stereotypic image of this situation is of a self-centered young adult returning home to place an unfair economic burden on parents who resent the invasion of their new-found privacy. While this image may represent the experience of some, boomerang children are for the most part well tolerated by parents as long as the return home is temporary and does not happen too many times (Bold, 2004).

Today, middle-aged parents of young adults are less likely to find themselves with empty nests than were their counterparts 30 years ago. More young adults are postponing marriage or are marrying and divorcing. A phenomenon called the **cluttered nest** occurs when adult children return to the parental nest to live after college graduation while they get established professionally and financially and save enough money to move into their own apartments or homes.

As one middle-aged mother in suburban Washington, D.C., asked rhetorically when recalling the time her daughter had returned home with two preschool-aged children after her divorce:

> *"What was I supposed to do? Slam the door in her face? She had no money. Her husband's lawyer was threatening to take the kids away, and she was so depressed I thought she might overdose on pills. I had to help. I love my daughter and I love my grandchildren.*
>
> *"I knew they wouldn't be with us forever. I knew she would be getting back on her feet soon enough. I knew I could help. What are families for?"*

Caught in the Middle: The Sandwich Generation

Besides struggling with adolescents, empty or cluttered nests, and boomerang kids, people in their middle years are also apt to have growing responsibilities for their aging parents. For this reason, middle-aged parents have been described as the **sandwich generation**. Researchers agree that daughters are more likely to assume the caregiving role than sons, and somewhere between half and two-thirds of adult women will assume this role at some time in their lives (Cicirelli, 2001, 2003).

Caring for an elderly family member can be a burden for the caregiver, but it can also increase intimacy between a parent and an adult child. One study of 133 pairs of adult caregiving daughters and their elderly mothers reported that about half the mothers and daughters saw their relationship as having been positively affected by the caregiving situation, whereas most of the rest reported no change in the quality of their relationships (Walker & McGraw, 1999).

For some middle-aged parents, though, the stress of caring for their children—whether adolescents or young adults—and for frail aging parents can be too great. Exhaustion and anger can reach a boiling point and can create intergenerational conflicts. These can also produce neglect or abuse of the elderly, which unfortunately is relatively common in the United States (National Center on Elder Abuse, 2004).

Caring for children and aging parents can cause stress for the marriage relationship (Skogrand et al., 2006). A married couple may be looking forward to freedom from caregiving responsibilities and to renewing that spark in their relationship. The opposite happens—instead there is added stress. There is evidence that having a healthy marriage going into the sandwich generation phase of life provides much needed support for the spouse who has the major responsibility for caring for two generations (Skogrand et al., 2006). It is, therefore, important to maintain a strong marriage relationship through the childrearing years, in preparation for what is sometimes a stressful time in life.

Grandparenthood

If I had known grandchildren would be this fun, I would have had them first.
—BUMPER STICKER

The most recent data available from a national survey of people aged 65 or older reveal that 75% have living grandchildren. Many people become grandparents long before age 65; the first grandchild is often born when grandparents are in their early or mid-40s (Aldous, 1998; Troll, 1997), with one-third of one's life being spent as a grandparent (Thiele & Whelan, 2006).

For most people, grandparent–grandchild interaction is very enjoyable. Three-fourths of all grandparents have contact with their grandchildren weekly. Although grandparents are not directly responsible for the well-being of their grandchildren, they do have a vested interest in their development (Westman, 1998).

In a summary of the current research about grandparents, several dimensions of the grandparent role have been identified by Thiele and Whelan (2006). These aspects or dimensions include grandparents' attitudes and expectations, grandparent behaviors, the symbolic meaning of grandparenthood, and the affective outcome or feeling of satisfaction of grandparents.

- *Grandparents' attitudes and expectations.* The role is ambiguous, and grandparents have little control over how it plays out. There may be an expectation that there will be frequent contact with their grandchildren and that may or may not happen.

- *Grandparent behavior.* There is no single way for grandparents to behave. In some cultures where the elderly are viewed as authority figures, the relationship with grandchildren may be very formal. In other cultures, the expectation is that grandparents are fun loving and warm.
- *Symbolic meaning of grandparenthood.* Some grandparents view their role as a source of status. Others view their role as emotional self-fulfillment. Still others see the grandparent role as their opportunity to be a teacher to the next generation.
- *Grandparent satisfaction.* How enjoyable or how happy grandparents are in their role varies. The vast majority are very satisfied and happy with their role, but a small minority are not. The greatest satisfaction seems to come when involvement is moderate, not detached, but not providing custodial care.

The role of grandparents may differ greatly in different cultural groups. As Thiele and Whelan (2006) noted, some cultures view the elderly in ways that affect their relationship with grandchildren. For example, in a study conducted with American Indian grandparents, researchers found that these grandparents did many of the typical things all grandparents do such as doing a variety of activities with their grandchildren and providing unconditional love (Robbins, Scherman, Holman, & Wilson, 2005). In addition, however, these grandparents also engaged in activities where they had the opportunity to pass on American Indian traditions and knowledge. Almost all of the participants in this study were concerned that tribal culture would be lost if their grandchildren did not learn about it and pass these traditions on to future generations.

Thinking about one's relationship with one's own grandparents might help clarify the dimensions described by Thiele and Whelan (2006). What was your relationship with your grandparents like? What kind of a grandparent do you want to be?

By and large, the grandparent role is mutually enjoyable for grandparents and grandchildren, and it gives the parents a welcome break. Although grandparenting can sometimes overwhelm and tire out grandparents, the role is generally pleasurable: "I can enjoy these kids so much now . . . so much more than I really could my own kids. I don't have to worry about them. Their mom and dad can do the worrying."

Grandparents Raising Grandchildren

The number of grandparents raising their grandchildren has grown in recent years and is expected to continue to grow. Current statistics show that 6.3% of all U.S. children are being parented by their grandparents (Dolbin-MacNab, 2006). Grandparents are typically raising their grandchildren because of problems that exist with the parents of the grandchildren such as substance abuse, HIV/AIDS, mental illness, neglect or abuse, incarceration, or divorce (Dolbin-MacNab, 2006). For many adults in the grandparenting role, it means that they can care for their grandchildren, spoil them, and then give them back to the parents. For other grandparents, however, grandparenting means caring for their grandchildren in the same way they cared for their own children—taking care of their physical and emotional needs 24/7 (Dolbin-MacNab, 2006). In some cases, grandparents are providing care for several grandchildren, who may come from several different families, and they also may be caring for their own children (Bachman & Chase-Lansdale, 2005).

The amount of stress experienced by grandparents raising grandchildren is extensive with concerns about finances, parenting issues, and their own health (Bachman & Chase-Lansdale, 2005; Goodman & Silverstein, 2006; Ross & Aday, 2006). These researchers indicate the need for financial and emotional support for grandparents as they are highly committed, but highly stressed as they care for their grandchildren.

African American children are more likely to be raised by their grandparents than children of other cultural groups, including Whites (Gibson, 2005; Goodman & Silverstein, 2006). Statistics show that 5% of White grandchildren are being raised by grandparents, 15% of African American children, and 9% of Latino children (Ross & Aday, 2006). One researcher suggests that custodial grandparenting is more prevalent in the African American community because, historically, members of this cultural group have cared for their own rather than have children placed in the social service system (Gibson, 2005). Black women are most likely to care for their grandchildren because of parental drug use and incarceration (Gibson, 2005).

Goodman and Silverstein (2006) studied the differences among African American, Latina, and White custodial grandmothers. They found that African American and Latina grandmothers raised their grandchildren more often because of financial reasons, and White grandmothers were more likely to raise their grandchildren because of some other dire parental circumstances such as parental substance abuse, child neglect, and parental mental health issues. These researchers also found that Latina and African American custodial grandparents were less likely to experience extreme stress than White grandmothers in raising their grandchildren. These authors suggest that White grandmothers are more likely to expect their adult children to be independent, and, therefore, when they must intervene and become caregivers of their grandchildren, it creates a sense of disappointment in their child, which adds to the stress.

Because they do not have to bother with the daily chores of childrearing, grandparents are free to develop a more creative relationship with their grandchildren, sharing activities and interests with them. For most grandparents, one of the greatest satisfactions of grandparenthood is seeing a continuation of their family through another generation.

Family Life in the Later Years

The later years of life can be bittersweet. For those who were successful in raising a family and planning for retirement, the later years are easier than for those who have family or financial problems. Some older adults experience loneliness and isolation. Many must make do on limited funds. And elder abuse by younger family members occurs in some families.

Although many studies of older people have focused on the negative aspects of aging, a recent study demonstrated that many people become happier as they age. Mroczek and Spiro (2003) found that older men, especially those who are married, are happier than are younger men. Older men seem to regulate their emotions more effectively and are more able to maximize the positive and minimize the negative. In a sample of 2,727 men from ages 25 to 74, the older men reported having fewer negative emotions and, in general, were happier than the younger men. Younger people reported feeling sad, nervous, hopeless, or worthless more often than did older participants. Thus, aging seems to have some positive aspects when it comes to emotions.

American society is going through a "demographic revolution" as the life span of the population increases. In 1900, the average life expectancy was 47 years; life span has increased to 77.2 now. The gap between males and females was 5.4 in 2001, and the average longevity was 74.4 for men and 79.8 for women (Arias & Smith, 2003).

Because of increased life expectancy, American society is growing older. Trends indicate that the population of older persons is increasing rapidly. The number of people over age 65 in the United States is currently 12.3%, and that percentage is expected to increase by 20% by the year 2030 (Karasik, 2005). In 1970, there were roughly 7.5 million people over the age of 75, and by 1999, that number had more than doubled to 16.3 million. Individuals over 85 years of age numbered about 1.4 million in 1970 and almost tripled to 4.17 million by 1999 (U.S. Bureau of the Census, 2000a, table 12, p. 13).

Defining Old Age

Old age is often said to begin at 65, which in our society is the typical age of retirement. But any exact chronological starting point for old age is bound to be arbitrary. In some parts of the world where life expectancy is lower, a person might be old at a much earlier age. Even in our own society, we see enormous variation among older adults. We all know active 75-year-olds and tired 50-year-olds.

Older adults are often divided into distinct groups: (1) the young-old, those between 55 and 65, who are still working and at the peak of their social and vocational status; (2) the middle-old, those between 65 and 75, who tend to be retired and in good health and have abundant time to follow their interests; (3) the old-old, those over age 75, who as a group tend to be the frailest, loneliest, and poorest of the old. Some observers add a fourth group, the frail old. Even though the old-old tend to have the most health problems as a group, there are frail old people represented among the young-old and middle-old groups as well. By adding this fourth category, one is signifying clearly the fact that human beings, for a variety of reasons, grow old at different rates.

Aging is in part a *psychological phenomenon*. How an older person feels depends to some degree on her or his mental attitude toward both the accomplishments of the past and the possibilities for the future. For most purposes, a person who feels "young at heart" is still young. Of course, aging is also a *biological reality*, and some variations among older adults are a result of their different genetic heritages. Aging is also a *social phenomenon*. If society forces people into retirement at 65, it is in effect declaring them to be old. Similarly, there are compelling data to argue that one's social standing or social class directly affects one's health and life expectancy. Similar to chickens, people have a pecking order, and the higher level of status one holds in the human pecking order, the longer, happier, and healthier one's life is likely to be (Marmot, 2004). Finally, aging is part of the family process, one that occurs in the context of ongoing interpersonal relationships with spouses, parents, children, and other family members whose attitudes help us define and redefine ourselves as we grow older.

Despite the challenges of aging—the lower energy levels, the failing eyesight or poor hearing, the serious health problems—many people adapt to these changes and continue to live fruitful lives. How we as individuals, and as members of families and communities, define the later years powerfully influences our well-being during this time.

Conventional Wisdom About Old Age

Grow old along with me! The best is yet to be, The last of life, for which the first was made.

—ROBERT BROWNING (1864/1970, p. 811)

Many people in our society accept the conventional wisdom about old age, most of which is negative. It is important, though, that we set the record straight about these false beliefs, which foster a form of prejudice known as **ageism**, prejudging an older person negatively solely on the basis of age. In the following discussion, we hope to deconstruct some of the most common myths about old age.

At 65, You're "Over the Hill." Attitude has a good deal to do with how "old" one is. People whose attitudes toward life remain positive generally lead happier and more fulfilling lives in their later years. Many symptoms popularly associated with old age—cognitive impairment, falling, dizziness, loss of bladder control, and loss of appetite—are symptoms of disease, not of normal aging.

Most Older Adults Are Poor. Actually, the financial situation for most people 50 and above is relatively good. The American Association of Retired Persons (AARP) reports that by looking at the entire 50-plus population over the last 20 years, one can see that incomes are up 18% and wealth has increased by 36%. Poverty has declined dramatically among older people, especially among older retirees. But AARP cites a major threat to financial security among older people: Many people retire middle class but die poor because of the cost of health care (Nicholson, 2001).

Government figures indicate that median annual income decreases after people reach about age 55. For example, households with adult members ages 45 to 54 have the highest median income before taxes: $54,148. In households with adult members ages 55 to 64, median income before taxes is $43,167; for the 65-and-older age group, median income falls to $21,729 (U.S. Bureau of the Census, 2001g). Keep in mind, though, that most of those over age 65 own their own home free and clear, and their household expenses are generally lower because their children no longer live with them.

Older couples often have more time to enjoy leisure activities together and see renewed happiness in their marriage. They may also return to hobbies or activities they previously did not have time to enjoy while working.

AARP argues that our culture swings back and forth, sometimes stereotyping all elderly as "being poor and having to eat dog or cat food to stay alive," and sometimes stereotyping all elderly "as living on golf courses and having yachts and fancy cars" (Deets, 1996). Since Social Security was created in the 1930s and Medicare in the 1960s, the poverty rate has dropped substantially among the elderly. In 1959 when the first data were collected on poverty and older Americans, rates have dropped from about 30% to 10.4% in 2002 (Proctor & Dalaker, 2003).

But group data do not tell the whole story. Some older people are doing relatively well. For example, White men who are able to hold onto good jobs throughout their whole careers have a much lower poverty rate, 7% or 8%, while single women have a higher poverty rate, and among single non-White women the poverty rate can be as high as 40% to 50% (Deets, 1996).

Older Adults Lose Their Sex Drive. Young people have a hard time imagining that their parents make love, let alone their grandparents and great-grandparents. Nonetheless, most older people enjoy sex, but they have sexual intercourse less often than when they were younger (AARP, 1999). In one study of 202 healthy retirement home residents ages 80 to 102, the researchers found that 88% of the men and 72% of the women fantasized about being intimate with a partner. Sexual feelings and sexual behaviors can continue across the life span. Notable exceptions are people who have some kind of physical disability and those who believe they shouldn't enjoy sex at their age.

The *Janus Report*, a national survey of sexual behavior, reported that sexual activity was higher in men than in women. There was some decrease in frequency as people became older, but the rate did not decrease as dramatically as many assumed.

An American Association of Retired Persons survey of 1,384 men and women found that about two out of three people were very satisfied or extremely satisfied with their physical relationships (AARP, 1999). As one 83-year-old widow said: "Physical satisfaction is not the only aim of sex. We seek the nearness of someone throughout the lonely nights of people in their 70s and 80s. We need someone to hold, hug and confide in" (Johnson, 2004, p. 1).

Older Adults Are Usually Sick. People over 65 have about half as many *acute* illnesses as those between 17 and 44. It is true, of course, that *chronic* conditions tend to accumulate over time, and older adults commonly suffer from sensory losses—hearing, vision, and taste. But as the American Association of Retired Persons points out, these problems do not keep most older adults from enjoying an active, healthy life. People who have adapted to change throughout life will likely find ways to cope with most of the changes that aging brings.

Older Adults Become Senile. The term *senility* is not often used by gerontologists today because it has little specific meaning. Although brain damage can be caused by a series of small strokes, most progressive organic brain impairment is caused by disease, such as Alzheimer's disease. Assuming that memory loss or change in behavior in older adults is a function of age can cause one to overlook a disease that might be successfully treated. All too often, people attribute an older person's anger or depression to old age, when, in fact, it may be due to a life occurrence that would cause similar symptoms in a younger individual (Rybash, 1999).

Most Older Adults End Up in Nursing Homes. Actually, about 43% of 65-year-olds are likely to spend some time in a nursing home before they die (a 52% chance for elderly women and a 33% chance for elderly men). The likelihood of being in a nursing home increases with age: 1.4% of those aged 65 to 74 are in a nursing home; 6% of those aged 75 to 84; and 24% of those 85 and older. Four out of five elderly with long-term care needs live in the community. Only one in five persons with such needs lives in a nursing home. Few families abandon their loved ones in their later years, and few families wantonly "warehouse" older members to a nursing home (American Association of Homes and Services for the Aging, 2004).

Older people are placed in a nursing home for a number of reasons: advancing age; a greater level of chronic disability; deteriorating mental and physical capacities; living alone, or lack of family members to provide help; female gender (women tend to outlive their husbands and end up alone); White race (Whites are twice as likely to enter nursing homes as Blacks); and time spent in a hospital or other health facility. About three out of four nursing home residents are aged 75 or older, and 7 out of 10 are women. The nursing home industry argues that the vast majority of nursing homes have dedicated staffs and try very hard to meet the needs of infirm older people (American Association of Homes and Services for the Aging, 2004).

Most Older Adults Are Lonely. The conventional wisdom brings to mind a picture of a frail old man sadly looking off into space, housed in a nursing home with no loved ones or friends visiting him until the day he quietly dies. There are certainly cases like this, but older adults as a group are not necessarily lonely. Some researchers studying loneliness have found that it increases with age, being the strongest among the oldest age groups. Some researchers have found that loneliness decreases with advancing age. And some researchers have found no statistical relationship between age and loneliness (Hall & Havens, 2004).

Loneliness is likely to increase in old age as family and friendship networks become smaller. Social contacts tend to decrease after retirement and may continue to decline with the death of family members, friends, change in residence after losing one's spouse, mobility difficulties, and poor health. To prevent feelings of isolation and loneliness, it is recommended that individuals keep in regular contact with older family members, friends, and neighbors and help them feel needed and valued. Local communities and groups are advised to increase the availability of programs and services for older people, enhance transportation programs for the elderly, develop low-cost leisure and educational activities, and involve older people in all levels of planning these services (Hall & Havens, 2004).

Older Adults Are Isolated from Younger Family Members. Research indicates that older people are usually not alienated from their families (Ikkink, van Tilburg, & Knipscheer, 1999). A national study (Troll, 1997) found that more than half of all people over age 65 who have children live either in the same household with an adult child or in the same neighborhood as a child. Contact with other family members, especially adult children, is rather frequent.

Most older adults enjoy their privacy, preferring not to live in the same house as their adult children and their grandchildren. Of older people who have adult children but live alone, however, half live within 10 minutes from a child. On the day they were interviewed for this study, half of the older people with children reported that they had seen one of their adult children the day they were interviewed, and about three-quarters reported having seen at least one of their adult children during the week preceding the interview. This study also revealed that even in those cases where the geographic distance between them is considerable, older and younger family members tend to stay in contact.

What about the quality of these contacts—a much more difficult characteristic to measure? One way to measure quality is to assess the amount of help family members give each other. In a national study, 7 out of every 10 older adults with children said they helped their children, and 7 out of every 10 older adults said they helped their grandchildren. Five out of every 10 said they even helped their great-grandchildren. Seven out of 10 older people also said they received help from their children. This help included home repairs and housework, care during an illness, and different kinds of gifts. In addition, older people reported that they helped their adult children by caring for grandchildren. In short, it appears that older people are not isolated from younger family members and that these contacts are generally happy ones (Allen, Blieszner, & Roberto, 2000).

Retirement

The stereotypical view of retirement is a dreary, downhill period of life in which people lose their self-esteem and immerse themselves in memories of better days; they stop being productive working citizens and slowly waste away. To the contrary, research shows that retired people are no more likely to be sick or depressed than people of the same age who are still on the job. In fact, most people adapt satisfactorily to retirement, with few long-term changes in their health, psychological well-being, or family relationships.

There are, of course, examples of people who find retirement difficult and depressing. One woman said of her recently retired husband, "He used to be a powerful executive with 200 employees under him. He would work long, hard hours and then come home to relax and enjoy his hobbies. He retired 5 years ago, and ever since he's been terribly depressed."

Fortunately, positive retirement stories are the general rule. Most men and women report they adjust quite well to voluntary retirement, and studies consistently find that satisfaction with life remains fairly high for the majority of retired people. Those who have difficulty with retirement are often people who have had difficulty making major transitions in life, people who are shy or lonely, and people with few instrumental (task-oriented or proactive) and communal (social) abilities (Fletcher & Hansson, 1991). Factors predicting a positive adjustment to retirement include good health (many older people leave the workforce because of poor health), economic security, and a supportive social network (Darkwa, 2004; Elderly Health Services, 2004).

Most older people adjust well to voluntary retirement, especially those who get involved in new activities.

As with any major life transition, retirement takes some adjustment. Retired people report a number of problems associated with this transition, including sleeplessness, aimlessness, and sadness over not seeing work friends and colleagues regularly. But other retirees are quick to point out that they have gotten involved in so many new activities that they have less free time than they did when they were working and would like to slow down a bit.

Retirement affects marriage in different ways. For couples who place a high value on intimacy and family relationships, retirement can bring more freedom to enjoy each other and the family. Some wives—especially those who always assumed traditional roles and traditional divisions of labor—are pessimistic about the husband's impending retirement, perhaps fearing the retiree will intrude on their domestic territory.

Long-Term Marriages

Stereotypes about older couples abound in our society. One common belief is that if you have survived many years together, you must be getting along extremely well. Counter to this opinion is the anonymous thought that, "Marriage is forever. And forever is a damned long time."

A number of family researchers have studied long-term marriages, trying to get closer to the truth. From their findings, George Rowe and Marcia Lasswell were able to divide **longevous marriages**—marriages that last 50 years or more—into three categories: (1) couples who are very happy and blissfully in love, (2) couples who are very unhappy but who continue the marriage out of habit or fear, and (3) couples in between, who are neither very happy nor very unhappy and accept the situation (cited in Sweeney, 1982). Lasswell estimated the "very happy" number at roughly 20% of the total and the "very unhappy" number at 20%. Both researchers also found a negative relationship between the number of children couples had and marital happiness: Couples with larger families tended to have less happy marriages. "We can't explain that, except the study indicated that a dip in marital happiness is almost always concurrent with the time the children are a heavy responsibility for parents," Rowe said (p. 23). He theorized that the more children a couple has, the longer this period of responsibility lasts and the more the relationship is drained by parenting responsibilities.

The death of a spouse is a difficult life transition for most, and for some it is a devastating personal crisis.

> After the loss of a loved one
>
> The years go fast
>
> But the days and nights are long.
>
> —Author Unknown

Brubaker (1990) outlined three characteristic stages of the grieving process:

1. **Crisis-loss stage of grief**. In the first few days and weeks after the loss, the survivor is in a chaotic state of shock. Common reactions are "I can't believe this is happening to me." "I'll do anything to bring her back." "What am I going to do now?"

2. **Transition stage of grief**. In the transition period, the survivor begins trying to create a new life. Grief lessens in its intensity, and the bereaved person sees the possibility of a life ahead.

3. **New-life stage of grief**. The survivor changes her or his lifestyle and proves to the world and to herself or himself that it is possible to live satisfactorily as a single person. The widow or widower develops an identity without the partner.

Grief lasts longer than was long believed to be the case—up to 2 years, according to research on widows. A widow's grief can include a range of feelings, from sadness and anger to fear and anxiety. The prevalence of anxiety in the first 3 years after a husband's death led one researcher to see its role in mourning as crucial. Other researchers see depression as a significant risk among bereaved spouses (Bruce, 2002).

In old age, loved ones with whom one had intimate relationships may no longer be alive, but this does not mean that people no longer feel intimate connections (Troll, 2001/2002). Many older people feel connected to their deceased intimate partners through prayer, photos, visits to the cemetery, and other ways they honor the dead. Commitment and caring are maintained after the death. Cognitive intimacy is maintained by thinking of the departed partner. Though physical encounters cannot continue, some individuals substitute heirlooms or pictures to preserve the physical presence of the loved one. And interdependent intimacy is maintained by hearing the voice of the dead speaking through one's own thoughts.

"Do you talk with Joan?" we asked one elderly husband who had lost his wife to cancer 7 years earlier. "Oh, yes," Bill replied. "She's right here in the kitchen with me now, helping get the coffee and cookies together." Bill maintained his intimate emotional connections with his wife after death and found strength in her presence.

Changes in Family Dynamics in the Later Years

Sibling relationships in middle and older adulthood have recently become a new area of research. Most sibling relationships remain strong and positive throughout the years and are important for the older adult's well-being. Research indicates in the later years that sisters are the closest, followed by cross-sex siblings, and then brothers (Van Volkom, 2006). Sometimes things trigger the opportunity to reconnect in later years, even when siblings had not been particularly close before. A spouse may have died, and relationships with siblings may become closer to fill the void. Here is how two sisters in their 80s developed a closer relationship:

> Two sisters, one age 80 and the other age 86, have always kept in touch but have not been especially close. They live 1,000 miles apart and have led very different lives. One was married to a chemist, and the other was married to a farmer. Over the years they would see each other once every year or two and would talk on the phone occasionally. In recent years, as they entered old age, they began calling each other regularly— usually every day—to talk about the mundane, but personal and real, events of daily life
>
> One was widowed 4 years ago after 56 years of marriage and did quite well in her grief with the help of family and friends in a very close-knit farming community. Recently her sister's husband died suddenly. Because the sister had no family nearby and lived in a large city, she has less family and community support. She began calling her sister in the farming community even more often—sometimes several times a day. They talked about losing husbands, with the one who has been widowed longer providing sage advice for the sister who just recently experienced her husband's death. They developed a very intimate emotional relationship with these frequent telephone conversations, even though they have not seen each other for 2 years.

Stepfamily relationships have also become a new but increasingly common aspect of family dynamics in later years, because people are living longer than ever before and because there are higher rates of divorce and remarriage (Sherman, 2006). Some couples are remarrying, and some are choosing to live together outside of marriage. The opportunity for a "second chance" is wonderful, but family relationships may be complicated. It is difficult to determine who is in the family and who is not when a person remarries in his or her 70s. There are conflicts over money, inheritance, and family possessions. Care of elderly stepparents can be challenging (Sherman, 2006). This is an area where there are few resources and models to help families navigate uncharted territory.

Summary

- Middle age roughly spans ages 35 to 65, a period during which many couples are (1) still raising teenagers, (2) launching young adults and then coping with their absence from or return to the home, and (3) entering retirement.

- For many, the challenges of middle age include coping with routinization in the job, developing a new or second career outside the home (especially for women), coping with the transition of menopause and "male menopause," maintaining the emotional and sexual health of the marriage, dealing with the empty or the cluttered nest, and managing the demands of aging parents.

- Marriages fail in the middle years for five main reasons: verbal, physical, or emotional abuse; alcohol or drug abuse; cheating; "falling out of love"; or different values or lifestyles.

- Recommendations for strengthening a marriage in the middle years include making one's spouse the number-one priority, being alert to warning signs of marital trouble, establishing an equal partnership, helping the spouse feel important and powerful, balancing togetherness and personal growth, working to keep the sexual relationship exciting, networking with other committed couples, evaluating the marriage and attending marriage enrichment workshops, changing frustrating job situations, and changing one's lifestyle rather than one's partner to revitalize the marriage. Happiness is key to a content spouse and is the best way to prevent infidelity from occurring.

- People in their middle years are often "sandwiched" between two or more competing responsibilities: caring for adolescents, dealing with boomerang kids (adult children returning to the parental nest), and caring for their own aging parents. The results can be both positive (a closer relationship between the caregiver and the aging parent) and negative (too much stress).

- Grandparenting reinforces continuity of the generations and brings pleasure to most grandparents. Of those 65 or older, 75% have living grandchildren.

- Today, 6.3% of children are being raised by their grandparents. These grandparents experience stress related to finances, parenting issues, and their own health.

- U.S. society is undergoing a "demographic revolution" due to the increasing life span of its population. Today, average life expectancy is over 77.

- Conventional wisdom about old age includes the following inaccurate beliefs: at 65, you're "over the hill"; most older adults are poor; older adults lose their sex drive; older adults are usually sick; older adults become senile; most older adults end up in nursing homes; most older adults are lonely; and older adults are isolated from younger family members.

- Contrary to stereotypes, retirement is not a negative period of life. Most people who retire voluntarily adapt satisfactorily to retirement, with few long-term effects on their health, psychological well-being, or family relationships.

- Not all marriages of long duration are happy. People stay married out of habit, or fear, or (in about 20% of these marriages) simply because they are very happy or in between or accepting, neither very happy nor unhappy. The fewer the number of children, the happier the marriage seems to be.

- The death of a spouse is a difficult life transition for most and a devastating personal crisis for some. More women than men will lose a spouse. Important factors in successfully coping with the loss of a spouse include maintaining a sense of autonomy (a belief in one's ability to direct one's own life) and being involved in social relationships and community affairs.

Key Terms

middle age	cluttered nest
midlife crisis	sandwich generation
routinization	old age
menopause	ageism
androgen	longevous marriage
male menopause	crisis-loss stage of grief
empty-nest syndrome	transition stage of grief
spacious nest	new-life stage of grief
boomerang kids	

Activities

1. Discuss career issues with a middle-aged man or woman. Ask the individual to trace her or his career development. What conclusions can you come to?
2. Interview your parents (if they are middle-aged) or other middle-aged individuals about the stresses of midlife and their means of coping with them.
3. Interview a middle-aged person who is "sandwiched" between trying to support adolescent or young-adult children and caring for an elderly family member. Prepare 10 or 15 questions for the interview and record 5 or 6 general conclusions.
4. After reading the section on grandparenthood, prepare some questions and interview a grandparent. This can be an easy and rewarding exercise because grandparents and young adults often have an automatic bond.
5. Interview an older couple. Ask them to tell you the story of their family, including information about their parents and grandparents. Focus part of the interview on intergenerational relationships.
6. Write down your feelings about death and share them in a small-group discussion. Record the similarities and differences in the group's observations.

Suggested Readings

AARP. (2001). Web site: http://www.aarp.org. AARP is a large and well-known organization providing information and advocacy for people age 50 and older.

AARP. (2004). AARP guide to Internet resources related to aging. Web site: http://www.aarp.org/internet/resources. Useful for seniors and professionals in gerontology.

Achenbaum, W. A. (2005). *Older Americans, vital communities*. Baltimore: Johns Hopkins University Press.

Aiken, L. R. (2004). *Dying, death, and bereavement* (4th ed.). Mahwah, NJ: Erlbaum. A brief but comprehensive survey of research, writings, and professional practices on death and dying.

Boston Women's Health Book Collective. (2006). *Our bodies, ourselves: Menopause*. New York: Touchstone/Simon & Schuster.

Dolbin-MacNab, M. L. (2006). Just like raising your own? Grandmothers' perceptions of parenting a second time around. *Family Relations, 55*, 564–575.

Kinsella, K., & Velkoff, V. A. (2001). An aging world: 2001. *International Population Reports*. Washington, DC: U.S. Bureau of the Census. Statistics on aging worldwide.

Kirasic, K. C. (2004). *Midlife in context*. New York: McGraw-Hill. Midlife in the context of culture; the impact of gender on how men and women experience midlife; and theoretical positions relating to midlife.

Kornhaber, A. (2004). *The grandparent solution: How parents can build a family team for practical, emotional, and financial success*. San Francisco: Jossey-Bass. Grandparenting lessons "from America's most outspoken grandpa."

Kübler-Ross, E. (2000). *Life lessons: Two experts on death and dying teach us about the mysteries of life and living/Elisabeth Kübler-Ross and David Kessler*. New York: Scribner.

Marmot, M. (2004). *Status syndrome: How your social standing directly affects your health and life expectancy*. New York: Times Books. People, like chickens, live in a pecking order. The higher in the social order, the longer and healthier one's life is likely to be.

Nadeau, J. W. (1998). *Families making sense of death*. Thousand Oaks, CA: Sage. "Well written and provides a rich qualitative analysis of how families make meaning after a significant death."

Skogrand, L., Henderson, K., & Higginbotham, B. (2006). Sandwich generation (fact sheet). Utah State University Cooperative Extension. Web site: http://extension.usu.edu/cooperative.

Van Volkom, M. (2006). Sibling relationships in middle and older adulthood: A review of the literature. *Marriage and Family Review, 40*, 151–170.

Visit the text-specific Online Learning Center at **www.mhhe.com/Olson6** for practice tests, chapter summaries, Web links, Internet exercises, key terms, and flashcards.

14. *Stress, Abuse, and Family Problems*

Intimacy, Strengths, and Diversity

Cross-Cultural Perspectives on Couple and Family Stress

Characteristics of Stress

Stress Across the Family Life Cycle

Family Coping Strategies

Domestic Violence

Physical Abuse and Neglect of Children

Sibling and Child-to-Parent Abuse

Alcohol Problems in Families

Summary

Key Terms

Activities

Suggested Readings

Intimacy, Strengths, and Diversity

Individuals, couples, and families have extraordinary abilities when it comes to facing the many problems in the world today. Couple and family intimacy is one of the most important components in successfully dealing with life's problems. We know that pulling together as a family—using close couple and family bonds—helps us get through difficult times. Developing and maintaining close and intimate relationships with friends and extended family, and relying on those relationships, is important in dealing with difficulties. Intimacy involves sharing feelings, sorrows, and joys, which helps people when there is stress in life.

> One individual had grown up learning to be very independent in life. She had learned that she could handle most crises in life, with little help from friends or family. At age 45 she is going through a divorce and a diagnosis of cancer. Even though she had handled most crises successfully, without relying on others for emotional support, she knew this was different—it was going to be more stressful than anything she had experienced thus far in her life.
>
> She approached two close friends and her sister and asked if she could rely on them as she went through the loss of her marriage and her diagnosis with cancer. She already had a close, intimate relationship with each of these people and now she needed to rely on them for support. Each of the people she approached had the same response of surprise. She had never asked for this kind of emotional support before and, of course, they would be there for as long as she needed.
>
> She called or got together with these close friends and family member when she needed to cry, needed to make decisions, or when she just needed the comfortable presence of someone who cared about her. Along the way she wished she had learned to rely on intimate relationships in getting through difficult times earlier in her life. Why did she wait until she was middleaged before she learned this important lesson?

Contrary to the notion that strength means facing a problem without any help, research indicates that the strength to cope with difficulties comes from the close and intimate relationships with friends and relatives.

Every couple and family will experience challenges. Strong marriages and strong families will be able to weather difficult times more successfully than people in marriages and families that are not strong. This chapter will describe a study about people who experienced a traumatic childhood and relied on their inner strengths along with using other strategies to become healthy adults. People will also tell you that going through difficult times often makes you a better, more caring person. Facing difficulties and coming through the crisis can also result in stronger marriages and families.

There is variability and diversity in how people define problems and difficulties. One of the models of family stress described in this chapter includes the definition the family or individual gives to the event. For example, some cultures have extended-family networks that provide care for children beyond the nuclear family. In such a culture, an adolescent leaving home to live with a relative may not be defined as a crisis. This may be true, for example, in American Indian families. In a culture where children are expected to live with their parents until they are grown, however, this event might be defined as a real crisis as a child running away from home.

Intimacy, strengths, and diversity all play a part in how people deal with family problems. Close relationships provide resiliency and strength in dealing with crises that is not available when one tries to go it alone, and this is likely to be true in all cultures.

Cross-Cultural Perspectives on Couple and Family Stress

The following are some of the aspects of family stress that are common across cultural groups. These are generalized principles that emerged from studying stress in different countries and cultures (Olson, 2004).

- *Families from all cultural groups experience couple and family stress.* Although the causes of couple and family stress and the types of issues that are most stressful may vary by cultural group, all couples and families seem to experience and understand the concept of stress.
- *All stressors either begin or end up in the family.* No matter what the origin of a stressor, it eventually affects the couple and family system and all its members.
- *All couples and families must find resources (internal and/or external) to help them cope with or manage the stress in their lives.* Couples and families from various cultural groups probably differ in the specific resources they use to manage stress. It is common for cultures with stronger extended families to rely on their family networks than on resources within their families. Conversely, families with a stronger nuclear family tend to rely on internal family resources rather than extended families.
- *All couples and families have some internal strengths for managing stress in their systems.* Cross-cultural studies of families have seldom sought to identify family strengths within a cultural group. Instead, they have focused on the problems in families from different cultures. By building on a strengths model, it is possible we will more clearly identify useful coping strategies across cultures.
- *To manage their stress, couples and families tend to first use internal resources (those inside the family system) before seeking external resources (those outside the family system).* Across many cultural groups, most families rely on their internal resources first, seeking external help only after internal resources have proven to be inadequate. In many cultures, the extended family system is considered "the family" rather than the nuclear family system. In families with strong extended-family structures, the major internal resources come from inside the extended family, often with fewer resources from the couple system.

Characteristics of Stress

The Curvilinear Nature of Stress

Hans Selye, a pioneer of stress research, defined stress as "the nonspecific response of the body to any demand made upon it" (1974, p. 14). It is immaterial whether the demand is positive or negative; both create the same physiological response. **Stress** is the body's reaction to the demands of life. **Stressors** are external events that cause an emotional and/or a physical reaction. Although people often think of stress as negative, its impact depends on how it is viewed by each individual. Stress is a very personal issue.

Stress has a **curvilinear relationship** with effective outcomes in that both too much and too little stress are problematic for individual and family functioning,

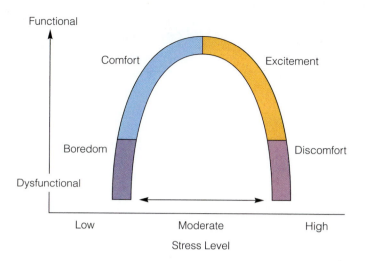

FIGURE 14.1

The Curvilinear Nature of Stress

but moderate levels of stress are usually positive (Figure 14.1). Thor Dahl (1980) described four reactions to different levels of stress: boredom, comfort, excitement, and discomfort. Too little stress is unhealthy and is associated with boredom and lack of motivation. Too much stress is also unhealthy and leads to feelings of discomfort, or **distress**. Low-to-moderate levels of stress are healthy and can feel comfortable. Moderate-to-high levels of stress can also be healthy, creating excitement and energy. This motivating, positive kind of stress is called **eustress**.

A paradoxical aspect of stress is that individuals continually need to seek an appropriate balance between too much and too little stress. This dynamic balance can often be difficult to achieve; most people feel pushed toward higher levels of stress. A major goal of life is to cope with stressors effectively. Happiness is not so much the absence of stress as it is the ability to manage stress effectively.

Stress and Life Events

The classic work of Thomas H. Holmes, Richard H. Rahe, and their colleagues (Holmes & Ella, 1989; Holmes & Rahe, 1967) has greatly influenced much of the current research on the relationship between life changes and signs of emotional and physiological stress in individuals. These researchers developed a scale of 43 "life events" that require some type of change of behavior, or readjustment. The scale is called the Holmes and Rahe Social Readjustment Rating Scale, but it is often referred to as the Holmes and Rahe Stress Test. These life events include personal, family, financial, and occupational stressors. Table 14.1 lists the top 14 stressors identified by Holmes and Rahe. It is noteworthy that 11 of the top 14 stressors are marriage and family issues. In fact, the scale could legitimately be called a Marriage and Family Stress Test.

Holmes and Rahe found a relationship between life changes and health. Of those people who scored between 0 and 150 points on the scale, more than 30% experienced a serious negative health change in the 2 years that followed. (A serious negative health change might be the development of rheumatoid arthritis, clinical depression, cancer, the onset of alcoholism, or a heart attack.) Of those who scored between 151 and 300 points, about 50% experienced a serious negative health change in the 2 years that followed. And of those who scored more than 300 points, almost 90% experienced a serious negative health change in the 2 years following the rating.

TABLE 14.1	Stress Test by Holmes and Rahe	
Event		**Points**
* 1. Death of spouse		100
* 2. Divorce		73
* 3. Marital separation		65
4. Jail term		63
* 5. Death of close family member		63
6. Personal injury or loss		53
* 7. Marriage		50
8. Fired at work/lost job		47
* 9. Marital reconciliation		45
*10. Retirement		45
*11. Change in health of family member		44
*12. Pregnancy		40
*13. Sex difficulties		39
*14. Gain of new family member		39

*Stressors related to couples and families.

Note: Impact points indicate the severity of the impact of the stressor on individuals, couples, or families.

Source: "The Social Readjustment Rating Scale" by T. H. Holmes and R. H. Rahe, *Journal of Psychosomatic Research, 11,* p. 213. Copyright 1967 by Elsevier Science Inc. Reprinted by permission of the publisher.

Holmes and Rahe found that physical and emotional problems are likely to occur when individuals experience a cluster of major and minor changes in life. As an example, a middle-aged woman scored above 700 on the Holmes and Rahe Stress Test. She received her divorce in January and remarried in August; her new husband moved out 3 months later; and by late November she had a new live-in companion. Her mother died during the year, and the woman started and lost two jobs. She had a sprinkling of other life changes during the year, including two car accidents and many bills. As might be predicted, she became very depressed and considered suicide.

Past life experiences based on culture or socioeconomic status also affect how people draw on resources and how they define the event. For example, low-income individuals and families may have had experiences with not having enough money to pay next month's rent. They know, however, that they have family and friends who will help them, since they have helped these family and friends in the past. They also know they have had experiences with not having rent money before and do not define it as a severe crisis. In contrast, middle-income individuals and families may be embarrassed to ask for help from friends and family and, therefore, will not rely on those resources. Because this does not happen often to middle-income individuals or families, it is likely they would define this as a severe crisis.

Stress Pileup

An important concept is **stress pileup,** which is the occurrence and aftereffects of several stresses within a few months. For example, stress in a couple's relationship is often taken by each person to his or her job, and stress at work is often brought home. In a study of stress in 400 people, Kenneth L. Stewart (1989; Olson & Stewart,

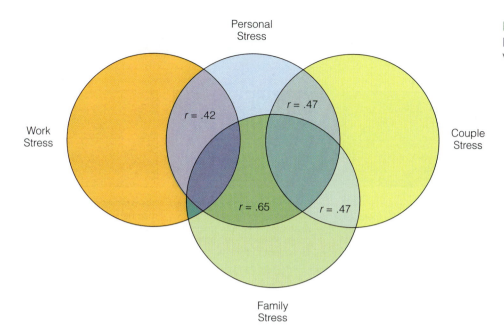

Personal
Stress

Work
Stress

Couple
Stress

Family
Stress

r = .42

r = .47

r = .65

r = .47

FIGURE 14.2

Interconnection in
Various Types of Stress

1991) asked questions about stress in each area of the person's life. He found that stresses in the various areas of life were interrelated. For example, family stress was highly related to personal stress, and couple stress and family stress were also related, as were couple stress and personal stress (Figure 14.2). This study clearly demonstrated that focusing on stress in only one area of life gives at best a partial picture of the total stress in a person's life.

Boundary Ambiguity and Family Stress

In a book called *Loss, Trauma, and Resilience: Therapeutic Work with Ambiguous Loss (2006)*, Pauline Boss vividly describes the effects of ambiguous loss on individuals and families. Another valuable contribution to family stress research is Boss's (1988) definition of **family coping** as "the management of a stressful event or situation by the family as a unit with no detrimental effects on any individual in that family" (p. 60). The family system uses cognitive, affective, and behavioral processes to manage the stress.

An understanding of stress is enhanced by Boss's (2002) use of the term **boundary ambiguity**, a lack of clarity about whether a person is in or out of the family system. The two related variables in boundary ambiguity are physical and psychological presence or absence. Boss also linked this concept to the level of stress that a given situation creates (Figure 14.3).

Low levels of boundary ambiguity (congruence between physical and psychological presence or absence) are related to low stress. When there is both physical and psychological absence, as in the death of a family member or an amicable divorce, it is possible for the family to grieve and then to move on with their lives. Likewise, situations in which there is both physical and psychological presence, as in a happy family or marriage, are also low in stress.

Physical presence and psychological absence creates high ambiguity, and it occurs when a family member suffers from alcoholism or has Alzheimer's disease. This type of situation is also very stressful because the member is physically avail-

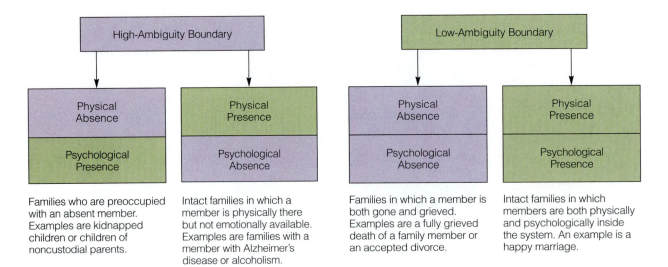

High-Ambiguity Boundary		Low-Ambiguity Boundary	
Physical Absence / Psychological Presence	Physical Presence / Psychological Absence	Physical Absence / Psychological Absence	Physical Presence / Psychological Presence
Families who are preoccupied with an absent member. Examples are kidnapped children or children of noncustodial parents.	Intact families in which a member is physically there but not emotionally available. Examples are families with a member with Alzheimer's disease or alcoholism.	Families in which a member is both gone and grieved. Examples are a fully grieved death of a family member or an accepted divorce.	Intact families in which members are both physically and psychologically inside the system. An example is a happy marriage.

FIGURE 14.3

Boundary Ambiguity and Family Stress

Source: Family Stress Management by P. Boss, 2001, Newbury Park, CA: Sage. Copyright © 2001 by Sage Publications. Reprinted by permission of Sage Publications.

able but is not emotionally available so family members cannot adequately resolve issues.

In the September 11, 2001, attack on America, the people who knew their family members were killed in the plane that went down near Pittsburgh were better able to accept the loss because they knew their family members were dead and there was low ambiguity. However, the people who had family members in the World Trade Towers who did not know if family members survived had high ambiguity, which Boss (2006) calls **ambiguous loss**. This was because the family member still had psychological presence, but was physically absent. Until the family knows whether the family member is alive or dead, there will be ambiguity. High levels of boundary ambiguity create high levels of family stress. In her book *Ambiguous Loss: Learning to Live with Unresolved Grief,* Pauline Boss (1999) describes how people need to find ways to accept the loss before they can move on through the grieving process.

After the destruction of the World Trade Towers, family members of many of those who were in the towers held vigils with pictures and candles. These people were suffering from ambiguous loss because they could not grieve until the status of their family member was verified. The problem with the World Trade Center destruction is that there were a large number of people who were cremated and their ashes were mixed in with the destroyed buildings.

Pauline Boss created a list of things that people can do to deal with grief and ambiguous loss (Cummins, 2001). First, keep looking for information on the missing person. Second, light a candle or make a memorial. Third, do not feel guilty about giving up hope. Fourth, talk with family, friends, and others who can be supportive. Fifth, do not blame yourself. Last, spend time with those close to you and be open to support from others.

Stress Across the Family Life Cycle

What stage of the family life cycle is most stressful for families? Most studies have found that the adolescent stage is the most challenging for both parents and adolescents. As indicated in Figure 14.4, families have an average of seven major stressors, and most of them are related to parent–adolescent conflict involving discipline, money, and homework. This stage also has the lowest level of family satisfaction.

There is an inverse relationship between family stress and family satisfaction. This is logical, but the evidence is rather clear in Figure 14.4. The highest stress and the lowest level of satisfaction occur at the adolescent stage. It is interesting that young couples begin marriage with about five major stressors and rather high levels of satisfaction. As stress increases in families with young children and adolescents, family satisfaction declines. The good news for families is that once the children are launched, the level of stress drops and the level of satisfaction rises again to the level similar to young couples.

Common Stressful Issues

The following are common life and family events that affected at least 10% of the families at all seven life cycle stages (Olson et al., 1989):

- *Uncompleted tasks.* The myth is that the "normal" intact American family is well-functioning, efficient, and effective. Uncompleted tasks are a problem in every stage of the life cycle for almost half of all families.
- *Emotional difficulties in family life.* At every stage of the family life cycle, an average of 15% to 20% of families reported experiencing emotional problems, with the highest rates at the adolescent (19%) and launching (28%) stages.
- *Unstable economic conditions.* Because this study was conducted during a period of some economic uncertainty, it is not surprising that 25% to 30% of families in all stages of the life cycle reported problems associated with hard economic times. High unemployment, crop failures that were due to weather, political turmoil leading to cuts in government budgets, and other conditions kept many families on edge.

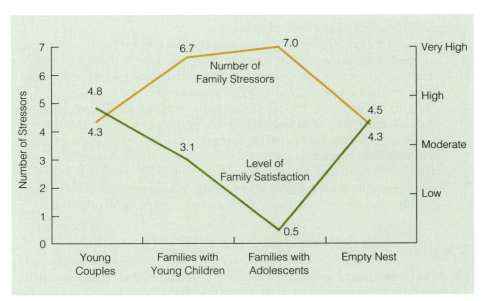

FIGURE 14.4
Family Stress and Family Satisfaction
Source: From *Families: What Makes Them Work* (2nd ed.) (pp. 122, 181) by D. H. Olson, H. I. McCubbin, H. Barnes, A. Larson, M.Muxen, and M. Wilson, Los Angeles, CA: Sage. Copyright © 1989 by Sage Publications. Reprinted by permission of the publisher.

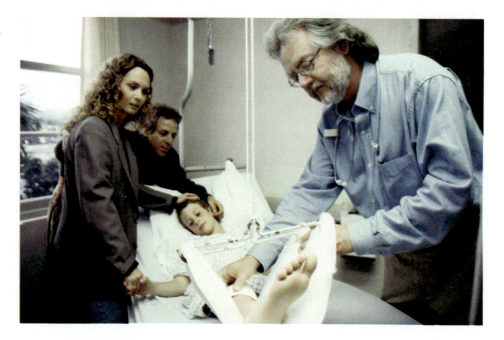

Medical care for families has become an increasingly costly expense, which contributes to stress for families.

- *Major economic investments and purchases*. Homes, children's educations, and business investments were other major financial expenses that caused worry for families across all stages, especially for those at the launching stage. Nearly half of all families had purchased a car or another major item for which they had taken out a loan.
- *Medical and dental expenses*. Rising interest rates, the higher cost of living, and increases in health care costs made it difficult for some families at every stage to adequately cover medical and dental bills, with 25% to 30% of families identifying these expenses as concerns. Health care expenses were especially troublesome during the childbearing and childrearing stages. Low-income families tended to sacrifice quality of care and preventive health care to reduce medical and dental expenses.
- *Money for the basics of family living*. Almost half of the families in every stage reported stress caused by the struggle to provide food and clothing, pay utilities, and cover housing costs. Families with adolescents were the most heavily burdened, with 62% reporting this concern.
- *Changing jobs or careers*. The challenges of the working world put a good deal of stress on families at all stages of the life cycle but especially at the young couple stage, where nearly half (46%) experienced this issue as they sought to establish themselves in a career. This challenge was also particularly stressful for one-third of the families at the launching stage; wives often were reentering the workforce after rearing children, and husbands were growing dissatisfied with the career they had been in for 10 or 20 years.

A Roller Coaster Course of Adjustment

The roller coaster model is very relevant for understanding the attacks on America that happened on September 11, 2001, when the World Trade Center in New York and a section of the Pentagon in Washington, D.C., were destroyed. Reuben Hill

(1958) initially developed the model in an attempt to understand the course of family adjustment to a crisis, but it can also be applied to other organizations or aspects of society. According to Hill, adjustment involves (1) a period of disorganization, (2) an angle of recovery, and (3) a new level of organization (see Figure 14.5).

In considering the attack on America, (September 11, 2001) this country was caught totally by surprise and this created a period of disorganization, both for the country and for the families who had family members in the area. Soon after the attack, the cities of New York and Washington, D.C., the country, and the families started to begin the process of recovery by mobilizing a large variety of resources. This process of recovery took months and eventually the families, the cities, and the country became reorganized. In the process, the reorganized cities and families became different and in some cases better than they were before the crisis. So a crisis can be problematic in the short run and in the long run can strengthen the various components that were initially attacked.

Another example is to consider how a stillbirth affects most families. Such an event is, of course, terribly painful for the parents, surviving siblings, and other family members; all of them initially experience loneliness and despair (DeFrain, Martens, Stork, & Stork 1986). The course of adjustment for the average parent of a stillborn child is charted in Figure 14.5.

The process of recovering from any crisis takes a long time. Two to three years seems to be about the average when there is a death of a family member. In many cases, the younger the family member, the longer the period of recovery. The recovery process lasts longer for families who believe it is not healthy to talk about death; this conspiracy of silence probably makes a couple's pain much greater than it might otherwise be. Couples who grieve openly, talking and crying with loved ones and friends, recover more quickly. It also appears that recovery takes about the same amount of time for men and women. A common myth is that men are "stronger" than women, that they can stand up better against pain. Men who act tough and do not have the courage to reach out for the help they need take longer to heal than those who are not afraid to admit they are hurt.

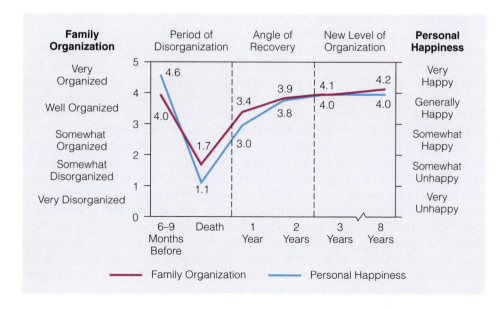

FIGURE 14.5

Family Recovery Process Following a Stillbirth (Couple Scores)

Source: Reprinted and adapted with permission from *Stillborn: The Invisible Death* by J. DeFrain, L. Martens, J. Stork, and W. Stork. Copyright © 1986 University Press of America. First published by Lexington Books. All rights reserved.

Chapter 14 | Stress, Abuse, and Family Problems   **395**

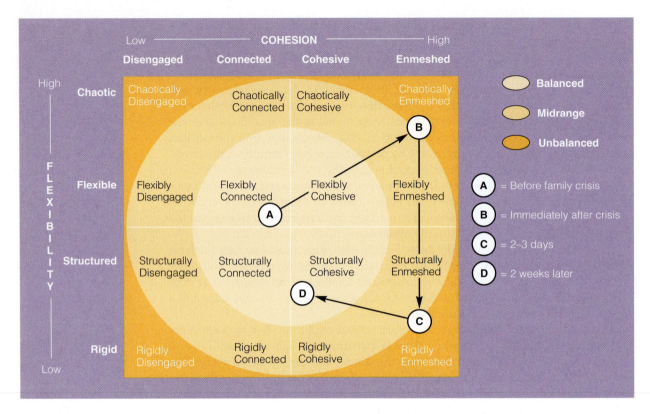

FIGURE 14.6
Family Changes in Response to the 9/11 Attacks

Family Systems Changes Before and After the 9/11 Attacks

An important aspect of family systems is that the family changes to deal with any crises. Let us consider the Greenberg family before and after the destruction of the Twin Towers (Figure 14.6). The father, Henry, worked on the 72nd floor, and it was initially unclear if he was able to escape. He was married for 26 years and had three children ages 22, 20, and 17.

Before 9/11 (point A), the family was *flexibly connected*, which is appropriate for their stage of the life cycle. Hours after the attack (point B), the family system became *chaotically enmeshed* because the family did not know if the father had escaped from his office. The family, along with close relatives and friends, gathered at their home and huddled together in a mutually supportive way. This high level of closeness and bonding created "enmeshment," and the fact that they did not know if he survived created a great deal of chaos in their family.

During the next day or two after the attack, the family continued to stay together and were emotionally enmeshed, but they developed a highly organized style of operating, creating a *rigidly enmeshed* system (point C). They got very organized as a group in an attempt to find out what happened to Henry. This rigidity was an attempt to bring some stability to the chaos by reorganizing some of their family. They decided that their home would be the headquarters and that everyone needed to be in touch by phone. They divided up into teams so they could better search to find out what happened to Henry. Some family members went to the site of the attack others went to check out the hospitals, and others stayed at home. They checked in with the home every few hours.

On the third day, a miracle happened from their point of view. They found that Henry was in a downtown hospital but was severely injured in one leg and arm and had some memory loss. He could not remember his phone number but did know his name. That enabled the hospital on the second day to post his name.

Two weeks later, he was home and the family then changed again, becoming a *structurally cohesive* system (point D). Some of the rigidity was no longer there, but they were still rather organized in order to care for him and to start to get back to their normal routines. Some of the closeness decreased and the family moved from being enmeshed to being cohesive. But the family was closer and more organized than before the attack, and this is a useful style while the family is recovering from the stress that they all experienced.

This example illustrates one family's ability to adapt to a crisis. The family changed system types several times over the 6-week period following the attack, and these changes were beneficial in helping the family more effectively deal with this major stressor.

After studying the impact of stress on several hundred couples and families by plotting the changes on the Couple and Family Map, the following general principles of change related to stress were developed (Olson, 1996). *First*, under stress couples and families often move in the direction of becoming more extreme on both flexibility (a move toward a more chaotic system) and cohesion (a move toward a more enmeshed system). *Second*, communication almost always increases

The death of a family member results in a difficult time for that family. The family is likely to experience family disorganization for some period following the death.

BOX 14.1   At Issue

The Impact of War on Families Left Behind

When you think about one country declaring war against another, your immediate concern is for the soldiers who will be fighting on the front lines and the civilians caught in the crossfire. It's easy to imagine—and often to see—the sacrifices they have made as part of their job and their duty. It is not so easy to see the sacrifices made by the families soldiers leave behind.

Since March 2003, when President George W. Bush declared war on Iraq, thousands of American soldiers have been deployed, leaving behind wives, husbands, children, parents, sisters, brothers, and grandparents who must learn to cope with their loved ones being at risk and so far from home.

By the end of 2004, almost 1,400 American troops had been killed and approximately 9,000 wounded, along with thousands upon thousands of Iraqis. Among the Americans killed were 27 women, 6 of whom were mothers. Their 10 children were a fraction of the more than 900 who have lost a parent in Iraq.

According to a December 15, 2004, release by Scripps Howard News Service (Hoffman & Rainville, 2004), more than 40% of the war dead through November of 2004 were married, and 429 had children, many of whom were under the age of 10. There are more "married with children" soldiers in this war than in past wars, partly because of the large numbers of reserve forces in Iraq, who tend to be older and more settled than active-duty soldiers.

The article quoted Charles Moskos, a leading military sociologist and Northwestern University professor, who said: "As much as we are concerned about veterans' programs, we now have to be concerned about orphan programs. This is the first time we crossed that threshold."

Military families have always had to face different challenges than those faced by civilian families. Often, military families move from city to city, or even country to country, as they follow military orders. Children (and spouses) have to learn to adapt quickly to new environments and to make new friends they may be with for only a few short months. Spouses must learn to be single parents while their husbands or wives are away for long periods. And these are challenges that occur during peacetime.

During wartime, the challenges are even greater as families cope with uncertainty and loss. An article in *Newsday* in December 2004 (Perez, 2004) described three families' struggles to deal with the holiday season. For one family, Christmas will never be the same, as Army Specialist Victor Martinez, 21, was buried on December 24. He had joined the army to help pay for college and to get a head start on his dream of becoming a police officer. In contrast, the family of Navy Hospital Corpsman Thomas Smith Jr., 23, was celebrating. Smith, wounded, returned home a hero and became a father just 5 days before Christmas. A third family waited and worried as their only child, Sergeant Francisco Soriano, stationed in Kuwait, waited for his orders to go to Iraq. His mother, who would not put up a tree until her son came home, said, "I don't sleep well. . . . I don't eat well. I can't watch the news. My only desire is to open the door and see his face again."

When soldiers are sent off to war, families undergo emotional cycles. In June 2004, the Department of Veterans Affairs' National Center for Post-Traumatic Stress Disorder published the *Iraq War Clinician Guide* (Waldrep,

during a stressful event. *Third*, once the stress has abated, couples and families usually return to a similar—but rarely to the same—type of system they had before the stress. *Fourth*, couples and families often require a minimum of 6 months to a year to adjust to a major stress. *Fifth*, balanced couple and family systems tend to become unbalanced during the stress and then return to another balanced system about a year later.

Posttraumatic Stress Disorder and War

With troops deployed in Iraq, Afghanistan, and other places where they are experiencing combat, we have many individuals affected by **Posttraumatic stress disorder (PTSD)** and the resulting symptoms. These symptoms are causing stress and disruption in marriage and family relationships (Greer, 2005). According to Sammons (2005), "PTSD can be a chronic and debilitating disorder—one closely associated with related problems such as substance abuse, depression, and domes-

Cozza, & Chen, 2004), which describes the cycle's five stages:

1. **Predeployment.** Between the time the family is notified and the time the soldier leaves, families often go through denial and then intense preparation for and anticipation of the departure.
2. **Deployment.** During the first few months of the soldier's absence, there can be significant emotional turmoil, including depression and feelings of abandonment. Families must find a new balance as they take on the responsibilities of the absent loved one.
3. **Sustainment.** While the soldier is away, families settle into a new routine. Some families, especially those with little outside support, have a more difficult time with this than others, and children may begin to act out in inappropriate ways.
4. **Redeployment.** Just before the soldier is due to return home, families often experience great excitement and anticipation along with great anxiety.
5. **Postdeployment.** While most homecomings are joyous occasions, they can also be accompanied by unrealistic fantasies about the reunion. Soldiers may find it hard to integrate into the family structure that has formed while they were away, and families may have a difficult time giving up new patterns they have created. It may also take time for couples to reestablish physical and emotional intimacy.

The five stages outline some of the emotional impacts on soldiers' families. But there are economic impacts as well. In August 2004, a *Money* magazine article entitled "Ephrata, Washington Pays for the War" (Caplin & McGirt, 2004) calculated some of the financial burdens families of deployed National Guard soldiers face. The article focused on members of 1161st Transportation Company, which had been on the longest deployment of any National Guard unit since World War II.

In rural areas like Ephrata, Washington, people often join the National Guard for a second income or as a way to pay for college. However, when a unit ships out, that economic advantage often disappears. Despite popular belief, the U.S. Army does not supply all of a soldier's needs, and it's up to the families to make up the difference. One soldier's wife said she had spent about $3,000 on hardware and supplies for her husband, and another $2,200 to ship it all to Iraq. Soldiers and their families also have to pay for phone calls home; although they get a discount rate, it often costs more than $1,000 a month to keep in touch.

And while federal law requires employers to hold jobs for National Guard troops on active duty, it does not require that their companies pay their salaries or continue to pay health benefits. The U.S. General Accounting Office issued a report in March 2003 stating that 41% of reservists reported that they earned less on active duty than in their civilian jobs. Spouses left at home often have to seek employment or second jobs in order to support their families.

The families in Ephrata, Washington, were planning a huge celebration when their loved ones returned home from the war. As one soldier's wife put it, "We deserve a party too. I truly believe anyone who was left behind serves their country too" (Caplin & McGirt, 2004).

tic and occupational dysfunction" (p. 902). It can result from combat or other traumatic events.

Soldiers are exposed to urban fighting, suicide bombers, and guerilla tactics. When these traumatic events are experienced consistently and over long periods of time, it is a predictor of later mental health problems (Greer, 2005). It makes sense, then, that mental health problems are the second most common reason for medical military discharge, second only to orthopedic injuries (Sammons, 2005). Some reports indicate that as many as 10% of those serving in combat may have a diagnosis of PTSD, which indicates that problems for family life are also substantial for these troops (Fals-Stewart & Kelley, 2005; Sammons, 2005).

A common symptom of PTSD is domestic violence, with one study indicating that the rate of violence for those diagnosed with PTSD was 5.4 times that of veterans who were not diagnosed with the disorder (Sherman, Sautter, Jackson, Lyons, & Han, 2006). Those veterans experiencing depression were also more likely to be violent than those veterans who did not experience depression.

Increased family separation has resulted from recent military deployment. Many families are having a difficult time responding to family members repeatedly being deployed to face difficult war-time combat.

Other mental health symptoms related to PTSD, such as substance abuse and occupational dysfunction, are not as well documented. These issues are also likely to be very disruptive to family life and personal well-being.

See Box 14.1 for a discussion of the impact of war on the families left behind.

Family Coping Strategies

The Chinese pictograph or symbol for the word *crisis* is a composite of two other pictographs: the symbols for *danger* and *opportunity* (Figure 14.7). For thousands of years, the Chinese have understood that a crisis can be a dangerous time but also a time to look for new opportunities. Strong families tend to agree with this idea. Professionals working with those under stress have commonly found that in the midst of the hurt and despair of a serious crisis, there are also some positive outcomes as people draw on their strengths.

What good could possibly come out of a disaster? Many families say that after they have weathered a crisis together, their relationships with each other are stronger, more positive, and more loving. People who have gone through a crisis often relate how they became stronger as individuals as well as closer to their partners and families. They grow to appreciate their families more and become more willing to share with them.

FIGURE 14.7
The Chinese Pictograph
for Crisis

Danger   Opportunity

Theoretical Perspectives

Pauline Boss (2001) clarified the difference between coping as a family resource and coping as a process. She explains why the concept of **managing stress** is a more accurate description of how families handle stressors than is *coping with stress:* A family's coping resources are considered strengths, but simply having these strengths available is no guarantee the family will use them to *manage* the stress. Boss (1992) also noted that resources are derived from all aspects of life: psychological, economic, and physical.

S. E. Hobfoll and C. D. Spielberger (1992) completed an excellent overview of family stress models and research, observing the commonalties and differences among family stress theories and identifying the important family resources across a variety of models. The major resources and strengths were cohesion rather than separateness, flexibility/adaptability rather than rigidity, communication rather than privacy, boundary clarity rather than boundary ambiguity, and order and mastery rather than chaos and helplessness.

Burr and Klein (1994) also provided an excellent summary evaluation of past studies of the most useful coping strategies for families. They identified six general coping strategies that encompass numerous specific strategies. The six general family coping strategies are cognitive, emotional, relationships, community, spiritual, and individual development (Table 14.2).

TABLE 14.2	Major Family Coping Strategies
General	**Specific**
Cognitive	Gain knowledge
	Reframe situation
Emotional	Express feelings
	Resolve negative feelings
	Be sensitive to others' emotional needs
Relationships	Increase cohesion
	Increase adaptability
	Increase trust and cooperation
Community	Seek help and support
Spiritual	Be involved in religious activities
	Maintain faith
Individual development	Develop autonomy, independence

Source: Adapted from *Reexamining Family Stress* (p. 133) by W. R. Burr and S. R. Klein, 1994, Thousand Oaks, CA: Sage. Copyright © 1994 by Sage Publications. Reprinted by permission of Sage Publications.

Coping with 9/11

In the September 11, 2001, attack by terrorists, many innocent people were killed. People used a variety of coping resources to deal with this major stress, and we will use this example to illustrate how coping resources are used by families.

In terms of cognitive coping resources, Burr and Klein (1994) described gaining knowledge and reframing the situation. Immediately after people learned of the attacks on the World Trade Center and the Pentagon, they wanted more and more information. Fortunately, the media dropped all other coverage and exclusively reported on the events related to this attack. This media coverage continued nonstop for several days.

Reframing is another cognitive resource, and it involves defining the situation as a challenge that can be conquered rather than denying it is a problem. Unfortunately, this attack was so dramatic that it immediately put people into a proactive mode that made them want to overcome the challenge.

In terms of emotional coping strategies, expressing feelings and being sensitive to others' emotional needs are important resources that help people cope. In the attack on America, we saw endless examples of New Yorkers and others around the country and world expressing their intense feelings about the events and being more open than normal to how others were feeling. With the attack came a dramatic shift in the level and intensity of feelings that were expressed and an interest in sharing with others.

Relationship coping resources include increasing cohesiveness or closeness, increasing flexibility or adaptability, and increasing trust and cooperation. Probably no recent event in our history has brought Americans together more dramatically than this attack. People sought out members of their family and often got reconnected with each other. During crises, people are also willing to forget their normal routine and to do whatever it takes to deal with the situation. Their trust and

Contrary to the notion that strength means facing a problem without any help, research indicates that the strength to cope with problems comes from close connections with friends, neighbors, and relatives. Human beings are, indeed, social beings. This African American church provides support in countless ways for its members in good times and in troubled times.

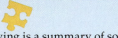

BOX 14.2 Putting It Together

Strategies for Managing Stress

The following is a summary of some of the major strategies for managing stress that were found across a variety of studies of couples and families.

- Look for something positive in every situation.
- Pull together rather than apart.
- Try to be open to sharing our feelings.
- Try to be flexible in handling roles and tasks.
- Try to focus on not worrying about what we cannot change.

- Take on the challenges head on.
- Be able to go with the flow.
- Be able to cry but also look for humor.
- Take on issues one at a time.
- Do not blame each other.
- Think about the meaning and purpose of life.
- Rely on our spiritual beliefs.
- Show our love to each other.

cooperation with each other increase as they bond together to deal with the major problem.

The value of the community as a source of support was clearly demonstrated after the attack. New Yorkers pulled together into a caring community, with strangers helping strangers. The city that had a reputation for being arrogant, distant, and noncaring was transformed into a caring network that rushed to help everyone in need.

The importance of spiritual beliefs was clearly evident from the time of the attack. People were comforted by clergy of all denominations, and prayers were offered by people around the country for those lost and their families. Religious services were packed with people who were there both to comfort and be comforted.

In summary, the terrorist attacks were so dramatic and powerful that it required that people use all the resources described above to begin to better manage the major stress that it created for all Americans. Because America and Americans are resilient and resourceful, they overcome crises and move on to become stronger people and a stronger country. Box 14.2 provides a summary of the most common strategies for managing stress.

Domestic Violence

> *The home is actually a more dangerous place for American women than the city streets.*
> —Dr. Antonia C. Novello, former U.S. Surgeon General
> ("Family Violence," 1991, p. 3)

Domestic violence can range from violent physical acts to coercive behavior toward a spouse or partner (Frias & Angel, 2005). It can be psychological or emotional abuse or physical violence to any family member, including pets. Domestic violence can also include the imposition and exploitation of economic dependence and isolation, as well as the destruction of property (Frias & Angel, 2005). Couple violence involves two adults who are intimate, regardless of their marital status, sexual orientation, or living arrangement (Frias & Angel, 2005).

When we hear the term "domestic violence," we often think about a man physically causing harm to his spouse or girlfriend. Many people think of men being the aggressors and women being the victims, with extensive physical harm being done. According to Michael Johnson (2005), domestic violence takes several forms and the aggressor is not always a male.

Johnson (2005) identifies three different types of domestic violence between couples. Intimate terrorism is violence enacted when taking control over one's partner. This will likely involve physical harm. This type of domestic violence is most often gender specific, with men being the aggressors. This type of violence is often frequent and brutal. Individuals often end up in shelters or hospitals; occasionally, murder is the result (Fergusson, Horwood, & Ridder, 2005; Holtzworth-Munroe, 2005; Johnson, 2005).

The second type of domestic violence involves violence resistance and may be in response to a partner's abuse. An example might be when a person inflicts harm on his or her partner in resisting assaults.

The third type of domestic violence identified by Johnson (2005) is situational couple violence, which results when there is a contentious situation or problem in the couple relationship. Situational couple violence is much more common than intimate terrorism. In this type of domestic violence, the aggressor is equally likely to be male or female (Holtzworth-Munroe, 2005; Johnson, 2005). Most studies do not distinguish among the different types of domestic violence, and these distinctions are more likely to be made in future research.

Incidence of Domestic Violence

Researchers estimate that approximately 3 million people, mostly women, are severely assaulted each year by their spouses (Gelles, 1997, 2000a). Most cases are not reported, for a variety of reasons. Victims often do not recognize the violence as abuse because in some ethnic and cultural groups violence toward women is the norm. Society's traditional respect for family privacy also inhibits reporting. Victims may feel guilt or shame for being abused or may fear the partner will retaliate if they report the incident.

Husband abuse occurs as well, but because men are generally bigger and stronger than women, husbands have higher rates of inflicting the most dangerous and injurious forms of violence on wives. Much violence by wives appears to be in self-defense (Straus, 1999).

A dating relationship is apparently more likely to be violent than a marital relationship. The National Family Violence Survey of 5,768 couples found that 20% of the dating couples had experienced a physical assault during the previous year, compared with 15% of the married couples (Stets & Straus, 1989). Courtship is a training ground for marriage and also, apparently, a training ground for spouse abuse.

As shown in Figure 14.8, attackers in violent crimes vary according to the type of violent crime—rape/sexual assault, robbery, and assault (both aggravated and simple assaults combined). Most robberies are committed by strangers (76%); relatives, well-known persons, and casual acquaintances are much less likely to rob

FIGURE 14.8
Victim–Offender Relationship in Crimes of Violence
Source: U.S. Bureau of the Census, 2003b, table 323, p. 208.

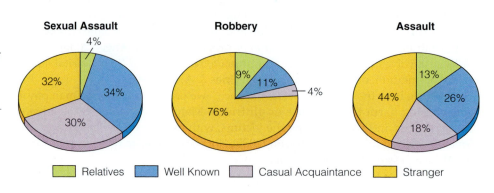

someone (24%). For rape/sexual assault and other types of assault, however, the story is different. In the case of rape/sexual assault, 32% are committed by strangers, 30% by casual acquaintances, 34% by well-known persons, and 4% by family members. In the case of other assaults, both aggravated assaults and simple assaults combined, 44% are committed by strangers, while 18% are committed by casual acquaintances, 26% by well-known persons, and 13% by relatives (U.S. Bureau of the Census, 2003b).

Spouse or partner abuse can be physical, sexual, or emotional. Spouse abuse and child abuse are closely linked. Seventy percent of the men who batter their partners also batter their children (Jouriles, Norwood, McDonald, & Peters, 2001; Vincent & Jouriles, 2000).

Diversity and Domestic Violence

We know that cultures where men are considered dominant are likely to have higher rates of domestic violence than cultures where men and women are considered equals. We also know that social class, migration, and female dependence on males affect the rates of domestic violence. These factors are very complex, but there are research findings that are beginning to make these relationships more clear.

Some studies show that domestic violence is more prevalent in Latino and African American cultures (Bornstein, 2006). Frias and Angel (2005) found that among poor women, women of Mexican origin reported similar rates of domestic violence to African American women. They found that Latina women from other countries such as Puerto Rico had significantly lower rates of violence. These authors concluded that there are differing cultural views that affect domestic violence for Latinos depending on on the country of origin.

Frias and Angel (2005) also found that Latina women who had immigrated to the United States when they were older than 15 years of age were at lower risk of domestic violence than those who immigrated before age 15. One can only speculate about the reason for this difference, but the timing of migration can also affect the incidence of domestic violence.

We also know that domestic violence is more common among low-income couples (Dingfelder, 2006; Frias & Angel, 2005). Low-income couples are likely to be experiencing considerable stress regarding meeting basic needs, which may affect one's ability to handle issues without violence. It is important to note, however, that domestic violence occurs at all income levels, and the degree to which domestic violence is reported may vary depending on income levels.

There are many factors that affect the willingness to report domestic violence. If a cultural group does not view domestic violence as negative, individuals are less likely to report violence to the police or even self-report violence in research studies. In fact, actions that may be viewed as domestic violence in one culture may not be viewed as domestic violence in another culture. Low-income couples may live in more crowded housing where domestic violence is reported to police by neighbors. Middle- or upper- income couples may live in homes where domestic violence is less likely to be noticed by neighbors and less likely to be reported. Therefore, we must be careful in assuming that reported incidences are an accurate assessment of what is really happening.

National Survey of Domestic Violence

One of the largest national surveys of marriage that also focused on spouse abuse was done by Shuji Asai and David Olson (2004) and is summarized in Table 14.3. This survey of 20,951 married couples from all 50 states had couples complete the

TABLE 14.3	National Survey of Spouse Abuse

- National sample of 20,951 married couples from all 50 states.
- Average age of 35 years for husbands and 32 years for wives who were married 2 to 30 years.
- Classified into nonabusive (61%), only wife abusive (8%), only husband abusive (17%), and volatile—both abusive (13%).
- Greater levels of alcohol use meant a higher level of partner abuse.
- Volatile couples saw more abuse between their parents, more abuse by their parents, and more abuse by others.
- Abused spouses had lower levels of assertiveness and self-confidence and higher levels of avoidance and partner dominance.
- Nonabusive marriages had significantly higher levels of couple closeness, communication, family and friends, personality strengths, couple flexibility, and conflict resolution.
- There are five couple types based on the ENRICH inventory: vitalized, harmonious, traditional, conflicted, and devitalized (with ranges from high couple satisfaction to low satisfaction).
- Levels of abuse were highly related to the five couple types: vitalized (5%), harmonious (11%), traditional (20%), conflicted (48%), and devitalized (73%).

Source: Asai & Olson, 2004.

ENRICH couple inventory. The average age was 35 for males and 32 for females, and they had been married from 2 to 30 years. Couples were classified into one of four groups based on their level of abuse: nonabusive (61%), only wife abusive (8%), only husband abusive (17%), and volatile—both abusive (13%).

Comparing nonabusive marriages with the other three abusive groups, couples in nonabusive marriages had lower levels of alcohol use and abuse, had less abuse from their parents, and saw less abuse between their parents. In terms of personality styles, couples in nonabusive marriages were more assertive, had higher levels of confidence, less often avoided issues, and less often dominated their partners. Nonabusive marriages had higher levels of couple closeness and flexibility, better communication and conflict resolution, and a more supportive family and friendship network.

In summary, in most ways nonabusive married couples had a much stronger marriage relationship in almost all the major dimensions compared to abusive marriages. This seems to demonstrate that having a strong marriage protects the couple from using more abusive approaches with the partner.

Relationship of Physical Abuse and Psychological Abuse

Marital violence has been found to be more common among young couples, among couples with low occupational status and income and job dissatisfaction, among couples who are socially isolated, among couples who have a greater number of dependent children in the home, and among couples who experienced violence in their family of origin. Violent couple relationships are associated with poor conflict resolution and communication skills and unequal decision-making responsibilities, which tend to be held solely by the husband (Arias & Pape, 1999; Street & Arias, 2001).

Physical abuse almost always is accompanied by psychological abuse, but psychological abuse is often present in relationships in which there is no physical violence (Arias & Pape, 1999; Street & Arias, 2001). However, abuse has been conceptualized as a developmental process in which psychological abuse occurs first and eventually may progress into physical aggression (Stets, 1990). Norina, a college co-ed, describes the escalation of abuse in her relationship with her boyfriend Jerry:

> "In the beginning I thought Jerry was abusive because he was drunk, but then it happened when he wasn't drunk, too. I ignored it at first. I guess I thought he would quit. I also loved him so much I tried to cover it up.
>
> "He became very demeaning toward me, and there was a lot of mental abuse. I wanted to quit seeing him, but he wouldn't accept it. I needed to get away, but he followed me wherever I went and watched every move I made. I didn't realize how bad the situation had become until one night at a party. He had followed me there but didn't speak to me most of the night. He left—or so I thought. Because I was upset, I started to talk with a male friend of mine. Out of the blue my boyfriend returned, picked me up, and carried me outside behind a building. I was scared and started crying. I was so upset I couldn't listen to him. He kept slapping me and telling me to shut up and listen. A few of my friends were watching. They confronted my boyfriend, and he started fighting with them too."

Although a woman who is psychologically abused will not have bruises or visible signs of injury, she will experience damage to her physical and psychological health. Psychologically abused women have an increased chance of serious or chronic illness, lower levels of relationship satisfaction, and lower levels of perceived power and control. These women experience psychological distress, including fear, low self-esteem, depression, an inability to trust others, nightmares, guilt, feelings of inferiority, pessimism, low ego strength, introversion, and helplessness. They also may experience psychophysiological symptoms such as fatigue, backache, headache, general restlessness, and insomnia. Psychological abuse also compromises mothering skills and thus puts children at risk. Psychological abuse has been found not only to be a major predictor of a mother's depression but also of her children's depression and low self-esteem (Arias & Pape, 1999; Street & Arias, 2001). In fact, data suggest that the psychological and behavioral dysfunction of children exposed to interparental psychological abuse is similar to that found in children exposed to interparental physical abuse.

Many symptoms experienced and reported by battered women mirror symptoms of PTSD (posttraumatic stress disorder). An investigation by Arias and Pape (1999) found psychological abuse to be a significant predictor of women's PTSD symptomatology and intentions to end an abusive relationship. Psychologically abused women with low-PTSD symptomatology were highly associated with intentions to terminate the abusive relationship, but there was no significant association for women in the high-PTSD symptomatology group. Arias and Pape suggest that because psychological abuse targets cognitions and is incorporated into self-concept, higher levels of abuse-related distress may decrease a woman's ability to leave the abusive relationship. Based on these findings, Arias and Pape argue that shelters need to increase the duration of stay for women to ensure affective and cognitive improvements and to increase the probability that these women will find the support and strength to leave the perpetrator.

Factors Contributing to Domestic Violence

Researchers and clinicians have hypothesized that a number of factors contribute to the likelihood of spouse abuse in a family. These factors are rather similar to those found in the national survey of spouse abuse previously described in Table 14.3 by Asai and Olson (2004).

Violence in the Family of Origin. The family systems theory attributes a tendency toward domestic violence as an adult to growing up in a violent home, where the child learns to be a victim as well as a potential **victimizer**. Abused male children typically learn to be victimizers. They often develop a sort of "pecking order" attitude toward violence: You get beaten up when you're small; then when you're big, you repeat what you learned. Female children typically learn to be victims in their family of origin and are likely to become victims again in their marriage (Frias & Angel, 2005; Gelles, 2000a). As with child abuse, however, growing up in a home where spouse abuse occurs does not guarantee that one will become a victim or a victimizer as an adult (Gelles, 2000a). People can and do make positive, life-affirming choices.

Theorists with a psychodynamically oriented approach might see some abusers as having a personality disorder that is facilitated by a "willing" victim. The abuser's sadism is reinforced by the victim's masochism. Another way to think of this is that the abuser is a dominating partner which is maximized because the abused person is passive rather than assertive.

In a similar vein, **learned helplessness theory** postulates that battered women often learned from childhood that they cannot afford to appear competent around competitive men who like to win. These women give power away to men, and this ingrained passivity leads to a lack of options in life. When abused, they feel they have no way out: nowhere to go, no job skills or career opportunities, no choice except to continue to take their punishment.

Low Self-Esteem. Low self-esteem is a factor in domestic violence. The abusive spouse may feel inadequate and may use violence to gain control. The abused spouse may passively accept the violence, feeling that she or he deserves nothing better.

Youth. Age and spouse abuse are statistically related. Marital violence is twice as likely among couples who are under age 30 than among those over age 30 (Gelles, 2000a).

Economic Stress. Although spouse abuse occurs in families at all income levels, economic stress increases the likelihood of wife battering. Spouse abuse is more likely in low-income families, and unemployed men are twice as likely to batter their wives as employed men are (Gelles, 2000a).

Financial Dependency. Financial dependency refers to the degree to which one person relies on another for financial support and in which one member of the couple has considerable control over financial resources (Bornstein, 2006). Financial dependency is positively related to the likelihood of domestic violence. Financial dependency creates an unequal balance of power, which makes it difficult for individuals to move out of the relationship and away from the violence because they have limited or no resources to do so (Bornstein, 2006).

Isolation. Social isolation is also a factor in abuse. Abusers often feel isolated and alone. They have fewer contacts with friends, neighbors, and relatives and engage in fewer social activities than nonabusers do. In stressful times, they have no social support network upon which to call (Gelles, 2000a).

Most women who are physically abused by their husbands or partners are reluctant to report the abuse and even more reluctant to end the relationship. One theory for this masochistic behavior is that these women were abused as children and know only the role of victim. Another theory is that throughout their lives they have been conditioned to act passively and as a consequence have few skills and little self-esteem and see no alternative to a brutal relationship.

Alcohol. Alcohol is implicated in a high percentage of domestic violence incidents. Many men who assault their wives are found to have been drinking (Gelles, 2000a; Substance Abuse and Mental Health Services Administration, 2004). Does drinking cause violence? Some observers argue that alcohol facilitates violence by helping break down the abuser's inhibitions. But alcohol is never the sole cause of a violent episode. Drinking is no more an excuse for assaulting another human being than it is for killing someone in a car accident. Our system of social justice would break down if people were not held responsible for their behavior.

Male Dominance. Professionals and clinicians studying abuse from a feminist perspective have identified clues as to why men batter women. They note that many in our culture believe that males have the right to control or try to control their partners. Men have also been socialized to believe that aggression is an acceptable, normal response to stress and anger. A patriarchal family system influences males to assume the head-of-the-household role and women to accept subordinate status. Egalitarian decision making is associated with nonviolence in families. Research shows that levels of wife beating and husband beating are higher among husband-dominant couples than among democratic couples (Gelles, 2000a).

Other Cultural Factors. In our culture the depersonalization and objectification of women are reinforced by pornography and by advertising that uses sexy women to sell products. Victim blaming is common, as rape trials often reveal. We live in a society with a high tolerance for overt coercion and the use of physical force to gain control over others (Pence & McDonnell, 2000). All of these social factors are viewed as contributing to the epidemic of domestic violence in this country.

Linkage of Animal Abuse and Domestic Violence. There is considerable evidence that mistreatment of animals is a powerful indicator that other forms of violence may be occurring in the home (Mickish & Schoen, 2004). Many abused women have companion animals, and many of these companion animals are abused by the perpetrators as a way to hurt and control the women or their children. Some women may choose not to leave the partner or stay separated for long because of their concern for the safety of their companion animals (Fawcett, Gullone, & Johnson, 2002). Other researchers have found that children who abuse animals often are cruel toward people, and they argue that we can intervene in the cycle of abuse by decreasing a child's potential to be abusive toward animals, and, consequently, promote prosocial behavior toward humans (Mickish & Schoen, 2004; Thompson & Gullone, 2003). One study found that half of all the youths surveyed had abused animals at some time in their lives with boys being more involved in abuse than girls (Baldry, 2003).

Patterns of Domestic Violence

Clinicians commonly see a three-phase, cyclical pattern to wife battering: (1) a tension-building phase; (2) an explosion phase, in which the actual beating occurs; and (3) a loving or honeymoon phase, in which the battered woman is rewarded for staying in the relationship (Walker, 2000). The third phase can be very pleasant. Many women stay with their spouses or boyfriends because of the promises and gifts that often follow a violent incident.

A common belief in our culture is that venting anger verbally can prevent physical violence. This theory of **catharsis conflict**, as it has been called, is simply not true. Verbal aggression is not a substitute for physical aggression but actually goes hand in hand with physical aggression. The more verbally aggressive a couple is, the more likely they are to be physically aggressive with each other (Gelles, 1997, 2000a).

Treatment and Prevention of Domestic Violence

Many clinicians and professionals who work in women's shelters are skeptical that batterers can alter their behavior without professional help and without the genuine desire to change. Some argue that battering men "have a good thing going," with a terrified wife and children who jump every time the batterer says jump.

Counselors commonly advise battered women to leave their husbands and go to a relative's or a friend's home or to a shelter for battered women. But this is easier said than done. Some men panic when women leave because they feel they are losing control. Panic can lead to even more violent behavior. "It's extremely rare that you read about a man who has beaten a woman to death while she's living with him," according to Ellen Pence, who works with battered women. "It's when she leaves him that he kills" (Pence & McDonnell, 2000).

Responding to pressure from the women's movement, police departments are now more likely to make arrests in cases of domestic violence. Assault against a spouse is seen as a serious offense. After studying research findings indicating that men who had spent time behind bars were less likely to assault their partners again, the Duluth, Minnesota, police department was the first in the United States to make arrest mandatory for suspected batterers. The Duluth program requires batterers to attend at least 6 months of counseling and classes. If a man misses two meetings, he risks serving up to 10 days in jail. Studies done 2 years after the program was initiated found that 80% of the women whose partners had completed the program were no longer being battered.

To help prevent the next generation from falling into the sexism/violence trap, Myriam Miedzian suggests encouraging schools to teach positive approaches to conflict resolution in the classroom and on the playground, to show children there are alternatives to violent behavior. Television should be prosocial and nonviolent rather than sexist and violent. We need to restrict violent pornography, which both demeans women and glorifies killing. Also boys should be encouraged from a young age to be empathetic rather than aggressive (Miedzian, 2002).

Physical Abuse and Neglect of Children

In a statistical sense, the American family is the most violent social institution in our society.

—MURRAY STRAUS AND RICHARD GELLES (1986, p. 466)

Child abuse is the physical or mental injury, sexual abuse, or negligent treatment of a child under the age of 18 by a person who is responsible for the child's welfare. Child abuse includes not only physical assault but also malnourishment, abandonment, neglect, emotional abuse, and sexual abuse. The U.S. Advisory Board on Child Abuse and Neglect (1990) stated, "Beating children, chronically belittling them, using them for sexual gratification, and depriving them of the basic necessities of life are repellent acts and cannot be permitted in a civilized society."

Professionals who work in the area of child abuse point out that abuse and neglect occur in families from all social classes and at all income levels. Being a child of rich, well-educated parents does not necessarily guarantee safety, but research does indicate that abuse is seven times more likely among low-income families (National Clearinghouse on Child Abuse and Neglect Information, 2004)—perhaps a reflection of the stress poorer families experience.

Incidence of Child Abuse

About 896,000 children were found to be victims of child maltreatment in 2002 (Administration for Children and Families, 2004). *Child neglect*, including medical neglect, the most commonly reported type of abuse, accounted for 60.5% of the victims. *Physical abuse* (major and minor physical injuries) accounted for 18.6% of verified cases; *sexual abuse* accounted for 9.9% of the cases; and *emotional abuse* or psychological maltreatment accounted for 6.5%. Many children were victims of more than one type of maltreatment. An estimated 1,400 children died as a result of mistreatment. Approximately two-fifths (40.3%) of child victims were maltreated by their mothers acting alone; 19.1% were maltreated by their fathers acting alone; 18.0% were maltreated by both mother and father; and 13.0% were abused by a nonparental perpetrator (Administration for Children and Families, 2004).

American society tends to condone violent rather than nonviolent approaches to the discipline of children. Research indicates that most American parents approve of spanking and slapping their children, and almost two out of three parents do so in a given year (Straus, 1994). Even though spanking and slapping are clearly

Child maltreatment includes child neglect, physical abuse, sexual abuse, and emotional abuse.

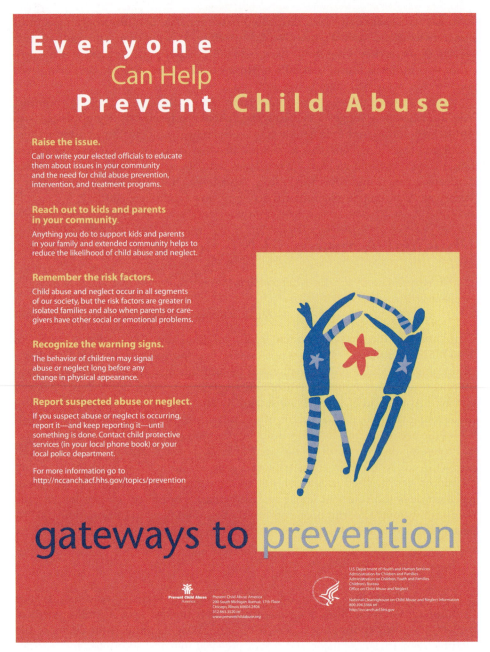

violent behaviors, they are not generally viewed as child abuse in our society. But why does our society consider it relatively acceptable to hit a child, a brother, or a spouse but unacceptable to hit an employee, a co-worker, or a salesperson?

Psychological aggression by American parents is also quite common. In a nationally representative sample of 991 parents, Straus and Field (2003) found that by the time the child reached age 2, 90% of the parents said they had used one or more forms of psychological aggression during the previous 12 months, and by age 5, 98% of the parents had done so. From ages 6 to 17 the rates of psychological aggression continued in the 90% range. Rates of what the researchers termed severe psychological aggression were lower: 10% to 20% for toddlers and about

50% for teenagers. Straus and Field found that psychological aggression cut across all social classes and ethnic and cultural groups, indicating that it is a near universal disciplinary tactic of American parents.

The Impact of Abuse on Children

Abused babies tend to be extremely difficult to nurture and to rear because of what they have experienced. Abuse between a parent and a child is a vicious cycle in which a negative act by the parent produces a negative response from the child, which, in turn, produces another negative response from the parent, and so on.

Researchers have found that abuse can compromise children's intellectual and social development in a variety of ways. Abused children tend to have lower IQ scores, learning problems, lower grades, and poorer school performance than do children who are not abused. Many abused children are aggressive, oppositional, and extremely wary. Other problems related to abuse include bedwetting; tantrums; inability to trust other people; difficulty relating to both peers and adults; generalized unhappiness; poor self-image; and the tendency to engage in juvenile delinquency, join a gang, run away from home, be truant from school, and become involved in violent crime (Straus & Field, 2003).

Transcending Abuse

Many abusive parents were themselves abused as children, but being abused as a child does not necessarily doom a person to pass the misery along to the next generation. Some abused children grow up to be happy and healthy adults, although transcending the pain of a violent childhood is very difficult. Since the early 1980s, researchers and clinicians have begun to focus on these resilient individuals. What they have found is that a nurturing relative, adult friend, or teacher often helped the troubled individual find a more positive approach to living.

Edward Zigler and his colleagues estimated that the rate of "cross-generational transmission" of child abuse is about 25% to 35%. This means that about one-quarter to one-third of those who are physically or sexually abused or neglected as children will subject their own children to similar abuse. However, the majority (65% to 75%) of people abused as children "will care for their offspring as well as the general population." According to the researchers, "many adults abused as children remember the agony they once suffered and have sworn to give their own children a better start." The research team did make it clear, however, that individuals with a history of abuse are still about six times more likely to abuse their own children than is the average person, who has about a 5% likelihood of doing so (Zigler, 2004). Clearly, the experience of childhood abuse does not predetermine that an abused child will grow up to abuse others later in life (Skogrand, DeFrain, DeFrain, & Jones, 2007). See Box 14.3 for coping strategies used by survivors of childhood trauma.

Families at Risk

A number of factors are related to the incidence of child abuse in a family (Gelles, 2000a):

- *Economic distress.* Unemployment, low income, illness in the family, and inability to pay for adequate medical care are stressors in the lives of many abusive parents.

BOX 14.3   Putting It Together

Surviving and Transcending a Traumatic Childhood: The Dark Thread

A study was conducted asking 90 volunteers who felt they had survived and transcended a traumatic childhood how they did it (Skogrand et al., 2007). The researchers wanted to know how, as young people, they survived the trauma and how, as adults, they transcended the trauma and became healthy. The participants decided for themselves whether they considered their childhood experience to be traumatic—with the definition of traumatic being that whatever happened to them had long-lasting psychological effects.

Some of the things that happened to the participants included the following:

- A high-school-age youth described how other students tried multiple times to burn her fat off with a Bunsen burner in chemistry class. Taunting and teasing were a routine part of her adolescent life—and no one did anything.
- A 15-year-old boy came home, one more time, to find his mother lying on the floor bleeding as a result of his father beating her up. The young man could not take it any more. He found a gun in the house and shot his father.
- One girl had 17 of her pet dogs killed by her father and stepbrothers—supposedly because she was "bad." She never knew what she had done wrong, but when she was "good" she got a new dog.

Almost all of the 90 who said they experienced trauma as children described abuse—someone abused them and most often they were abused by one or more family members. The trauma/abuse was usually multifaceted. For example, a person may have been sexually and physically abused, lived with a family member who was an alcoholic, and experienced abandonment all over the same time period. These things often went on for years.

As children, they could only survive, getting through life as best they could. They did not have the emotional or cognitive abilities or the physical strength to do anything but live through it. Looking back, the participants in this study said they did several things to survive:

- *They drew on spiritual resources.* They turned to a higher being that loved and cared about them. Usually, this was God, the protector. They believed in angels and did lots of praying. Religious institutions and leaders were typically not helpful.
- *They disassociated.* When they were being beaten or sexually abused, they mentally left their bodies and tuned out the pain. Some said it was like they were watching what was happening to them from a distance.
- *They escaped.* They read books, did well in school, developed their skills in music, or came up with other forms of diversion to get away from what was happening to them.

- *Inadequate parenting skills.* Abusive parents often have unrealistic expectations of their children, have little knowledge of child development, and demonstrate an inability to bond with infants (Azar & Bober, 1999; Azar & Gehl, 1999).
- *Parental personality problems.* Abusive parents often have low self-esteem and are likely to be more immature, less empathetic, and more self-centered than nonabusive parents. They also tend to be rigid, domineering, self-righteous, moralistic, and prone to anger.
- *Chemical abuse as a means of coping with stress.* Abusive parents often have high stress in their lives but have a difficult time dealing with that stress in a proactive, rational manner. Many turn to alcohol and other drugs to forget their troubles.
- *Social isolation.* Abusive families tend to be isolated from their community, with few friends or sources of outside support.
- *A special child.* Children with a chronic illness, an emotional disturbance, hyperactivity, mental retardation, or a physical handicap are at higher risk for abuse. Children who were unplanned and are unwanted are also more likely to be abused, as are children whose birth was difficult.

- *They accepted life as it was.* The participants in this study often did not realize, at the time, that what was happening to them was abnormal. They had never known anything else, and they accepted it as part of life.
- *They survived by default.* Later, they realized that, as children, things had happened that kept them afloat. Something happened that kept them from the one beating that could have resulted in death or having their spirit broken to the point that they could not put themselves back together. Someone came to the door when they were being beaten, or someone came into their lives who made things better.

As adults, they could begin the process of healing, transcending, and becoming healthy. They now had the emotional, cognitive, and physical abilities to do things to become healthy, even though it was a long, slow process:

- *They sought out spiritual resources.* They, again, relied on a loving higher being or God to be there for them. Organized religion was helpful for some, but for most it was a personal spiritual connection that helped.
- *They sought out therapy and support groups.* About half of the participants went to counseling and/or attended support groups to help them heal.
- *They got married to a loving spouse.* Many found a loving supportive spouse through a first marriage. Their spouse listened to them, supported them, and some-

times taught them how to become healthy. Others married someone who was also abusive and eventually got out of the marriage. Participants would say that even this first step of marrying someone who was abusive was a first step in getting away from the abuse.
- *They escaped from the abuse.* As adults, many had to literally move away from the abuser/abusers to become healthy. Others did not physically move but stopped having contact with those who harmed them.
- *They looked forward, not back.* At some point, many of the participants said they had to let go of what happened to them. This was usually after much healing had already taken place. They had to focus on the future.

We often hear about those who had traumatic childhoods growing up to further the cycle of abuse. But many draw on strengths and are, for a variety of reasons, able to become healthy and have healthy family lives. The "dark thread" of abuse will always be there, but it can become less pervasive in their lives.

A large number of the participants in this study became professionals who helped others in their work. Although no one said they were glad this trauma happened to them, they said it was all part of what made them who they are today.

Source: Surviving and Transcending a Traumatic Childhood: The Dark Thread by Linda Skogrand, Nikki DeFrain, John DeFrain, and Jean Jones, 2007, New York: Haworth Press.

- *Family size.* Researchers have found that the likelihood of child abuse tends to increase with family size. Parents of two children are 50% more likely to abuse their children than are parents of a single child. The rate of child abuse has been found to peak at five children and to decline in larger families (Gelles, 2000a).
- *Domestic violence in the family of origin.* Many abusive parents witnessed domestic violence between their own parents and were likely to have been physically punished themselves as children.
- *A violent subculture.* Some cultures and subcultures appear to be more tolerant of violent behavior toward children. For example, children who live in an unsafe neighborhood characterized by high levels of violence are at greater risk of being abused than are children growing up in a more peaceful neighborhood.
- *A violent marriage.* Parents who abuse their spouse are more likely to abuse their children than are parents whose marriage is peaceful.
- *Single parent.* Children who live with a single parent are more likely to suffer abuse than are those who live with two parents, perhaps because of the stresses often associated with single parenthood.

Children are more likely to suffer abuse when their parents are under stress because of unemployment, low income, or illness, especially if the parents are immature and know little about the development of children. During stressful times, parents need friends and other sources of support to help them cope with frustrations, and they need to relate to their children in a positive way.

- *Stepparent*. A child living with a stepparent is more likely to be abused than is a child living with both natural parents, perhaps because the stepparent's lack of a biological tie with the child can foster intolerance. One study of preschoolers found the likelihood for abuse to be 40 times greater for stepchildren.

Treatment and Prevention of Child Abuse

A growing body of professional literature demonstrates that Americans can do something about child abuse (Gelles, 2000b). Parents can learn how to deal more positively and effectively with their children. Education is the key to preventing abuse; education and therapy are needed to help abusive families.

Professionals see child abuse as a family and societal problem. Treating the problem involves three interrelated strategies: (1) increasing the parent's self-esteem, (2) increasing the parent's knowledge of children and positive childrearing techniques, and (3) devising community support networks for families under stress.

Parents who mistreat children are commonly viewed as people who need more positive ways of coping with their many problems. Counselors working with abusive parents are often quite successful in facilitating positive behavioral changes. By focusing on these parents' strengths, a therapist can enhance the development of the parents' self-esteem and parenting skills. A counselor can also provide referrals to other community services: financial aid for families in economic distress, food stamps, aid in finding better housing, family planning and adoption services, and day care.

Many programs for troubled parents include a parent discussion and support group among the treatment offerings. A group of parents, often facilitated by a professional, gets together to share stories about life's ups and downs and to offer advice and support to each other. Child abuse hotlines are also available to parents around the clock for help in dealing with difficult childrearing situations.

There are a number of things we as a society can do to prevent the abuse of children (Baumrind, 2004). They include working to reduce sources of social stress, such as poverty, racism, inequality, unemployment, and inadequate health care; eliminating sexism in the workplace and the home; providing adequate child care; promoting educational and employment opportunities for both men and women; supporting sex education and family planning programs in an effort to reduce unplanned and unwanted pregnancies; and working to end the social isolation of families in our culture.

Sibling and Child-to-Parent Abuse

Domestic violence is not initiated only by adults, and it is not directed only at children and partners. Siblings also engage in violence, and children sometimes attack their parents.

Sibling Abuse

One of the most common forms of family violence is **sibling abuse**. Seventy-five percent of siblings experience at least one violent episode a year. Fifty percent of siblings are punched, kicked, or bitten each year, and 16% beat each other up. Guns or knives are used or their use is threatened in less than 1% of these incidents (Gelles, 2000a).

Siblings often learn physical violence in the home, usually from their parents. One study found that of the children who were repeatedly abused by their parents, 76% severely assaulted a sibling; only 15% of children whose parents used no physical punishment or other violence over the course of a year assaulted a sibling (Gelles, 2000a).

To prevent sibling violence, parents can do the following things: (1) not be violent toward each other, (2) be supportive of and nurturing toward their children,

Child-to-parent abuse is devastating to a family. Children who abuse their parents are likely to be in their teen years or older.

(3) give their children a strong, clear message that violence is not acceptable, (4) monitor their children's behavior and be watchful, and (5) avoid coercive discipline, which is associated with higher rates of fighting between siblings.

In sum, parents need to take the time to teach their children nonviolent ways of relating to each other. Older children, in particular, can be instructed to sit down together and come up with a nonviolent solution to a conflict. Their efforts at conflict resolution can be surprisingly creative (Sibling Abuse Survivors' Information and Advocacy Network, 2004).

Child-to-Parent Abuse

Although some authorities in our culture believe that it is acceptable for parents to hit children, few believe it is all right for children to hit parents. Because parents are usually physically and socially more powerful than their children, we assume that parents are immune to abuse by their children. But **child-to-parent abuse** occurs in many families.

In a nationwide survey of family violence, nearly 10% of the parents reported that they had been hit, bitten, or kicked at least once by their children. Three percent of the parents reported that they had been a victim at least once of severely violent behavior on the part of a child 11 years old or older. The researchers concluded that "children are capable of violent behavior that is as devastating as violence inflicted by adults" (Gelles & Straus, 1988; Ulman & Straus, 2003). The research team heard stories of children pushing parents down stairs, setting the house on fire with the parents in it, and attacking parents with guns or knives in an effort to seriously injure or kill them. The majority of children who attack their parents are between the ages of 13 and 24.

Mothers are abused more often than fathers, probably because women usually are not as physically strong as men and because women are commonly viewed as acceptable targets for aggression. Mothers who have been abused by their husbands are more likely to be abused by their children (Gelles, 2000a). Teenagers who were once victims of parental violence often grow up to fight back.

Finally, family caseworkers report many situations in which an adult child physically or emotionally abuses her or his elderly parents. The stress of caring for an aging parent can be great, and abusive adult children sometimes argue that they are paying their parents back for abuse they suffered as children: "He did it to me. Now I have my chance to get even." Fortunately, many treatment programs are available to help people find positive and satisfying ways to relate to one another across the generations (see Bergeron, 2002; Carp, 2000; Tatara, 1998).

Alcohol Problems in Families

A family with a drinking problem is always a family in trouble.
—Marcia Lasswell and Thomas Lasswell (1991, p. 256)

Alcohol is a drug that acts as a depressant to the central nervous system. It is the mood-altering ingredient in wine, beer, and liquor. Alcohol is absorbed into the bloodstream and travels to virtually every part of the body. When ingested in large amounts or over a long period of time, alcohol can kill. It can damage the liver, heart, and pancreas; other consequences include malnutrition, stomach irritation, lowered resistance to disease, and irreversible brain or nervous system damage.

Alcohol abuse is a generic term that encompasses both **alcoholism**, which is the addiction to alcohol characterized by compulsive drinking, and **problem drinking**, which is alcohol consumption that results in a functional disability. More than one-half of American adults have a close family member who has or has had alcoholism or was a problem drinker. That is to say, about half of all adults in this country grew up with an alcoholic or problem drinker or had a blood relative who was an alcoholic or problem drinker (Dawson & Grant, 1998; Physician Leadership on National Drug Policy, 2000).

Alcohol is the most widely used psychoactive drug in the United States. It contributes to 100,000 deaths annually, making it the third leading cause of preventable death in this country after tobacco and diet/activity patterns.

Based on victim reports, 37% of the rapes and sexual assaults in America involve alcohol use by the offender. Fetal alcohol syndrome (FAS), which can occur when women drink during pregnancy, is the leading known environmental cause of mental retardation in Western countries. An estimated 6.6 million children under age 18 live in households with at least one alcoholic parent (U.S. Department of Health and Human Services, 2004). To see if you have a problem with alcohol, review the warning signs in Table 14.4.

Alcohol as a "Cause" of Family Violence

Alcohol is commonly associated with marital disruption, domestic violence, and many other family problems (National Council on Alcoholism and Drug Dependence, 2004; Roosa, Tein, Groppenbacher, Michaels, & Dumka, 1993; U.S. Department of Health and Human Services, 2004). Alcohol abuse is far more common among men than among women, although alcohol abuse by women is growing. Most literature has focused on the husband as the alcohol abuser and the wife and children as victims, but statistics show that alcohol dependence problems among wives are on the rise.

Alcohol abuse and family violence are statistically related. A national sample of more than 2,000 couples found, in general, that the more often a spouse was drunk, the greater likelihood there was of physical violence in the marital relationship. The exception to this finding was when the alcohol abuse was extreme. In this case, when the spouse was "almost always" drunk, the level of physical violence dropped to a lower level (Straus, 1990).

TABLE 14.4	Warning Signs for Alcohol Abuse

The following are some common warning signs of alcohol abuse. The more warning signs that apply, the greater the severity of the problem with alcohol use.

1. Drinking alone or secretively.

2. Using alcohol deliberately and repeatedly to perform or to get through difficult situations.

3. Feeling uncomfortable on occasions when alcohol is not available.

4. Escalating alcohol consumption beyond an already established drinking pattern.

5. Consuming alcohol heavily in risky situations (e.g., before driving).

6. Getting drunk regularly or more frequently than in the past.

7. Drinking in the morning or at other unusual times.

Source: Core Concepts in Health (9th ed.) (p. 268) by P. M. Insel and W. T. Roth, 2004, New York: McGraw-Hill. Reprinted by permission.

Even if there is no violence in the family of an alcoholic, there is likely to be a high degree of marital dissatisfaction and a large number of disagreements. Tension and verbal conflict are likely to be frequent. Researchers have estimated that half the divorces and half the juvenile arrests for delinquency in the United States occur in families with at least one alcohol-abusing member.

Spouses and children of alcohol abusers are at risk for developing serious physical and emotional problems. Although the majority of children reared in alcoholic homes are no more prone to suffer some kind of pathology, they are more likely to exhibit a variety of behavioral and emotional problems than are children from families without an alcoholic member. These problems include conduct disorders or delinquency, alcohol abuse, hyperactivity, difficulties with school work, anxiety, depression, or other health problems.

The Family's Reaction to Alcohol Abuse

In a classic article, Joan K. Jackson (1954) was the first to describe how families attempt to live with an alcohol-abusing father. Jackson studied a sample of families of Alcoholics Anonymous members and outlined a seven-stage process. It is widely recognized today that there are many families with alcohol-abusing mothers or other members, and Jackson's insights are useful for understanding these families. These stages are also applicable to other chemical dependence problems.

- *Stage 1: The family attempts to deny the problem.* The problem drinker, when confronted by the sober adult about the drinking behavior, denies there is a problem. The family accepts this statement and tolerates or rationalizes the abuser's drinking episodes.
- *Stage 2: The family tries to eliminate the problem.* When the drinking can no longer be ignored, the sober spouse tries to control the problem drinker with threats, bribes, and/or by hiding the alcohol. Marital conflict increases, and family members isolate themselves from friends and neighbors in a futile effort to conceal the drinker's problem.
- *Stage 3: The family becomes disorganized.* The sober spouse realizes that the problem cannot be rationalized away or concealed from the children or the drinker's employer and co-workers. The sober spouse also recognizes that it is futile to try to curtail the drinker's alcohol consumption. Conflict increases, with the children often caught between arguing parents.
- *Stage 4: The family makes a first attempt at reorganization.* The sober spouse recognizes that the drinker cannot function adequately in the family—a recognition often precipitated by the drinker's mismanagement of family funds or by the drinker's violence toward the sober spouse or the children—and takes action. The sober spouse may assume the alcohol abuser's role in the family or may decide to leave the alcohol abuser. The sober spouse may seek assistance from various public agencies, counselors, and self-help groups such as Al-Anon. This network of support helps the sober partner gradually regain self-esteem and find the strength to go on. During this stage, the problem drinker is likely to bargain with the family, hoping to regain the lost family role and stature. If the family accepts the drinker's bargain but the drinker continues or resumes drinking, the destructive cycle begins again.
- *Stage 5: The family attempts to escape the problem.* The sober spouse seeks a legal separation or divorce. The alcohol abuser often gives up drinking for a while, but the sober spouse has already shifted from inaction to action.

- *Stage 6: The family makes a second attempt at reorganization.* After legal separation or divorce, the sober spouse assumes the roles formerly held by the problem drinker, and family life without the problem drinker is generally much better for all family members. The sober spouse may feel guilty for having left the troubled partner. The problem drinker may attempt to reenter the family or may try to "get even" with the family.
- *Stage 7: The family reorganizes, with the substance abuser seeking help.* If the alcohol-abusing member seeks help and learns to control the drinking, the family may be able to reunite successfully. The process can be difficult; family roles will have to be reassigned once again, and family members will need to reassess their feelings toward the alcohol abuser.

Later therapists built on Jackson's work and outlined a number of coping strategies women commonly use when dealing with alcohol-abusing husbands. These include emotional withdrawal from the marriage; infantilizing the husband; threatening separation or divorce or locking the spouse out of the house; trying to avoid family conflict; assuming control over family finances; and acting out themselves by drinking, threatening suicide, or becoming involved with other men.

Treatment and Prevention of Alcoholism

Some family therapists have been critical of programs that treat the alcoholic outside the context of the family, whereas some alcoholism treatment therapists have criticized family therapists for assuming that alcoholism can be cured simply by eliminating dysfunctional family patterns (Fenell & Weinhold, 1997). It is probably safe to say that problems in families can contribute to alcohol abuse in individual members and that the alcohol abuse then contributes to problems for that family. Those who work with alcohol abusers are becoming increasingly aware that family therapy is an important tool in the treatment of alcoholics and their family system (O'Farrell & Fals-Stewart, 2001; Rowe, 2003).

Self-help groups such as **Alcoholics Anonymous (AA)** (for alcoholics) and **Al-Anon** (for families of alcoholics) have chapters in most U.S. cities and towns. In some metropolitan areas, many different AA meetings are held at a variety of

Alcoholics need to be confronted about their condition by people they trust and in a form they can receive. Even in the most advanced phases, alcoholics can recognize and accept some reality.

locations each week. These groups offer advice and support for troubled individuals and families. **Alateen**, founded on the AA model, is a support group for young people with alcoholic parents. In weekly meetings, members discuss their problems and learn from others in similar situations.

The National Council on Alcoholism and Drug Dependence (NCADD; 2004) in New York City argues that the disease can be stopped, citing the fact that 1.5 million Americans are in recovery. Some of NCADD's recommendations for people dealing with an alcoholic are as follows:

- *Recognize that alcoholism is a disease.* It is not a moral failure or a simple lack of willpower.
- *Learn as much as possible about alcoholism.* Most libraries have many books and articles on alcoholism and other addictions.
- *Do not become an enabler.* Do not support someone's drinking by pretending there is no problem (denial) or by protecting or lying for the alcoholic.
- *Avoid home treatments.* Do not try to solve the loved one's problem by preaching, complaining, acting like a martyr, or trying to reason with the drinker. Alcoholics need expert help from organizations such as Alcoholics Anonymous.
- *Get help for yourself.* The illness of alcoholism affects everyone close to the alcoholic. Many organizations help not only the alcoholic but family members and friends as well.

Acknowledging the Dangers of Legal Drugs

Our national fervor to stamp out use of and addiction to illegal drugs has in some ways overshadowed the serious harm legal drugs cause in our society. Alcohol and tobacco cause many times the number of deaths attributable to illegal drugs—and the associated costs, in terms of lost time from work and medical bills, are much greater.

About 100,000 Americans die each year from alcohol abuse, including alcohol-related medical problems, motor vehicle crashes, homicides, suicides, and other unintentional injuries (U.S. Department of Health and Human Services, 2004). The Centers for Disease Control and Prevention (2004b) reports 478,000 deaths each year linked to smoking. More than 440,000 deaths each year are caused by tobacco use, making smoking the leading cause of death in our country. Because of exposure to secondhand smoke, an estimated 3,000 nonsmoking Americans die of lung cancer, and more than 35,000 die of heart disease. Also, an estimated 150,000 to 300,000 children younger than 18 months of age have respiratory tract infections because they have been exposed to smoke.

There are about 20,000 deaths each year in this country from drug-induced causes. "Drug-induced causes" include not only deaths from dependent and nondependent use of drugs (legal and illegal use) but also poisoning from medically prescribed drugs and other drugs (Minino, Arias, Kochanek, Murphy, & Smith, 2002).

Medically, alcohol and cigarette addictions are the most difficult habits to break, according to Dr. William Brostoff. It is easier to withdraw or undergo detoxification from cocaine or even heroin than from alcohol or cigarettes ("Nation's Legal Drugs," 1986). It has been found that actively involving the spouse in the smoking cessation program increases the program's success (Whitehead & Doherty, 1989).

Almost all adult smokers begin to smoke before age 20, researchers have found. Recent studies indicate that family functioning is related to adolescent cigarette smoking. For example, William J. Doherty and William Allen (1994) found that families who were low in family cohesion (togetherness) and had a parent who smoked were the most likely to have a young adolescent who smoked. Similarly, Janet N. Melby and her colleagues found that harsh and inconsistent parenting was related to adolescent tobacco use and that nurturant and involved parenting was not (Melby, Conger, Conger, & Lorenz, 1993).

The family clearly is a major influence in our lives, either as a foundation for health and happiness or as an unhappy battleground. Emotional, physical, and sexual abuse does occur in families, and many families are plagued by alcoholism and addiction to other legal and illegal drugs. But these problems can be treated effectively. Fortunately, most families find ways to create relatively supportive and satisfying relationships among their members, which helps prevent many family problems of all sorts.

Summary

- Families in all cultures experience stress, even though the types of issues that cause the stress vary by cultural group. All stressors, regardless of their origin, eventually affect family members. All families have some internal resources for managing stress, which they tend to use before turning to resources outside the family.
- The relationship between stress and functioning is curvilinear. Too little stress creates boredom; too much stress creates discomfort and frustration. Eustress, a low-to-moderate or a moderate-to-high level of stress, is positive, motivating, and exciting.
- New stressors appear at each stage of the family life cycle; others are common across all stages. Financial issues concern families at all stages and all income levels. Intrafamily and work/family strains and the death of a family member or relative are also seen at all stages of the family life cycle.
- Stress is highest and family satisfaction is lowest among families with adolescents. Young and older couples without children in the home tend to have the least stress and highest couple satisfaction.
- The roller coaster course of adjustment to stressors, described by Hill, involves a period of disorganization, an angle of recovery, and a new level of organization.
- In families who cope successfully with stress, the parents possess these resources: good financial management skills, appreciation for the personality of the partner, a strong social support network of family and friends, a good sexual relationship, a happy marriage, and satisfaction with the quality of their lives.
- Families draw on a variety of resources and related coping strategies to deal with stressful issues: cognitive resources (reframing the situation), emotional resources (expressing feelings), relationship resources (increasing cohesion), community resources (seeking help and support from outside the family), spiritual resources (praying; seeking help from a pastor, priest, or rabbi), and individual resources (developing autonomy).
- According to family systems theory, family members' behaviors are all interrelated; each member's actions affect the other members and their actions. As such, the family systems approach focuses on helping families resolve relationship issues rather than on identifying "causes" of family problems.
- Based on a national survey of spouse abuse with 20,951 married couples, nonabusive marriages were compared with abusive marriages. Couples in nonabusive marriages had used less alcohol, had higher levels of couple closeness and flexibility, had better communication and conflict resolution, and had a stronger network of family and friends. In terms of personality, nonabusive marriages had partners who were more assertive, had higher levels of self-confidence, and less often tried to dominate their partners.
- Many of the risk factors for spouse abuse in a family are similar to those for child abuse: victimization as a child, low self-esteem, youth, economic stress, social isolation, alcohol abuse, and a male-dominated relationship. Cultural factors that implicitly support the objectification and denigration of women may also play a part.
- Counselors generally advise battered women to leave their husbands. Shelters for abused women and their children offer emotional support and counseling as well as practical help. Police arrest of perpetrators of domestic violence is more common today, and research indicates that men who spend time behind bars are less likely to assault their partners again.
- Child abuse encompasses not only physical assault resulting in injury but also abandonment, neglect, emotional abuse, and sexual abuse. Abuse and neglect

occur across all socioeconomic levels, although they are far more prevalent among low-income families.

- Many abusive parents were themselves abused as children, but only about one-quarter to one-third of all children who are abused grow up to abuse their own offspring.
- Parental and family risk factors for child abuse include economic distress, inadequate parenting skills, parental personality problems, chemical abuse, social isolation, a special child, family size, domestic violence in the abuser's family of origin, a violent subculture or marriage, and single parenthood or stepparenthood.
- Sibling abuse and child-to-parent abuse are more common than might be expected. An estimated 75% of siblings are involved in a violent episode each year, and 10% of parents are victims of their children's violent behavior.
- An estimated 100,000 Americans die each year from alcohol abuse, and about 478,000 Americans die from diseases linked to smoking.

Key Terms

stress	learned helplessness
stressor	theory
curvilinear relationship	catharsis conflict
distress	child abuse
eustress	sibling abuse
stress pileup	child-to-parent abuse
family coping	alcohol abuse
boundary ambiguity	alcoholism
ambiguous loss	problem drinking
managing stress	Alcoholics
posttraumatic stress	Anonymous (AA)
disorder (PTSD)	Al-Anon
victimizer	Alateen

Activities

1. Identify a major stressor experienced by you and your family and plot how your family changed over time to deal with this major stressor on the Couple and Family Rating Form, Table A.2 in Appendix A. Identify your family's position at four points in time: before the event, during the event, 1 to 2 months after the event, and 6 months after the event. (Review Figure 14.6 if necessary.)
2. List the family stressors and strains you recognize at the launching stage of the family life cycle. Then discuss family stressors and strains at the launching stage with your parents. Have each parent describe what the stressors are (or were) for her or him. Look at those areas in which your mother's response differs from your father's. Also compare their descriptions with yours.
3. Select a major stressor in your family and describe how your family reacted as a group. It can be the same stressor as the one you identified in Activity 1, or it can be a different one. Indicate what your family did that was helpful and not helpful in dealing with the stressor. What resources did you and your family find most useful for managing your stress?
4. In small groups, discuss the extent of alcohol and other drug abuse on campus. Also discuss any violent incidents, such as date rape, related to chemical abuse.

Suggested Readings

Al-Anon/Alateen. (2004). Welcome to Al-Anon and Alateen. Web site: http://www.al-anon.alateen.org. For spouses and children of alcoholics and problem drinkers.

Alcoholics Anonymous. (2004). Web site: http://www.alcoholics-anonymous.org. Information from the pioneering organization.

Bancroft, L. (2002). *Why does he do that? Inside the minds of angry and controlling men*. New York: Putnam's Sons. Helps us understand the mind and motives of the batterer.

Bonanno, G. A. (2004). Loss, trauma, and human resilience: Have we underestimated the human capacity to thrive after extremely adverse events? *American Psychologist, 59*(1), 20–28. Many people are exposed to loss or potentially traumatic events at some point in their lives, and yet they continue to have positive emotional experiences in life and show only minor disruptions in their ability to function.

Boss, P. (2002). *Family stress management: A contextual approach*. Thousand Oaks, CA: Sage. Why do some families survive stressful situations while others fall apart?

Boss, P. (2006). *Loss, trauma, and resilience: Therapeutic work with ambiguous loss*. Dunmore, PA: Norton.

Bushman, B. J., & Anderson, C. A. (2001). Media violence and the American public: Scientific facts versus media misinformation. *American Psychologist, 56*(6/7), 477–489. Media violence is clearly linked to violence in our society, but the media do not clearly report this fact.

Ennett, S. T., Bauman, K. E., Foshee, V. A., Pemberton, M., & Hicks, K. A. (2001). Parent–child communication about adolescent tobacco and alcohol use: What do parents say and does it affect youth behavior? *Journal of Marriage and the Family, 63*, 48–62. Parents have to be careful about how they advise their teenagers, because the young people sometimes do the exact opposite of what parents suggest.

Frias, S. M., & Angel, R. J. (2005). The risk of partner violence among low-income Hispanic subgroups. *Journal of Marriage and the Family, 67*, 552–564.

Graham-Bermann, S. A., & Edleson, J. L. (Eds.). (2001). *Domestic violence in the lives of children: The future of research, intervention, and social policy.* Washington, DC: American Psychological Association. For researchers, policymakers, and those who care about the effects of domestic violence on children.

Koenig, L. J., Doll, L. S., O'Leary, A., & Pequegnat, W. (2004). *From child sexual abuse to adult sexual risk: Trauma, revictimization, and intervention.* Washington, DC: American Psychological Association. The relationship between child sexual abuse and adult sexual health outcomes in men and women.

Malley-Morrison, K. (2003). *Family violence in a cultural perspective: Defining, understanding, and combating abuse.* Thousand Oaks, CA: Sage. Focuses on family violence from four major ethnic populations in the United States: Native Americans, African Americans, Latinos, and Asian Americans.

Polivy, J., & Herman, C. P. (2002). If at first you don't succeed: False hopes of self-change. *American Psychologist, 57*(9), 677–689. Despite repeated failure at attempts to change their behavior, people make repeated attempts to do so. Why?

Sammons, M. T. (2005). Psychology in the public sector: Addressing the psychological effects of combat in the U.S. Navy. *American Psychologist, 162,* 123–129.

Schewe, P. A. (2002). *Preventing violence in relationships: Interventions across the life span.* Washington, DC: American Psychological Association. Focuses on healthy interpersonal relationship skills as the basis for preventing violence.

Skogrand, L., DeFrain, N., DeFrain, J., & Jones, J. (2007). *Surviving and transcending a traumatic childhood: The dark thread.* New York: Haworth.

van Wormer, K., & Bednar, S. G. (2002). Working with male batterers: A restorative-strengths perspective. *Families in Society: The Journal of Contemporary Human Services, 83*(5/6), 557–565.

Wright, K. (2003). Relationships with death: The terminally ill talk about dying. *Journal of Marital and Family Therapy, 29*(4), 435–454.

Visit the text-specific Online Learning Center at **www.mhhe.com/Olson6** for practice tests, chapter summaries, Web links, Internet exercises, key terms, and flashcards.

15 *Divorce, Single-Parent Families, and Stepfamilies*

Intimacy, Strengths, and Diversity

Divorce in Today's Society

Understanding Divorce

Adjusting to Divorce

Single-Parent Families and Stepfamilies

Types of Single-Parent Families

Stepfamilies

Summary

Key Terms

Activities

Suggested Readings

Intimacy, Strengths, and Diversity

This chapter is about intimacy and the roller coaster ride of loss of intimacy in divorce and new found intimacy in remarriage resulting in stepfamilies. Intimacy becomes complicated in divorce, when what was once a close relationship turns to the deterioration of the marriage. There was a history of intimacy, and children may have resulted from a close, intimate emotional and sexual relationship. Even though that may be gone in divorce, it is never forgotten. Stepfamily relationships require new and usually more complicated intimate relationships with the addition of stepchildren and new extended-family relationships.

People seek inner strength as they go through a divorce and also as single parents. All types of families can be strong. In fact, single mothers and single fathers can create wonderfully strong family relationships. There is not doubt that life is

Stepfamilies are becoming increasingly common as the number of single parents and divorced parents marry.

often more complicated and stressful for single parents and stepfamilies, but many families do well in meeting the challenges.

This chapter is also about the diversity of family forms. This growing family complexity creates challenges for family members, extended-family members, therapists, and policymakers as we try to navigate new territory.

Divorce in Today's Society

Divorcees are people who have not achieved a good marriage—they are also people who would not settle for a bad one.

—PAUL BOHANNAN (1970, p. 54)

Marriage continues to be popular in our society; unfortunately, the likelihood of a marriage being successful is not particularly high. Whereas half of first marriages end in divorce, about 60% of second marriages are likely to end in divorce. Figure 15.1 illustrates the divorce–remarriage patterns that can be expected with a 50% divorce rate.

Statistical and Historical Trends

Before the mid-1800s, people married for physical and economic survival. Divorce for most people was not an option (Joanning & Keoughan, 2006). Many marriages were arranged, or women married the farmer down the road with only two or three potential marriage partners available. Very few marriages ended in divorce during this time (Coontz, 2005). By the late 1800s and early 1900s, young people moved from viewing marriage as a way to stay alive to marrying for love (Joanning &

FIGURE 15.1

Estimated Divorce and Remarriage Rates for 1,000 Individuals Married in 1990

Source: Family Science (p. 445) by W. R. Burr, R. D. Day, and K. S. Bahr. Copyright © 1993 Wesley Burr, Randal Day, Kathleen Bahr. Reprinted by permission of the authors.

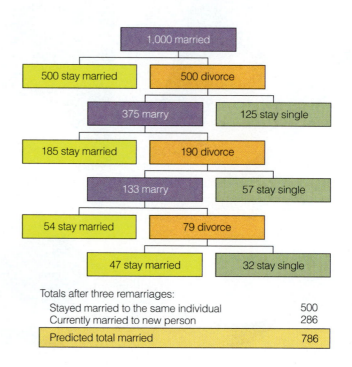

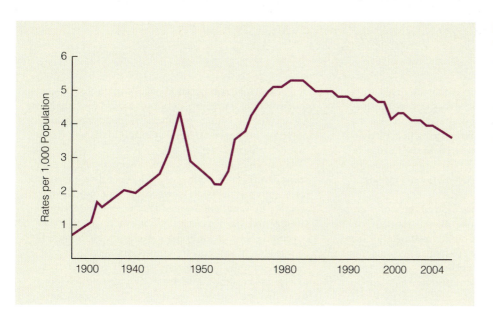

FIGURE 15.2
Divorce Rate: 1900–
2005

*Source: Statistical Abstract of the
United states,* 1951, no. 57; 1999
no 91; 2004–2005, no. 70; 2006,
table 117; National Vital Statistics
Reports, vol. 54, no. 17.

Keoughan). Today, about 50% of marriages end in divorce (Cole & Broussard, 2006).
As can be seen by Figure 15.2, the divorce rate has been increasing and then leveling off.

Divorce rates can change as a result of societal events. Notice the peak in divorce
that occurred in 1946 after the end of World War II (see Figure 15.2). The Vietnam
War also created an increase in divorce in the 1970s (Cole & Broussard, 2006).
Divorces decreased during the recession of the 1950s, because people may not have
felt divorce was an option when money was tight. Some researchers, although not
all, believe that part of the increase in divorce in the 1970s was also related to a
change in divorce laws, which made it easier to get divorced (Cole & Broussard,
2006). During this time, many states went from fault-based divorce to no-fault
divorce, which meant that divorces could be granted without either partner finding fault with their spouse. The highest divorce rates in history occurred in 1979
and 1981, with the rates beginning a decline and then leveling off through 2005
(Cole & Broussard, 2006). But the divorce rate could increase again as a result of the
Iraq War like it did after other wars.

Another factor that also seems to have had a significant effect on divorce rates
was women entering the workforce and earning salaries that allowed for economic
independence. This earning ability was spurred on by the feminist movement in
the 1960s and 1970s, which increased the awareness of equity in economic opportunities (Cole & Broussard, 2006). Some suggest that contraception options, which
became more available in the 1970s, also contributed to divorce rates, because
women could chose not to have children, and without children they were able to
get out of unhappy marriages (Cole & Broussard, 2006).

The average age at divorce is 36 for men and 33 for women. The average length
of first marriages that end in divorce is about 7 years. So, of the half of all first marriages that end in divorce, half of those end within the first 7 years. In terms of first
marriages, divorce most often occurs during the first year or two. By the end of
5 years of marriage, 19% of couples are divorced; by the end of 10 years, 14% more
are divorced. Another 7% divorce before 15 years of marriage; 7% more divorce

BOX 15.1   Diversity in Families

The Globalization of Divorce

Although America ranks high in the rate of divorce, the rest of the world is catching up. Across Europe, for instance, marriage rates are declining and divorce rates are climbing steadily, with Belgium reporting in 2002 that it had the fewest number of marriages in the European Union (3.9 per 1,000 people) and the highest number of divorces (3.0 per 1,000 people) (UK National Statistics, 2004).

Cultural changes taking place around the world are influencing divorce rates in almost every country. One of the countries changing most rapidly is the Republic of Korea, which in the past 10 to 15 years has become an increasingly open, westernized society.

Prior to 1990, divorce was a cultural and legal taboo in the Republic of Korea (known as South Korea by Westerners), and Korea's divorce rate was one of the lowest in the world (1.1 per 1,000 people). A divorced woman would be ostracized and had a very slim chance of marrying again. She usually lost custody of her children and had a difficult, if not impossible, time finding employment. A divorced man would also have had a hard time finding a job, or if he already had one, would not get promoted. His career path was definitely cut short. His chances at remarriage were not good either, as few women wanted to marry a man who had already shown he could not keep a stable relationship or take care of his family (Lankov, 2004).

The situation began to change in the early 1990s. Within 12 years, Korea's divorce rate rose from 11% in 1990 to 47% in 2002, ranking the country among the top 10 in the world. Some of the reasons for this swift-spreading change include "the collapse of traditional patriarchic values, rise of a new generation of college-educated women, the growth of employment opportunities for female workers and their ensuing economic independence, and the powerful influence of Western individualism and feminism" (Lankov, 2004).

As a symbol of just how much Korean attitudes toward divorce have changed, in 2004 nearly a quarter of the country's television viewers tuned in once a week to watch a show called *Love and War,* where actors dramatized actual divorce cases and marital conflicts. Viewers could then vote online on whether they thought the couple should stay together or get divorced.

The Republic of Korea isn't the only Asian country to experience a dramatic rise in divorce rates. Below are some divorce statistics and their cultural significance in several other Asian countries:

- *India.* Not so long ago, a woman was so tied to her husband's fate that if he died before she did, she was thrown onto his funeral pyre. Today, that practice is no longer legal, and women in unhappy marriages are now seeking divorce. In 2004, the divorce rate was estimated at 11 per 1,000 people (versus 7.41 in 1991). However, divorce is still not socially accepted by everyone. One divorced woman related to *Time Asia* that divorced women in India always feel a sense of isolation and that "women like her are widely viewed as inferior to those with husbands" (Fitzpatrick, 2004).
- *Japan.* Statistics showed that in 2004 a couple married every 42 seconds in Japan—and that every 2 minutes another couple got divorced. The divorce rate rose from 22% in 1990 to 38% in 2002. The biggest change

before their 25th anniversary; and 3% more divorce before their 50th anniversary (U.S. Bureau of the Census, 2004a).

Legal Trends

Since 1970, when the state of California introduced no-fault divorce, major changes have occurred in divorce laws across the United States. These changes came about as a direct response to the rising number of divorces and to the changing roles of women in this country. Today, all 50 states have laws similar to California's (Parkman, 2000).

No-fault divorce abolished fault ("guilt" of one party) as the basis for dissolving a marriage. Under no-fault law, one party's assertion that "irreconcilable differences have caused the irremediable breakdown of the marriage" is sufficient for the granting of a divorce.

in Japan, where 70% of all divorces are initiated by women, was the increase in the number of couples getting divorced after 20 years or more of marriage. In 1975, there were 6,810 such divorces; in 2002, there were 45,536 (Fitzpatrick, 2004).

- *China.* In the past 20 years, the divorce rate in mainland China has doubled—and has tripled in Taiwan. As in Japan, many of these divorced couples are in their 40s and 50s and have been married for many years. People over the age of 50 seeking divorce made up 9% of all divorces in 1980, as compared to 14.7% in 2003. The Association for Asian Research suggested four reasons for increased divorce rates among middle-aged Chinese: (1) the concept of marriage is changing and individual pursuit of happiness is seen as more important than stability; (2) the demands of professional success coupled with the demands of raising a family cause strain on relationships; (3) social acceptance of divorce has increased, and more opportunities exist to meet new partners; and (4) familial support systems—where extended families all lived together and shared responsibilities—are weaker than ever before ("Divorce Rate Climbs," 2004).

In Shanghai, where divorce rates increased by 30% in the 1-year period from 2003 to 2004, the government sent out notices to couples seeking divorce asking them to reconsider the correctness of their decision. One reason for the sharp increase was that procedures for divorce were greatly simplified in 2004, and couples who previously had to wait a month for their divorce agreement now had to wait about 10 minutes ("Divorce Rate on the Increase in Shanghai," 2004).

Elsewhere around the world divorce rates and attitudes toward divorce vary markedly. Africa, for instance, exhibits great disparities. In Morocco, a law was passed in February 2004, stating that women were no longer legally required to obey their husbands. Divorce, however, still brings a woman great shame. In contrast, when a woman in the western Sahara gets a divorce, she throws a party, and men who seek the hand of the newly available women bring presents like camels, perfume, or money (Harter, 2004).

In another part of the continent, Egypt is struggling to find a more equitable system of granting divorce by changing some of its centuries-old laws and traditions. However, as reported by Human Rights Watch (2004), even the new laws are still biased toward the male population. Egyptian men have an unconditional right to divorce without ever having to go to court; they simply have to make an oral renunciation that can later be ratified by a member of the clergy. Women, on the other hand, must go through complicated legal procedures. If they wish to keep full financial rights, they must show evidence that their husbands inflicted physical harm, a claim they are usually required to support with eyewitness testimony. A woman can file for "no-fault" divorce—if she agrees to forfeit all her financial rights and repay the dowry given to her by her husband when they were wed (Human Rights Watch, 2004).

As the westernization of the world continues, as economic growth in poor countries increases, and as women's rights take on greater dimensions, we can expect the rising global divorce rate to continue to be an unintentional byproduct.

Traditional Divorce Law. Lenore Weitzman and Ruth Dixon have identified the four major elements of traditional divorce law that were transformed by the no-fault system of divorce (Weitzman & Dixon, 1992):

- *Gender-based divisions of role responsibilities.* Traditional family law assumed that the husband would provide financial support in a lifelong marriage. If the marriage ended and if the wife had been virtuous, she was granted **alimony**—continued financial support. This gender-based division of labor was also recognized in regard to children. The husband remained responsible for their economic support after the divorce, and the wife was the preferred custodial parent.
- *Grounds for divorce.* Traditionally, fault—legal blame for the end of a marriage—had to be assigned, and only serious offenses were considered sufficient grounds for divorce. Evidence for misbehavior varied from state to

Because divorce can be a traumatic experience for adults and children, lawyers should not act as adversaries doing battle for their clients but should try to facilitate responsible communication. The lawyer's most important task is to help divorcing parents restructure the family and minimize the emotional damage to both themselves and their children.

state, but husbands charged with cruelty were often alleged to have caused bodily harm to their wives. Wives were more likely to be charged with neglecting their husbands or their homes. In practice, many couples wishing to divorce simply agreed privately to an **uncontested divorce**—one in which one party, often the wife, would charge the other party, generally the husband, with mental cruelty, and the "accused" would agree not to challenge the "accuser" in court. Even though the parties colluded in the matter and often perjured themselves in court, the courts considered the grounds "appropriate violations" of the marriage contract.

- *Adversarial proceedings.* In the traditional system, lawyers "did battle" for their clients, and divorces had to be "won." One partner was "guilty", and the other was "innocent."
- *Linkage of the financial settlement to determination of fault.* A finding of "guilty" or "innocent" had important financial consequences. Alimony could be awarded only to an innocent spouse: A wife found guilty of adultery, for example, could not receive alimony. Property awards were also linked to the determination of fault. This linkage produced heated accusations and counteraccusations.

No-Fault Divorce Law. Weitzman and Dixon (1992) have also explained how no-fault divorce law altered the four elements of traditional divorce law just listed:

- *Redefinition of the traditional duties of husbands and wives and establishment of equality between the genders as a norm.* Under no-fault laws, the husband is no longer considered by law to be the head of the family. Both spouses are presumed to be equal partners, with equal obligations for financial support and care of their children. Spouses are treated equally with respect to child custody, as well as finances and property. The so-called **tender years doctrine,** which presumed that young children would do better with their mother than with their father, has been replaced by the notion of joint custody as being in the "best interests of the child." Fathers are at least theoretically equal to mothers in questions of custody. In a small number of cases, fathers are winning not only custody but also child support.

- *Elimination of fault-based grounds for divorce.* Under no-fault laws, one spouse does not have to prove the other's adultery, cruelty, or desertion. The concept of *irreconcilable differences* recognizes the irrelevancy of discussing the reasons for the marital dissolution in court.
- *Elimination of the adversarial process.* Proponents of divorce reform argued that the adversarial nature of traditional divorce proceedings was harmful to all parties involved, especially to the children. Under no-fault, by facilitating accurate and responsible communication rather than doing battle, lawyers can help divorcing parents restructure the family and prepare to fulfill their postdivorce parenting responsibilities. Many spouses neither love nor hate each other at the end of a marriage; they are capable of an *amicable divorce* and are good candidates for joint custody of their children.
- *Basing of financial decisions on equity, equality, and economic need rather than on fault or gender-based role assignments.* In a no-fault system, each spouse's economic circumstances are assessed under the principle of equality between the sexes. No-fault laws adhere to the notion that divorced women should be self-supporting but that if that is not possible, they should receive fair compensation. Under the newer no-fault divorce laws, older homemakers are more likely to receive alimony than are younger homemakers. In some cases, a woman might receive support while she goes back to school for retraining. Attorneys have been forcefully arguing that women who previously put their husbands through professional school are entitled to a share of their earnings for a period of time after the divorce.

Reformers of traditional divorce law argued that with an increasing number of women entering the labor force, alimony was rapidly becoming an anachronism. This, however, ignored the fact that female workers earn on average only about 80% of what male workers earn (U.S. General Accounting Office, 2003).

There has been a backlash to the financial aspects of no-fault divorce. Many see these reforms as antiwomen measures that punish women financially for divorce. Divorced women and their children suffer an immediate drop of 27% in their standard of living, whereas their ex-husbands experience an increase of 10% in their standard of living (Parkman, 1995).

No-fault divorce laws are based on the theory that equality results in a more positive outcome for all involved. How the theory works in practice depends on the decisions of individual judges who must adjudicate the 1.1 million divorces in the United States each year.

Effects of the Change. In evaluating the results of the no-fault divorce system, researchers over the years have reported a mixture of expected and unexpected findings. Researchers continue to dispute whether the divorce rate did increase as a result of no-fault divorce (Binner & Dnes, 2001; Nakonezny, Shull, & Rodgers, 1995; Rodgers, Nakonezny, & Shull, 1997). The mandatory counseling feature of the system apparently did not bring about many reconciliations; it proved too late, too late for most marriages. And lawyers have been cautioned to support marriage in their work with troubled couples, though the role of money cannot be overlooked in the lawyer/client dynamics because lawyers receive more money for divorces than for marital reconciliations (Muller, 2002).

Indeed, no-fault has eliminated the hypocrisy of the old system, which forced spouses into pointing the finger whether they wished to or not, and it seems to have somewhat reduced the bitterness of the battles. The number of hearings before a final decree of divorce has declined markedly, and it was at these hearings when many of the most bitter battles were fought. Property settlements and spousal and child support appear to be fairer under the new guidelines. However, no-fault did eliminate one benefit of traditional divorce law for those who have a valid grievance: Because men can no longer be faulted for obvious wrongdoing, women, in particular, have lost a bargaining advantage in negotiating property settlements and alimony (Weitzman & Dixon, 1992).

Judges wryly comment that divorce court service is like a sentence in Siberia. Despite changes in divorce laws, divorce court remains "one of the saddest rooms in America." But no-fault laws have alleviated some of the tremendous pain of divorce and have facilitated greater cooperation in coparenting after the divorce.

Understanding Divorce

No emptiness on earth can compare with the loss of love..

—PAUL THEROUX (1996, p. 425)

Both partners in a divorce often spend considerable time trying to unravel the reasons why their marriage ended. Although the task is difficult, it is essential to the postdivorce recovery process. The search for the "causes" of a divorce must take into consideration a number of factors and many points of view. In this section we will look at several important issues to understand why people divorce.

The Culture of Divorce

Divorce culture, a term Barbara Dafoe Whitehead (1997) so poignantly describes in her book of the same name, is the notion that divorce has now become so accepted that it is almost the expected outcome of marriage. Before the 1950s, divorce was rare, and there was considerable social pressure to stay married, even if it was a bad and abusive marriage. But now divorce is linked with the pursuit of individual satisfaction, and there is less social pressure to stay married. Even the presence of children is not a deterrent to getting divorced as it was in the past. The challenges of divorce are even fodder for comedy, as in the movie *Mrs. Doubtfire,* in which a mother unknowingly hires the separated father (dressed up as a woman) as a nanny to care for their children.

Why Couples Divorce

"Marriage causes divorce!" is the facetious reply to the question "What causes divorce?" The stresses and strains of living together are simply too difficult for many couples. But the picture is more complicated. What are some of the interwoven factors that cause divorce? Why do some people divorce while others in apparently more troubled relationships stay married? Family researchers and family therapists have spent considerable time exploring what causes divorce.

In a national study of marital therapists who work with couples, Whisman, Dixon, and Johnson (1997) identified the most common problems reported by couples (Table 15.1). The results of their study demonstrate that poor communication, power struggles, unrealistic expectations about marriage, sexual relationship problems, and difficulties in decision making top the list.

TABLE 15.1	Couples' Problems as Reported to Marital Therapists				
Type of Problem	**Frequency of Problem**	**Rank of Problem**	**Difficulty Treating**	**Damaging Impact**	**Composite Ranking**
Communication	87%	1	7	6	4.7
Power struggle	62	2	4	7	4.3
Unrealistic expectations	50	3	8	8	6.3
Sex	47	4	17	17	12.7
Decision making	47	5	14	14	11
Demonstrating affection	45	6	13	13	10.7
Money management	43	7	15	16	12.7
Lack of loving feelings	40	8	1	4	4.3
Children	38	9	18	18.5	15.2
Individual problems	38	10	5	9	8
Value conflicts	35	11	12	11	11.3
Role conflicts	32	12	16	15	14.3
Extramarital affairs	28	13	3	2	6

Source: Adapted from Whisman, Dixon, & Johnson (1997, table 1, p. 364). *Journal of Family Psychology, 11*, 361–366. Copyright © 1997 by the American Psychological Association. Adapted with permission.

The study also provided an overall ranking based on the frequency, difficulty of treating, and the damaging impact of each problem. Based on the overall ranking, the top five issues were power struggles, lack of loving feelings, communication, extramarital affairs, and unrealistic expectations. The most difficult problems for therapists to treat were lack of loving feelings, alcoholism, and extramarital affairs. The issues with the most damaging impact on the marriage were physical abuse, extramarital affairs, and alcoholism.

Infidelity was the most commonly reported cause for divorce in another study (Amato & Previti, 2003), followed by incompatibility, drinking or drug use, and growing apart. Former husbands and wives were more likely to blame their ex-spouses than themselves for the problems that led to the breakup. Both former husbands and wives said that the women were more likely to initiate the divorce (Amato & Previti, 2003).

Unhappy Versus Happy Couples

To learn more about the characteristics of happily married versus unhappily married couples, David Olson and Amy Olson (2000) studied a national sample of 21,501 married couples from across the United States. They compared 5,127 very unhappy couples in the study, most of whom were in marriage counseling, with 5,153 happily married couples who had attended a marriage enrichment program. To confirm how satisfied the couples were, spouses were asked whether they had considered getting divorced. As expected, among the happy couples, 96% of the spouses said they had not considered divorce, whereas among the unhappy couples, 97% of the spouses had considered divorce.

In terms of background characteristics, the mean age was 35 for males and 32 for females. The couples had been married an average of 9.7 years; they had an average of 2.9 children; and the majority of the spouses had some college education.

Happy couples share fun and laughter together. This is because they have good relationship skills and are able to resolve any problematic issues.

The surprising thing about the background characteristics was the similarity in age, years married, and number of children among the couples, whether happy or unhappy.

All the couples took the ENRICH marital inventory, which focuses on 15 important relationship areas like communication, conflict resolution, role relationship, and sexual relationship. Analysis was done to determine how well the couple agreement scores on the ENRICH scales could discriminate between the happily and the unhappily married couples. The analysis showed that the scales could discriminate with about 90% accuracy between happily and unhappily married couples.

Happily married couples had significantly higher scores than unhappy couples on five scales that were most predictive of marital happiness. They were, in order of importance, *communication, flexibility, closeness, personality compatibility,* and *conflict resolution.* Whereas happy and unhappy couples differed significantly on almost all areas of their relationship, the next group of areas that showed a significant difference between them was their sexual relationship, family and friends, and financial management. Figure 15.3 illustrates the average scores for the happily and the unhappily married couples.

Couple Flexibility and Couple Closeness. This study was the first to identify the importance of couple flexibility and closeness as very important for happy couples today in our society. This is because couples are often so stressed out and busy that they need to be flexibile and be able to reconnect when they are together (see Figure 15.3). Most happily married couples had high levels of couple agreement on closeness (91%) and flexibility (75%), and unhappy couples had low levels of couple closeness (27%) and flexibility (20%).

Communication and Conflict Resolution. Some authorities might say that communication problems are the central reason for divorce. Most divorcing people relate how communication, including the ability to resolve conflict and deal with problems, broke down in their marriage. Communication and conflict resolution are interrelated. Happy couples had very high couple agreement in communication (75%), whereas it was only 11% for unhappy couples. Also, happy couples had generally high couple agreement on conflict resolution (61%), whereas it was only 12% for unhappy couples.

The Impact of Divorce on Parents

In the largest follow-up study of divorce to date, Mavis Hetherington and John Kelly (2002) followed over 1,400 people who experienced divorce for up to 30 years. In their book *For Better or Worse: Divorce Reconsidered,* they found that the majority of parents (70%) who divorced felt that they were doing at least as well or better than before the divorce.

They identified six different styles of adjusting to the divorce. The first three types (70%) were doing better, and they were called the enhanced, competent loners, and good enoughs. The *enhanced type* (20%) felt that the divorce helped them focus on their strengths and develop themselves more fully. The *competent loners* (10%) never remarried but led rather full and happy lives as single persons. The largest group was the *good enoughs* (40%), who felt that divorce was like a speed bump, but that they were survivors and it did not negatively impact their lives.

Less than one-third of the parents (30%) felt their lives were more negatively impacted by the divorce. The *seekers* (13%) felt that remarriage brought them the security and meaning that they wanted in their lives. The *libertines* (6%) coped by living life in the fast lane and not focusing on the past but enjoying the present.

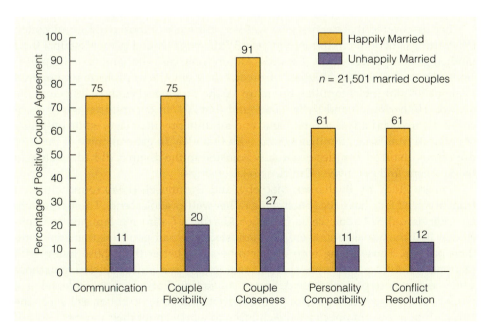

FIGURE 15.3

Satisfaction in Happy and Unhappy Marriages

The *defeateds* (11%) were most negatively impacted and experienced poverty, depression, drug abuse, and bitterness.

This major study provides the best evidence to date that most parents who get divorced eventually adjust and manage well over time. This study is important because it used a large sample, followed people for many years, and was done well. It is in striking contrast to many other studies, which have been limited in scope and have focused on the more negative impact of divorce.

The Impact of Divorce on Children

A significant question that parents face when considering divorce is what impact the divorce will have on their children. In many child custody cases, children often become the pawns of divorcing parents who want to get back at each other, thus forcing the courts to intervene and decide what is in the children's best interests.

Some of the most vocal professionals describing the negative impact of divorce on children include Judith Wallerstein and her colleagues (Wallerstein & Blakeslee, 2003, Wallerstein & Lewis, 2004). They conducted a longitudinal study of children of divorce using a small sample of families and concluded that divorce has a long-term impact on children. Even 5 years after a divorce, they found more than one-third of the children showed signs of moderate-to-severe depression. After 10 years, some of the adult children were underachieving and having emotional problems, and after 15 years, some adult children were having problems in their love relationships. This study had a small and biased sample of 60 families and no control group, although it did follow the same people over time, and provided a negative perspective on divorce.

While most of the studies have emphasized the negative impact of divorce on children, Hetherington and Kelly (2002) identified both the negative and the more positive aspects of divorce on children. In their study, *For Better or Worse: Divorce Reconsidered,* they investigated the impact of divorce on children with over 1,400 adults and 2,500 children. They found that between 75% and 80% of the children were doing rather well 6 years after the divorce. So resiliency was much more prominent than pathology in the children.

They discovered that the first year was very difficult for most children, although many things got better in the second year. While boys tended to rebel against their mother, girls experienced greater stress and in some cases became sexually precocious. About 20% of the children of divorce had emotional problems, compared to about 10% for intact families, but many of the problems began years before the divorce. Hetherington and Kelly also found that 70% of the children who experienced divorce said it was acceptable to end an unhappy marriage, while only 40% of children from intact families agreed with that idea. In general, most of the children from divorced families eventually adjusted to the divorce, did adequately in their careers, and got involved in close relationships.

A major study by Buchanan, Maccoby, and Dornbusch (1996) found children from divorced families to be functioning rather well as adolescents. These researchers interviewed 522 adolescents from 365 Northern California families and concluded that the adolescents were well adjusted and had good relationships with their parents. Those living with their mothers did better than those living with their fathers. Adolescents whose parents remarried were better adjusted than those adolescents whose parents were dating or cohabiting. Furthermore, adolescents of parents who shared feelings with their children seemed to do better, as long as the parents' openness did not cause the children to worry about their parents. Most of the adolescents continued to stay in touch with the noncustodial parent, but contact tended to drop off over time (Buchanan & Heiges, 2001).

Constance Ahrons, a long-time researcher of divorce, concludes that the affect of divorce on children varies depending on a multitude of interactive factors (Ahrons, 2006). These factors take into account the child, the parents, the pre- and postdivorce family, and the environmental and social factors. She concludes that most children of divorced parents grow up to be healthy and well adjusted, while another smaller group does less well.

The personalities of children affect how they react and response to divorce (Ahrons, 2006). For example, the child's temperament and ways of coping have an impact on his or her ability to deal with this major family change. Is the child easy going, or does he or she respond dramatically to family transitions? Has the child developed ways of coping with difficulties? A child's emotional health before the divorce also affects his or her ability to deal with divorce. In addition, the relationship the child had with each parent before the divorce has an impact on the child's divorce experience.

A major factor in children's adjustment to divorce is also how well the parents deal with the divorce (Ahrons, 2006). The parents may lack the emotional health to handle the divorce in a mature way, and children get caught in the middle of parents who may not realize the impact of their behavior on the children. In addition, parents experience anger and grief and many other emotions and may not be able to help their children with those same feelings. As a result, the children can be left to fend for themselves.

Since the 1970s, there have been increasing numbers of services and programs for families going through divorces (Blaisure, 2006). Increasingly, court systems have required that parents go through educational programs to help them help their children adjust to divorce. Currently, 11 states have legislation requiring divorcing parents of minor children to attend such education. In addition, programs for children are being provided in schools and other community organizations.

Divorce in High-Conflict Versus Low Conflict Marriages

Amato and Booth (1997) conducted a longitudinal study on divorce, which they reported on in their book *A Generation at Risk.* These researchers interviewed parents and their children before and after divorce, and the national sample consisted of 471 parents who had a 7-year-old child in 1980. When the child was 19, the researchers interviewed the adult children along with their parents, bringing the total sample to 942 adults.

One significant and consistent finding was that parents' marital quality in 1980 was related to the adult childrens' dating and marriage relationship quality 12 years later. The adult children had more problems with dating and, if married, had less happy marriages. Amato and Booth (1997) stated that "parents' marital unhappiness and discord have a broad negative impact on virtually every dimension of offspring well-being" (p. 219). They found that problems in the parent–child relationship often occurred prior to the divorce and that the divorce increased the problems in parenting. They also found that divorce had a negative impact on the fathers' affection for their children but not the mothers' (Amato & Booth, 1996).

A surprising finding was that low-conflict marriages that ended in divorce (about two-thirds of the marriages) had a more negative impact on the adult children's development than did high-conflict marriages that ended in divorce. Low-conflict couples do have some conflict and quarrels, but at a much lower level than high-conflict couples. The findings suggest that in the case of high-conflict marriages, the divorce was good for the children in terms of their mental health. However, offspring of divorced couples who had low levels of marital conflict showed increased levels of psychological distress, fewer ties with kin and friends, less happy marriages, and a greater probability of divorcing (Amato & Booth, 1997).

These findings have fueled the debate about whether parents with low levels of marital conflict should divorce. One study found support for divorce in high-conflict marriages but not in low-conflict marriages (McLanahan & Sandefur, 1994). Researchers concluded that children living in homes with high-conflict marriages (persistent and severe abuse) were better off if the parents divorced. They maintained, however, that children from low-conflict marriages would be better off if the parents remained together.

A study by Chase-Lansdale, Cherlin, and Kiernan (1995) found that divorce seems to have a more negative impact on children who have fewer, rather than greater, emotional problems. This longitudinal study of over 17,000 children was done in Great Britain. This study and those by Amato and Booth (1996, 1997) and McLanahan and Sandefur (1994) seem to support the idea that divorce is more detrimental to children who are doing well in general as compared to those who are already having more serious emotional and behavior problems.

Amato and Booth (1997) also studied the consequences of divorce on income level and educational attainment in adult children of divorced parents. Their findings clearly demonstrate that higher levels of education in the parents had a positive impact on the children. Children of parents with higher levels of education were more socially active, had more friends, were happier, and had higher levels of self-esteem. Higher levels of education in the parents were also directly linked to the level of education achieved by their adult children, which subsequently had an impact on other quality-of-life outcomes for the adult children, including income level.

Amato and Booth's research (1997) also revealed that adult children of divorce had higher rates of cohabitation than did children from stable marriages and those from unstable marriages (Amato & Booth, 1997). At each age level from 20 to 26 years, adult children from divorced parents had the highest rate of cohabitation, followed by adult children from unstable marriages; adult children from stable marriages had the lowest rate of cohabitation. With adult children of divorce, the rate of cohabitation was 30% at age 20, 40% at age 23, and 48% at age 26; these rates were significantly lower for the other groups (Amato, 2003).

A single mother tells about her struggles over the divorce and how she tries to communicate honestly with her children:

> "The best thing I can do is to tell the kids, 'Look, I do have some unhappy feelings about your father, but this is only natural because we did get a divorce, you know. Please forgive me for this. Don't expect me to talk about him with affection or say how good he is. But really, I don't think he's a bad person so much as we just weren't right for each other. I do think your father loves you very much, though I agree with you that he doesn't show it very often. He does send your support checks more regularly now, and I think he sees this as a way of showing how he loves you.
>
> 'You also need to know that I was not a perfect wife, just as he wasn't a perfect husband. And today, I'm not a perfect mother, either. I tried to be a good wife, and I try very hard to be a good mother. But I won't be permissive with you, or overly indulgent as a mother. I am trying to find a balance between patience and flexibility on the one hand, and rules and limits on the other hand.
>
> 'No, I'm not perfect, but if you'll accept me with my faults, I will accept yours. Most important, I love you and as much as humanly possible I will be around to listen, to care, to help you deal with the challenges life brings you.'"

Adjusting to Divorce

To fall in love is awfully simple, but to fall out of love is simply awful.

—BESS MYERSON (1987)

The divorce process is stressful and even traumatic for many. The most difficult time is the period leading up to the decision to divorce. After the divorce, most generally feel good about the property settlement, and they generally feel that their life is better overall than it was during the marriage. After divorce, some people withdraw for awhile but gradually become involved with others again.

Using a religious metaphor, Paul Bohannan (1970) has described the divorce process as an intense journey that encompasses "six stations." These stations, or experiences, often overlap, occur in different sequences, and vary in intensity for each individual. The six experiences are:

- **Emotional divorce.** The deterioration of the marriage and the breakdown of bonding and communication, which are replaced by feelings of alienation.
- **Legal divorce.** The dissolution of the marriage by the legal system and the courts.
- **Economic divorce.** The division of money and property and the establishment of two separate economic units.
- **Coparental divorce.** Decisions about child custody, single parenting, and visitation rights.
- **Community divorce.** Changes in relationships with friends and community members.
- **Psychological divorce.** The regaining of individual autonomy.

Emotional Divorce

When two people decide to marry, they feel so good because of the love they share. Divorce feels so awful because that love has been lost. Divorce involves a vast spectrum of emotions, and no two individuals react to it the same way. There are, however, some common patterns that appear in most divorces.

Anger and violence are very common with divorced couples. Many people who feel anger over the loss of a mate try to escape this pain or rage through chemicals. Even individuals who are not prone to abusing drugs can find no other way to cope. "I just needed to turn my brain off for a while," one husband said. "It hurt too much to think, and I couldn't stop thinking painful thoughts any other way."

Other people may fall into total emotional disrepair and depression, finding it impossible to function. They may sleep a lot and possibly think about suicide. One woman who lost her husband to her best friend put it this way, "I was so depressed I wanted to kill myself, but for three days I couldn't find the energy to get out of bed to get the pills in the bathroom to do it." Many physicians argue that the misery of a dissolving marriage can also weaken the body's resistance to disease.

The crisis of divorce, like many other crises in life, often adds to the common human feeling of loneliness. In the words of one divorced mother of two young children, "This weekend is pretty lonely. All my weekday friends have weekend husbands. I've painted Billy's room, baked 10 dozen oatmeal cookies (Elizabeth's request), and got 2 weeks of shopping done and it is still only Saturday. Maybe I got married because weekends are so long."

The decision to divorce is rarely reached easily or quickly, and it may be fraught with ambivalence. Even when a spouse has moved out of the home, there is still a chance that he or she will return. Emotions run deep. Hate may exist in tandem with love. One minute a spouse thinks, "There's no way that I can survive this marriage," and the next, "Oh, I miss her so much."

Legal Divorce

When Bohannan first conceived his six stations of divorce, he identified the traditional adversarial legal process as a significant challenge. No-fault laws have eliminated the element of blame, or fault, to some degree, but they have not removed all conflict from the proceedings. Competing attorneys do battle for their clients, and these "hired guns" try to get the most they can for whoever is paying the fee.

The adversarial approach may work reasonably well for resolving disputes between businesses or strangers, but families with children thrive on trust and cooperation. Divorcing parents have to deal with each other because they remain connected by their children. Rather than helping mend the wounds of a broken family, the legal system often makes things worse. One judge commented, "Criminal court is easier, and a lot more fun."

In recent years, a nationwide movement toward the mediation of divorces has gained ground in the United States. A network of professional and volunteer medi-

Divorce has resulted in a growing number of single mothers, many of whom have less money than before the divorce.

ators is growing, with the intent of keeping family disputes out of the legal system to minimize the emotional damage to ongoing family relationships. Rather than partners' each hiring legal representation, families can go to a trained mediator, who tries to work out the dispute in the best interest of everyone involved. The mediator works to find a win–win solution, as opposed to the win–lose approach of the courtroom (Smith, 2003).

Economic Divorce

Some spouses simply don't want to argue about the money, the house, the cars, the furniture. The pain of divorce seems too much to bear, and the financial details exceed their coping abilities. But the economic realities must be faced and resolved. Lawyers are useful for sorting out all the complications—and to represent divorcing partners' interests when they don't have the energy to do so themselves. Many people are so relieved to get out of an unhappy marriage that they don't want to think about the details. "Let him have anything he wants," many a lawyer has heard. "I just want to forget the whole thing."

Divorce can have a crippling financial legacy. Drastic downward mobility, a sort of reverse American dream, is one major consequence of divorce for many. One research team found, for example, that the incomes of divorced people are lower than the incomes of married people, by 30% for women and by 10% for men (Stroup & Pollock, 1994). Because children still usually remain with their mother after a divorce, it's especially important for women to get a fair income and property settlement.

After a divorce, some women are forced into the job market. They may have little job experience because they've been home caring for children. Their self-esteem may be low as a result of the breakup of the marriage, and they may have little confidence in their ability to find and hold a good job in a tight job market.

The term **feminization of poverty** refers to the statistical fact that the percentage of female single parents in the total percentage of people who are poor in this country is increasing. This increase of women in poverty is primarily due to the increasing divorce rate and the severe reduction in divorced women's income. The divorced woman, especially the mother with young children, is in a difficult situation. Her marriage proved unworkable and ending it was probably a good idea, but life after divorce often proves to be financially punishing (Myers & Gill, 2004).

Coparental Divorce

Spouses may divorce each other, but parents cannot divorce their children. Children play a role in making a satisfactory marriage relationship more difficult to achieve in some respects, but they are also a bond between parents, even in divorce and after it. About 60% of divorces involve children (U.S. Bureau of the Census, 2000e). The most difficult dilemma facing many divorcing partners is the question of what will happen to the children. The coparental divorce experience reflects the reality that parents must work out how they will coparent even though they will no longer be married or live together.

It has been estimated that 80% of the children in divorced families live with their mothers, 12% live with their fathers, and 8% live with other relatives (U.S. Bureau of the Census, 2000e). Traditionally, women have taken the lion's share of the responsibility for the children in a divorce. Fathers have often found themselves with minimal visitation rights and little control. Such an outcome does not foster coparenting.

The majority of children wish to have continued contact with both parents after divorce. The youngsters, in essence, continue to love both parents even though the parents don't love each other. Ensuring that both parents have ongoing contact with their children is a difficult goal to achieve. If hostilities continue between the parents and the mother has been granted custody of the children, the father often finds himself in an uncomfortable situation. Although he may want to see his children, the visits can be punishing emotionally both for him and for the children. Many fathers simply fade out of the picture in this type of arrangement. They find that going to the zoo or on a picnic with their kids a few days a month is too bittersweet an experience. The father in this type of situation often charges that the mother has poisoned his relationship with his children. The mother often maintains that the father showed no interest in the children before the divorce and that this pattern continued after the divorce. She may say that the children want to be with their friends on the weekend rather than with their father.

Objectively judging who is to blame in these circumstances is difficult, but the end result is generally quite clear. The father often drifts away from his children emotionally and feels little inclination to pay child support because he doesn't feel connected to them anymore. If he marries again, he is likely to marry a woman with

Coparenting has become increasingly popular and has resulted in more fathers having quality time with their children.

children of her own and may feel pressure from his new wife to be involved with "their" children. "I've got two sets of kids to support now," one father said. "One set isn't even really mine, and my own set, I can only see every other weekend."

As we discussed earlier, numerous studies have looked at the effects of divorce on children (Wallerstein & Lewis, 2004). These studies reveal three conclusions.

First, divorce is a very difficult crisis in the lives of the vast majority of children who experience it. Most children grieve over the divorce and wish it were not happening. This is especially true in the case of marriage devitalization or burnout, in which the divorce may have come as a complete surprise to the children.

Second, many children are angry at their parents, and many are angry at themselves. When parents break up, children often feel responsible. It takes sensitive parents to help guide the children through their grief. Some parents, overburdened with their own anger and sadness, are of little help to their children. "My best friend's parents got a divorce, and I felt so sorry for her," 11-year-old Jenna said. "I imagined once what it would be like if my parents got a divorce. I did this so I could understand what my friend was going through. Then when my parents got a divorce, I felt so guilty. I thought they got a divorce because I had imagined they got one."

Third, although divorce is difficult for almost all children, subjection to highly conflicted marital hostilities is even worse. Amato and Booth (2001) found that a high-conflict home can have negative consequences for all family members. Children, in particular, respond to this type of environment with depression, anger, troubles in school, and various physiological symptoms.

Community Divorce

Divorce comes as a shock not only for members of the nuclear family but also for relatives, friends, neighbors, and colleagues at work. Many people are unsure of how to respond to divorcing friends and relatives. The best approach is to listen when they want to share and to be caring and supportive. Friends, parents, sisters, and brothers are often the most supportive. Conversely, most in-laws become out-laws; they tend to support and defend their relative, regardless of the reasons for the divorce. Parents are particularly stressed when their adult children divorce. The effects of divorce spread outward like vibration rings caused by dropping a stone in a quiet pond. Our attention is drawn to the point where the stone hits the water, and less interest is given the larger area which is also disturbed by the impact.

Divorce research has tended to focus on the impacts on the divorcing couple and on their children, but not on the effects on others, such as grandparents (Barth, 2004). But when talking with parents of divorcing individuals, researchers and clinicians often find that even though some might be glad their child was getting a divorce, the overwhelming emotions most of them describe are feelings of sorrow. In the words of one mother, "At first it was like a death in the family to think that our son-in-law would not be a part of the family any longer."

The couple's friends also have difficulty responding to a divorcing couple. Which of the partners should the couple friends continue to have contact with? It would be difficult to keep both ex-partners as friends, and it would seem awkward to invite just one person to a social occasion. The divorcing couple often feel bitter about losing their couple friends. However, couples who were primarily connected to only one of the partners often offer valuable support after a divorce.

Psychological Divorce

Many people getting divorced find it useful to talk with a marriage and family therapist or another professional skilled in working with personal and relationship problems. Counselors can provide insights and suggestions for adjusting to the single life. Many people also join support groups. Parents Without Partners and similar groups across the country can provide help to divorcing people seeking to grow through their crisis. These support groups bring together people with similar problems who can be mutually supportive and caring. Groups of divorced people also set up educational programs and social activities (dances, potlucks, camping trips). The main thing is to become actively involved with other people again (Parents Without Partners, 2004).

When they are ready, many divorced people look forward to dating again. Friends and relatives are often a valuable source for identifying potential dating partners. It is important, however, that divorced individuals begin dating gradually rather than rushing the process. The worst thing a newly divorced person can do is to marry again quickly, "on the rebound."

How Long Does It Take to Adjust?

How long does the divorce journey take? The answer is different for each person. The emotional process of divorce may last from several months to a few years after the divorce. The legal process may take only 6 months, but if children are involved and a custody fight occurs, the struggle could last several years. One father, who had been fighting for custody of his youngsters for 6 years, had incurred legal costs of close to $100,000.

The economic process of divorce may also last a long time. For example, if the ex-wife goes back to school after the divorce, she may be in school for 3 or 4 years. Both spouses suffer financially, but usually the wife is the primary financial loser.

Dating after a divorce can be both scary and enjoyable. However, newly divorced people should not rush the emotional process of divorce, which can take anywhere from several months to a few years. They should ease into dating slowly, and they definitely should not rush into another marriage on the rebound.

The coparental divorce process can last from several months to years. If the couple is on friendly terms, they may work out a joint-custody arrangement that functions well in a few months. If not, battles over custody and child visitation may last a long time. The psychological divorce may also take a long time: Some people take several years to shift to a more independent lifestyle; others make the transition in a few months. As mentioned, these stations of divorce usually run concurrently and often overlap.

Divorce is often less problematic for people who can talk openly about it. When individuals accept the divorce as an important part of their lives, they can then move on as independent and happy single people. Divorce is something that most people do not willingly choose, but it can often be a very valuable learning experience. As one man said, "Going through a divorce was an important part of my life that I wouldn't let anyone take away from me for a million dollars. And it was something I wouldn't want to go through again for a million dollars!"

A single mother explains how a professional counselor played a key role in the healthy resolution of a number of difficult situations the divorcing spouses encountered:

> *"My ex-husband and I went to counseling immediately upon recognition of our marital problems. Counseling helped us a great deal. It helped us reach an understanding of what happened in our marriage and why. We still attribute our good relationship after the divorce to the fact that we did go to a counselor and were able to really understand each other and the problems we had. Without this understanding, I think I would still feel very bitter and vengeful."*

Single-Parent Families and Stepfamilies

The majority of divorces today involve children, and the challenges single parents face can be daunting: loneliness and isolation, financial problems, and work overload can be especially distressing. In spite of these difficulties, though, researchers and clinicians consistently find that many single parents develop healthy and functional families. Meanwhile, the noncustodial parent is also working to establish a new identity and figure out how to maintain a relationship with the children that he or she has "lost" in the process of divorce (Bailey, 2003; Manning, Stewart, & Smock, 2003).

In this section we will consider how parents "pick up the pieces" of their lives after divorce and establish new and functional family systems. We will compare these systems to the nuclear family and explore stresses and strengths for both single-parent families and stepfamilies.

The Increase in Single-Parent Families

Over the past three decades in the United States, there has been a significant increase in single-parent families. In 1970, there were 30 million family groups including children in the United States. In 2000, there were 37 million family groups with children. Single-mother families increased from 3 million in 1970 to 10 million in 2000. Single-father families increased from 393,000 to 2 million.

The proportion of all families that were married-couple families with children declined from 87% in 1970 to 69% in 2000. During the same 30-year period, the proportion of single-mother families grew from 12% to 26%, and single-father families grew from 1% to 5% (Fields & Casper, 2001). The percentage of single-parent families varies by ethnic group, with the highest rate being in African American families at 64% (see Figure 15.4).

Some observers have suggested that single-parent families—also called one-parent, lone-parent, and solo-parent families—are problem families, but this generalization is inaccurate. Indeed, many divorced single parents do an excellent job of raising children who thrive at home and at school. So do many stepfamilies. This is not to say that single-parent families and stepfamilies are problem free. Single-parent families and stepfamilies face many of the same challenges that other families face, yet they must also cope with additional, unique challenges.

Family Terminology

The changing nature of the family in our society has given rise to new terminology, which we will discuss and define in this section.

Binuclear Families Compared to Single-Parent Families. Constance Ahrons (2004) sometimes prefers the term *binuclear family* to *single-parent family* because it acknowledges the positive outcome that results from divorce. Divorce is a process that results in family reorganization rather than disintegration of the family system. This reorganization of the nuclear family after divorce frequently results in the establishment of two households, the mother's and the father's. If one ex-spouse does not drop out of the family after the divorce and the two households continue to interrelate, then a **binuclear family** has been established.

In some binuclear families, children have a primary and a secondary home: One parent has **sole custody,** and the children live with that parent in the primary home; the other parent in the secondary home has rights of visitation with the

FIGURE 15.4

Two-Parent and Single-Parent Families

Source: U.S. Bureau of the Census (2001e).

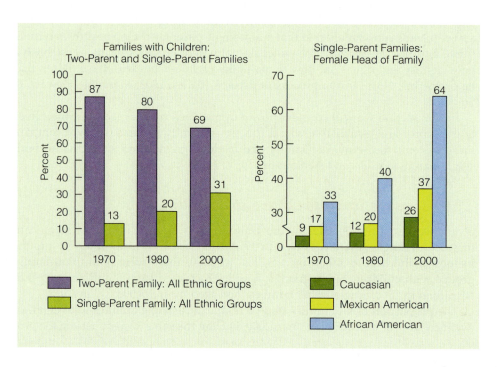

Many people who remarry have children from a previous marriage, and the resulting combination can be a large stepfamily with complex dynamics. The children must establish relationships with their stepparent and their stepsiblings, and the adults must learn new roles as stepparents.

children. In a smaller proportion of families, the homes of both divorced parents have equal importance—"one child, two homes." This arrangement has been termed **joint custody**. In an even smaller proportion of families, one parent has sole custody of one or more of the children, and the other parent has sole custody of the other child or children—an arrangement called **split custody** (McBride, 2003).

In binuclear families, relationships between the two households can vary greatly. Some ex-spouses continue the predivorce wars into the postdivorce years, whereas others get along wonderfully. A few binuclear families even share some holidays. The majority, however, rarely get together as a group. Ahrons (2003) identified four types of relationships in binuclear families: *perfect pals, cooperative colleagues, angry associates,* and *fiery foes;* Ahrons also uses the term *dissolved duo* to describe a relationship that is completely over.

Marriage and Remarriage. A few words need to be said at this point about the term **remarriage.** The dictionary definition includes both marrying the same person again (a rare occurrence) and marrying a second (or subsequent) time after the death of or divorce from the first partner. In this text, *remarriage* refers exclusively to two spouses who have never been married to each other before.

Blended Families and Stepfamilies. Emily Visher and John Visher (1998), well known for their research on stepfamilies, object to the term **blended family** for a variety of reasons. First and foremost, the label fosters unrealistic expectations that the new family will quickly and easily blend together into a harmonious family. Second, the term assumes a homogeneous unit without a previous history or background. On the other hand, the terms **stepfamily** and **stepparent** have suffered from a number of stereotypes, often bringing to mind fairy-tale visions of "wicked stepmothers" (Claxton-Oldfield, 2000; Recker, 2001). In fact, most stepparent–stepchild relationships function relatively well.

Growing Family Complexity

The joining together of two families in a second or subsequent marriage adds considerable complexity to a family system. A child of divorced parents who both remarry will have two stepparents; a range of possible combinations of biological siblings, stepsiblings, and half-siblings; up to eight grandparents; and numerous extended relatives (aunts, uncles, cousins, etc.).

Figure 15.5 illustrates one example of a binuclear family, with a child in the center. This figure is relatively complicated, and yet it shows only the relationships between the child and her or his parents, stepparents, stepsiblings, and half-siblings. If the child's relationships with the rest of the family—siblings, grandparents, and other relatives in the extended family—were added, the figure would become even more complicated. Of course, complexity in a family system is neither good nor bad in itself. Some binuclear families of enormous complexity function quite well. As one 7-year-old girl said, "I love my new family. I now have a whole lot more grandpas and grandmas, and they all give me presents!"

As important new people are added to a family system, the number of potentially positive and negative human relationships increases geometrically. Take, for example, a man from a relatively small family who married a woman with a huge extended family. The fellow's mother-in-law has nine brothers and sisters and countless nieces and nephews. His father-in-law has four brothers and sisters, and these folks also have a considerable number of progeny. "I have to have a program in hand when I go to a family picnic," the fellow chuckles. "Sometimes there will

FIGURE 15.5

Sample Model of a Binuclear Family

Source: Divorced Families: A Multidisciplinary View (p. 155) by C. Ahrons and R. Rodgers, 1987, New York: Norton. Copyright 1987 Constance R. Ahrons and Roy H. Rodgers. Reprinted by permission of W. W. Norton and Company. (Also Ahrons, 2004.)

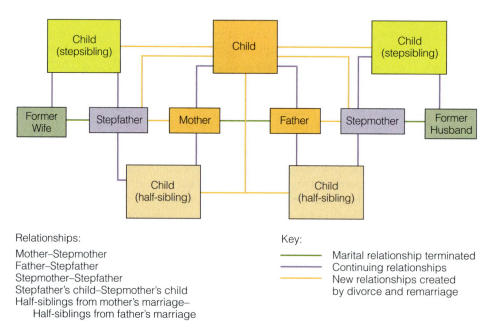

Relationships:
Mother–Stepmother
Father–Stepfather
Stepmother–Stepfather
Stepfather's child–Stepmother's child
Half-siblings from mother's marriage–
   Half-siblings from father's marriage

Key:
——— Marital relationship terminated
——— Continuing relationships
——— New relationships created
    by divorce and remarriage

TABLE 15.2	Differences Between Nuclear Families and Stepfamilies	
Characteristic	**Nuclear Family**	**Stepfamily**
Role as parent	Two parents	Two adults; one is a parent
	Marital dyad are parents	Marital dyad plus previous partner(s) are parents
	May be single parents	
Biological relationship	Biological family	Nonbiological family
	Biological relationship between both parents and children and between siblings	Biological relationship between one parent and children
		Children of both parents might be included in family
	Physical similarity often present	Lower level of physical similarity
Marriage history	Ongoing marriage	New marriage partner
	Often first marriage	One or both previously married
	Parents influence marriage	Parents and previous partner(s) influence marriage
Balancing marriage and parenting	Marriage came before child(ren)	Marriage came after child(ren)
	Maintaining marriage is goal	Developing marriage is goal
	Parenting often given priority over marriage	Marriage often given priority over parenting
Bonding	Bond is primarily to nuclear family and both parents	Bond often greater to one parent
		Stepparent bond takes time to develop
	Family rituals and celebrations increase bonding	Rituals must be developed and may create conflicts
	Extended families can support bonding	Extended families can create issues and decrease bonding
Loyalty issues	Roots are stable	Roots are disrupted; can be rebuilt
	General sense of loyalty and belonging	Loyalty and belonging more difficult to develop
	Loyalty to both parents more common	Initial loyalty to one parent is common
Parenting issues	Roles and responsibilities tend to develop gradually	Roles and responsibilities disrupted and often must be redefined
	Child(ren) can play two parents off each other	Child(ren) can play two parents plus stepparents off against each other
	Parenting roles can be shared and can be conflictual	Parent and stepparent roles often create conflict
		Grandparents' and stepgrandparents' roles are unclear
	Power hierarchy clear among siblings	Power struggles to develop hierarchy among siblings and stepchildren
Financial issues	Parental income to own children	Parents' and stepparents' income to own and/or stepchildren
	No financial support expected from others	Child support payments can create issues
	Financial demands more predictable	More financial demands from new marriage and new family

Source: Adapted from *Treating the Remarried Family* (pp. 23–27) by C. J. Sager, H. S. Brown, H. Crohn, T. Engel, E. Rodstein, and L. Walker, 1983, New York: Brunner/Mazel. Copyright 1983 by Brunner/Mazel. Reprinted by permission of Taylor and Francis Inc.

be more than 200 people at these gatherings. It's almost like going to a soccer game. They should all wear jerseys with numbers."

Differences Between Nuclear Families and Stepfamilies

Many stepfamilies falsely assume that they are like nuclear families. Table 15.2 highlights some of the salient differences between nuclear families and stepfamilies. First of all, there are usually two biological parents in a nuclear family, and the children are clearer about their biological heritage. In a stepfamily, one parent is not a biological parent, which can increase children's feelings of attachment to their biological parent. In a nuclear family the parents' marriage is ongoing and may have lasted many years, but in a stepfamily, one marriage partner has changed. The new couple have to balance their investment in the new marriage with the handling of parenting and stepparenting issues.

The bonds that children feel with their parents and vice versa are often stronger in nuclear families than in stepfamilies. There are often loyalty issues in stepfamilies, with children, particularly adolescents, feeling greater loyalty to their biological parents than to the stepparent. Many stepfamilies struggle with complex and sometimes conflictual dynamics. Issues regarding grandparents and stepgrandparents add to the complexity. There can also be struggles between stepsiblings when both spouses bring children to the new family. Financial issues can also be complex. When both parents in a stepfamily have children, the financial resources available for child support payments and for meeting the financial demands of all the children can be limited.

A study that compared stepfamilies and biological families in terms of marital conflict found no significant differences between them using nationally representative data on 2,655 Black and White married couples with children and comparing the frequency of marital conflict. The researchers found, contrary to their expectations, that remarriage and stepchildren are not necessarily associated with more frequent marital conflict and that, in some cases, they are associated with less frequent conflict (MacDonald & DeMaris, 1995). More research comparing the two family types is necessary, but some observers are skeptical of its usefulness, arguing that the comparison is like one between apples and oranges (Barta, 2001; Gamache, 2001; Hornik, 2001).

Types of Single-Parent Families

Single-parent households, headed either by a mother or a father, are continuing to increase; they now constitute 32% of all households nationwide. As we mentioned earlier, in 1970, there were 3 million single-parent households headed by mothers in the United States; in 2000, the number was 10 million. There were 393,000 single-parent households headed by fathers in 1970; in 2000, there were 2 million. The percentage of single-parent families headed by fathers increased from 10% of the total in 1970 to 16% of the total in 2000 (Fields & Casper, 2001, p. 7).

Much of the literature on single-parent families since the 1960s has accentuated the negative. We will try to take a more balanced view of these families by identifying both the stresses and the strains unique to single parents as well as by looking at the positive aspects of growing up in a healthy single-parent family.

Divorced single-parent families can be put in four categories: (1) mothers with sole custody; (2) fathers with sole custody; (3) split-custody families, in which the father has sole custody of one or more children and the mother has sole custody of one or more children; and (4) joint-custody families, in which both the mother and the father share decision making. John DeFrain, Judy Fricke, and Julie Elmen (1987) analyzed these four types of single-parent families in their study of 738 single parents in 45 states: 528 mothers with sole custody, 114 fathers with sole custody, 40 fathers with split custody, and 56 mothers and fathers with joint legal and physical custody. Their findings are summarized below.

Mothers with Custody

Divorced mothers who head single-parent families must cope with many stresses. Nonetheless, they also experience many joys.

Stresses. One of the major problems for mothers with sole custody is limited finances, a situation often made worse by a father's failure to pay child support. In a study of 492 court records, K. D. Rettig, D. H. Christensen, and C. M. Dahl (1991) found that court-ordered awards met only 58% of the children's income needs when measured against poverty-level support. As expected, the parent with whom the children lived spent a much higher proportion of her (or his) income to support the children than did the parent with whom the children did not live. This serious problem in our country is made worse by the fact that only about half (48%) of noncustodial parents make full child support payments, 26% make partial payments, and 26% make no payments at all (see Rettig, Leichtentritt, & Stanton, 1999).

Loneliness is also a common problem for most single parents. One mother commented, "The only real sorrow we feel about the arrangement [single parenthood] is that her father isn't with us to share in the daily goings on of family life." The other parent is not there to kiss the child's scraped knee, to celebrate in the loss of the first tooth, or to join in the birthday parties—in short, the ups and downs of daily childrearing. "I bleed for my children when I see their loneliness in being

Healthy single-parent families share the same strengths that contribute to the well-being of strong two-parent families. This father genuinely enjoys spending leisure time with his children.

away from Dad and former friends. I regret seeking more conversation and support from them in my own loneliness than they can give me," a mother said. Some mothers worry that the day may come when the children will no longer know their father. Some divorced mothers with custody also lament the loss of positive grandparent relationships. In many families, ties with grandparents are severed by the divorce.

For some single parents, battles with the ex-spouse continue for years. Many mothers with custody dread continued contact with the ex-partner. In the words of Ahrons (2003), these parents are not "perfect pals" or "cooperative colleagues" but rather "angry associates" and "fiery foes" who often square off against each other. In one mother's words, "Because their father sees them as often as he does, they're put in a heavy loyalty dilemma. Consequently, they return home feeling confused by guilt and wanting to blame or hate. This is all happening because their father is trying to get them to live with him. I will never have total peace as long as he's alive!"

Strengths. Strong single-parent families exhibit the same constellation of qualities as two-parent families exhibit: appreciation and affection for each of the family members; commitment to the family; open, honest, and straightforward communication patterns; adequate amounts of enjoyable time together; a sense of spiritual well-being; and the ability to manage stress and crisis effectively. Besides facing many challenges, mothers with sole custody experience a number of specific joys, such as the freedom to make decisions about their own lives and the lives of their children without interference or harassment from hostile fathers. Also, in many families, divorce does not mean the end of meaningful relationships with grandparents. One single mother reported, "My ex-spouse's parents are extremely helpful. They take my preschool daughter some weekends, and having the time to myself is wonderful."

For some mothers with custody, the burden of almost total responsibility for the children is nearly unbearable, but others thrive on the responsibility. "The joy that is unique to being a single parent is the all-engulfing satisfaction when things are going well. You not only take all of the responsibility, but you receive all of the joy from the growth and new discovery that the child is experiencing."

Finally, some mothers with sole custody are thankful for fathers who stay involved with their children after the divorce. "The girls are always excited to see Dad. Dad is excited to see the girls. And I'm glad to be alone for a while." Former spouses sometimes remain friends, or at least neutral colleagues, in the challenge of rearing children after divorce. Their collaboration contributes to the health, happiness, and adjustment of the children. Sometimes both parents attend band concerts, Girl Scout meetings, open houses at school, and so forth.

Fathers with Custody

Family researchers and clinicians have found that many fathers do a good job raising children after a divorce, just as many mothers who were formerly full-time homemakers successfully work outside the home after a divorce (Coles, 2003; Emmers-Sommer, Rhea, Triplett, & O'Neil, 2003; Greif, 2000). When comparing a group of divorced single fathers and divorced single mothers, researchers are likely to find that statistically the two groups look quite similar: They describe the process of divorce they went through in similar ways, talk about the same types of stresses they encounter as single parents, describe similar childrearing philosophies and behaviors, report the adjustment of their children to the divorce as being similar, describe the effectiveness of their relationship with the ex-spouse in relatively the same way, and describe the challenges of developing new intimate relationships in a similar fashion. Divorced single fathers, however, do differ from divorced single mothers in a significant way: They tend to earn more money. Most studies that have, in essence, asked the question, "Can fathers do a good job as solo parents?" have answered yes. It also appears that the sorrows and joys of solo parenting for fathers are very similar to those related by mothers with custody.

Stresses. Single-parent fathers often feel sorrow over the fact that the family unit has been broken up. Even though fathers see the new single-parent family as a family, it is not, in the eyes of many fathers, a complete family. "I feel sorry for my children because they don't have their mother anymore," one father said.

Many single fathers miss their ex-wives and find loneliness and balancing work and family difficult. Many also report that both time and money are limited. Single fathers with custody generally make more money than single mothers with custody, but time and money pressures are still common complaints among them. "I don't seem to have much time or money to do the things that I would like. It is difficult for me to meet women." Fathers often complain that they have no one with whom to share the joys of parenting. Also, many fathers report that the children

Although fewer men than women have sole custody of the children after a divorce, research shows that single fathers do just as good a job of childrearing as single mothers do and that they experience the same stresses of loneliness and limited time and money.

miss their mother. "It is difficult when she asks, 'Why doesn't my mom call me or want to see me?'"

Strengths. Many single fathers report a considerable number of joys, such as being able to watch their children grow. "To see my son's mind develop" is a great joy. "He is quite intelligent, and his ambitions are much greater with me. The environment around his mother is extremely negative and shameful." Fathers also enjoy the love between themselves and their children. "Now there are only two in our family, and it's much harder on me but well worth it. We have more love and a stronger bond now." Having custody also means having control. Many single fathers, having been through lengthy and painful divorce and custody battles with their ex-wives, feel great relief.

For many fathers, single parenthood means getting closer to their children. One father proudly related how he had become closer to his children after adjusting his priorities in life by putting the children before his job and the housework. Fathers with custody have the opportunity to really enjoy their children in a more natural environment. "I get great pleasure from being with my son. This gives me a sense of accomplishment since I do have him and am making it work."

Some fathers do get along with their ex-spouses. One 54-year-old father who was caring for nine children said he was especially pleased that "my ex-wife and I get along. If there is a problem—and we do have some—I get on the phone, and we talk it out and resolve it. That's something we didn't do too well when we were married." Although the marriage is over, ex-spouses can sometimes build a solid partnership for the good of their children.

Split Custody

Split custody is a child custody arrangement that involves both divorced parents separately (Bauserman, 2002; DeFrain et al., 1987; Hawthorne, 2000; McBride, 2003). Each parent has responsibility for at least one of their children and thus has all the stresses and strains of solo parenting.

Split custody is apparently the rarest of all parenting options after divorce, but it works quite well for many. Perhaps the most interesting question about split custody is why parents choose this arrangement. Many split-custody parents indicate that the child or children wanted it. A number of fathers said that their sons wanted to live with them, especially during adolescence.

"My oldest [14] told [my ex-wife] he'd rather live with me," related Edward, a 48-year-old contractor. "I told him it would be all right. She brought him to my house and asked me if he could stay. When I told her yes, she said, 'Good, you take him. I can't handle him anymore.' About 6 months later, she wanted him back, but he refused to go."

Mothers have told researchers of "losing" not only sons to their ex-husbands but daughters as well. Some "switching" of households may almost be inevitable after divorce; adolescents need to balance their fantasies with the realities of life in the other home with the other parent. They may find that the other home is no better than the home in which they currently live.

For many, split custody is a family decision, involving input from every family member. One parent commented, "Ever since the separation we have tried to do the right thing for the children and put aside our own differences. Therefore, the decision on custody was negotiated among the four of us, with no outsider involved."

Joint Custody

Joint custody is defined as either physical custody, where the child spends about equal time with both parents, or shared legal custody where the child spends more time with one parent but both parents are involved in the child's life. In general, joint custody can be successful only if both parents are willing and able to work together in the best interests of the child or children.

Joint custody has been found to have more positive outcomes for children than sole custody. In a meta-analysis of 33 studies that examined 1,846 sole-custody and 814 joint-custody families, Robert Bauserman (2002) found that child adjustment was more positive with joint custody than with sole custody. Children in joint custody had fewer emotional problems, higher self-esteem, better school performance, and more positive family relationships than children under sole custody.

Joint custody works only when both parents are able to work together. Also, it does not work when one parent is abusive, has emotional problems, or has a noncooperative attitude. Bauserman (2002) found that parents in joint custody reported less conflict and did not spend much time arguing over issues related to the child.

While no particular custody arrangement is best for all families, joint custody can work if parents can work together (DeFrain et al., 1987). What is best for the children has to be decided on the basis of answers to numerous questions, including (1) Do the children and both parents feel it best that both parents continue contact with the children after the divorce? (2) Are both parents capable of maintaining an adequate home for the children? (3) Can the parents get along with each other well enough to manage a joint-custody arrangement after the divorce? If all members of the family can honestly answer yes to all three questions, then joint custody can potentially be successful.

Joint-custody parents report less stress than single-custody parents. Joint-custody parents also have more time to pursue their own interests because the ex-spouse assumes a share of the child care responsibilities. Joint-custody parents are more likely to come from a devitalized or burned-out marriage; they are likely to neither love nor hate each other but are able to deal rationally with each other.

Coping Successfully as a Single Parent

Single parents have developed a number of successful strategies for coping with their unique station in life and offer the following suggestions for other single parents:

- Don't rush into a new couple relationship, particularly in an attempt to transfer your dependence onto another person. Let go of the past and move on.
- Realistically face what has happened. Learn from it; don't repeat it.
- Don't succumb to feelings of failure and worthlessness. Make the best of the situation and don't blame yourself completely.
- Keep busy with constructive activities. Take up new (or old) activities you always wanted to find time to enjoy.
- Listen to others but make your own decisions.
- Take one day at a time, setting small goals at first.
- Consider going back to school.
- Be flexible, adaptable, and independent.

Stepfamilies

Though they may be fearful of entering into a new relationship, and perhaps skeptical of the institution of marriage itself, most single parents want to find a new mate. Even more difficult than finding a new partner is finding one who cares about the children, and one whom the children like also. Single parents who marry again then face the challenge of developing a stepfamily system that works.

Stages in the Formation of a Stepfamily

People go through three stages in the process of forming a new family through remarriage: (1) entering a new relationship, (2) planning the new marriage and family, and (3) developing a stepfamily (Carter & McGoldrick, 1999). These stages are summarized in Table 15.3.

Entering a New Relationship. Before beginning this stage, divorced individuals should feel that they have recovered from the loss of the first marriage. A full recovery from a crisis such as divorce can take a long time; many people marry again before they have completely recovered from a divorce. To successfully bond with the second partner, however, one must be divorced emotionally as well as legally from the first partner.

TABLE 15.3	Stages in the Formation of a Stepfamily	
Stage	**Prerequisite Attitudes**	**Developmental Issues**
1. Entering a new relationship	Achieving complete recovery from the loss of first marriage (adequate emotional divorce)	Recommitting to marriage and to forming a family, with a readiness to deal with the complexity and amount of effort required
2. Planning the new marriage and family	Accepting one's own fears and those of the new spouse and children about remarriage and forming a stepfamily	Working on openness in the new relationship to avoid pseudomutuality
	Accepting the need for time and patience to adjust to the complexity and ambiguity of	Planning for the maintenance of cooperative coparent relationships with ex-spouses
	a. Multiple new roles	Planning to help the children deal with fears, loyalty conflicts, and membership in two systems
	b. Boundaries: space, time, membership, and authority	Realigning relationships with the extended family to include the new spouse and children
	c. Affective issues: guilt, loyalty, conflicts, desire for mutuality, unresolvable past hurts	Planning the maintenance of connections for the children with the extended family of the ex-spouse(s)
3. Developing a stepfamily	Finally resolving one's attachment to the previous spouse and to the ideal of an "intact" family	Restructuring family boundaries to allow for the inclusion of new spouse/stepparents
	Accepting a different model of family with permeable boundaries	Realigning relationships throughout subsystems to permit the interweaving of several systems
		Making room for relationships of all the children with biological (noncustodial) parents, grandparents, and other extended family
		Sharing memories and histories to enhance stepfamily integration

Source: Adapted from "Forming a Remarried Family" by B. Carter and M. McGoldrick. In *The Expanded Family Life Cycle: Individual, Family, and Social Perspectives,* 3rd ed., edited by B. Carter and M. McGoldrick, 1999, Boston: Allyn & Bacon. Copyright © 1999 by Allyn & Bacon. Reprinted by permission.

The major developmental issue during this stage of the process is a recommitment to the institution of marriage itself and to the idea of forming a new partnership and family. Before marrying again, individuals need to decide whether they want a new intimate relationship that requires closeness and personal commitment.

Planning the New Marriage and Family. In the second stage of this process, both spouses-to-be and their children must learn to accept their own fears about the new marriage and the formation of a stepfamily. This stage also requires acceptance of the fact that much time and patience are needed to adjust to the complexity and ambiguities of a new family.

One difficulty during this stage is dealing with multiple new roles: that of being a new spouse, a new stepparent, and a new member of a new extended family. The family will also need to make adjustments in terms of space, time, membership, and authority and to deal with affective issues, including feelings of guilt, loyalty conflicts, the desire for mutuality, and unresolvable past hurts. These feelings can come in a multitude of forms. For example, those planning to marry again often feel guilty because they must spend time and energy developing relationships with members of their soon-to-be family, often at the expense of time spent with the "old" family. One new stepfather acknowledged, "By spending so much time, money, and energy on my new spouse and stepchildren, I am neglecting my biological children."

During this second stage of planning the new marriage and family, a number of developmental issues or tasks must be addressed. All members of the new family need to work to build open, honest, straightforward communication patterns in order to avoid **pseudomutuality**, a false sense of togetherness. Other issues include building and planning to maintain cooperative coparenting relationships with ex-spouses, for the benefit of all parents and the children. It is also necessary to realign relationships with both extended families so that there is a place for the new spouse. If family members can manage to do all these things relatively well, the remarriage will have a better chance of succeeding.

Developing a stepfamily. In the third stage of the process of forming a new family, the newly married partners need to strengthen their couple relationship so that they can function as coparents. Family members need to see that the new marriage is genuine and that the stepfamily that the couple has begun to build together is a good family.

There are a number of developmental issues or tasks during this third stage of the remarriage process. Family boundaries must be restructured to include the new spouse/stepparent. Relationships throughout the different subsystems of the "old" families may need to change to permit the interweaving of this new family system. In short, there must be room in the family for stepchildren, half-siblings, new sets of grandparents, and extended kin. It is also important to make room for relationships between all the children and their biological (noncustodial) parents, grandparents, and other extended family members. Sharing memories and histories from each side of the new stepfamily can enhance integration.

Boundary Ambiguity in Stepfamilies

Family boundary ambiguity refers to a lack of clarity regarding who is included and who is not included in the family, and this lack of clarity regarding family composition is associated with stress for family members (Stewart, 2007). Because of the multiple and complex family compositions that can result in stepfamilies, boundary ambiguity is likely to result.

Stewart (2007) found that boundary ambiguity is rare in remarriages where couples only have shared children with no other children being brought into the marriage. However, boundary ambiguity is more prevalent where there are non-residential stepchildren. It seems that people have a tendency to define family as those who live with you, and those who are out of sight are also out of mind. In addition, when the stepfamily is structurally more complex, there is likely to be more boundary ambiguity, such as when parents have multiple sets of children.

Stepfamilies in Later Life

Stepfamilies are increasing as a family structure in later life which adds complexity to relationships with adult stepchildren, care of elderly stepparents, and inheritance issues. Couples are experiencing the opportunity for a second chance as they find love and remarriage in later years, but they are also faced with unique and complex challenges in the new multifamily relationships. There are no clear rules for these relationships because it is a relatively new phenomenon (Sherman, 2006). Family members may not know who they are to each other. For example, if the remarriage occurs after all the children are adults, are they still stepbrothers and -sisters to their stepparent's children? They are faced with new responsibilities. Who cares for an aging stepmother? They are also faced with issues around finances and inheritance. Who inherits the family business? These relationships require increased patience, communication, and commitment to navigate this new territory.

Strengths of Stepfamilies

Research findings on stepfamilies are generally positive. In spite of the presumption that stepfamilies will fail to succeed because of the many unique challenges they face, most stepfamilies do relatively well. Research on stepfamilies (Coleman, Ganong, & Fine, 2000; Ganong & Coleman, 1994, 1999, 2000) indicates that investigators have often failed to take into account the complexity of stepfamily relationships because of the number of people involved—extra parents, extra siblings, extra grandparents, extra sets of aunts and uncles, and so forth. Some stepfamily studies have also erred in using small samples of stepfamilies and nonrandom samples. Much of the data have been gathered through self-report questionnaires rather than through interviews or professional observations. And much of the data have come from only one family member, despite the fact that husbands, wives, children, and grandparents often have very different perceptions of what is going on in a family.

The goal of a study by Noel Schultz, Cynthia Schultz, and David Olson (1991) was to identify the major strengths of **simple stepfamilies**, which include children from only one parent, and compare them with those of **complex stepfamilies**, which include children from both parents. The researchers hypothesized and found that simple stepfamilies have more strengths than complex stepfamilies, reasoning that there is less complexity and conflict in simple stepfamilies than in complex stepfamilies. Figure 15.6 summarizes the data, which indicate that simple stepfamilies have more strengths than complex stepfamilies in the areas of personality issues, communication skills, ability to resolve conflict, parenting skills, and adjustment to the process of being a stepfamily.

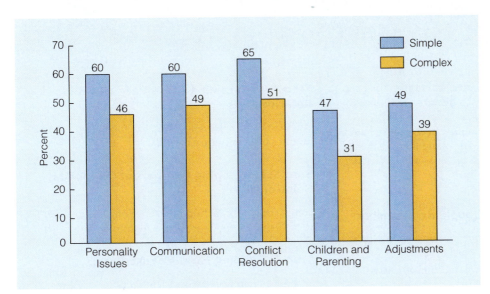

FIGURE 15.6

Strengths of Simple Versus Complex Stepfamilies (based on ENRICH)

Source: Data from "Couple Strengths and Stressors in Complex and Simple Stepfamilies in Australia" by N. C. Schultz, C. L. Schultz, and D. H. Olson, 1991, *Journal of Marriage and the Family*, 53, p. 560. Copyright 1991 by the National Council on Family Relations. Reprinted by permission.

Just because a first marriage ended in divorce does not mean a new marriage will also fail. In fact, the painful process of divorce can be a tremendous learning experience and can help provide the foundation for a successful new marriage and a strong stepfamily.

Guidelines for Stepfamilies

Emily Visher and John Visher developed an excellent set of helpful guidelines for both stepparents and stepfamilies. The **Stepping Ahead Program** (Visher & Visher, 1998), an eight-step program (described in more detail in Box 15.2), was designed to help stepfamilies avoid some common pitfalls and to get their new families off to a positive start.

The program involves nurturing the couple relationships so that the new marriage survives and thrives, finding personal space and time to relax and unwind, nourishing family relationships by spending time with each of the new members, maintaining close parent–child relationships, developing the stepparent–stepchild relationship, building family trust, strengthening stepfamily ties through regular family discussion, and working with the children's other household.

Developing stepfamily relationships after divorce and remarriage is difficult. Stepparents face many challenges in dealing with the offspring of their new spouse (Ahrons, 2003, 2004; Visher & Visher, 1996, 1998; Visher, Visher, & Pasley, 1997). Stepparents must remember that they are taking on someone else's child and many of the childrearing responsibilities formerly held by a biological parent. Stepparents often find themselves either overidealized by their stepchildren early in the relationship or the victim of displaced hostility.

Not all members of a stepfamily are biologically related. This is an obvious enough fact and one that should, in theory, be relatively simple to deal with. But our culture considers biological family ties special. "Blood is thicker than water," the old saying goes. Biological family bonds are difficult to break. Many children of divorce keep hoping that Mom and Dad will reunite, and the new marriage of one of the parents dashes those hopes. When a stepparent enters the family,

BOX 15.2   Putting It Together

The Stepping Ahead Program

Stepfamilies have endured negative stereotypes since the days of Cinderella and the ugly stepsisters. While stepfamilies do face complicated issues, there are steps parents can take to help separate families become integrated into one well-functioning unit. Emily and John Visher developed the eight steps below as guidelines to help make that happen.

Step 1: Nurturing Your Couple Relationship

Plan a weekly activity away from your household that you both enjoy doing together.

Arrange to have 20 minutes of relaxed time alone with each other every day.

Talk together about the running of your household for at least 30 minutes each week.

Step 2: Finding Personal Space and Time

Take time to make a special "private" place for each of the adults and children in your household.

Each of you should take 2 hours a week doing something for yourselves that you would like to do.

Step 3: Nourishing Family Relationships

Share with family members what you each appreciate about one another.

Step 4: Maintaining Close Parent–Child Relationships

Parent and child: Do something fun together for 15 to 20 minutes once or twice a month.

Step 5: Developing Stepparent–Stepchild Relationships

Stepparent and stepchild: Do something fun together for 15 to 20 minutes once or twice a month.

Step 6: Building Family Trust

Schedule a family event once a month.

Step 7: Strengthening Stepfamily Ties

Hold a family discussion once every 2 weeks.

Step 8: Working with the Children's Other Household

Give the adults in the children's other household positive feedback once a month.

Source: Adapted from "The Stepping Ahead Program" (pp. 58–89) by E. Visher. In Stepfamilies Stepping Ahead, edited by M. Burt, 1989, Lincoln, NE: Stepfamilies Press. Copyright 1989 by Stepfamily Association of America. Adapted by permission. (See Visher & Visher, 1998.)

children truly know that their mother and father will never get back together. This can cause despair and bitterness toward the stepparent. The stepparent can become the personification of evil in the child's mind: "If only *she* weren't around, Mom and Dad would get back together."

Even though the relationships between biological parent and child are well established, the couple in a stepfamily are newlyweds. It can be very difficult for the couple to balance marital needs and the children's needs. Family members' loyalties are divided in new and complex ways when a new family member comes on the scene. If a stepparent does not recognize the stepchildren's long-standing bonds with the biological parent and move carefully, the stepparent can end up in a very difficult love triangle.

A common example is a single mother who lives alone with her children for a number of years before marrying again. The mother may have developed strong ties and a comfortable pattern of parenting with her children. If she has an adolescent son or daughter, the mother's relationship with the child may be more like that of a big sister than that of a parent. The adolescent may become very jealous of the new spouse. "She always used to want to talk to me after school. Now she spends all her time with him!"

In the case of single-parent families headed by a male, girls may develop an almost "wifelike" relationship with their father during the single-parent period, according to Geoffrey Greif (2000). Daughters often serve as confidante and household manager for their father, and many enjoy their new status. When the father marries again, the daughter may see the stepmother as a competitor for Dad's time and affection and an intruder on her wifelike roles.

Stepparents must avoid the tendency to try too hard; bonding takes a good deal of time. Newlyweds generally go out of their way to please each other, but the same approach taken with the stepchildren can create problems for the new stepparent. The stepparent knows that his or her new spouse's children are a major hurdle in establishing a successful marriage and feels that if she or he can only get along with the children, the chances for success in this new marriage are vastly improved. But children do not easily forsake the love of their birth parent for a stepparent. Adolescents, in particular, are often not very open to including an "outsider" in their family.

The stepparent needs to avoid the trap of trying to replace the former parent. In reality, the stepparent is not so much a new parent in the family as a new adult in the family. The parent role has to develop slowly. The urge to build a solid new marriage can spur stepparents to play the "superstepmother" or "superstepfather" role, which is neither realistic nor beneficial.

Stepparents must also avoid favoritism in dealing simultaneously with their "real" children and their stepchildren. Children are not always pleasant to be around; they can at times be selfish, whiney, disobedient, and intrusive. Just as many parents have difficulty loving their own children when they are not acting lovable, so it is difficult for stepparents to love someone else's children at times. It is also important that stepparents not overcompensate for their tendency to favor their biological children by being more lenient with their stepchildren.

Stepparents also need to develop skills in dealing with complex financial realities in their new families. Although people who are marrying again are usually painfully aware of how challenging family money problems can be, few feel comfortable discussing money matters and financial planning before remarriage (Pasley & Ihinger-Tallman, 1994). Some even prefer to avoid talking about minor financial issues until they become more serious problems. Money problems are common in stepfamilies. For example, a father who remarries is sometimes in the difficult position of sending child support payments to his biological children, supporting his new family, and hoping that his new spouse's former husband will continue to provide financial support for the stepchildren.

Summary

- Though about half of first marriages end in divorce, marriage is so popular in the United States that more than 80% of younger people divorcing before age 25 will marry again.
- No-fault divorce laws eliminated (1) fault as grounds for divorce, (2) gender-based division of responsibilities, (3) the adversarial nature of divorce, and (4) linkage of the financial settlement to the determination of fault. Some argue, however, that no-fault's principle of equity between the sexes penalizes divorced women financially.
- The most prominent problems reported by couples seeking marital therapy are poor communication, power struggles, unrealistic expectations about marriage, sexual relationship problems, and difficulties in decision making. For marital therapists, the most difficult problems to treat are lack of loving feelings, alcoholism, and extramarital affairs.
- Research on the effects of marital discord and divorce on children suggests that divorce is a crisis in the lives

of most children who experience it. In addition to sadness and regret, many children experience anger at their parents and at themselves.

- Divorce has a broad, long-term negative impact on most aspects of a child's well-being. Research shows that children who have experienced divorce have higher rates of cohabitation and more unstable marriages than do children from stable marriages.

- A surprising research finding suggests that low-conflict marriages that end in divorce have a more negative impact on children than do high-conflict marriages that end in divorce.

- Bohannan identified six different but overlapping "stations" of the divorce process: emotional divorce, legal divorce, economic divorce, coparental divorce, community divorce, and psychological divorce.

- The duration and experience of the entire process of divorce vary with each individual. It appears, however, that when people can talk openly about divorce and accept it as an important part of their lives, they can move on as happy single individuals.

- In 2000, nearly one-third of all U.S. families were headed by a single parent, most of whom were female.

- Differences between nuclear families and stepfamilies include biological parent–child ties, the nature and length of the couple's marriage, parent–child emotional bonds, loyalty issues, extended-family issues, power struggles between children, and the degree of demands on financial resources.

- There are four types of divorced single-parent families, or binuclear families: mothers with sole custody, fathers with sole custody, split-custody families (in which the father has custody of one or more children and the mother has custody of one or more children), and joint-custody families (in which mother and father share decision making and childcare responsibilities after the divorce in relatively equal time segments). Researchers have concluded that the type of relationship the ex-spouses have often determines which single-parent family style will work best.

- Divorced single parents face challenges that include loneliness and isolation, money problems, and work overload. Joys of single parenting include the freedom to make decisions without interference, the satisfaction of watching the children grow and develop, and increased closeness with the children.

- Single parents advise newly single parents to take time to get to know themselves before rushing into new relationships; not to succumb to feelings of failure, worthlessness, or self-pity; to keep busy with constructive activities; to listen to others but make their own decisions; to set small goals; to consider going back to school; and to remain flexible, adaptive, and independent.

- Many divorced individuals with children are extremely cautious about entering a new marriage. Remarriage involves letting go of the old relationship and any pain associated with it; planning for the complexities involved in the new couple and family relationship; and then making room for the new spouse, the new spouse's children, one's own children, and all the children's relationships with their biological parents and extended families.

- Stepparenting is challenging. Some of the pitfalls associated with stepparenting include trying too hard to establish a successful relationship with their stepchildren, provoking resentment or jealousy in their stepchildren, trying to replace the absent biological parent, and favoring their own children over their stepchildren.

- Steps in building a strong stepfamily include nurturing the couple, family, parent–child, and stepparent–stepchild relationships; building stepfamily trust and ties; keeping bridges open to the children's biological parents; and finding personal space and time for all family members.

- Research indicates that the majority of stepfamilies have strengths similar to those of other types of families. In terms of personality issues, communication skills, ability to resolve conflict, parenting skills, and adjustment to being part of a stepfamily, research indicates that simple stepfamilies have more strengths than complex stepfamilies.

Key Terms

no-fault divorce	binuclear family
alimony	sole custody
uncontested divorce	joint custody
tender years doctrine	split custody
divorce culture	remarriage
emotional divorce	blended family
legal divorce	stepfamily
economic divorce	stepparent
coparental divorce	pseudomutuality
community divorce	simple stepfamily
psychological divorce	complex stepfamily
feminization of poverty	Stepping Ahead Program

Activities

1. Interview someone who has been divorced. Ask her or him to recount experiences encountered throughout the entire divorce process. Use Bohannan's six stations of divorce as a guide for your questions. Compare and contrast the results of your interview with others in a small-group discussion.

2. Interview a member of a single-parent family. Ask not only about the stresses the family faces but also about the strengths in the family. How is the family different from a two-parent family? How is it similar? Discuss your findings with other students.

3. Interview a member of a stepfamily, focusing on both the strengths and the stresses in the family. Compare and contrast the family with a nuclear family. Share your findings with other students.

4. Review Table 15.2 and discuss the differences between a nuclear family and a stepfamily. What consequences do these differences have for the parents and the children in each type of family?

Suggested Readings

Barnes, S. L. (2001). Stressors and strengths: A theoretical and practical examination of nuclear, single-parent, and augmented African American families. *Families in Society: The Journal of Contemporary Human Services, 82*(5), 449–460. Academic studies of African American families have focused on the negative for many years. This study takes a more balanced approach, looking at both family problems and successes.

Clapp, G. (2000). *Divorce and new beginnings: A complete guide to recovery. Solo parenting, co-parenting, and step-families* (2nd ed.). New York: Wiley. Offers guidelines for navigating the difficult straits of loss, growth, and resolution.

Coontz, S. (2005). *Marriage, a history: From obedience to intimacy or how love conquered marriage.* New York: Viking.

Deal, R. L. (2002). *The smart step-family.* Minneapolis: Bethany House.

Hetherington, E. M., & Stanley-Hagan, M. M. (2000). Divorce. In A. E. Kazdin (Ed.), *Encyclopedia of psychology* (Vol. 3, pp. 61–65). Washington, DC: American Psychological Association/Oxford University Press. A useful synopsis.

Joanning, H., & Keoughan, P. (2006, May/June). The divorce process and therapeutic interventions. *Family Therapy Magazine,* pp. 14–16.

Wallerstein, J. S., & Blakeslee, S. (2003). *What about the kids? Raising your children before, during, and after divorce.* New York: Hyperion. Wallerstein and her colleagues have devoted many years to learning about the process of divorce and its effects on family members.

Visit the text-specific Online Learning Center at **www.mhhe.com/Olson6** for practice tests, chapter summaries, Web links, Internet exercises, key terms, and flashcards.

16. *Strengthening Marriages and Families*

Couple and Family Strengths

Premarital and Marriage Programs

Marital and Family Therapy

Strengthening Your Marriage and Family Relationships

The Future of Your Family

Summary

Activities

Suggested Readings

To build strong marriages and families, we need to focus on developing couple and family strengths. A prominent marriage research, project conducted by John Gottman and colleagues clearly demonstrated that in healthy and happy marriages there is a ratio of five positive statement to one negative (Gottman & Notarius, 2000). The study of over 20,000 marriages by David Olson and Amy Olson (2000) also clearly demonstrated that focusing on positive communication and developing the positive feeling of couple closeness was the core of happy marriages. In families, John DeFrain and Nick Stinnett (2002) identified the six strengths that are characteristic of healthy and happy families: positive communication, commitment, appreciation and affection, spiritual well-being, enjoying time together, and ability to manage stress. Studies from over 30 countries have demonstrated the salience of these family strengths.

Couple and Family Strengths

Our emphasis on strengths is rare in the marriage and family field, yet it is becoming more popular in the fields of psychology and even business. In psychology, the groundbreaking work of Martin Seligman (2002) focuses on the importance of positive experiences, positive personality traits, and positive feelings and optimism in helping improve emotional and physical health.

In business, a good example of the positive approach is reflected in the work of Donald Clifton who said that psychology was based too much on what was wrong with people instead of what is right with them. In their book *Now, Discover Your Strengths*, a popular book in the business world, Marcus Buckingham and Donald Clifton (2005) include assessment created by the Gallup Organization called the *Strength Finder* that measures 34 areas or themes for a person and identifies the top five most prominent personal strengths.

This book has emphasized couple strengths by identifying the major strengths of happily married couples at the beginning of most of the chapters. Our goal has been to describe what happy couples are doing well to make them succeed and to illustrate it with specific examples. A subtheme could be "Building on Your Couple Strengths." This does not mean ignoring issues, and so we have also described in most chapters the common stumbling blocks that all couples have—happy and unhappy. The difference is that happy couples are better able to resolve these issues. Another subtheme is "Turn Your Stumbling Blocks (issues) Into Stepping Stones (strengths)." The ultimate goal is to help identify how couples can build on their strengths and create new ones by overcoming problematic issues.

The family strengths we have emphasized are illustrated in the world globe because they are relevant across all cultures and societies (see Figure 16.1). The six specific strengths are *commitment to family, enjoyable time together, ability to manage stress and crisis effectively, spiritual well-being, positive communication,* and *appreciation and affection.*

Kenneth Boulding (1985), an economist and philosopher, believes that human betterment is the end toward which we individually and collectively should strive. It is an increase in the "ultimate good," that which is good in itself. Four great virtues make up this ultimate good, and they are also illustrated in Figure 16.1.

- *Economic adequacy:* "riches," in contrast to poverty; nourishment, in contrast to starvation; adequate housing, clothing, health care, and other essentials of life.

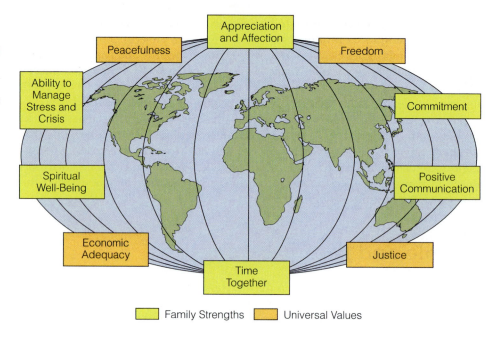

FIGURE 16.1

Family Strengths and Universal Values Around the World: A Proposed Model

Source: Adapted with permission from an illustration by Amie DeFrain.

Appreciation and Affection

Peacefulness

Freedom

Ability to Manage Stress and Crisis

Commitment

Spiritual Well-Being

Positive Communication

Economic Adequacy

Justice

Time Together

☐ Family Strengths   ☐ Universal Values

- *Justice,* in contrast to injustice; equality, rather than inequality, in access to work, education, and health.
- *Freedom,* in contrast to coercion and confinement.
- *Peacefulness,* in contrast to war and strife.

We offer strengths to each other as individuals, family members, and citizens of our communities. Novelist James A. Michener, a self-described "citizen of the world," dedicated a lifetime to understanding people around the world, living in an area for months or years and writing about what he saw and heard. He concluded:

> We are all brothers [and sisters]. We all face the same problems and find the same satisfactions. We are united in one great band. I am one with all of them, in all lands, in all climates, in all conditions. Since we brothers [and sisters] occupy the entire earth, the world is our home. (Michener, 1991, p. 249)

The family strengths perspective cautions that if you look only for problems in families, you will find only problems. If you look for strengths, however, you will find strengths. A family's strengths become the foundation upon which its members build even more successful ways of relating to one another.

As folk singers Peter, Paul, and Mary sang in the song "River of Jordan":

> We are only one river: We are only one sea.
>
> And it flows through you, and it flows through me.
>
> We are only one people. We are one and the same.
>
> We are all one spirit. We are all one name.
>
> We are the father, mother, daughter and son.
>
> From the dawn of creation, we are one.
>
> We are one. (Yarrow, 1972)

Premarital and Marriage Programs

Programs and services for couples and families range from informal networks to couple and family therapy. Table 16.1 lists program types in order of their therapeutic impact, from least to most intensive. As couple and family issues become more serious and chronic, a higher intensity of treatment is recommended. For example, it would be more appropriate for a couple who has been having marital problems for several years and has seriously considered divorce to see a couple therapist rather than to attend a self-help group.

Couple education programs can be very useful resources for couples without serious problems. These programs can help couples meet and learn from other couples. They can also learn from skill-building programs that focus on communication and conflict-resolution skills. These are relationship skills that couples can use to improve their relationships and resolve the differences that inevitably arise in any close relationship.

Couple therapy and family therapy are recommended when relationship problems between partners or among family members are chronic and intense. When problems involve the children, family therapy is called for. In families headed by two parents, the parents may also benefit from couple therapy, because parenting can put a great deal of stress on the couple relationship. Couple therapy and family therapy are most effective when begun before problems become severe and chronic.

Premarital Programs for Marriage

Failing to prepare is like preparing to fail.

This quote emphasizes the importance of being prepared for marriage, which is one of the most challenging tasks that you will experience in your life. Because the risk of divorce is about 50% and because of the high value couples place on a happy marriage, more couples are seeking premarital counseling from the clergy performing their marriage ceremony or from a professional counselor.

There is increasing evidence that a good premarital program can help improve a couple's relationship and reduce their chances of divorce. As discussed in Chapter 11, an effective premarital program has at least three essential components: (1) a premarital inventory with individual feedback for each couple, (2) a skill-building component that focuses on communication and problem solving, and (3) small-group

TABLE 16.1	Programs for Couples and Families		
	Service	**Goal**	**Provider**
Education courses for students	Functional marriage and family courses	Awareness and knowledge	High school and college teachers
Couple education programs	Premarital and marital programs	Insight and skills in communication and conflict resolution	Clergy, counselors, and marital therapists
Couple and family therapy	Marital and family therapy	Insight and change in relationship dynamics	Marital and family therapists, psychologists

Educational programs for couples are increasingly popular, both as a means for helping couples learn new relationship skills and as a way to strengthen an already effective relationship. There is always room for improvement.

discussions in which couples can air their mutual issues. The program should last 6 to 8 weeks and should be started a year before the marriage so that the partners have time to develop their relationship skills and deal with any important issues.

Premarital counseling is popular with most clergy. In a national study of 231 clergy from several Protestant denominations, 94% said they thought that all premarital couples should have counseling before marriage, and 100% said they provided premarital counseling to all couples before they would marry them (Jones & Stahmann, 1994).

One of the most popular premarital programs in the United States is the *PREPARE Program,* which is offered by over 65,000 counselors and clergy. As mentioned in Chapter 11, more than 2 million couples have participated in this program over the past 10 years. The six goals of the program are to (1) help the couple explore their relationship strengths and growth areas; (2) teach the couple the communication skills of assertiveness and active listening; (3) help the couple learn to resolve conflict effectively using a 10-step conflict resolution model; (4) help the couple discuss their families of origin; (5) develop a workable budget and financial plan; and (6) develop personal, couple, and family goals. The PREPARE Program focuses on 20 important relationship areas, including communication, conflict resolution, financial management, and egalitarian roles. For more information on the PREPARE Program and the location of a professional in your community, and to take a sample *Couple Quiz,* visit the Web site at www.prepare-enrich.com.

Couple Education Programs

Interest in couple programs is on the rise (Hunt, Hof, & DeMaria, 1998). There are two types of couple programs. One type, referred to simply as a couple enrichment program, usually lasts 1 or 2 days and often takes place on a weekend. The focus is on motivating the couple to increase the amount of personal information they share with each other. These relatively brief programs are helpful to some couples who already have a good marriage and want to improve it. However, for couples with more serious relationship issues, such programs can create problems by raising expectations for a better relationship, but not providing the relationship skills to achieve it.

The second type of program, couple education, focuses on teaching communication and conflict resolution skills (Berger & Hannah, 1999). These programs are more effective than the 1- or 2-day couple enrichment programs. They usually last about 6 weeks and meet each week for about 2 hours. Skill-building programs have demonstrated their effectiveness and value to couples.

The following five marriage education programs are high quality and have developed and been refined over the last 20 years:

- *Couple Communication Program*—Sherod and Phyllis Miller (2000)
- *PAIRS Program*—Lori Gordon (Gordon & Durana, 1999)
- *PREP Program*—Howavd Markman and Scott Stanley (2004)
- *PREPARE/ENRICH Program*—David Olson, David Fournier, and Joan Druckman (2001)
- *Relationship Enhancement Program*—Bernard Guerney (Cavedo & Guerney, 1999)

To learn more about these programs and other couple education programs, go to the Smart Marriages Web site at www.smartmarriages.com.

A study compared three couple education programs for newlywed couples (Hawley & Olson, 1995). The programs were Preston Dyer and Genie Dyer's *Growing Together*, Edward Bader's *Learning to Live Together*, and Don Dinkmeyer and Jon Carlson's *Training for Marriage Enrichment (TIME)*. Seventy-one newlywed couples were assigned to the three programs, and 28 couples were assigned to a control group. All three programs were about 6 weeks long, and all focused on communication, conflict resolution, finances, role relationship, family of origin, and sexuality. Couples met in a small group with about six other couples and a trainer on a weekly basis for about 2 hours.

Ninety-eight percent of the couples in the couple programs said they would recommend the program to another couple, and 96% said they would repeat the experience. More than 85% felt the topics were very relevant, and 75% felt their group leader was helpful. There were significant improvements in the couples' scores on communication, conflict resolution, personality issues, financial management, dealing with family and friends, and marital satisfaction on some statistical tests, though not on others. The couples really enjoyed the experience and felt it was very beneficial to their marriage.

Marital and Family Therapy

If you did nothing more when you have a family together than to make it possible for them to really look at each other, really touch each other, you would have already swung the pendulum in the direction of a new start.

—Virginia Satir (1988)

Couples with persistent relationship problems should seek marital therapy as early as possible. Couples and families who receive help with problems before they become too severe have a much better chance of overcoming the difficulties and building a stronger relationship than do those who wait. An analogy can be made

TABLE 16.2	Top 10 Stumbling Blocks for Couples

A nationwide survey of 21,501 married couples from newlyweds to retirees uncovered the 10 most common difficulties they face:

Issue/Problem	Percentage of Couples
1. We have problems sharing leadership equally.	93%
2. My partner is sometimes too stubborn.	87
3. Having children reduces our marital satisfaction.	84
4. My partner is too negative or critical.	83
5. I wish my partner had more time and energy for recreation with me.	82
6. I wish my partner were more willing to share feelings.	82
7. I always end up feeling responsible for the problem.	81
8. I go out of my way to avoid conflict with my partner.	79
9. We have difficulty completing tasks or projects.	79
10. Our differences never seem to get resolved.	78

Source: Olson & Olson, 2000.

to treating cancer and a problematic marriage: the sooner you seek treatment, the more effective the treatment and the better the outcome.

Common Problems in Couple Relationships

The national survey of 21,501 married couples identified 10 of the most common marital problems for married couples from newlyweds to retired couples (Olson & Olson, 2000). The top 10 issues or stumbling blocks were obtained across both happy and unhappy couples and they are summarized in Table 16.2.

In reviewing the common stumbling blocks for married couples, it is striking that a high percentage of both happy and unhappy couples (ranging from 78% to 93%) have these problems. The most problematic issue for couples is sharing leadership equally, with 93% agreeing that this is a problem. Over 80% of the couples agreed that their partner was too stubborn, that children reduced their marital satisfaction, that their partner was too negative or critical, that they wish they had more time to be together, that they wish their partner would share more feelings, and that they often ended up feeling responsible for problems. Three other very common issues were avoiding conflict with their partner, having difficulty completing tasks, and that differences never seemed to get resolved.

When clustering these 10 items into topic areas, the most common areas were regarding conflict resolution (3 items); couple flexibility (2 items); personality issues (2 items); and 1 item in communication, leisure activities, and parenting. These are issues that marital and family therapists often observe when working with couples having marital problems.

Problem Related to Closeness and Flexibility

Marital and family therapists working with couples and families with problems often use the Couple and Family Map. Because it focuses on the key dimensions of cohesion, flexibility, and communication, the Couple and Family Map provides a

Family gatherings can be a great way for different generations to connect and build a stronger family network.

useful framework for diagnosing and treating several common problems in marital and family systems.

One frequent problem couples seeking counseling describe is the feeling that they are at opposite extremes on the same dimension of the model. On the cohesion dimension, for example, one partner may want more togetherness, whereas the other partner may want more autonomy. Similarly, on the flexibility dimension, one partner may desire more flexibility in the family, whereas the other partner may want more rules (i.e., rigidity). When couples disagree on the balance of separateness (autonomy) and togetherness in their relationship, they can negotiate by jointly planning their schedules. When couples disagree on flexibility issues (rules or roles), they might try reversing roles at home for a week.

Another common problem for couples occurs when both partners are at the same extreme on one or both model dimensions. Both may be disengaged from the relationship because they are so heavily involved in career or outside interests that they have little time or energy for the marriage. Or both may be enmeshed, so invested in the partner that they have little room to develop personal interests and skills. When couples are disengaged, it is important for them to assess their commitment to the relationship. When couples are too enmeshed, one solution is for each of them to develop more separate interests and spend more time apart.

This all may sound quite simple, but difficulties arise because people see their relationships differently and have conflicting expectations about them. For example, the wife and the husband often offer different couple and family descriptions and goals. Add a teenage child, and the child's description will tend to be different from that of the parents. In fact, adolescents will describe their family as more extreme on the dimensions of cohesion and flexibilty (to unbalanced levels), whereas their parents will tend to see their family as more healthy and balanced on the Couple and Family Map (Figure 16.2).

There is no avoiding this dilemma of differing family perceptions. By interviewing only one person in the family, the husband or wife or adolescent, a coun-

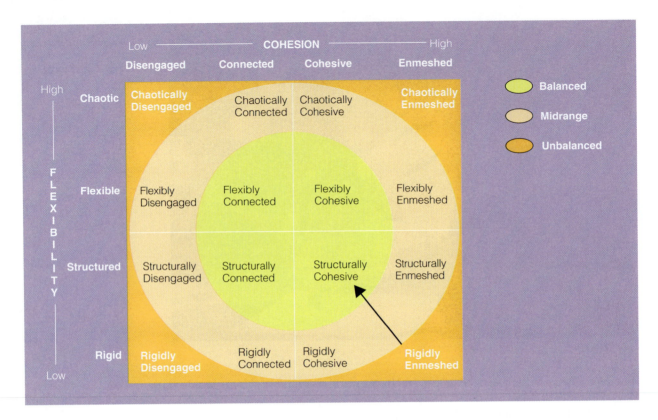

FIGURE 16.2

Couple and Family Map

selor would get only a snapshot rather than a panoramic view of the entire family and its complexity. The solution lies in getting everyone together, asking countless questions, and dealing with the conflicting perspectives of all the family members. This approach produces a more valid—and also a more complex—picture of the family's dynamics.

How Effective Is Marital and Family Therapy?

In a national survey of the practice of 526 marital and family therapists, therapists from 15 states commented on therapy with 1,422 clients (Doherty & Simmons, 1996). In addition, 492 clients rated their satisfaction with their marital and family therapies.

Marital and family therapists spent about half their time working with couples and families and half working with individuals. They spent about 20 hours a week seeing clients in therapy and carried a total caseload of about 24 clients. The common presenting problems were depression (44%), other psychological problems (35%), marital problems (30%), anxiety (21%), parent–child problems (13%), alcohol/drug problems (8%), child behavior issues (8%), and family-of-origin issues (7%). The most frequent DSM-IV (Diagnostic and Statistical Manual of Mental Disorders, Fourth Edition) diagnostic codes were adjustment disorder (25%), depression (23%), and anxiety disorders (14%).

Marital and family therapy is a relatively short process, as compared to traditional individual therapy provided by psychiatrists and some psychologists. The median number of sessions for the marital and family therapists was 12. The average length of therapy was 11 sessions for couples, 9 for families, and 13 for individuals. Most clients were seen biweekly. Based on the therapists' records, the average cost of therapy was $80 for each 1-hour session, for a total of $780. Individual therapy was the most expensive ($845), couple therapy was next ($748), and family therapy was the least expensive ($585).

The outcome of the therapy was usually very successful from the perspective of both the client and the therapist. Overall, 83% of the clients felt the therapeutic goals had been achieved; 89% felt their emotional health had improved; 78% said their family relationships had gotten better; and 63% felt their relationships with their partners had also improved. In addition, most clients were very satisfied with their therapy: 98% rated the service as good to excellent; 97% said they got the kind of help they wanted; 98% said they were able to deal with their problems more effectively; 93% said their needs were met; 94% said they would return to the same therapist again; and 97% said they would recommend the therapist to a friend. In summary, it appears that marital and family therapy is a rather cost-effective and efficient approach to dealing with a range of emotional and relationship problems in individuals, couples, and families (Doherty & Simmons, 1996).

Choosing a Marital and Family Therapist

Marital and family therapists are specifically trained to deal with relationship problems and to work directly with couples and families. Although some psychologists, psychiatrists, and social workers have some additional training with couples and families, they are in the minority. Licensed marital and family therapists are certified by the American Association for Marriage and Family Therapy (AAMFT) and have received specialized training in relationship issues. Psychologists typically have a doctorate or a master's degree in psychology and their initial training tends to emphasize work with individuals with emotional problems. Psychiatrists are medical doctors who have additional training in the field of mental health and their speciality is to administer drugs for emotional problems. Last, social workers receive some training in working with couples and families.

The most highly trained marital and family therapists are certified members of AAMFT or are licensed by the state in which they work. In most localities, the yellow pages of the telephone directory list marital and family therapists under "marital and family counseling." One can also consult a family service agency or the United Way for suggestions. Physicians or clergy may also be able to assist in the search for a qualified professional.

Following are some specific questions potential clients should ask a therapist *before* beginning marital or family therapy:

- What is your professional training and degree?
- How much specialized training and experience have you had in marital and family therapy?
- Do you usually see couples and families together or as individuals?
- What procedure will you use to evaluate our relationship?
- How much will you charge for that assessment?
- How frequently will we have sessions, and how long will they last?
- Can we establish a contract for a specific number of sessions?
- What will each session cost?

The more comfortable you feel about the therapist's answers to these questions, the more confidence you can have in the therapist's ability to help you as a couple or family.

Keys to Family Resiliency

The goal of family therapists is to help families with problems develop relationship skills that will promote resilience. Froma Walsh (2006) identified the key characteristics of healthy families that are usually missing from problem families (Table 16.3).

The *family organizational patterns* that are important are connectedness, flexibility, and social and economic resources. In terms of connectedness, healthy families are able to support each other emotionally and to collaborate with each other. Healthy families are also flexible; they are open to change and are able to adapt to challenges over time. Finally, healthy families often can rely on extended kin and a support network in times of need.

The *family communication processes* comprise clear communication, open expression of emotion, and collaborative problem solving. Healthy families exhibit skills in each of these areas, whereas families with problems tend to be lacking in these skills. As a result, family communication skills are often the focus of treatment with problem families.

The *family belief systems* that are important for family resiliency are making meaning of adversity, having a positive outlook, and having spiritual resources. Healthy families are able to face adversity directly and maintain a positive outlook. They are able to transcend their problems, often by drawing on their spiritual beliefs.

Family Therapy Case Study

The Davis family has five members: Mary and Don, the parents; 18-year-old Ann; 16-year-old Julie; and 9-year-old Peter. Mary drank to relieve feelings of inadequacy in a family dominated by high achievers: Don and the oldest daughter, Ann. The middle daughter, Julie, also felt inadequate but tried to console her mother and was responsible enough to be a surrogate mother to Peter, the youngest child. The family came in for therapy shortly after Mary began treatment for her dependence on alcohol. Ann subsequently left home, angry at Mary for all the problems she had caused. Julie felt lost because her mother was being "taken care of" by other people and Julie's role as chief counselor had been usurped.

In terms of the Couple and Family Map, the Davis family would be classified as a "rigidly enmeshed" family, which is an unbalanced family type because they

TABLE 16.3	Keys to Family Resiliency

Family Organizational Patterns
- Connectedness
- Flexibility
- Social and economic resources

Family Communication Processes
- Clarity
- Open emotional expression
- Collaborative problem solving

Family Belief System
- Making meaning
- Positive outlook
- Transcendence and spirituality

Source: Strengthening Family Resilience (2nd ed.) by F. Walsh, 2006, New York: Guilford Press. Reprinted with permission of Guilford Press.

Although the challenges can be formidable, families are capable of dramatic and positive change. Marital and family therapists can be helpful guides on the journey toward healing.

are at the extreme levels of both cohesion and flexibility. The goal for therapy in terms of their family system is to move them one level toward the balanced part of the model, which would move them to the "structurally cohesive" family type (see Figure 16.2).

Diagnosis. In terms of cohesion, the Davis family was *enmeshed*. They evidenced high emotional bonding as well as high mutual dependency. The mother and the two daughters competed intensely for approval from each other and from Dad. The family's external boundaries were closed. No one felt free to interact with people outside the family, partly because they were afraid Mary would be drunk and embarrass everyone. Friends and relatives were kept at a distance. The only time husband and wife made contact was when one of the children misbehaved. Then the two would team up as parents and support each other; otherwise, they did not interact much. The father–daughter coalitions, especially that between Don and Ann, were strong. In many ways, Don and Ann played the role of parents in the family, because Mary's drinking often made her incapable of parenting.

Individual activities were permitted but only within family-approved guidelines. Don and Ann spent a lot of time playing tennis together, but Julie's desire to spend the same amount of time away from the family "partying" with friends was not approved. Close friends, especially males, were not allowed. The family tried desperately to have fun at their cabin on the weekends. Everyone was required to go, and the implicit message was, "You *will* have fun!" The result was that nobody enjoyed the weekends at the cabin. Tending to Peter's needs kept Julie connected to the family after she became adrift when her mother entered the alcohol treatment program.

Much of the conflict in the family seemed to stem from its *rigidity*. The family system and each of its members could seldom think of new ways to solve problems. Also, no one in the family knew how to be appropriately assertive. Rather than making their point firmly but without malice or yelling, family members resorted to aggressive behaviors: screaming, throwing things, and occasionally striking each other.

Family roles were stereotypic and rigid. Mary saw herself as being in charge of the house, and she saw Don as the boss of the children, the rule enforcer. Mary made many threats but rarely carried them out. When things got out of hand, Don delivered punishment in a heavy-handed manner. When Mary felt upset about life, she tended to clean house or drink. She made life difficult for everyone by insisting that each be as compulsive about housekeeping standards as she was.

All in all, family leadership, rules, and roles were very rigid. As new situations developed in the family, the members did not have the flexibility to negotiate and create solutions that were reasonable. Ann and Julie could not discuss possible changes in a rational fashion with their parents. The Davises were locked in a dysfunctional family system that was the *rigidly enmeshed*.

Treatment. The family therapist sought to focus on those issues in the family on which some positive movement was already under way. On the dimension of cohesion, the goal was to increase the level of individual autonomy in the family—in short, to give each member more space. A related goal was to strengthen the marriage.

In terms of flexibility, the family therapist taught family members how to negotiate and compromise with each other, rather than alternating between quiet passivity and conflict. Members were taught to see family rules as general guidelines to be discussed and interpreted as new situations arose in day-to-day living. This gave the children a chance to argue their points and even to change their parents' minds occasionally. When the family as a whole had improved on these dimensions, the focus shifted to the marriage.

Don and Mary continued in marital therapy as a couple. The therapist focused on ways the couple could learn to enjoy each other's company again. They were encouraged to go out on dates without the children and to do things they felt they hadn't had time to do together for many years. As the marriage improved, the number of disagreements with the children diminished. Why was this? As the marital coalition strengthened and Mary took back her rightful place on the parental team, it was less necessary for Julie and Ann to struggle for a position in coalition with Dad, and Julie no longer felt it necessary to try to fill the vacuum.

The family therapist got a good deal of help from Mary's alcohol counselors and from Alcoholics Anonymous. The chemical dependence specialists were adept at helping Mary maintain sobriety once she had attained it. Al-Anon, which focuses on the family of the alcoholic, gave Don and the children support and ideas in their struggle to live with an alcoholic. As Mary became more secure in her marriage with Don, she was able to be more supportive of Julie in her growth as an individual. The family became more adept at both separating from and connecting with each other.

As a result of couple therapy to strengthen the marriage and family therapy to improve the family functioning, after about 10 sessions the family was now functioning as a "structurally cohesive" family (see the Couple and Family Map, Figure 16.2). In terms of cohesion, they had moved from being "enmeshed" to being less connected as a "cohesive" family. Don and Mary became more emotionally connected to each other, and this helped to reduce the dysfunctional parent–adolescent coalition of Don and daughter Ann. In terms of flexibility, the family moved from

Families have a variety of ways that they interact with the outside world. Spending time with other families is a healthy way to teach children about the world outside of their own family.

being "rigid" to being "structured." The parents started to work more as a cooperating team and gave their adolescents a little more freedom and autonomy. All family members were much happier with how the family had changed, and they were more clear about how they could continue to improve their family over time.

Strengthening Your Marriage and Family Relationships

There are a variety of ways to build stronger marriage and family relationships. First, you need to make the choice of a good partner and then prepare for your marriage by seeking out premarital counseling. Second, you need to do things to continually build a stronger couple and marital relationship. Last, you need to work on building your family strengths, which ultimately impact the quality of the individual, couple, and parent–child relationships.

Building a Stronger Marriage

The couple relationship is the foundation of a strong family, so it is important that the couple develop a strong and healthy relationship. If the marriage is strong, it also has a positive impact on the emotional and physical health of the individuals (Waite & Gallagher, 2000).

There are a variety of specific things that couples can do to build a stronger relationship. Box 16.1 lists 10 suggestions that have been found to be important across numerous studies. These include giving compliments, finding time to dialogue, having a weekly date, being assertive, listening with care, resolving issues before they become serious, and seeking help if you have problems that you are unable to resolve. Because marriage changes over time, it is important to keep working on

BOX 16.1   Putting It Together

Building a Stronger Marriage

Relationships, like children, need to be nurtured and protected in order to grow and remain healthy. One of the natural consequences of long-term relationships is that couples become complacent about each other and about the strengths upon which their relationship was built. The 10 suggestions listed here can help couples keep relationships vital and healthy.

1. Give one or two compliments to your partner each day.
2. Find time to dialogue for 5 minutes each day about your relationship.
3. Have a weekly meeting for about 15 minutes with your partner and discuss one or two issues and one or two strengths of your relationship.
4. One night a week, have a date with each other, just as you did before marriage.
5. Be assertive—ask for what you want—so your partner does not have to guess.
6. Share feelings with each other and remember to listen, listen, and listen.
7. Resolve issues as soon as possible.
8. If a problem persists for 2 to 3 months, use the six steps for resolving couple conflict (see Chapter 5 on conflict resolution).
9. If you are unable to resolve your conflict, seek professional counseling from a marital therapist.
10. At least once a year, try to attend a workshop to enrich your marriage.

improving the relationship. One way is to look for opportunities to attend couple enrichment programs with other couples.

Building a Stronger Family

In numerous studies, we have found that strong families successfully manage life's difficulties in a variety of ways. These are some of their strategies:

- *Look for something positive in difficult situations.* No matter how difficult, most problems teach us something about ourselves and others that we can draw on in future situations.
- *Pull together.* Think of the problem not as one family member's difficulty but as a challenge for the family as a whole.
- *Create open channels of communication.* Challenges cannot be met when communication shuts down.
- *Keep things in perspective.* "These things, too, shall pass."
- *Adopt new roles in a flexible manner.* Crises often demand that individuals learn new approaches to life and take on different responsibilities.
- *Focus to minimize fragmentation.* Look at the big picture. Focusing on the details rather than the essentials can make people edgy, even hysterical.
- *Create a life full of meaning and purpose.* We all face severe crises in life. These challenges are simply unavoidable. Our aim should be to live a useful life of service to our community. Giving of ourselves brings a richness and dignity to our lives, in spite of the troubles we endure.
- *Actively meet challenges head on.* Life's disasters do not go away when we look in another direction.

Building Family Rituals. Most families operate in a reactive rather than a proactive manner and simply drift through life without a clear direction or meaning. But families can become more intentional, which means becoming more con-

BOX 16.2　Putting It Together

Building a Stronger Family

Families today are often mix-and-match affairs with any number—and type—of parents, grandparents, children, and siblings. In order for any family to work, no matter what its makeup, there has to be a conscious effort to instill positive feelings and a sense that every family member is equally important. Here are 10 suggestions for keeping families strong.

1. Give at least one compliment to each family member each day.
2. Do a daily dialogue for 5 to 10 minutes each day about what is happening with each family member.
3. Try to have your family meal together with everyone present.
4. Have a weekly family meeting for about 30 to 45 minutes with all family members attending. Each member should say one thing they like about the family and one issue they have with their family that everyone will work on during the session.
5. Give top priority to your marriage.
6. Be as assertive as your children are with you.
7. Remember to listen, listen, and listen.
8. Spend 1 hour of quality time each week with each child (one on one).
9. If a problem persists, bring it to the family meeting and use the six-step Model for resolving the conflict (see Chapter 5).
10. If a parenting problem lasts for 2 to 3 months, seek professional help from a family therapist.

nected with each other and sharing meanings and experiences. William Doherty, a respected family therapist, wrote a useful book entitled *The Intentional Family: How to Build Family Ties in Our Modern World* (1997) to help families to become more intentional.

One very useful way to build an intentional family is to develop family rituals, which are repeated and coordinated activities that have significance for the family (Doherty, 1997). Three types of family rituals and the function they serve are described. *Connection rituals* facilitate bonding and include everyday activities like family meals and bedtime rituals. *Love rituals* increase intimacy in the couple and family and include celebration of special days like birthdays, Valentine's Day, Mother's Day, and Father's Day. *Community rituals* help bond the family with the broader community of kin and friends and include such activities as weddings, funerals, and graduations.

Strengthening Your Family. Although the foundation of a strong family is a strong marriage, more families today are composed of single parents and also are stepfamilies, where children and parenting came before the marriage. The following are specific suggestions that single-parent families, stepfamilies, and two-parent families can use to strengthen their families. (DeFrain, 2006).

Specific suggestions for building more strengths in your family are summarized in Box 16.2. Some of these suggestions are similar to those proposed for building a strong marriage, but the focus is on all family members. Giving compliments and doing dialogue is very important in families and a family meal together can help family members get reconnected. A family meeting is very desirable for families using good communication skills of assertiveness and conflict resolution. Spending some quality time with each family member on a one-to-one basis is a good way to decrease the probability of having serious problems. Again, it is important to resolve problematic issues and, if they persist, to seek out a professional therapist.

The Future of Your Family

The future of families in the United States begins with each of us as we create the future in our own family.

The following are comments from students who took this course and were asked to describe their families or plan for their own marriages and families.

"For the future," said 26-year-old Allan, "I want to raise my family like my family did. We were a close family and had good communication. We had fun together and got much love from one another, because our family cared for each other."

* * * * *

"I think we're a happier family than we were in the past because we laugh a lot," answered Marta, a 40-year-old divorced mother of three who was completing her college degree. "The children think I'm really a liberated woman, and that's pretty exciting. I'd tell young people to hang in there with your parents and try and understand them, because they love you and they just want the very best for you."

* * * * *

"The future for my family?" 19-year-old Rachel replied. "I'm not sure. My parents have been divorced for about 15 years, and they're both remarried. My mom's happily remarried. My dad is not so happy. He always talks about my mom and what she's doing and what they'd be like if they were still together.
"My mom has done a really good job of showing us things are okay, even with stressful events. She has raised us very well, I believe. My father . . . he screwed up, and he's realizing it now. And I just don't know what to say to him. Yeah, Dad, you blew it. And I think he's going to get divorced again. For myself, I have the biggest hopes. I know everyone does."

* * * * *

"As far as where we're going," 21-year-old Tanya noted, "I think we'll be okay because my partner, Darren, has a strong family. But I don't want my dysfunctional family to overshadow our life because that's something I want to overcome. I want to overcome the statistics and have a strong marriage. I know I can count on my mom and dad who have a great marriage."

In summary, these students provided insights into their life experiences and their thoughts and dreams about their families in the future. Life inevitably brings challenges. The key to life is to build strong relationship with others and have a caring network of family and friends to help you enjoy life and deal with life's challenges.

Summary

- Economist Kenneth Boulding believes that there are four great virtues that make up the "ultimate good," and we should individually and collectively strive to achieve these: *economic adequacy, justice, freedom,* and *peacefulness*.
- Within the world, focusing on our similarities as human beings can help unite us and understand one another. Within families, focusing on family strengths emphasizes these strengths and helps us build successful ways of relating to one another.
- There are many ways individuals, couples, and families seek support, advice, and education, ranging from *informal networks* to *professional therapy*. The intensity level of the program should correspond to the level of need.
- A good premarital program can reduce a couple's chances of divorce and improve their overall relationship. One important way we can strengthen marriages

is to offer good premarital programs that give couples the skills to help them through their lives together.

- There are two types of couple programs: *couple enrichment programs* and *couple education programs*. Couple enrichment programs typically last 1 or 2 days and improve the couple relationship by increasing the sharing between the couple. Couple education programs are skill based, more comprehensive, and more effective in helping couples build stronger relationships.

- The top five stumbling blocks identified by couples in a national survey were the following: They have problems sharing leadership equally, they feel their partner is sometimes too stubborn, they are less satisfied with their marriage since having children, they feel their partner is too negative or critical, and they wish their partner had more time and energy for recreation.

- Family members often have different perceptions of the issues, events, and dynamics in their family. This is one reason the Couple and Family Map is helpful in assessing each family member's perceptions and providing a reference point for therapy.

- In a national survey of the practice of marital and family therapists, Doherty and Simmons (1996) found that through therapy 83% of clients felt that their therapeutic goals had been achieved, 89% said their emotional health had improved, 78% said their family relationships had gotten better, and 63% felt their relationship with their partner had also improved.

- Froma Walsh (2006) identified characteristics of healthy families that are usually not present in problem families: *family organizational patterns, family communication processes,* and *family belief systems.*

- Building strong marriages begins with your being proactive about your relationship skills and developing good relationships with others. Choosing a good partner and premarital education are the first steps you can take to develop a strong marriage. Then, as a couple, seek out couple education programs. When you have a family, remember to build on your strengths as individuals, as a couple, and as a family.

- William Doherty identified three types of family rituals that help families become more connected within the family as well as within the community, with friends, and with extended family. They are *connection rituals, love rituals,* and *community rituals.*

- Ways to build a strong family are to compliment each family member at least once each day; have a 5- to 10-minute daily dialogue about what is happening with each family member; try to have the family meal with everyone present; have a 30- to 45-minute weekly family meeting with all family members attending; give top priority to your marriage; be assertive like your children are with you; listen, listen, listen; spend 1 hour of quality time each week with each child one on one; if problems persist, use the 10-step model for resolving the conflict; seek professional help if a parenting problem lasts 2 or 3 months.

Activities

1. Write down the strengths in your current couple relationship.
2. Write down the strengths in your family of origin that you want to bring into your marriage.
3. Write down the problematic issues in your family of origin and think about ways you can avoid bringing them into your marriage.
4. What are the pros and cons of premarital counseling?
5. Will cohabitation help you prepare for marriage?
6. Would you attend a couple program or go to marital therapy?

Suggested Readings

Berger, R., & Hannah, M. T. (1999). *Preventive approaches in couples therapy.* Philadelphia: Brunner/Mazel.

DeFrain, J. (2006). *Family treasures: Creating strong families.* Lincoln: University of Nebraska Press.

Doherty, W. J. (1997). *The intentional family: How to build family ties in our modern world.* Reading, MA: Addison-Wesley.

Doherty, W. J. (2000). *Take back your kids.* Notre Dame, IN: Sorin Books.

Doherty, W. J. (2001). *Take back your marriage.* New York: Guilford.

Hunt, R. A., Hof, L., & DeMaria, R. (Eds.). (1998). *Marriage enrichment: Preparation, mentoring, and outreach.* Philadelphia: Brunner/Mazel.

Olson, D. H., & Olson, A. K. (2000). *Empowering couples: Building on your strengths.* Minneapolis: Life Innovations.

Walsh, F. (2006). *Strengthening family resilience* (2nd ed.). New York: Guilford.

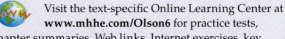 Visit the text-specific Online Learning Center at **www.mhhe.com/Olson6** for practice tests, chapter summaries, Web links, Internet exercises, key terms, and flashcards.

Couple and Family Scales

Couple and Family Map

Couple and Family Map

The Couple and Family Map can be used to define the way in which a couple or a family interacts—that is, to describe the family system. The Couple and Family Scales are the tools an interviewer uses to place the couple or family in the Couple and Family Map. In this resource section we will outline the instructions for using these scales. The process consists of six steps:

1. Understanding the dimensions and concepts of the Couple and Family Map.
2. Interviewing the couple or family.
3. Completing the Coalition Rating Scale.
4. Assigning a scale value for each concept.
5. Assigning a global rating for each dimension.
6. Plotting the global ratings on the Couple and Family Map.

Step 1: Dimensions and Concepts

There are three primary dimensions in the Couple and Family Map: family cohesion, family flexibility, and family communication. Each dimension has several concepts that help define and describe it. Before doing an assessment of a couple or a family, the interviewer reviews all the concepts and their descriptions for each of the three dimensions.

Step 2: Interview Questions

To assess a couple or a family, the interviewer, usually through a semistructured interview, evaluates the couple's or family's interactions in terms of each of the concepts for each dimension. Those experienced in using the Family and Couple Scales find it helpful to encourage the couple or family to discuss with each other the interview questions in Table A.1. The questions focus on the two dimensions of cohesion and flexibility but not on communication. To assess communication, the interviewer simply observes how the couple or family communicate while they are discussing the interview questions. The interviewer should encourage the couple or the family to talk directly to each other—*not* to the interviewer—so that the interviewer can observe how they interact with each other.

Step 3: The Coalition Rating Scale

After the interview, the interviewer first completes the Coalition Rating Scale (shown in Table A.2), if it applies. It is necessary to use this scale if one or more family members function differently from the rest of the family. For example, it is possible to have a *rigidly enmeshed* family with a *chaotically disengaged* husband. If there is a disengaged member or a coalition (see definitions given in Table A.2), these family members are rated separately from the rest of the

---

TABLE A.1	Interview Questions for Assessing Family Cohesion and Flexibility

Questions for Assessing Family Cohesion

1. *Separateness/togetherness:* How much do family members go their own way versus spending time with the family?
2. *I–we balance:* Do family members have a good balance of time apart and together?
3. *Closeness:* Do people feel close to each other?
4. *Loyalty:* Is the family a top priority compared with work or friends?
5. *Activities:* Do people spend much time having fun together?
6. *Dependence/independence:* Do family members stay in close contact?

Other Useful Questions to Assess Family Cohesion

1. How does your family celebrate birthdays and holidays?
2. Describe your typical dinnertime meal in terms of who is present, who prepares the meal, who cleans up, and the type of family interaction that occurs.

3. What is a typical weekend like in your family?
4. Do you have special times when you get together as a family?

Questions for Assessing Family Flexibility

1. *Leadership:* Is leadership shared between parents?
2. *Discipline:* Is (was) discipline strict?
3. *Negotiation:* How do you negotiate differences in your family?
4. *Roles:* Does each spouse do only certain tasks?
5. *Rules:* Do rules change in your family?
6. *Change:* Is change upsetting to your family?

Other Useful Questions to Assess Family Adaptability

1. How open is your family to change?
2. Is your family good at problem solving?
3. Does your family seem disorganized?
4. Who is in charge—the parent(s) or the child(ren)?

Instructions

The functioning of most families can be adequately described on the basis of their assessment as a unit or group. However, some families include individuals or dyadic units (coalitions) whose functioning may be markedly different from that of the rest of the family as a group.

This Coalition Rating Scale provides a way of noting coalitions' or disengaged individuals' patterns in family systems. After observing the family's interactions, any coalitions or disengaged individuals should be identified by checking the relevant categories below.

Definitions

Coalition. A coalition is two or more people with a high degree of emotional closeness to one another. During family interaction, the members of a coalition are very connected to one another and may at times exclude other family members.

Disengaged individual(s). A disengaged individual is emotionally separated from the rest of the family. Disengaged individuals often exhibit a low degree of involvement and interaction with other family members.

Coalitions

____ Mother–son
____ Mother–daughter
____ Father–son
____ Father–daughter
____ Son–daughter
____ Same-sex siblings
____ Other

Disengaged Individuals

____ Disengaged mother
____ Disengaged father
____ Disengaged child(ren)
____ Other

(A husband–wife coalition is considered a positive dyad and is therefore not listed.)

family system. The interviewer completes the Coalition Rating Scale *first*, before completing the other scales.

Step 4: Assigning Scale Values

After interviewing the couple or family, the interviewer rates them on each of the concepts that make up the three dimensions, using the scales in Table A.3. Before selecting a value, the interviewer carefully reads the descriptions for each concept and then selects a value from 1 to 8 that most closely represents the couple or family as a unit.

Step 5: Assigning Global Ratings

After assigning a rating for each concept in each of the three dimensions and recording those ratings on Table A.4, the interviewer makes a global rating for each of the three dimensions (cohesion, flexibility, and communication) and records the global ratings on Table A.4. The global rating for each dimension should be based on an overall evaluation rather than on a sum of the subscale (concept) ratings.

Step 6: Plotting a Family System Type on the Couple and Family Map

Finally, the interviewer plots the couple's or the family's global ratings on cohesion and flexibility on the Couple and Family Map (Figure A.1). This determines the marital or family system type. If, for example, the interviewer assigns a family a global rating of 5 on the cohesion dimension and 4 on the flexibility dimension, the model will identify the family as *structurally cohesive*, one of the four balanced family types on the Couple and Family Map. If the family contains a coalition or a disengaged member, the interviewer also plots the coalition or member on the map.

TABLE A.3 Couple and Family Scales

Levels of Family Cohesion

COHESION

Score	Disengaged (Unbalanced) 1 2	Connected (Balanced) 3 4	Cohesive (Balanced) 5 6	Enmeshed (Unbalanced) 7 8
Separateness/togetherness	High separateness	More separateness than togetherness	More togetherness than separateness	Very high togetherness
I–we balance	Primarily "I" / Primarily "we"	More "I" than "we"		More "we" than "I"
Closeness	Little closeness	Low-to-moderate closeness	Moderate-to-high closeness	Very high closeness
Loyalty	Lack of loyalty	Some loyalty	Considerable loyalty	High loyalty
Activities	Mainly separate	More separate than shared	More shared than separate	Mainly shared
Dependence/independence	High independence / High dependence	More independence than dependence	More dependence than independence	High dependence

Levels of Family Flexibility

FLEXIBILITY

Score	Rigid (Unbalanced) 1 2	Structured (Balanced) 3 4	Flexible (Balanced) 5 6	Chaotic (Unbalanced) 7 8
Leadership	Authoritarian	Sometimes shared	Often shared	Lack of leadership
Discipline	Strict discipline	Somewhat democratic	Democratic	Erratic/inconsistent
Negotiation	Limited discussion	Organized discussion	Open discussion	Endless discussion
Roles	Roles very stable	Roles stable	Role sharing	Dramatic role shifts
Rules	Unchanging rules	Few rule changes	Some rule changes	Frequent rule changes
Change	Very little change	Moderate change	Some change	Considerable change

Levels of Family Communication

COMMUNICATION

Score	Poor 1 2	Good 3 4	Very Good 5 6
Listening skills	Poor listening skills	Appears to listen, but feedback is limited	Gives feedback, indicating good listening skills
Speaking skills	Often speaks for others	Speaks for oneself more than for others	Speaks mainly for oneself rather than for others
Self-disclosure	Low sharing of feelings	High sharing of feelings	Moderate sharing of feelings
Clarity	Inconsistent messages	Clear messages	Very clear messages
Staying on topic	Seldom stays on topic	Often stays on topic	Mainly stays on topic
Respect and regard	Low to moderate	Moderate to high	High

TABLE A.4	Couple and Family Rating Form

COHESION

Score	Disengaged		Connected		Cohesive		Enmeshed	
	1	2	3	4	5	6	7	8
Separateness/togetherness	☐	☐	☐	☐	☐	☐	☐	☐
I–we balance	☐	☐	☐	☐	☐	☐	☐	☐
Closeness	☐	☐	☐	☐	☐	☐	☐	☐
Loyalty	☐	☐	☐	☐	☐	☐	☐	☐
Activities	☐	☐	☐	☐	☐	☐	☐	☐
Dependence/independence	☐	☐	☐	☐	☐	☐	☐	☐
Global rating	☐	☐	☐	☐	☐	☐	☐	☐

FLEXIBILITY

Score	Rigid		Structured		Flexible		Chaotic	
	1	2	3	4	5	6	7	8
Leadership	☐	☐	☐	☐	☐	☐	☐	☐
Discipline	☐	☐	☐	☐	☐	☐	☐	☐
Negotiation	☐	☐	☐	☐	☐	☐	☐	☐
Roles	☐	☐	☐	☐	☐	☐	☐	☐
Rules	☐	☐	☐	☐	☐	☐	☐	☐
Change	☐	☐	☐	☐	☐	☐	☐	☐
Global rating	☐	☐	☐	☐	☐	☐	☐	☐

COMMUNICATION

Score	Poor		Good		Very Good	
	1	2	3	4	5	6
Listening skills	☐	☐	☐	☐	☐	☐
Speaking skills	☐	☐	☐	☐	☐	☐
Self-disclosure	☐	☐	☐	☐	☐	☐
Clarity	☐	☐	☐	☐	☐	☐
Staying on topic	☐	☐	☐	☐	☐	☐
Respect and regard	☐	☐	☐	☐	☐	☐
Global rating	☐	☐	☐	☐	☐	☐

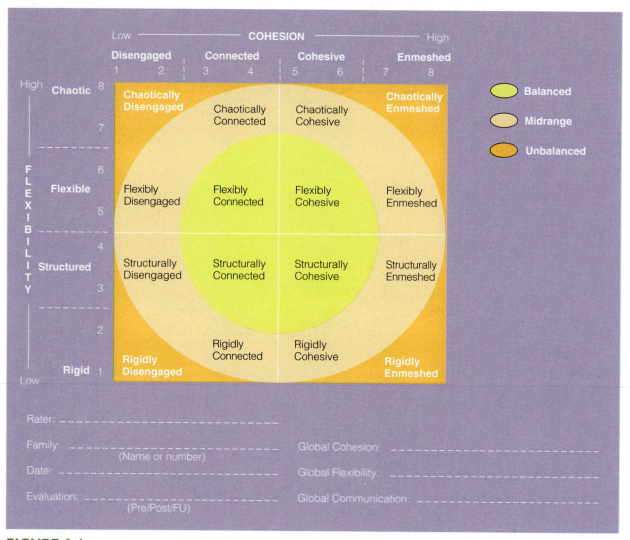

FIGURE A.I
Couple and Family Map

Family Science and Family Research Methods

A Knowledge Explosion
Family Research Methods
Research Designs
A Final Word About Research

Family science is growing rapidly, as a profession and as a social science. In recent years, research on the family has improved in both quality and quantity. Family researchers use many of the same methods as other social scientists, but they tailor these methods to their own interests and purposes as they focus on couple and family issues. This section describes several research methods, including questionnaires, interviews, case studies, and observational approaches.

A Knowledge Explosion

Family science is a multidisciplinary field, which has an impact on many disciplines. These disciplines in turn contribute to the understanding of families (Table B.1). Over the past 30 years, this science has emerged as a genuine discipline unto itself. Its primary goal is to achieve a better understanding of families in order to enhance the quality of family life. Professionals whose main interests are research, theory, and the development of programs for families tend to call themselves *family scientists*. Those who develop educational programs for couples and families call themselves *family life educators*. Those who work clinically with troubled families are called *marital and family therapists*.

Family scientists have backgrounds in a wide variety of disciplines: human development, family science programs, human ecology, home economics, social work, nursing, educational psychology, psy-chology, sociology, psychiatry, and anthropology. Family scientists may be researchers, professors, teachers, family life educators, family therapists, ministers, nurses, social workers, or attorneys.

Family Research Methods

The whole of science is nothing more than a refinement of everyday thinking.

—Albert Einstein

It is primarily through research that new ideas and facts are discovered. The word *research* is derived from the Middle French word *recherché*, meaning "to investigate thoroughly." Science, in the final analysis, is an examination of events or information in an attempt to make new discoveries.

It has been argued that the family is the most difficult institution in human society to study. The reason for this is that families tend to be closed to outsiders; they often "put their best foot forward." To study important issues and to solve family problems, researchers and practitioners have to get below the surface and deal with both the positive and the negative aspects of family life.

Family researchers have a creative mix of tools and techniques for learning more about family realities, using both "insider" and "outsider" perspectives. An **insider perspective** is provided by family members when they describe how they see their relationships. An **outsider perspective** is provided by researchers

TABLE B.I	Disciplines Contributing to Family Science	
Discipline	**Topics in Family Science**	
Anthropology	Cross-cultural studies; kinship; diversity in families	
Biology	Conception and reproduction; growth, development, and aging	
Child development	Development of infant and child; interpersonal skills	
Economics	Family finances; consumer behavior	
Education	Family life education; marriage preparation	
English	Marriages and families in literature (present and past)	
History	Historical perspectives on the family throughout time	
Human ecology	Ecosystem perspectives on family, nutrition, housing, clothing	
Law	Marriage and divorce laws; child custody laws	
Medicine and nursing	Families and health	
Psychiatry	Family therapy	
Psychology	Family psychology; assessment of couples and families	
Social work	Treating problem families; family policy	
Sociology	Marriage and divorce statistics; sociological theories about families	

or therapists observing and describing the activity from their point of view. Methods that tap the insider perspective are questionnaires, interviews, and case studies. Outsider perspectives are obtained through observational approaches. Family researchers often use only one method in a particular study, but there are advantages to a multimethod approach that uses both insider and outsider perspectives.

Family researchers study couple and family issues from both quantitative and qualitative perspectives. **Quantitative research** typically uses structured questionnaires and scales to assess people's description of their relationship (i.e., couple, marriage, family) attitudes and behaviors. Their responses are typically converted to numbers that can be summed and analyzed using statistical methods. **Qualitative research** tends to be based on more or less open-ended interviews of people talking about how they see their relationships. Their verbal responses are analyzed looking for themes in their comments. Ultimately, quantitative studies produce numbers that can be analyzed, whereas qualitative studies are more often looking for themes in stories from persons about a given topic.

Because quantitative studies rely on questionnaires and scales rather than personal interviews, quantitative studies usually have a larger sample of participants than qualitative studies. In qualitative research, data collection is often more involved and time consuming, because the interviews or written testimony can be much longer and in depth. This usually requires a great deal more time to transcribe into written testimony from the participants. This is why it has been said that, "Quantitative research learns a little about a lot of people, and qualitative research learns a lot about a few." This statement is an oversimplification of the difference between these two different research traditions, but it does highlight their differences.

Neither approach is "better" than the other. They are simply two different ways to study families. There is a growing movement today to use so-called **mixed-methods research** approaches, which rely on both qualitative and quantitative methods in the same study. For example, a research team focusing on marital quality might want to begin with 10 in-depth, face-to-face interviews, in which time is spent talking with couples about their marriages in a relatively unstructured and open-ended fashion. The researcher might ask a few broad, leading questions and then listen as the couple talk about how

they view the particular issues, all of which is tape recorded or videotaped.

After completing a series of these in-depth interviews and transcribing the data—that is to say, the couples' thoughts about the issues—the researchers can then design the quantitative phase of the study. The open-ended interview questions can then be transformed into a more structured questionnaire with closed-end questions, that is, questions that have a series of fixed responses. The questionnaire can then be mailed to hundreds of couples in a wide geographic area. By using a qualitative approach, the researchers develop an in-depth understanding of the dynamics of marital quality based on a small sample of couples. Expanding the sample size and the breadth of the study to many more couples using the quantitative approach then increases the sample size and the ability to use statistical analysis with the data. The mixed-methods approach gives the investigator, in sum, "the best of both worlds."

Research methods need to be suitable for the population being studied. Written questions, for example, are inappropriate for people whose culture is predominantly oral.

Questionnaires

Perhaps the most common method of studying families is the questionnaire. The researcher carefully prepares a series of questions based on a review of previous research on the topic. *Fixed-response questions* require an individual to pick his or her response from a selection of possible responses; *open-ended questions* allow the individual to respond in her or his own words. A questionnaire might contain either or both types of questions.

Developing a questionnaire is a challenge. What questions one asks and the manner in which the questions are phrased can greatly influence the results of a study. Researchers are wise to do a trial run with a small sample of families to see whether the questions are clear and precise. Next, the process of **validating** a survey instrument—ensuring that the instrument measures what it is intended to measure—often takes researchers several months or even a number of years, depending on the complexity of the problem they are studying.

After the questionnaire is deemed satisfactory by the research team, it is distributed to a sufficiently large sample of family members. A number of factors determine the size of the sample, including how much money the research team has to spend on the project, how important the topic is to the researchers, and how difficult it is to find a group of families who are willing to participate in the study.

In the past, it was quite common for family researchers to limit their studies to what mothers thought was going on in their families. Fathers and children were often ignored. Researchers assumed that one individual could speak for the family as a whole. Furthermore, researchers favored this approach to studies of multiple family members because the latter were much more time consuming, expensive, and difficult to analyze. Today, most researchers recognize that fathers, mothers, and children often differ in their perceptions of family life and that a good study demands information and perceptions gathered from multiple family members.

Interviews

The interview—whether face to face or by telephone—is another family research method. Some investigators believe that interview data are more valid than data from questionnaires because the researcher can ask follow-up questions and get more information. On the other hand, some research has found that people are more honest on questionnaires. Furthermore, interviews tend to take more time, cost more money, and thus reach fewer people than is possible with questionnaires. Variation from one interviewer to another may also taint the results; questionnaires, of course, are standardized. Perhaps the best approach is to use both questionnaires and interviews. The results can then be compared with each other to provide **cross-validation**.

Case Studies

Some of the most emotionally gripping research findings have come from family therapists and researchers using the case study method. A **case study** is a detailed description of a person or family whose interactions illustrate some specific idea, concept, or principle of family science. Using this method, researchers record in narrative form and analyze the complexities of family dynamics. Great care is taken to protect the privacy and anonymity of the family members, in part by concealing their names and disguising any identifying family characteristics.

The major problem with case studies is that the families described are probably not representative of all American families. For example, if a researcher were to analyze the case of a stepfamily in treatment at a counseling agency, the researcher might conclude that stepfamilies have numerous problems. This conclusion would be biased, however, because it was based on a family who had come for help. If the researcher were to question stepfamilies by randomly telephoning people in the community, the result would be a more **representative sample**—that is, a random selection—of stepfamilies and probably a more positive description of interactions in this type of family.

Observational Approaches

Social psychologists who study families and family therapists who deal with problem families tend to work by observing family interactions in natural settings, such as the home. Observational approaches, which tap the outsider perspective, have both strengths and limitations. One strength is that the researcher does not have to rely on family members' self-reports of their own behavior. One major limitation is that the presence of a stranger (the therapist or researcher) influences family members' behavior, making it less natural. Researchers also need to consider whether families who volunteer for such studies differ in some ways from families who do not. These are important issues in any research study, but they are more problematic in observational studies.

Sometimes a family is brought into a research laboratory for a study. Often the laboratory is set up like a living room or a dining room, and the family is asked to perform a particular task together, such as playing a game. The researchers videotape the interaction and later study the video to analyze and evaluate the family members' communication styles. Many families are not willing to participate in such studies, of course, and those who do may act differently than they do when behind closed doors. Despite the difficulties associated with observational research, however, many creative observational family studies have contributed significantly to the field of family science.

Historical and Multicultural Studies

Studies of families from earlier generations are often useful and interesting to us today. As historians point out, we cannot know where we are going in the future unless we know where we have been. Historical research, which often relies on diaries and historical statistics about families, can help us understand families in the past.

Feminists argue that much of what has been presented as family history in the past has focused on the lives of men (*his*-story) and has neglected the lives of women (*her*-story). The history of the family, in many cultures traditionally the domain of women, has received little attention from historians (who have for the most part been men). But in recent decades, a resurgent feminist history movement has begun to look at the past from women's perspectives.

Similarly, multicultural studies of families can contribute rich insights into family life and family interactions. The United States has innumerable family cultures: African American, Caucasian, Latino, Italian American, Chicago suburban, inner-city Boston, gay-male, lesbian, middle class, upper class, rural, urban, and so forth. Family life is different in each of these cultures. A family in the commuter culture of Los Angeles, for example, lives a life quite different from that of a family in rural Iowa. Diversity in families is discussed in greater detail in Chapter 2.

Research Designs

Researchers are often interested in how particular families grow and change over time. Three types of research designs that take the passage of time into consideration are longitudinal studies, cross-sectional studies, and cross-sectional cohort studies.

Longitudinal Studies

In a longitudinal study, the researcher interviews or observes a family several times over a period of months or years. This approach obviously takes a considerable amount of time, effort, and money. For those reasons, only a small proportion of family research is longitudinal. The results of such projects, however, are often well worth the effort because they provide valuable information about long-term processes, such as the effect of the birth of a child on a marriage.

One longitudinal study focused on couples who took a premarital inventory—called PREPARE—3 months before marriage and were followed up 3 years after marriage (Larsen & Olson, 1989). PREPARE is a 125-item questionnaire that focuses on 12 important areas of a couple's relationship, including communication, conflict resolution, role relationships, and sexual intimacy. Couples who were separated or divorced at the 3-year follow-up were compared with couples who remained happily married. The scores on the PREPARE inventory were found to predict with about 80% to 85% accuracy which couples would later divorce and which would be happily married. The findings indicate that problems experienced by couples before marriage can lead to more serious problems after marriage. This study also demonstrates the predictive validity of PREPARE and the value of longitudinal research.

Cross-Sectional Studies

In a cross-sectional study, a researcher selects couples or families at various stages of the family life cycle and compares the differences between the various stages. For example, a researcher could compare four stages of the life cycle by selecting some newlywed couples, some couples with young children, some couples with adolescents, and some older couples whose children had left home. The aim of this approach is to describe the similarities and differences between couples and families at these four stages.

The advantage of the cross-sectional design is efficiency: Data can be collected from all four groups at about the same time and then immediately compared. A disadvantage of this type of study is that it is not possible to know if identified similarities and differences are due only to the stage of the life cycle or to the characteristics of these specific families—a question that could only be answered by a longitudinal study that followed the same families over time. Furthermore, cross-sectional studies cannot reveal whether the historical context for each group (past experiences, crises, etc.) influenced the findings.

Cross-Sectional Cohort Studies

Because of the problems with both longitudinal and cross-sectional studies, researchers have designed a shortcut known as the cross-sectional cohort study. Using this approach, researchers do not follow a group of families for many years; instead, they study various families at different stages of the family life cycle for shorter periods. They might, for example, study a group of families with a 10-year-old, another group with a 12-year-old, a third group with a

14-year-old, and a fourth group with a 16-year-old. If they follow these families for 5 years, they could analyze changes from age 10 to 15, 12 to 17, 14 to 19, and 16 to 21. The result would be an overview of an 11-year period (age 10 to age 21) achieved in only 5 years of research.

A Final Word About Research

No single study can provide definitive answers to important questions in family science. In fact, each study almost invariably raises new questions that are complex and difficult to answer. The advancement of scientific knowledge is a slow and painstaking process. People researching a particular topic in family science have to examine data from many related studies on the topic.

Sometimes studies produce findings that conflict with the results of other studies. These discrepancies may be due to variations in the type of questions asked, the method of research used, or the specific sample studied. For example, a sample of families drawn from the Midwest may look at gender-role issues in families somewhat differently from a sample of families drawn from Latino families living in California. Likewise, two-parent traditional American families may have a different way of looking at certain issues than do single-parent families.

Although studies on similar topics may have differing results, good studies tend to complement each other. When dozens of researchers from various parts of the United States look at a problem from many different theoretical approaches, using different research methods and different statistical analyses, a fairly comprehensive picture emerges. When the findings are similar in spite of all the differences in the sample, method, and analysis, the results are more conclusive and help build more valid findings and theories about couples and families.

Contraception and Abortion Options

Contraception
Abortion

Contraception

In the United States, there are 3.6 million births each year. It has been estimated that half the births result from unintentional pregnancies. Among the other 50%—the intentional conceptions—many are undertaken with little planning (Insel & Roth, 2004). Although parenthood is a challenge that lasts a lifetime, it's clear that many pregnancies occur by accident or with little forethought.

Why are unintentional pregnancies so common in our society? The answer, in short, is that effective contraception takes a good deal of planning and thought, and sex for most people simply does not. Social psychologist Donn Byrne (1983) outlines five steps involved in effective contraception. Our commentary follows each of Byrne's steps:

1. *The individual must acquire and remember accurate information about contraception.* This is no small task.
2. *The individual must acknowledge the likelihood of engaging in sexual intercourse.* Many in our society—in particular, women—receive the message that nonmarital sex is wrong. Preparing for nonmarital sex thus seems doubly wrong.
3. *The individual must obtain the contraceptive.* This involves a visit to a physician, a drugstore, or a clinic. This also involves admitting both to oneself and to others that one is planning to have sex.
4. *The individual must communicate with her or his partner about contraception.* Partners who do not communicate cannot assume the other has taken preventive measures. Unfortunately, the likelihood of communication about contraception is relatively low.
5. *The individual must actually use the contraceptive method.* People sometimes resist using contraceptives because they consider some methods to be messy, interruptive, or unromantic.

Byrne's five steps make it clear that there are many barriers to the effective understanding and use of contraception. It is little wonder that so many pregnancies are unplanned.

The science of **contraception**—which focuses on the prevention of conception, or pregnancy—has from its very beginnings been an embattled research area. Pressure from conservative religious groups and politicians has impeded progress in this area in the United States.

The ideal contraceptive would be harmless, reliable, free of objectionable side effects, inexpensive, simple, reversible in effect, removed from the sexual act, and protective against sexually transmitted disease. Unfortunately, there is no such contraceptive.

Methods of Contraception

Birth control methods used by women and men in this country fall into six broad categories: sterilization, oral contraceptives, barrier methods, intrauterine devices (IUDs), spermicides, and hormone implants (Hatcher et al., 1994, 1997, 1998; Hyde & DeLamater, 2003; Insel & Roth, 2004; Kelly, 2004). Fertility awareness methods, which involve avoiding intercourse during the fertile phase of a woman's menstrual cycle, are also used by some.

Sterilization

Sterilization, or voluntary surgical contraception, is the contraceptive method of choice for 29% of U.S. women and for 11% of U.S. men. This method is used by men and women who do not wish to have children or who have had all the children they desire. The sterilization procedure for women, called **tubal ligation**, involves cutting or tying and sealing the woman's fallopian tubes to prevent passage of the ova into the uterus; the procedure is difficult to reverse. The male sterilization procedure, called **vasectomy**, involves surgically severing the vasa deferentia; it is also usually irreversible and should be considered permanent. Sterilization is a more complex procedure in women than in men. In actual practice, sterilization is typically 99.6% effective for women and 99.85% effective for men.

Oral Contraceptives

Oral contraceptives, or birth control pills, are favored by 28% of U.S. women. Oral contraceptives are 97% effective in preventing pregnancy. The *pill*, a combination oral contraceptive, contains the hormones **estrogen** and **progestin**. In addition to preventing pregnancy, the pill makes the menstrual cycle more regular, tends to reduce menstrual cramping, and is associated with lower incidences of breast and ovarian cysts and pelvic inflammatory disease (PID). Potential negative side effects of the pill include nausea, weight gain, fluid retention, breast tenderness, headaches, missed menstrual periods, acne, mood changes, depression, anxiety, fatigue, decreased sex drive, and circulatory diseases.

The *minipill* contains progestin only. Besides reliability, the minipill brings increased regularity to the menstrual cycle, tends to reduce menstrual cramping, and is associated with a lower incidence of breast and ovarian cysts and PID.

Emergency oral contraception refers to methods used after unprotected sexual intercourse. An emergency contraceptive may be appropriate after a regularly used method has failed (e.g., if a condom breaks). Emergency contraception is designed to be used for just that and should not be relied on as a regular method. The most commonly used emergency contraceptive is a two-dose regimen of certain oral contraceptives that have been used for more than a decade in Great Britain, Germany, and other countries.

The American Medical Association and 59 other medical and women's groups petitioned the U.S. Food and Drug Administration (FDA) to allow the sale of emergency oral contraception over the counter without a prescription from a doctor. This move was opposed by some antiabortion groups (Goodman, 2001).

The controversy continued into 2004 when the FDA rejected a drug maker's application to sell the morning-after contraceptive pill over the counter because of concerns about whether young girls would use it safely. The product, called Plan B, consists of two high doses of a hormone used for birth control and is argued to be 89% effective if taken within 72 hours after sexual intercourse. It is not considered to be an abortion pill, because it prevents pregnancy from starting (Harris, 2004).

Advocates of the morning-after contraceptive pill argued that making it more broadly available would prevent unwanted pregnancies and decrease the rate of abortions. Opponents argued it would encourage promiscuity and risky sex. (One plan is to restrict sales to women over age 16.)

Barrier Methods

Barrier methods of contraception, favored by 20% of U.S. women, include condoms, diaphragms, and cervical caps. Failure rates are 14% to 18%.

Condom. Worn by the male over the penis during intercourse, a **condom**, made of latex rubber, catches semen and prevents it from entering the vagina. Condoms are available without a prescription and offer protection against sexually transmitted diseases (STDs). Although condom use is a contraceptive method a man can take responsibility for, one-third of all condoms are purchased by women. Condoms can fail for a variety of reasons: breakage; not leaving a space at the tip of the condom to collect the semen; lubrication with petroleum jelly, which weakens latex; seepage of semen around the opening of the condom or if the condom slips off in the vagina after coitus; storing the condom for more than 2 years or storing it at temperature extremes; and not placing the condom on the penis at the beginning of intercourse. Some people are allergic to rubber condoms. (Other "natural" kinds are also available.) Some men complain that condoms reduce sensation on the penis. The failure rate for condoms is about 14%.

Diaphragm. A **diaphragm** is a dome-shaped cup of thin rubber stretched over a collapsible metal ring. The diaphragm, which must be used with a spermicidal (sperm-killing) cream or jelly, is inserted into the vagina to cover the mouth of the cervix, blocking sperm from entering the uterus. Inexpensive and reusable, a diaphragm must be fitted by a physician. Common reasons for failure of a diaphragm to prevent pregnancy include improper fitting or insertion of the diaphragm, removal of the diaphragm too soon (sooner than 6 to 8 hours) after intercourse, insufficient use of spermicide with the diaphragm, damage to the diaphragm, leakage around the diaphragm, or dislodging of the diaphragm. Some people are allergic to the rubber in diaphragms (plastic diaphragms are also available), and some people are allergic to spermicides. Diaphragm users also have an increased risk of toxic shock syndrome, bladder infection, and vaginal soreness caused by pressure from the rim of the diaphragm. The failure rate for diaphragms is about 18%.

Cervical Cap. A thimble-shaped rubber or plastic cup, the **cervical cap** fits over the cervix and is held in place by suction. Like the diaphragm, it must be fitted by a clinician and is used with a spermicide; it can, however, be left in place for longer periods of time than the diaphragm. Potential problems that can result in pregnancy include improper fitting, insertion, or placement. Women using cervical caps also have a possible risk of toxic shock syndrome or of an allergic reaction to the rubber or the

Contraception and Abortion Options   **A-15**

spermicide. Also the cervical cap may abrade or irritate the vagina or cervix. The failure rate for cervical caps is about 18%.

Intrauterine Devices

Intrauterine devices (IUDs) are made of molded plastic and are inserted by a physician into a woman's uterus through the vagina. The IUD apparently works by causing an inflammatory reaction inside the uterus that attracts white blood cells. The white blood cells then produce substances that are poisonous to sperm and thus prevent fertilization of the egg. The inflammatory reaction can be halted by removing the IUD (Berkow, 1997).

Most U.S. manufacturers have stopped making IUDs because of the fear of costly lawsuits over their safety. Although they are still favored by 2% of women, IUDs have caused pelvic infections, some serious enough to have resulted in the death of about 21 women. Other negative side effects include uterine cramping, abnormal bleeding, and heavy menstrual flow. IUDs come in a variety of shapes. An IUD is inserted through the vagina and cervix into the uterus by a medical professional, where it remains until the woman wishes to have it removed. So that the wearer can be sure the IUD has not been expelled by the uterus, a slender string attached to the IUD protrudes through the cervical opening just far enough into the vagina so that the woman can feel it with her finger. IUD failure rates are typically about 2%, mostly resulting from expulsion of the IUD without the woman's notice.

Spermicides

Favored by 3% of women, **spermicides** include foams, creams, jellies, and vaginal inserts (also called vaginal suppositories). They are available without a prescription. Spermicides must be inserted with an applicator into the vagina before intercourse and are only effective for a short time. Many couples dislike having to interrupt the sexual act to insert a spermicide. Failure rates are about 21%. Pregnancy can result when too little spermicide is used, if the spermicide is placed in the vagina too long before intercourse, if the woman douches within 6 to 8 hours after intercourse, or, in the case of suppositories, if the spermicide fails to melt or foam properly. Some people are allergic to the chemicals in spermicides. Some say they taste unpleasant during oral-genital sex.

Hormone Implants and Depo-Provera Injections

Norplant is the trade name of an implant that is placed under the skin on the inside of a woman's upper arm and releases the hormone progestin. It provides 99.9% protection from pregnancy for up to 5 years. Norplant was approved by the FDA in 1990. It was the newest, most effective contraceptive method to become available in the United States in many years. Women who cannot take birth control pills for various medical reasons are cautioned not to consider Norplant.

The most common side effects of contraceptive implants are menstrual irregularities, including longer menstrual periods, spotting between periods, or having no bleeding at all. After a year of use, the menstrual cycle usually becomes more regular. Less common side effects are headaches, weight gain, breast tenderness, nausea, acne, and mood swings. More serious health concerns are similar to those experienced with oral contraceptives (Insel & Roth, 2004).

Depo-Provera (DMPA), a progestin administered by injection, became available in this country in 1992. DMPA injections must be repeated every 3 months for maximum effectiveness. DMPA is used in more than 90 nations around the world (Hatcher et al., 1998). Planned Parenthood staff report it is becoming more popular than Norplant and may become more popular than the pill. DMPA works like other progestin-only methods by inhibiting ovulation, thickening cervical mucus, and inhibiting the growth of the endometrium. It is very effective, with a typical user failure rate of less than 1%, which is slightly less effective than Norplant but more effective than the pill (Hyde & DeLamater, 2003).

Withdrawal

Withdrawing the penis before ejaculation is a highly unreliable way to prevent pregnancy. An estimated 19% of women whose partners use this approach will become pregnant in any given year.

Douching

Flushing the vagina with vinegar or some other type of acidic liquid such as *Coca-Cola* is also an ineffective birth control method. Although it is true that some acidic solutions will kill sperm, it can take sperm only a minute to reach the cervical mucus; once there, they move freely into the uterus, where no douching solution can reach them. The douche itself, in fact, may even push some sperm into the uterus.

Fertility Awareness Methods

For many users of these methods, their main advantage is that they are considered acceptable by the Roman Catholic Church. The four contraceptive methods known as **fertility awareness** are based on avoiding intercourse during the fertile phase of a woman's menstrual cycle. The methods differ in the way in which they identify the woman's fertile period.

The least-effective fertility awareness approach—even for women who have regular menstrual cycles—is the *calendar method*. To use this method, a woman must carefully keep records of her cycles for 12 months. Then, to figure out when to abstain from intercourse, the woman subtracts 18 days from the shortest and 11 days from the longest of her previous 12 menstrual cycles. If, for example, her cycles last from 26 to 29 days, she needs to avoid intercourse from day 8 through day 18 of each cycle (Berkow, 1997).

The second fertility awareness method, the *basal body temperature method*, is based on the knowledge that a woman's body temperature drops slightly before ovulation and rises slightly after ovulation. After about 3 months of daily record keeping, a woman's temperature patterns usually become apparent.

A third fertility awareness approach, the *cervical mucus (ovulation) method*, is based on changes in cervical secretions throughout the menstrual cycle. Before ovulation, cervical mucus increases and is clear and slippery. During ovulation, some women can detect a slight change in the texture of the mucus, finding that it can be formed into an elastic thread that can be stretched between thumb and finger. After ovulation, cervical secretions become cloudy and sticky and decrease in quantity. One problem with this approach is the potential misreading of changes in the composition of the cervical mucus because of vaginal infections and vaginal products or medications.

A fourth fertility awareness approach, the *sympto-thermal method*, combines two rhythm methods to gain better effectiveness. The woman records changes in her cervical mucus (symptoms) and her basal body temperature (thermal). Combining the two is thought to give a more accurate method of determining the time of ovulation (Hyde & DeLamater, 2003).

Home tests for detecting ovulation have been developed recently. The tests detect hormone levels in urine. Developed for couples wanting to conceive, these tests, like the temperature method, determine only when ovulation has occurred, and then the safe period after ovulation. They do not warn a woman several days in advance when ovulation will occur, which she needs to know to prevent pregnancy. Researchers are trying to develop tests that will do this (Hyde & DeLamater, 2003).

Fertility awareness methods of contraception are not recommended for women who have very irregular menstrual cycles (about 15% of all women) and for women for whom pregnancy would be a serious problem. Proponents of fertility awareness methods argue that they are about 90% effective. In practice, however, an estimated 25% of women using these methods become pregnant in any given year.

Making Contraceptive Decisions

In making rational choices about contraceptive methods, individuals and couples should take into account several considerations (Allgeier & Allgeier, 2000; Hyde & DeLamater, 2003; Kelly, 2004). First, people need to consider the health risks of each method in terms of personal and family medical history. IUDs are not recommended for young women without children, for example, because they increase the risk of pelvic infection and possible infertility. Oral contraceptives should be used only after an evaluation of a woman's medical history.

Individuals must ask themselves, How important is it to me to avoid pregnancy at this point in life? Oral contraceptives offer by far the best protection against pregnancy, but there are some risks associated with them. Condoms, diaphragms, and cervical caps have fewer related health problems than oral contraceptives, but the risk of pregnancy is greater with these methods. To maximize their effectiveness, they need to be used in combination with a spermicide and used every time a couple has intercourse.

The type of relationship one is involved in should also be considered. Barrier methods require more motivation than the pill because they generally must be used at or close to the time of intercourse. Both partners must have a well-developed sense of responsibility to ensure the success of these methods. Barrier methods often require cooperation between partners. If one has sexual intercourse only infrequently, barrier methods may make more sense than oral contraceptives.

Condom use, preferably with a spermicide, is critically important if there is any possibility of the presence of a sexually transmitted disease. Condoms are especially important for those who are not in an exclusive, long-term relationship. They are also useful for women taking oral contraceptives, because cervical changes that occur during hormone use can increase the likelihood of contracting certain diseases.

Both partners should consider convenience and comfort. Oral contraceptives rank high in both regards, although, again, the possible negative side effects and health risks of the pill need to be factored into the equation. If a woman has difficulty remembering to take her pills, another method might be better.

The ease and cost of obtaining and continuing each method also need to be considered. Oral contraceptives require an annual pelvic exam and periodic medical checkups. Pills are also more expensive than barrier methods. Diaphragms and cervical caps require an initial examination and fitting. Norplant requires implantation by a physician.

Finally, religious and philosophical beliefs should be taken into consideration. Abstinence is the only acceptable approach for some individuals before marriage.

For those who wish to make responsible contraceptive choices, it is important to discuss the options with competent professionals. Both men and women should be knowledgeable in this very important subject area.

Abortion

In 1973, the U.S. Supreme Court overturned by a 7-to-2 vote laws that had made abortion in America a criminal act. Since that decision, approximately 21 million American women have chosen to have 35 million abortions, according to the Alan Guttmacher Institute (AGI). Forty-nine percent of pregnancies among American women are unintended; half of these are terminated by abortion. Researchers estimate that 48% of women in this country will have at least one unplanned pregnancy between the ages of 15 and 44 and that at current rates, 43% of

American women will have had an abortion by age 45. In 1997, there were 1.33 million abortions in the United States, down from an estimated 1.61 million in 1990 (AGI, 2000).

Strictly defined, **abortion** is the expulsion of a fetus from the uterus before the fetus has developed sufficiently to survive outside the mother (before viability). In common usage, abortion refers only to artificially induced expulsions, those caused by mechanical means or drugs. Spontaneous abortions, those that occur naturally and are not induced by mechanical means or drugs, are commonly called *miscarriages* (Insel & Roth, 2004).

Abortion Laws

For more than two centuries in early U.S. history (from the 1600s to the early 1900s), abortion was not a crime if it was performed before *quickening* (fetal movement, which begins at approximately 20 weeks). United States abortion laws followed English common law during this period. An antiabortion movement began in the early 1800s. It was led by physicians who argued against the validity of the concept of quickening and who opposed the performing of abortions by untrained people, who also threatened physician control of medical services. The controversy over abortion attracted minimal attention until the mid-1800s, when newspapers began advertising abortion preparations. Opponents of such medicines argued that women were using them as birth control measures and that women could also hide extramarital affairs through their use. The medicines were seen by some as evidence that immorality and corruption threatened America. By the early 1900s, virtually all states (at the urging of male politicians; women could not vote at the time) had passed antiabortion laws (Insel & Roth, 2004).

Social pressure for the legalization of abortion grew in the 1960s. Despite laws against abortion, many illegal abortions were being performed. Women sometimes died because of nonsterile or medically inadequate procedures. During this period, courts began to invalidate many of the state laws on the grounds of constitutional vagueness and a violation of the right to privacy (Francoeur, 1982, 1997; Insel & Roth, 2004).

In the 1973 landmark case *Roe* v. *Wade*, the U.S. Supreme Court made abortion legal by denying the states the right to regulate early abortions. The high court replaced the restrictions most states still imposed at that time with new standards governing abortion decisions. The Court conceptualized pregnancy in three parts (trimesters) and gave pregnant women more options in regard to abortion in the first trimester (3 months) than in the second or third trimester. The Court ruled that during the first trimester, the abortion decision must be left to the judgment of the woman and her physician. The Court ruled that during the second trimester, the right to abortion remained but that a state could regulate certain factors in an effort to protect the health of the woman, such as the type of facility in which an abortion could be performed. The Supreme Court ruled that during the third trimester, the period of pregnancy in which the fetus is viable outside the uterus, a state could regulate and even ban all abortions except in situations in which they were necessary to preserve the mother's life or health (Hyde & DeLamater, 2003; Insel & Roth, 2004). In addition, in 1976, the Supreme Court decided in *Planned Parenthood* v. *Danforth* that neither the parents of a minor nor the husband of a woman had the right to veto a woman's decision to have an abortion.

Today, opponents of abortion remain unsuccessful in their efforts to overturn *Roe* v. *Wade* or amend the U.S. Constitution to outlaw abortion. Recent controversy has focused on a late-term abortion procedure referred to by abortion opponents as "partial birth abortion." This is a nonmedical term for a rarely used late abortion method.

Research indicates that babies born at or before 24 weeks rarely survive, that babies born at 25 to 26 weeks have a 50% chance of survival, and that a baby's chance of survival increases to 90% at 30 weeks ("Abortion Foes Vow to Fight," 1991).

After the Supreme Court's 1973 decision, the number of abortions performed each year rose steadily. The decision did not end the controversy over abortion; indeed, in many ways it seemed to intensify it (Francoeur, 1982, 1997; Insel & Roth, 2004).

Campaigns were begun on the national, state, and local levels by many groups hoping to overturn the decision and restore the ban on abortion. Some favored amending the U.S. Constitution; others worked to weaken the decision by chipping away at its edges in a variety of ways. The Supreme Court, hearing arguments against abortion nearly every year, continued to uphold its 1973 decision. In the original decision the Court had voted 7 to 2 in favor of legalizing abortion; by the mid-1980s conservative appointments to the high court had cut the abortion

rights majority on the Court to an unpredictable 5-to-4 margin (Insel & Roth, 2004).

The controversy boiled over in July 1989, when the Supreme Court handed down its decision in the case of *Webster* v. *Reproductive Health Services*. Although the Court did not overturn *Roe* v. *Wade*, it permitted several key abortion restrictions enacted by the Missouri state legislature in 1986 to stand. Two of the most significant restrictions upheld in *Webster* v. *Reproductive Health Services* were the prohibition of the use of all public facilities, resources, and employees for abortion services and the requirement for costly and time-consuming tests to determine fetal viability if a physician estimated the fetus to be 20 weeks or older.

In the 1989 decision, the majority of the Supreme Court justices also rejected *Roe*'s framework of trimesters, which had been an attempt by the justices in 1973 to balance women's rights and fetal rights. The 1989 decision did not, however, replace the trimester framework with any other standard for balancing these rights. The justices declined to address the preamble of the Missouri law, which stated that "the life of each human being begins at conception," arguing that this was only a "value judgment" and that this value judgment did not "regulate abortion" (Insel & Roth, 2004).

In 1992, tensions mounted again as the nation awaited a Supreme Court decision on *Planned Parenthood* v. *Casey*. Pro-choice activists feared the high court would overturn *Roe* v. *Wade* and make abortion an issue for state regulation. But in a narrow 5-to-4 decision in early July, the Supreme Court once more upheld the spirit of *Roe* v. *Wade* but once again restricted its reach. States were now free to restrict abortion as long as the restrictions did not place an "undue burden" on women. The Supreme Court held that the state of Pennsylvania could (1) impose a 24-hour waiting period before an abortion, (2) require doctors to tell women about other options besides abortion, (3) require women to sign an "informed consent" form before the procedure, (4) mandate parental notification for minors, and (5) make doctors provide statistical information about patients. However, the Court also held that the state of Pennsylvania could not force a woman to tell her husband that she was having an abortion (Clift, 1992; Insel & Roth, 2004).

Today, pro-life groups on the local, state, and national levels continue to seek legislation that would make abortion a crime; at the same time, pro-choice groups work to ensure a woman's right to an abortion if she so chooses. Although the outcome of the abortion controversy cannot be predicted, it is unlikely that either side will give up the fight.

The American public in general is also divided on the issue. A random sample of 1,513 adults taken 28 years after the *Roe* v. *Wade* decision found that 21% said abortion should be legal in all cases; 38% said it should be legal in most cases; 25% said it should be illegal in most cases; 14% said it should be illegal in all cases; and 2% had no opinion or refused to answer (*ABC News–Washington Post*, 2001).

Unsuccessful at this point in their efforts to ban abortion by overturning *Roe* v. *Wade* or passing a constitutional amendment against it, abortion opponents recently have focused on specific methods of abortion. One method of late-term abortion referred to by opponents as "partial birth abortion" has been targeted but was struck down in a June 2000 Supreme Court decision (*Stenberg* v. *Carhard*). The judges in a 5-to-4 majority view argued the ban placed an undue burden on women seeking abortion and failed to take into consideration the need to protect women's health (Insel & Roth, 2004).

Abortion Procedures

About 90% of the abortions in the United States are performed within the first trimester (Kelly, 2004). The type of procedure used generally depends on how far along a woman is in her pregnancy. We will explain a variety of abortion procedures in this section, beginning with those used early in pregnancy and concluding with those employed later in pregnancy.

Mifepristone. The drug mifepristone (commonly known as RU-486) combined with misoprostol has been used widely in Europe for early abortions and is now used routinely in the United States (Kelly, 2004). Mifepristone blocks uterine absorption of the hormone progesterone, causing the uterine lining and any fertilized egg to shed (Insel & Roth, 2004). Combined with misoprostol 2 days later, which increases contractions of the uterus and helps expel the embryo, this method has fewer health risks than surgical abortion and is effective 95% of the time. Researchers in Europe report few serious medical problems associated with this method. Some of the side effects include cramping, abdominal pain, and bleeding like that of a heavy period (Strong, DeVault, & Sayad, 1999).

Both pro-choice activists and pro-life activists see mifepristone with misoprostol as an important development in the abortion controversy. If abortion can be induced simply, safely, effectively, and privately, the nature of the controversy surrounding abortion will change dramatically. Clinics that perform abortions are regularly picketed by anti-abortion protesters in the United States, making the experience of obtaining a legal abortion difficult for many women. If use of this method spreads in spite of opposition from antiabortion groups, abortion will become an almost invisible, personal, and relatively private act.

RU-486 was used by more than 600,000 women in Europe in the 1990s with only one known death, a French woman in poor health. More than half the obstetrician-gynecologists who do not provide surgical abortions in the United States said they would be willing to offer mifepristone to their patients, according to a Kaiser Family Foundation survey. This would expand women's access to abortion, because abortion is unavailable in 86% of U.S. counties (McCullough, 2000).

In France, more than one in four women who decide to terminate an early pregnancy choose RU-486 rather than conventional abortion methods. The drug was approved for use in this country by the FDA in 2000 after years of bitter debate, and it is now widely available. Pro-choice adherents called the approval a historic occasion, similar to the development of the birth control pill. Pro-life advocates vowed to continue the fight against abortion (Berkow, 1997; Insel & Roth, 2004; Kaufman, 2000; Kelly, 2004).

Vacuum Aspiration. Also called *vacuum suction* or *vacuum curettage*, **vacuum aspiration** is a method of abortion that is performed during the first trimester of pregnancy, up to 12 weeks from the beginning of the last menstrual period. It is the most common abortion procedure used during the first trimester in the United States. Vacuum aspiration is performed on an outpatient basis and requires a local or a general anesthetic. It takes about 10 to 15 minutes, although the woman stays in the doctor's office, clinic, or hospital for a few hours afterward.

Medical professionals prepare the woman for the procedure in a manner similar to preparing for a pelvic examination. An instrument is then inserted into the vagina to dilate the opening of the cervix. The end of a nonflexible tube connected to a suction apparatus is inserted through the cervix into the uterus. The contents of the uterus, including fetal tissue, are then sucked out.

Vacuum aspiration is the most common method of early abortion in the United States for two reasons: It is simple, and complications are rare and usually minor. It does, however, pose a risk of uterine perforation; infection, with fever and chills; hemorrhaging; unsuccessful abortion, in which the fetus continues to grow; and failure to remove all the fetal material. Complications are most likely when the procedure is performed by an unqualified person who lacks professional training. Infection may occur if the woman fails to follow postprocedure instructions (Hatcher et al., 1998; Hyde & DeLamater, 2003; Kelly, 2004).

Dilation and Curettage. **Dilation and curettage (D & C)** is similar to vacuum aspiration but must be performed in a hospital under general anesthetic. It is performed between 8 and 20 weeks after the last menstrual period. By the beginning of the second trimester, the uterus has enlarged and its walls have become thinner. The contents of the uterus cannot be as easily removed by suction, and therefore the D & C procedure is used.

In a D & C, the cervix is dilated, and a sharp metal loop attached to the end of a long handle (the curette) is inserted into the uterus and used to scrape out the uterine contents. D & Cs are also performed to treat infertility and menstrual problems.

Vacuum aspiration is preferable to a D & C because the former is done on an outpatient basis, eliminating the expense of hospitalization and often the risk involved in the use of general anesthetics. D & Cs also cause more discomfort than vacuum aspiration, and the risks of uterine perforation, infection, and hemorrhaging are greater.

Dilation and evacuation (D & E) is a related procedure used between 13 and 16 weeks after the last menstrual period. D & E is similar to both D & C and vacuum aspiration, but it is a bit more complicated, requiring the use of forceps and suction. It is performed in a hospital or at a clinic (Kelly, 2004).

Induced Labor. Induced labor is a method of abortion performed late in the second trimester, generally in a hospital. In *saline-induced abortion*, the most common type of induced labor, a fine tube is inserted through the abdomen into the amniotic sac, and some amniotic fluid is removed. An equal amount of saline solution is then injected through the tube,

causing labor and miscarriage to occur within a few hours. In *prostaglandin-induced abortion*, hormonelike substances called prostaglandins are injected into the amniotic sac, injected intravenously, or inserted by means of a vaginal suppository with similar results (Hyde & DeLamater, 2003).

Induced labor is the most common method of abortion for those pregnancies that have progressed late into the second trimester. Induced labor is both more costly and more hazardous than the methods explained earlier. Although serious complications are rare, they can occur. If the technique is done carelessly, saline solution can enter a blood vessel, inducing shock and possibly death. Also, a blood disorder is a possible, although rare, complication from induced labor.

Prostaglandin-induced abortion is preferable to saline-induced abortion because labor begins more quickly and is shorter. But saline-induced abortions do have advantages over prostaglandin-induced abortions: less risk of excessive bleeding, less risk of a retained placenta, less risk of a torn cervix as a result of too-rapid dilation, and less risk of the delivery of a live although nonviable fetus. Nausea, vomiting, and diarrhea are also more common with the prostaglandin method (Hyde & DeLamater, 2003).

Induced labor is physically more uncomfortable than the methods of abortion used earlier in pregnancy. It is also often more emotionally upsetting for the woman, because she experiences contractions for several hours and then expels a lifeless fetus (Kelly, 2004). Induced labor accounts for only 1% of abortions in the United States (Koonin, Kochanek, Smith, & Ramick, 1991).

Hysterotomy. A surgical method of abortion, **hysterotomy** is performed between 16 and 24 weeks after the last menstrual period. A cesarean section is performed, and the fetus is removed. Hysterotomies are relatively rare, but they are useful if the pregnancy has progressed to the late second trimester and the woman's health leads physicians to conclude that neither of the induction methods is appropriate (Hyde & DeLamater, 2003).

Physical and Emotional Aspects of Abortion

The chance of dying as a result of a legal abortion in the United States is far lower than the chance of dying during childbirth. Before the 9-week point in

TABLE C.1	Abortion Risks
	Risk of Death in Any Given Year
Legal abortion	
Before 9 weeks	1 in 500,000
9–12 weeks	1 in 67,000
13–16 weeks	1 in 23,000
After 16 weeks	1 in 8,700
Illegal abortion	1 in 3,000
Pregnancy and childbirth	1 in 14,300

Source: The Harvard Guide to Women's Health by K. J. Carlson, S. A. Eisenstat, and T. Ziporyn, 1996, Cambridge, MA: Harvard University Press.

pregnancy, a woman has a 1 in 500,000 chance of dying as a result of an abortion. This compares to a 1 in 14,300 chance of dying as a result of pregnancy and childbirth. (See Table C.1.)

Infection is a possibility after an abortion, however. Women are advised to consult a physician if they have an elevated temperature, experience severe lower abdominal cramps or pain, experience heavy bleeding (heavier than their normal menstrual period), or if their menstrual period does not begin within 6 weeks after the abortion. Women are also advised to follow directions for prescriptions faithfully, to avoid strenuous physical activity, to rest as much as possible for several days, and to avoid sexual intercourse for 2 to 3 weeks following an abortion (Boston Women's Health Book Collective, 1998).

Some women experience feelings of guilt after an abortion; others feel great relief that they are no longer pregnant. Still other women are ambivalent: happy not to be pregnant but sad about the abortion. Some of the emotional highs and lows may be related to hormonal adjustments and may cease after the woman's hormone levels return to normal. The intensity of feelings associated with an abortion generally diminishes as time passes, but some women experience anger, frustration, and guilt for many years (Boston Women's Health Book Collective, 1998; Kelly, 2004).

Those experiencing severe, negative psychological reactions to abortion are rare, according to a review of research findings by a panel commissioned by the American Psychological Association (Adler et al., 1992; Landers, 1989). The psychologists concluded that there is no such thing as "postabortion syndrome." They also noted that it is important to keep in mind that "the question is not simply whether abortion has some harmful psychological effects, but whether those effects are demonstrably worse than the psychological consequences of unwanted childbirth" (Landers, 1989). The investigators argued that abortion is not likely to be followed by severe psychological response but is best understood "within a framework of normal stress and coping rather than a model of psychopathology" (Adler et al., 1992, p. 1194). Many women find it helpful to talk about the experience with sympathetic family members, friends, and professional counselors.

An 8-year study of nearly 5,300 women confirmed what earlier researchers had found (Russo & Dabul, 1997). Researchers at Arizona State University and Phoenix College found that abortion does not lead to lasting emotional trauma in young women who are psychologically healthy before they become pregnant; in contrast, women who are in poor emotional health after an abortion are likely to have been feeling bad about their lives before ending their pregnancies.

Adolescents and Abortion

One of the controversies swirling around abortion is whether parents have the right to give consent or be notified when their adolescent child seeks an abortion. Though abortion is legal in the United States, many states require consent or notification. Legislators passing these laws argue that parental consent is justified by a number of assumptions, including the high risk of psychological harm from abortion; the adolescents' inability to make an informed decision; and the benefits of having parents involved in the decision-making process (Adler, Ozer, & Tschann, 2003).

Researchers argue, however, that empirical data raise questions about the high risk of psychological harm. The data do not suggest that legal minors are at heightened risk for serious psychological harm when compared to adult abortion patients or peers who have not had an abortion. Further, research indicates that adolescent abortion patients actually may be more competent than pregnant adolescents not considering an abortion. Researchers also question adolescents' supposed inability to make informed decisions about abortion. In locations where it has been studied, virtually all adolescents' requests for a judge's approval to have an abortion without notifying parents have been granted by judges assessing the adolescent's competence and reasons for requesting the judicial bypass. Finally, although parental involvement laws aim to promote family communication and functioning, there are few data to actually demonstrate this contention (Adler et al., 2003).

Decision Making and Unintended Pregnancy

When a woman suspects she is unintentionally pregnant, she should first confirm the pregnancy through a formal laboratory test. A physical examination by a physician will help establish how long she has been pregnant. After pregnancy has been conclusively established, she can weigh her options carefully: carrying the child to term and keeping it, carrying the child to term and relinquishing it for adoption, or having an abortion. This is a decision that can greatly affect an individual's life. A woman facing this difficult decision should talk with several people she respects and trusts and who can remain calm and objective during the discussion (Insel & Roth, 2004; Kelly, 2004).

Married couples commonly choose to keep an unplanned baby, although abortion remains an option for many married women, especially those who feel they already have as many children as they can care for properly. Couples who are not married may choose to get married, although many authorities believe that pregnancy is not by itself a sufficient reason for marriage. Some young parents receive help rearing their babies from their own parents and other relatives while they complete their educations and become more capable of assuming parental responsibilities. However, grandparents are often less than excited about becoming "parents" once again.

Adoption agencies today have difficulty finding babies for all the couples who wish to adopt. The high rate of abortion has contributed to this situation, along with society's generally negative attitude toward relinquishing babies for adoption. Social attitudes are reflected in the expression "giving up the child for adoption." The majority of adolescent mothers who carry their babies to term thus choose to keep them, despite the difficulties young mothers face in this situation. Adoption is seen as a viable al-

ternative by many people, however. Some agencies are making an effort to ease the pain young mothers may feel by allowing them to have continued contact with the child and its adoptive parents.

Many people have strong feelings about the dilemma of unintended pregnancy and are eager to influence the decision in one direction or another. The individual or couple experiencing the dilemma, however, carries the responsibility for the decision. Whatever the decision, an unintended pregnancy is often a very lonely and stressful time in a woman's life.

Preventing Abortion

The Planned Parenthood Federation of America argues that reducing the number of unintended pregnancies in this country will reduce the number of abortions. Using this line of thought, Planned Parenthood (1985; Moglia & Knowles, 1997) advocates the following ways to prevent abortion:

- *Make contraceptives more easily available.* Every public dollar spent on family planning saves at least two tax dollars in the next year alone in reduced health and welfare services associated with unintended births.
- *Provide young people with a better teacher than experience.* Support sex education programs instead of hoping that sex will disappear if no one talks about it.
- *Increase the involvement of men.* No woman ever made herself pregnant. Help men recognize equal responsibility in all aspects of sexuality, including obtaining and using contraception.
- *Develop new birth control methods that are temporary, safe, effective, easy to use, and without side effects.* Increase government support for research in this area.
- *Make America friendlier to children.* Research by the Alan Guttmacher Institute indicates that the United States has one of the highest teen pregnancy rates among the developed nations of the world. Countries with lower rates were found to be more realistic about the accepting of sexuality and to have open access to family planning services.

Pregnancy and Childbirth

The Process of Reproduction
Pregnancy and Preparation
    for Birth
Labor and Delivery
Caring for an Infant
Miscarriage, Stillbirth, and
    Infant Death

In this section we will discuss reproduction, infertility, and pregnancy. We will then look at the birth process and childbirth practices. Finally, we will discuss the changes a new baby brings to the family and the impact on the family of miscarriage, stillbirth, or infant death.

The Process of Reproduction

Conception is a complicated process. In this section we will discuss how conception occurs, the nature of infertility, and signs of pregnancy.

Conception

The average woman's menstrual cycle lasts 28 days. For as long as she is fertile (approximately 35 years, from about age 12 to about age 47), each cycle prepares her body for **conception** and childbearing. The most fertile period occurs about midway through the menstrual cycle, or 14 days before the next **menses** begins. This is the point at which **ovulation** occurs.

Estimates of women's fertility have ranged from 2 days in a menstrual cycle to 10 or more. Research published in the *New England Journal of Medicine* indicates there are 6 days in every menstrual month when a woman can get pregnant. Dr. Arthur Wilcox, who teaches at the University of North Carolina, argues that conception is possible if a woman has intercourse on the 5 days before ovulation as well as on the day her ovaries release a new egg. Sex before the 6-day period almost certainly will not result in pregnancy, nor will intercourse just one day after ovulation. The researchers at the National Institute of Environmental Health Sciences in Research Triangle Park, North Carolina, also found that 94% of pregnancies resulted from sperm that had lingered less than 3 days. There were no pregnancies from sperm more than 5 days old (Insel & Roth, 2004).

There are approximately a half-million eggs in the female ovaries at birth. Only 400 to 500 of them will ripen and be released into the oviducts during a woman's lifetime. Unfertilized eggs live about 24 hours; then they disintegrate and are expelled along with the uterine lining during **menstruation**. Each egg—made up of 23 chromosomes, fat droplets, protein substances, and nutrient fluid—is about the size of a pinpoint (1/250 inch in diameter; Insel & Roth, 2004).

Sperm cells are even smaller than eggs (1/8,000 inch in diameter). One average male ejaculation contains approximately 300 million to 400 million sperm. Sperm contain 23 chromosomes and have a tail for mobility. When a male ejaculates during intercourse, the sperm are propelled into the woman's vagina. Unless a sperm reaches and fertilizes an egg, it will die within about 72 hours. Many sperm cells die in the acidic environment of the vagina. The survivors migrate to the cervix, or "neck" of the uterus, where secretions are more alkaline and hospitable to sperm. Once inside the uterus, many sperm fail to reach an oviduct or to enter the oviduct that contains the egg. If an egg is not present in the oviduct, the sperm swim erratically. If the sperm have found the oviduct with the egg, they swim directly toward it, apparently drawn by chemicals released by the egg. Those sperm that come in contact with the egg must penetrate the tough membrane that encases it.

Each sperm cell that makes contact with the egg deposits an enzyme that helps to dissolve this membrane. About 2,000 sperm manage to make it this far. The first sperm cell that meets a dissolved, bare spot on the egg cell can swim into the cell and merge with the nucleus of the egg. This union is called **fertilization.** The sperm's tail, which has served as a propeller during this journey, gets stuck in the outer membrane and drops off. The head of the sperm cell is implanted inside the egg, and no more sperm can enter, perhaps because on fertilization the egg releases a chemical making it impregnable (Insel & Roth, 2004). The fertilized egg travels for 3 to 4 days through an **oviduct** (fallopian tube) into the uterus (Figure D.1). The lining of the uterus has already become puffed out, which aids the implantation of the fertilized egg, the **zygote.**

The egg carries the hereditary characteristics of the mother and her ancestors; sperm cells carry the hereditary characteristics of the father and his ancestors. Each parent cell, the egg and the sperm, contains 23 chromosomes, and each chromosome has at least 1,000 genes. These genes are the genetic code, the chemical instructions for the design of every part of a new baby. These genes specify whether the new human being will be male or female, short or tall, blonde or brunette, and so on.

Environmental influences also affect the fetus's development a great deal during pregnancy. Health

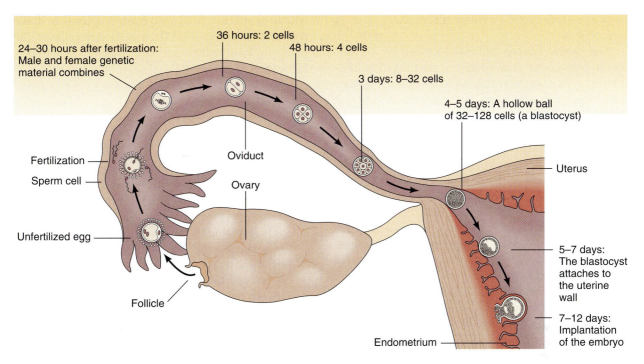

24–30 hours after fertilization: Male and female genetic material combines

36 hours: 2 cells

48 hours: 4 cells

3 days: 8–32 cells

4–5 days: A hollow ball of 32–128 cells (a blastocyst)

Oviduct

Ovary

Fertilization

Sperm cell

Unfertilized egg

Follicle

Uterus

Endometrium

5–7 days: The blastocyst attaches to the uterine wall

7–12 days: Implantation of the embryo

FIGURE D.1
Conception

Source: Core Concepts in Health, 2004 update (9th ed.) (p. 198) by P. M. Insel and W. T. Roth, 2004, New York: McGraw-Hill. Copyright 2004 by McGraw-Hill. Reprinted by permission.

authorities urge a prospective mother to eat well; avoid alcohol, drugs, and smoking; get adequate rest and exercise; have medical checkups regularly; build intimate emotional relationships with a network of other people; and generally live a healthy lifestyle (Insel & Roth, 2004).

Infertility

Infertility is defined as the inability of a couple to achieve pregnancy after repeated intercourse without contraception for 1 year. Infertility affects about one in five couples in the United States, and it is becoming increasingly common because couples are waiting longer to have children. About 60% of couples who have not conceived in a year do conceive later, with or without infertility treatment (Beers, 2003).

Up to 40% of the factors contributing to infertility are male, and in about 15% of couples who are infertile, both partners have problems. For this reason, both individuals should be evaluated (Insel & Roth, 2004).

Female infertility has two key causes: tubal blockage (in 40% of the cases) or failure to ovulate (40%). An additional 10% of infertility cases are caused by anatomical abnormalities, benign growths in the uterus, thyroid disease, and other uncommon conditions. The remaining 10% of infertility cases cannot be explained (Beers, 2003; Insel & Roth, 2004).

Tubal blockage is a common result of pelvic inflammatory disease (PID), a complication of several sexually transmitted diseases. Most cases are associated with untreated chlamydia or gonorrhea. Other PID causes include unsterile abortions and certain types of older intrauterine devices (IUDs). Other causes of tubal blockages include prior surgery and endometriosis, a condition in which endometrial (uterine) tissue grows outside the uterus. This endometrial tissue responds to hormones, causing pain, bleeding, scarring, and adhesions (Beers, 2003; Insel & Roth, 2004).

Age also affects infertility. Around age 30, a woman's fertility naturally begins to decline. The main factor in ovulation failure is probably age. Toxic chemicals, radiation, and cigarette smoking also appear to reduce female fertility (Beers, 2003; Insel & Roth, 2004).

The main causes of male infertility include low sperm count, lack of sperm motility (the ability to move spontaneously), misshapen sperm, and blocked passageways between the testes and urethra. Smoking may reduce sperm counts and cause abnormal sperm. From 1938 to 1971, millions of women took diethylstilbestrol (DES), a synthetic hormone thought to help prevent miscarriage. Sons of these mothers may have increased sperm abnormalities and fertility problems. Some prescription and illegal drugs also affect a man's sperm count. Heavy use of marijuana, for example, reduces sperm counts and suppresses certain reproductive hormones. Several other causes of sperm problems have been noted, including injury to the testicles, infection (especially from the mumps during adulthood), birth defects, and having the testes subjected to high temperatures (Beers, 2003; Insel & Roth, 2004).

Some research indicates that sperm counts worldwide have dropped as much as 50% in the past 30 years. Toxic substances such as lead, chemical pollutants, and radiation may be responsible for this decrease. Researchers are also looking at substances found widely in the environment that may interfere with the body's hormones, therefore causing problems with reproduction and development. These substances, called *endocrine disrupters*, include dioxin, PCBs (polychlorinated biphenyls), DDT (dichloro-diphenyl-trichloroethane), and compounds used in certain plastics. Though animal studies have linked prenatal exposure to endocrine disrupters with feminized genitalia and other reproductive problems in male offspring, scientists do not know yet what effects they have on human health and fertility (Insel & Roth, 2004).

About 90% of couples diagnosed with infertility have a physical problem; for the remaining 10% the cause is uncertain. Conventional medical therapies are relied on in most cases. These include surgery to repair oviducts, clear up endometriosis, and correct anatomical problems in both men and women. Fertility drugs also are used to help women ovulate, but there is the risk of causing multiple births. If these more conventional treatments do not work, there are more advanced techniques. Infertility treatments are expensive and emotionally draining, and success for a couple is uncertain. Some couples choose not to try to have children, and others turn to adoption. One

way to avoid infertility is to protect against sexually transmitted diseases (STDs) and to seek prompt and complete treatment if an STD is contracted (Beers, 2003; Insel & Roth, 2004).

"Am I Pregnant?"

Common early indicators of pregnancy include the following:

- A missed menstrual period (although a woman can miss a period for many reasons, including stress, illness, and emotional upset).
- Slight bleeding may follow implantation of the fertilized egg. Women sometimes mistake this bleeding for menstrual flow because it happens about the time the period is expected. This slight bleeding usually lasts only a few days.
- Nausea, usually but not always in the morning. **Morning sickness** tends to disappear by the 12th week of pregnancy.
- Changes in the shape, coloration, and sensitivity of the breasts. The breasts become fuller; the area around the nipples darkens; veins become more prominent; and the swelling causes tingling, throbbing, or minor pain.
- An increased need to urinate, resulting from pressure from the growing uterus on the bladder and hormonal changes.
- Fatigue and sleepiness caused by hormonal changes.
- An increase in vaginal secretions, either clear and nonirritating or slightly yellow and itchy.
- Retention of body fluids, including some swelling of the face, hands, and feet.

A woman who wants a reliable answer to the question "Am I pregnant?" can consult her physician, who can then perform a pregnancy test. The woman can also purchase a pregnancy test at a pharmacy. If the woman adheres precisely to the directions for administering the test, the home test can determine pregnancy within a week after conception with reasonable reliability. If the test kit indicates the woman is pregnant, she should follow up with a visit to a healthcare provider for confirmation. If the test kit results are negative but the conditions that led her to believe she was pregnant persists, she also should visit with a healthcare provider (Allgeier & Allgeier, 2000).

Pregnancy and Preparation for Birth

Not more than 36 hours after fertilization, the egg has divided in half; by 48 hours, the egg has divided again into four. The process of division continues as the egg moves down the oviduct. Within 3 to 4 days, the tiny fertilized mass, containing anywhere from 64 to 128 cells, reaches the uterus. The mass, called a **blastocyst**, is hollow at the center. The outer shell of cells (*trophoblast*) multiplies faster than the inner cells and eventually grows into the **placenta, umbilical cord**, and **amniotic sac**. The inner cells grow into three distinct layers: The innermost layer (*endoderm*) becomes the inner body parts; the middle layer (*mesoderm*) becomes muscle, bone, blood, kidneys, and sex glands; and the outermost layer (*ectoderm*) eventually grows into the skin, hair, and nervous tissue. Five or seven days after fertilization, the blastocyst begins implanting itself in the wall of the uterus, and its cells start to take nourishment from the uterine lining (Insel & Roth, 2004). Figure D.2 illustrates the stages of fetal development.

Pregnancy progresses over the course of three **trimesters**, periods of 13 weeks each. During each trimester, important prenatal milestones occur (Figure D.3). During the first trimester, the external appearance of the mother's body changes very little, although she may experience some or all of the common signs of pregnancy listed earlier. In the second trimester, which some women consider the most peaceful part of a pregnancy, the mother gains weight, and it becomes clear to others that she is pregnant. Women who are happy about the upcoming birth often report a sense of well-being during the second trimester. The third trimester is often the most difficult part of the pregnancy. The increased demands the growing fetus places on the woman's body may make her lethargic and gradually intensify her impatience to give birth (Beers, 2003; Insel & Roth, 2004).

The pregnant woman has a great deal of responsibility, because everything that enters or comes in contact with her body can potentially affect the fetus (Insel & Roth, 2004). Her partner, family, and friends also have major responsibilities to support the mother in her efforts to maintain physical and mental health and, thus, aid in the baby's development. Prenatal care includes appropriate diet, exercise, rest, and the avoidance of alcohol and drugs not prescribed by a physician. There are many things to learn during pregnancy. Medical professionals and health educators specializing in pregnancy, labor, and delivery can be very helpful.

Although pregnancy and childbirth are clearly "natural" processes, numerous problems can arise, some of them life-threatening to the infant and the mother. Because of the potential for problems, women should receive regular medical evaluation and care during pregnancy.

Education for Childbirth

Education is extremely important during this period in a woman's and a couple's life. Expectant couples generally have many questions and sometimes fears that they can address with the help of resources such as books, films, and classes.

One positive development over the past 25 to 30 years has been the growth of childbirth classes. In most communities, the vast majority of pregnant women and their partners attend a series of educational sessions at a local hospital or clinic to help them prepare for the delivery. Sessions often involve presentations on prenatal development; nutrition and exercise during pregnancy; the role of fathers,

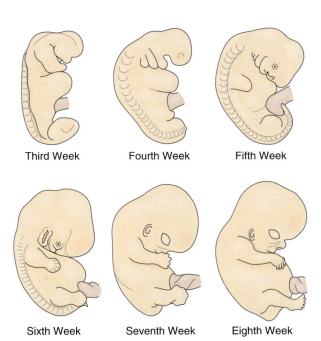

Third Week   Fourth Week   Fifth Week

Sixth Week   Seventh Week   Eighth Week

FIGURE D.2
The Fetal Development Process

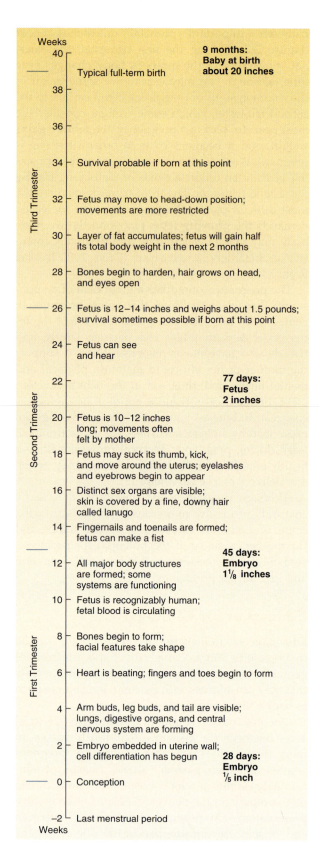

Weeks

40 —
Typical full-term birth

9 months:
Baby at birth
about 20 inches

38 —

36 —

34 — Survival probable if born at this point

32 — Fetus may move to head-down position; movements are more restricted

30 — Layer of fat accumulates; fetus will gain half its total body weight in the next 2 months

28 — Bones begin to harden, hair grows on head, and eyes open

26 — Fetus is 12–14 inches and weighs about 1.5 pounds; survival sometimes possible if born at this point

24 — Fetus can see and hear

22 —
77 days:
Fetus
2 inches

20 — Fetus is 10–12 inches long; movements often felt by mother

18 — Fetus may suck its thumb, kick, and move around the uterus; eyelashes and eyebrows begin to appear

16 — Distinct sex organs are visible; skin is covered by a fine, downy hair called lanugo

14 — Fingernails and toenails are formed; fetus can make a fist

12 — All major body structures are formed; some systems are functioning

45 days:
Embryo
1⅛ inches

10 — Fetus is recognizably human; fetal blood is circulating

8 — Bones begin to form; facial features take shape

6 — Heart is beating; fingers and toes begin to form

4 — Arm buds, leg buds, and tail are visible; lungs, digestive organs, and central nervous system are forming

2 — Embryo embedded in uterine wall; cell differentiation has begun

28 days:
Embryo
⅕ inch

0 — Conception

−2 — Last menstrual period

Weeks

Third Trimester / *Second Trimester* / *First Trimester*

grandparents, and other supporters; and many other issues. Question-and-answer sessions and practice drills of techniques that will be useful during labor and delivery are also common in these programs. The goal of these classes is to reduce fear and to manage discomfort and pain during this challenging time. Some people attend refresher sessions for subsequent pregnancies.

Fewer people take parenting classes after the baby is born, but these programs can be very helpful to new parents. Successful labor and delivery are only the first important steps in the journey of parenthood.

Nutrition and Exercise During Pregnancy

An adequate diet during pregnancy greatly improves a mother's chance of remaining healthy and of delivering a healthy baby. Inadequate diet has been associated with a variety of diseases mothers can develop during pregnancy. One goal of a healthy diet is to promote a full-term pregnancy: A normal-birthweight baby has a better chance of survival and of a healthy childhood than does a low-birthweight baby. Not only does a baby get all of its nutrients from its mother, but it competes for her nutrients when there are not enough to meet both of their needs (Beers, 2003; Insel & Roth, 2004).

A healthy weight gain for a mother during pregnancy is anywhere from 24 to 27 pounds. The average gain is about 1.5 to 3 pounds a month for the first 3 months, and 1 pound every 9 days for the last 6 months. Approximately 80,000 calories are required during the course of a pregnancy. This may sound like a lot, but it is only 300 additional calories per day—the equivalent of one scoop of ice cream.

Medical authorities agree that moderate physical activity during pregnancy contributes to the mother's mental and physical well-being. Exercise

FIGURE D.3

The Three Periods of Prenatal Development
The baby's anatomy is almost completely formed during the first 3 months of prenatal life, although the fetus is only a few inches long at the end of this period (called the first trimester). During the second 3 months (the second trimester), the fetal heartbeat can be heard with a stethoscope, and the mother feels vigorous kicking and turning in her abdomen. The largest weight gain occurs during the last few months of prenatal development (the third trimester).

keeps the muscles toned, which is helpful during delivery and in regaining a nonpregnant shape after childbirth. Unless their job is too stressful physically or emotionally, most women can continue working at their jobs into the final stages of pregnancy. A woman's need for rest and sleep increases during pregnancy, which puts great demands on her body (Insel & Roth, 2004).

Drug Use During Pregnancy

Although the placenta serves as a filter to protect the embryo from dangerous substances in the mother's blood, the so-called placental barrier is not foolproof. Many drugs pass easily through the placenta and can cause fetal damage. Alcohol is one of those drugs. **Fetal alcohol syndrome (FAS)** has been a subject of considerable concern recently. In fact, the Centers for Disease Control and Prevention has labeled it the leading cause of birth defects in the United States (Kelly, 2004). A small body, facial malformation, and poor mental capabilities are some of the ways FAS presents itself in children. Large-scale surveys indicate that babies of mothers who drink excessively are exposed to considerable risk of serious malformation during both the early, embryonic stage and the later phases of fetal development. In particular, alcohol easily damages eyes and vision (Masters, Johnson, & Kolodny, 1998). Pregnant women can eliminate the possibility of damage to the fetus by not drinking *any* alcohol during pregnancy.

Smoking is also dangerous to the developing fetus. Nicotine and carbon monoxide from smoking pass through the placental barrier into the fetal bloodstream. Babies born to women who smoked heavily during pregnancy almost always weigh less at birth than babies born to women who stopped smoking at the beginning of pregnancy. A smokeless working environment during pregnancy is also important for the mother's and baby's health.

Sex During Pregnancy

Pregnancy generates mixed emotions: joy, discomfort, wonder, fear, insecurity, curiosity, and enthusiastic expectation. Because this is an emotion-filled time, maintaining a healthy sexual relationship is important for pregnant women and their partners. With reasonable caution, couples can make love until the birth process begins. Most couples resume inter-

course within 3 to 6 weeks after the birth of a child (Beers, 2003; Kelly, 2004).

Labor and Delivery

The first sign of impending birth is **labor**, contractions of the uterus that occur at regular intervals. During labor, the uterine muscles gradually stretch the cervical opening in preparation for birth, and those muscles also push the baby down into the vagina so that it can be born. Signs of the beginning of labor vary from individual to individual. In many mothers, it is accompanied by a discharge of the bloody mucus that has plugged the cervix during pregnancy and prevented bacteria from entering the uterus. In some women, the amniotic sac ruptures ("the breaking of the waters") during early labor (Beers, 2003).

Three Stages of Labor

Medical tradition divides labor into three stages (Figure D.4).

Stage 1. During the first stage of labor, the uterus contracts in rhythmic waves, and the cervical opening dilates (expands) to about 4 inches in diameter and effaces, or thins out. Early in stage 1, contractions occur every 15 to 20 minutes and last approximately 1 minute. **Contractions**—tightenings of the uterine muscles—are followed by periods of relative relaxation. Later in stage 1, the contractions increase in frequency and in length. By the time contractions are about 5 minutes apart, the woman should be in the hospital to begin preparation for the birth. (Later in this resource section we will take a look at some alternatives to the traditional hospital birth.) Most women spend all of stage 1 in a labor room at the hospital. Labor lasts 2 to 24 hours or more, and during long labors, labor pains may stop and start up again. During a first birth, labor averages about 10 hours. For subsequent babies, labor may average about 8 hours or less, often decreasing with each birth (Beers, 2003).

Stage 2. The second stage of labor—the **delivery**, or birth, itself—usually takes place in the delivery room and lasts a few minutes to an hour or more. Ninety-nine percent of all babies enter the world lengthwise, with 96% entering the cervix and traveling through

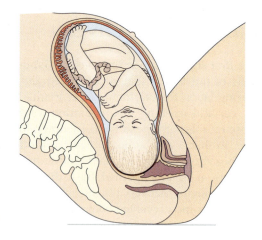

(a)

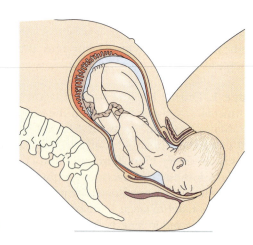

(b)

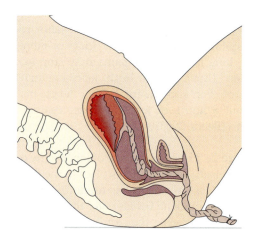

(c)

the vagina headfirst. Three percent of babies are born buttocks first, called a *breech birth*. The remaining 1% of babies are in a transverse position, with the back near the cervix. In these cases, the medical team tries to rotate the baby lengthwise; if they do not succeed, a cesarean section must be performed.

When the baby's head reaches the entrance to the vagina, this is called *crowning*. The physician or nurse-midwife encourages the mother to "bear down," to help push the child out through the vagina (Boston Women's Health Book Collective, 1998).

The vagina can stretch a great deal to allow the baby to emerge, but the *perineum* (the tissue between the anus and the vagina) can stretch only so far before it tears. Physicians often prestretch the perineum early in labor to reduce the risk of tearing; extensive tearing makes infection more likely and slows recovery. Some physicians make a minor surgical incision in the perineum—an **episiotomy**—to prevent tearing. After the birth, the episiotomy is repaired with a few surgical stitches and usually heals in about 3 weeks. Although episiotomy has been a relatively routine medical practice in the United States for many years, some controversy surrounds the practice; pregnant women may want to learn more about the pros and cons of the procedure before delivery. Many feminists and childbirth groups consider episiotomies to be unnecessary in most deliveries (Insel & Roth, 2004).

As the baby's head passes through the birth canal, its body rotates somewhat so that the shoulders can exit. After the shoulders are delivered, the rest of the body slips out easily. Shortly after delivery, mucus is removed from the baby's mouth, and the baby begins breathing through its lungs, sometimes after a gentle slap from the physician. The umbilical cord is painlessly cut about 3 inches from the baby's body; the stub dries up and falls off in a few days. In many states, the newborn's eyes are treated against gonorrhea with silver nitrate or an antibiotic (Beers, 2003).

Stage 3. The third stage of labor is the expulsion of the **afterbirth**, or placenta and fetal membranes, by mild contractions from the uterus. To avoid infection, the physician or nurse examines the placenta

FIGURE D.4

Birth: Labor and Delivery
(a) the first stage of labor; (b) the second stage of labour: delivery of the baby; (c) the third stage of labor: expulsion of the placenta.

carefully to ascertain that all of it has been expelled from the uterus. This third stage of labor may take only a few minutes or up to an hour. If an episiotomy was performed, it is repaired during this time.

After delivery, the baby is bathed, and in many hospitals the baby is then taken to the recovery room for a visit with the mother, father, and perhaps a few other very special people. Mothers are encouraged to be active reasonably soon after delivery—to walk around or use the bathroom, for example. (If the mother received anesthesia during delivery, she may not begin to walk around for 12 to 24 hours.) Some hospitals provide a "rooming-in" option for mothers who want their baby nearby all the time or at least when they are awake. Another option is to bring the baby to the mother every 3 to 4 hours to be breast- or bottle-fed. If all goes well, mother and baby go home in a few days (Allgeier & Allgeier, 2000). The first major challenge of parenthood has been met.

Cesarean Section

When normal vaginal birth is impossible or undesirable for some reason, a **cesarean section** (C-section), a surgical procedure, is performed to deliver the baby. C-sections are used in a variety of situations: if the baby is too large or the mother's pelvis is too small to allow the baby to move into the vagina; if labor has been very long and hard and the cervix has not dilated or if the mother is near exhaustion; if the umbilical cord has prolapsed (is preceding the baby through the cervix); if there is an Rh (blood factor) incompatibility; if there is excessive bleeding; or if the mother's or baby's condition takes a turn for the worse (Hyde & DeLamater, 2003).

C-sections are performed by making an incision through the mother's abdomen and then through the wall of the uterus. The baby is lifted out, and the uterine and abdominal walls are sewn up. Normal vaginal births are sometimes possible after a woman has delivered by cesarean; other women have two or three cesarean deliveries. The rate of complications related to C-sections is low, but recovery is somewhat longer than for vaginal birth, requiring 3 to 4 days in the hospital rather than 1 to 2 (Hyde & DeLamater, 2003).

The number of cesarean deliveries in the United States increased steadily in the 1970s and 1980s, peaking at 24% in 1989 (Taffel, Placek, Moien, & Kasary, 1991). Cesarean rates then fell slightly to 20.6% by 1996. The decline was attributed almost entirely to the increase among women giving birth vaginally after an earlier C-section.

C-sections can be safer for both mother and baby when labor is prolonged and stressful, advocates say. They cite lower rates of maternal and neonatal mortality and of infant brain damage due to trauma during labor and delivery. Critics of C-sections argue that many cesareans are unnecessary, that they are simply more convenient for the physician in terms of anticipating and scheduling deliveries. The debate is likely to continue on a situation-by-situation basis (Hyde & DeLamater, 2003).

Alternative Approaches to Birth

In the past and in many parts of the world today, childbirth has been viewed as a natural phenomenon requiring little fanfare or special attention. In developed countries, however, beginning about 100 years ago, medical intervention became more and more common. Childbirth came to be viewed more as a medical condition or emergency. Reliance on drugs and anesthetics to reduce pain grew, as did the time for recovery from the birth experience. Labor and delivery became the sole province of physicians and nurses in hospitals. From a feminist perspective, women lost control to medical experts (Kelly, 2004).

Natural Childbirth. In 1932, British physician Grantly Dick-Read published *Childbirth Without Fear* (1932/1984), and women and their partners began to regain some of the control they had formerly held over the birth process. Dick-Read believed that medical intervention generated fear, and fear created more tension and pain. His approach, which he called *natural childbirth*, educated women about labor and delivery and taught them relaxation techniques to reduce tension.

The Lamaze Method. The French obstetrician Fernand Lamaze introduced a similar method in the 1950s. The *Lamaze method* of "prepared childbirth" is widely popular today. In this method, the baby's father or a friend or relative serves as a coach for the mother. In prenatal classes, the mother and her coach learn relaxation and breathing techniques for dealing with the intensity of labor. The woman remains active and alert during the birth of her baby (Kelly, 2004).

The Lamaze approach does not prohibit the use of painkillers during labor but usually reduces the need for them. Routine use of anesthesia during child-birth has been criticized, primarily because drugs can slow the progress of labor and affect the baby's well-being during the first several hours of life (Allgeier & Allgeier, 2000). One rational approach to the controversy over anesthesia and other painkillers is for a pregnant woman to participate in prepared childbirth classes and use the breathing and relaxation techniques of the Lamaze method during labor. If she discovers that she cannot control her pain and wishes an anesthetic, she can request it without guilt. The anesthetic should then be administered with great caution (Hyde & DeLamater, 2003).

Leboyer's "Gentle Birthing." The French physician Frederick Leboyer (1995) advocated methods for reducing the shock of birth to the baby. Instead of a bright, noisy delivery area, Leboyer recommended a quiet, dimly lit, warm setting. In the Leboyer method, the baby lies on the mother's abdomen for a while before the umbilical cord is cut and then receives a gentle, warm bath.

Home Birth. Because medical complications occur in approximately 1 out of 20 births, most professionals recommend delivery in a hospital, where there is access to advanced technology and professional assistance. Some couples choose to have their baby born at home, however. A trained and licensed **midwife** or certified nurse-midwife can assist in the process. It is also recommended that a cooperating physician be on call in case of an emergency (Allgeier & Allgeier, 2000; Kelly, 2004).

Birthing Rooms and Birthing Centers. In response to the desire that birth be a cooperative process between professionals and families and a balance of technology and tenderness, many hospitals have established birthing rooms and birthing centers. Birthing rooms are decorated more like bedrooms than like hospital rooms. Sometimes children and family members are allowed to be present for the birth, as is common in many societies. When a birthing room is used, the mother stays in the same room for labor and delivery. After delivery, the baby is checked for signs of distress, weighed and measured, and kept warm (Kelly, 2004).

Birthing centers humanize the birth process even further. Birthing centers are separate healthcare facilities affiliated with hospitals. They have not only birthing rooms but also kitchens and other rooms in which visitors and family members can stay. Birthing centers are usually staffed by nurses and nurse-midwives, although physicians are often in attendance for deliveries. They have emergency equipment and arrangements with a hospital if transfer for emergency care is necessary (Allgeier & Allgeier, 2000). Procedures and philosophy vary widely from institution to institution, and prospective parents are advised to consider their options carefully.

Physical and Psychological Changes After Birth

After the baby is born, the mother's body undergoes drastic physiological changes. Levels of the hormones estrogen and progesterone, having increased during pregnancy, drop sharply when the placenta is expelled and gradually return to normal over a few weeks to a few months. Other endocrinic changes include an increase in hormones associated with breast-feeding. As a result of the considerable stress a woman undergoes during labor and delivery, she may feel exhausted. Discomfort from delivery and from the episiotomy, if one was performed, is also common for the first few weeks after childbirth (Hyde & DeLamater, 2003).

For a day or two after birth, the mother often feels elated. Most highs in life, however, are often followed by lows. In terms of energy expended, mother and baby have indeed been through an ordeal. Within a few days after delivery, many women experience some depression and periods of crying.

Mood swings can range from mild to severe. The *maternity blues* or *baby blues* are the mildest form of depression, with sadness and tears lasting 24 to 48 hours. It is estimated that 50% to 80% of mothers experience mild baby blues after delivery. **Postpartum depression**, which affects 1% of mothers and lasts 6 to 8 weeks, is a bit more serious. It is characterized by a depressed mood, insomnia, tearfulness, feelings of inadequacy, an inability to cope, irritability, and fatigue (Insel & Roth, 2004).

A number of factors are thought to contribute to the depression women commonly feel after birth. Being in the hospital is stressful, and when the mother returns home, she faces a new set of stressors. Her energy level is low, yet she must care for a newborn, an exhausting task involving almost constant attentiveness. She may get up several times at night to attend to the baby, who may be hungry or sick, may need a diaper change, or may be crying for some unknown reason. Although pregnancy and childbirth are natural processes, the stresses of the associated physiological and physical changes disrupt a woman's life.

Over the years, however, many fathers have become actively involved in the challenging process of parenthood. During pregnancy, labor, and delivery, the father can be a friend, coach, and supporter. After the birth, fathers have a chance to share in the considerable stresses of parenthood. They can get up at night to feed the baby and can share in other caregiving tasks.

One very positive development over the past two decades has been the increase in support services for new parents. Many services were developed to help so-called at-risk families, those in which there is a potential for abuse or neglect of the baby. Among the risk factors commonly cited are high family stress, a parent who becomes angry easily, a very depressed parent, a parent with little extended-family support, a teenage mother, and alcohol or other drug abuse in the family.

There are also programs for parents who are not at risk for abuse or neglect of their infant but who are simply experiencing the everyday stresses and strains of parenthood. Childbirth and parenting classes are generally available and meet on a regular basis. Typically, a professional gives a short talk on a relevant topic, and a group discussion follows. Churches, synagogues, and other organizations also sponsor forums for parents to get together socially to share their insights and the challenges they are facing. These programs help parents realize that they are not alone and that they can find ways to cope during this difficult time.

Caring for an Infant

When the infant arrives, a new set of challenges faces the parents. They quickly learn that their baby is more in charge of their life than they are. During the early weeks, the important process of creating a new family begins.

Bonding with the Baby

For most women, the attachment process begins even before the baby is born. During pregnancy, most women develop a sense of the baby as a separate individual and form an emotional attachment to that individual (Leifer, 1980). Many parents-to-be give the fetus a name—some serious, some funny—and mothers and fathers occasionally talk to the baby in the womb, play music for it, massage it. Even before birth, the baby is part of the family. For most parents, bonding develops quickly after birth as they care for this dependent child.

Breast-Feeding

In the early part of the 20th century, **breast-feeding** declined in popularity; many viewed it as somehow "lower class." Bottled formula was considered antiseptic, scientific, sophisticated, and dignified. By the mid-1960s, only about 20% of women breast-fed their babies. A renewed interest in breast-feeding began soon after; by the mid-1980s, the percentage had risen to 60%, which it is today (Insel & Roth, 2004).

One advantage breast-fed babies receive is a temporary immunity (so-called passive immunity) from antibodies in their mothers' milk; this protects them from a variety of diseases, including respiratory infections, colds, bronchitis, pneumonia, German measles, scarlet fever, and polio Olds, London, & Ladewig, 2004. Most studies comparing the benefits of bottle-feeding and breast-feeding conclude that breastfeeding is usually better for the physical well-being of the baby. Human milk is more easily digested than is milk from other animals or from vegetable-based formulas (such as those made from soybeans). Although human milk contains less protein than cow's milk, human infants can utilize almost all of the protein in their mother's milk but only about half the protein in cow's milk. Breast-fed babies are less likely to have diarrhea or to be constipated than are bottle-fed babies; they also tend to have healthier teeth and are less likely to be obese or to get premature atherosclerosis. These apparent advantages led the American Pediatric Society to conclude that breast milk is superior to formula. For those women who simply cannot or prefer not to breast-feed their babies but wish the nutritional advantages of human milk, human milk banks now operate in many large metropolitan areas (Allgeier & Allgeier, 2000).

The average baby ingests about 1,000 calories a day from breast milk, and this can be a great help to a mother who gained more weight than she wished during pregnancy. Breast-feeding mothers generally can lose weight quite steadily without denying themselves food by nursing for 6 months or so

(Allgeier & Allgeier, 2000). By about 6 months of age, however, breast milk alone cannot meet the growing baby's needs for calories and protein. It becomes necessary to supplement breast milk with solid food at that time or even earlier.

Although its advantages are many, breast-feeding causes stress and inconvenience for many women working outside the home. More important than the feeding choice is the quality of the relationship between a mother and her baby: A baby raised in a loving home can grow up to be a healthy, psychologically secure individual whether bottle-fed or breast-fed. Breast-feeding can be a happy experience for both mother and child, but the woman who nurses grudgingly may communicate feelings of resentment and unhappiness to her baby. The infant would be better off with a relaxed, loving, bottle-feeding mother.

Miscarriage, Stillbirth, and Infant Death

Fewer than 1% of infants born in the United States die in the first year after birth. The infant mortality rate is at a record low level in U.S. history: 6.8 deaths per 1,000 live births (Arias, Anderson, Kung, Murphy, & Kochanek, 2004). About ½% of infants are stillborn in this country (National Institutes of Health, 2002). Slightly more than 15% of all known pregnancies end in miscarriage, and one-third of all women experience a miscarriage at some time in their reproductive years (Insel & Roth, 2004; National Center for Health Statistics, 1999).

Miscarriage, or in medical terminology, spontaneous abortion, is the termination of a pregnancy from natural causes before the time the fetus can survive for even a few minutes outside the uterus. (Induced abortion is the term used for those expulsions of an embryo or fetus that are artificially induced by mechanical means or drugs.) Miscarriage generally occurs before the 20th week of pregnancy. A fetus born dead from natural causes after 20 weeks is called *stillborn*. Perhaps 50% to 78% of all fertilized eggs spontaneously abort. Only about 10% to 15% of the time are women aware that they have miscarried. Spontaneous abortions often seem to be functional in that they naturally eliminate many defective fetuses (Beers, 2003; Hyde & DeLamater, 2003; Olds et al., 2004).

About 85% of miscarriages happen in the first 12 weeks of pregnancy; the remaining 15% occur during weeks 13 to 20. The most likely reason is an abnormality in fetal development, usually as a result of extra chromosomes (about 60% of miscarriages). Occupational exposure to some chemicals may increase the chances of having a miscarriage. Other possible causes include chronic infections, unrecognized diabetes in the mother, and defects in the uterus. About one-third of the time there is no known cause for the miscarriage. Many studies have indicated that emotional disturbances in the mother's life usually are not linked with miscarriage (Beers, 2003; Insel & Roth, 2004).

Miscarriage does, however, cause emotional disturbance in the lives of many mothers. Women tend to blame themselves: "I exercised too hard"; "Stress at work caused this"; "I fell down and hurt the baby." But stress or physical trauma rarely results in a miscarriage, and women are advised to try not to blame themselves (Insel & Roth, 2004).

American society tends to define the loss of the fetus as "just a miscarriage," but most women who experience a miscarriage see the loss as a death—the death of a baby or the death of a dream. Research indicates that losing a baby due to miscarriage can be a devastating experience for family members. Some mothers will consider suicide after a miscarriage. Some couples' relationships are thrown into turmoil as a result of the loss. Some surviving siblings will feel guilt that they somehow caused the death and will grieve in silence. But families who support each other through these difficult times are likely to end up feeling stronger and more deeply committed to each other (DeFrain, Millspaugh, & Xie, 1996).

Stillbirth is the death of a so-called viable fetus, a fetus that was mature enough developmentally to have lived outside the womb but for some reason or reasons was born dead. Stillbirths occur in the seventh to ninth months of pregnancy (the third trimester). Before this time, the event is called a miscarriage. Some causes of stillbirth are known. These include problems with the placenta, birth defects, growth restrictions, and infections. But in about one-third to one-half of all stillbirths, the cause of death is undetermined.

The chances of infant mortality before the first birthday are under 1% in the United States. About 2,500 of these deaths are attributed to **sudden infant death syndrome (SIDS)**, for which the cause is unknown. A common scenario is that the parent or another caretaker puts the seemingly healthy infant in the crib for a nap and comes back a few minutes or hours later to find the baby has died. An autopsy reveals no apparent cause (DeFrain, Ernst, Jakub, & Taylor, 1991).

It is possible for parents to reduce factors known to increase SIDS risk:

- Always place a baby to sleep on her or his back, even at naptime.
- Don't smoke around the baby.
- Don't smoke if you're pregnant.
- Place a baby on a firm mattress, such as one in a safety-approved crib.
- Remove soft, fluffy bedding and stuffed toys from the baby's sleep areas.
- Keep blankets and other coverings away from the baby's nose and mouth.
- Don't put too many layers of clothing or blankets on the baby.
- Make sure all the baby's caretakers know that infants should be placed to sleep on their backs to reduce SIDS risk (National Institutes of Health, 2003).

Although the chance of losing a baby to miscarriage, stillbirth, SIDS, or the baby dying in the first year of life outside the mother is relatively small, the loss is a severe crisis in the lives of most families who experience it. When a baby dies, the family begins a long and difficult journey. Many parents and even some grandparents consider suicide after the loss of a baby; the pain and guilt can be overwhelming. Marriages are often strained by the loss, and parental relationships with surviving children sometimes suffer (DeFrain et al., 1996; DeFrain, Ernst, & Nealer, 1997).

Research indicates that family members who have experienced the death of an infant are at serious risk for major emotional and physical problems. Immediate and effective community support from relatives, friends, and professionals is essential. Most families recover from the death of an infant, but the road back to emotional well-being is long, difficult, and often very lonely. Three to five years of "recovery" is very common among bereaved parents, although as many point out, one never really recovers from such a tragedy (DeFrain et al., 1996, 1997).

Glossary

A

ability to manage stress and crisis One of the six major qualities (commonly found in emotionally healthy families) identified by researchers working within the family strengths framework.

abortion Expulsion of a fetus from the uterus before it is sufficiently developed to survive on its own; commonly used to describe only artificially induced terminations of pregnancy.

accommodating style A style of conflict resolution characterized by nonassertive but cooperative behavior; accommodaters subjugate their own wants and needs to those of others.

acculturation The intermeshing of cultural traits and values with those of the dominant culture.

afterbirth The placenta and fetal membranes, which are expelled from the uterus during the third stage of labor.

ageism A form of prejudice or discrimination in which one judges an older person negatively solely on the basis of age.

aggressive communication A style of interpersonal communication that attempts to hurt or put down the receiver while protecting the aggressor's self-esteem.

agreeing to disagree A negotiating strategy in which two people are unable to agree on opposing courses of action and decide to take neither course of action.

Al-Anon A self-help group for families of alcoholics.

Alateen A support group for young people with alcoholic parents, based on the Alcoholics Anonymous model.

alcohol abuse A generic term that encompasses both alcoholism (addiction to alcohol characterized by compulsive drinking) and problem drinking (alcohol consumption that results in functional disability).

Alcoholics Anonymous (AA) A self-help group for alcoholics.

alcoholism Addiction to alcohol characterized by compulsive drinking.

alimony Court-ordered financial support to a spouse or former spouse following separation or divorce.

ambiguous loss When a family member is physically absent but psychologically present, the family experiences highly stressful feelings. People need to find ways to accept a loss before they can move on through the grieving process, but this is difficult when there is significant ambiguity in the situation. *See also* boundary ambiguity.

amniotic sac The membrane that encloses the fetus and holds the amniotic fluid, which insulates the fetus.

androgen Any of the hormones that develop and maintain male secondary sex characteristics.

anorgasmia A sexual dysfunction that prevents a woman from having an orgasm.

appreciation and affection One of the six major qualities (commonly found in emotionally healthy families) identified by researchers working within the family strengths framework.

arranged marriage *See* parent-arranged marriage.

assertive communication A style of interpersonal communication that involves expressing one's self-interests and wishes without degrading or putting down the other person.

assertiveness A person's ability to express her or his feelings and desires.

assimilation Adopting the cultural traits and values of the dominant culture.

attentive listening A style of listening focused on fully understanding the speaker's point of view; characterized by encouragement rather than trying to direct or control the speaker.

authoritarian parenting A parenting style characterized by the demand for absolute obedience to rigid rules and the use of punitive, forceful disciplinary measures.

autonomic power pattern A power pattern in a marriage in which both partners have about equal authority but in different areas of life; both make decisions in their particular domains independent of each other.

avoidance A person's tendency to minimize issues and a reluctance to deal with issues directly.

avoidance style A style of conflict resolution characterized by nonassertive and passive behavior; avoiders often withdraw from the conflict or change the subject.

B

balanced families Families who fit into the four central categories of the Couple and Family Map: families who are flexibly connected, flexibly cohesive, structurally connected, or structurally cohesive. *See also* midrange families; unbalanced families.

bankruptcy The state of being financially insolvent or unable to pay one's bills.

barrier methods of contraception Devices that prevent pregnancy by physically blocking the sperm from entering the uterus, including condoms, diaphragms, and cervical caps.

behaviorist A clinician who, based on learning theories, has developed practical, positive ways of dealing with children's behavior; rather than focusing on punishment, behaviorists encourage "accentuating the positive." *See also* reinforcement.

belief system One of the four major components of the sociocultural context in which families live, centering on religious/spiritual/ethical beliefs and other ideas about how to live successfully and happily in the world. *See also* extended-family system; family system; social system.

bidirectional effects Both the influence of the child on the parent and the influence of the parent on the child; child development specialists and family scientists concur that studying these effects is important to an understanding of parent–child dynamics.

bilateral descent A method of tracing the lineage of children equally through ancestors of both mother and father.

binuclear family A postdivorce family in which both parents participate in the raising of their children despite living in separate households; the children generally reside with one of the parents.

bisexual Sexual orientation toward members of both sexes.

blamer A person whose style of anger management is characterized by a short temper, emotionally intense responses to stress, and the belief that others are responsible for her or his feelings and problems.

blastocyst An early stage of the fertilized egg, containing about 100 cells; implants itself in the uterine lining (endometrium).

blended family A term used to describe a stepfamily. Some researchers object to the term because it creates unrealistic expectations that the new family will quickly and easily "blend" together harmoniously and because it assumes a homogeneous unit, one without a previous history or background. *See also* stepfamily.

boomerang kids Adult children who come back to their parents' home to live as a result of divorce, job loss, or an inability to make it in the "real world."

boundaries The lines that both separate systems from and connect systems to each other. The notion of a boundary implies a hierarchy of interconnected systems, each larger than the one before it.

boundary ambiguity Lack of clarity about whether a person is either in or out of the family system; related to family stress levels. The concept includes two variables: physical and psychological presence or absence. High ambiguity (conflicting variables) produces high levels of stress.

brainstorming A conflict resolution strategy that involves thinking of as many solutions to a problem as possible.

breast-feeding Feeding a baby from the mother's breast rather than from a bottle; usually better than bottle-feeding for the physical well-being of the baby.

budgeting The regular, systematic balancing of income and expenses.

C

Caring Cluster One of two groups of characteristics that distinguish romantic relationships from friendships; includes being an advocate for one's partner and giving the utmost. *See also* Passion Cluster.

case study A detailed description of a person or a family that illustrates a specific idea, concept, or principle of family science.

catharsis conflict The false belief that venting anger verbally prevents physical violence. Researchers who study family violence have found that verbal and physical violence are related.

centrifugal interaction Behavior that pushes system components away from one another, decreasing the system's connectedness.

centripetal interaction Behavior that pulls system components toward one another, resulting in the system's increasing connectedness.

cervical cap A thimble-shaped contraceptive device that fits snugly over the cervix; must be fitted by a physician and used with a spermicide.

cesarean section (C-section) Surgical delivery of the fetus by incising the mother's abdominal and uterine walls.

child abuse The physical or mental injury, sexual abuse, or negligent treatment of a child under the age of 18 by a person who is responsible for the child's welfare.

child-free alternative The decision by married or cohabiting adults not to have children.

child-to-parent abuse Violence directed at a parent by a child.

circular causality model An interpersonal communication model that describes an interaction pattern in which both parties view their behavior as a reaction to the other's behavior rather than as something for which they are each responsible. The first person sends out a message that causes a change in and a response from the second person. That response causes a new response in the first person, whose response initiates another response from the second person, and so on. This type of communication cycle can escalate into conflict.

closed system A family system that has the capacity to maintain the status quo and avoids change; also called a *morphostatic system*.

closure The resolution of an issue.

cluttered nest The period during which young adults return to their parental home until they are established professionally and financially and can move into an apartment or home of their own.

coculture A distinct cultural or social group living within a dominant culture but also having membership in another culture, such as gay men and lesbians.

cognitive development theory A model of child development that views growth as the mastery of specific ways of perceiving, thinking, and doing; growth occurs at discrete stages.

cohabitation Two unrelated adults sharing the same living quarters.

cohesion *See* family cohesion.

collaborative style A style of conflict resolution characterized by a high degree of assertiveness about reaching one's own goals coupled with a concern for the other person.

collective worldview The group is viewed as more important than the individual.

commitment Attachment to another. One of the six major qualities (commonly found in emotionally healthy families) identified by researchers working within the family strengths framework; also, the cognitive component of Sternberg's three dimensions of love.

communication The way humans create and share meaning, both verbally and nonverbally; the foundation for developing and maintaining human relationships, especially intimate relationships. *See also* family communication; positive communication.

community divorce One of Bohannan's six different but overlapping experiences of divorce; involves changes in friendships and community relationships.

companionate love A type of love relationship characterized by commitment and intimacy but lacking intense passion; common between partners who have been together for many years.

competitive style A style of conflict resolution characterized by aggression, lack of cooperation, pursuit of personal concerns at the expense of the other, and the desire to "win" at all costs.

competitive symmetry A style of communication in which partners attempt to control the situation and the other by escalating the level of hostilities in a competitive manner.

complementary interaction A style of communication in which the partners adopt two different tactics: One is dominant and one is submissive. *See also* symmetrical interaction.

complementary needs theory The supposition that people are attracted to partners whose personalities

differ from but complement their own. Family researchers have not found much support for this theory.

complex stepfamily A stepfamily that includes children from both parents. *See also* simple stepfamily.

compromise style A style of conflict resolution characterized by a willingness to give up something to resolve an issue.

conception The union of a sperm cell and the nucleus of an ovum (egg), which begins the development of the fetus; also called *fertilization*.

conceptual framework A set of interconnected ideas, concepts, and assumptions that helps organize thinking from a particular perspective. The field of family science includes a variety of major conceptual frameworks: family systems theory (or the family systems framework), the family strengths framework, the family development framework, the symbolic interaction framework, the social construction framework, and the feminist framework.

condom A rubber sheath placed over the penis before intercourse to prevent pregnancy and protect against sexually transmitted diseases.

conflicted couple A type of premarital and married couple characterized by few relationship strengths, low levels of relationship satisfaction, and a high risk of divorce.

conjugal family system A family consisting of a husband, a wife, and children; also called a *nuclear family*.

consanguineal family system A family system that emphasizes blood ties more than marital ties.

constructive intimacy games Games, or exercises, designed to increase intimacy in a relationship; people participate voluntarily, and they know the rules and goals of the game. *See also* destructive intimacy games.

consummate love A type of love relationship characterized by commitment, intimacy, and passion.

contraception A deliberate action (use of a device, drug, or technique) taken to prevent conception (pregnancy).

contractions Tightenings of the muscles, especially those of the uterus, during labor.

convenience A type of cohabiting relationship in which one partner takes and the other gives. A relationship of convenience is usually based on sexual, caretaking, economic, or social needs rather than on love.

coparental divorce One of Bohannan's six different but overlapping experiences of divorce; involves decisions about custody of the children, single parenting, and visitation rights for the noncustodial parent.

coparenting A style of parenting in which both parents take on tasks and roles traditionally associated with only the mother or the father.

Couple and Family Map A graphic representation of dynamic relationships within families, comprising three central dimensions: cohesion (togetherness), flexibility (ability to change), and communication (a facilitating dimension that helps families move between the extremes on the cohesion and flexibility dimensions). Identifies 16 types of family relationship.

couple-arranged marriage Freedom of choice in marriage. This approach is sometimes referred to as the *love match*, though love is not always the goal of marriage in Western industrialized societies. *See also* parent-arranged marriage.

crisis-loss stage of grief A period of chaotic shock; the first of Brubaker's three stages of the grieving process. *See also* new-life stage of grief; transition stage of grief.

cross-cultural family study A research study focused on how cultural context influences family issues, among them, values and behaviors, courtship and marriage patterns, communication, roles, work and the family, childrearing patterns, and sexuality.

cross-validation A comparison of the results from one research method with those of another research method to see if the findings are similar or identical.

cultural competence The ability to be effective in working with a variety of cultural groups. This ability involves awareness, knowledge, and skills.

cultural group A set of people who embrace core beliefs, behaviors, values, and norms and transmit them from generation to generation.

cultural identity A feeling of belonging that evolves from the shared beliefs, values, and attitudes of a group of people; the structure of the group's marital, sexual, and kinship relationships.

curvilinear relationship Researchers have found that the relationship between stress and effective outcomes for people is curvilinear—both too much and too little stress are problematic for individual and family functioning, but moderate levels of stress are usually positive.

D

dance of anger Lerner's metaphor to describe styles of managing anger and ways in which these styles interact.

dating A form of courtship involving a series of appointed meetings for social interaction and activities during which an exclusive relationship may evolve between two people. Also called *individual-choice courtship*.

definition of the situation The concept that a situation is based on a person's subjective interpretation; hence, people can have different views of the same situation.

delivery The second stage of labor, lasting from the time the cervix is completely dilated until the fetus is expelled or removed by cesarean section.

democratic parenting A parenting style that establishes the parents' legitimate power to set rules while also recognizing the child's feelings, individuality, and need to develop autonomy; uses positive reinforcement, seldom punishment, to enforce standards. Also called *authoritative parenting*.

Depo-Provera (DMPA) A progestin that is administered by injection.

destructive intimacy games Games that reduce intimacy because people are often unaware of the game, do not voluntarily participate, and are often manipulated to behave in certain ways. *See also* constructive intimacy games.

devitalized couple The unhappiest type of married couple; characterized by few couple strengths and the highest risk for divorce.

diaphragm A cup-shaped rubber contraceptive device that is inserted in the vagina before intercourse to cover the cervical opening and block sperm from entering the uterus; must be fitted by a physician and used with a spermicide.

dilation and curettage (D & C) An abortion technique used in the second trimester of pregnancy; performed in a hospital under general anesthetic. After the cervix is dilated (opened), the embryo is removed from the uterus with a sharp instrument (curette).

dilation and evacuation (D & E) An abortion technique used in the second trimester of pregnancy. Suction and forceps are used to remove the embryo or fetus.

DINS dilemma Inhibited or hypoactive sexual desire in couples with many demands on their time. DINS stands for double income, no sex.

directive listening A style of listening in which the listener attempts to control the direction of the conversation through the use of questions.

distancer An individual who (1) wants emotional space when stress is high, (2) is self-reliant rather than a help-seeker, and (3) values privacy.

distress Feelings of discomfort caused by high levels of stress.

divorce culture The notion that divorce has become so accepted in the United States that it is almost expected as the outcome of marriage.

double bind A situation in which the message relayed by the speaker calls into question the type of relationship the receiver has with the speaker.

double standard Different standards of appropriate sexual and social behavior for the two sexes; the belief that premarital sex is more acceptable for males than for females.

E

ecology The study of how all the organisms in a system relate to one another.

economic divorce One of Bohannan's six different but overlapping experiences of divorce; involves the division of money and property and the establishment of two separate economic units.

egalitarian roles Social equality between the sexes; equal sharing of practical responsibilities and decision making by men and women. Also called *equalitarian roles.*

ejaculatory incompetence A sexual dysfunction that prevents a man from ejaculating in his partner's vagina despite a firm erection and a high level of sexual arousal.

emancipation A type of cohabiting relationship based on the desire to break free of parental values and influence rather than on love.

emic perspective The analysis of a society from the inside. *See also* etic perspective.

emotional divorce One of Bohannan's six different but overlapping experiences of divorce; involves the deterioration of the marriage and the breakdown of bonding and communication, which are replaced by feelings of alienation.

empty love A type of love relationship involving commitment but no passion or intimacy.

empty-nest syndrome Feelings of malaise, emptiness, and lack of purpose that some parents experience when their last child leaves home. *See also* spacious nest.

endogamy The practice of choosing a mate from within one's own ethnic, religious, socioeconomic, or general age group.

enjoyable time together One of the six major qualities (commonly found in emotionally healthy families) identified by researchers working within the family strengths framework.

ENRICH A comprehensive marital inventory containing 125 questions in categories that are relevant to married couples and their satisfaction with their relationship. ENRICH is an acronym for **EN**riching **R**elationship **I**ssues, **C**ommunication, and **H**appiness.

episiotomy A surgical incision from the vagina toward the anus, performed to prevent tearing of the perineum during child-birth.

erectile dysfunction A sexual dysfunction in which a man has difficulty achieving or maintaining penile erection that is firm enough for intercourse.

estrogen Although often called the *female hormone,* any of a group of hormones, produced primarily by the ovaries, that are significant in controlling female physiological functions and directing the development of female secondary sex characteristics at puberty.

ethnic group A set of people who are embedded within a larger cultural group or society and who share beliefs, behaviors, values, and norms that are transmitted from generation to generation.

ethnic identity The geographic origin of a minority group within a country or culture; cultural identity transcends ethnic identity.

ethnocentrism The assumption that one's own culture is the standard by which to judge other cultures.

etic perspective The analysis of a society from the outside. *See also* emic perspective.

eustress A moderate-to-high level or a low-to-moderate level of stress that is energizing, motivating, positive, and healthy.

exogamy The practice of choosing a mate from outside one's own group.

expressive role According to Parson and Bales's model of the modern family, the wife-mother's role—caring for the emotional well-being of the family, providing nurturing and comfort. *See also* instrumental role.

extended family A nuclear family and those related to its members by blood, such as aunts, uncles, cousins, and grandparents.

extended-family system One of the four major components of the sociocultural context in which families live; focuses on the degree of importance relatives outside the nuclear family have on the family's life. *See also* belief system; family system; social system.

F

family Two or more people who are committed to each other and who share intimacy, resources, decision-making responsibilities and values; people who love and care for each other.

family cohesion The togetherness or closeness of a family; one of the three dimensions of the Couple and Family Map.

family communication Interaction; sharing of thoughts and feelings; the facilitating dimension of the Couple and Family Map.

family coping A family's ability to manage stressful events or situations as a unit with minimal or no detrimental effects on any individual members.

family coping resources Resources of a healthy family system on which the family can draw in times of stress, including cohesion, adaptability, and a willingness to adopt nontraditional family roles in the face of changing economic circumstances. *See also* personal coping resources.

family development framework A conceptual framework that focuses on how family members deal with roles and developmental tasks within the family unit as they move through the stages of the life cycle.

family flexibility A family's ability to change and adapt in the face of stress or crisis; one of the three dimensions of the Couple and Family Map.

family of origin The family in which a person is raised during childhood.

family power The ability of one family member to change the behavior of the other family members.

family science An interdisciplinary field whose primary focus is to better understand families in order to enhance the quality of family life. Professionals whose main focus of applied or action research is the family tend to call themselves *family scientists;* those who develop educational programs for families sometimes call themselves *family life educators* or *family educators*; those who work clinically with troubled families are called *marriage* (or *marital*) *and family therapists*.

family strengths framework A conceptual framework proposing that if researchers study only family problems, they will find only problems in families, but that if they are interested in family strengths, they must study strong families; identifies six qualities that strong families commonly demonstrate: commitment, appreciation and affection, positive communication, enjoyable time together, spiritual well-being, and the ability to manage stress and crisis effectively.

family system One of the four major components of the sociocultural context in which families live; focuses on the interconnectedness of family members. *See also* belief system; extended-family system; social system.

family systems theory (or family systems framework) A conceptual framework that views everything that happens to any family member as having an impact on everyone else in the family, because family members are interconnected and operate as a group, or family system.

family therapy An approach to helping families; based on the belief that the roots of an individual's problems may be traced to troubled family dynamics, and solutions can come by working with the whole family.

fatuous love A type of love relationship in which commitment is based on passion but in which there has not yet been time to develop true intimacy.

femininity A gender-linked constellation of personality traits and behavioral patterns traditionally associated with females in a society.

feminist framework A conceptual framework that emphasizes the value of women's perspectives on society and the family, that recognizes women's subordination, and that promotes change in that status.

feminization of poverty The statistical fact that the percentage of female single parents in the total percentage of those who are poor in the United States has increased.

fertility awareness A variety of contraceptive methods based on predicting a woman's fertile period and avoiding intercourse during that interval (or using an additional method of contraception during that time).

fertilization The union of a sperm cell and the nucleus of an ovum (egg); also known as *conception.*

fetal alcohol syndrome (FAS) Serious malformations (particularly of the facial features and the eyes) seen in children whose mothers drank excessively during their pregnancy.

flexibility *See* family flexibility.

G

gender The learned characteristics and behaviors associated with biological sex in a particular culture. *See also* sex.

gender identity A person's internal sense of being female or male, which is expressed in personality and behavior.

gender role The traits and behaviors assigned to males and females in a culture.

gender-role stereotype A rigid, simplistic belief about the distinctive psychological characteristics and behavioral patterns attributable to a man or woman based exclusively on sex.

general systems theory A set of principles and concepts that can be applied to all types of systems, living and nonliving.

goals Specific, achievable objectives or purposes.

gunnysacking An alienating ("dirty") fighting tactic in which a person saves up unresolved grievances until he or she explodes, resulting in a major confrontation.

H

harmonious couple A type of premarital and married couple characterized by many couple strengths, relationship satisfaction, and a low risk of divorce.

heterosexual Sexual orientation toward members of the other sex.

HIV *See* human immunodeficiency virus.

homogamy The tendency to marry someone of the same ethnic group, educational level, socioeconomic status, religion, and values.

homosexual Sexual orientation toward members of the same sex.

human ecosystem A model showing how various human subsystems interrelate among each other. To really understand a specific family system, one also needs to consider the various system levels it influences and that influence it.

human immunodeficiency virus (HIV) The virus that causes AIDS.

husband-dominant power pattern A power pattern in a marriage in which the man is the boss.

hypothesis An assertion subject to verification or proof; a presumed relationship between variables.

hysterotomy A relatively rare surgical method of abortion, performed in the late second trimester of pregnancy, in which a cesarean section is performed to remove the fetus.

I

idiographic approach A theoretical approach that focuses on the study of individuals and individual differences. *See also* nomothetic approach.

incest taboo The nearly universal societal prohibition of intercourse between parents and children and between siblings.

incongruity humor Humor that points out things in life that don't fit together logically; a tool for couples and families who want to "fight fair."

individualistic worldview The individual is viewed as more important than the group.

induced labor A method of abortion performed in the late second trimester, generally in a hospital, in which a saline solution or prostaglandins are injected into the amniotic sac to cause the woman's body to expel the fetus.

infatuation A type of love relationship characterized by passion and lacking both intimacy and commitment.

insider perspective How people inside the family describe their relationships. *See also* outsider perspective.

instrumental role According to Parson and Bales's model of the modern family, the husband-father's role—being the breadwinner, the manager, and the leader of the family. *See also* expressive role.

interdependence of parts A characteristic of systems; the parts or elements of a system are interconnected in such a way that if one part is changed, other parts are automatically affected.

intimacy Sharing intellectually, physically, and/or emotionally with another person; the emotional component of Sternberg's three dimensions of love.

intimacy need fulfillment The satisfaction one receives from having personal needs fulfilled.

intimate experience An experience in which one feels close to another or shares oneself in one area of life, such as intellectually, socially, emotionally, or sexually.

intimate relationship A partnership involving an emotional bond between two people, with proven mutual commitment and trust, that provides personal and relationship security and rewards; a relationship in which one shares intimate experiences in several areas of life over time, with expectations that this sharing will continue.

intrauterine device (IUD) A contraceptive device inserted by a physician into a woman's uterus to prevent conception from occurring.

J

jealousy The condition of being resentful and suspicious of a rival.

joint custody A legal child custody arrangement following a divorce in which children divide their time between the homes of both parents, with both homes having equal importance: "one child, two homes."

K

kinship The relatedness of certain individuals within a group. Cultures have norms and expectations that structure and govern kin behavior.

L

labor The stages of delivering a baby, consisting of contractions of the uterine muscles and dilation of the cervix, the birth itself, and the expulsion of the placenta.

learned helplessness theory A theory that a learned passivity develops from giving power over oneself to another; that passivity increases helplessness, reduces problem-solving abilities, and limits options.

learning theories Approaches to understanding human development that focus on how people learn to behave the way they do.

legal divorce One of Bohannan's six different but overlapping experiences of divorce; involves the dissolution of the marriage by the legal system and the courts.

liking A type of love relationship characterized by intimacy but lacking passion and commitment.

lineage Line of descent, influenced by cultural norms. Lineage determines membership in a kinship group, patterns of inheritance, and kinship obligations or responsibilities. *See also* matrilineal society; patrilineal society.

linear causality model An interpersonal communication model that assumes a direct, or linear, relationship between cause and effect.

Linus blanket A type of cohabiting relationship in which one of the partners is so dependent or insecure that he or she prefers a relationship with anyone to being alone.

longevous marriage A long-term marriage that lasts 50 years or more.

looking-glass self The idea that you learn about yourself based on the feedback you receive from others.

M

male menopause Physical changes in men related to age, similar to those that occur in women during menopause.

managing stress Pauline Boss's alternative to the phrase *coping with stress*; individual family members' use of their own resources to help their family deal with a stressor or work through a crisis.

marriage An emotional and legal commitment between two people to share emotional and physical intimacy, various tasks, and economic resources.

masculinity A gender-linked constellation of personality traits and behavioral patterns traditionally associated with males in a society.

masturbation Self-stimulation of the genitals; also called *autoeroticism*.

mating gradient The tendency of women to marry men who are better educated or more successful than they are.

matriarchal group A group in which the mother or eldest female is recognized as the head of the family, kinship group, or tribe. Descent is traced through this woman.

matrilineal society A society in which descent, or lineage, is traced through females.

matrilocal society A society that encourages newly married couples to live with or near the wife's kin, especially her mother's kinship group.

menopause The cessation of ovulation, menstruation, and fertility in women as a result of aging.

menses The menstrual flow in which the endometrial tissue is discharged.

menstruation The discharge from the uterus through the vagina of blood and the unfertilized ova; occurs about every 28 days in nonpregnant women between puberty and menopause.

metacommunication Communicating about communicating.

middle age Generally speaking, the years between the ages of 35 and 65; from the standpoint of the family development conceptual framework, the middle years of the family life cycle are the launching period for young-adult children and the period before the parents' retirement.

midlife crisis A period of questioning one's worth, values, and contributions in life, usually beginning in a person's 40s or early 50s.

midrange families Families who are extreme on one dimension of the Couple and Family Map but balanced on the other dimension. There are eight midrange family types. For example, a family might be structurally enmeshed: extreme on cohesion (enmeshed) but balanced on flexibility (structured). *See also* balanced families; unbalanced families.

midwife A nonphysician who attends and facilitates a birth.

minority group A social group that differs from the rest of the population in some ways and that often experiences discrimination and prejudice.

miscarriage The termination of a pregnancy from natural causes before the fetus is viable outside of the mother (during the first or second trimester of pregnancy).

mixed message A message in which there is a discrepancy between the verbal and the nonverbal components: The receiver hears one thing but simultaneously feels something else.

mixed-methods research This is a type of study in which family researchers use both qualitative and quantitative research techniques, thus benefiting from the strengths of both approaches to research.

monogamy A relationship in which a man or a woman has only one mate.

morning sickness Nausea experienced by many women during the first trimester of pregnancy, often but not exclusively in the morning.

morphogenic system A system that is open to growth and change; also called an *open system.*

morphostatic system A system that has the capacity to maintain the status quo, thus avoiding change; also called a *closed system.*

multiple system levels General systems theory holds that systems are embedded within other systems, layer upon layer.

multiracial marriage Marriage between people from two different cultural or ethnic groups.

mutual dependency A relationship in which each person wants and needs the other person.

N

negative feedback Information or communication that is intended to minimize change in a system.

neutralized symmetry A style of communication in which partners respect each other, approach each other as equals, and avoid exerting control over each other.

new-life stage of grief The period during which the bereaved establishes a new lifestyle and exhibits to society and himself or herself that he or she can live satisfactorily as a single person; the last of Brubaker's three stages of the grieving process. *See also* crisis-loss stage of grief; transition stage of grief.

no-fault divorce Divorce laws that do not place blame (fault) for the divorce on either spouse. One party's assertion that irreconcilable differences exist is sufficient grounds for dissolving the marriage.

nomothetic approach A theoretical approach that focuses on developing a theory that works for a great number of cases. Researchers using this approach believe it is possible to develop a general family theory. *See also* idiographic approach.

non-love A type of love relationship characterized by the absence of commitment, intimacy, and passion.

nonverbal communication The communication of emotions by means other than words, such as touch, body movement, facial expression, and eye contact.

Norplant The trade name of a contraceptive implant placed under the skin on the inside of a woman's upper arm; releases the hormone progestin.

nuclear family A kinship group in which a husband, a wife, and their children live together in one household; also called a *conjugal family system.*

O

old age Arbitrarily defined as beginning at age 65, which coincides for most people with retirement.

open system A family system that is open to growth and change; also called a *morphogenic system.*

oral contraceptives Birth control pills taken by mouth that contain hormones that suspend ovulation and thus prevent conception.

organic sexual dysfunction Impairment of the ordinary physical responses of sexual excitement or orgasm as the result of physical or medical factors, such as illness, injury, or drugs.

organismic theory Developed by Jean Piaget and expanded by later theorists, a theory of child development emphasizing that children's minds develop through various stages and that children think very differently from adults; sees child-thought as primitive and mystical, with logical reasoning developing slowly into adulthood.

outsider perspective How researchers or therapists perceive a family, in contrast with how family members perceive the family. *See also* insider perspective.

overfunctioner An individual who knows what is best not only for herself or himself but for everybody else as well; they cannot let others solve their problems themselves.

oviduct In the female reproductive system, one of a pair of tubes through which ova (eggs) travel from an ovary to the uterus. Also called *fallopian tube*.

ovulation The regular monthly release in the female of one or more eggs from an ovary.

P

painful intercourse A sexual dysfunction characterized by intense discomfort during sex; experienced by both women and men and often related to physical problems with the sex organs.

parent-arranged marriage A practice, common in non-industrialized societies, in which the parents of the bride and groom select the future spouse and arrange the marriage ceremony. Based on the principle that the elders in a community have the wisdom to select an appropriate spouse, this type of marriage generally extends existing family units rather than creating new units. *see also* couple-arranged marriage.

parent education A lecture-and-discussion format for small or large groups of parents that is aimed at helping them learn how to raise children successfully.

parental control The degree of flexibility exhibited by a parent in terms of enforcing rules and disciplining her or his child(ren).

parental support The amount of caring, closeness, and affection a parent exhibits or gives to his or her child(ren).

partner dominance The degree to which a person feels her or his partner tries to be controlling and dominant in their relationship.

passion Intense physiological arousal; the motivational component of Sternberg's three dimensions of love.

Passion Cluster One of two groups of characteristics that distinguish romantic relationships from friendships; includes fascination, sexual desire, and exclusiveness. *See also* Caring Cluster.

passive–aggressive behavior Feigning agreement or acting as if everything is okay but later becoming hostile or aggressive; an indirect way of expressing anger.

passive communication A style of interpersonal communication characterized by an unwillingness to say what one thinks, feels, or wants.

patriarchal group A group in which the father or eldest male is recognized as the head of the family, kinship group, or tribe. Descent is traced through this man.

patrilineal society A society in which descent, or lineage, is traced through males.

patrilocal society A society that encourages newly married couples to live with or near the husband's kin, especially his father's kinship group.

permissive parenting A style of parenting in which the parents (1) permit the child's preferences to take over their ideals and (2) rarely force the child to conform to their standards.

permissiveness The extent to which couples are physically intimate before marriage.

personal coping resources Qualities that help people deal with stressors across the life cycle, such as an individual's self-esteem and mastery (confidence in personal abilities). *See also* family coping resources.

personification The belief that everything one's partner does is a reflection on oneself; leads to attempts to control the partner's behavior.

persuasive listening A style of listening in which the "listener" is looking only for an opportunity to take over and control the direction of the conversation.

placenta A vascular organ that joins the fetus with the mother's uterus and through which the fetus receives nutrients and discharges wastes; expelled in the final stage of labor, following the birth of the baby.

plural marriage A marriage in which a man has more than one wife (polygyny) or a woman has more than one husband (polyandry).

polyandry A plural marriage in which a woman has more than one husband.

polygamy A marriage in which a man or a woman has more than one mate; a plural marriage.

polygyny A plural marriage in which a man has more than one wife.

positive communication One of the six major qualities (commonly found in emotionally healthy families) identified by researchers working within the family strengths framework.

positive feedback Information or communication that is intended to create change in a system.

postmodernism A belief system that emphasizes multiple perspectives or "truths." Postmodernists are extremely skeptical in regard to questions of truth, meaning, and historical interpretation. No objective, universal truth can be seen, once and for all, and readily agreed upon. Instead, there is only a collection of subjective truths shaped by the particular subcultures in which we live. These multiple subjective truths are constantly competing for our attention and allegiance.

postpartum depression A feeling of depression after giving birth, characterized by irritability, crying, loss of appetite, and difficulty sleeping; thought to be a result of the many physiological changes that occur after delivery.

posttraumatic stress disorder (PTSD) A severe stress reaction characterized by the reexperiencing of past traumatic events.

power The ability of an individual in a social system to change the behavior of other members of the system through will, influence, or control.

prejudice Negative judgment or opinion having no or limited basis in fact; hostility to a person or a group based on physical characteristics.

premature ejaculation A sexual dysfunction in which a man is unable to control his ejaculation reflex voluntarily and reaches orgasm sooner than he or his partner wishes.

PREPARE A comprehensive premarital inventory that assesses a couple's relationship and determines how idealistic or realistic each person is in regard to marriage, how well the couple communicates, and how well the couple resolves conflicts and financial issues; acronym for **PRE**-marital **P**ersonal **A**nd **R**elationship **E**valuation.

problem drinking Alcohol consumption that results in functional disability.

progestin A hormone connected with pregnancy and contained in oral contraceptives.

pseudo–kin group A type of kinship group in which relationships resembling kinship ties develop among "unrelated" individuals.

pseudomutuality A false sense of togetherness.

psychodynamic theory Developed by Freud and his followers, a theory of human development that emphasizes the importance of providing a positive emotional environment during early childhood, when the foundation for later life is laid down.

psychological divorce One of Bohannan's six different but overlapping experiences of divorce; involves the regaining of individual autonomy.

psychosocial sexual dysfunction Impairment of the ordinary physical responses of sexual excitement or orgasm as a result of psychological, developmental, interpersonal, environmental, or cultural factors.

pursuer An individual who wants a very high degree of togetherness and expression of feelings in a relationship.

Q

qualitative research Qualitative research in the field of family science tends to focus on family members' perceptions of their world and how they live in it. Data are recorded in the form of words and stories that the family members tell. These verbal or written perceptions are analyzed by researchers looking for common themes that explain the processes of life in families.

quantitative research Quantitative research in the field of family science reduces family members' attitudes and behaviors to numbers that can be analyzed using statistical methods. Rather than work with the words and stories collected in qualitative investigations, quantitative researchers work with data that are numerical.

quid pro quid A strategy for negotiating differences in which one person gets to do what he or she wants in exchange for doing something another person requests; "this for this."

quid pro quo A strategy for negotiating differences in which one person agrees to do something in exchange for the other person's agreement to do something else of equal value or importance; "this for that."

R

race A group of people with similar and distinctive physical characteristics.

racism Discrimination or prejudice based on the belief that people's physical characteristics determine their human capacities and behaviors and that groups of people with certain characteristics are inferior to others.

rapid orgasm A sexual dysfunction in which a woman consistently reaches orgasm sooner than she or her partner wishes; the counterpart of premature ejaculation in the male.

rapport The process of communication in which two people develop understanding and a sense of closeness.

reinforcement Rewarding desired behavior to increase the likelihood that it will be repeated.

rejecting parenting A style of parenting in which parents pay little attention to their children's needs and set few or no expectations for their children's behavior.

remarriage A marriage in which one or both partners marry following divorce or the death of a spouse; in this book, remarriage refers to couples who have never been married to each other before.

representative sample A random selection of individuals who accurately reflect the characteristics of a particular group.

research study Careful, systematic, and patient investigation in a field of knowledge to establish facts or principles, test hypotheses, or better understand processes.

resource theory of family power A theory that the balance of power in a marriage is related to the relative resources (especially money, level of education, and occupational prestige) each spouse has in the relationship.

retarded ejaculation A sexual dysfunction in which prolonged and strenuous effort is needed to reach orgasm.

role The expected behavior of a person or group in a given social category, such as husband, wife, supervisor, or teacher.

role making The process of creating new roles or revising existing roles.

role taking The process whereby people learn how to play roles correctly by practicing and getting feedback from others.

romantic love A type of love relationship characterized by intimacy and passion but lacking commitment.

routinization A situation, often encountered in middle age, in which one's job lacks the challenge it once offered and becomes boring.

S

sandwich generation Parents, usually in their 50s and older, who are simultaneously responsible for child rearing and for caring for their own aging parents; individuals who are "caught in the middle" between two generations.

segregation Isolation of an ethnic group within the dominant culture.

self-confidence A measure of how a person feels about herself or himself and the ability to control things in her or his life.

self-disclosure Revealing to another person personal information or feelings that that individual could not otherwise learn.

self-revelation The disclosing of personal information about oneself.

sex Being biologically male or female; also, sexual activity or behavior. *See also* gender.

sex educator A trained teacher who provides information and principles about sex and sexuality, generally in a group setting.

sex ratio The relationship between the number of men and the number of women of a given age.

sex therapist A trained individual who teaches and counsels clients individually, in pairs, or in small groups about sex and sexuality.

sex therapy A process of education and counseling designed to help people overcome sexual problems.

sexual dysfunction A state in which one's sexual behavior or lack of it is a source of distress; any malfunction of the human sexual response that inhibits the achievement of orgasm, either alone or with a partner.

sexual orientation A person's self-identification as a heterosexual, homosexual, bisexual, or transgender.

sexuality The set of beliefs, values, and behaviors by which one defines oneself as a sexual being.

sibling abuse Physical violence between siblings; probably the most common form of abuse of children.

SIDS *See* sudden infant death syndrome.

simple stepfamily A stepfamily that includes children from only one parent. *See also* complex stepfamily.

singlehood The state of being unmarried, divorced, or unattached to another person.

social construction framework A conceptual framework that proposes that human beings are profoundly immersed in the social world and that our understanding of this world and beliefs about this world are social products.

social environment All the factors, both positive and negative, in society that impact individuals and their relationships, such as mass media, the Internet, changing gender roles, and growing urban crowding.

social learning theory A psychological theory of development that focuses on learning through observation, imitation, and reinforcement.

social system One of the four major components of the sociocultural context in which families live; encompasses the influence of the community, laws, economic resources, educational opportunities, and other external factors on the family. *See also* belief system; extended-family system; family system.

sole custody A child custody arrangement following a divorce in which only one parent has legal and physical custody of the child or children; the other parent generally has visitation rights.

spacious nest A positive descriptive term for the time in a marriage when the children have left home. *See also* empty-nest syndrome.

sperm The male reproductive cells produced by the testes.

spermicide A contraceptive substance (gel, cream, foam, or vaginal insert) that is toxic to sperm; usually used with a barrier device; may protect against certain sexually transmitted diseases.

spiritual well-being One of the six major qualities (commonly found in emotionally healthy families) identified by researchers working within the family strengths framework.

split custody A legal child custody arrangement following a divorce in which each parent has sole custody of one or more of the children.

STD *See* sexually transmitted disease.

stepfamily The family created when one or both partners in a marriage have a child or children from a previous marriage. *See also* blended family.

stepparent An adult who is married to one's biological parent but who is not one's birth parent.

Stepping Ahead Program An eight-step program designed to build strengths in stepfamilies.

stereotype A standardized, oversimplified, often foolish and mean-spirited view of someone or something.

sterilization Any procedure, but usually a surgical one, by which an individual is made incapable of reproduction.

stress The nonspecific response of the body to any demand made upon it.

stress pileup The occurrence and after-effects of several stresses within a short period of time, which can strain an individual's or a family's coping abilities.

stressor An external event that causes an emotional and/or a physical response and that can precipitate a crisis.

submissive symmetry A style of communication in which each participant tries to give control of the situation, and responsibility for it, to the other.

subsystem In the general systems theory, a small system that is part of a larger suprasystem.

sudden infant death syndrome (SIDS) The sudden, unexpected death of an infant, which cannot be explained by postmortem examination or tests.

suprasystem In the general systems theory, a large system that incorporates smaller subsystems.

symbolic interaction framework A conceptual framework that focuses on the internal perceptions of family members and examines how they learn roles and rules in society through interaction and shared meaning.

symmetrical interaction A style of communication in which partners send similar messages designed to control how the relationship is defined. *See also* complementary interaction.

syncratic power pattern A power pattern in a marriage in which both partners share authority equally and make decisions jointly.

system A set of interconnected components that form a whole; what happens to one component affects all the other components.

T

tender years doctrine The legal presumption under traditional divorce laws that young children would do better with their mother than with their father after a divorce.

testing A type of cohabiting relationship undertaken as a trial in a situation closely resembling marriage.

theory Systematically organized knowledge applicable in a wide variety of circumstances; especially, a system of assumptions, accepted principles, and rules of procedure devised to analyze, predict, or otherwise explain the nature or behavior of a specified set of phenomena.

traditional couple A type of premarital and married couple characterized by some external strengths (such as religion and friends) but fewer internal strengths (such as communication and conflict resolution skills).

transgender An individual who believes that he or she is a victim of a biologic accident that occurred before birth and has been living within a body incompatible with his or her real gender identity. A majority of transgender persons are biologic males who identify themselves as females, usually early in childhood.

transition stage of grief The period during which the bereaved's grief lessens and he or she begins to recognize that a new life is possible; the second of Brubaker's three stages of the grieving process. *See also* crisis-loss stage of grief; new-life stage of grief.

trimester One of three periods of about 3 months each into which pregnancy is divided.

tubal ligation A female sterilization procedure in which the oviducts (fallopian tubes) are cut or tied and sealed.

U

umbilical cord A flexible structure that connects the fetus to the placenta and through which nutrients pass to the fetus and waste products are discharged.

unbalanced families Families who fall at the extremes on both the flexibility and the cohesion dimensions of the Couple and Family Map: chaotically enmeshed, chaotically disengaged, rigidly enmeshed, or rigidly disengaged, families. *See also* balanced families; mid-range families.

uncontested divorce Under traditional divorce law, a divorce in which one party would charge the other party with an infraction that was considered by the court as grounds for granting a divorce and the accused party would agree not to challenge the accuser in court. In many cases, parties were forced to collude and to perjure themselves in order to divorce.

underfunctioner An individual who is too highly flexible and disorganized and becomes less competent under stress.

uninvolved parenting A style of parenting in which parents ignore their children and let them do what they wish unless it interferes with the parents' activities.

V

vacuum aspiration An abortion method, used during the first trimester of pregnancy, in which the uterine contents are removed by suction.

vaginismus A sexual dysfunction in which a womans' vaginal muscles involuntarily constrict, preventing intercourse.

validation The process of ensuring that a research instrument measures what it is intended to measure.

vasectomy A male sterilization procedure in which the vasa deferentia are severed and tied.

victimizer One who victimizes others. Children who grow up with violence often learn the potential for victimizing others as adults.

vitalized couple A type of premarital and married couple characterized by many couple strengths, high marital satisfaction, and a low risk of divorce.

vulva The external female genital organs.

W

wholeness A characteristic of systems; general systems theorists believe that the whole is more than the sum of its parts.

wife-dominant power pattern A power pattern in a marriage in which the woman is the boss.

Z

zero-sum game A game in which one side's margin of victory equals the other side's margin of defeat, producing a final sum of zero; what one person wins, the other loses.

zygote The fertilized ovum (egg).

Photo Credits

References

AARP. (1999). The Modern Maturity sexuality study. Web site: http://www.aarp.org/mmaturity/sept_oct99/greatsex.html.

AARP. (2005). Sexuality at midlife and beyond. Web site: http://www.aarp.org.

Abbott, D. A., & Meredith, W. H. (1988). Characteristics of strong families: Perceptions of ethnic parents. *Home Economics Research Journal, 17*(2), 140–147.

ABC News–Washington Post. (2001, January 11–15). Poll: Views about abortion. Cited in T. Raum. Associated Press (2001, January 23). Bush's early gamble: The new president will find it hard to finesse the thorny issue of abortion. Lincoln [NE] *Journal Star,* p. 5A.

Abma, J. C., Martinez, G. M., Mosher, W. D., & Dawson, B. S. (2004, December). Teenagers in the United States: Sexual activity, contraceptive use, and childbearing, Series 23, Number 24. Washington, DC: Centers for Disease Control and Prevention.

Abortion foes vow to fight: Maryland's governor OKs abortion-rights law. (1991, February 19). Lincoln [NE] *Journal Star,* p. 2.

Addis, M. E., & Mahalik, J. R. (2003). Men, masculinity, and the context of help seeking. *American Psychologist, 58*(1), 5–14.

Adler, N. E., David, H. P., Major, B. N., Roth, S. H., Russo, N. F., & Wyatt, G. E. (1992). Psychological factors in abortion: A review. *American Psychologist, 47,* 1194–1204.

Adler, N. E., Ozer, E. J., & Tschann, J. (2003, March). Abortion among adolescents. *American Psychologist,* 211–217.

Administration for Children and Families. (2003). Child maltreatment 2001. U.S. Department of Health and Human Services. Washington, DC: http://www.acf.hhs.gov/programs/cb/publications/cm01/index.htm.

Administration for Children and Families. (2004). Child maltreatment 2002. U.S. Department of Health and Human Services. Washington, DC: http://www.acf.hhs.gov.programs/cb/publications/cm02/chapterthree.htm.

Administration for Children and Families. (2007). The Healthy Marriage Initiative. Web site: http://www.acf.hhs.gov/healthymarriage/about/mission.html#ms.

AFL-CIO and the Institute for Women's Policy Research. (1999). Equal pay for working families: National and state data. http://www.aflcio.org/issuepolitics/women/equalpay/EqualPayForWorkingFamilies.cfm.

Ahlburg, D. A., Jensen, E. R., & Perez, A. E. (1997). Determinants of extramarital sex in the Philippines. *Health Transition Review,* Suppl. to Vol. 7, pp. 467–479.

Ahrons, C. R. (2003). *The binuclear family study 1979–2000.* Harvard University, The Radcliffe Institute for Advanced Study, Murray Research Center.

Ahrons, C. R. (2004). *We're still family: What grown children have to say about their parents' divorce.* New York: HarperCollins.

Ahrons, C. R. (2006, May/June). Long-term effects of divorce on children. *Family Therapy Magazine,* pp. 24–27.

Ahrons, C. R., & Rodgers, R. H. (1987). *Divorced families: A multidisciplinary view.* New York: Norton.

Alan Guttmacher Institute. (1999). *Teenage pregnancy: Overall trends and state-by-state information* (Table 1). New York: Author.

Alan Guttmacher Institute. (2000). *Induced abortion.* New York: Author (http://www.agi-usa-org/pubs/fb_induced_abortion.html).

Alan Guttmacher Institute. (2002). Teen pregnancy: Trends and lessons learned. *The Guttmacher Report on Public Policy, 5*(1), 2.

Aldous, J. (1998). Public policy and grandparents: Contrasting perspectives. In M. E. Szinovacz (Ed.), *Handbook on grandparenthood* (pp. 230–246). Westport, CT: Greenwood.

Allen, K. R., Blieszner, R., & Roberto, K. A. (2000). Families in the middle and later years: A review and critique of research in the 1990s. *Journal of Marriage and the Family, 62*(4), 911–926.

Allen, W. D., & Olson, D. H. (2001). Five types of African-American marriages based on ENRICH. *Journal of Marital and Family Therapy, 27*(3), 301–314.

Allgeier, E. R., & Allgeier, A. R. (2000). *Sexual interactions: Basic understandings* (6th ed.). Boston: Houghton Mifflin.

Alliance for Children and Families. (2004). 11700 West Lake Park Drive, Milwaukee, WI 53224-3099: http://www.info@alliance1.org.

Altura, J. (1974). Poem. In J. Gillies, *My needs, your needs.* New York: Doubleday.

Amato, P. R. (2003). Reconciling divergent perspectives: Judith Wallerstein, quantitative family research, and children of divorce. *Family Relations: Interdisciplinary Journal of Applied Family Studies, 52*(4), 332–339.

Amato, P. R., & Booth, A. (1996). A prospective study of divorce and parent–child relationships. *Journal of Marriage and the Family, 58,* 356–365.

Amato, P. R., & Booth, A. (1997). *A generation at risk: Growing up in an era of family upheaval.* Cambridge, MA: Harvard University Press.

Amato, P. R., & Booth, A. (2001). The legacy of parents' marital discord: Consequences for children's marital quality. *Journal of Personality and Social Psychology, 81*(4), 627–638.

Amato, P. R., & Previti, D. (2003). People's reasons for divorcing: Gender, social class, the life course, and adjustment. *Journal of Family Issues, 24*(5), 602–626.

American Association for Marriage and Family Therapy. (2004). Infidelity. Web site: http://www.aamft.org/families/Consumer_Updates/Infidelity.asp.

American Association of Family and Consumer Sciences. (2004). 1975 definition of families. Cited in AAFCS Call for 2004 Program Proposals, 2. Web site: http://www.aafcs.org.

American Association of Homes and Services for the Aging. (2004). Nursing home statistics. Web site: http://www.aahsa.org/public/backgrd1.htm.

American Heritage Dictionary of the English Language (4th ed.). (2000). Boston: Houghton Mifflin.

American Psychological Association. (2004). *Resolution on sexual orientation, parents and children.* Web site: www.apa.org/pi/lgbc.

amFAR AIDS Research. (2004). Global initiatives. Web site: http://www.amfar.org/cgi-bin/iowa/programs/globali/record.html?record=87.

Anderson, J. R., & Doherty, W. J. (2005). Democratic community initiatives: The case of overscheduled children. *Family Relations, 54,* 654–665.

Arias, E., Anderson, R. N., Kung, H., Murphy, S. L., & Kochanek, K. D. (2004). Deaths: Final data for 2001. *National Vital Statistics Reports, 50*(15). Hyattsville, MD: National Center for Health Statistics. Web site: http://www.cdc.gov/nchs/data/nvsr/nvsr52/nvsr52_03.pdf.

Arias, E., & Smith, B. L. (2003). Deaths: Preliminary data for 2001. *National Vital Statistics Reports, 52*(3), 21. Hyattsville, MD: National Center for Health Statistics. Web site: www.cdc.gov.

Arias, I., & Pape, K. T. (1999). Psychological abuse: Implications for adjustment and commitment to leave violent partners. *Violence and Victims, 14*(1), 55–67.

Arond, M., & Pauker, S. L. (1987). *The first year of marriage.* New York: Warner Books.

Asai, S. G. (2004). Culturally sensitive adaptation of PREPARE with Japanese premarital couples. *Journal of Marital and Family Therapy, 30*(4), 411–426.

Asai, S. G., & Olson, D. H. (2004). *National couple abuse study.* Roseville, MN: Life Innovations. Web site: http://lifeinnovations.com.

Avenevoli, S., Sessa, F. M., & Steinberg, L. (1999). Family structure, parenting practices, and adolescent adjustment. In E. M. Hetherington (Ed.), *Coping with divorce, single parenting and remarriage* (pp. 65–90). Mahwah, NJ: Erlbaum.

Axtell, R. G. (1999). *Do's and taboos of humor around the world: Stories and tips from business and life.* New York: Wiley.

Azar, S. T., & Bober, S. L. (1999). Children of abusive parents. In W. K. Silverman & T. O. Ollendick (Eds.), *Developmental issues in the clinical treatment of children* (pp. 371–392). Needham Heights, MA: Allyn & Bacon.

Azar, S. T., & Gehl, K. S. (1999). Physical abuse and neglect. In R. T. Ammerman et al. (Eds.), *Handbook of prescriptive treatments for children and adolescents* (2nd ed., pp. 329–345). Needham Heights, MA: Allyn & Bacon.

Baca-Zinn, M. (1995). Social science theorizing for Latino families in the age of diversity. In R. E. Zambrana (Ed.), *Understanding Latino families: Scholarship, policy, and practice* (Vol. 2, pp. 177–189). Thousand Oaks, CA: Sage.

Bach, G., & Wyden, P. (1969). *The intimate enemy: How to fight fair in love and marriage.* New York: Morrow.

Bachman, H. J., & Chase-Lansdale, P. L. (2005). Custodial grandmothers' physical, mental, and economic well-being: Comparisons of primary caregivers from low-income neighborhoods. *Family Relations, 54,* 475–487.

Bailey, S. J. (2003). Challenges and strengths in nonresidential parenting following divorce. *Marriage and Family Review, 35*(1/2), 59–80.

Baldry, A. C. (2003). Animal abuse and exposure to interpersonal violence in Italian youth. *Journal of Interpersonal Violence, 18*(3), 258–281.

Baldwin, S. E., & Baranoski, M. V. (1990). Family interactions and sex education in the home. *Adolescence, 25,* 573–582.

Bámaca, M. Y., Umaña-Taylor, A. J., Shin, N., & Alfaro, E. C. (2005). Latino adolescents' perception of parenting behaviors and self-esteem: Examining the role of neighborhood risk. *Family Relations, 54,* 621–632.

Barry, E. (2007, February). Eagerness and some resignation as Civil Union Law takes effect. *The New York Times.* Web site: http://www.nytimes.com/2007/02/20/nyregion/20civil.html.

Barta, P. L. (2001). Blended families: How to make sense of your new stepfamily. *In Touch.* Missoula, MT: APS Healthcare.

Barth, J. C. (2004). Grandparents dealing with the divorce of their child: Tips for grandparents and therapists. *Contemporary Family Therapy: An International Journal, 26*(1), 41–44.

Bateson, G., Jackson, D. D., Haley, J., & Weakland, J. (1956). Toward a theory of schizophrenia. *Behavioral Science, 1,* 251–264.

Bateson, M. C. (1994). *Peripheral visions.* New York: HarperCollins.

Batson, C. D., Qian, Z., & Lichter, D. T. (2006). Interracial and intraracial patterns of mate selection among

America's diverse Black population. *Journal of Marriage and the Family, 68*, 658–672.

Bauer, J. W., & Wollen, B. J. (1990). *Financial management extension consultant program: Young singles and young couples.* St. Paul: Minnesota Extension Service.

Baumrind, D. (1991). The influence of parenting style on adolescent competence and substance abuse. *Journal of Early Adolescence, 11*(1), 56–95.

Baumrind, D. (1995). *Child maltreatment and optimal caregiving in social contexts.* New York: Garland.

Baumrind, D. (1996). The discipline controversy revisited. *Family Relations, 45*, 405–414.

Baumrind, D. (2004). Publications. Institute of Human Development Web site: http://ihd.berkeley.edu/baumpub.htm.

Bauserman, R. (2002). Child adjustment in joint-custody versus sole-custody arrangements: A meta-analytic review, *Journal of Family Psychology, 16*(1), 23–35.

BBC News. (2004, November 16). STUC urges gender pay gap action. Web site: http://news.bbc.co.uk/go/pr/fr/-/2/us_news/scotland/4013675.stm.

Bean, R. A., Barber, B. K., & Crane, D. R. (2006). Parental support, behavioral control, and psychological control among African American youth. *Journal of Family Issues, 27*(10), 1335–1355.

Becvar, D. S., & Becvar, R. J. (2006). *Family therapy: A systematic integration* (6th ed.). Boston: Pearson/Allyn & Bacon.

Beers, M. H. (Ed.). (2003). *The Merck manual of medical information.* Whitehouse Station, NJ: Merck Research Laboratories.

Beers, M. H. (Ed.). (2007). Intimacy and dating. Web site: http://www.merck.com/pubs/mmanual_ha/contents.html.

Bell, R. Q. (1977). *Child effects on adults.* Hillsdale, NJ: Erlbaum.

Belsky, J., & Hsieh, K. H. (1998). Patterns of marital change during the early childhood years: Parent personality, coparenting and division-of-labor correlates. *Journal of Family Psychology, 12*(4), 511–528.

Belsky, J., & Kelly, J. (1994). *The transition to parenthood: How a first child changes a marriage: Why some couples grow closer and others apart.* New York: Delacorte.

Bem, S. L. (1995). Dismantling gender polarization and compulsory heterosexuality: Should we turn the volume down or up? *Journal of Sex Research, 32*(4), 329–334.

Bent-Goodley, T. B. (2005). An African-centered approach to domestic violence. *Families in Society, 86*, 197–206.

Bepko, C., & Johnson, T. (2000). Gay and lesbian couples in therapy: Perspectives for the contemporary family therapist. *Journal of Marital and Family Therapy, 26*(4), 409–419.

Berger, R., & Hannah, M. T. (1999). *Preventive approaches in couples therapy.* Philadelphia: Brunner/Mazel.

Bergeron, L. R. (2002). Family preservation: An unidentified approach in elder abuse protection. *Families in Society, 83*(5/6), 547–556.

Berkow, R. (Ed.). (1997). *The Merck manual of medical information: Home edition.* White House Station, NJ: Merck Research Laboratories.

Bernard, J. (1970). Women, marriage, and the future. *Futurist, 4*, 41–43.

Bernard, J. (1972). *The future of marriage.* New York: World.

Bernstein, R. (2005). Texas becomes the nation's newest "majority–minority" state, Census Bureau announces. News Release CB05-118. Web site: http://www.census.gov/Press-Release.

Berscheid, E. (1999). The greening of relationship science. *American Psychologist, 54*(4), 260–266.

Berscheid, E. (2006). Seasons of the heart. In M. Mikulincer & G. S. Goodman (Eds.), *Dynamics of romantic love: Attachment, caregiving, and sex* (pp. 404–422). New York: Guilford.

Berscheid, E., & Reis, H. T. (1998). Attraction and close relationships. In D. T. Gilbert, S. T. Fiske, & G. Lindzey (Eds.), *The handbook of social psychology* (4th ed., pp. 193–281). New York: McGraw-Hill.

Bhopal, K. (1997). South Asian women within households: Dowries, degradation and despair. *Women's Studies International Forum, 20*(4), 489–492.

Bierstedt, R. (1950). An analysis of social power. *American Sociological Review, 6*, 7–30.

Billingsley, A. (1986). *Black families in White America.* Englewood Cliffs, NJ: Prentice Hall.

Billingsley, A. (1992). *Climbing Jacob's ladder: The ending legacy of African-American families.* New York: Touchstone.

Binner, J. M., & Dnes, A. W. (2001). Marriage, divorce, and legal change: New evidence from England and Wales. *Economic Inquiry, 39*(2), 298–306.

Binson, D., Michaels, S., Stall, R., Coates, T. J., Gagnon, J. H., & Catania, J. A. (1995). Prevalence and social distribution of men who have sex with men: United States and its urban centers. *Journal of Sex Research, 32*(3), 245–254.

Biracial couples find more tolerance. (2001, July 6). Lincoln [NE] *Journal Star,* p. 5A.

Bissell, M. (2000). Socio-economic outcomes of teen pregnancy and parenthood: A review of the literature. *Canadian Journal of Human Sexuality, 9*(3), 191–204.

Blackman, L., Clayton, O., Glenn, N., Malone-Colon, L., & Roberts, A. (2005). *The consequences of marriage for African Americans: A comprehensive literature review.* New York: Institute for American Values.

Blackwell, D. L., & Lichter, D. T. (2000). Mate selection among married and cohabiting couples. *Journal of Family Issues, 21*(3), 275–302.

Blaisure, K. (2005, May/June). Separation and divorce. *Family Therapy Magazine,* pp. 10–13.

Blankenhorn, D. (1999, December 6). Fatherhood on the rebound. *Christianity Today,* pp. 70–71.

Blankenhorn, D. (2004). About David Blankenhorn. American Values.org Web site: http://www.americanvalues.org/htmolabout_david_blankenhorn.html.

Blood, R. O., & Wolfe, D. M. (1960). *Husbands and wives.* Glencoe, IL: Free Press.

Blow, A. J., & Hartnett, K. (2005). Infidelity in committed relationships II: A substantive review. *Journal of Marital and Family Therapy, 31,* 217–233.

Bock, J. D. (2000). Doing the right thing? Single mothers by choice and the struggle for legitimacy. *Gender and Society, 14*(1), 62–86.

Bohannan, P. (1970). The six stations of divorce. In P. Bohannan (Ed.), *Divorce and after* (pp. 29–55). New York: Doubleday.

Bold, M. (2004). Boomerang kids. University of North Texas, Center for Parent Education. Web site: http://www.unt.edu/cpe/module1/blk5boom.htm.

Boonstra, H. (2000). Promoting contraceptive use and choice: France's approach to teen pregnancy and abortion. *The Guttmacher Report on Public Policy, 3*(3).

Borcherdt, B. (1996). *Head over heart in love: 25 guides to rational passion.* Sarasota, FL: Professional Resource Press.

Borcherdt, B. (2000). *You can control your anger! 21 ways to do it.* Sarasota, FL: Professional Resource Press.

Borders, L. D., Penny, J. M., & Portnoy, F. (2000). Adult adoptees and their friends: Current functioning and psychosocial well-being. *Family Relations, 49,* 407–418.

Bornstein, R. F. (2006). The complex relationship between dependency and domestic violence. *American Psychologist, 61,* 595–606.

Boss, P. (1988). *Family stress management.* Newbury Park, CA: Sage.

Boss, P. (1992). Primacy of perception in family stress theory and measurement. *Journal of Family Psychology, 6*(2), 113–119.

Boss, P. (1999). *Ambiguous loss: Learning to live with unresolved grief.* Cambridge, MA: Harvard University Press.

Boss, P. (2001). *Family stress management* (2nd ed.). Newbury Park, CA: Sage.

Boss, P. (2002). *Family stress management.* Thousand Oaks, CA: Sage.

Boss, P. (2006). *Loss, trauma, and resilience: Therapeutic work with ambiguous loss.* Dunmore, PA: Norton.

Boston Women's Health Book Collective. (1998). *Our bodies, ourselves for the new century: A book by and for women.* New York: Touchstone/Simon & Schuster.

Boulding, K. (1985). *Human betterment.* Beverly Hills, CA: Sage.

Bowen, G. L., Pittman, J. F., Pleck, J. H., Haas, L., & Voydanoff, P. (Eds.). (1995). *The work and family interface: Toward a contextual effects perspective.* Minneapolis: National Council on Family Relations.

Brandeis University Institute for Health Policy. (1993). Substance abuse: The nation's number one health problem. Cited by National Council on Alcoholism and Drug Dependence: http://www.ncadd.org.

Brandeis University Institute for Health Policy. (2001). Substance abuse: The nation's number one health problem. Cited by National Council on Alcoholism and Drug Dependence: http://www.ncadd.org.

Brick, P., & Taverner, B. (2001). *Positive images: Teaching abstinence, contraception, and sexual health* (3rd ed.). Morristown, NJ: Planned Parenthood of Greater Northern New Jersey.

Broderick, C. B. (1992). *Marriage and the family* (4th ed.). Englewood Cliffs, NJ: Prentice Hall.

Broderick, C. B. (1993). *Understanding family process: Basics of family systems theory.* Newbury Park, CA: Sage.

Brown, E. (2000b). Working with marital affairs: Learning from the Clinton triangles. In L. Vandecreek & T. L. Jackson (Eds.), *Innovations in clinical practice: A source book* (Vol. 18, pp. 471–478). Sarasota, FL: Professional Resource Press/Professional Resource Exchange.

Brown, K. G. (2003). Perceived parental authority style and the quality of father–child and stepfather–stepchild relationships. *Dissertation Abstracts International-A, 63*(11), 4091.

Brown University Center for Alcohol and Addiction Studies. (2000). Position paper on drug policy. Physician Leadership on National Drug Policy. Cited by National Council on Alcoholism and Drug Dependence: http://www.ncadd.org.

Browning, R. (1970). Grow old along with me! In I. Jack (Ed.), *Browning: Poetical works.* Oxford, UK: Oxford University Press. (Original work published 1864.)

Brubaker, T. H. (Ed.). (1990). *Family relationships in later life* (2nd ed.). Newbury Park, CA: Sage.

Bruce, M. L. (2002). Psychosocial risk factors for depressive disorders in late life. *Biological Psychiatry, 52*(3), 175–184.

Bryan, A. A. (1998). *Facilitating couple relationships during the transition to parenthood.* Unpublished doctoral dissertation, University of Wisconsin, Eau Claire, Department of Family Health Nursing.

Buchanan, C. M., & Heiges, K. L. (2001). When conflict continues after the marriage ends: Effects of postdivorce conflict on children. In J. H. Grych & F. D. Fincham (Eds.), *Interparental conflict and child development: Theory, research, and applications* (pp. 337–362). New York: Cambridge University Press.

Buchanan, C. M., Maccoby, E. E., & Dornbusch, S. M. (1996). *Adolescents after divorce.* Cambridge, MA: Harvard University Press.

Buckingham, M., & Clifton, D. O. (2005). *Now, discover your strengths.* Lincoln, NE: Gallup Press.

Bulcroft, K., & O'Conner-Roden, M. (1986, June). Never too late. *Psychology Today,* pp. 66–69.

Bumpass, L. (1999, March). (Interviewed by Nadya Labi.) A bad start: Living together may be the road to divorce. *Time,* p. 61.

Bumpass, L., & Lu, H. H. (1998). *Trends in cohabitation and implications for children's family contexts.* Unpublished manuscript, University of Wisconsin, Madison, Center for Demography.

Bumpass, L., & Lu, H. H. (2000a). Cohabitation: How the families of U.S. children are changing. *Focus, 21*(1), 5–8.

Bumpass, L., & Lu, H. H. (2000b). Trends in cohabitation and implications for children's family contexts in the United States. *Population Studies, 54,* 29–41.

Burgess, E. W., & Wallin, P. (1943). Homogamy in social characteristics. *American Journal of Sociology, 49*(2), 109–124.

Burr, W. R., Day, R. D., & Bahr, K. S. (1993). *Family science.* Pacific Grove, CA: Brooks/Cole.

Burr, W. R., & Klein, S. R. (1994). *Reexamining family stress.* Thousand Oaks, CA: Sage.

Buss, D. M., Shackelford, T. K., Kirkpatrick, L. A., & Larsen, R. J. (2001). A half century of mate preferences: The cultural evolution of values. *Journal of Marriage and the Family, 63,* 491–503.

Byrne, D. (1983). Sex without contraception. In D. Byrne & W. A. Fisher (Eds.), *Adolescents, sex, and contraception.* Hillsdale, NJ: Erlbaum.

Caldwell, J., Du Bois, B., Erickson, J., Goins, R., Hillabrant, W., Kendall, E., et al. (2005). Culturally competent research with American Indians and Alaska Natives. *American Indian and Alaska Native Mental Health Research: The Journal of the National Center, 12,* 1–21.

Cameron, S. C., & Wycoff, S. M. (1998). The destructive nature of the term race: Growing beyond a false paradigm. *Journal of Counseling and Development, 76,* 277–285.

Caplin, J., & McGirt, E. (2004, August 1). Ephrata, Washington pays for the war: A small town's National Guard soldiers trained hard for duty in Iraq. No one trained their families for the financial burden of their absence. *Money.* Web site: www.guardfamily.org/A00_admin/A0017_news%5Chtm%5CNYCU_07_12_2004.htm#Homefront_dealing_with_deployment.

CardWeb.com. (2004). Median net worth. Survey of consumer finances. Web site: http://www.CardWeb.com.

Carp, F. M. (2000). *Elder abuse in the family: An interdisciplinary model for research.* New York: Springer.

Carson, D. K., Dail, P. W., Greeley, S., & Kenote, T. (1990). Stresses and strengths of Native American reservation families in poverty. *Family Perspective, 24*(4), 383–400.

Carter, B., & McGoldrick, M. (1999). *The expanded family life cycle: Individual, family, and social perspectives* (3rd ed.). Boston: Allyn & Bacon.

Castro, R. (2001). "When a man is with a woman, it feels like electricity": Subjectivity, sexuality and contraception among men in central Mexico. *Culture, Health and Sexuality, 3*(2), 149–165.

Caughy, M. O., O'Campo, P. J., Nettles, S. M., & Lohrfink, K. F. (2006). Neighborhood matters: Racial socialization of African American children. *Child Development, 77,* 1220–1236.

Cavedo, C., & Guerney, B. G. (1999). Relationship enhancement, enrichment and problem prevention. In R. Berger & M. T. Hannah (Eds.), *Preventive approaches in couple therapy* (pp. 73–105). Philadelphia: Brunner/Mazel.

Centers for Disease Control and Prevention. (2004a). Actual causes of death in the United States, 2000. National Center for Chronic Disease Prevention and Health Promotion. Web site: http://www.cdc.gov/nccdphp/factsheets/death_causes2000.htm.

Centers for Disease Control and Prevention. (2004b). Targeting tobacco use: The nation's leading cause of death. National Center for Chronic Disease Prevention and Health Promotion. Web site: http://www.cdc.gov/nccdphp/aag/aag)_osh.htm.

Centers for Disease Control and Prevention. (2004c, May 21). Youth risk behavior surveillance—United States, 2003. *Morbidity and Mortality Weekly Report, 53*(SS-2).

Centers for Disease Control and Prevention. (2005). Injury and violence. Web site: http://222.cdc.gov.

Centers for Disease Control and Prevention. (2006). *HIV/AIDS Surveillance Report, 2005.* Atlanta: Author. Web site: http://www.cdc.gov/hiv/topics/surveillance/resources/reports.

Chamberlin, J. (2005). "A critical time " for LGB research. *Monitor in Psychology, 36,* 84–85.

Chapman, M., & Perreira, K. (2005). The well-being of immigrant Latino youth: A framework to inform practice. *Families in Society, 86,* 104–111.

Chase-Lansdale, P. L., Cherlin, A. J., & Kiernan, K. E. (1995). The long-term effects of parental divorce on the mental health of young adults: A developmental perspective. *Child Development, 66,* 1614–1634.

China Internet Information Center. (2004, June 4). Liu Dalin and his sex museum. Web site: http://www.china.org.cn/english/NM-e/97295htm.

China.Org.CN. (2001). Extramarital sex top threat to marriage; and Unfaithful husband sentenced to prison. Web site: http://www.china.org.cn.

Christopher, F. S. (2001). *To dance the dance: A symbolic interactional exploration of premarital sexuality.* Mahwah, NJ: Erlbaum.

Chu, K. (2006, December 15). How to escape card debt. *USA Today,* p. 3B.

Cicirelli, V. G. (2001). Intergenerational decision making by mother and adult child: Effects of adult child gender and age of dyad. *The Gerontologist, 41*(1), 12.

Cicirelli, V. G. (2003). Caregiving decision making by older mother and adult child: Process and expected outcome. *The Gerontologist, 43*(1), 364.

Cinotto, S. (2006). "Everyone would be around the table": American family mealtimes in historical perspective, 1850–1960. In R. W. Larson, A. R. Wiley, & K. R. Branscomb (Eds.), *Family mealtimes as a context of development and socialization* (pp. 17–34). San Francisco: Jossey-Bass.

Clark, R., Anderson, N. B., Clark, V. R., & Williams, D. R. (1999). Racism as a stressor for African Americans. *American Psychologist, 54*(10), 805–816.

Claxton-Oldfield, S. (2000). Deconstructing the myth of the wicked stepparent. *Marriage and Family Review, 30*(1–2), 51–58.

Clift, E. (1992, July 13). Abortion angst: How the court's ruling will affect women, doctors and activists on both sides. *Newsweek*, pp. 16–19.

Cole, C. L., & Broussard, J. (2006, May/June). The social context and history of divorce in the U.S. *Family Therapy Magazine*, pp. 6–9.

Cole, W., Dickerson, J. F., & Smilgis, M. (1994, October 17). Now for the truth about Americans and sex: The first comprehensive survey since Kinsey smashes some of our most intimate myths. *Time*, pp. 62–70.

Coleman, M., & Ganong, L. H. (2004). *Handbook of contemporary families: Considering the past, contemplating the future.* Thousand Oaks, CA: Sage.

Coleman, M., Ganong, L., & Fine, M. (2000). Reinvestigating remarriage: Another decade of progress. *Journal of Marriage and the Family, 62*(4), 1288–1307.

Coles, R. L. (2003). Black single custodial fathers: Factors influencing the decision to parent. *Families in Society: The Journal of Contemporary Human Services, 84*(2), 247–258.

Coley, R. L., & Chase-Lansdale, P. L. (1998). Adolescent pregnancy and parenthood: Recent evidence and future directions. *American Psychologist, 53*(2), 152–166.

Connidis, I. A., & McMullin, J. A. (1999). Permanent childlessness: Perceived advantages and disadvantages among older persons. *Canadian Journal on Aging, 18*, 447–465.

Cook, R., & DeFrain, J. (2005). Using discourse analysis to explore family strengths: A preliminary study. *Marriage and Family Review, 38*(1), 3–12.

Coontz, S. (2005). *Marriage, a history: From obedience to intimacy or how love conquered marriage.* New York: Viking.

Cooper, M. L. (2002). Alcohol use and risky sexual behavior among college students and youth: Evaluating the evidence. *Journal of Studies of Alcohol, 14*, 101–117.

Cowan, C. P. (1996). Becoming parents: What has to change for couples? In C. F. Clulow (Ed.), *Partners become parents.* Northvale, NJ: Aronson.

Cowley, G. (1989, March 13). How the mind was designed: Evolutionary theory is yielding rich new insights into everything from cognition to sexual desire. *Newsweek*, pp. 56–58.

Crockenberg, S. C. (2003). Rescuing the baby from the bathwater: How gender and temperament (may) influence how child care affects child development. *Child Development, 74*(4), 1034–1038.

Crosby, J. F. (1991). *Illusion and disillusion: The self in love and marriage.* Belmont, CA: Wadsworth.

Csikszentmihalyi, M. (1999). If we are so rich, why aren't we happy? *American Psychologist, 54*(10), 821–827.

Cummins, H. J. (2001). *Advice for those experiencing ambiguous loss.* Minneapolis: Minneapolis Star and Tribune.

Dahl, T. (1980). *Model of stress.* Unpublished manuscript University of Minnesota, Minneapolis.

Dailard, C. (2001). Sex education: Politicians, parents, teachers and teens. *The Guttmacher Report, 4*(1).

Danes, S. (1992). Parental perceptions of children's financial socialization. In R. Imas (Ed.), *Proceedings of the Association for Financial Counseling and Planning Education* (pp. 16–35). Charleston, SC: Association for Financial Counseling and Planning Education.

Darkwa, O. (2004). Social welfare services for the aged. Chicago: University of Illinois. Web site: http://www.uic.edu/classes/socw/socw550/AGING/sld001.htm.

Davis, K. E. (1985, February). Near and dear: Friendship and love compared. *Psychology Today, 19*, 22–30.

Davis, K. E. (2004). *Love's many faces apprehended.* Washington, DC: American Psychological Association.

Davis, K. E. (2007). Professional profile. Web site: http://keith.davissocialpsychology.org.

Dawson, D. A., & Grant, B. F. (1998). Family history of alcoholism and gender: Their combined effects on DSM-IV alcohol dependence and major depression. *Journal of Studies on Alcohol, 59*(1), 97–106.

Dee, T. S. (2001). The effects of minimum legal drinking ages on teen childbearing. *Journal of Human Resources 36*(4), 824–838.

Deen, M. R. (2005, June). Family values reconsidered. *Family Focus*, pp. 5–6.

Deets, H. B. (1996). Aging in America: A women's issue. Workshop on social protection, poverty, and older persons at risk, American Association of Retired Persons and UN/ECE. Web site: http://www.unece.org/spot/deets.htm.

DeFrain, J. (1999). Strong families around the world. *Family Matters: Journal of the Australian Institute of Family Studies, 53*, 6–13.

DeFrain, J. (2006). *Family treasures: Creating strong families.* Lincoln, NE: University of Nebraska Press.

DeFrain, J., & Asay, S. (Eds.). (2007). *Strong families around the world: The family strengths perspective.* New York: Haworth.

DeFrain, J., Ernst, L., Jakub, D., & Taylor, J. (1991). *Sudden infant death: Enduring the loss.* New York: Lexington Books/Macmillan.

DeFrain, J., Ernst, L., & Nealer, J. (1997). The family counselor and loss. In J. R. Woods, Jr. (Ed.), *Loss in pregnancy or the neonatal period: Principles of care with clinical cases and analyses* (pp. 499–520). Pitman, NJ: Jannetti.

DeFrain, J., Fricke, J., & Elmen, J. (1987). *On our own: A single parent's survival guide.* Lexington, MA: Lexington Books/Heath.

DeFrain, J., Martens, L., Stork, J., & Stork, W. (1986). *Stillborn: The invisible death.* Lexington, MA: Lexington Books/Heath.

DeFrain, J., Millspaugh, E., & Xie, X. (1996). The psychosocial effects of miscarriage: Implications for health professionals. *Families, Systems, and Health: Journal of Collaborative Family Health Care, 14*(3), 331–347.

DeFrain, J., & Stinnett, N. (2002). Family strengths. In J. J. Ponzetti et al. (Eds.), *International encyclopedia of marriage and family* (2nd ed.). New York: Macmillan Reference Group.

DeLuccie, M. (1995). Mothers as gatekeepers: A model of maternal mediators of father involvement. *Journal of Genetic Psychology, 156*(1), 115–131.

DeNavas-Walt, C., Proctor, B., & Lee, C. (2006). Income, poverty, and health insurance coverage in the United States: 2005. *Current population reports.* Washington, DC: Government Printing Office.

DePaulo, B. (2004, November 21). Singles shall overcome. Web site: http://www.unmarriedamerica.org/News-About-Us/singles_shall_overcome.htm.

DiCenso, A., Guyatt, G., Willan, A., & Griffith, L. (2002). Interventions to reduce unintended pregnancies among adolescents: Systematic review of randomized controlled trials. *British Medical Journal, 324*(7351), 1426–1430.

Dick-Read, G. (1984). *Childbirth without fear: The original approach to natural childbirth.* New York: Harper & Row. (Original work published 1932.)

Dienhart, A. (2001). Make room for daddy: The pragmatic potentials of the tag-team structure for sharing parenting. *Journal of Family Issues, 22*(8), 973–999.

Dindia, K. (2000). Self-disclosure, identity, and relationship development: A dialectic perspective. In K. Dindia & S. Duck (Eds.), *Communication and personal relationships* (pp. 147–162). New York: Wiley.

Dinger, M. K., & Parsons, N. (1999). Sexual activity among college students living in residence halls and fraternity or sorority housing. *Journal of Health Education, 30*(4), 242–246.

Dingfelder, S. (2006). Violence in the home takes many forms. *Monitor in Psychology, 37,* 18.

Dirie, W. (1998). *Desert flower.* New York: Morrow.

Divorce rate climbs among middle-aged Chinese. (2004, February 1). *The Epoch Times.* Web site: http//www.asianresearch.org/articles/1846.htm.

Divorce rate on the increase in Shanghai. (2004, December 16). *Shanghai Daily.* Web site: http://www.china.org.cn/english/Life/115127.htm.

Dobson, J. C. (1999). *Love must be tough: New hope for families in crisis.* Nashville: Word.

Doherty, W. J. (1997). *The intentional family. How to build family ties in our modern world.* Reading, MA: Addison-Wesley.

Doherty, W. J. (2000). *Take back your kids.* Notre Dame, IN: Sorin Books.

Doherty, W. J. (2001). *Take back your marriage: Sticking together in a world that pulls us apart.* New York: Guilford.

Doherty, W. J., & Allen, W. (1994). Family functioning and parental smoking as predictors of adolescent cigarette use: A six-year prospective study. *Journal of Family Psychology, 8*(3), 347–353.

Doherty, W. J., & Anderson, J. R. (2004). Community marriage initiatives. *Family Relations, 53,* 425–432.

Doherty, W. J., Erickson, M. F., & LaRossa, R. (2006). An intervention to increase father involvement and skills with infants during the transition to parenthood. *Journal of Family Psychology, 20*(3), 438–447.

Doherty, W. J., Kouneski, E. F., & Erickson, M. F. (1998). Responsible fathering: An overview and conceptual framework. *Journal of Marriage and the Family, 60*(2), 277–292.

Doherty, W. J., & Simmons, D. S. (1996). Clinical practice patterns of marriage and family therapists: A national survey of therapists and their clients. *Journal of Marital and Family Therapy, 22,* 9–25.

Dolbin-MacNab, M. L. (2006). Just like raising your own? Grandmothers' perceptions of parenting a second time around. *Family Relations, 55,* 564–575.

Downs, B. (2003). *Fertility of American women: June 2002.* Current Population Reports, P20-548. Washington, DC: U.S. Bureau of the Census.

Duke, J. T. (1999, March 6). Mormon family life and cohabitation. Reported by Bob Mims, *Salt Lake Tribune.*

Duly, A. (2003). Consumer spending for necessities. *Consumer Expenditure Survey Anthology,* pp. 35–38.

Duvall, E. M. (2001). Evelyn Duvall's life. *Marriage and Family Review, 32*(1/2), 7–23.

Duvander, A.-Z. E. (1999). The transition from cohabitation to marriage: A longitudinal study of the propensity to marry in Sweden in the early 1990s. *Journal of Family Issues, 20*(5), 698–717.

Educational Fund to Stop Gun Violence. (2005). Issues and campaigns. Web site: http://www.csgv.org.

Einstein, A. (1988). Cosmic religion. In L. D. Eigen & J. P. Siegel (Eds.), *The Macmillan dictionary of political quotations.* New York: Macmillan. (Original work published 1931.)

Elderly Health Services. (2004). Self-help tips for the elderly. Hong Kong, People's Republic of China: Elderly Health Services Head Office. Web site: http://www.info.gov.hk/elderly/english/healthinfo/selfhelptips/adjustmenttoretirement-e.htm.

Emmers-Sommer, T. M., Rhea, D., Triplett, L., & O'Neil, B. (2003). Accounts of single fatherhood: A qualitative study. *Marriage and Family Review, 35*(1/2), 99–115.

Encyclopedia Britannica. (2004). Biography: Dirie, Waris. Web site: http://www.britannica.com/eb/article?eu=368479.

Enright, E. (2004, July and August). A house divided. *American Association of Retired Persons Magazine,* pp. 60, 64–66, 68, 81.

Erickson, R. (2005). Why emotion work matters: Sex, gender, and the division of household labor. *Journal of Marriage and the Family, 67,* 337–351.

Erikson, E. H. (1950). *Childhood and society.* New York: Norton.

Erisman, M. (2004) Spiritual and moral identity formation within the family. *The Family Psychologist, 20*(2), 9–12.

Fadiman, G., & Bernard, A. (2000). *Bartett's book of anecdotes.* Boston: Little, Brown.

Faiola, A. (2004, August 31). Japanese women live, and like it, on their own. *The Washington Post,* p. A01.

Falicov, C. J. (1996). Mexican families. In M. McGoldrick, J. Giordano, & J. K. Pearce (Eds.), *Ethnicity and family therapy* (pp. 169–182). New York: Guilford.

Fals-Stewart, W., & Kelley, M. (2005). When family members go to war—A systemic perspective on harm and healing. *Journal of Family Psychology, 19,* 233–236.

Family Focus. (2005, June). American families: By the numbers. *Family Focus,* pp. 6, 14.

Family violence tops health issue (1991, October 17). Lincoln [NE] *Journal Star,* p. 3.

Fawcett, N. R., Gullone, E., & Johnson, J. (2002, March). The relationship between animal abuse and domestic violence: Implications for animal welfare agencies and domestic violence. *Australian Domestic and Family Violence Clearinghouse Newsletter, 10,* 4–7.

Fay, R., Turner, C., Klassen, A., & Gagnon, J. (1989). Prevalence and patterns of same-gender sexual contact among men. *Science, 246,* 338–348.

Fergusson, D. M., Horwood, L. J., & Ridder, E. M. (2005). Rejoinder. *Journal of Marriage and the Family, 67,* 1131–1136.

Fehr, B. (2004). A prototype model of intimacy interactions in same-sex friendships. In D. J. Mashek & A. Aron (Eds.), *Handbook of closeness and intimacy* (pp. 9–26). Mahwah, NJ: Erlbaum.

Fenell, D. L., & Weinhold, B. K. (1997). *Counseling families: An introduction to marriage and family therapy* (2nd ed.). Denver, CO: Love.

Fields, J. (2003, June). *Children's living arrangements and characteristics: March 2002.* Current Population Reports, P20-547. Washington, DC: U.S. Bureau of the Census.

Fields, J., & Casper, L. M. (2001). *America's families and living arrangements: March 2000.* Current Population Reports, P20-537. Washington, DC: U.S. Bureau of the Census.

Fill, S. K. (2002). Single mothers by choice: An exploratory study. *Masters Abstracts International, 40*(06), 1420.

Fincham, F. D., Hall, J., & Beach, S. R. (2006). Forgiveness in marriage: Current status and future directions. *Family Relations, 55,* 415–427.

Fitzpatrick, L. (2004, March 29). Getting out. *Time Asia.* Web site: http://www.time.com/time/asia/magazine/printout/0,13675,501040405-605534,00.html.

Fitzpatrick, M. H. (1988). *Between husbands and wives: Communication in marriage.* Beverly Hills, CA: Sage.

Fletcher, W. L., & Hansson, R. O. (1991, March). Assessing the social components of retirement anxiety. *Psychology and Aging, 6,* 76–85.

Flynn, C. P. (2000a). Why family professionals can no longer ignore violence toward animals. *Family Relations, 49*(1), 87–95.

Flynn, C. P. (2000b). Woman's best friend: Pet abuse and the role of companion animals in the lives of battered women. *Violence Against Women, 6*(2), 162–177.

Fowers, B., & Davidov, B. (2006). The virtue of multiculturalism: Person transformation, character, and openness to the other. *American Psychologist, 61,* 581–594.

Fowers, B. J., Montel, K. H., & Olson, D. H. (1996). Predicting marital success for premarital couple types based on PREPARE. *Journal of Marital and Family Therapy, 22*(1), 103–119.

Fowers, B. J., & Olson, D. H. (1986). Predicting marital success with PREPARE: A predictive validity study. *Journal of Marital and Family Therapy, 12*(4), 403–413.

Fowers, B. J., & Olson, D. H. (1992). Four types of premarital couples: An empirical typology based on PREPARE. *Journal of Family Psychology, 6*(1), 10–21.

Fox, G. L., & Murry, V. M. (2000). Gender and families: Feminist perspectives and family research. *Journal of Marriage and the Family, 62*(4), 1160–1172.

Francoeur, R. T. (1982). *Becoming a sexual person.* New York: Wiley.

Francoeur, R. T. (Ed.). (1997). *International encyclopedia of sexuality.* New York: Continuum.

Franklin, C. W., II. (1989). The male sex drive. In L. Richardson & V. Taylor (Eds.), *Feminist frontiers II* (pp. 274–278). New York: Random House.

Fravel, D. L. (1995). *Boundary ambiguity perceptions of adoptive parents experiencing various levels of openness in adoption.* Unpublished doctoral dissertation, University of Minnesota, St. Paul.

Frias, S. M., & Angel, R. J. (2005). The risk of partner violence among low-income Hispanic subgroups. *Journal of Marriage and the Family, 67,* 552–564.

Friedan, B. (1963). *The feminine mystique.* New York: Norton.

Friedan, B. (1997). *Beyond gender: The new politics of work and family.* Washington, DC: The Woodrow Wilson Center Press, book jacket.

Friedlin, J. (2002). Second and third wave feminists clash over the future. *Women's E-News.*

Fromm, E. (2000). *The art of loving.* New York: Continuum.

Gagnon, J. H. (2004). *An interpretation of desire: Essays in the study of sexuality.* Chicago: University of Chicago Press.

Gallup, Inc. (1989). *Love and marriage.* Princeton, NJ: The Gallup Organization.

Gallup, Inc. (2004, June 22). The cultural landscape: What's morally acceptable? Web site: http://www.gallup.com/content/login.aspx?ci=12061.

Gallup poll. (1996). *Gender and society: Status and stereotypes.* Princeton, NJ: The Gallup Organization.

Gallup poll. (2001, February 21). *Americans see women as emotional and affectionate, men as more aggressive.* Princeton, NJ: The Gallup Organization.

Galvin, K. M., & Brommel, B. J. (1986). *Family communication: Cohesion and change* (2nd ed.). Glenview, IL: Scott, Foresman.

Gamache, S. (2001). Stepfamily life . . . and then some. British Columbia Council for Families, Vancouver, BC. Web site: http://www.bccf.bc.ca/learn/fl_stepfam.html.

Ganong, L. H., & Coleman, M. (1994). *Remarried family relationships.* Thousand Oaks, CA: Sage.

Ganong, L. H., & Coleman, M. (1999). *Changing families, changing responsibilities: Family obligations following divorce and remarriage.* Mahwah, NJ: Erlbaum.

Ganong, L. H., & Coleman, M. (2000). Remarried families. In C. Hendrick & S. S. Hendrick (Eds.), *Close relationships: A sourcebook* (pp. 155–168). Thousand Oaks, CA: Sage.

Garbarino, J. (2000). The soul of fatherhood. *Marriage and Family Review, 29*(2/3), 11–21.

Gardyn, R. (2002, July/August). The mating game. *American Demographics,* pp. 33–37.

Garman, E. T., & Forgue, R. E. (1997). *Personal finance* (5th ed.). Boston: Houghton Mifflin.

Garman, E. T., & Forgue, R. E. (2002). *Personal finance* (7th ed.). Boston: Houghton Mifflin.

Gary, L. E., Beatty, L. A., & Berry, G. L. (1986). Strong Black families: Models of program development for Black families. In S. Van Zandt, H. Lingren, G. Rowe, P. Zeece, L. Kimmons, P. Lee, D. Shell, & N. Stinnett (Eds.), *Family strengths 7: Vital connections* (pp. 453–468). Lincoln: University of Nebraska Press.

Gay and Lesbian Times. (2003, October 9). Sex clampdown proposed in Indonesia. Web site: http://www.gaylesbiantimes.com/?id=1167&issue=824.

Gelles, R. J. (1997). *Intimate violence in families* (3rd ed.). Thousand Oaks, CA: Sage.

Gelles, R. J. (2000a). Family violence. In M. H. Tonry (Ed.), *The handbook of crime and punishment* (pp. 178–206). New York: Oxford University Press.

Gelles, R. J. (2000b). Treatment resistant families. In R. M. Reece (Ed.), *Treatment of child abuse: Common ground for mental health, medical, and legal practitioners* (pp. 304–312). Baltimore: Johns Hopkins University Press.

Gelles, R. J., & Straus, M. A. (1988). *Intimate violence.* New York: Simon & Schuster.

Gibbs, N. (2001, July 30). Who's in charge here? *Time,* pp. 40–49.

Gibran, K. (1976). *The prophet.* New York: Knopf. (Original work published 1923.)

Gibson, P. A. (2005). Intergenerational parenting from the perspective of African American grandmothers. *Family Relations, 54,* 280–297.

Glenn, N., & Marquardt, E. (2001). *Hooking up, hanging out, and hoping for Mr. Right.* New York: Institute for American Values.

Glenn, N. D. (1996). Values, attitudes, and the state of marriage. In D. Popenoe, J. B. Elshtain, & D. Blankenhorn (Eds.), *Promises to keep* (pp. 15–33). Lanham, MD: Rowman & Littlefield.

Glick, P. (1989). Remarried families, stepfamilies, and stepchildren: A brief demographic analysis. *Family Relations, 38,* 24–27.

Goldenberg, H., & Goldenberg, I. (2007). *Family therapy: An overview.* Belmont, CA: Brooks/Cole.

Gomel, J. N., Tinsley, B. J., Parke, R. D., & Clark, K. M. (1998). The effects of economic hardship on family relationships among African American, Latino, and Euro-American families. *Journal of Family Issues, 19*(4), 436–476.

Goodman, C. C., & Silverstein, M. (2006). Grandmothers raising grandchildren. *Journal of Family Issues, 27,* 1605–1626.

Goodman, E. (2001, February 26). Clear up contraceptive issue before it's 2-LATE. Lincoln [NE] *Journal Star,* p. 4B.

Gordon, K., Baucom, D. H., & Snyder, D. K. (2005). Forgiveness in couples: Divorce, infidelity, and couples therapy. In E. L. Worthington (Ed.), *Handbook of forgiveness* (pp. 407–422). New York: Routledge.

Gordon, L., & Durana, C. (1999). The PAIRS Program. In R. Berger & M. T. Hannah (Eds.), *Preventive approaches in couples therapy.* Philadelphia: Brunner/Mazel.

Gordon, P. A. (2003). The decision to remain single: Implications for women across cultures. *Journal of Mental Health Counseling, 25*(1), 33–45.

Gordon, S., & Gordon, J. (2000). *Raising a child responsibly in a sexually permissive world* (2nd ed.). Cincinnati, OH: Adams Media.

Gottman, J. M., & DeClaire, J. (2001). *The relationship cure: A five-step guide for building better connections with family, friends, and lovers.* New York: Crown.

Gottman, J. M., & Notarius, C. I. (2000). Decade review: Observing marital interaction. *Journal of Marriage and the Family, 62,* 927–947.

Gottman, J. M., Schwartz Gottman, J., & DeClaire, J. (2006). *Ten lessons to transform your marriage: America's love lab experts share their strategies for strengthening your relationship.* New York: Crown.

Gottman, J. M., & Silver, N. (1994a, March/April). What makes marriage work. *Psychology Today.* Web site: www.neicenet.com/script/main/art .asp?articlekey=34927&pf=3.

Gottman, J. M., & Silver, N. (1994b). *Why marriages succeed or fail.* New York: Simon & Schuster.

Gottman, J. M., & Silver, N. (1999). *The seven principles for making marriage work.* New York: Crown.

Graham, L. (1998, December 13). Where have all the small towns gone? *Parade,* pp. 6–9.

Gray, P. (1998, January 18). Paradise found. *Time,* p. 67.

Green, R.-J., Bettinger, M., & Zacks, E. (1996). Are lesbian couples fused and gay male couples disengaged? Questioning gender straightjackets. In J. Laird & R.-J. Green (Eds.), *Lesbians and gays in couples and families: A handbook for therapists* (pp. 185–230). San Francisco: Jossey-Bass.

Greenspan, S. I. (2003). Child care research: A clinical perspective. *Child Development, 74*(4), 1064–1068.

Greer, M. (2005). A new kind of war. *Monitor on Psychology, 36,* 38.

Greif, G. L. (2000). How do I involve fathers? In D. DePanfilis (Ed.), *Handbook for child protection practice.* Thousand Oaks, CA: Sage.

Grotevant, H. D. (2003). Counseling psychology meets the complex world of adoption. *The Counseling Psychologist, 31*(6), 753–762.

Gustafson, R. (2005). Is pornography addictive? Web site: http://www.parentstov.org.

Haddock, S. A., Zimmerman, T. S., Ziemba, S. J., & Lyness, K. P. (2006). Practices of dual earner couples successfully balancing work and family. *Journal of Family and Economic Issues, 27,* 207–234.

Haley, J. (1959). The family of the schizophrenic: A model system. *Journal of Nervous and Mental Disorders, 129,* 357–374.

Hall, M., & Havens, B. (2004). Social isolation and social loneliness. Division of Aging and Seniors, Health Canada. Web site: http://www.hc-sc.gc.ca/seniors-aines/naca/writings_gerontology/writ18/writ18_3_e.htm.

Halpern, D. F. (2005). Psychology at the intersection of work and family. *American Psychologist, 60,* 397–409.

Hamilton, B. E., Martin, J. A., & Ventura, S. J. (2006). Births: Preliminary data for 2005. National Center for Health Statistics. Web site: http://www.cdc.gov/nchs.

Harmon, A. (1998, August 30). Researchers say cyberspace sad, lonely: People who spend time online are more depressed. Lincoln [NE] *Journal Star,* p. 5A.

Harris, A. H., & Thoresen, C. E. (2005). Forgiveness, unforgiveness, health and disease. In E. L. Worthington (Ed.), *Handbook of forgiveness* (pp. 321–334). New York: Routledge.

Harris, G. (2004, May 1). FDA restricts pill's availability. *New York Times* report in the Minneapolis *Star Tribune,* p. A2.

Harris, J. (2003). *I kissed dating goodbye.* Sisters, OR Multnomah.

Hart, A. D., Weber, C. H., & Taylor, D. (1998). *Secrets of Eve: Understand the mystery of female sexuality.* Nashville: Word.

Harter, P. (2004, August 4). Divorce divides Morocco and W Sahara. *BBC News.* Web site: http://news.bbc.co.uk/go/pr/fr/-/1/hi/world/africa/3532612.stm.

Hatcher, R. A., et al. (1997). *The essentials of contraceptive technology.* Baltimore: Johns Hopkins School of Public Health, Center for Communication Programs, Population Information Program.

Hatcher, R. A., Trussell, J., Stewart, F., Stewart, G. K., Kowal, D., Guest, F., Cates, W., & Policar, M. S. (1994). *Contraceptive technology 1992–1994* (16th ed.). New York: Irvington.

Hatcher, R. A., Trussell, J., Stewart, F., Stewart, G. K., Kowal, D., Guest, F., Cates, W., & Policar, M. S. (1998). *Contraceptive technology* (17th ed.). New York: Irvington.

Hawley, D. R., & Olson, D. H. (1995). Enriching newlyweds: An evaluation of three enrichment programs. *American Journal of Family Therapy, 23,* 129–147.

Hawthorne, B. (2000). Split custody as a viable post-divorce option. *Journal of Divorce and Remarriage, 33*(4), 1–19.

He, W., Sengupta, M., Velkoff, V. A., & DeBarros, K. A. (2005). 65+ in the United States: 2005. *Current population reports.* Washington, DC: Government Printing Office.

Hellmich, N. (1990, April 4). Marriage is no. 1 with men. *USA Today,* p. 1D.

Hendrick, S. S., & Hendrick, C. (2000). Romantic love. In C. Hendrick & S. S. Hendrick (Eds.), *Close relationships: A sourcebook* (pp. 203–215). Thousand Oaks, CA: Sage.

Henry J. Kaiser Family Foundation/ABC Television. (1998, September). Sex in the 90s: 1998 National survey of Americans on sex and sexual health. Web site: http://www.kff.org.

Henshaw, S. K. (1999). *U.S. teenage pregnancy statistics with comparative statistics for women aged 20–24* (p. 5). New York: Alan Guttmacher Institute.

Herbert, W. (1999, February 22). Not tonight, dear: Americans say their sex lives leave a lot to be desired. *U.S. News and World Report,* pp. 57–59.

Herbst, P. G. (1952). The measurement of family relationships. *Human Relations, 5,* 3–35.

Herek, G. M. (2006). Legal recognition of same-sex relationships in the United States. *American Psychologist, 61*(6), 607–621.

Hernandez, D. J. (1997). Child development and the social demography of childhood. *Child Development, 68*(1), 149–169.

Hetherington, E. M., & Kelly, J. (2002). *For better or worse: Divorce reconsidered.* New York: Norton.

Higginson, J. G. (1998). Competitive parenting: The culture of teen mothers. *Journal of Marriage and the Family, 60,* 135–149.

Hill, R. (1958). Generic features of families under stress. *Social Casework, 49,* 139–150.

Hill, Z. E., Cleland, J., & Ali, M. M. (2004). Religious affiliation and extramarital sex among men in Brazil. *International Family Planning Perspectives, 30*(1), 20–26.

Hines, P. M., & Boyd-Franklin, N. (1996). African American families. In M. McGoldrick, J. Giordano, & J. K. Pearce (Eds.), *Ethnicity and family therapy* (pp. 66–84). New York: Guilford.

Hingson, R. W., & Howland, J. (2002). Comprehensive community interventions to promote health: Implications for college-age drinking problems. *Journal of Studies on Alcohol,* Suppl. No. 14, 226–240.

Hird, M. J., & Abshoff, K. (2000). Women without children: A contradiction in terms? *Journal of Comparative Family Studies, 31*(3), 347–366.

Hobfoll, S. E., & Spielberger, C. D. (1992). Family stress: Integrating theory and measurement. *Journal of Family Psychology, 6*(2), 99–112.

Hochschild, A. R. (1997). *The time bind: When work becomes home and home becomes work.* New York: Metropolitan Books.

Hoffman, L., & Rainville, A. (2004, December 15). Children of the fallen. Scripps Howard News Service. Web site: www.shns.com/shns/warkids.

Hogan, M. J. (1993). Family futures: Possibilities, preferences and probabilities. *Marriage and Family Review, 18,* 255–262.

Holmes, T. H., & Ella, D. M. (Eds.). (1989). *Life change, life events, and illness: Selected papers.* New York: Praeger.

Holmes, T. H., & Rahe, R. H. (1967). The social readjustment rating scale. *Journal of Psychosomatic Research, 11,* 213–218.

Holtzman, M. (2005, June). The family definitions continuum. *Family Focus,* pp. 1, 3.

Holtzworth-Munroe, A. (2005). Male versus female intimate partner violence: Putting controversial findings into context. *Journal of Marriage and the Family, 67,* 1120–1125.

Holzner, C., Jameson, K., Maloney, T., Abebe, B., Lund, M., & Schaub, K. (2006). *The economic impact of the Mexico–Utah relationship.* University of Utah. Web site: http://www.ipia.utah.edu/utah_mexico_final_version.pdf.

Horn, W. F. (1995). *Father facts.* Lancaster, PA: The National Fatherhood Initiative.

Hornik, D. (2001). Can the church get in step with stepfamilies? *US Catholic, 66*(7), 30–31.

Houseknecht, S. K., & Lewis, S. K. (2005). Explaining teen childbearing and cohabitation: Community embeddedness and primary ties. *Family Relations, 54,* 607–620.

Houseknecht, S. K., & Sastry, J. (1996). Family decline and child well-being: A comparative analysis. *Journal of Marriage and the Family, 58,* 726–739.

Howard, J. (2002). In A. Gore and T. Gore, *The spirit of family.* New York: Henry Holt (back cover).

Human Rights Watch. (2004, November 29). Divorced from justice: Women's unequal access to divorce in Egypt. Web site: http://hrw.org/reports/2004/egypt1204/1.htm.

Hunt, R. A., Hof, L., & DeMaria, R. (Eds.). (1998). *Marriage enrichment: Preparation, mentoring and outreach.* Philadelphia: Brunner/Mazel.

Hunter, A. G. (1997). Counting on grandmothers: Black mothers' and fathers' reliance on grandmothers for parenting support. *Journal of Family Issues, 18*(3), 251–269.

Husseini, R. (2000). Crimes of honor. *Al-Raida, 17*(89), 19–21.

Hyde, J. S., & DeLamater, J. D. (2003). *Understanding human sexuality* (8th ed.). Dubuque, IA: McGraw-Hill.

Ihinger-Tallman, M., & Pasley, K. (1987). *Remarriage.* Newbury Park, CA: Sage.

Ihinger-Tallman, M., & Pasley, K. (1997). Stepfamilies in 1984 and today: A scholarly perspective. *Marriage and Family Review, 27*(1–2), 19–40.

Ikkink, K. K., van Tilburg, T., & Knipscheer, K. C. P. M. (1999). Perceived instrumental support exchanges in relationships between elderly parents and their adult children: Normative and structural explanations. *Journal of Marriage and the Family, 61,* 831–844.

Insel, P. M., & Roth, W. T. (2004). *Core concepts in health, 2004 update* (9th ed.). New York: McGraw-Hill.

Jaccard, J., Dittus, P. J., & Gordon, V. V. (1998). Parent–adolescent congruency in reports of adolescent sexual behavior and in communications about sexual behavior. *Child Development, 69*(1), 247–261.

Jackson, J. K. (1954). The adjustments of the family to the crisis of alcoholism. *Quarterly Journal of Studies on Alcohol, 15,* 562–586.

Janus, S. S., & Janus, C. L. (1993). *The Janus report on sexual behavior.* New York: Wiley.

Joanning, H., & Keoughan, P. (2006, May/June). The divorce process and therapeutic interventions. *Family Therapy Magazine,* pp. 14–16.

Johansen, A. S., Leibowitz, A., & Waite, L. J. (1996). The importance of child-care characteristics to choice of care. *Journal of Marriage and the Family, 58,* 759–772.

Johnson, B. (2004). Older women talk about sex. *Selfhelp.* Web site: http://www.selfhelpmagazine.com/articles/aging/eldersex.html.

Johnson, M. P. (2005). Domestic violence: It's not about gender—Or is it? *Journal of Marriage and the Family, 67,* 1126–1130.

Jones, E. F., & Stahmann, R. F. (1994). Clergy beliefs, preparation, and practice in premarital counseling. *Journal of Pastoral Care, 48,* 181–186.

Jouriles, E. N., Norwood, W. D., McDonald, R., & Peters, B. (2001). Domestic violence and child adjustment. In J. H. Grych & F. D. Fincham (Eds.), *Interparental conflict and child development: Theory, research, and applications* (pp. 315–336). New York: Cambridge University Press.

Julien, D., Chartrand, E., Simard, M., Bouthillier, D., & Begin, J. (2003). Conflict, social support, and relationship quality: An observational study of heterosexual, gay male and lesbian couples' communication. *Journal of Family Psychology, 17*(3), 419–428.

Kagan, J. (1964). *The nature of the child.* New York: Basic Books.

Karasik, R. J. (2005, September). Aging: Everybody's doing it. *Family Focus,* p. 3.

Kaufman, M. (2000, September 30). RU-486 user: It's easier, but not easy. *Washington Post* article published in the Lincoln [NE] *Journal Star,* p. 6A.

Keillor, G. (1994, October 17). It's good old monogamy that's really sexy. *Time,* p. 71.

Keillor, G. (2005). *Lake Wobegon days.* New York: Viking Penguin.

Kelly, G. F. (2004). *Sexuality today: The human perspective* (7th ed.). New York: McGraw-Hill.

Kennedy, J. F. (1990). Inaugural address. In D. B. Baker (Ed.), *Political quotations.* Detroit: Gale Research. (Original work published 1961.)

Kiang, L., Gonzales-Backen, M., Yip, T., Witkow, M., & Fuligni, A. (2006). Ethnic identity and the daily psychological well-being of adolescents from Mexican and Chinese backgrounds. *Child Development, 77,* 1338–1350.

Kilmann, R., & Thomas, K. (1975). Interpersonal conflict: Handling behavior as reflections of Jungian personality dimensions. *Psychological Reports, 37,* 971–980.

Kindlon, D. (2001). *Too much of a good thing: Raising children of character in an indulgent age.* New York: Talk Miramax.

Klein, D. M., & White, J. M. (1996). *Family theories.* Thousand Oaks, CA: Sage.

Klein, M., & Gordon, S. (1992). Sex education. In C. E. Walker & M. C. Roberts (Eds.), *Handbook of clinical child psychology* (2nd ed., pp. 933–949). New York: Wiley.

Kline, G. H., Stanley, S. M., Markman, H. J., Olmos-Gallo, P. A., St. Peters, M., Whitton, S. W., & Prado, L. M. (2004). Timing is everything: Pre-engagement cohabitation and increased risk for poor marital outcomes. *Journal of Family Psychology, 18*(2), 311–318.

Knutson, L., & Olson, D. H. (2003). Effectiveness of PREPARE Program with premarital couples in a community setting. *Marriage and Family, 6*(4), 529–546.

Kohlberg, L. (1966). Cognitive stages and preschool education. *Human Development, 9,* 5–17.

Koonin, L. M., Kochanek, K. D., Smith, J. C., & Ramick, M. (1991). Abortion surveillance, United States, 1988. *Morbidity and Mortality Weekly Report, 40* (SS-1), 15–42. Washington, DC: National Office of Vital Statistics.

Kornblum, J. (2004, May 27). No blind eye to a roving one: Older women increasingly ask unfaithful spouses for divorce. *USA Today,* p. 9D.

Kostelnik, M. (2005). *What is a high quality early childhood program?* Lincoln: University of Nebraska, College of Education and Human Sciences.

Kottak, C. P. (2004). *Anthropology: The exploration of human diversity* (10th ed.). Boston: McGraw-Hill.

Kraut, R., Patterson, M., Lundmark, V., Kiesler, S., Mukopadhyay, T., & Scherlis, W. (1998). Internet paradox: A social technology that reduces social involvement and psychological well-being? *American Psychologist, 53*(9), 1017–1031.

Kulthau, K., & Mason, K. O. (1996). Market child care versus care by relatives: Choices made by employed and nonemployed mothers. *Journal of Family Issues, 17*(4), 561–578.

Kurdek, L. A. (1998). The nature and predictors of the trajectory of change in marital quality over the first 4 years of marriage for first-married husbands and wives. *Journal of Family Psychology, 12*(4), 594–510.

Kurdek, L. A. (2000). Attractions and constraints as determinants of relationship commitment: Longitudinal evidence from gay, lesbian, and heterosexual couples. *Personal Relationships, 7*(3), 245–262.

Kurdek, L. A. (2001). Differences between heterosexual-nonparent couples and gay, lesbian, and heterosexual-parent couples. *Journal of Family Issues, 22*(6), 727–754.

Kurdek, L. A. (2003). On being insecure about the assessment of attachment styles. *Journal of Social and Personal Relationships, 19*(6), 811–834.

Kurdek, L. A. (2005). Gender and marital satisfaction early in marriage: A growth curve approach. *Journal of Marriage and the Family, 67,* 68–84.

Kurdek, L. A. (2006). Differences between partners from heterosexual, gay, and lesbian cohabiting couples. *Journal of Marriage and the Family, 68,* 509–528.

Lacayo, R. (1997, April 14). The kids are all right: Day care—A new study says it's mostly harmless, sometimes helpful and less important than home. *Time,* p. 76.

Laird, J., & Green, R.-J. (1996). *Lesbians and gays in couples and families: A handbook for therapists.* San Francisco: Jossey-Bass.

LaMastro, V. (2001). Childless by choice? Attributions and attitudes concerning family size. *Social Behavior and Personality, 29*(3), 231–243.

Landers, A. (1997, June 30). How to tell if a date or mate is a potential batterer. Minneapolis [MN] *Star Tribune,* p. 16.

Landers, S. (1989, March). Koop will not release abortion effects report. *American Psychological Association Monitor,* p. 1.

Langer, G., Arnedt, C., & Sussman, D. (2004). ABC News: Primetime Live poll: American sex survey. Web site: http://abcnews.go.com/Primetime/News/story?id=156921@page=1.

Lankov, A. (2004, August 9). The dawn of modern Korea: Changes for better or worse. *The Korea Times.* Web site: http://times.hankooki.com/cgi-bin/hkiprn.cgi?pa=/1page/opinion/200408/kt2004080916572054130.htm&ur=times.hankooki.com&fo=print_kt.htm.

Lansky, B. (1986). *Mother Murphy's law.* New York: Meadowbrook/Simon & Schuster.

Larsen, A. S., & Olson, D. H. (1989). Predicting marital satisfaction using PREPARE: A replication study. *Journal of Marital and Family Therapy, 15,* 311–322.

Larson, P. J., & Olson, D. H. (2004). Spiritual beliefs and marriage: A national survey based on ENRICH. *The Family Psychologist, 20*(2), 4–8.

Larson, R. W., Branscomb, K. R., & Wiley, A. R. (2006). Forms and function of family mealtimes: Multidisciplinary perspectives. In R. W. Larson, A. R. Wiley, & K. R. Branscomb (Eds.), *Family mealtimes as a context of development and socialization* (pp. 1–15). San Francisco: Jossey-Bass.

Larson, R. W., Wilson, S., Brown, B. B., Furstenberg, F. F., Jr., & Verma, S. (2002). Changes in adolescents' interpersonal experiences: Are they being prepared for adult relationships in the twenty-first century? *Journal of Research on Adolescence, 12*(1), 31–68.

Lasswell, M., & Lasswell, T. (1991). *Marriage and the family* (3rd ed.). Belmont, CA: Wadsworth.

Laumann, E. O., et al. (Eds.). (2004). *The sexual organization of the city.* Chicago: University of Chicago Press.

Laumann, E. O., Gagnon, J. H., Michael, R. T., & Michaels, S. (1994). *The social organization of sexuality: Sexual practices in the United States.* Chicago: University of Chicago Press.

Laumann, E. O., Gagnon, J. H., Michael, R. T., Michaels, S., & Kolata, G. (1995). *Sex in America: A definitive survey.* Boston: Little, Brown.

Laumann, E. O., & Michael, R. T. (2000). *Sex, love, and health in America: Private choices and public policies.* Chicago: University of Chicago Press.

Laumann, E. O., Paik, A., & Rosen, R. C. (1999). Sexual dysfunction in the United States: Prevalence and predictors. *Journal of the American Medical Association, 28*(6), 537–544.

Lazarony, L. (2002, August 15). Credit cards: Big debt on campus. Web site: http://www.bankrate.com/brm/news/cc/20020815a.asp.

Leboyer, F. (1995). *Birth without violence: The book that revolutionized the way we bring our children into the world.* Rochester, VT: Healing Arts Press.

Lee, G. R., Peek, C. W., & Coward, R. T. (1998). Race differences in filial responsibility expectations among older parents. *Journal of Marriage and the Family, 60,* 404–412.

Lee, V. (1996). Asian American families: An overview In M. McGoldrick, J. Giordano, & J. K. Pearce (Eds.), *Ethnicity and family therapy* (pp. 227–248). New York: Guilford.

Lee, Y., & Waite, L. (2005). Husbands' and wives' time spent on housework: A comparison of measures. *Journal of Marriage and the Family, 67,* 328–336.

Leiblum, S., & Rosen, R. (2000). *Principles and practices of sex therapy.* New York: Guilford.

Leiblum, S. R. (2002). *Getting the sex you want: A woman's guide to becoming proud, passionate, and pleased in bed.* New York: Crown.

Leifer, M. (1980). *Psychological effects of motherhood: A study of first pregnancy.* New York: Praeger.

LeMasters, E. E. (1957). Parenthood as crisis. *Marriage and Family Living, 19,* 325–355.

Leon, K., & Jacobvitz, D. B. (2003). Relationships between adult attachment representations and family ritual quality: A prospective, longitudinal study. *Family Process, 42*(3), 419–432.

Lerner, H. G. (2005). *The dance of anger: A woman's guide to changing the patterns of intimate relationships.* New York: Perennial Currents.

Levine, J. A., & Pitt, E. W. (1995). *New expectations: Community strategies for responsible fatherhood.* New York: Families and Work Institute.

Levine, J. R., & Markman, H. J. (Eds.). (2001). *Why do fools fall in love? Experiencing the magic, mystery, and meaning of successful relationships.* San Francisco: Jossey-Bass.

Levy, K., Kelly, K. M., & Jack, E. L. (2006). Sex differences in *Jealousy:* A matter of evolution or attachment theory? In M. Mikulincer & G. S. Goodman (Eds.), *Dynamics of romantic love: Attachment, caregiving, and sex* (pp. 128–145). New York: Guilford.

Lino, M. (2004). *Expenditures on children by families, 2003.* U.S. Department of Agriculture, Center for Nutrition Policy and Promotion. Miscellaneous Publication No. 1528-2003. Washington, DC. Web site: http://www.cnpp.usda.gov.

Lisle, J. (2004, November 24). Single women become a force in home buying. Web site: http://www.realestatejournal.com/buysell/salestrends/20041124-lisle.html.

Liu, D., Ng, M. I., & Haeberle, E. J. (1997). *Sexual behavior in modern China—Report on the nationwide survey of 20,000 men and women.* New York: Continuum.

Lunneborg, P. (1999). *The chosen lives of childfree men.* Westport, CT: Bergin & Garvey/Greenwood.

Luthra, R., & Gidycz, C. A. (2006). Dating violence among college men and women: Evaluation of a theoretical model. *Journal of Interpersonal Violence, 21*(6), 717–731.

Lykken, D. (1999). *Happiness.* New York: Golden Books.

Maccoby, E. E., & Lewis, C. C. (2003). Less day care or different day care? *Child Development, 74*(4), 1069–1075.

MacDonald, W. L., & DeMaris, A. (1995). Remarriage, stepchildren, and marital conflict: Challenges to the incomplete institutionalization hypothesis. *Journal of Marriage and the Family, 57,* 387–398.

Mace, D. (1982). *Love and anger in marriage.* Grand Rapids, MI: Zondevan.

Mace, D., & Mace, V. (1980). Enriching marriages: The foundation stone of family strength. In N. Stinnett, B. Chesser, J. DeFrain, & P. Knaub (Eds.), *Family strengths: Positive models for family life.* Lincoln: University of Nebraska Press.

Malinowski, B. (1929). *The sexual life of savages.* New York: Harcourt.

Manning, R. D. (2001). Credit cards on campus. Web site: http://www.newdream.org/newsletter/creditcards.php.

Manning, W., & Brown, S. (2006). Children's economic well-being in married and cohabiting parent families. *Journal of Marriage and the Family, 68,* 345–362.

Manning, W., & Smock, P. (2005). Measuring and modeling cohabitation: New perspectives from qualitative data. *Journal of Marriage and the Family, 67,* 989–1002.

Manning, W. D., Stewart, S. D., & Smock, P. J. (2003). The complexity of fathers' parenting responsibilities and involvement with nonresident children. *Journal of Family Issues, 24*(5), 645–667.

Manzi, C., Vignoles, V. L., Regalia, C., & Scabini, E. (2006). Cohesion and enmeshment revisited: Differentiation, identity, and well-being in two European cultures. *Journal of Marriage and the Family, 68,* 673–689.

Marelich, W. D., Gaines, S. O., & Banzet, M. R. (2003). Commitment, insecurity and arousability: Testing a transactional model of jealousy. *Representative Research in Social Psychology, 27,* 23–31.

Markman, H. J., & Stanley, S. M. (2004). PREP Program overview. Web site: www.smartmarriages.com/prep.overview.html.

Markman, H. J., Stanley, S. M., Jenkins, N. H., & Blumberg, S. L. (2004). *12 hours to a great marriage: A step-by-step guide for making love last.* San Francisco: Jossey-Bass.

Marmot, M. (2004). *Status syndrome: How your social standing directly affects your health and life expectancy.* New York: Times Books.

Marsh, J. C. (2003). Arguments for family strengths research. *Social Work, 48*(2), 147–149.

Masters, W. H., Johnson, V. E., & Kolodny, R. C. (1995). *Human sexuality* (5th ed.). New York: HarperCollins.

Masters, W. H., Johnson, V. E., & Kolodny, R. C. (1998). *Heterosexuality.* New York: Gramercy Books.

May, R. (1969). *Love and will.* New York: Norton.

McAdoo, H. P. (Ed.). (1997). *Black families* (3rd ed.). Thousand Oaks, CA: Sage.

McAdoo, H. P. (Ed.). (1999). *Family ethnicity: Strength in diversity* (2nd ed.). Thousand Oaks, CA: Sage.

McAdoo, H. P. (Ed.). (2002). *Black children: Social, educational, and parental environments* (2nd ed.). Thousand Oaks, CA: Sage.

McAdoo, H. P. (Ed.). (2007). *Black families* (4th ed.). Thousand Oaks, CA: Sage.

McBride, E. K. (2003). Splitting heirs: Reforming the custodial treatment of identical twins in divorce. *Family Law Quarterly, 37*(3), 515–526.

McCarthy, B. (2001). Male sexuality after fifty. *Journal of Family Psychotherapy, 12*(1), 29–37.

McCarthy, B. (2003). Marital sex as it ought to be. *Journal of Family Psychotherapy, 14*(2), 1–12.

McCullough, M. (2000, September 29). RU-486 wins FDA approval: Abortion pill available in a month. Knight Ridder Newspapers article published in the Lincoln [NE] *Journal Star,* p. 1A.

McGinley, E., & Sabbadini, A. (2006). *Play Misty for Me* (1971): The perversion of love. *International Journal of Psychoanalysis, 87*(2), 589–597.

McGoldrick, M., Giordano, J., & Pearce, J. K. (1996). *Ethnicity and family therapy* (2nd ed.). New York: Guilford.

McGoldrick, M., Giordano, J., & Preto, N. G. (2005). *Ethnicity and family therapy.* New York: Guilford.

McKinnon, J., & Bennett, C. (2005). We the people: Blacks in the United States. Report CNSR-25, U.S. Bureau of the Census.

McLanahan, S., & Sandefur, G. (1994). *Growing up with a single parent: What hurts, what helps.* Cambridge, MA: Harvard University Press.

McLeod, B. (1986, July). The oriental express. *Psychology Today,* pp. 48–52.

Mead, M. (1935). *Sex and temperament in three primitive societies.* New York: Morrow/Quill.

Meezan, W., & Rauch, J. (2005). Gay marriage, same-sex parenting, and America's children. *The Future of Children, 15*(2), 98–107.

Meier, J. A., McNaughton-Cassill, M., & Lynch, M. (2006). The management of household and childcare tasks and relationship satisfaction in parenting couples. *Marriage and Family Review, 40,* 61–88.

Meier, P. (1991, January 6). War of words: Women talk about how men and women talk. Minneapolis *Star Tribune,* p. 8.

Melby, J. N., Conger, R. D., Conger, K. J., & Lorenz, F. O. (1993). Effects of parental behavior on tobacco use by young male adolescents. *Journal of Marriage and the Family, 55,* 439–454.

Mendenhall, T. J., Grotevant, H. D., & McRoy, R. G. (1996). Adoptive couples: Communication and changes made in openness levels. *Family Relations, 45,* 223–229.

Mertensmeyer, C., & Fine, M. (2000). ParentLink: A model of integration and support for parents. *Family Relations, 49,* 257–265.

Michener, J. A. (1991). *The world is my home.* New York: Random House.

Mickish, J., & Schoen, K. (2004). Colorado Alliance for Cruelty Prevention: Safe pets, safe families, safe communities. *The Colorado Lawyer, 33*(1), 37–40.

Miedzian, M. (2002). *Boys will be boys: Breaking the link between masculinity and violence.* New York: Lantern Books.

Milanese, M. (2002). Hooking up, hanging out, making up, moving on. *Stanford Magazine.* Web site: http://www.stanfordalummus.org/news/magazine.

Miller, B. C. (2002). Family influences on adolescent sexual and contraceptive behavior. *Journal of Sex Research, 39*(1), 22–26.

Miller, B. C., Benson, B., & Galbraith, K. A. (2001). Family relationships and adolescent pregnancy risk: A research synthesis. *Developmental Review, 21*(1), 1–38.

Miller, R. B. (2000). Misconceptions about the U-shaped curve of marital satisfaction over the life course. *Family Science Review, 13*(1–2), 60–73.

Miller, S., & Miller, P. A. (1997). *Core communication: Skills and processes.* Littleton, CO: Interpersonal Communication Programs.

Miller, S., & Miller, P. (2000). *Couple communication—Thriving together.* Evergreen, CO: Interpersonal Communication Programs.

Mindel, C. H., Habenstein, R. W., & Wright, R., Jr. (Eds.). (1988). *Ethnic families in America: Patterns and variations* (3rd ed.). New York: Elsevier.

Minino, A. M., Arias, E., Kochanek, K. D., Murphy, S. L., & Smith, B. L. (2002). Deaths: Final data for 2000. *National Vital Statistics Reports, 50*(15). Hyattsville, MD: Centers for Disease Control and Prevention/National Center for Health Statistics.

Moglia, R. F., & Knowles, J. (Eds.). (1997). *All about sex: A family resource on sex and sexuality.* New York: Three Rivers Press.

Mohatt, G., & Thomas, L. (2006). "I wonder, why would you do it that way?" In J. E. Trimble & C. B. Fisher (Eds.), *The handbook of ethical research with ethnocultural populations and communities.* Thousand Oaks, CA: Sage.

Montagu, A. (1964). *Man's most dangerous myth: The fallacy of race.* Cleveland: World.

Moore, K. A. (1998). What a difference a dad makes. *Child trends report.* Washington, DC: Child Trends.

Morbidity and Mortality Weekly Report. (2006, June). Epidemiology of HIV/AIDS—United States, 1981–2005. *Morbidity and Mortality Weekly Report, 55,* 589–592.

Morgan, S. P., & Chen, R. (1992). Predicting childlessness for recent cohorts of American women. *International Journal of Forecasting, 8,* 477–493.

Morrill, P. (2006). *Couples in great marriages with a traditional structure and egalitarian relationship.* Unpublished master's thesis, Utah State University, Logan.

Mroczek, D. K., & Spiro, A., III. (2003). Modeling intraindividual change in personality traits: Findings from the Normative Aging Study. *Journals of Gerontology: Series B: Psychological Sciences and Social Sciences, 58B*(3), 153–165.

Muller, D. (2002). Fault or no fault? *Christian Century, 119*(12), 28–31.

Mulvihill, G. (2007, February). N.J. civil union law goes into effect with gay couples vowing to push for marriage. *StarTribune.* Web site: http://www.startribune.com/484/v-print/story/1013013.html.

Murstein, B. I. (1980). Mate selection in the 1970s. *Journal of Marriage and the Family, 42,* 52–54.

Murstein, B. I. (1987). A classification and extension of the SVR theory of dyadic pairing. *Journal of Marriage and the Family, 42,* 777–792.

Mussen, P. H. (1969). Early sex-role development. In D. A. Goslin (Ed.), *Handbook of socialization theory and research.* Chicago: Rand McNally.

Mydans, S. (2004, November 20). There she is, "Miss Spinster of Thailand" and proud of it. *The New York Times.*

Myers, J. E., & Gill, C. S. (2004). Poor, rural and female: Under-studied, under-counseled, more at-risk. *Journal of Mental Health Counseling, 26*(3), 225–242.

Myerson, B. (1987). *Miss America, 1945: Bess Myerson's own story.* New York: Newmarket Press.

Nakonezny, P. A., Shull, R. D., & Rodgers, J. L. (1995). The effect of no-fault divorce law on the divorce rate across the 50 states and its relation to income, education, and religiosity. *Journal of Marriage and the Family, 57*(2), 477–488.

National Center for Injury Prevention and Control. (2005). Violence. Web site: http://www.cdc.gov/ncipc/default.htm.

National Center on Elder Abuse. (2004). NCEA: The source of information and assistance on elder abuse. U.S. Administration on Aging. Web site: http://www.elderabusecenter.org.

National Child Care Information Center. (2004a, September). Hispanics and child care: The changing landscape. U.S. Department of Health and Human Services, Washington, DC.

National Child Care Information Center. (2004b). National Leadership Forum on Child Care Issued of the Hispanic Community. Child Care Bulleting Issue 24. U.S. Department of Health and Human Services, Washington, DC.

National Clearinghouse on Child Abuse and Neglect Information. (2004). Child abuse and neglect fatalities: Statistics and interventions. U.S. Department of Health and Human Services. Washington, DC. Web site: http://nccanch.acf.hhs.gov/pubs/factsheets/fatality.cfm.

National Coalition for the Homeless. (2004, September). How many people experience homelessness? NCH Fact Sheet #2. Washington, DC. Web site: http://www.nationalhomeless.org/numbers.html.

National Coalition for the Protection of Children and Families. (2007). The effects of pornography and sexual messages. Web site: http://www.nationalcoalition.org.

National Council on Alcoholism and Drug Dependence. (2004). Alcohol and drug dependence are America's number one health problem. Web site: http://www.ncadd.org/facts/numbroneproblem.html.

National Crime Victimization Survey. (2002). *Crime and victims statistics.* Washington, DC: U.S. Department of Justice, Office of Justice Programs. Web site: http://www.ojp.usdoj.gov/bjs/cvict.htm.

National Institute of Child Health Research Network. (2003). *Child Development, 74*(4), 976–1005.

National Opinion Research Center. (1996). *General social survey.* Chicago: University of Chicago.

Nation's legal drugs may be its worst drugs. (1986, November 23). Lincoln [NE] *Journal Star,* pp. 1D, 3D.

Neugarten, B. (1968). The awareness of middle age. In B. Neugarten (Ed.), *Middle age and aging.* Chicago: University of Chicago Press.

Neumaier, J. (2001). Coronary heart disease patients and sex: Death in the extramarital bed. *MMW—Fortschritte der Medizin, 143*(20), 18–19.

New York State Administrative Regulations. (1995). 9 N.Y.C.R.R. 2104.6(d)(3).

Nicholson, T. (2001). 50+ world—Bright scene with shadows. *AARP Bulletin,* p. 25.

Niebuhr, R. (1988). Serenity prayer. In G. Carruth & E. Ehrlich (Eds.), *Harper book of American quotations.* New York: Harper & Row. (Original work published 1951.)

Niehuis, S., Skogrand, L., & Houston, T. (2006). When marriages die: Premarital and early marriage precursors to divorce. *Forum of Family and Consumer Issues, 11.* Online journal: http://www.ces.ncsu.edu/depts/fcs/pub/forum.html.

Nord, C. W., & Zill, N. (1996). Non-custodial parents' participation in their children's lives: Evidence from the

Survey of Income and Program Participation. Washington, DC: U.S. Department of Health and Human Services. Web site: ftp://aspe.os.dhhs.gov/cyp.

Norris, C. (1990). *What's wrong with postmodernism: Critical theory and the ends of philosophy.* Baltimore: Johns Hopkins University Press.

Norwood, E. (1998). Poor folks have dreams. In C. L. Nelson & K. A. Wilson (Eds.), *Seeding the process of multicultural education* (pp. 73–78). Plymouth, MN: Minnesota Inclusiveness Program.

Ochs, E., & Shohet, M. (2006). The cultural structuring of mealtime socialization. In R. W. Larson, A. R. Wiley, & K. R. Branscomb (Eds.), *Family mealtimes as a context of development and socialization* (pp. 35–49). San Francisco: Jossey-Bass.

O'Farrell, T. J., & Fals-Stewart, W. (2001). Family-involved alcoholism treatment: An update. *Recent Developments in Alcoholism, 15,* 329–356.

Ogunwole, S. (2006). We the people: American Indians and Alaska Natives in the United States. Report CENSR-28, U.S. Bureau of the Census.

Olds, S. B., London, M. L., & Ladewig, P. (2004). *Maternal–newborn nursing and women's healthcare* (7th ed.). Upper Saddle River, NJ: Pearson/Prentice Hall.

Olson, A., & Olson, D. H. (2001). Ten traits of love. In J. R. Levine & H. J. Markman (Eds.), *Why do fools fall in love? Experiencing the magic, mystery, and meaning of successful relationships.* San Francisco: Jossey-Bass.

Olson, D. H. (1996). Clinical assessment and treatment using the Circumplex Model. In F. W. Kaslow (Ed.), *Handbook in relational diagnosis* (pp. 59–80). New York: Wiley.

Olson, D. H. (1997). Family stress and coping: A multisystem perspective. In S. Dreman (Ed.), *The family on the threshold of the 21st century: Trends and implications* (pp. 259–280). Mahwah, NJ: Erlbaum.

Olson, D. H. (2003). Circumplex model of marital and family systems. In F. Walsh (Ed.), *Normal family processes: Growing diversity and complexity* (3rd ed., pp. 514–548). New York: Guilford.

Olson, D. H. (2004). Multisystem assessment of stress and health (MASH) model. In D. R. Catherall (Ed.), *Handbook of stress, trauma and the family* (pp. 325–346). New York: Brunner-Routledge.

Olson, D. H., & Cromwell, R. E. (1975). Power in families. In R. E. Cromwell & D. H. Olson (Eds.), *Power in families* (pp. 3–11). Newbury Park, CA: Sage.

Olson, D. H., Fournier, D. G., & Druckman, J. M. (2001). *PREPARE, PREPARE-MC and ENRICH inventories* (4th ed.). Minneapolis: PREPARE/ENRICH.

Olson, D. H., Fye, S., & Olson, A. (1999). *National survey of happy and unhappy married couples.* Minneapolis: Life Innovations.

Olson, D. H., & Gorall, D. (2002). Circumplex model of marital and family systems. In F. Walsh (Ed.), *Normal families* (3rd ed.) New York: Guilford.

Olson, D. H., McCubbin, H. I., Barnes, H., Larsen, A., Muxen, M., & Wilson, M. (1989). *Families: What makes them work* (2nd ed.). Los Angeles: Sage.

Olson, D. H., & Olson, A. K. (2000). *Empowering couples: Building on your strengths.* Minneapolis: Life Innovations.

Olson, D. H., & Stewart, K. L. (1991). Family systems and health behaviors. In H. E. Schroeder (Ed.), *New directions in health psychology assessment. Series in applied psychology: Social issues and questions* (pp. 27–64). Washington, DC: Hemisphere.

Olson, S. (2001, April). The genetic archaeology of race. *Atlantic Monthly,* pp. 69–80.

Onah, H. E., Iloabachie, G. C., Obi, S. N., Ezugwu, F. O., & Eze, J. N. (2002). Nigerian male sexual activity during pregnancy. *International Journal of Gynecology and Obstetrics, 76*(2), 219.

Ooms, T. (1998). *Toward more perfect unions: Putting marriage on the public agenda.* Washington, DC: Family Impact Seminar.

Ooms, T., Bouchet, S., & Parke, M. (2004). *Beyond marriage licenses: Efforts in states to strengthen marriage and two-parent families.* Washington, DC: Center for Law and Social Policy.

Orwell, G. (1951). *Animal farm.* New York: Penguin.

Padgett, D. (1997). The contribution of support networks to household labor in African American families. *Journal of Family Issues, 18*(3), 227–250.

Pan, P. A. (2000, December 26). Thoroughly modern women disconcert many in China. *The Washington Post,* p. A20.

Pan, Y. (2002). *On the freedom of mate selection.* Paper presented at the Building Family Strengths Conference, Shanghai Academy of Social Sciences, Shanghai, China.

Parents Without Partners. (2004). What is Parents Without Partners? Web site: http://www.parentswithoutpartners.org/about.htm.

Parkman, A. M. (1995). The deterioration of the family: A law and economics perspective. In G. B. Melton (Ed.), *The individual, the family, and social good: Personal fulfillment in times of change* (pp. 21–52). Lincoln: University of Nebraska Press.

Parkman, A. M. (2000). *Good intentions gone awry: No-fault divorce and the American family.* Lanham, MD: Rowman & Littlefield.

Parsons, T. (1955). The American family: Its relations to personality and the social structure. In T. Parsons & R. F. Bales (Eds.), *Family socialization and interaction process* (pp. 3–21). Glencoe, IL: Free Press.

Parsons, T. (1965). The normal American family. In S. M. Farber, P. Mustacchi, & R. H. L. Wilson (Eds.), *Man and civilization: The family's search for survival* (pp. 31–50). New York: McGraw-Hill.

Parsons, T., & Bales, R. F. (1955). *Family socialization and interaction process.* Glencoe, IL: Free Press.

Pasley, K., & Ihinger-Tallman, M. (Eds.). (1994). *Stepparenting: Issues in theory, research, and practice.* Westport, CT: Greenwood.

Patterson, C. J. (2000). Family relationships of lesbians and gay men. *Journal of Marriage and the Family, 62,* 1052–1069.

Pawelski, J., Perrin, E. C., Foy, J. M., Allen, C. E., Crawford, J. E., Del Monte, M., et al. (2006). *Pediatrics, 118,* 349–363.

Peele, S., with Brodsky, A. (1991). *Love and addiction.* New York: Taplinger.

Pence, E. L., & McDonnell, C. (2000). Developing policies and protocols in Duluth, Minnesota. In J. Hanmer & C. Itzin (Eds.), *Home truths about domestic violence: Feminist influences on policy and practice* (pp. 249–268). London: RoutledgeFalmer.

Pensanti, H. (2001). *Better sex for you: A natural approach to finding new levels of sexual satisfaction.* Lake Maru, FL: Siloam Press.

Peplau, L. A. (2001). Rethinking women's sexual orientation: An interdisciplinary, relationship-focused approach. *Personal Relationships, 8*(1), 1–19.

Peplau, L. A., Cochran, S. D., & Mays, V. M. (1997). A national survey of the intimate relationships of African American lesbians and gay men: A look at commitment, satisfaction, sexual behavior, and HIV disease. In B. Green (Ed.), *Ethnic and cultural diversity among lesbians and gay men: Psychological perspectives on lesbian and gay issues* (Vol. 3, pp. 11–38). Thousand Oaks, CA: Sage.

Peplau, L. A., & Spalding, L. R. (2000). The close relationships of lesbians, gay men, and bisexuals. In C. Hendrick & S. S. Hendrick (Eds.), *Close relationships: A sourcebook* (pp. 111–123). Thousand Oaks, CA: Sage.

Peplau, L. A., Veniegas, R. C., & Campbell, S. M. (1996). Gay and lesbian relationships. In R. C. Savin-Williams & K. M. Cohen (Eds.), *The lives of lesbians, gays, and bisexuals: Children to adults* (pp. 250–273). Ft. Worth, TX: Harcourt.

Perez, L. (2004, December 26). In three city homes, grief for the ultimate loss, fear for a son sent to Iraq, and relief for one who is back. *Newsday.* Web site: www.newsday.com/news/printedition/newyork/nyc-nyiraq264096646dec26,0,7962315.print.story?coll=nyc-nynews-print.

Perreira, K., Chapman, M., & Stein, G. (2006). Becoming an American parent: Overcoming challenges and finding strength in a new immigrant Latino community. *Journal of Family Issues, 27,* 1383–1414.

Peters, M. F. (1981). Strengths of Black families. In N. Stinnett, J. DeFrain, K. King, P. Knaub, & G. Rowe (Eds.), *Family strengths 3: Roots of well-being* (pp. 73–91). Lincoln: University of Nebraska Press.

Peterson, G. W., Steinmetz, S., & Wilson, S. M. (2005). *Parent–youth relations: Cultural and cross-cultural perspectives.* New York: Haworth.

Peterson, K. S. (1992a, March 12). Adults should know status of parents. *USA Today,* p. 1D.

Peterson, K. S. (1992b, March 12). Parents hand down financial attitudes. *USA Today,* p. 4D.

Pew Research Center for the People and the Press. (2005, August 3). Abortion and rights of terror suspects top court issues. Web site: http://people-press.org/reports/display.php3?ReportID=253.

Physician Leadership on National Drug Policy. (2000). Position paper on drug policy. Providence, RI: Brown University Center for Alcohol and Addiction Studies.

Pieve, L. (2001). An ethnographic study of the perceptions of Puerto Rican pregnant teenagers. *Dissertation Abstracts International-A, 62*(03), 1226.

Pines, A. M. (1998). *Romantic jealousy: Causes, symptoms, cures.* New York: Routledge.

PlanetSave.com. (2001, August 13). Women sentenced to 100 lashes for extramarital sex in Nigeria. Web site: http://www.planetsave.com/ViewStory.asp?ID=1165.

Planned Parenthood Federation of America. (1985, Spring). Five ways to prevent abortion (and one way that won't). In *Family matters* (p. 2). Lincoln, NE: Planned Parenthood of Lincoln.

Poduska, B. (2001, August). The credit trap. *Marriage and Families,* pp. 22–28.

Popenoe, D., & Whitehead, B. D. (1999a). *Should we live together? What young adults need to know about cohabitation before marriage.* New Brunswick, NJ: Rutgers University, National Marriage Project.

Popenoe, D., & Whitehead, B. D. (1999b). *The state of our unions.* New Brunswick, NJ: Rutgers University, National Marriage Project.

Popenoe, D., & Whitehead, B. D. (2000). *The state of our unions.* New Brunswick, NJ: Rutgers University, National Marriage Project.

Popenoe, D., & Whitehead, B. D. (2004). *The state of our unions.* New Brunswick, NJ: Rutgers University, National Marriage Project.

Popenoe, D., & Whitehead, R. D. (2005). *The state of our unions.* Piscataway, NJ: Rutgers University, National Marriage Project.

Population Reports. (1999, April). Condom use. Baltimore: Johns Hopkins School of Public Health, Center for Communication Programs, Population Information Program.

Porter, J. (1999, January 10). It's time to start thinking about electing a female president. Lincoln [NE] *Journal Star,* p. 6D.

Proctor, B. D., & Dalaker, J. (2003). *Poverty in the United States: 2002.* Current Population Reports, Consumer Income. Washington, DC: U.S. Bureau of the Census.

Puente, S., & Cohen, D. (2003). Jealousy and the meaning (or nonmeaning) of violence. *Personality and Social Psychology Bulletin, 29*(4), 449–460.

Qian, Z. (2005). Breaking the last taboo: Interracial marriages in America. *Contexts, 4*, 33–37.

Qian, Z., Blair, S. L., & Ruf, S. D. (2001). Asian American interracial and interethnic marriages: Differences by education and nativity. *International Migration Review, 35*(2), 557–586.

Raffaelli, M., Bogenschneider, K., & Flood, M. F. (1998). Parent–teen communication about sexual topics. *Journal of Family Issues, 19*(3), 315–333.

Raley, S. B., Mattingly, M. J., & Bianchi, S. (2006). How dual are dual-income couples? Documenting change from 1970–2001. *Journal of Marriage and the Family, 68*, 11–28.

Raven, B. H., Centers, R., & Rodrigues, A. (1975). The bases of conjugal power. In R. E. Cromwell & D. H. Olson (Eds.), *Power in families* (pp. 217–232). Newbury Park, CA: Sage.

Recker, N. K. (2001). The wicked stepmother myth. Family Life Month Packet. Columbus: Ohio State University Extension Web site: http://ohioline.osu.edu/flm01/FS04.html.

Reinisch, J., & Beasley, R. (1994). *The Kinsey Institute new report on sex* (p. 45). New York: St. Martin's.

Reiss, I. L., & Lee, G. R. (1988). *Family systems in America* (4th ed.). New York: Holt, Rinehart & Winston.

Remez, L. (1998). In Turkey, women's fertility is linked to education, employment and freedom to choose a husband. *International Family Planning Perspectives, 24*(2), 97–98.

Rennison, C. M. (2003, February). Intimate partner violence, 1993–2001. U.S. Department of Justice, Office of Justice Programs. Web site: http://www.ojp.usdoj.gov/bjs.

Rettig, K. D., Christensen, D. H., & Dahl, C. M. (1991). Impact of child support guidelines on the economic well-being of children. *Family Relations, 40*, 167–175.

Rettig, K. D., Leichtentritt, R. D., & Stanton, L. M. (1999). Understanding noncustodial fathers' family and life satisfaction from resource theory perspective. *Journal of Family Issues, 20*(4), 507–538.

Reynolds, M. (2002, April 3). Kandahar's lightly veiled homosexual habits. *Los Angeles Times.* Web site: http://www.globalgayz.com/g-afghanistan.html.

Rich, J. (2003). *The couple's guide to love and money.* Oakland, CA: New Harbinger.

Ridley, C. A., Peterman, D. J., & Avery, A. W. (1978, April). Cohabitation: Does it make for a better marriage? *Family Coordinator*, pp. 129–136.

Risman, B. J., & Johnson-Sumerford, D. (1998). Doing it fairly: A study of postgender marriages. *Journal of Marriage and the Family, 60*, 23–40.

Robbins, C. C. (1987, May 25). Expanding power for Indian women. *New York Times*, pp. III, 1.

Robbins, R., Scherman, A., Holman, H., & Wilson, J. (2005). Roles of American Indian grandparents in times of cultural crises. *Journal of Cultural Diversity, 12*, 62–68.

Roberts, L. (2005). Alcohol and the marital relationship. *Family Focus*, pp. 12–13.

Roberts, S. (2006, October 15). To be married means to be outnumbered in America. *The New York Times*, p. A22.

Roberts, S., Sabar, A., Goodman, B., & Balleza, M. (2007, January 16). 51% of women are now living without spouse. NYTimes.com. Web site: http://select.nytimes.com.

Robles, B. J. (2003). *Latino families: Net worth.* Baltimore: Annie Casey Foundation.

Rodgers, J. L., Nakonezny, P. A., & Shull, R. D. (1997). The effect of no-fault divorce legislation on divorce rates: A response to a reconsideration. *Journal of Marriage and the Family, 59*(4), 1026–1030.

Rokach, A. (2005). Coping with loneliness during pregnancy and motherhood. *Psychology and Education, 42*(1), 1–12.

Rokach, A. (2006). Loneliness in domestically abused women. *Psychological Reports, 98*(2), 367–373.

Roosa, M. W., Tein, J.-Y., Groppenbacher, N., Michaels, M., & Dumka, L. (1993). Mothers' parenting behavior and child mental health in families with a problem drinking parent. *Journal of Marriage and the Family, 55*, 107–118.

Root, M. P. P. (Ed.). (1992). *Racially mixed people in America.* Newbury Park, CA: Sage.

Root, M. P. P. (2002). The color of love. *The American Prospect, 13*(7), 54–55.

Ross, M. E., & Aday, L. A. (2006). Stress and coping in African American grandparents who are raising their grandchildren. *Journal of Family Issues, 27*, 912–932.

Rowe, C. L. (2003). Family-based interventions for substance abuse: A profile of two models. *The Family Psychologist, 19*(4), 4–9.

Rudy, D., & Grusec, J. E. (2006). Authoritarian parenting in individualist and collectivist groups: Associations with maternal emotion and cognition and children's self-esteem. *Journal of Family Psychology, 20*(1), 68–78.

Russell, B. (1938). *Power: A new social analysis.* New York: Norton.

Russo, N. F., & Dabul, A. J. (1997). The relationship of abortion to well-being: Do race and religion make a difference? *Professional Psychology: Research and Practice, 28*(1), 23–31.

Rybash, J. M. (1999). Aging and autobiographical memory: The long and bumpy road. *Journal of Adult Development, 6*(1), 1–10.

Sager, C. J., Brown, H. S., Crohn, H., Engel, T., Rodstein, E., & Walker, L. (1983). *Treating the remarried family.* New York: Brunner/Mazel.

Sammons, M. T. (2005). Psychology in the public sector: Addressing the psychological effects of combat in the U.S. Navy. *American Psychologist, 162*, 123–129.

Sarkisian, N., Gerena, M., & Gerstel, N. (2006). Extended family ties among Mexicans, Puerto Ricans, and

Whites: Superintegration or disintegration? *Family Relations, 55,* 331–344.

Satir, V. (1988). *The new peoplemaking.* Palo Alto, CA: Science and Behavior Books.

Scheinkman, M. (2005). Beyond the trauma of betrayal: Reconsidering affairs in couples therapy. *Family Process, 44,* 227–244.

Schmitt, D. P., & Buss, D. M. (2001). Human mate poaching: Tactics and temptations for infiltrating existing mateships. *Journal of Personality and Social Psychology, 80*(6), 894–917.

Schnell, R. (2000). The representation and treatment of adultery in medieval literature. *International Academy for Marital Spirituality Review, 6,* 17–33.

Schramm, D. G. (2006). Individual and social costs of divorce in Utah. *Journal of Family and Economic Issues, 27,* 133–151.

Schramm, D. G., Marshall, J. P., Harris, V. W., & Lee, T. R. (2005). After "I do": The newlywed transition. *Marriage and Family Review, 38,* 45–67.

Schultz, N. C., Schultz, C. L., & Olson, D. H. (1991). Couple strengths and stressors in complex and simple stepfamilies in Australia. *Journal of Marriage and the Family, 53,* 555–564.

Schwartz, J., Raine, G., & Robins, K. (1987, May 11). A "superminority" tops out. *Newsweek,* pp. 48–49.

Search Institute. (2006). *Introduction to assets.* Minneapolis: Author. Web site: http://www.search-institute.org/assets.

Seligman, M. E. (2002). *Authentic happiness.* New York: Free Press.

Selle, R. (1998, May). People in the news: Feminism's matriarch. *The World and I,* p. 51.

Selye, H. (1974). *The stress of life* (2nd ed.). New York: McGraw-Hill.

Sen, A. (2001, October 27–November 9). Many faces of gender inequality. *Frontline.* Web site: http://www.flonnet.com/fl18220040.htm.

Sex Information and Education Council of the U.S. (2001). Community action kit. Web site: http://www.siecus.org/advocacy/kits0005.html.

Sex Information and Education Council of the U.S. (2004). Adolescence and abstinence fact sheet. Web site: http://www.siecus.org/pubs/fact/fact0001.html.

Sharma, A. R., McGue, M. K., & Benson, P. L. (1998). The psychological adjustment of United States adopted adolescents and their nonadopted siblings. *Child Development, 69*(3), 791–802.

Sheehy, G. (1998). *New passages: Mapping your life across time.* New York: Pocket Books.

Sherman, C. W. (2006, December). Remarriage and stepfamily in later life. *Family Focus,* pp. 8–9.

Sherman, M. D., Sautter, F., Jackson, M. H., Lyons, J. A., & Han, X. (2006). Domestic violence in veterans with posttraumatic stress disorder who seek couples therapy. *Journal of Marital and Family Therapy, 32,* 479–490.

Shorris, E. (1992). *Latinos: A biography of the people.* New York: Norton.

Shostak, A. (1987). Singlehood. In M. Sussman & S. Steinmetz (Eds.), *Handbook of marriage and the family.* New York: Plenum.

Sibling Abuse Survivors' Information and Advocacy Network. (2004). Sasian. Web site: http://www.sasian.org.

Silva, M. (2002). The effectiveness of school-based sex education programs in the promotion of abstinent behavior: A meta-analysis. *Health Education Research, 17*(4), 471–481.

Silverman, J. (2001). Dating violence against adolescent girls. *Journal of the American Medical Association, 286*(5), 572–579.

Silverstein, L. B., & Auerbach, C. F. (2000). Continuing the dialogue about fathers and families. *American Psychologist, 55*(6), 683–684.

Singh, S., & Darroch, J. E. (2000). Adolescent pregnancy and childbearing: Levels and trends in developed countries. *Family Planning Perspectives, 32*(1), 14–23.

Singletary, M. (2003, August 27). Do college students need credit cards? Hardly. *The Washington Post.* Web site: http://www.washingtonpost.com/ac2/wp-dyn/A56633-2003Aug27.

Singletary, M. (2004, October 20). College students should steer clear of credit cards. *The Washington Post.* Web site: http://washingtonpost.com/wp-dyn/articles/A50054-2004(ct20.html).

Skinner, K. B., Bahr, S. J., Crane, D. R., & Call, V. R. A. (2002). Cohabitation, marriage and remarriage. *Journal of Family Issues, 23*(1), 74–90.

Skogrand, L. (2004). A process for learning about and creating programming for culturally diverse audiences. *Forum of Family and Consumer Issues, 9.* Online journal: http://www.ces.ncsu.edu/depts/fcs/pub/forum.html.

Skogrand, L., DeFrain, N., DeFrain, J., & Jones, J. (2007). *Surviving and transcending a traumatic childhood: The dark thread.* New York: Haworth.

Skogrand, L., Hatch, D., & Singh, A. (2008). Strong marriages in Latino culture. In R. Dalla, J. DeFrain, J. Johnson, & D. Abbott (Eds.), *Strengths and challenges of new immigrant families: Implications for research, policy, education, and service.* Lanham, MD: Lexington Books.

Skogrand, L., Henderson, K., & Higginbotham, B. (2006). Sandwich generation (fact sheet). Utah State University Cooperative Extension. Web site: http://extension.usu.edu/cooperative.

Skogrand, L., Schramm, D. G., Marshall, J. P., & Lee, T. (2005). The effects of debt on newlyweds and implications for education. *Journal of Extension, 43.* Web site: http://www.joe.org/joe/2005june/rb7.shtml.

Skolnick, A. S., & Skolnick, J. H. (1977). *Family in transition.* Boston: Little, Brown.

Skutch, L. P. (2001). Childless-by-choice women and mothers-by-choice: A comparative study of attitudes and behaviors on quality of life and feminist perspectives. *Dissertation Abstracts International-B*, 62(2), 1145.

Smith, J. (2003). The adopted child syndrome: A methodological perspective. *Families in Society: The Journal of Contemporary Human Services*, 82(6), 491–497.

Smith, K. (2002). *Who's minding the kids? Child care arrangements: Spring 1997* (pp. 70–86). Washington, DC: U.S. Bureau of the Census.

Smock, P. (2000). Cohabitation in the United States. *Annual Review of Sociology*, 26, 1–20.

Solot, D., & Miller, M. (2000). Ten ways to improve your chances for a good marriage after cohabitation. *Florida Times-Union*.

Somers, M. S. (1993). A comparison of voluntarily child-free adults and parents. *Journal of Marriage and the Family*, 55, 643–650.

Spencer, M. (2006). Revisiting the 1990 *Special Issue on Minority Children:* An editorial perspective 15 years later. *Child Development*, 77, 1149–1154.

Sprey, J. (1990). Theoretical practice in family studies. In J. Sprey (Ed.), *Fashioning family theory: New approaches* (pp. 9–33). Newbury Park, CA: Sage.

Stanley, S. M., Whitton, S. W., Sadberry, S. L., Clements, M. L., & Markman, H. J. (2006). Sacrifice as a predictor of marital outcomes. *Family Process*, 45, 289–303.

Stauss, J. H. (1986). The study of American families: Implications for applied research. *Family Perspective*, 20(4), 337–350.

Stauss, J. H. (1993). Reframing and refocusing American Indian family strengths. *Family Perspective*, 27(4), 311–321.

Sternberg, R. J. (2007a). Triangular theory of love. Web site: http://en.wikipedia.org/wiki/Triangular_theory _of_love.

Sternberg, R. J. (2007b). Robert J. Sternberg homepage. Web site: http://yale.edu/rjsternberg.

Sternberg, R. J., & Barnes, M. (Eds.). (1988). *The psychology of love*. New Haven, CT: Yale University Press.

Sternberg, R. J., & Weis, K. (Eds.). (2006). *The new psychology of love*. New Haven, CT: Yale University Press.

Stets, J. E. (1990). Verbal and physical aggression in marriage. *Journal of Marriage and the Family*, 52, 501–514.

Stets, J. E., & Straus, M. A. (1989). The marriage as a hitting license: A comparison of assaults in dating, cohabiting, and married couples. In M. A. Pirog-Good & J. E. Stets (Eds.), *Violence in dating relationships* (pp. 33–52). New York: Greenwood.

Stewart, K. L. (1989). Stress and adaptation: A multisystem model of individual, couple, family, and work systems. *Dissertation Abstracts International-A*, 49(08).

Stewart, S. D. (2007). *Brave new stepfamilies*. Thousand Oaks, CA: Sage.

Stinnett, N., & DeFrain, J. (1985). *Secrets of strong families*. Boston: Little, Brown.

Straus, M. A. (1990). The national family violence surveys. In M. Straus & R. J. Gelles (Eds.), *Physical violence in American families* (pp. 3–16). New Brunswick, NJ: Transaction.

Straus, M. A. (1994). *Beating the devil out of them: Corporal punishment in American families*. New York: Lexington Books.

Straus, M. A. (1998). Impulsive corporal punishment by mothers and antisocial behavior and impulsiveness of children. *Behavioral Sciences and the Law*, 16(3), 353–374.

Straus, M. A. (1999). *The benefits of avoiding corporal punishment: New and more definitive evidence*. Unpublished manuscript, University of New Hampshire, Family Research Laboratory.

Straus, M. A. (2001). *Beating the devil out of them: Corporal punishment in American families*. New Brunswick, NJ: Transaction.

Straus, M. A. (2002). Communicating the no-spanking message to parents. *Journal of Family Communication*, 21(5), 3–5.

Straus, M. A., & Field, C. J. (2003). Psychological aggresion by American parents: National data on prevalence, chronicity, and severity. *Journal of Marriage and the Family*, 65, 795–808.

Straus, M. A., & Gelles, R. J. (1986). Societal change and change in family violence from 1975 to 1985 as revealed by two national surveys. *Journal of Marriage and the Family*, 48, 465–479.

Straus, M. A., & Mathus, A. K. (1996). Social change and trends in approval of corporal punishment by par-ents from 1968 to 1994. In D. Frehsee, W. Horn, & K. Bussman (Eds.), *Violence against children* (pp. 91–105). New York: de Gruyter.

Straus, M. A., & Stewart, J. H. (1999). Corporal punishment by American parents: National data on prevalence, chronicity, severity, and duration, in relation to child and family characteristics. *Clinical Child and Family Psychology Review*, 2(2), 55–70.

Street, A. E., & Arias, I. (2001). Psychological abuse and posttraumatic stress disorder in battered women: Examining the roles of shame and guilt. *Violence and Victims*, 16(1), 65–78.

Strong, B., DeVault, C., & Sayad, B. W. (1999). *Human sexuality: Diversity in contemporary America* (3rd ed.). Mountain View, CA: Mayfield.

Stroup, A., & Pollock, G. E. (1994). Economic consequences of marital dissolution. *Journal of Divorce and Remarriage*, 22(1/2), 37–54.

Struthers, C. B., & Bokemeier, J. L. (2000). Myths and realities of raising children and creating family life in a rural county. *Journal of Family Issues*, 21(1), 17–46.

Substance Abuse and Mental Health Services Administration. (2004). The complicated relationship between substance abuse and violence. Center for Substance Abuse Prevention. Washington, DC: U.S. Department of Health and Human Services. Web site: http://www .samhsa.gov.

Sureender, S., Khan, A. G., & Radharkrishnan, S. (1997). The dowry system and education of female children:

Attitudes examined in Bihar, India. *Demography India*, 26(1), 109–122.

Sutton, C. E. T., & Broken Nose, M. A. (1996). American Indian families: An overview. In M. McGoldrick & J. Giordano (Eds.), *Ethnicity and family therapy* (2nd ed., pp. 31–44). New York: Guilford.

Sweeney, J. (1982, June 21). Taking the long view of marriage: Why do some endure? *Los Angeles Times*, pp. 1, 21–23.

Switala, K. (2007). The feminist theory Web site: http://www.cddc.vt.edu/feminism/enin.html.

Taffel, S. M., Placek, P. J., Moien, M., & Kosary, C. L. (1991). 1989 U.S. cesarean section rate steadies—VBAC rate rises to nearly one in five. *Birth*, 18, 73–77.

Tannen, D. (2001). *You just don't understand: Women and men in conversation*. New York: Quill.

Tannen, D., & Aries, E. (1997). Conversational style: Do women and men speak different languages? In M. R. Walsh (Ed.), *Women, men, and gender: Ongoing debates* (pp. 79–100). New Haven, CT: Yale University Press.

Tatara, T. (Ed.). (1998). *Understanding elder abuse in minority populations*. Philadelphia: Brunner/Mazel.

Taylor, H. (1998, March 11). The Harris poll #14: Differences in American and Japanese attitudes to extramarital sex, divorce—and Princess Diana. The Harris Poll: http://www.harrisinteractive.com/harris_polll/index.asp?PID=193.

Taylor, R. J., Jackson, J. S., and Chatters, L. M. (Eds.). (1997). *Family life in Black America*. Thousand Oaks, CA: Sage.

Taylor, R. J., Lincoln, K. D., & Chatters, L. M. (2005). Supportive relationships with church members among African Americans. *Family Relations*, 54, 501–511.

Theroux, P. (1996). *My other life: A novel*. Boston: Houghton Mifflin.

Thiele, D. M., & Whelan, T. A. (2006). The nature and dimension of the grandparent role. *Marriage and Family Review*, 40, 93–108.

Thomas, V., & Olson, D. H. (1993). Problem families and the Circumplex Model: Observational assessment using the clinical rating scale. *Journal of Marital and Family Therapy*, 19(2), 159–175.

Thompson, K. L., & Gullone, E. (2003). Promotion of empathy and prosocial behaviour in children through humane education. *Australian Psychologist*, 38(3), 175–182.

Tichenor, V. J. (1999). Status and income as gendered resources: The case for marital power. *Journal of Marriage and the Family*, 61, 638–650.

Trimble, J., & Fisher, C. (2006). Our shared journey: Lessons from the past to protect the future. In J. Trimble & C. Fisher (Eds.), *The handbook of ethical research with ethnocultural populations and communities* (pp. xv–xxix). Thousand Oaks, CA: Sage.

Troll, L. E. (1997). Growing old in families. In I. Deitch & C. Ward Howell (Eds.), *Counseling the aging and their families* (pp. 3–16). Alexandria, VA: American Counseling Association.

Troll, L. E. (2001/2002). When the world narrows: Intimacy with the dead? *Generations*, 25(2), 55–58.

Tubbs, C. Y., Roy, K. M., & Burton, L. M. (2005). Family ties: Constructing family time in low-income families. *Family Process*, 44, 77–91.

UK National Statistics. (2004, January 24). Marriage and divorce rates: EU comparison, 2002. Web site: http://www.statistics.gove.uk/STATBASE/ssdataset.asp?vlnk+17625&More=Y.

Ulman, A., & Straus, M. A. (2003). Violence by children against mothers in relation to violence between parents and corporal punishment by parents. *Journal of Comparative Family Studies*, 34(1), 41–60.

United Nations AIDS. (2004). A global overview of the AIDS epidemic. Web site: http://www.unaids.org/EN/resources/epidemiology.asp.

United Nations International Labour Office. (2004a). *Breaking through the glass ceiling: Women in management—update 2004*. Geneva: Author.

United Nations International Labour Office. (2004b). *Global employment trends for women 2004*. Geneva: Author.

University of Michigan. (2003). Monitoring the future: National results on adolescent drug use: Overview of key findings, 2002. Cited by the U.S. Department of Justice, Office of Justice Programs, Bureau of Justice Statistics. Web site: http://www.ojp.us.doj.gov/bjs/dcf/du.htm.

Urban Institute. (2000, February 1). A new look at homelessness in America. Web site: http://www.urban.org.

U.S. Advisory Board on Child Abuse and Neglect. (1990). *Child abuse and neglect: Critical first steps in response to a national emergency*. Washington, DC: U.S. Government Printing Office.

U.S. Bureau of the Census. (2000a). Census Bureau facts for features. Web site: http://www.census.gov/Press-Release/www/2000/cb00ff13.html.

U.S. Bureau of the Census. (2000b). Census 2000 brief: Overview of race and Hispanic origin, 2000. Web site: http://www.census.gov.

U.S. Bureau of the Census. (2000c). Census 2000. Web site: http://www.census.gov.

U.S. Bureau of the Census. (2000d, June). Fertility in American women: Population characteristics. Web site: http://www.census.

U.S. Bureau of the Census. (2000e). *Statistical abstract of the United States* (120th ed.). Washington, DC: U.S. Government Printing Office.

U.S. Bureau of the Census. (2001a). Age: 2000. Census 2000 brief. Web site: http://www.census.gov.

U.S. Bureau of the Census. (2001b). *Census 2000 shows America's diversity*. Web site: http://www.census.gov/Press-Release/www.2001/cb01cn61.html.

U.S. Bureau of the Census. (2001c, March). Current population survey. Web site: http://www.census.gov.

U.S. Bureau of the Census. (2001d). *Population by race and Hispanic/Latino status*. Web site: http://census.gov/statab/www/part1a.html.

U.S. Bureau of the Census. (2001e). *Population change and distribution*. Web site: http://www.census .gov/population/cen2000/c2kbr01-2.pdf.

U.S. Bureau of the Census. (2001f). Population profile of the United States: 2000. Web site: http://www.census .gov.

U.S. Bureau of the Census. (2001g). *Statistical abstract of the United States* (121st ed.). Washington, DC: U.S. Government Printing Office.

U.S. Bureau of the Census. (2002a). Money income in United States—2001. Web site: http://www.census .gov.

U.S. Bureau of the Census. (2002b). Press release. Web site: http://www.census.gov/Press-Release/www/2002/ cb02cn173.html.

U.S. Bureau of the Census. (2002c). *Statistical abstract of the United States* (122nd ed). Washington, DC: U.S. Government Printing Office.

U.S. Bureau of the Census. (2002d). Summary File 3 (SF 3). Poverty status in 1999 by sex by age. Web site: http:// factfinder.census.gov.

U.S. Bureau of the Census. (2003a). American Indian and Alaska Native heritage month: November 2003. Web site: http://www.census.gov.

U.S. Bureau of the Census. (2003b). *Statistical abstract of the United States* (123rd ed.). Washington, DC: U.S. Government Printing Office.

U.S. Bureau of the Census. (2004a). Census Bureau projects tripling of Hispanic and Asian populations in 50 years; non-Hispanic Whites may drop to half of total population. Web site: http://www.census.gov/Press-Release/ www/releases/archives/population/001720.html.

U.S. Bureau of the Census. (2004b). Population profile of the United States: 2000. Web site: http://www.census .gov.

U.S. Bureau of the Census. (2004c). *Statistical abstract of the United States* (120th ed.). Washington, DC: U.S. Government Printing Office.

U.S. Bureau of the Census. (2004d, July 19). Unmarried and Single Americans Week. Web site: http://census .gov/Press-Release/www/releases/archives/facts _for. . . .

U.S. Bureau of the Census. (2005a). Educational attainment in the United States: 2005. Web site: http://www .census.gov/population/www/socdemo/education/ cps2005.html.

U.S. Bureau of the Census. (2005b). Family groups with children under 18 years old by race and Hispanic origin. *Statistical abstract or the United States*. Web site: http://www.census.gov/compendia/statab/tables/ 07s0062.xls.

U.S. Bureau of the Census. (2005c, May). Indicators of marriage and fertility in the United States from the American Community Survey: 2000–2003. Web site: http://census.gov/population/www/socdemo/ fertility/mar-fert-sli. . . .

U.S. Bureau of the Census. (2005d). Internet access and usage and online service usage: 1997–2005. *Statistical abstract of the United States*. Web site: http://www.census .gov/compendia/statab.

U.S. Bureau of the Census. (2005e). Marital status of the population by sex, race and Hispanic origin: 1990– 2005. *Statistical abstract of the United States*. Web site: http://www.census.gov/compendia/statab.

U.S. Bureau of the Census. (2005f). 2005 American community survey: Data profile highlights. *Fact sheet*. Web site: http://factfinder.census.gov.

U.S. Bureau of the Census. (2006a). Hispanic heritage month. *Facts for features*. Web site: http://www.census .gov/Press-Release.

U.S. Bureau of the Census. (2006b, February). Valentine's Day: February 14. Web site: http://census.gov/Press -Release/www/releases/archives/facts_for. . . .

U.S. Census Bureau News. (2004). Hispanic and Asian American increasing faster than overall population. (June 14, 2004).

U.S. Department of Health and Human Services. (2004). 10th special report to the U.S. Congress on alcohol and health: Highlights from current research, June 2000. National Institutes of Health, National Institute on Alcohol Abuse and Alcoholism. Washington, DC. Web site: http://www.niaaa.nih.gov.

U.S. Department of Justice. (2005). Victims of crime. Web site: http://www.usdoj.gov.

U.S. Department of Labor. (2003). *Highlights of women's earnings in 2002,* Report 972. Bureau of Labor Statistics, Washington, DC.

U.S. General Accounting Office. (2003). *Women's earnings: Work patterns partially explain difference between men's and women's earnings.* Report to Congressional requesters. Washington, DC: Author.

Van As, C. F. (2003). Facilitating the optimal academic achievement of the adolescent through parenting. *Dissertation Abstracts International-A, 63*(08), 2794.

Van Dorn, R. A., Bowen, G. L., & Blau, J. R. (2006). The impact of community diversity and consolidated inequality on dropping out of high school. *Family Relations, 55,* 105–118.

van Dulmen, M., Miller, B. C., Grotevant, H. D., Fan, X., & Christensen, M. (2000). Comparisons of adopted and nonadopted adolescents in a large, nationally representative sample. *Child Development, 71*(5), 1458–1473.

Van Volkom, M. (2006). Sibling relationships in middle and older adulthood: A review of the literature. *Marriage and Family Review, 40,* 151–170.

van Wormer, K., Wells, U., & Boes, M. (2000). *Social work with lesbians, gays, and bisexuals: A strengths perspective.* Needham Heights, MA: Allyn & Bacon.

Vega, W. A. (1995). The study of Latino families: A point of departure. In R. E. Zambrana (Ed.), *Understanding Latino families: Scholarship, policy, and practice* (Vol. 2, pp. 3–17). Thousand Oaks, CA: Sage.

Vega, W. A., Patterson, T., Sallis, J., Nader, P., Atkins, C., & Abraham, I. (1986). Cohesion and adaptability in Mexican American and Anglo families. *Journal of Marriage and the Family, 48*, 857–867.

Veniegas, R. C., & Peplau, L. A. (1997). Power and the quality of same-sex friendships. *Psychology of Women Quarterly, 21*(3), 279–297.

Vincent, J. P., & Jouriles, E. N. (2000). *Domestic violence: Guidelines for research-informed practice.* London: Jessica Kingsley.

Visher, E. B. (1989). The Stepping Ahead Program. In M. Burt (Ed.), *Stepfamilies stepping ahead* (3rd ed., pp. 57–89). Lincoln, NE: Stepfamilies Press.

Visher, E. B., & Visher, J. S. (1992). *How to win as a stepfamily* (2nd ed.). New York: Brunner/Mazel.

Visher, E. B., & Visher, J. S. (1996). *Therapy with stepfamilies.* New York: Brunner/Mazel.

Visher, E. B., & Visher, J. S. (1998). Stepparents: The forgotten family members. *Family and Conciliation Courts Review, 37*(4), 444–451.

Visher, E. B., Visher, J. S., & Pasley, K. (1997). Stepfamily therapy from the client's perspective. *Marriage and Family Review, 27*(1–2), 191–213.

von Bertalanffy, L. (1968). *General system theory: Foundation, development, applications.* New York: Braziller.

Vosburg, E. S. (2004). Toward triadic communication: A crisis in Japanese family relationships. In W. C. Nichols (Ed.), *Family therapy around the world* (pp. 105–117). Binghamton, NY: Haworth.

Voydanoff, P. (2005). Work demands and work-to-family and family-to-work conflict: Direct and indirect relationships. *Journal of Family Issues, 26*, 707–726.

Waite, L. J. (1998). Why marriage matters. In T. Ooms (Ed.), *Strategies to strengthen marriage* (pp. 1–22). Washington, DC: Family Impact Seminar.

Waite, L. J. (2001, April). 5 marriage myths, 6 marriage benefits. *Marriage and Families*, pp. 19–25.

Waite, L. J. (2003, April). Uncommitted cohabitation versus marriage. *Terskel, 76*, 17–20.

Waite, L. J., & Gallagher, M. (2000). *The case for marriage: Why married people are happier, healthier, and better off financially.* New York: Doubleday.

Waite, L. J., & Lehrer, L. (2003). The benefits from marriage and religion in the United States: A comparative analysis. *Population and Developmental Review, 29*(2), 255–275.

Waldrep, D. A., Cozza, S. J., & Chen, R. S. (2004, June). The impact of deployment on the military family. In *Iraq War Clinician Guide* (2nd ed., pp. 83–86). Washington, DC: Department of Veterans Affairs, National Center for PTSD.

Walker, A. J., & McGraw, L. A. (1999). Interdependence between mothers and daughters in middle and later life: Patterns of connection and autonomy. Poster presented at the 61st Annual Conference of the National Council on Family Relations, Irvine, CA, November 12–15.

Walker, L. E. (2000). *The battered woman syndrome* (2nd ed.). New York: Springer.

Waller, W. (1951). *The family* [revised by R. Hill]. New York: Dryden.

Wallerstein, J. S., & Blakeslee, S. (2003). *What about the kids? Raising your children before, during, and after divorce.* New York: Hyperion.

Wallerstein, J. S., & Lewis, J. M. (2004). The unexpected legacy of divorce: Report of a 25-year study. *Psychoanalytic Psychology, 21*(3), 353–370.

Walsh, F. (1998). *Strengthening family resilience.* New York: Guilford.

Walsh, F. (2006). *Strengthening family resilience* (2nd ed.). New York: Guilford.

Wang, R., Bianchi, S., & Raley, S (2005). Teenagers' Internet use and family rules: A research note. *Journal of Marriage and the Family, 67*, 1249–1258.

Watamura, S. E., Sebanc, A. M., & Gunnar, M. R. (2002). Rising cortisol at childcare: Relations with nap, rest, and temperament. *Developmental Psychobiology, 40*(1), 33–42.

Weitzman, L. J., & Dixon, R. B. (1992). The transformation of legal marriage through no-fault divorce. In A. S. Skolnick & J. H. Skolnick (Eds.), *Family in transition: Rethinking marriage, sexuality, child rearing, and family organization* (7th ed., pp. 217–289). New York: HarperCollins.

Westman, J. C. (1998). Grandparenthood. Parenthood in America, General Library System, University of Wisconsin–Madison. Web site: http://parenthood.library.wisc.edu/Westman/Westman-Grandparenthood.html.

Whisman, M. A., Dixon, A. E., & Johnson, B. (1997). Therapists' perspectives of couple problems and treatment issues in couple therapy. *Journal of Family Psychology, 11*(3), 361–366.

Whitaker, C. (1992). Symbolic experiential family therapy: Model and methodology. In J. K. Zeig (Ed.), *Evolution of psychotherapy: The second conference* (pp. 13–23). Philadelphia: Brunner/Mazel.

Whitam, F. L., Daskalos, C., Sobolewski, C. G., & Padilla, P. (1998). The emergency of lesbian sexuality and identity cross-culturally: Brazil, Peru, the Philippines, and the United States. *Archives of Sexual Behavior, 27*(1), 31–56.

White, M., & Epston, D. (1990). *Narrative means to therapeutic ends.* New York: Norton.

White, M., & Morgan, A. (2006). *Narrative therapy with children and their families.* Adelaide, Australia: Dulwich Centre Publishers.

Whitehead, B. D. (1997). *The divorce culture.* New York: Knopf.

Whitehead, B. D. (2003). *Why there are no good men left.* New York: Broadway Books.

Whitehead, B. D., & Popenoe, D. (2001). *The states of our unions.* Rutgers University, National Marriage Project.

Whitehead, D., & Doherty, W. J. (1989). Systems dynamics in cigarette smoking: An exploratory study. *Family Systems Medicine, 7*(3), 264–273.

White House. (2004). Summary fact sheet on HIV/AIDS. Web site: http://www.whitehouse.gov/onap/facts.html.

Whitman, C. T. (1995, May 31). Wheaton College commencement address. *Good Morning America.* New York: ABC Television.

Wiener, N. (1956). *I am a mathematician.* New York: Doubleday.

Wilmot, W. W., & Hocker, J. L. (2007). *Interpersonal conflict* (7th ed.). Boston: McGraw-Hill.

Winch, R. F. (1958). *Mate selection: A study of complementary needs.* New York: Harper.

Wind, R. (2006, December). Premarital sex is nearly universal among Americans, and has been for decades. Media Center, Alan Guttmacher Institute. Web site: http://www.guttmacher.org/media/nr/2006/12/19/index.html.

Winslow, S. (2005). Work–family conflict, gender, and parenthood, 1977–1997. *Journal of Family Issues, 26,* 727–755.

Wolak, J., Mitchell, K., & Finkelhor, D. (2006). Online victimization of youth: Five years later. Web site: http://www.missingkids.com.

Wolfe, A. (1999, September). The mystique of Betty Friedan. *The Atlantic Online*: http://www.theatlantic.com/issues/99sep/9909friedan.htm.

Woodward, B. (2000). *Maestro: Greenspan's Fed and the American boom.* New York: Simon & Schuster.

Woodward, J. C. (1988). *The solitude of loneliness.* Lexington, MA: Lexington Books/Heath.

Worthington, E. L. (Ed.). (2005). *Handbook of forgiveness.* New York: Routledge.

Wrobel, G. M., Ayers-Lopez, S., Grotevant, H. D., & McRoy, R. G. (1996). Openness in adoption and the level of child participation. *Child Development, 67*(5), 2358–2374.

Wuerffel, J., DeFrain, J., & Stinnett, N. (1990, Fall). How strong families use humor. *Family Perspective,* pp. 129–142.

Wynne, L. (1958). Pseudo-mutuality in the family relations of schizophrenics. *Psychiatry, 21,* 205–222.

Xu, X., Ji, J., & Tung, Y.-Y. (2000). Social and political assortative mating in urban China. *Journal of Family Issues, 21*(1), 47–77.

Yarrow, P. (1972). River of Jordan. *PP&M Lifelines.* Mary Beth Music, ASCAP. Burbank, CA: Warner Bros. Records.

Zambrana, R. E. (Ed.). (1995). *Understanding Latino families.* Thousand Oaks, CA: Sage.

Zambrana, R. E., & Capello, D. (2003). Promoting Latino child and family welfare: Strategies for strengthening the child welfare system. *Children and Youth Services Review, 25*(10), 755–780.

Zaslow, M., & Eldred, C. (1998). Parenting behavior in a sample of young mothers in poverty. *APA Monitor.* Washington, DC: American Psychological Association.

Zeig, J. K. (Ed.). (2001). *Changing directives: The strategic psychotherapy of Jay Haley.* Chandler, AZ: Zeig, Tucker and Theisen.

Zigler, E. F. (2004). Research interests. Yale University, Department of Psychology, New Haven, CT. Web site: http://www.yale.edu/psychology/FacInfo/Zigler.html.

Credits

TEXT

Definition of "family" Copyright © 2006 by Houghton Mifflin Company. Reproduced by permission from *The American Heritage Dictionary of the English Language,* Fourth Edition. **Kahlil Gibran: "On Marriage"** "On Marriage" from *The Prophet* by Kahlil Gibran. Copyright © 1923 by Kahlil Gibran and renewed 1951 by Administrators C.T.A. of Kahlil Gibran Estate and Mary G. Gibran. Used by permission of Alfred A. Knopf, a division of Random House, Inc. **"Extreme Togetherness Poem" by Judy Altura**, copyright © 1974 by Judy Altura, from MY NEEDS, YOUR NEEDS, OUR NEEDS by Jerry Gillies. Used by permission of Doubleday, a division of Random House, Inc. **Kahlil Gibran: "On Children"** "On Children" from *The Prophet* by Kahlil Gibran. Copyright © 1923 by Kahlil Gibran and renewed 1951 by Administrators C.T.A. of Kahlil Gibran Estate and Mary G. Gibran. Used by permission of Alfred A. Knopf, a division of Random House, Inc. **Lyrics from "River of Jordan"** RIVER OF JORDAN. Words and music by PETER YARROW © 1972 (Renewed) MARY BETH MUSIC. All rights reserved. Used by permission of ALFRED PUBLISHING CO., INC.

FIGURES

Figure 1.1 U.S. Census Bureau, 2005, Table 54. **Figure 1.2** U.S. Census Bureau, 2005, Table 62. **Figure 1.4** Adapted from "Family Decline and Child Well-Being: A Comparative Analysis" by S. K. Houseknecht and J. Sastry, 1966, *Journal of Marriage and Family, 58,* p. 734. http://www.blackwell-synergy.com/loi/jomf. **Figure 2.1** *U.S. Census (2005), Statistical Abstract Table 677, 696, and 62. **U.S. Census Data (2005), Educational Attainment, Table 1a. **Figure 2.2** U.S. Census Bureau (2004a). **Figure 5.2** Reproduced with permission of authors and publisher from: R. H. Kilmann and K. W. Thomas, "Interpersonal Conflict-Handling Behavior as Reflections of Jungian Personality Dimensions," 1975, *Psychological Reports, 37,* 971–980. © Psychological Reports 1975. **Figure 6.1** From SEX IN AMERICA by John Gagnon. Copyright © 1994 by CSG Enterprises, Inc., Edward O. Laumann, Robert T. Michael, and Gina Kolata. By permission of LITTLE, BROWN AND COMPANY. **Figure 6.2** From SEX IN AMERICA by John Gagnon. Copyright © 1994 by CSG Enterprises, Inc., Edward O. Laumann, Robert T. Michael, and Gina Kolata. By permission of LITTLE, BROWN AND COMPANY. **Figure 6.3**

From SEX IN AMERICA by John Gagnon. Copyright © 1994 by CSG Enterprises, Inc., Edward O. Laumann, Robert T. Michael, and Gina Kolata. By permission of LITTLE, BROWN AND COMPANY. **Figure 6.4** THE SOCIAL ORGANIZATION OF SEXUALITY: Sexual Practices in the United States (pp. 370–371) by E. O. Laumann, J. H. Bagnon, R. T. Michael, and S. Michaels, 1994, Chicago: University of Chicago Press. Reprinted with permission. **Figure 7.1** Reproduced with permission from P. G. Herbst, *The Measurement of Family Relationships,* Copyright (© 1952 The Tavistock Institute, London, UK, 1952), by permission of Sage Publications Ltd. **Figure 8.1** U.S. Census Bureau (2003b). **Figure 8.2** U.S. Census Bureau, Current Population Survey, March 2001. **Figure 8.3** U.S. Census Bureau (2003b). **Figure 9.1** "Near and Dear: Friendship and Love Compared" by K. E. Davis 1985 (February). *Psychology Today,* p. 24. Copyright 1985 by Sussex Publishers, Inc. Reprinted by permission from *Psychology Today* magazine. **Figure 9.2** *The Psychology of Love* (p. 37) edited by R. Sternberg and M. Barnes, 1988, New Haven, CT: Yale University Press. Copyright 1988 by Yale University Press. Reprinted by permission. **Figure 9.3** *The Psychology of Love* (p. 51) edited by R. Sternberg and M. Barnes, 1988, New Haven, CT: Yale University Press. Copyright 1988 by Yale University Press. Reprinted by permission. **Figure 9.4** *Empowering Couples: Building on Your Strengths* by D. H. Olson and A. K. Olson. © 2000 Life Innovations. Reprinted with permission. **Figure 10.2** From *Family Systems in America,* 4th edition, by Reiss. Reprinted with permission of Wadsworth, a division of Thomson Learning: www.thomsonrights.com. Fax 800-730-2215. **Figure 11.2** *Empowering Couples: Building on Your Strengths* by D. H. Olson and A. K. Olson. © 2000 Life Innovations. Reprinted with permission. **Figure 12.1** Mark Lino, 2004. *Expenditures on Children by Families,* 2003, U.S. Dept. of Agriculture, Center for Nutrition Policy and Promotion. **Figure 12.3** "Frequency of Adolescent Sons and Daughters Being Hit by a Parent" from *Beating the Devil Out of Them: Corporal Punishment in American Families* by M. A . Straus. Copyright © 2001 Transaction Publishers. Reprinted with permission of the publisher. **Figure 12.4** "Relationship Between Corporal Punishment Received as a Teenager and Adult Depression" from *Beating the Devil Out of Them: Corporal Punishment in American Families* by M. A. Straus. Copyright © 1994 Transaction Publishers. Reprinted with permission of the publisher. **Figure 13.1** General Social Survey, National Opinion Research Center

at the University of Chicago, 1996. Used with permission. **Figure 14.3** P. Boss, *Family Stress Management,* copyright © 2001 by Sage Publications. Reprinted by permission of Sage Publications, Inc. **Figure 14.4** From Olson, McCubbin, Barnes, Larson, Muxen, and Wilson, *Families: What Makes Them Work,* 2/e, copyright © 1989 by Sage Publications. Reprinted by permission of Sage Publications, Inc. **Figure 14.5** Reprinted and adapted from *Stillborn: The Invisible Death* by J. DeFrain, L. Martens, J. Stork, and W. Stork. Copyright © 1986 by Lexington Books. Reprinted with permission of Lexington Books, an imprint of Rowman & Littlefield Publishing Group. **Figure 14.8** U.S. Census Bureau (2003b, table 323, p. 208). **Figure 15.1** "Estimated Divorce and Remarriage Rates for 1,000 Individuals Married in 1990" from *Family Science* (p. 445) by W. R. Burr, R. D. Day, and K. S. Bahr. Brooks/Cole © 1993 by Randal Day. Reprinted with author's permission. **Figure 15.2** Statistical Abstract of the United States: 1951, no. 57; 1999, no. 91; 2004–2005, no. 70; 2006, table 117. National Vital Statistics Reports, vol. 54., no. 17. **Figure 15.4** U.S. Census Bureau (2001e). **Figure 15.5** From DIVORCED FAMILIES: A Multidisciplinary View by Constance R. Ahrons and Roy H. Rodgers. Copyright © 1987 by Constance R. Ahrons and Roy H. Rodgers. Used by permission of W. W. Norton & Company, Inc. **Figure 15.6** Data from "Couple Strengths and Stressors in Complex and Simple Stepfamilies in Australia" by N. C. Schultz, C. L. Schultz, and D. H. Olson, 1991, *Journal of Marriage and the Family, 53,* p. 560. Copyright 1991 by the National Council on Family Relations. Reprinted by permission. **Figure 16.5** Adapted with permission from an illustration by Amie De Frain.

TABLES

Table 1.1 U.S. Census Bureau (2003b). **Table 2.1** World Citizen Update (Winter, 1998). Updated from "State of the Village Report" by Donella Meadows (1990). For more information about Donella (Dana) Meadows, see Sustainability Institute's Donella Meadows Archive, http://sustainer.org/dhm_archive/. **Table 4.1** *Empowering Couples: Building on Your Strengths* by D. H. Olson and A. K. Olson. © 2000 Life Innovations. Reprinted with permission. **Table 4.2** *Empowering Couples: Building on Your Strengths* by D. H. Olson and A. K. Olson. © 2000 Life Innovations. Reprinted with permission. **Table 5.1** *Empowering Couples: Building on Your Strengths* by D. H. Olson and A. K. Olson. © 2000 Life Innova-

Name Index

Abbott, D., 45, 63
Abebe, B., 242
Abma, J. C., 173, 174
Abraham, I., 254
Abshoff, K., 337, 338
Aday, L. A., 375
Addis, M. E., 193
Ahlburg, D. A., 180
Ahrons, C. R., 439, 448, 449, 450, 454, 461
Aiken, L. R., 385
Alberti, R. E., 133, 149
Aldous, J., 373
Alfaro, E. C., 16
Ali, M. M., 180
Allen, C. E., 156, 157
Allen, K. R., 380
Allen, W., 423
Allen, W. D., 200, 319
Allgeier, A. R., A-17, A-28, A-33, A-34, A-35, A-36
Allgeier, E. R., A-17, A-28, A-33, A-34, A-35, A-36
Altura, J., 85
Alvarez, R., 50
Amato, P. R., 295, 339, 435, 439, 440, 445
Anderson, C. A., 424
Anderson, J. R., 26, 59, 309, 327
Anderson, N. B., 59
Anderson, R. N., A-36
Angel, R. J., 403, 405, 408, 424
Annunziata, J., 361
Anthony, J., 242, 267
Arias, E., 376, 422, A-36
Arias, I., 406, 407
Aries, E., 106
Arnedt, C., 165
Aron, A., 272
Arond, M., 224, 225, 316
Asai, S. G., 199, 202, 405, 406, 407
Asay, S., 73, 74
Auerbach, C. F., 355
Avery, A. W., 295
Axtell, R. G., 108, 124
Ayers-Lopez, S., 336
Azar, S. T., 414

Baca-Zinn, M., 200
Bach, D., 242
Bach, G., 133

Bachman, H. J., 374, 375
Bader, E., 471
Bahr, K. S., 428
Bahr, S. J., 295
Bailey, S. J., 447
Baldry, A. C., 410
Baldwin, S. E., 172
Bales, R. F., 82
Balleza, M., 264
Bámaca, M. Y., 16
Bancroft, L., 424
Banzet, M. R., 252
Baranoski, M. V., 172
Barber, B. K., 339
Barnes, H., 393
Barnes, M., 249, 250
Barnes, S. L., 465
Barnett, R. C., 214
Barry, E., 177, 178, 305
Barta, P. L., 452
Barth, J. C., 445
Bateson, G., 112
Bateson, M. C., 199
Batson, C. D., 38, 60
Baucom, D. H., 323
Bauer, J. W., 241
Bauman, K. E., 424
Baumrind, D., 339, 341, 342, 417
Bauserman, R., 456, 457
Beach, S. R., 323
Bean, R. A., 339
Beasley, R., 170
Beatty, L. A., 50
Becvar, D. S., 72
Becvar, R. J., 72
Bednar, S. G., 425
Beers, M. H., 282, 369, 370, A-27, A-28, A-29, A-30, A-31, A-32, A-36
Bell, R., 343
Belsky, J., 321, 334
Bem, S., 106
Bennett, C., 37, 38
Benson, B., 171
Benson, P. L., 337
Bent-Goodley, T. B., 31
Bepko, C., 167
Berger, R., 311, 312, 327, 471, 483
Bergeron, L. R., 418
Bergmann, B. R., 360

Berkow, R., A-16, A-17, A-20
Bernard, A., 190
Bernard, J., 7, 14, 80
Bernstein, R., 36
Berry, G. L., 50
Berscheid, E., 66, 67, 284, 285
Berzon, B., 186
Bettinger, M., 155
Bhopal, K., 274, 275
Bianchi, S., 23, 194
Bierstedt, R., 207
Billingsley, A., 48
Binner, J. M., 433
Binson, D., 167
Bissell, M., 168
Blackman, L., 304, 306
Blackwell, D. L., 289
Blair, S. L., 53
Blaisure, K., 439
Blakeslee, S., 438, 465
Blankenhorn, D., 354
Blau, J. R., 16
Blieszner, R., 380
Blood, R. O., 207, 208
Blow, A. J., 152, 179, 186
Blumberg, S. L., 108, 124, 150
Bober, S. L., 414
Bock, J. D., 352
Boes, M., 167
Bogenschneider, K., 170
Bohannan, P., 428, 441, 442, 464
Bokemeier, J. L., 24
Bold, M., 372
Bonanno, G. A., 424
Boonstra, H., 168
Booth, A., 149, 295, 339, 439, 440, 445
Borcherdt, B., 131, 132, 150
Borders, L. D., 337
Bornstein, R. F., 405, 408
Boss, P., 344, 391, 392, 401, 424
Bouchet, S., 325
Boulding, K., 467, 482
Bouthillier, D., 137
Bowen, G. L, 16, 216, 221, 222
Boyd-Franklin, N., 200, 360
Branscomb, K. R., 107
Brick, P., 168
Brinkley, D., 234
Broderick, C., 3

Broken Nose, M. A., 200
Brommel, B. J., 206
Brostoff, W., 422
Broussard, J., 429
Brown, B. B., 351
Brown, E., 179, 186
Brown, H. S., 451
Brown, K. G., 341
Brown, S., 15
Browning, R., 377
Brubaker, T. H., 382
Bruce, M. L., 335, 383
Bryan, A., 322
Bryant, J., 28
Buchanan, C. M., 438, 439
Buckingham, M., 467
Bulcroft, K., 282
Bumpass, L., 8, 294, 299
Burgess, E. W., 7, 80
Burr, W. R., 401, 402, 428
Burt, M., 462
Burton, L. M., 18
Bush, G. W., 398
Bushman, B. J., 424
Buss, D. M., 180, 198, 271, 285
Byrne, D., A-14

Cabrera, N., 361
Caldwell, J., 32, 38
Call, V. R. A., 295
Cameron, S. C., 33, 34
Campbell, R., 24
Campbell, S. M., 167
Capello, D., 50
Caplin, J., 399
Carey, M. P., 186
Carlson, K. J., A-22
Carp, F. M., 418
Carson, D. K., 54, 56
Carter, B., 458
Cashmore, E., 63
Casper, L. M., 448, 452
Castro, R., 180
Caughy, M. O., 16
Cavedo, C., 471
Centers, R., 208, 209
Chamberlin, J., 156, 157
Chang, I., 63
Chapman, M., 31, 40
Chartrand, E., 137
Chase-Lansdale, P. L., 168, 374, 375, 440
Chatters, L. M., 48, 50
Chen, R., 337
Chen, R. S., 399
Cherlin, A., 372, 440
Christensen, A., 124
Christensen, D. H., 453
Christensen, M., 337
Christopher, F. S., 172, 186
Chu, K., 235, 237
Ciaramigoi, A. P., 271

Cicirelli, V. G., 373
Cinotto, S., 107
Clapp, G., 465
Clark, K. M., 24
Clark, R., 59
Clark, V. R., 59
Claxton-Oldfield, S., 450
Clayton, O., 304
Cleland, J., 180
Clements, M., 149, 324, 327
Clift, E., A-19
Clifton, D. O., 467
Cluck, K., 242
Cochran, S. D., 167
Cohen, D., 251, 272
Cole, C. L., 429
Cole, W., 161, 162
Coleman, M., 265, 460
Coles, R. L., 454
Coley, R. L., 168
Conger, K. J., 423
Conger, R. D., 423
Connidis, I. A., 271, 339
Cook, R., 81
Cooley, C., 80
Coontz, S., 264, 428
Cooper, M. L., 174
Cowan, C. P., 334
Coward, R. T., 50
Cowley, G., 198
Cozza, S. J., 399
Crane, D. R., 295, 339
Crittenden, A., 360
Crockenberg, S. C., 350
Crohn, H., 451
Cromwell, R. E., 206, 207, 209
Crosby, J., 139, 141, 149
Crose, R., 214
Crouter, A. C., 149
Csikszentmihalyi, M., 216
Cummins, H. J., 392

Dabul, A. J., A-22
Dahl, C. M., 453
Dahl, T., 389
Dail, P. W., 54
Dailard, C., 169
Dalaker, J., 378
Danes, S., 335
Darkwa, O., 381
Darroch, J. E., 168
Daskalos, C., 159
Davidov, B., 39, 40, 41, 42
Davis, K. E., 244, 245, 247, 248, 476, 477
Dawson, B. S., 173
Dawson, D. A., 419
Day, R. D., 361, 428
DeBarros, K. A., 282
DeClaire, J., 2, 28, 113, 124, 138, 150
Dee, T. S., 176
Deen, M. R., 4, 155

Deets, H. B., 378
DeFrain, A., 468
DeFrain, J., 2, 13, 45, 47, 57, 63, 79, 81, 107, 258, 395, 413, 415, 425, 452, 457, 467, 481, 483, A-36, A-37
DeFrain, N., 413, 415, 425
Delamater, J. D., A-14, A-16
DeLuccie, M., 355
DeMaria, R., 470, 483
DeMaris, A., 452
DeNavas-Walt, C., 38
DePaulo, B., 266
Devahastin, S., 267
DiCenso, A., 173
Dickerson, J. F., 161
Dick-Read, G., A-33
Dienhart, A., 351
Dindia, K., 114
Dinger, M. K., 174
Dingfelder, S., 405
Dinkmeyer, D. C., 471
Dirie, W., 159
Dittus, P. J., 170
Dixon, A. E., 431, 432, 434, 435
Dnes, A. W., 433
Dobson, J., 251, 270
Doherty, W. J., 26, 309, 322, 323, 327, 345, 346, 354, 355, 358, 360, 422, 423, 474, 475, 481, 483
Dolbin-MacNab, M. L., 374, 385
Dole, B., 190
Dole, E., 190
Doll, L. S., 425
Dornbusch, S. M., 438
Douglas, S. J., 45, 89, 360
Downs, B., 337, 352, 416, 453
Druckman, J., 471
Duke, J., 295
Dumka, L., 419
Durana, C., 471
Duvall, E. M., 79, 80
Duvander, A.-Z. E., 277
Dyer, G., 471
Dyer, P., 471

Edleson, J. L., 425
Einstein, A., 143, 234, A-8
Eisenstat, S. A., A-22
Eldred, C., 358
Ella, D. M., 389
Elmen, J., 452
Emmers-Sommer, T. M., 454
Emmons, M. L., 133
Engel, E., 451
Ennett, S. T., 424
Enright, E., 371, 372
Erickson, M. F., 354, 358
Erickson, R., 191
Erikson, E., 364
Erisman, M., 78
Ernst, L., 357, A-37

Eze, J. N., 180
Ezugwu, F. O., 180

Fadiman, G., 190
Faiola, A., 267
Falicov, C. J., 200
Fals-Stewart, W., 399, 421
Fan, X., 337
Fawcett, N. R., 410
Fay, R., 93, 167
Fehr, B., 253
Fenell, D. L., 421
Ferguson, F. I. T., 272
Fergusson, D. M., 404
Field, C. J., 34, 412, 413, 467, 475
Fields, J., 448, 452
Fill, S. K., 352
Fincham, F. D., 323
Fine, M., 265, 358
Finkelhor, D., 23
Fisher, C., 39, 63
Fitzpatrick, L., 430, 431
Fitzpatrick, M. H., 211
Fletcher, W. L., 381
Flood, M. F., 170
Florsheim, P., 186
Flynn, C. P., 347
Forgue, R. E., 220, 234, 238, 239, 241
Foshee, V. A., 424
Fournier, D., 471
Fowers, B., 39, 40, 41, 42, 255, 313, 320, 321
Fowler, O. S., 289
Fox, G. L., 82, 204
Francoeur, R. T., A-18, A-19
Frank, R., 92
Franklin, A., 360
Franklin, B., 178
Franklin, C. W., 201
Fravel, D. L., 337
Frias, S. M., 403, 405, 408, 424
Fricke, J., 452
Friedan, B., 27, 82
Fromer, J. E., 63
Fromm, E., 251, 270
Fuligni, A., 39
Furstenberg, F. F., Jr., 351
Fye, S., 128

Gagnon, J. H., 161, 163, 167, 181, 182
Gaines, S. O., 252
Galbraith, K. A., 171
Gallagher, M., 13, 14, 15, 27, 29, 301, 304, 305, 327, 479
Galvin, K. M., 206
Gamache, S., 452
Ganong, L. H., 265, 460
Garbarino, J., 354
Garcia, A. M., 63
Garcia, M., 49
Gardyn, R., 285, 288, 289

Garman, E. T., 220, 234, 238, 239, 241
Gary, L. E., 50, 128, 129
Gehl, K. S., 414
Gelles, R. J., 29, 404, 408, 409, 410, 411, 413, 415, 416, 417, 418
Gerena, M., 31
Gerstel, N., 31
Gibbs, N., 345
Gibran, K., 84, 262, 358, 360
Gibson, P. A., 375
Gidycz, C. A., 292
Gill, C. S., 443
Giordano, J., 33, 287
Glass, S. P., 186
Glenn, N., 9, 278, 279, 301, 304
Glick, P., 9, 266
Goldenberg, H., 67, 68, 69, 70, 71, 72, 98
Goldenberg, I., 67, 68, 69, 70, 71, 72, 98
Gomel, J. N., 24
Gonzales-Backen, M., 39
Goodman, B., 264
Goodman, C. C., 375
Goodman, E., A-15
Gorall, D., 44
Gordimer, N., 186
Gordon, C., 125
Gordon, J., 172
Gordon, K., 323
Gordon, L., 471
Gordon, P. A., 266, 267
Gordon, S., 172
Gordon, V. V., 170
Gottman, J. M., 2, 28, 110, 113, 122, 124, 138, 150, 312, 313, 327, 467
Graham, L., 24
Graham-Bermann, S. A., 425
Grant, B. F., 138, 324, 419
Gray, J. W., 34, 36, 105
Greeley, S., 54
Green, R. J., 155, 156
Greenfield, P., 29
Greenspan, S. I., 350
Greer, M., 398, 399
Greif, G. L., 454, 463
Griffith, L., 173
Groppenbacher, N., 419
Gross, E., 29
Grotevant, H. D., 336, 337
Grusec, J. E., 341
Guerney, B. G., 471
Guest, F., 316
Gullone, E., 410
Gunnar, M. R., 350
Gustafson, R., 23
Guyatt, G., 173

Haas, L., 216
Habenstein, R. W., 338
Haddock, S. A., 194
Haeberle, E. J., 159
Haley, J., 88, 112

Hall, J., 323
Hall, M., 380
Halpern, D. F., 10, 28, 194, 195
Ham, J., 155
Hamilton, B. E., 11
Han, X., 399
Hannah, M. T., 311, 312, 327, 471, 483
Hansson, R. O., 381
Harmon, A., 23
Harris, A. H., 323
Harris, G., A-15
Harris, J., 277
Harris, S., 274
Harris, V. W., 316, 327
Hart, A. D., 182
Hartnett, K., 152, 179, 186
Harvey, J. H., 186
Hatch, D., 39, 63, 218, 309
Hatcher, R. A., A-14, A-16, A-21
Havens, B., 380
Hawley, D. R., 471
Hawthorne, B., 456
He, 282
Heiges, K. L., 439
Helburn, S. W., 360
Hellmich, N., 177
Henderson, K., 363, 385
Hendrick, C., 248, 249
Hendrick, S. S., 248, 249
Henshaw, S. K., 168
Herbst, P. G., 209, 210
Herek, G. M., 4, 156, 157, 353
Herman, C. P., 425
Hertwig, O., 155
Hetherington, E. M., 437, 438, 465
Hicks, K. A., 424
Higginbotham, B., 363, 385
Higginson, J. G., 168
Hill, R., 79, 394, 395, 423
Hill, Z. E., 180
Hines, P. M., 200
Hingson, R. W., 175
Hird, M. J., 337, 338
Hobfoll, S. E., 401
Hochschild, A., 18
Hocker, J. L., 144, 145
Hof, L., 470, 483
Hoffman, L., 398
Hogan, M. J., 355
Holman, H., 374
Holmes, T. H., 389, 390
Holtzman, M., 6
Holtzworth-Munroe, A., 404
Holzner, C., 219, 242
Horn, W., 354
Hornik, D., 452
Horwood, L. J., 404
Houseknecht, S. K., 16, 25
Houston, T., 316
Howard, J., 6, 50, 114, 122, 198, 398
Howland, J., 175

Hsieh, K-H., 321
Hunt, R. A., 470, 483
Hunter, A. G., 48
Husseini, R., 180
Hyde, J. S., 157, 158, 185, 294, 370, A-14, A-16, A-17, A-19, A-21, A-33, A-34, A-36

Ihinger-Tallman, M., 463
Ikkink, K. K., 380
Iloabachie, G. C., 180
Insel, P. M., 183, 419, A-14, A-16, A-18, A-19, A-20, A-23, A-26, A-27, A-28, A-29, A-30, A-31, A-32, A-34, A-35, A-36

Jaccard, J., 170
Jack, E. L., 42, 93, 147, 252
Jackson, D. D., 112
Jackson, J., 48
Jackson, J. K., 420, 421
Jackson, M. H., 399
Jacobvitz, D. B., 77
Jakub, D., A-37
Jameson, K., 242
Janus, C. L., 167, 168, 170, 176, 379
Janus, S. S., 167, 168, 170, 176, 379
Jenkins, N. H., 108, 124, 150
Jennings, J., 63
Jensen, E. R., 180
Ji, J., 289
Joanning, H., 428, 465
Johansen, A. S., 349
Johnson, B., 379, 434
Johnson, J., 410
Johnson, M. P., 403, 404
Johnson, T., 167
Johnson, V. E., 158, 176, 177, A-31
Johnson-Sumerford, D., 351
Jones, E. F., 470
Jones, J., 413, 415, 425
Jouriles, E. N., 405
Julien, D., 137

Kagan, J., 202
Karasik, R. J., 376
Kaufman, M., A-20
Kazdin, A. E., 465
Keillor, G., 164, 193
Kelley, M., 399
Kelly, G. F., 184, A-14, A-17, A-20, A-21, A-22, A-23, A-31, A-33, A-34
Kelly, J., 334, 437, 438
Kelly, K. M., 252
Kendall, E., 125
Kennedy, J. F., 145
Kenote, T., 54
Keoughan, P., 428, 429, 465
Ketcham, K., 271
Khan, A. G., 275
Kiang, L. 39, 40
Kiernan, K. E., 440

Kiesler, S., 28
Kilmann, R., 144
Kindlon, D., 345, 346
King, 94, 114, 198
Kinsella, K., 385
Kinsey, A., 160, 170
Kirasic, K. C., 385
Klassen, A., 167
Klein, M., 172
Klein, S. R., 401, 402
Kline, 295
Knipscheer, K. C. P. M., 380
Knowles, J., A-23
Knutson, L., 311, 327
Kobliner, B., 242
Kochanek, K. D., 422, A-21, A-36
Koenig, L. J., 425
Kohlberg, L., 203
Kolata, G., 161, 162, 163, 164
Kolodny, R., 158, 176-177, A-31
Koonin, L. M., A-21
Kornblum, J., 371, 372
Kornhaber, A., 385
Kostelnik, M., 350, 351
Kottak, C. P., 34
Kouneski, E. F., 354
Kraut, R., 23, 28, 29
Kübler-Ross, E., 385
Kulthau, K., 349
Kurdek, L. A., 155, 156, 157, 317, 320

Lacayo, R., 350
Laird, J., 155, 156
LaMastro, V., 337, 338
Lamaze, F., A-33, A-34
Landers, A., 142, 294
Landers, S., 176, A-22
Langer, G., 165
Lankov, A., 430
Lansky, B., 335
LaRossa, R., 358
Larsen, A., 313, 393, A-11
Larson, J., 301
Larson, P. J., 78
Larson, R. W., 107, 351
Lasswell, M., 214, 382, 418
Lasswell, T., 418
Laumann, E. O., 161, 162, 163, 164, 181, 182
Lazarony, L., 236
Leboyer, F., A-34
Lee, G. R., 290, 291
Lee, T., 218, 242, 327
Lee, T. R., 316
Lee, V., 202
Lee, Y., 191
Lehrer, L., 13
Leiblum, S., 182
Leibowitz, A., 349
LeMasters, E. E., 333, 334
Leo, J., 93

Leon, K., 77
Lerner, H. G., 134, 135, 136, 137, 149, 150
Levine, J., 246, 356
Levy, K., 252
Lewis, C. C., 350
Lewis, J. M., 438, 445
Lewis, S. K., 16
Lichter, D. T., 38, 289
Lincoln, K. D., 50, 254, 351, 462, 483
Lino, M., 334, 335
Lippa, R. A., 214
Liu, D., 159
Lohrfink, K. F., 16
Lorenz, F. O., 423
Lu, H. H., 8, 294
Lund, M., 242
Lundmark, V., 28
Lunneborg, P., 337, 338
Luthra, R., 292
Lykken, D., 216
Lynch, M., 191, 214
Lyness, K. P., 194
Lyons, J. A., 399

Maccoby, E. E., 350, 438
MacDonald, W. L., 452
Mace, D., 7, 133, 134, 309
Mace, V., 7, 309
Mahalik, J. R., 193
Malinowski, B., 157
Malley-Morrison, K., 425
Malone-Colon, L., 304
Maloney, T., 242
Mankiller, W., 200
Manning, R. D., 236
Manning, W., 8, 15
Manning, W. D., 447
Manzi, C., 339
March, K., 360
Marelich, W. D., 252
Markman, H. J., 108, 109, 122, 124, 150, 246, 324, 327, 471
Marmot, M., 377, 385
Marquardt, E., 278, 279, 301
Marsh, J. C., 74
Marshall, J. P., 218, 242, 316, 327
Martens, L., 395
Martin, J. A., 11, 170, 271, 363, 364, 467
Martinez, G. M., 173
Martinez, V., 398
Mashek, D. J., 272
Mason, K. O., 349
Masters, W. H., 158, 176, 177, 182, 183, A-31
Mathus, A. K., 346
Mattingly, M. J., 194
May, R., 131
Mays, V. M., 167
McAdoo, H. P., 46, 48, 63
McBride, E. K., 449, 456
McCarthy, B., 177, 178

McCubbin, H. I., 63, 393
McCullough, M., A-20
McDonald, R., 405
McDonnell, C., 410
McGinley, E., 251
McGirt, E., 399
McGoldrick, M., 33, 287, 288, 458
McGraw, L. A., 373
McGue, M. K., 337
McKinnon, J., 37, 38
McLanahan, S., 440
McLaughlin, M., 117
McLeod, B., 52
McManus, M. J., 327
McMullin, J. A., 339
McNaughton-Cassill, M., 191, 214
McRoy, R. G., 336, 337
Mead, G., 80
Mead, M., 9, 197, 198, 320
Meadows, D. H., 32
Meezan, W., 156, 352
Meier, J. A., 191, 192, 194, 214
Meier, P., 101, 102,
Melby, J. N., 423
Mendenhall, T. J., 336
Meredith, W., 45
Mertensmeyer, C., 358
Miall, C., 360
Michael, R. T., 92, 133, 161, 162, 163, 164,
    181, 182, 244, 403
Michaels, M., 419
Michaels, M. W., 326
Michaels, S., 161, 162, 181
Michener, J. A., 468
Mickish, J., 410
Miedzian, M., 411
Miller, B. C., 171, 172, 337
Miller, M., 297
Miller, P., 334, 471
Miller, P. A., 117, 118, 124
Miller, S., 117, 118, 124
Millspaugh, E., A-36
Mindel, C. H., 338
Minino, A. M., 422
Mitchell, K., 23
Moglia, R. F., A-23
Mohatt, G., 39, 63
Moien, M., A-33
Montagu, A., 33, 34
Montel, K. H., 320
Moore, K. A., 356
Morgan, A., 81
Morgan, S. P., 337
Mori, Y., 267
Morrill, P., 324
Morrison, T., 35
Mosher, W. D., 173
Moskos, C., 398
Mroczek, D. K., 376
Mukopadhyay, T., 28
Muller, D., 433

Mulvihill, G., 305
Murphy, S. L., 335, 422, A-36
Murry, V. M., 82, 204
Murstein, B., 289, 290
Mussen, P., 203
Muxen, M., 393
Myers, J. E., 443
Myerson, B., 441

Nadeau, J. W., 385
Nakonezny, P. A., 433
Nealer, J., 357, A-37
Nelsen, J., 224
Nemiroff, M., 361
Nettles, S. M., 16
Neugarten, B., 364
Neumaier, J., 180
Newton, R. H., 308
Ng, M. I., 159
Niebuhr, R., 138
Niehuis, S., 316
Nord, C. W., 354
Norris, C., 81
Norwood, E., 219
Norwood, W. D., 405
Notarius, C., 110, 111, 467
Novello, A. C., 403

O'Campo, P. J., 16
O'Conner-Roden, M., 282
O'Farrell, T. J., 421
O'Leary, A., 425
O'Neil, B., 454
Obi, S. N., 180
Ochs, E., 107
Ogunwole, S., 38
Olds, S. B., A-35, A-36
Olson, A. K., 100, 101, 108, 119, 125, 127,
    128, 150, 152, 153, 190, 191, 210, 211,
    216, 217, 220, 221, 245, 246, 255, 256,
    260, 311, 313, 319, 320, 327, 329, 330,
    337, 339, 340, 388, 390, 393, 397, 405,
    406, 407, 435, 460, 461, 467, 471, 472,
    483
Olson, D. H., 44, 46, 78, 83, 87, 88, 89, 91,
    100, 101, 108, 119, 120, 122, 123, 125,
    127, 128, 150, 152, 153, 190, 191, 200,
    206, 207, 209, 210, 211, 216, 217, 220,
    221, 245, 246, 255, 256, 260, 311, 313,
    319, 320, 327, 329, 330, 337, 339, 340,
    388, 390, 393, 397, 405, 406, 407, 435,
    460, 461, 467, 471, 472, 483, A-11
Olson, S., 36
Onah, H. E., 180
Ooms, T., 325, 326, 327
Orwell, G., 188
Ozer, E. J., A-22

Padgett, D., 48
Padilla, P., 159
Paik, A., 182

Palacio, J., 72
Pan, P. A., 267
Pan, Y., 276
Pape, K. T., 406, 407
Parke, M., 325
Parke, R. D., 24
Parkman, A. M., 430, 433
Parsons, N., 174
Parsons, T., 82, 193, 194, 213
Pasley, K., 463
Patterson, C. J., 167
Patterson, M., 28
Pauker, S. L., 224, 225, 316
Pawelski, J., 156, 157
Pearce, J. K., 33
Peek, C. W., 50
Peele, S., 251, 270
Pemberton, M., 424
Pence, E. L., 410
Penny, J. M., 337
Pensanti, H., 182
Peplau, L. A., 167
Pequegnat, W., 425
Perez, A. E., 180
Perez, L., 398
Perreira, K., 31, 39, 40
Peterman, D., 295
Peters, B., 405
Peters, H. E., 361
Peters, M., 48
Peterson, G. W., 108
Peterson, K. S., 220, 224
Piaget, J., 343
Pieve, L., 168
Pines, A. M., 85, 252, 272
Pitt, E., 356
Pittman, J. F., 216
Placek, P. J., A-33
Pleck, J. H., 216
Polivy, J., 425
Pollock, G. E., 443
Popenoe, D., 6, 7, 8, 9, 10, 29, 266, 294,
    298, 299, 301
Porter, J., 23
Portes, A., 63
Portnoy, F., 337
Preto, N. G., 287
Previti, D., 435
Proctor, B., 38
Proctor, B. D., 378
Puente, S., 251, 272

Qian, Z., 38, 53, 60, 63

Radharkrishnan, S., 275
Raffaelli, M., 170
Rahe, R. H., 389, 390
Raine, G., 52
Rainville, A., 398
Raley, S. B., 23, 194
Ramick, M., A-21

Rauch, J., 156, 157, 352
Raven, B. H., 208, 209
Recker, N. K., 450
Reddick, R. J., 63
Regalia, C., 339
Reinisch, J., 170
Reis, H. T., 66, 283, 285
Reiss, I. L., 290, 291, 292
Remez, L., 274
Rennison, C. M., 20
Rettig, K. D., 453
Reynolds, M., 157
Rhea, D., 454
Rich, J., 216
Ridder, E. M., 404
Ridley, C. A., 295
Risman, B. J., 351
Rivers, C., 124, 214
Robbins, C. C., 201
Robbins, R., 374
Roberto, K. A., 380
Roberts, A., 304
Roberts, L., 21
Roberts, S., 7, 264
Robins, K., 52
Robles, B. J., 231
Rodgers, J. L., 433
Rodgers, R., 450
Rodrigues, A., 208, 209
Rodstein, E., 451
Rokach, A., 255
Roosa, M. W., 419
Root, M. P. P., 34
Rosen, R., 182
Ross, M. E., 375
Roth, W. T., 183, 419, A-14, A-16, A-18, A-19, A-20, A-23, A-26, A-27, A-28, A-29, A-30, A-31, A-32, A-34, A-35, A-36
Rowe, C. L., 421
Rowe, G., 382
Roy, K. M., 18, 450
Rozema, H. R., 105
Rudy, D., 341
Ruf, S. D., 53
Rumbaut, R., 63
Russell, B., 206
Russell, C., 89
Russo, N. F., A-22

Sabar, A., 264
Sabbadini, A., 251
Sadberry, S. L., 324, 327
Sager, C. J., 451
Sammons, M. T., 398, 399, 425
Sandefur, G., 440
Sarkisian, N., 31
Sastry, J., 25
Sautter, F., 399
Savin-Williams, R. C., 186
Scabini, E., 339
Schaub, K., 242

Scheinkman, M., 152
Scherlis, W., 28
Scherman, A., 374
Schewe, P. A., 425
Schmitt, D. P., 180
Schnell, R., 180
Schoen, K., 410
Schramm, D. G., 218, 222, 223, 242, 306, 316, 317, 327
Schultz, C. L., 460, 461
Schwartz, J., 52, 53, 113, 124, 138, 150
Schwartz, P., 214
Schwartz Gottman, J., 113, 124, 138, 150
Scott, M., 122, 471
Sebanc, A. M., 350
Seligman, M. E., 467
Selle, R., 27
Selye, H., 388
Sen, A., 205
Sengupta, M., 282
Sharma, A. R., 337
Sheehy, G., 369
Sherman, C. W., 384, 460
Sherman, M. D., 399
Shin, N., 16
Shohet, M., 107
Shorris, E., 50
Shostak, A., 265
Shull, R. D., 433
Silva, M., 173
Silver, N., 2, 28, 122, 312–313, 327
Silverman, J., 293
Silverstein, L. B., 355
Silverstein, M., 375
Simard, M., 137
Simmons, D. S., 474, 475, 483
Singh, A., 39, 63, 218, 309
Singh, S., 168
Singletary, M., 236, 237
Skinner, K. B., 295
Skogrand, L., 39, 41, 51, 52, 63, 107, 218, 242, 309, 316, 363, 373, 385, 413, 414, 415, 425
Skolnick, A. S., 7
Skolnick, J. H., 7
Skutch, L. P., 338
Slap, G. B., 294
Smilgis, M., 161
Smith, B. L., 376, 422
Smith, J., 337, 443
Smith, J. C., A-21
Smith, K., 349
Smith, N. R., 206
Smith, T., Jr., 398
Smock, P., 8, 294, 447
Snyder, D. K., 323
Sobolewski, C. G., 159
Solot, D., 297
Somers, M. S., 339
Soriano, F., 398
Sorokin, P., 7

Spalding, L. R., 167
Spencer, M., 39
Spielberger, C. D., 401
Spiro, A., III, 376
Sprecher, S., 186
Sprenkle, D. H., 89
Sprey, J., 81
St. Augustine, 207, 231
Stahmann, R. F., 470
Stanley, S. M., 108, 122, 124, 150, 324, 327, 471
Stanley-Hagan, M. M., 465
Stauss, J. H., 54, 55
Stein, G., 31
Steinmetz, S., 29, 108
Sternberg, R. J., 249, 250, 270, 272
Stets, J. E., 404, 407
Stewart, J. H., 345, 348
Stewart, K. L., 390
Stewart, S. D., 220, 447, 459, 460
Stinnett, N., 46, 74, 76, 79, 467
Stork, J., 395
Stork, W., 395
Straus, M. A., 29, 345, 346, 347, 348, 404, 411, 412, 413, 418, 419
Street, A. E., 406, 407
Stroup, A., 443
Struthers, C. B., 24
Stuart, R. B., 162
Subrahmanyam, K., 29
Sureender, S., 274
Sussman, D., 165
Sutton, C. E. T., 200
Switala, K., 82, 98

Taffel, S. M., A-33
Tamis-LeMonda, C. S., 361
Tannen, D., 102, 103, 104, 105, 106, 125
Tatara, T., 418
Taylor, D., 182
Taylor, H., 180
Taylor, J., A-37
Taylor, R. J., 48, 49
Tear, J., 101, 102, 124
Tein, J.-Y., 419
Theroux, P., 434
Thiele, D. M., 373, 374
Thomas, K., 144
Thomas, L., 39, 63
Thomas, V., 91
Thomas, W., 80
Thompson, A. I., 63
Thompson, K. L., 410
Thoresen, C. E., 323
Thornton, J., 214
Tichenor, V. J., 208
Tinsley, B. J., 24
Todd, M. J., 244, 245, 247, 248
Tomlin, L., 117
Toussaint, P., 360
Trimble, J., 39, 63

Triplett, L., 454
Troll, L. E., 373, 380, 383
Tschann, J., A-22
Tubbs, C. Y., 18
Tung, Y.-Y., 289
Turner, C., 167
Twain, M., 131

Ulman, A., 418
Umaña-Taylor, A. J., 16

Van As, C. F., 341
Van Dorn, R. A., 16
van Dulmen, M., 337
van Leeuwenhoek, A., 155
van Tilburg, T., 380
Van Volkom, M., 383, 385
van Wormer, K., 167, 425
Velkoff, V. A., 282, 385
Veniegas, R. C., 167
Ventura, S. J., 11
Verma, S., 351
Vignoles, V. L., 339
Vincent, J. P., 405
Visher, E., 449, 461, 462
Visher, J., 449, 461, 462
von Bertalanffy, L., 68
Vosburg, E. S., 202
Voydanoff, P., 194, 195, 214, 216

Waite, L., 191
Waite, L. J., 13, 14, 15, 27, 29, 301, 304, 305,
    327, 349, 479
Waldrep, D. A., 398
Walker, A. J., 373
Walker, L., 451

Walker, L. E., 410
Waller, W., 208
Wallerstein, J. S., 438, 445, 465
Wallin, P., 80
Walsh, F., 44, 98, 476, 483
Wang, R., 23
Watamura, S. E., 350
Watson, J. B., 7
Weakland, J., 112
Weber, C. H., 182
Weinhold, B. K., 421
Weis, K., 249, 272
Weitzman, L., 431, 432, 434
Wells, U., 167
Whelan, T. A., 373, 374
Whisman, M. A., 434, 435
Whitaker, C., 67
Whitam, F. L., 159
White, J. M., 80
White, M., 81
Whitehead, B. D., 6, 7, 8, 9, 10, 29, 266,
    286, 294, 298, 299, 301, 434
Whitehead, D., 422
Whitman, C. T., 329
Whitton, S. W., 324, 327
Wiener, N., 309
Wiley, A. R., 93, 107, 124, 465
Willan, A., 173
Williams, D. R., 59
Willie, C. V., 63
Wilmot, W. W., 144, 145
Wilson, J., 374
Wilson, M., 393
Wilson, S., 351
Wilson, S. M., 108
Wilson, T., 251

Winch, R., 289
Wincze, J. P., 186
Wind, R., 70, 172, 176
Winslow, S., 194
Witkow, M., 39
Wolak, J., 23
Wolfe, A., 27
Wolfe, D. M., 207, 208
Wollen, B. J., 241
Woodward, J. C., 226, 269, 270
Worthington, E. L., 323, 327
Wright, K., 425
Wright, R., Jr., 338
Wrobel, G. M., 336
Wuerffel, J., 76
Wyatt, G. E.
Wycoff, S. M., 33, 34
Wyden, P., 133
Wynne, L., 88

Xie, X., A-36
Xu, X., 289

Yarrow, P., 468
Yip, T., 39

Zacks, E., 155
Zambrana, R. E., 50
Zaslow, 358
Zeig, J. K., 88
Ziemba, S. J., 194
Zigler, E., 413
Zill, N., 354
Zimmerman, C., 7
Zimmerman, T. S., 194
Ziporyn, A-22

Subject Index

Page numbers in italics refer to figures and tables.

AARP sexual intimacy survey, 166–167
ABC News survey of sexual behavior, 164–166
Abortion
    adolescents and, A-22–A-23
    defined, A-18
    emotional aspects of, A-22
    laws on, A-18–A-20
    married couples and, A-23
    physical aspects of, A-21–A-22
    preventing, A-23
    procedures used, A-20–A-21
    public opinion on, A-20
    risk of death from, A-21–A-22, *A-22*
    statistics on, A-18
Abrazo (hug), 108
Abstinence, A-19
Abstinence-only sex education, 169, 172–173
Abuse, jealousy and, 252
Abused children, 408. *See also* Child abuse and neglect
Acceptance, 245
Accommodating style, 145
Acculturation
    defined, 58
    intercultural marriages and, 287
Achievement, African American families and, 50
Acquired immune deficiency syndrome (AIDS), 159–160, 180
Acute illnesses, 379
Adaptability, in Mexican American families, 52
Addictive love relationships, 251
Administration for Children and Families (ACF), 325
Adolescent pregnancy, 168
Adolescents
    abortion and, A-22–A-23
    adopted, 337
    authoritarian parenting and, 341
    cigarette smoking and, 422–423
    corporal punishment and, 346, *347,* 348
    dating violence and, 293
    impact of divorce on, 438–439

sexual behavior among, 173–176
    split custody and, 456
Adopted child syndrome, 337
Adoptees, 337
Adoption, 336–337, A-23
Adult caregiving, 373
Adult children, parental divorce and, 439, 440
Adult depression, 347, *348. See also* Depression
Adult position, 139
Adults, personal satisfaction by age group, *368*
Adversarial divorce proceedings, 432, 442
Affection
    family communication and, 45
    in strong families, 74–75
    White families and, 48
Afghanistan, 157
Africa
    divorce in, 431
    female circumcision in, 159
African American children, 306
African American churches, 50
African Americans
    benefits of marriage to men, 306
    children being raised by grandparents, 375
    demographics, 37–38
    domestic violence and, 405
    family strengths, 48, 50
    family structure, *10,* 11
    gender roles, 200
    marriage and, 304–306
    median family income level, 227, *227*
    net family worth, 231
    single-parent families, 448
    types of marriages, 319–320, *320*
African American women
    domestic violence and, 405
    experiences in marriage, 306
    feminism and, 200
    oppression and, 200
    power of mothers, 48
    raising grandchildren, 375
Afterbirth, A-32–A-33
Age
    domestic violence and, 408
    infertility and, A-27

Ageism, 377
Aggressive communication, 119–120
Aggressiveness, 119–120, 208–209
Aging, 376–377. *See also* Old age
Aging parents. *See* Elderly
Agreeing to disagree, 148
Agreements
    negotiating, 147–148
    reviewing and renegotiating, 148
    solidifying, 148
Al-Anon, 421
Alaska Natives, 38, 54–56
Alateen, 422
Alcohol abuse
    deaths per year related to, 422
    defined, 419
    family reaction to, 420–421
    societal effects of, 419
    treatment and prevention, 421–422
    warning signs of, 419
Alcoholics Anonymous (AA), 421–422
Alcoholism, 419
Alcohol use
    as a "cause" of family violence, 419–420
    domestic violence and, 409
    physiological effects of, 418
    pregnancy and, A-31
    problems associated with, 21
    and sexual behavior among college students, 174–176
    societal effects of, 419
    trends in, 20–21
Alimony, 431, 432, 433
Ambiguous loss, 391, 392
Ambiguous Loss: Learning to Live with Unresolved Grief (Boss), 392
American Association for Marriage and Family Therapy (AAMFT), 66, 179, 181, 475
American Association of Sexuality Educators, Counselors, and Therapists (AASECT), 184
American Indians
    areas of greatest concentration, 54
    challenges of families, *54*
    communal living, 201
    demographics, 38
    family strengths, 54–56
    gender roles, 200–201

grandparents, 374
historical experience affecting family lives, 31–32
notions of time and, 201
number of recognized tribes, 54
American Sex Survey, 164–166
American sexual behavior. *See* Sex and sexual behavior
Amicable divorce, 433
Amniotic sac, A-29, A-31
Androgen, 370
Anesthesia, childbirth and, A-33–A-34
Anger
dance of anger concept, 134–137
divorce and, 441
facts and myths about, 132, 133
keeping in balance with love, 133–134
perspectives on the nature of, 131–132
reasons for suppressing, 130–131
See also Conflict
Anger management, 134–137
Angry associates, 449
Animal abuse, 347, 410
Annie Hall (movie), 177
Annual household expenses, 230, *231*
Anorgasmia, 183
Antiabortion laws, A-18
Antiabortion movement, A-18
Apinayean society, 158
Appreciation
family communication and, 45
in strong families, 74–75
White families and, 48
Aranda society, 158
Arapesh people, 197
Arranged marriages, 274–277
The Art of Loving (Fromm), 251
Asian Americans
acculturation and, 54
demographics and demographic trends, 38
discrimination against, 53
family strengths, 52–54
family structure, *10*, 11
gender roles, 202
median family income level, 227, *227*
Asian Indians, 38
Assault, victim–offender relationship in, 404, *404*, 405
Assertive communication, 119, 120
Assertiveness
in communication, 119, 120
defined, 121, 208–209
marital success and, 308
positive influence of, 122, 123
Assimilation, 58
Assistance, in friendship, 245
Association for Couples in Marriage Enrichment, 309

Attentive listening, 118
Attractiveness, mate selection and, 284–285
Attractiveness capital, 285
Authoritarian parenting, 341, 342
Authority, 208, *209*
Autonomic power pattern, 210, *210*
Avoidance
defined, 121
negative influence of, 122–123
Avoidant style
in conflict resolution, 145
in couples' relationships, 122–123
Awareness, cultural competence and, 40

Babies
bonding with, A-35
breast-feeding, A-35–A-36
See also Infants
Baby blues, A-34
Baby Boom, childlessness rate and, 337
Baby Boomers, 366
Bad to worse couples, 321
Balanced families, 89–91, *91*
Bankruptcy, 240
Barrier methods of contraception, A-15–A-16, A-18–A-19
Basal body temperature method, A-17
Battered women, 407, 408
Battered women shelters, 407
Batterers, 294
Behaviorism, 344
Belgium, divorce in, 430
Best-friend couples, 178
Better Sex for You (Pensanti), 182
Bidirectional effects, 343
Bilateral descent, 43
Bilingualism, 55, 56
Binuclear families
compared to single-parent families, 448–449
growing complexity of, 450–451
Biracial couples, 60
Birth control. *See* Contraception
Birth control pills, A-14–A-15
Birthing centers, A-34
Birthing rooms, A-34
Birth(s)
act of, A-31–A-32
out-of-wedlock, 352
trends in, 10, 12
See also Childbirth
Bisexuality, 154
Black Americans. *See* African Americans
Black–White marriages, 286–287
Blame game, 109
Blamers, 136–137
Blastocyst, *A-27*, A-29
Blended families, 449–450
Body language, men and, 312

Boomerang kids, 372
Boredom, 389
Bottle-feeding, A-35
Boundaries, 68
Boundary ambiguity, 337, 391–392, *392*, 459–460
Brainstorming, 147
Brazil, extramarital sex and, 180
Breast-feeding, A-35–A-36
Breast milk, A-35–A-36
Breech birth, A-32
Budgeting, 232–233

Calendar method, A-17
Carbon monoxide, A-31
Career
childlessness and, 338
marriage as a predictor of success in, 14
middle age and, 367–368
Career change, family stress and, 394
Caregiving
by adults, 373
for aging parents, 195
Caring, nonpossessive, 308
Caring Cluster, 245, 247, *247*
The Case for Marriage (Waite & Gallagher), 13, 14
Case studies, A-10
Catharsis conflict, 410
Centrifugal interactions, 71
Centripetal interactions, 71
Cervical cap, A-15–A-16, A-18
Cervical mucus method, A-17
Cervix, A-26
Cesarean section, A-33
Change
as affected by relationship flexibility, *88*
balancing with stability, 70–71
in relationships over time, 94–95
stress and, 17–18
Chaotic relationships, 87, 88, 93–94
Chemical abuse/dependence
child abuse and, 414
family reaction to, 420–421
Cherokee Nation, 38, 201
Chicanos/Chicanas, 50, 71–72
Child abuse and neglect
cross-generational transmission, 413
defined, 411
families at risk for, 413–416
impact on children, 413
incidence of, 411–413
surviving and transcending, 413, 414–415
treatment and prevention, 416–417
trends in, 20
See also Abused children
Child behavior, parenting style and, *340*

Childbirth
  alternative approaches to, A-33–A-34
  cesarean section, A-33
  labor and delivery, A-31–A-35
  physical and psychological changes
    following, A-34–A-35
Childbirth classes, A-29–A-30, A-35
Childbirth Without Fear (Dick-Read), A-33
Child care, 19, 348–350
Child development
  child care and, 349–350
  in gay and lesbian families, 352–353
  impact of abuse on, 413
  parenting programs and, 358
  positive impact of fathers on, 356
  theories of, 343–344
Child Effects on Adults (Bell), 343
Child-free alternative, 337–339
Child neglect, 411. *See also* Child abuse
  and neglect
Child position, 139
Childrearing
  conventional wisdom about, 331–333
  cost of, 334–335, *335*
  Mother Murphy's Law for, *335*
  theories of, 343–345
  See also Parenting and parenthood
Children
  being raised by grandparents,
    374–375
  boomerang kids, 372
  of cohabiting relationships, 299
  connectedness to elderly parents,
    380
  consequences of the death of, 356–
    357, A-37
  conventional wisdom about, 331–333
  coparental divorce and, 443–445
  cost of raising, 334–335, *335*
  impact of divorce on, 438–439, 440,
    445
  importance in Latino families, 51–52
  of intercultural marriages, 287
  Internet use and, 23
  interparental psychological abuse
    and, 407
  joint custody and, 457
  married parents as predictor for suc-
    cess in, 15
  poverty and, 24–25, *25*
  responsibility for finances and,
    335–336
  from same-sex couples, 157
  self-concept and, 80–81
  sibling abuse, 417–418
  stepfamilies and, 452
  from two-parent families, 304, 325
  See also Adult children; Parent–child
    relationship
Child support, 354, 356, 453
Child-thought, 344

Child-to-parent abuse, 418
Child Trends, 356
China
  changes in sexuality, 159
  divorce in, 431
  extramarital sex and, 180
  male and female traits identified in,
    192–193
  marriage and dating in, 276
  single women in, 267
Chlamydia, A-27
Chromosomes, A-26
Chronic illnesses, 379
  psychological abuse and, 407
Cigarette smoking, 422–423
Circular causality model, 109
Circumplex Model of Marital and Fam-
  ily Systems, 89
Civil unions, 4, 305
Clarity, 89
Clergy, premarital education and, 309,
  470
Closed system, 70
Closeness
  in happy couples, 436–437
  problems related to in couples and
    families, 472–474
Closure, 143
Cluttered nest phenomenon, 372
Coalition, *A-3*
Coalition Rating Scale, A-2–A-3, *A-3*
Cocultures, 33
Coercive power, 208, *209*
Cognitive coping strategies, *401,* 402
Cognitive development theory, 203–204
Cohabitation
  adult children of divorce and, 440
  arguments for and against, 297
  compared to marriage, 15
  considerations before cohabiting, 297
  defined, 293
  factors affecting rates of, 295
  increase in, 293–295, 306
  multicultural couples and, 60
  as preparation for marriage, 298–300
  pros and cons of, 140
  reasons for, 295
  self-assessment quiz, 298–299
  trends in, 8
  types of, 295–297
Cohesion
  balance of separateness and con-
    nectedness, 71–72
  in couples and families, 83–86
  defined, 44, 83
  family communication and, 89
  healthiness of relationships bal-
    anced on, 90–91
  levels of, *83*
  See also Family cohesion
Cohesive relationships, *83,* 84, *85*

Collaborative style, 144–145
Collective worldview, 218
College students
  alcohol use and sexual behavior
    among, 174–176
  credit cards and, 235, 236
  dating, 278–280
Comic relief, 142
Command component, 110
Commitment
  to the family, 44
  in love relationships, 249, *250*
  in strong families, 75–76
  in White families, 46
Communal living, 201
Communication
  aggressive, 119–120
  assertive, 119, 120
  content and relationship messages
    in, 109–110
  as a cooperative endeavor, 109
  in couples, 88–89, 100, *101,* 437, 472
  cultural differences in, 106–108
  dimensions for assessing, 88–89
  double binds, 111–113
  in families, 88–89
  family cohesion and, 89
  as feedback, 72–73
  gender differences in, 101–106
  importance of, 100, 108
  intimacy and, 253–254
  listening and, 117–118
  mealtime practices and, 107
  meaning and, 100
  mixed messages, 111
  passive, 119, 120
  positive and negative cycles of,
    120–123
  power dynamics and, 211–212
  self-disclosure, 113–117
  using to increase intimacy, 121
  See also Metacommunication; Non-
    verbal communication; Positive
    communication
Communication skills
  in developing intimacy, 256
  in gay and lesbian couples, 156
Communication styles, gender and,
  101–102
Community coping resources, *401,* 403
Community divorce, 441, 445
Community life, 16
Community rituals, 481
Companionate love, 250
Compatibility, 257
Competent loners, 437
Competitive interactions, 211
Competitive style, 144
Competitive symmetry, 211
Complementary couples, 178
Complementary interactions, 212

Complementary needs theory, 289
Complex stepfamilies, 460, *461*
Compromise style, 145
Compulsive spending, 240
Conception, A-26–A-27, *A-27*
Conceptual frameworks, 65
Condoms, A-15, A-18, A-19
Confidential adoption, 336
Confiding, in friendship, 245
Conflict
    African American marriages and, 306
    in dating, 292–293, 294
    in gay and lesbian couples, 137
    hierarchy of, 128–129
    intimacy breeds, 132–133
    love–hate relationship and, 131
    reasons for being suppressed, 130–131
    stepfamilies and, 452
    See also Anger
Conflict-avoiding couples, 312
Conflicted couples, 319, 320, 322
Conflict flexibility, 472
Conflict-minimizing couples, 178
Conflict resolution
    constructive and destructive approaches, 143
    in couples, *127*, 127–128, *128*, 138, 437, 472
    developing intimacy and, 256
    fighting fairly, 138–143
    positive communication and, 137–138
    steps in, 145–148
    styles of, 143–145, *144*, 312
Conjugal family systems, 43
Connectedness
    balancing with separateness, 71–72
    family resiliency and, 476
Connected relationships, *83*, *84*, *85*
Connection rituals, 481
Consanguineal family systems, 43
Constructive intimacy games, 259–260
Consumer Credit Counseling Service (CCCS), 241
Consummate love, 250
Contempt, 138, 312
Contentment, American Indians and, 55
Contraception
    making choices about, A-17–A-18
    methods of, A-14–A-17
    overview of, A-14
Contractions, A-31
Control, 209, 224
Convenience cohabitation, 296–297
Cooperative colleagues, 449
Coparental divorce, 443–445, 447
Coparenting, 350–352
Coping, 44
Corporal punishment, 346–348, 411–412

Counseling
    divorce and, 446, 447
    financial, 240–241
    strong families and, 78
    See also Family therapy; Marital therapy; Parent counseling; Premarital education
Couple and Family Map
    dance of anger concept and, 135
    mapping couples and families in closeness and flexibility, 472–474
    mapping relationship changes over time, 94–95
    overview of, 89–91
    parenting styles and, 339–343
    steps in using, A-2–A-3
    value of, 91–92
Couple-arranged marriages, 276
Couple closeness, 257, 436–437
Couple Communication Program, 471
Couple education programs, 469, 470–471
Couple enrichment programs, 470–471
Couple flexibility, 257, 436–437
Couple rating form, *A-5*
Couple relationships
    change in dynamics over time, 94–95
    common problems in, 472, *472*
    developing intimacy in, 256–258
    effect of societal factors and values on, 19–20
    focusing on the strengths of, 467–468
    impact of the social environment on, 16–26
    programs for, *469*
    strengthening, 479–480
    See also Intimate relationships; Love relationships
Couple scales, *A-4*
Couples Communication, 309, 311
Couple stress, 388. *See also* Stress
Couple therapy, 469
Couple violence, 403. *See also* Domestic abuse and violence
Courtship, violence in, 404
Courtship patterns
    dating, 277–278
    hanging out and hooking up, 278–280
    Internet dating, 281
    matchmaking services, 280–281
    parent-arranged marriages, 274–277
Credit
    advantages and disadvantages, 235
    avoiding debt and bankruptcy, 240
    financial counseling, 240–241
    overextension, 238–240
    purchasing a home, 237–238
Credit cards, 235, 236–237
Credit clinics, 241

Credit history, 236
Credit spending, 240
Criminal victimization, 20
Crisis, Chinese pictograph for, 400, *401*
Crisis-loss stage of grief, 382
Crisis management, 78–79
Crisis resolution, 129
Crisis spending, 240
Criticism, 138, 312
Cross-cultural family studies, 56–58
Cross-sectional cohort studies, A-11–A-12
Cross-sectional studies, A-11
Cross-validation, A-10
Crowning, A-32
C-section, A-33
Cultural competence, 40–42
Cultural groups
    applying the concept of, 36
    defined, 33
    financial style and, 218–219
Cultural identity, 32–33
Culture
    applying the concept of, 36
    gender roles and, 197–198
Culture of divorce, 434
Curvilinear relationships, 388–389

Dance of anger concept, 134–137
The Dance of Anger (Lerner), 134
Dating
    among older people, 282–284
    conflict and violence in, 292–293, 294, 404
    contemporary vs. traditional patterns, *196*
    divorced individuals and, 446
    do's and don'ts, 281
    emergence of, 277–278
    hanging out and hooking up, 278–280
    limitations of, *277*
Dating services, 280–281
Daughters
    corporal punishment and, 346, *347*, 348
    impact of parenting style on, 339
Day care. *See* Child care
Debit cards, 237
Debt
    above normal limits, 238
    avoiding, 240
    effects on newlyweds, 218
    of families, 25
    reasons for, 240
Decision making
    in the hierarchy of conflict, 128–129
    the power process and, 212
Defeateds, 438
Defensiveness, 138, 312
Definition of the situation, 80
Delinquency, 285

Delivery, A-31–A-32
Democratic parenting, 340–341, 342
Demographics
    African Americans, 37–38
    American Indians and Alaska Natives, 37
    Asian Americans, 38
    ethnic diversity in America, 36
    family characteristics by ethnic group, *37*
    Hispanics, 36–37
    majority–minority states, 36
    trends in, 38–39, *41*
Dental expenses, 394
Depo-Provera (DMPA), 174, A-16
Depression
    corporal punishment during adolescence and, 347, *348*
    divorce and, 441
    in mothers following childbirth, A-34–A-35
Descent. *See* Lineage
Desert Flower (Dirie), 159
Destructive intimacy games
    limiting, 262–263
    overview of, 258–259
    types of, 260–262
Devitalized couples, 319–320, 322
Diaphragms, A-15, A-18
Diet, during pregnancy, A-30
Diethylstilbestrol (DES), A-28
Dilation and curettage (D & C), A-21
Dilation and evacuation (D & E), A-21
DINS dilemma, 176
Directive listening, 117–118
Disagreement, agreeing to, 148
Discipline
    as affected by relationship flexibility, *88*
    Asian Americans and, 53
    corporal punishment, 346–348, 411–412
    current trends in the use of, 345–346
Disclosure, 113–117
Discrimination
    against Asian Americans, 53
    differences in income and, 229–230
Disengaged individuals, *A-3*
Disengaged relationships, *83*, 84, *85*, 86
Disguised objectives, 263
Dissolved duo, 449
Distancers, 135
Distress, 389
Diversity
    in America, 36
    in family and couple relationships, 2
    financial style and, 218–220
    increasing the appreciation of, 31
    interconnection to strengths, 31
    intimacy in families and, 31–32
    trends in, *41*

Divorce
    absent fathers and, 354
    adjusting to, 446–447
    alcohol abuse and, 420
    arranged marriages and, 275
    cohabitation and, 294–295, 300
    cross-cultural perspective on, 61
    culture of, 434
    economic costs of, 222–223
    ethnically mixed couples and, 287
    experiences of, 441–446
    family reorganization and, 448
    globalization of, 430–431
    grounds for, 431–432
    happy vs. unhappy couples, 435–437, *437*
    in high- vs. low-conflict marriages, 439–440
    impact on children, 438–439, 440, 445
    impact on parents, 437–438
    legal trends, 430–434
    marriage difficulties and, 306
    during middle age, 371–373
    predicting, 312
    reasons for, 434–435, *435*
    statistical and historical trends in, 8–9, *10*, *428*, 428–430, *429*
    women filing for, 15
Divorce law
    traditional, 432–433
    See also No-fault divorce
DMPA, A-16
Domestic abuse and violence
    childhood corporal punishment and, 347
    diversity and, 405
    factors affecting the willingness to report, 405
    factors contributing to, 407–410
    incidence, 404–405
    later acts of child abuse and, 415
    less likely in marriages, 15
    National Survey of Domestic Violence, 405–406, *406*
    overview of, 403
    patterns of, 410
    prevention and treatment, 410–411
    relationship of physical and psychological abuse, 406–407
    as a symptom of PTSD, 399
    types of, 404
Double-binds
    metacommunication and, 112–113
    overview of, 111–112
Double income, no sex (DINS) dilemma, 176
Double standard
    decline in, 197
    for sexual and social behavior, 278
Douching, A-16–A-17

Drug-induced deaths, 422
Drugs and drug abuse, 20, 21, A-31
Duluth, Minnesota, 410–411
Dysfunctional families, 76

Early-childhood programs, 351
Eclectic approach, 65
Ecological approach, 68, *69*
Ecology, defined, 68
Economic adequacy, 467
Economic assets, married people and, 304
Economic divorce, 441, 443, 446–447
Economic inequality, 226, *227*
Economic purchases, family stress and, 394
Economic stress
    child abuse and, 413
    coping with, 221–222
    domestic violence and, 408
    as a family problem, 220–221
    family stress and, 393
Ectoderm, A-29
Education
    African American families and, 50
    Asian Americans and, 53
    by ethnic group, *37*
    gender differences in income and, 228–229
Educational homogamy, 289
Egalitarian decision making
    in gay and lesbian couples, 156
    Latino families and, 51
Egalitarian groups, 43–44
Egalitarian marriages, 48, 50
Egalitarian relationships, 200–201
Egalitarian roles
    marital satisfaction and, 210–211, *211*
    trend toward, 195, 197
Egg, A-26, *A-27*
Egypt, divorce in, 431
Ejaculatory incompetence, 183
Elderly
    abuse and neglect of, 373
    American Indians and, 55, 56
    child-to-parent abuse and, 418
    dating among, 282–284
    demographics, 282
    family caregiving for, 195
    sexuality and, 166–167
    See also Old age
Emancipation cohabitation, 296
Emergency oral contraception, A-15
Emic perspective, 58
Emotional child abuse, 411
Emotional coping strategies, *401*, 402
Emotional difficulties, family stress and, 393
Emotional divorce, 441–442
Emotionally expressive couples, 178
Emotion work, 191

Empty love, 250
Empty-nest syndrome, 333, 372
Endocrine disrupters, A-28
Endoderm, A-29
Endogamy, 286
Endometriosis, A-27
Endometrium, *A-27*
Enhanced type, 437
Enjoyment
   in friendship, 245
   money and, 224
Enmeshed relationships, *83, 84, 85,*
   85–86, 92–94
Enmeshment, 85–86
ENRICH, 255–256, 313
"Ephrata, Washington Pays for the
   War" (Caplin & McGirt), 399
Episiotomy, A-32, A-34
Equalitarian roles. *See* Egalitarian roles
Equal Pay Act of 1963, 205
Erectile dysfunction, 183
Estrogen, A-14
Ethnic diversity. *See* Diversity
Ethnic families, challenges to, 58–62
Ethnic groups
   applying the concept of, 36
   characteristics of strong families, 45
   defined, 33
   differences in family income levels,
     227, *227*
   family strengths and challenges,
     46–56
   marriage between, 60
Ethnicity/ethnic identity
   applying the concept of, 36
   defined and described, 32–33
   Latino families and, 50
Ethnocentrism, 56–57, 59
Etic perspective, 57–58
Eustress, 389
Everybody Loves Raymond (TV show),
   92–93
Evolutionary theory, concept of race
   and, 34
Exercise, during pregnancy, A-30–A-31
Exogamy, 286
Expert power, 208, *209*
Explosive couples, 178
Expressive role, 82
Expressivity, 194
Extended family
   American Indians and, 54, 55
   Asian Americans and, 53
   defined, 43
   intercultural marriages and, 288
Extramarital friendships, 178–179
Extramarital sex, 180. *See also* Infidelity
Eye contact, 108

FACES scale, 52
Fair fighting, 138–143

Fallopian tube, A-26
Families
   African Americans and, 48
   Asian Americans and, 53
   characteristics of continuity in, 12
   connectedness during old age, 380
   death of an infant and, A-37
   definitions of, 4–6
   emotion work in, 191
   expenses, 230, *231*
   impact of community life on, 16
   intimacy in diverse cultures, 31–32
   loyalty in Asian Americans, 53
   mental work in, 192
   net worth, 231
   nonindulgent, 346
   past predictions about, 6–7
   power in, 206–213
   programs for, *469*
   qualities of strength in, *74,* 74–79
   resiliency, 476, *476*
   spending time together, 18
   strengthening, 480–481
   strengths perspective on, 2, *13,*
     467–468
   terminology, 448–450
   well-being and mealtime practices,
     107
Families and Democracy Model, 26
Familism, Latino families and, 50
Family Adaptability and Cohesion
   Evaluation Scales, 52
Family belief systems, resiliency and,
   476, *476*
Family cohesion
   American Indians and, 55
   defined, 44
   interview questions for assessing,
     A-2
   Latino families and, 50
   levels of, A-4
   Mexican Americans and, 52
   See also Cohesion
Family communication
   characteristics of, 45
   levels of, *A-4*
   resiliency and, 476, *476*
Family coping
   defined, 391
   resources, 221
   strategies, 400–403
Family counseling. *See* Family therapy
Family debt, 25
Family development framework, 67,
   79–80
Family expenses, 230, *231*
Family flexibility
   defined, 44
   interview questions for assessing,
     A-2
   Latino families and, 50

   levels of, *A-4*
   Mexican Americans and, 52
Family income
   by ethnic group, 37, 227, *227*
   gender differences, 228–229
   patterns of unequal distribution in,
     226, *227*
   of the poor, 226
   ranges of, 226
   See also Income; Money; Wealth
Family life educators, 66, A-8
Family net worth, 231
Family of origin
   later domestic violence and, 408
   marriage and, 313–315
Family organizational patterns, resiliency and, 476, *476*
Family power
   bases of, 207–208
   characteristics of, 206
   defined, 206
   outcomes, 209
   processes, 208–209
   See also Power
Family practice, 66
Family rating form, *A-5*
Family relationships
   effect of societal factors and values
     on, 19–20
   intimacy within couples and,
     257–258
Family resiliency, 476, *476*
Family rituals
   building, 480–481
   in strong families, 77
Family satisfaction, family stress and,
   393
Family scales, A-4
Family science
   disciplines contributing to, *A-8*
   overview of, 65–67, A-8
Family science research
   complementary studies and, A-12
   designs, A-11–A-12
   methods, A-8–A-11
Family scientists, A-8
Family size, child abuse and, 415
Family strengths framework, 67, 73–79
Family Strengths Inventory, 47
Family stress
   boundary ambiguity and, 391–392,
     392
   common stressful issues, 393–394
   coping strategies, 400–403
   cross-cultural perspectives on, 388
   the family life cycle and, 392–393
   family satisfaction and, *393*
   general principles of change related
     to, 397–398
   in military families, 398–399
   roller coaster model of, 394–395

September 11 attacks and, *396*, 396–398

war-related posttraumatic stress disorder and, 398–400

Family structure

and parenting style in affecting child development, 343

percentage of children in poverty and, 25, *25*

trends in, 10–12

Family systems

changes before and after the September 11 attacks, *396*, 396–398

characteristics of, 44–45

defined, 67

growing complexity of, 450–451

sociocultural context and, *45*, 45–46

Family systems theory

on change, 204

Couple and Family Map and, 89

overview of, 67–73

on parent–child dynamics, 343

Family therapy

case study, 476–479

choosing a therapist, 475

creation of family systems theory and, 68

divorce and, 446

effectiveness, 474–475

overview of, 357–358

statistics on, 474–475

times to use, 469

using early on, 471–472

See also Marital and family therapists

Family time

promotes family cohesion, 44

in strong families, 77

White families and, 46

See also Time

Family-to-work influence, 194–195

Family trees, 43

Family violence, alcohol and, 419–420

Family work

distribution by gender, 191

See also Housework

Fathers

absent, 354

during childbirth and with newborns, A-35

coparental divorce and, 443, 444

coparenting and, 351–352

with custody, 454–456

involvement with infants, 357–358

as nurturers, 354–355

positive impact on child development, 356

responsible, 355–356

Fatuous love, 250

Federal Trade Commission, 237

Feedback, 72–73

Female circumcision, 159

Female genital mutilation (FGM), 159

Female infertility, A-27–A-28

Female traits, survey of, *192*, 192–193

Femininity, 188–189

Feminism

African American women and, 200

family relationships and, 82–83

historical studies of families and, A-11

overview of, 82, 204, 206

Feminist framework, 67, 82–83

Feminization of poverty, 443

Fertility, in women, A-26

Fertility awareness methods, A-17

Fertility drugs, A-28

Fertilization, A-26, *A-27*

Fetal alcohol syndrome (FAS), 419, A-31

Fetus, conception and development, A-26–A-27, A-29, *A-29*, *A-30*

Fiery foes, 449

Fighting, marriage and, 312

Fighting fairly, 138–143

Filial piety, 53, 202

Finances

couple strengths and, 217

divorce and, 443

domestic violence and, 408

effects of problems in, 24–25

importance of, 216

reasons for causing problems for families, 223–224

stress of, 220–222 (*see also* Economic stress)

Financial counseling, 240–241

Financial dependency, domestic violence and, 408

Financial management

budgeting, 232–233

issues for married couples, 217, *217*

pooling money, 233–234

saving, 234–235

styles in, 218–220

Financial stress. *See* Economic stress

Firearm-related violence, 20

Fixed-response questions, A-9

Flexibility

balancing stability and change, 70–71

in couples, 87–88, 436–437

defined, 87

in families, 87–88

family resiliency and, 476

healthiness of relationships balanced on, 91

problems related to in couples and families, 472–474

Flexible relationships, 87, *88*

Flexibly disengaged family, 314–315

Florida, marriage legislation, 325–326

For Better or Worse: Divorce Reconsidered (Hetherington & Kelly), 437, 438

Forgiveness, 323–324

Fouls, 142

Frail old, 376

France, use of RU-486 in, A-20

Freedom, 468

Friends

contrasting with lovers, 247–249

divorcing couples and, 445

Friendships

elements of, 245

intimacy within couples and, 257–258

negative aspects, 248

outside of love relationships, 255

positive aspects, 247

that turns into love, 248–249

vs. love, 244–245

Fully disclosed adoption, 336

The Future of Marriage (Bernard), 14

Gay couples and families

characteristics of, 155–157

civil unions, 305

conflict and supportiveness in, 137–138

increasing number of, 155

issues in studying, 156–157

parenting, 352–353

trends in, 4

Gay men

infidelity and, 179

sexual behavior, 167–168

Gay parenting, 352–353

Gender

communication and, 101–106

definitions of, 82, 154

differences in income and, 228–229

disclosure and, 113–114

distribution of family work by, 191

traditional divorce law and, 432

work–family interface, 194–195

Gender communication quotient, 105

Gender identity, 188

Gender inequality

feminist framework, 204, 206

overview of, 205

Gender roles

in African American culture, 200

in American Indian culture, 200–201

in Asian American culture, 202

changing nature of, 23–24

contemporary view of, 194–195

culture and, 197–198

defined, 188

egalitarian, 195, 197

international perspective on, 197–199

marriage and, 190–199

in Mexican American culture, 199–200

overview of, 188–189
perspective on differences in, 106
stereotypes in, 188
theories about, 202–206
traditional view of, 193–194
Gender-role stereotypes, 188
General systems theory, 68–70, 72–73
A Generation at Risk (Amato & Booth), 439
Genes, A-26
Genetics, concept of race and, 34
Gentle birthing, A-34
Germany, extramarital sex in, 180
"Giving Compliments" game, 260
Global economy, effect on American families, 25–26
"Global Employment Trends for Women 2004," 205
Goals, economic, 216
Gonorrhea, A-27, A-32
Good enoughs, 437
Good gets worse couples, 321
Grandchildren, 374–375
Grandparents and grandparenthood
American Indian families and, 56, 374
child care and, 348
demographics, 373
dimensions of, 373–374
divorced children and, 454
raising grandchildren, 374–375
Grieving, stages of, 382–383
Growing edge, 133
Growing Together Program, 471
Gun homicides, 20
Gunnysacking, 141

Handbook of Forgiveness (Worthington), 323
Hanging out, 278–280
Happiness
management of stress and, 389
in married people, 14
Harmonious couples, 319, 320, 322
Hate, and love, 131
Health
African American marriages and, 305, 306
impact of psychological abuse on, 407
life changes and, 389
marriage and, 304
Health care expenses, 394
Healthy Marriage Initiative, 324–325
Healthy relationships, 90–91
Heterosexuality, 154
Hispanic families
child care and, 349
demographics, 349
median income level, 227, *227*
trends in family structure, *10*, 11

See also Latino families
Hispanics, demographic trends, 36–37, 38
Historical studies, A-10–A-11
Hmong, 38
Holmes and Rahe Social Readjustment Rating Scale, 389, *390*
Holmes and Rahe Stress Test, 389, *390*
Home birth, A-34
Homelessness, 25
Home loans, 238
Homes
purchasing, 237–238
renting vs. buying, 237–238, *239*
Homicides, gun-related, 20
Homogamy, 289–290
Homosexuality
across cultures, 157, 158–159
defined, 154
Hooking up, 278–280
Hormone therapy, for menopause, 369
Household expenses, 230, *231*
Household income. *See* Family income
Household inequality, 205
Housework, 190, 191. *See also* Family work
Housing costs
determining, 237
for divorcing families, 223
Hugging, 108
Human ecology, 68, *69*
Human immunodeficiency virus (HIV), 159–160
Human mate poaching, 180
Human milk, A-35–A-36
Human reproduction, A-26–A-28
Humor
in conflict resolution, 142
in family communication, 76
power and, 208
as a quality for mate selection, 285
Hunger, 25
Husband abuse, 404
Husband-dominant power pattern, 209, *210*
Husbands and Wives (Blood & Wolfe), 207
Hypoactive sexual desire, 176
Hypotheses, 65
Hysterotomy, A-21

Idiographic approach, 65
"I Don't Care; You Decide" game, 261–262
"If You Really Love Me, You'll Know What I Want" game, 263
Illegal abortions, A-18
Illness, in old age, 379
Implantation, *A-27*
Implicit rules, 263
Impotence, 183
Impulsive–aggressive behavior, 341

Impulsive spending, 240
Incest taboos, 157
Income
African American marriages and, 305
mothers with custody and, 453
in old age, 377–378
See also Family income; Money; Wealth
Incongruity humor, 142
Independence
balanced with intimacy in communication, 103
within families, 71–72
marital success and, 307
India
arranged marriage in, 276
divorce in, 430
Individual-choice courtship, 277–278
Individualistic worldview, 218
Indonesia, extramarital sex in, 180
Induced labor, A-21
Infants
caring for, A-35–A-36
mortality rates, A-36
See also Babies
Infatuation, 250, 251
Infertility, A-27–A-28
Infibulation, 159
Infidelity, 178–181
Informational power, 208, *209*
Inhibited sexual desire, 176
Insider perspective, A-8, A-9
Institutional inequality, 205
Instrumentality, 193
Instrumental role, 82
Intelligence, as a quality for mate selection, 285
The Intentional Family (Doherty), 481
Interaction component, 111
Intercultural marriage, 286–288
Interdependence, 130
Interdependence of parts, 70
Interest-free credit cards, 235
Interfaith marriage, 286–288
Intermarriage, 36
Internet
dating, 281
human relationships and, 21–23
pornography and the sexual exploitation of children, 23
psychological affect on individuals, 23
trends in adult use of, 22
Internet dating, 281
Interracial marriage, 286–288
Interviews, A-10
Intimacy
breeds conflict, 132–133
communication and, 103, 119–120, *120, 121*, 253–254

defined, 2, 253
developing, 255–258
increasing, 121
in love relationships, 249–250, *250*
marriage and, 255
in men and women, 253
self-disclosure and, 114–115
Intimacy games
constructive, 259–260
destructive, 258–259, 260–263
dimensions of, *260*
Intimacy need fulfillment, 291
The Intimate Enemy: How to Fight Fair in Love and Marriage (Bach & Wyden), 133
Intimate experience, 254
Intimate partner violence, 20
Intimate relationships
diversity and, 2
impact of the social environment on, 16–26
intimacy and, 2
partner violence, 20
self-disclosure in, 116–117
strengths perspective, 2
traits of, 255–256
vs. intimate experience, 254–255
See also Couple relationships; Love relationships
Intimate terrorism, 404
Intrauterine devices (IUDs), A-16, A-18
Iraq war, 398–399, 429
Iraq War Clinician Guide (Waldrep, Cozza, & Chen), 398–399
Irreconcilable differences, 433
Islamic courts, 180
Isolation
child abuse and, 414
domestic violence and, 408
"I" statements, 141

Japan
divorce in, 430–431
extramarital sex in, 180
marriage in, 276
nonverbal communication in, 108
premarital couples in, 202
single women in, 267
Japanese Americans, 52–53
Jealousy, 85, 251–252
Jews, concept of ethnicity and, 36
Job change, family stress and, 394
Joint custody, 432–433, 449, 457
Jordan, extramarital sex in, 180
Justice, 468
"Just Say No" programs, 172
Juvenile delinquency, 285, 420

Keraki society, 158
Kin relationships, 42–44
Kinship
African American families and, 48

defined, 42
Latino families and, 51
Kinship groups, 42–43
Kissing, 158
Knowledge, cultural competence and, 40–41
Knowledge-positions, 81
Korea. *See* South Korea
Kwoma society, 157

Labor
features of, A-31
induced, A-21
stages of, A-31–A-33, *A-32*
Lamaze method, A-33–A-34
Language, gender bias and, 189
Latinas
domestic violence and, 405
raising grandchildren, 375
Latino families
children being raised by grandparents, 375
domestic violence in, 405
financial style, 219
net worth, 231
strengths of, 50–52
See also Hispanic families
Law of enlightened self-interest, 308
Leadership
as affected by relationship flexibility, *88*
as a problem in couples, 472
Learned helplessness theory, 408
Learning theories, 344
Learning to Live Together Program, 471
Legal divorce, 441, 442–443
Legal drugs, 422–423
Legitimate power, 208, *209*
Leisure activities, as a problem in couples, 472
Lesbian couples and families
characteristics of, 155–157
conflict and supportiveness in, 137–138
increasing number of, 155
infidelity and, 179
issues in studying, 156–157
parenting, 352–353
trends in, 4
Lesbians, sexual behavior, 167–168
Libertines, 437–438
Life events/changes, stress and, 389–390
Life expectancy, 376
Liking, 250
Lineage, 43
Linear causality model, 109
Lines of descent, 43
Linus blanket cohabitation, 296
Listening, 88, 89, 117–118
Living together. *See* Cohabitation

Loneliness
divorce and, 441
mothers with custody and, 453–454
in old age, 380
Lone-parent families. *See* Single-parent families
Longevity, marriage as a predictor for, 13–14, 304
Longevous marriages, 382–383
Looking-glass self, 80
Loss, Trauma, and Resilience (Boss), 391
Love
comments on the nature of, *244*
dynamic connection to hate, 131
jealousy and, 251–252
keeping in balance with anger, 133–134
negative aspects of, 248
perspectives on, 251
positive aspects of, 247
that develops from friendship, 248–249
traits of, 246
unique characteristics of, 245, 247
vs. friendship, 244–245
Love and Addiction (Peele), 251
Love and War (Korean TV show), 430
Love match, 276
Love Must Be Tough (Dobson), 251
Love relationships
jealousy in, 251–252
outside friendships and, 255
See also Couple relationships; Intimate relationships
Love rituals, 481
Lovers, contrasting with friends, 247–249
Love triangle, 249–250
Lower-middle-income families, 226
Low-income couples and families
child abuse and, 411
collective worldview, 218
domestic violence and, 405, 408
financial style, 218–219
housing costs during divorce and, 223
income levels, 226, *227*
Loyalty, 53
Lunelle, 174

Machismo, 199–200
Majority culture, advantages of being in, 59
Majority–minority states, 36
Male dominance, domestic violence and, 409
Male menopause, 370
Male traits, *192*, 192–193
Managing stress. *See* Stress management
Mangaian society, 158

Man's Most Dangerous Myth: The Fallacy of Race (Montagu), 34
Maori society, 157
Marital and family therapists, 39–40, 66, A-8. *See also* Family therapy; Marital therapy
Marital conflict, stepfamilies and, 452
Marital satisfaction
    changes in over time, 320–322
    the transition to parenting and, 334
Marital success
    cohabitation and, 294–295
    predicting, 312
Marital therapy
    choosing a therapist, 475
    divorce and, 446
    effectiveness, 474–475
    statistics on, 474–475
    using in a timely manner, 471–472
    See also Marital and family therapists
Marital violence
    couples more likely to experience, 406
    See also Domestic abuse and violence
Marriage
    abortion and, A-23
    advantages of, 13–16
    African Americans and, 304–306
    American Indians and, 56
    Asian American families and, 202
    benefits of, 303–304
    changes before and after having a child, 322
    changes in satisfaction over time, 320–322
    characteristics of, 3–4
    compared to cohabitation, 15
    components of success in, 307–308
    contemporary vs. traditional patterns in, *196*
    continuity in, 12
    defined, 3
    delay in, 303
    difficulties and divorce, 306
    drifting apart in, 322
    effects of parenthood on, 333–334
    emotion work in, 191
    facts about, *307*
    family of origin and, 313–315
    forgiveness in, 323–324
    gender roles and, 189–199
    intimacy and, 255
    keeping as a top priority, 322–323
    long-term, 382–383
    median age for, 266, 286
    mental work in, 192
    middle-aged, 370
    outside the group, 59–60
    past predictions about, 6–7

planning after a divorce, 459
    predicting success in, 312–313
    premarital fantasies vs. marital realities, *318*
    retirement and, 382
    role relationships in happy vs. unhappy couples, 190, *190*
    sacrifice in, 324
    self-disclosure in, 116, 117
    sex within, 176–178
    singlehood as an alternative to, 266–268
    strengthening, 479–480
    strengths perspective on, 2
    styles in, 178
    top relationship issues, *191*
    transition to, 316–319
    trends in, 6, 7–8, *10*, 264, *264*, 303, 306–307
    types of, 319–320, *320*
    the wedding, 315–316
Marriage brokers, 275
Marriage counseling. *See* Marital therapy
Marriage education, 308–313, 317, 319
Marriage Encounter, 309
Marriage movement, 309
Marriage Preparation and Reservation Act (Florida), 325–326
Masculinity, 188
Masturbation, 158
Matchmakers, 276, 280–281
Materialism, 18
Maternity blues, A-34
Mate selection
    challenges for contemporary women, 286
    dating, 277–278
    interracial and interfaith marriages, 286–288
    mating gradient, 285
    physical attractiveness in, 284–285
    theories of, 289–292
    See also Courtship patterns
Mating gradient, 285
Matriarchal group, 43
Matrilineal societies, 43
Matrilocal society, 44
Matrimony (Fowler), 289
Maturity, marital success and, 307
Mealtime practices, 107
Meaning, shared, 80
Mediated adoption, 336
Mediation, of divorces, 442–443
Medical expenses, 394
Medicine, concept of race and, 34
Memories, 344–345
Men
    alcohol abuse and, 419
    body language and, 312
    causes of divorce in middle age, 372

changing nature of gender roles and, 24
    communication and, 101–106
    contemporary notions of gender and, 194–195
    coparenting and, 351–352
    disclosure and, 114
    feminist notions of the family and, 82–83
    gender differences in income, 228–229
    happiness in old age, 376
    infertility in, A-28
    instrumentality and, 193
    intimacy and, 253
    jealousy and, 252
    marriage as a predictor of career success, 14
    mate selection and, 285
    median age for marriage, 286
    minimizing power issues and, 213
    relationship power balances and, 24
    reluctance to seek professional help for problems, 193
    sex ratio, 286
    styles in anger management, 137
    survey of male traits, *192*, 192–193
    views of sex and love, 152
Menopause
    in men, 370
    in women, 369–370
Menses, A-26
Menstrual cycle, A-26
Menstruation, A-26
Mental retardation, 419
Mental work, 192
Men–women relationship, 60–61
Mesoderm, A-29
Mestizo, 200
Metacommunication, 112–113
Mexican Americans
    diversity within, 50–51
    family strengths, 52
    gender roles and, 199–200
Mexico, extramarital sex in, 180
Middle age
    boomerang kids and, 372
    cluttered nest, 372
    as crisis and opportunity, 367
    defining, 364, 366
    demographic trends, 366
    divorce and, 371–373
    empty-nest syndrome, 372
    family stress in, 365
    grandparenthood, 373–374
    levels of personal satisfaction, *368*
    sandwich generation families, 363–364, 373
    sexuality in, 368–370
    strengthening marriage in, 370
    the working world and, 367–368
Middle Ages, extramarital sex in, 180

Middle-income families, 226, 227
Middle-old, 376
Middlescence, 364
Midlife crisis, 367
Midrange families, 90
Midwives, A-34
Mifepristone, A-20
Military families, 398–399
Milk, human, A-35–A-36
Minipill, A-15
Minnesota Science Museum, 34
Minority groups
   in America, 33
   practice with, 39–40
   research with, 39
Miscarriages, A-18, A-36
Miscommunication, 141
Misoprostol, A-20
"Miss Spinster," 267
Mixed messages, 111
Mixed-methods research, A-9
Models of couples and families
   family development framework, 79–80
   family strengths framework, 73–79
   family systems theory, 67–73
   feminist framework, 82–83
   social construction framework, 81–82
   symbolic interaction framework, 80–81
Money
   common orientations toward, 224
   family stress and, 394
   fathers with custody and, 455
   happiness and, 216
   pooling, 233–234
   saving, 234–235
   self-assessment quiz, 225
   stepfamilies and, 463
   strategies in management, 232–235
      (see also Financial management)
   as a taboo subject, 223–224
   as a top priority in society, 333
   See also Finances; Income; Wealth
Monogamy, 43
Morning-after contraceptive pill, A-15
Morning sickness, A-28
Morocco, divorce in, 431
Morphogenic system, 70
Morphostatic system, 70, 71
Mortality inequality, 205
Mortality rates, effect of marriage on, 13–14
Mortgages, 238
Mothers
   child-to-parent abuse and, 418
   with custody, 453–455
   physical and psychological changes following childbirth, A-34–A-35
   power issues with fathers and, 355

Movies, family dynamics in, 93
Mrs. Doubtfire (movie), 434
MTV, 93–94
Multicultural studies, A-11
Multiple system levels, 68
Multiracial marriages, 60
Mundugumor people, 197
Mutual dependency, 291

Nagging, 103
Nakode (matchmaker), 276
Narrative therapy, 81
Natality inequality, 205
National Council on Alcoholism and Drug Dependence, 422
National Council on Family Relations (NCFR), 66
National Survey of Domestic Violence, 405–406, 406
National Survey of Sexual Behavior, 161–164
Native Americans. See Alaska Natives; American Indians
Natural childbirth, A-33
Navajos, 38, 201
Nawa culture, 157
Negative feedback, 72–73
Negotiation
   as affected by relationship flexibility, 88
   strategies in, 147–148
Neolocal society, 44
Neutralized interactions, 211
Neutralized symmetry, 211–212
New Chance parenting program, 358
New Jersey, same-sex civil union law, 305
New-life stage of grief, 383
Newlyweds, 218, 316–319
Nicotine, A-31
Nigeria, extramarital sex in, 180
No-fault divorce
   conflict and, 442
   defined, 430
   effects of, 433–434
   in Egypt, 431
   features of, 432–433
Nomothetic approach, 65
Noncommunication, 108
Nonindulgent families, 346
Nonintimate relationships, 255–256
Non-love, 250
Nonmarital childbearing, absent fathers and, 354
Nonmarket work, 205
Nonparenthood, 337–339
Nonpossessive caring, 308
Nonverbal communication
   cultural differences in, 106–108
   overview of, 110–111
Norplant, A-16

Now, Discover Your Strengths (Buckingham & Clifton), 467
Nuclear families
   defined and described, 42–43
   differences with stepfamilies, 451, 451–452
   trends in, 10
Nurse-midwives, A-34
Nursing homes, 379
Nutrition, during pregnancy, A-30

Observational approaches, A-10
Old age
   attitude and, 377
   changes in family dynamics and, 383–384
   connectedness to other family members, 380
   death of a spouse and, 382–383
   defining, 376–377
   demographics of life expectancy, 376
   happiness and, 376
   illness and, 379
   intimacy in, 363
   loneliness and, 380
   nursing homes and, 379
   personal satisfaction and, 368
   retirement and, 380–382
   senility and, 379
   sexuality and, 283, 378–379
   wealth and income in, 377–378
   See also Elderly
Old-old, 376
One-parent families. See Single-parent families
Online dating, 281
"On Marriage" (Gibran), 84
Open adoption, 336–337
Open-ended interviews, A-9
Open-ended questions, A-9
Open system, 70
Oral contraceptives, A-14–A-15, A-18, A-19
Organic sexual dysfunctions, 182
Organismic theory, 343–344
The Osbournes (TV show), 93–94
Out-of-wedlock births, 352
Outsider perspective, A-8–A-9
Ovary, A-27
Overcrowding, 24
Overfunctioners, 136
Oviduct, A-26, A-27
Ovulation, A-26
Ovulation method, A-17
Ownership inequality, 205

Painful intercourse, 183
Painkillers, childbirth and, A-33–A-34
PAIRS program, 311
Parental control, 339
Parental support, 339

Parent-arranged marriages, 274–277
Parent–child relationship
    cross-cultural perspective on, 61–62
    destructive intimacy games and, 262
    in gay and lesbian couples, 156
Parent counseling, for child abuse, 416
Parent education, 357–358, A-30, A-35
"Parenthood as Crisis" (LeMasters),
    333–334
Parenting and parenthood
    child care issues, 348–350
    conventional wisdom about, 331–333
    corporal punishment issues,
        346–348
    cost of raising a child, 334–335, 335
    couples and, 329–330, 330, 472
    as crisis, 333–334
    discipline issues, 345–346
    fatherhood and, 354–356
    gay and lesbian, 352–353
    issues in, 345–349
    single mothers, 352
    strengths of happy vs. unhappy
        married couples, 329, 330
    styles in, 339–343
    teaching children about money and
        finances, 335–336
    translating philosophy into action,
        358–359
    transmission of adult problems to
        children, 331
    when a child dies, 356–357, A-37
    See also Childrearing; Coparenting;
        Parents
Parent position, 139
Parents
    abusive, 414
    child-to-parent abuse and, 418
    death of an infant and, A-37
    divorcing children and, 445
    impact of divorce on, 437–438
    prevention of sibling abuse of,
        417–418
    sex education and, 170–172
    support for new parents, A-35
Parents Without Partners, 446
PARIS Program, 471
Partial birth abortion, A-19, A-20
Partner dominance, 121, 123
Pashtun culture, 157
Passion, in love relationships, 250, 250
Passion Cluster, 245, 247, 247
Passive–aggressive behavior, 142
Passive communication, 119, 120
Passive immunity, A-35
Passiveness, 119, 120
Patriarchal group, 43
Patrilineal societies, 43
Patrilocal society, 44
Peacefulness, 468
Pelvic inflammatory disease (PID), A-27

Perfect pals, 449
Perineum, A-32
Permissiveness, 278
Permissive parenting, 341, 342–343
Personal coping resources, 221
Personality compatibility, 257
Personality problems, abusive parents
    and, 414
Personal satisfaction, by age group, 368
Personification, 85
Perspective, etic and emic, 57–58
Persuasive listening, 117
Philippines, extramarital sex in, 180
Physical abuse
    of children, 411 (see also Child abuse
        and neglect)
    relationship to psychological abuse,
        406–407
    See also Domestic abuse and violence
Physical attractiveness, mate selection
    and, 284–285
Pill (oral contraceptive), A-14–A-15, A-19
Placenta, A-29, A-31, A-32–A-33
Placental barrier, A-31
Plan B, A-15
Planned Parenthood Federation of
    America, 170, A-23
Planned Parenthood v. Casey, A-19
Planned Parenthood v. Danforth, A-19
Plural marriage, 43
Police departments, prevention of do-
    mestic abuse and, 410–411
Polyandry, 43
Polygamy, 43
Polygyny, 43
Pooling money, 233–234
Pornography, 23
Positive communication
    characteristics of, 45
    conflict resolution and, 137–138
    in strong families, 76
    White families and, 48
Positive feedback, 72
Positive reinforcement, 344
Postabortion syndrome, A-22
Postmodernism, 81–82
Postpartum depression, A-34–A-35
Posttraumatic stress disorder (PTSD),
    398–400, 407
Poverty
    annual income levels, 226
    children and, 24–25, 25
    demographics, 226
    by ethnic group, 37
    feminization of, 443
    the meaning of living in, 226
    old age and, 377–378
    problems frequently related to, 216
Power
    characteristics of, 206
    communication and, 211–212

    defined, 206
    major aspects of, 207–209
    minimizing issues in, 212–213
    in relationships, 24
    types of patterns in, 209–210
    A Prairie Home Companion (Keillor),
        193
Pregnancy
    childbirth classes, A-29–A-30
    drug use and, A-31
    early indicators, A-28
    exercise during, A-30–A-31
    fetal development, A-29, A-29, A-30
    labor and delivery, A-31–A-35
    nutrition during, A-30
    sex during, A-31
    unintentional, A-14
    See also Unintended pregnancy
Pregnancy tests, A-28
Prejudice, 59, 377
Premarital couples
    in Japan, 202
    types of, 320, 321
Premarital education
    components of, 310–312, 469–470
    Healthy Marriage Initiative and,
        324–325
    overview of, 309–310
    predicting the success of a marriage,
        312–313
    usefulness of, 469
Premarital inventory, 310
Premarital sexual behavior, 173–176
Premature ejaculation, 183, 185
Prepaid credit cards, 235
PREPARE, 309, 311, 313, 470, A-11
Prepared childbirth, A-33
PREPARE/ENRICH Program, 471
PREP program, 122, 309, 311, 471
Preschoolers, child care and, 348–350
Prevention and Relationship Enhance-
    ment Program (PREP), 122, 309, 311,
    471
Preventive Approaches in Couples-Therapy
    (Berger & Hannah), 311
Principle of least interest, 208
Problem drinking, 419
Problem families. See Unbalanced
    families
Problem solving, 129
Professional inequality, 205
Progesterone, A-20
Progestin, A-14, A-16
Prostaglandin-induced abortion, A-21
Prostaglandins, A-21
Pseudo–kin groups, 43
Pseudomutuality, 459
Psychodynamic theory, 343
Psychological abuse, 406–407
Psychological aggression, against chil-
    dren, 412–413

Psychological divorce, 441, 446
Psychology, taking a positive approach in, 467
Psychosocial sexual dysfunctions, 182
PTSD. *See* Posttraumatic stress disorder
Purchases, family stress and, 394
Pursuers, 135
Putting Family First Initiative, 26

Qualitative research, A-9
Quantitative research, A-9
Questionnaires, A-9–A-10
Quickening, A-18
Quid pro quid, 147–148
Quid pro quo, 147

Race
    antiquated concept of, 33–36
    intercultural marriages and, 287–288
Racial characteristics, 34
Racism, 59, 229–230
Rape and sexual assault
    differences across cultures, 157–158
    victim–offender relationship in, 404, *404,* 405
Rapid ejaculation, 183
Rapid-fire questioning, 142
Rapid orgasm, 183
Rapport, 290–291
Reality television, 93–94
Reconciliation, 323
Referent power, 208, *209*
Reframing, *401,* 402
Regard, 89
Reinforcement, 344
Reiss's wheel theory of love, 290–292
Rejecting parenting, 341
Relationship component, 110, 111
Relationship coping resources, *401,* 402–403
Relationship Enhancement Program, 309, 311, 471
Relationship fusion, 85–86
Relationships
    changing nature of power balances, 24
    entering after a divorce, 458–459
    as the essence of life, 67
    family science and, 66
    See also specific relationship types
Relationship science, 66–67
Relationship services, 280
Religion
    African American families and, 50
    intercultural marriages and, 287
    Latino families and, 52
    See also Clergy
"Religious," distinguished from "spiritual," 78
Religious orientation, cohabitation and, 295

Remarriage
    defined, 449
    stepfamilies and, 452
    trends in, 8–9, *10,* 265, 306
Renting, vs. buying a home, 237–238, *239*
Report component, 109
Representative samples, A-10
Reproduction, A-26–A-28
Republic of Korea. *See* South Korea
Research
    complementary studies and, A-12
    conducting within cultural contexts, 39
    defined, 65
    designs, A-11–A-12
    meaning of term, A-8
    methods, A-8–A-11
Resiliency. *See* Family resiliency
Resource theory of family power, 207–208
Respect, 89, 245
Retarded ejaculation, 183
Retirement, 380–382
Reward power, 208, *209*
Rigid relationships, 87, 88, 93
"River of Jordan" (song), 468
Robbery, *404,* 404–405
Roe v. Wade, A-18–A-19
Role complementarity, 290
Role making, 80
Roles
    as affected by relationship flexibility, *88*
    flexibility in gay and lesbian couples, 156
    instrumental and expressive, 82
    in the symbolic interaction framework, 80
Roller coaster model, 394–395
Romantic love, 250
Routinization, 367
RU-486, A-20
Rules, relationship flexibility and, *88*
Rural communities, urban migration and, 24

Sacrifice, 324
Saline-induced abortion, A-21
Same-sex couples
    civil unions, 305
    marriage rights and, 4
    See also Gay couples and families;
        Lesbian couples and families
Same-sex marriages, 4
Sandwich generation families, 363–364, 373
Satisfaction, by age group, *368*
Saving, 234–235
Scandinavia, marriage in, 276–277
Scotland, wage gap in, 205

Search Institute, 26
Secured credit cards, 237
Security, money and, 224
Seekers, 437
Segregation, 58
Self-awareness, cultural competence and, 40
Self-concept, 80–81
Self-confidence, 121
Self-disclosure, 88–89, 113–117
Self-esteem
    abusive parents and, 414
    domestic violence and, 408
    marital success and, 307
Self-revelation, 291
Semiarranged marriages, 276
Senegal, extramarital sex in, 180
Senility, 379
Sensate focus, 184
Separateness, balancing with connectedness, 71–72
Separateness–togetherness
    balanced and unbalanced, *83,* 84–85
    in extremes, 85–86
September 11 attacks
    coping with, 402–403
    experiences of ambiguous loss and, 392
    family adjustment to, 394–395
    family system changes before and after, *396,* 396–398
Serial monogamy, 9
Sex and sexual behavior
    advice on sexual health, 177
    and alcohol use among college students, 174–176
    among adolescents, 173–176
    among Americans, 160–168
    attitudes across cultures, 158–159
    defined, 154
    in developing intimacy, 256–257
    differences across cultures, 157–158
    frequency of intercourse across cultures, 158
    gender views on sex and love, 152
    historical perspective on, 154–155
    HIV/AIDS and, 159–160
    infidelity, 178–181
    intercultural marriages and, 288
    marital styles, 178
    married couples and, 14, 152–153, *153,* 176–178, 304
    in middle age, 368–370
    in old age, 166–167, 283, 378–379
    open communication about in society, 152
    during pregnancy, A-31
    self-assessment, 170
    in strong families, 75, 76
    techniques across cultures, 158

using to smooth over disagreements, 141

Sex and Temperament in Three Primitive Societies (Mead), 197–198

Sex and the City (TV series), 266

Sex educators, 184

Sex ratio, 286

Sex roles, intercultural marriages and, 288

Sex therapists, 184

Sex therapy, 183–185

Sexual addiction, 23

Sexual assault. *See* Rape and sexual assault

Sexual attractiveness, 157

Sexual child abuse, 411

Sexual dysfunctions, 182–183

Sexual health, 181–185

Sexuality. *See* Sex and sexual behavior

Sexuality education

    approaches to programs in, 168–170

    consequences when inadequate, 168

    issues of effectiveness in, 172–173

    parents and, 170–172

Sexually transmitted diseases (STDs), A-28

Sexual orientation, 154

Sexual problems

    dysfunctions, 182–183

    frequency of, 181, *181*

    lack of sexual desire, 182

    sex therapy and, 183–185

Shanghai, divorce in, 431

Shared meaning, 80

Should We Live Together? (Popenoe & Whitehead), 298

Sibling abuse, 417–418

Sibling relationships, in old age, 383–384

Significant others, spending time with, 18

Silent passage, 369

Silent treatment, 142

Silver nitrate, A-32

Simple stepfamilies, 460, *461*

Single-father families

    fathers with custody, 454–456

    trends in, *10*, 11, 447, 452

Singlehood

    in American history, 267–268

    as an alternative to marriage, 266–268

    in Asian countries, 267

    characteristics of success in, 268–269

    coping with loneliness in, 269–270

    demographics, 264

    diversity in, 269

    increase in, 265–266

    new definitions of, 266–267

    problems of, 268–269

    See also Unmarried people

Single-mother families

    mothers with custody, 453–454

    parenting and, 352–353

    trends in, *10*, 11, 447, 452

Single-parent families

    child abuse and, 415

    conventional wisdom about, 333

    fathers with custody, 454–456

    increase in, 447–448, *448*

    joint custody, 457

    mothers with custody, 453–454

    percentage of children in poverty, 25, *25*

    split custody, 456

    strengthening, 481

    successful coping strategies, 457

    trends in, *10*, 11

    types of, 452–457

Single women

    poverty rate in old age, 378

    singlehood and, 268

    See also Single-mother families

Sisterhood, in old age, 383–384

Situational couple violence, 404

Skin color, 34

Slapping

    of children, 411–412

    See also Corporal punishment

Smoking, 422–423, A-31

Social construction framework, 67, 81–82

Social environment

    changing, 26

    defined, 16

    impact on relationships, 16–26

    positive responses to, 26–27

Social isolation

    child abuse and, 414

    domestic violence and, 408

Social learning theory, 202, 203

Social psychologists, use of observational approaches, A-10

Social shame, 56

Social support, 221–222

Sociocultural context family system characteristics and, 45, *45–46*

Sole custody, 448–449

Solo-parent families. *See* Single-parent families

Sons

    corporal punishment and, 346, *347*, 348

    impact of parenting style on, 339

South Korea

    divorce in, 430

    single women in, 267

Spacious nest phenomenon, 372

Spanking, 411–412. *See also* Corporal punishment

Speaking skills, 88, 89

Special-needs children, 414

Special opportunity inequality, 205

Sperm cells, A-26, *A-27*

Sperm counts, A-28

Spermicides, A-15, A-16, A-18, A-19

Sperm problems, A-28

"Spiritual," distinguished from "religious," 78

Spiritual coping resources, *401*, 403

Spiritual values, intimacy within couples and, 258

Spiritual well-being, 44, 47, 78

Split custody, 449, 456

Spontaneity, 245

Spontaneous abortions, A-18, A-36

Spouse abuse, 347. *See also* Domestic abuse and violence

Squeeze technique, 185

Stability, balancing with change, 70–71

Stability–change

    balanced and unbalanced, 87

    in extremes, 87–88

Status, money and, 224

Stay-at-home mothers, 12

Staying on topic, 89

Stays good couples, 321

STEEP program, 357–358

Stenberg v. Carhard, A-20

Stepchildren, 416, 450, 452

Stepfamilies

    boundary ambiguity in, 459–460

    child abuse and, 416

    developing, 459

    differences with nuclear families, *451*, 451–452

    financial style, 219–220

    guidelines for, 461–463

    in later life, 460

    money problems and, 463

    notions of blended family and, 449–450

    relationships in the later years, 384

    stages in the formation of, *458*, 458–459

    stepchildren in, 452

    strengthening, 481

    strengths of, 460–461

Stepparents, 416, 450

Stepparent-stepchild relationship, 450

Stepping Ahead Program, 461, 462

Steps Toward Effective Enjoyable Parenting (STEEP) program, 357–358

Stereotypes, 58–59

Sterilization, A-14

Stillbirths, *395*, 395, A-36

Stillborns, A-36

Stimulus, 290

Stimulus–value–role (SVR) theory, 290

Stonewalling, 122, 138, 312

Stop-and-go technique, 184–185

Strength Finder assessment, 467

Strengths perspective

on families, 13
value of, 2
Stress
  African American marriages and, 306
  boundary ambiguity and, 391–392, *392*
  change and, 17–18
  cross-cultural perspectives on, 388
  curvilinear nature of, 388–389
  defined, 388
  interconnection in types of, *391*
  life events and, 389–390
  in middle age, 365
  parenting and, 334
  past life experiences and, 390
  stress pileup, 390–391
  See also Economic stress; Family stress
Stress management
  families and, 401
  in middle age, 365
  strategies for, 403
  in strong families, 78–79
  White families and, 47
Stressors
  defined, 388
  in middle age, 365
Stress pileup, 390–391
Stress-related symptoms, 365
Strong families, qualities of, *74*, 74–79
Structurally enmeshed families, 313–314
Structured questionnaires, A-9
Structured relationships, 87, *88*
Subculture violence, child abuse and, 415
Submissive interactions, 211
Submissive symmetry, 211
Substance abuse
  child abuse and, 414
  trends in, 20–21
Subsystem, 68
Sudden infant death syndrome (SIDS), A-36–A-37
Supportive couples, 178
Suprasystem, 68
Sweaty-palm syndrome, 282
Sweden
  marriage in, 277
  no-spanking law, 347–348
Symbolic interaction framework, 67, 80–81
Symmetrical interactions, 211
Sympto-thermal method, A-17
Syncratic power pattern, 209–210, *210*
Systems, defined, 68

Take Back Your Kids (Doherty), 346
Take Back Your Marriage (Doherty), 322
Tchambuli people, 198
Teaser rates, 237

Teenage pregnancy, 168
Television shows, family dynamics in, 92–94
Tender years doctrine, 432
Terrorist attacks. *See* September 11 attacks
Testing cohabitation, 297
Thailand, single women in, 267
Theory, 65
Thonga society, 158
"The Tie That Binds" game, 262
Time
  American Indians and, 201
  for oneself and significant others, 18
  See also Family time
Time-outs, 142
TLC approach, 346
Tobacco, 422–423
Tobacco use, 21
Togetherness, 52. *See also* Family cohesion; Separateness–togetherness
Too Much of a Good Thing: Raising Children of Character in an Indulgent Age (Kindlon), 346
Tough love, 251
Traditional beliefs, 54
Traditional couples, 178, 319, 320, 322
Training for Marriage Enrichment Program, 471
Transgender, 154
Transition stage of grief, 382
Tribal community, 56
Tribal support systems, 55
Trimesters, A-19, A-29, *A-30*
Trobriand Island society, 157–158
Trophoblast, A-29
Trukese society, 158
Trust, 245
Truth statements, 81
Tubal blockage, A-27
Tubal ligation, A-14
12 Hours to a Great Marriage (Markham et al.), 122
Twin Cities Youth, 34
Two-income couples and families
  advantages and disadvantages of, 231–232
  pooling money, 233–234
Two-marriages concept, 14–15
Two-parent families
  decrease in, *448*
  by ethnic group, *37*
  percentage of children in poverty, 25, *25*
  strengthening, 481

Ultimate good, 467
Ultimatums, 139
Umbilical cord, A-29, A-32
Unbalanced families, 89–91, *91*
Uncompleted tasks, 393

Uncontested divorce, 432
Underfunctioners, 136
Understanding, in friendship, 245
Unemployment, domestic violence and, 408
Unintended pregnancy, A-14, A-23
Uninvolved parenting, 341–342, 343
Unmarried people
  increase in, 306
  See also Singlehood
Upper-income families, *227*
Urban migration, 24
U.S. Supreme Court, abortion cases, A-18–A-19, A-20
Uterus, A-26

Vacuum aspiration, A-20–A-21
Vacuum curettage, A-20–A-21
Vacuum suction, A-20–A-21
Vaginal suppositories, A-16
Vaginismus, 183
Validating couples, 178, 312
Validation, of survey instruments, A-9
Value complementarity, 290
Values, intercultural marriages and, 287
Value systems, 12
Vasectomy, A-14
Verbal abuse, 142
Verbal aggression, 410
Victim blaming, 409
Victimizers, 408
Victim–offender relationship, *404*, 404–405
Vietnam War, divorce rates and, 429
Violence
  in dating, 292–293, 294
  divorce and, 441
  in society, 20
Violence resistance, 404
Violent crimes, victim–offender relationship in, *404*, 404–405
Violent marriages, child abuse and, 415
Vitalized couples, 319, 320, 322
VOICES (play), 34
Volatile couples, 178, 312
Voluntary childlessness, 337–339
Voluntary surgical contraception, A-14

Wage gap, 205
Wars
  divorce rates and, 429
  impact on families left behind, 398–399
  posttraumatic stress disorder and, 398–400
Wealth
  marriage as a predictor for, 15
  married people and, 304
  in old age, 377–378
  See also Finances; Income; Money

Webster v. Reproductive Health Services, A-19
Weddings, 315–316
What About Bob? (movie), 93
"What Makes Marriage Work" (Gottman & Silver), 312
Wheel theory of love, 290–292
White families
    median income level, 227, *227*
    net worth, 231
    strengths of, 46–48, 52
    trends in family structure, *10,* 11
White women
    childless, 337
    raising grandchildren, 375
Whole family system, 69
Wholeness, 69
Widows, grief and, 383
Wife-dominant power pattern, 209, *210*
"Willing" victims, 408
Withdrawal method, A-16
Women
    alcohol abuse and, 419
    alcohol-abusing spouses and, 421
    anger management styles, 137
    births per woman, 10, 12
    childless, 337
    communication and, 101–106
    coparental divorce and, 443
    couple-arranged marriage and, 276
    cross-cultural perspective on opportunity, 60–61
    dating process and, 278
    disclosure and, 113–114
    divorce, filing for, 5
    divorce, global trends in, 430, 431
    divorce in middle age, 372
    divorce law and, 432, 433, 434
    divorce rates and, 429
    economic divorce and, 443
    emotion work and, 191
    expressivity and, 194
    female traits survey, *192,* 192–193
    fertility in, A-26
    gender differences in income, 228–229
    gender roles and, 23–24, 194–195
    hanging out and hooking up, 278–280
    homogamy and, 289
    infertility in, A-27–A-28
    intimacy and, 253
    jealousy and, 252
    marriage trends, 264, 286
    mate selection and, 285–286
    the mating gradient and, 285
    mental work and, 192
    miscarriages and, A-36
    no-fault divorce and, 433, 434
    objectification of, 409
    out-of-wedlock births, 352
    power in families and, 208
    power in relationships and, 24
    power issues with fathers and, 355
    raising grandchildren, 375
    sex ratio, 286
    sexual experimentation in dating and, 278
    singlehood and, 266–267
    two-marriages concept and, 14–15
    valuing of marriage and parenthood, 265
    views of sex and love, 152
    wage gap, 205
    and work at middle age, 367–368
    work outside the home, 19, 194, 231–232
Work
    African American families and, 48
    marital success and, 307–308
    middle age and, 367–368
    outside the home, women and, 19, 194, 231–232
Work–family interface, 194–195
Work-to-family influence, 194
World Trade Center attack. *See* September 11 attacks
World War II, divorce rates and, 429
Written communication, 110

You Just Don't Understand: Women and Men in Conversation (Tannen), 102
Young-old, 376
"You" statement, 141

Zero-sum games, 259
Zygote, A-26